HUMAN DEVELOPMENT 95/96

Twenty-Third Edition

Editor

Karen L. Freiberg
University of Maryland, Baltimore

Dr. Karen Freiberg has an interdisciplinary educational and employment background in nursing, education, and developmental psychology. She received her B.S. from the State University of New York at Plattsburgh, her M.S. from Cornell University, and her Ph.D. from Syracuse University. She has worked as a school nurse, a pediatric nurse, a public health nurse for the Navajo Indians, an associate project director for a child development clinic, a researcher in several areas of child development, and a university professor. She is the author of an award-winning textbook, *Human Development: A Life-Span Approach*, which is now in its fourth edition. She is currently on the faculty at the University of Maryland, Baltimore County.

Cover illustration by Mike Eagle

Annual Editions
A Library of Information from the Public Press

The Dushkin Publishing Group, Inc.
Sluice Dock, Guilford, Connecticut 06437

The Annual Editions Series

Annual Editions is a series of over 65 volumes designed to provide the reader with convenient, low-cost access to a wide range of current, carefully selected articles from some of the most important magazines, newspapers, and journals published today. Annual Editions are updated on an annual basis through a continuous monitoring of over 300 periodical sources. All Annual Editions have a number of features designed to make them particularly useful, including topic guides, annotated tables of contents, unit overviews, and indexes. For the teacher using Annual Editions in the classroom, an Instructor's Resource Guide with test questions is available for each volume.

VOLUMES AVAILABLE

Africa
Aging
American Foreign Policy
American Government
American History, Pre-Civil War
American History, Post-Civil War
Anthropology
Archaeology
Biology
Biopsychology
Business Ethics
Canadian Politics
Child Growth and Development
China
Comparative Politics
Computers in Education
Computers in Business
Computers in Society
Criminal Justice
Developing World
Drugs, Society, and Behavior
Dying, Death, and Bereavement
Early Childhood Education
Economics
Educating Exceptional Children
Education
Educational Psychology
Environment
Geography
Global Issues
Health
Human Development
Human Resources
Human Sexuality
India and South Asia

International Business
Japan and the Pacific Rim
Latin America
Life Management
Macroeconomics
Management
Marketing
Marriage and Family
Mass Media
Microeconomics
Middle East and the Islamic World
Money and Banking
Multicultural Education
Nutrition
Personal Growth and Behavior
Physical Anthropology
Psychology
Public Administration
Race and Ethnic Relations
Russia, the Eurasian Republics, and Central/Eastern Europe
Social Problems
Sociology
State and Local Government
Urban Society
Violence and Terrorism
Western Civilization, Pre-Reformation
Western Civilization, Post-Reformation
Western Europe
World History, Pre-Modern
World History, Modern
World Politics

Cataloging in Publication Data
Main entry under title: Annual Editions: Human development. 1995/96.
    1. Child study—Periodicals. 2. Socialization—Periodicals. 3. Old age—Periodicals.
I. Freiberg, Karen L., *comp.* II. Title: Human development.
ISBN 1–56134–359–5   155'.05   72–91973
HQ768.A55

© 1995 by The Dushkin Publishing Group, Inc., Guilford, CT 06437

Twenty-Third Edition

Printed in the United States of America

Editors/ Advisory Board

EDITORS

Karen L. Freiberg
University of Maryland, Baltimore

ADVISORY BOARD

Judith E. Blakemore
Indiana University-Purdue University

Karen Duffy
State University College Geneseo

Bonnie Duguid-Siegal
University of Western Sydney

Mark Greenberg
University of Washington

Don Hamacheck
Michigan State University

Gregory F. Harper
SUNY College, Fredonia

Jan L. Hitchcock
University of Southern Maine

Alice S. Honig
Syracuse University

Helen Lemay
SUNY, Stony Brook

Judith K. Lepuschitz
University of Central Oklahoma

David S. McKell
Northern Arizona University

Carroll Mitchell
Cecil Community College

Martin Murphy
University of Akron

Harriett Ritchie
American River College

Gary M. Schumacher
Ohio University

William H. Strader
Fitchburg State College

Harold R. Strang
University of Virginia

Margaret Varma
Rutgers University

James R. Wallace
St. Lawrence University

Karen Zabrucky
Georgia State University

Members of the Advisory Board are instrumental in the final selection of articles for each edition of Annual Editions. Their review of articles for content, level, currentness, and appropriateness provides critical direction to the editor and staff. We think you'll find their careful consideration well reflected in this volume.

STAFF

Ian A. Nielsen, Publisher
Brenda S. Filley, Production Manager
Roberta Monaco, Editor
Addie Raucci, Administrative Editor
Cheryl Greenleaf, Permissions Editor
Deanna Herrschaft, Permissions Assistant
Diane Barker, Proofreader
Lisa Holmes-Doebrick, Administrative Coordinator
Charles Vitelli, Designer
Shawn Callahan, Graphics
Steve Shumaker, Graphics
Lara M. Johnson, Graphics
Laura Levine, Graphics
Libra A. Cusack, Typesetting Supervisor
Juliana Arbo, Typesetter

To the Reader

In publishing ANNUAL EDITIONS we recognize the enormous role played by the magazines, newspapers, and journals of the *public press* in providing current, first-rate educational information in a broad spectrum of interest areas. Within the articles, the best scientists, practitioners, researchers, and commentators draw issues into new perspective as accepted theories and viewpoints are called into account by new events, recent discoveries change old facts, and fresh debate breaks out over important controversies.

Many of the articles resulting from this enormous editorial effort are appropriate for students, researchers, and professionals seeking accurate, current material to help bridge the gap between principles and theories and the real world. These articles, however, become more useful for study when those of lasting value are carefully *collected, organized, indexed,* and *reproduced* in a *low-cost format*, which provides easy and permanent access when the material is needed. That is the role played by *Annual Editions*. Under the direction of each volume's *Editor*, who is an expert in the subject area, and with the guidance of an *Advisory Board*, we seek each year to provide in each *ANNUAL EDITION* a current, well-balanced, carefully selected collection of the best of the public press for your study and enjoyment. We think you'll find this volume useful, and we hope you'll take a moment to let us know what you think.

This anthology has been developed to make the study of human development more exciting. A student should be more than an information processing-storage-retrieval system. To study means to pursue knowledge, to attentively scrutinize scientific data, to consider the opinions of others, to ask one's own questions, to ponder, to reflect, to be involved. This book is intended to promote mental exercise. Many of the articles included in *Annual Editions: Human Development 95/96* ask questions that have no answers. A controversy is presented. Several sides of the issue are considered. Ultimately, the reader must choose to accept or reject the proposals which have been advanced, or to be eclectic and incorporate parts of several theories into his or her belief system.

The articles included in this anthology are theoretically eclectic. They employ elements from a variety of sources. While the field of psychology is represented more than other disciplines, psychology's debt to the other sciences is well documented. Psychological development is an interaction of genes, anatomy, neural networks in the brain, physiology, nutrition, health, personal influences, environmental influences, cognitions, and a multitude of other continually changing life circumstances. The reader is encouraged to consider the plasticity and the multiple permutations of experiences possible in each unique human being's life.

Eight stages of life are delineated (prenatal, infancy, early childhood, school-age, adolescence, and early, middle, and late adulthood), but the continuity of life and the whole person are paramount.

The selections for this anthology were chosen to represent both the classic topics of life span human development—physical development, cognitive and language development, and personal and social development and some "hot" topics within these areas—gene probing, AIDS, infant memory, multiculturalism, homelessness, date rape, and family violence. In keeping with the trend to look at human development from an ecological perspective, we have carefully included articles that represent microsystems (family, school, work); exosystems (television, community concerns); macrosystems (economics, government); mesosystems (home visiting health programs); and the unique individual's own contribution to development (genes, brain organization, health).

The six units of this anthology are arranged chronologically from genetic and prenatal development through late adulthood. The units have also been subordinated topically so that within each unit are included articles about physical, cognitive, and personal-social development. Units three and four are further ordered and subordered topically. Unit three contains articles that primarily deal with childhood physical development, health, cognition, language, and school. Unit four concludes the coverage of child development with articles focusing on social and personal development. It includes research data and discussions of the influence of parenting practices, parents' career pressures, societal mores, peer pressures, drugs, sex, violence, television, divorce, child abuse, homelessness, and other personal-social factors impinging on children's psyches.

We hope that each reader will not only be interested in, but will also be enriched by, the selections in this anthology. Please use the article rating form on the last page of this book to express your opinions. We hope to maximize both the usefulness of and your enjoyment of each revision of *Annual Editions: Human Development*.

Karen Freiberg

Karen Freiberg
Editor

Unit 1

Genetic and Prenatal Influences on Development

Ten selections discuss genetic influences on development, reproductive technology, and the effects of substance abuse on prenatal development.

The concepts in bold italics are developed in the article. For further expansion please refer to the Topic Guide and the Index.

Unit 2

Development during Infancy and Early Childhood

Eight selections profile the impressive abilities of infants and young children, examine the ways in which children learn, and look at sex differences.

The concepts in bold italics are developed in the article. For further expansion please refer to the Topic Guide and the Index.

Unit 3

Development during Childhood – Cognition and Schooling

Eight selections examine human development during
childhood, paying specific attention to social and
emotional development, cognitive and language
development, and development problems.

Unit 4

Development during Childhood — Family and Culture

Eleven selections discuss the impact of home and culture on childrearing and child development. The topics include parenting styles, family structure, and cultural influences.

The concepts in bold italics are developed in the article. For further expansion please refer to the Topic Guide and the Index.

The concepts in bold italics are developed in the article. For further expansion please refer to the Topic Guide and the Index.

Unit 5

Development during Adolescence and Early Adulthood

Eight selections explore a wide range of issues and topics concerning adolescence and early adulthood.

The concepts in bold italics are developed in the article. For further expansion please refer to the Topic Guide and the Index.

Unit 6

Development during Middle and Late Adulthood

Eight selections review a variety of biological and psychological aspects of aging, questioning the concept of set life stages.

The concepts in bold italics are developed in the article. For further expansion please refer to the Topic Guide and the Index.

Topic Guide

This topic guide suggests how the selections in this book relate to topics of traditional concern to students and professionals involved with the study of human development. It is useful for locating articles that relate to each other for reading and research. The guide is arranged alphabetically according to topic. Articles may, of course, treat topics that do not appear in the topic guide. In turn, entries in the topic guide do not necessarily constitute a comprehensive listing of all the contents of each selection.

TOPIC AREA	TREATED IN:	TOPIC AREA	TREATED IN:
Adolescence	38. Much Riskier Passage 39. Teenage Turning Point 40. Teenagers and AIDS 41. Date and Acquaintance Rape 53. Getting Older and Getting Better	Depression	37. Impact of Homelessness 39. Teenage Turning Point 45. When Violence Hits Home 46. New Middle Age 48. Miserable Working Woman
Adoption	44. Lifelong Impact of Adoption	Divorce	30. Effects of Divorce on Children 33. Alienation 35. Miracle of Resiliency 43. Is There Love after Baby? 45. When Violence Hits Home
Aggression	14. Mental Health for Babies 18. Sizing Up the Sexes 36. Televised Violence and Kids 37. Impact of Homelessness on Children 45. When Violence Hits Home		
		Drug Abuse	5. Eugenics Revisited 6. What Crack Does to Babies 8. When a Pregnant Woman Drinks 9. Sperm under Siege 13. Clipped Wings 38. Much Riskier Passage 45. When Violence Hits Home
AIDS	10. Moms, Kids, and AIDS 34. Why Kids Have a Lot to Cry About 38. Much Riskier Passage 40. Teenagers and AIDS		
Attachment	6. What Crack Does to Babies 14. Mental Health for Babies	Education/School	23. Learning from Asian Schools 24. Tracked to Fail 25. The Good, the Bad, and the Difference 26. Trying to Explain AIDS 31. Lasting Effects of Child Maltreatment 33. Alienation 36. Televised Violence and Kids 37. Impact of Homelessness on Children
Child Abuse	31. Lasting Effects of Child Maltreatment 34. Why Kids Have a Lot to Cry About 35. Miracle of Resiliency		
Cognitive Development	11. New Perspective on Cognitive Development 12. Amazing Minds of Infants 15. Home Visiting Programs 16. "I Forget" 19. Human Mind 20. Adaptive Nature of Cognitive Immaturity 21. Bilingual/Bicultural Young Children 22. Life in Overdrive 25. The Good, the Bad, and the Difference 49. Midlife Myths	Emotional Development/ Personality	12. Amazing Minds of Infants 14. Mental Health for Babies 22. Life in Overdrive 25. The Good, the Bad, and the Difference 26. Trying to Explain AIDS 29. Same Family, Different Lives 30. Effects of Divorce on Children 31. Lasting Effects of Child Maltreatment 32. Your Loving Touch 35. Miracle of Resiliency 52. Unlocking the Secrets of Aging
Creativity	19. Human Mind 22. Life in Overdrive 49. Midlife Myths 53. Getting Older and Getting Better	Ethics/Morality	3. Cloning 4. Choosing a Perfect Child 25. The Good, the Bad, and the Difference 26. Trying to Explain AIDS 39. Teenage Turning Point 52. Unlocking the Secrets of Aging
Culture	21. Bilingual/Bicultural Young Children 23. Learning from Asian Schools 28. Bringing Up Father 33. Alienation 34. Why Kids Have a Lot to Cry About 35. Miracle of Resiliency 38. Much Riskier Passage 42. Psychotrends 50. Prime of Our Lives	Family/Parenting	14. Mental Health for Babies 15. Home Visiting Programs 25. The Good, the Bad, and the Difference 27. Can Your Career Hurt Your Kids? 28. Bringing Up Father 29. Same Family, Different Lives 30. Effects of Divorce on Children 31. Lasting Effects of Child Maltreatment 32. Your Loving Touch 33. Alienation 35. Miracle of Resiliency 43. Is There Love after Baby?
Day Care	13. Clipped Wings 14. Mental Health for Babies 27. Can Your Career Hurt Your Kids?		

TOPIC AREA	TREATED IN:	TOPIC AREA	TREATED IN:
Fertility	3. Cloning 4. Choosing a Perfect Child 44. Lifelong Impact of Adoption	Peers/Cohorts (cont'd)	49. Midlife Myths 50. Prime of Our Lives
Genetics	1. Biologists Find Key Genes 2. New Genetic Code 3. Cloning 4. Choosing a Perfect Child 5. Eugenics Revisited 29. Same Family, Different Lives 35. Miracle of Resiliency	Physical Development	15. Home Visiting Programs 20. Adaptive Nature of Cognitive Immaturity 37. Impact of Homelessness on Children 51. On Growing Old
Health	15. Home Visiting Programs 22. Life in Overdrive 26. Trying to Explain AIDS 28. Bringing Up Father 34. Why Kids Have a Lot to Cry About 35. Miracle of Resiliency 36. Televised Violence and Kids 37. Impact of Homelessness on Children 40. Teenagers and AIDS 48. Miserable Working Woman	Prenatal Development	1. Biologists Find Key Genes 2. New Genetic Code 3. Cloning 6. What Crack Does to Babies 7. War Babies 8. When a Pregnant Woman Drinks 9. Sperm under Siege 10. Moms, Kids, and AIDS
High Risk Infants	6. What Crack Does to Babies 7. War Babies 13. Clipped Wings	Self-Esteem	15. Home Visiting Programs 24. Tracked to Fail 35. Miracle of Resiliency 39. Teenage Turning Point 41. Date and Acquaintance Rape 45. When Violence Hits Home 48. Miserable Working Woman 53. Getting Older and Getting Better
Language/ Communication	15. Home Visiting Programs 17. Toddler Talk 21. Bilingual/Bicultural Young Children	Sex Differences	18. Sizing Up the Sexes 30. Effects of Divorce on Children 35. Miracle of Resiliency 39. Teenage Turning Point 42. Psychotrends 48. Miserable Working Woman
Late Adulthood	47. Building a Better Brain 50. Prime of Our Lives 51. On Growing Old 52. Unlocking the Secrets of Aging 53. Getting Older and Getting Better	Stress	23. Learning from Asian Schools 27. Can Your Career Hurt Your Kids? 33. Alienation 34. Why Kids Have a Lot to Cry About 35. Miracle of Resiliency 38. Much Riskier Passage 43. Is There Love after Baby? 46. New Middle Age 48. Miserable Working Woman
Marriage	42. Psychotrends 43. Is There Love after Baby? 45. When Violence Hits Home 48. Miserable Working Woman 49. Midlife Myths	Television	33. Alienation 34. Why Kids Have a Lot to Cry About 36. Televised Violence and Kids 38. Much Riskier Passage
Middle Adulthood	46. New Middle Age 47. Building a Better Brain 48. Miserable Working Woman 49. Midlife Myths 50. Prime of Our Lives	Teratogens	6. What Crack Does to Babies 8. When a Pregnant Woman Drinks 9. Sperm under Siege
Nutrition	7. War Babies 13. Clipped Wings 37. Impact of Homelessness on Children 46. New Middle Age 51. On Growing Old 52. Unlocking the Secrets of Aging	Violence/Rape	5. Eugenics Revisited 27. Can Your Career Hurt Your Kids? 31. Lasting Effects of Child Maltreatment 34. Why Kids Have a Lot to Cry About 36. Televised Violence and Kids 38. Much Riskier Passage 41. Date and Acquaintance Rape 45. When Violence Hits Home
Occupation/Work	27. Can Your Career Hurt Your Kids? 31. Lasting Effects of Child Maltreatment 33. Alienation 48. Miserable Working Woman	Young Adulthood	42. Psychotrends 43. Is There Love after Baby? 44. Lifelong Impact of Adoption 45. When Violence Hits Home
Peers/Cohorts	27. Can Your Career Hurt Your Kids? 33. Alienation 40. Teenagers and AIDS 41. Date and Acquaintance Rape 48. Miserable Working Woman		

Genetic and Prenatal Influences on Development

- **Genetic Influences (Articles 1–5)**
- **Prenatal Influences (Articles 6–10)**

Erik Erikson became renown as the first major theorist to discuss human development over the entire life span. His "eight ages of man" began with infancy and ended with late adulthood. Missing from his theory were the first nine months of human development (prenatal period), and any reflections about the influence of genes on human behavior. This is understandable, given his emphasis on psychosocial development, and given the dearth of information about the impact of genetic and prenatal factors on the totality of postnatal human development in the 1950s and 1960s when he was developing his theory.

Today there is a burgeoning field of research that deals with genetic and prenatal influences on development. Embryology and fetology have documented that behavior occurs in the embryo and fetus within the uterus. Geneticists have provided ample evidence that genes play an important role, not only in the structure of organisms but also in functions and behaviors.

For many years, psychologists were involved in what became known as the nature-nurture controversy. Was human behavior controlled more by heredity and genes (nature) or by environmental factors (nurture)? The subject is debated or argued as an exercise, but it is of no practical importance for the furthering of the scientific study of human behavior. Carefully controlled studies of identical twins raised either together or apart have made us aware that behavior is multifactorial. Both genes and environment influence all behavior. Any simple behavior can be altered by many different environmental factors in many ways. In addition, most behaviors are influenced by many genes in many ways (polygenic causations). The influences of nature and nurture cannot realistically be looked at separately in the total world of complex human beings.

Genetics, the branch of biology dealing with heredity, moved from Gregor Mendel's speculations about dominance and recessiveness of sweet pea strains to speculations about cloning humans, or at least altering genetic diseases prenatally with genetic replacement therapy, in a brief 100 years. What does the future hold in the way of genetic engineering?

The basic mechanisms of heredity—chromosomes, genes, DNA molecules, nucleotides, dominant and recessive traits, intermediate and polygenic traits, mutations, mitosis and meiosis, extra chromosomes, and absent chromosomes—have been known for about 30 years. Genetic maps and genetic markers are currently emerging as geneticists are determining the presence of specific chromosomes and the nucleotide sequences of DNA that are associated with specific genes. As more precise knowledge of the location and nature of normal and abnormal genes becomes known, genetic testing can increasingly be used to determine if an unborn baby has inherited specific disorders. Genetic counseling is currently suggested to couples with family histories of certain genetic disorders. Soon it may be possible to replace abnormal genes with cultivated sequences of DNA, "good genes," during in vitro fertilization, before an embryo is implanted in the uterus. What are the implications of gene replacement therapy for human development?

The rate of development between fertilization of an ovum by a sperm and the birth of a human being nine and one-half short months later is astronomical. Never again in the life span of the human will growth and development occur as rapidly. Infant development and adolescent development pale in comparison to prenatal development. Because prenatal growth and change is so rapid, it is also fragile. Many substances that are relatively harmless from infancy through late adulthood are extremely poisonous to the developing embryo/fetus. Teratology, the study of malformations of an embryo or a fetus, has revealed thousands of possible teratogens, or substances that cause embryonic or fetal malformations. Fortunately, nature provides some protections to the organism developing within its mother's uterus. Only very small substances will diffuse across the sinus spaces between the mother's uterus and the placenta surrounding the developing embryo/fetus. This filter-like defense system is called the placental barrier.

The small substances that will cross the placental barrier include nutrients, waste products, radiation, some medications, some illicit drugs, alcohol, caffeine, the tars, nicotine, and carbon monoxide from tobacco smoking, viruses, and some very small bacteria. Most of these are teratogenic. The obvious exceptions are nutrients, which must cross from mother to embryo/fetus, and waste products, which must cross back in order to be eliminated through the mother's body.

Malnutrition of a mother is one of the more common reasons for poor growth and development of an embryo/fetus. Malnourished mothers tend to give birth to low-birth-weight infants with a high rate of infant disabilities or death. Recent research suggests that the deleterious effects of prenatal malnutrition can last a lifetime.

The more common prenatal teratogens, which have long lasting deleterious effects on human development, are radiation, drugs, and viral infections. While most humans are always careful to avoid any unnecessary exposure to radiation, the same cannot be said of drugs and viral infections. Alcohol, cocaine, tobacco, AIDS, herpes, syphilis, and many other drugs and viruses are associated with high rates of low birthweight infants and infants born with physical, cognitive, and personal-social disabilities.

The articles selected for this unit reflect the newest information about genetics and prenatal influences on development. The first five articles deal with embryogenesis, morphogens, mutant genes, cloning, in vitro fertilization, gene probing, and future gene replacement therapy. The last five articles deal with the teratogenic effects of crack, malnutrition, alcohol, tobacco, chemical substances, and the AIDS virus.

Looking Ahead: Challenge Questions

What are hedgehog morphogens? Why are they important to understanding genetic and prenatal development?

How many exceptions have been found to Mendel's laws of inheritance? How dangerous are these exceptions?

Where should we draw the line on cloning research?

Would you elect to have in vitro fertilization and gene replacement therapy to create a perfect child?

How many human exceptionalities have genetic markers?

What does prenatal crack exposure do to babies?

How long does prenatal malnutrition affect human development?

How much alcohol is teratogenic? What does it do to the embryo/fetus?

How do sperm contribute to the hazards of prenatal development?

Explain why HIV positive mothers should or should not be treated for AIDS during pregnancy.

Biologists Find Key Genes That Shape Patterning of Embryos

A gene named hedgehog directs the development of cells in the limbs and brain.

Natalie Angier

Rare indeed are the scientific findings that make jaws drop and spirits do cartwheels. But the discovery of a class of genes, given the cheeky name hedgehog, has aroused the passions of developmental biologists so vigorously that their normal reserve and skepticism have dissolved, leaving them groping for ever-stronger ways to express the beauty and consequence of what has been divulged.

Three teams of scientists report in the current issue of the journal Cell that they have finally unearthed what developmental scientists have been seeking for the last 25 years, as they studied the implausibly complex sequence of events that allow a single cell, the fertilized egg, to efflorescc into a complete animal. They have identified the genes that act on the early embryo to lend it shape and pattern, transforming a nondescript comma of tissue into a vertebrate animal, with limbs and digits, brain and spinal cord, the body shape set from head to heel.

These genes produce so-called morphogens, molecules of celebrated stature that researchers have known must exist but have had tremendous difficulty isolating. The word morphogen means "maker of structure," and the hedgehog proteins are just that. Once switched on inside the embryo, the molecules sweep slowly across the primordial buds of tissue and begin generating identifiable form, sculpturing arms, hands and fingers on the sides of the embryo, vertebrae and ribs along its midline, a brain within the skull. The morphogen tells the cells it touches where they are situated in the body and what they are destined to become. It gives them their address, their fate, their identity, their purpose in life.

First detected in fruit flies, the hedgehog genes earned their name for their ability, when mutated, to give a fly the bristly appearance of a hedgehog. Their normal function in the fruit fly is to dictate growth, and the latest trio of reports establish that the same genes also dictate structural design in vertebrates.

The papers describe the isolation of hedgehog genes from mice, zebra fish and chickens, three staple organisms of laboratory research, widely separated in evolutionary time.

"This new class of signaling molecules will probably end up being the most important molecules in vertebrate development," said Dr. Clifford J. Tabin, a developmental biologist at Harvard Medical School and the principle author of one of the three reports. When the results on the hedgehog work first became apparent, he said, "I was bouncing off the walls."

Scientists have yet to look for the genes in humans, but they are certain that hedgehog is performing the same role in human embryos as it is in little fish. If this turns out not to be the case, said Dr. Philip W. Ingham, a senior scientist at the Molecular Embryology Laboratory at the Imperial Cancer Research Fund in Oxford, England, and the head investigator on another of the new papers, "I'll resign from science."

And with such a big segment of the puzzle of development now snapped into place, researchers said they can begin filling in the rest of the confounding picture of embryogenesis. They can start to decipher how the hedgehog molecules interact with other essential players known to participate slightly later in development, including the famed Hox genes, also assiduous builders of bodies, which themselves are found across the evolutionary scale.

"This is extraordinary work, it's fantastic, and I wish I'd done it," said Dr. Jim Smith, head of the developmental biology laboratory at the National Institute for Medical Research in London. "When I started working on limb development in 1976, we all knew there had to be something like this, but we didn't necessarily think we'd live to see it."

Dr. Smith, who has written a review of research on the hedgehog genes that will appear in the next issue of Cell, could not contain his enthusiasm. "It's the sort of thing that brings tears to your eyes," he said.

The work is of an exquisitely basic nature, born more of curiosity about nature than of specific clinical goals. But scientists said the findings may prove useful in the quest for better ways to treat head and spinal cord injuries, as well as degenerative diseases of the brain.

"People these days are very interested in molecules that mediate important decisions in the early development of the central nervous system," said Dr. Andrew P. McMahon, a developmental biologist at Harvard University and the principal researcher on the third of the latest papers. "There are a lot of diseases for which one would like to be able to grow new neurons," and understanding the basic signals of nervous system development is one road toward the shimmering Oz of neurological regeneration.

The protein made by the hedgehog gene organizes the fates of neighboring cells.

The hedgehog morphogens also offer relief to developmental biologists who lately had grown dissatisfied with another proffered candidate for the role of omnipotent morphogen: retinoic acid, or vitamin A. In widely publicized reports a few years ago, scientists suggested that retinoic acid could be the long-sought morphogen that sets up a body plan. However, there were sizable gaps in the data and doubts in the minds of many biologists that retinoic acid worked at such a fundamental level in the embryo.

In the new work, the hedgehog genes pass all the litmus tests that vitamin A had failed, displaying with extraordinary precision the properties that scientific theories about morphogens had predicted. It is turned on, or expressed, at precisely the right times of development, and in all the right places. And when scientists manipulate embryos and subtly alter the ways in which hedgehog genes are expressed, they get the sort of macabre developmental mutations they are expecting. For example, they can prompt a growing chick to sprout mirror-image sets of wings simply by inserting active hedgehog genes in the tissue abutting that where the genes are normally expressed.

'Exciting Breakthrough'

With the new results, said Dr. Ingham, "we can forget about retinoic acid" as an architect of the body.

For scientists who work on fruit flies, or Drosophila, the new discoveries prove once again how prescient they were to focus on simple animals as a way of comprehending more complex societies.

"It's a very exciting breakthrough and a vindication of the power of model organisms," said Dr. Matthew P. Scott, a professor of developmental biology and genetics at Stanford University School of Medicine. "Here we have a molecule that was found for its role in determining segmentation in insects, and it's turned out to be extremely important in understanding the most interesting properties of vertebrate growth."

Yet with all the enthusiasm surrounding the new finding, scientists admit they have much to learn. For example, they know that in humans, hedgehog in all likelihood switches on sometime around day 15 of pregnancy, to help shape the central nervous system, and is largely finished with that task by day 28. It comes into play shortly afterward in molding the limbs of the body. However, scientists do not yet have a clue as to what activates hedgehog to get morphogenesis rolling.

Nor do they know much about the hedgehog molecules themselves, what sort of proteins they are and how they manage to communicate with embryonic cells to persuade them to adopt a particular fate. The hedgehog proteins are unlike any detected before, which is both a blessing and a hurdle—a blessing because scientists like novel things and because they knew the molecules they were familiar with were not sufficient to explain the mysteries of development; and a hurdle because they must start from scratch in understanding the molecules. So far, they have found four different hedgehog genes in vertebrate animals, but they suspect there may be more.

The fourth variety, which scientists call Sonic hedgehog, has an illustrious history. Scientists were first inspired to seek morphogens by the seminal research of Dr. John Saunders and others who, in the 1960's and 1970's, painstakingly grafted parts of embryos together to see what resulted. The work yielded a bizarre set of mutant animals with excess or abnormal digits and limbs, but the results were consistent and revealing. Together they indicated that in certain key regions of the primordial embryo, there are what are known as zones of polarizing activity, local headquarters that disseminate essential information about how surrounding cells are supposed to behave.

Scientists' Fantasies Exceeded

"The idea was that these signaling centers sent out a protein that affected neighboring cells and organized their fates," said Dr. Scott.

The signaling protein seems to work in a gradient fashion. By this theory, the protein diffuses from a central zone, getting less concentrated as it spreads. Depending on how much of the informational protein they receive, cells will choose one course of action over another. In the embryonic limb, for example, a heavy dose of the diffusing signal will instruct the cells to prepare to assume the role of a pinkie, while a lighter concentration will inform the cells they are destined to become a thumb.

Neurobiologists also gathered evidence from grafting experiments that a central signaling system helps knead the developing brain into shape. In this case, the zones of information were thought to be located in two embryonic structures, one called the notochord, a stiff rod that serves as the developing creature's temporary backbone, and the other called the floor plate, a bulge of tissue that eventually gives rise to the adult spinal cord. Scientists proposed that the structures jointly secrete a powerful information molecule able to tell surrounding cells whether they are destined to become part of the hind brain, the forebrain, motor nerves or other constituents of the nervous system.

Thus was born the notion of the morphogen, the diffusible conductor of cell fates. Finding it, however, was another matter.

> Scientists suspect that the protein stimulates the response of a master gene inside the cells; this potent gene may in turn set off a string of other genes.

Because recent work in fruit flies indicated that the hedgehog gene helps determine the growth of body segments in the larvae, the three research teams thought it worth the effort to seek the vertebrate equivalents of the gene and check whether hedgehog was somehow involved in animal growth.

The results exceeded their fantasies. The Sonic hedgehog molecule proved to be the desperately sought shaper of bodies. It is expressed in the limb at exactly the site known to be the zone of polarizing activity. It is activated exactly where it should be

A Gene That Signals Direction and Location

Scientists have discovered a class of genes, called hedgehog genes, that lend shape and pattern to the early embryo. Once turned on, these genes make proteins that give neighboring cells signals telling them their position and roles in forming a leg, wing or fin. At other sites, the hedgehog proteins direct development of the the central nervous system.

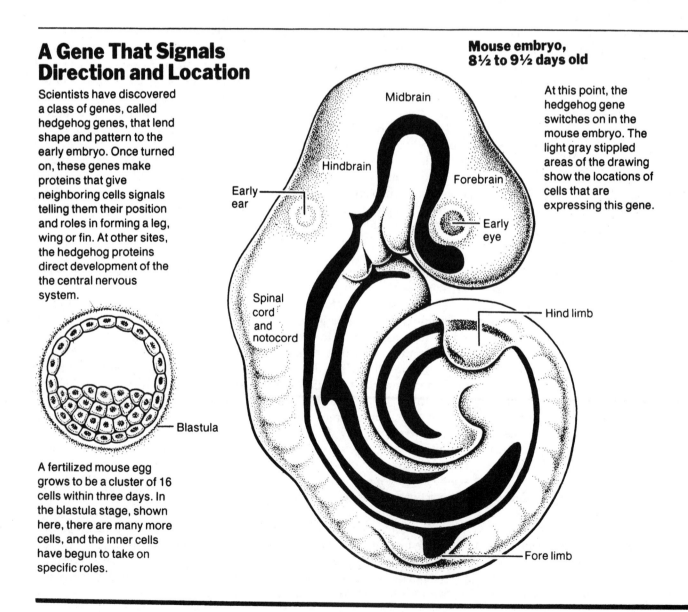

Mouse embryo, 8½ to 9½ days old

At this point, the hedgehog gene switches on in the mouse embryo. The light gray stippled areas of the drawing show the locations of cells that are expressing this gene.

Midbrain

Hindbrain

Forebrain

Early ear

Early eye

Spinal cord and notocord

Hind limb

Fore limb

Blastula

A fertilized mouse egg grows to be a cluster of 16 cells within three days. In the blastula stage, shown here, there are many more cells, and the inner cells have begun to take on specific roles.

in the notochord and floor plate in the early central nervous system.

Sonic Hedgehog's Modus Operandi

By manipulating the sonic hedgehog gene alone, the researchers have been able to recapitulate the suite of deformities seen in the older grafting experiments, thus demonstrating they have pinpointed the legendary morphogen.

The scientists have yet to clarify the roles of the three other hedgehog genes they have detected, but these seem more limited in their scope, toiling in specific regions like the sex cells of the body.

The challenge now is to understand the modus operandi of the Sonic hedgehog protein, how it persuades cells to do its bidding as it oozes by them. Scientists suspect that the protein stimulates the response of a master gene inside the cells, perhaps a member of the Hox gene family. That potent gene may in turn set off a string of other genes, which jointly realize the cell's destiny.

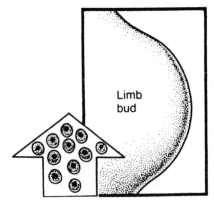

Within the early nervous system, the signals arising from the top and from the bottom are involved in formation of specific neurons at specific sites. Neurons at the top are associated with sensory functions, while neurons at the bottom control movement.

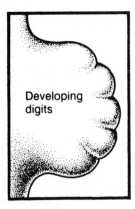

Limb bud

Developing digits

In the limb bud, the positional information from the hedgehog protein makes the cells start defining the arrangement of digits of a future paw.

Sources: Dr. Andrew McMahon, Harvard University; "Molecular Biology of the Cell" (Garland)

Mouse embryo, 14 days old

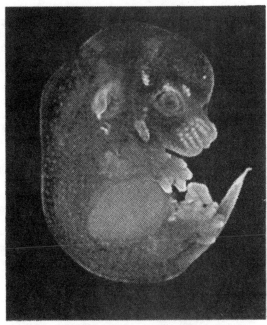

Dr. Bradley R. Smith, Dr. Elwood Lenny, Dr. G. Allan Johnson, Center for In Vivo Microscopy, Duke University Medical Center (N.I.H. National Resource)

Scientists suspect the hedgehog protein stimulates a master gene inside cells that sets off a cascade of other genes. The response to a signal, they think, depends on the local concentration of the hedgehog protein. Biologists expect to find the hedgehog gene in humans, too.

Nancy Sterngold, The New York Times; Illustration by Michael Reingold

A New Genetic Code

The ABCs of DNA are changing radically. And that can bring tragedy.

SHARON BEGLEY

Puttering about the abbey garden 130 years ago, Gregor Mendel wasn't content to leave the birds and the bees to the birds and the bees. The Austrian monk carefully sprinkled pollen from a purple-flowered plant onto a white-flowered plant. He brushed pollen from a plant that grew wrinkled peas onto one that made smooth peas. He crossed whites with whites and purples with purples, smooth with smooth and wrinkled with wrinkled. Besides harvesting enough peas to turn the monks green and the abbey into allergen heaven, Mendel also discovered the rules of biological inheritance. His lessons were simple and, in their modern version, seemingly infallible. Babies inherit 23 chromosomes from each parent. Some genes (for blue eyes, say) are recessive and others (brown eyes) dominant; an offspring shows the recessive trait only if he inherits two copies of that gene and one of the dominant one. So went the rule book.

Well, even Newton had his Einstein, and now genetics revolutionaries are showing that Mendel's laws can be broken. Genes, it turns out, act so perversely they would have shocked the monk into a vow of perpetual silence. Mutant genes grow from one generation to the next like a sci-fi escapee, so that Grandma's tiny and innocuous mutation becomes Grandson's tragic birth defect. Genes costume themselves so that one inherited from Mom has a markedly different effect from the exact same gene inherited from Dad. "It's the sort of stuff that's just not supposed to happen," says geneticist and pediatrician Judith Hall of the University of British Columbia. "But it does."

The violations of Mendel's laws represent a true paradigm shift for genetics. They also have sobering clinical implications. Prenatal testing and genetic counseling both rely on Mendel's rules. Because Mendel wasn't 100 percent right, neither are they. Scientists don't know how often the rules fail "because we pick it up only when it leads to disease," says Hall. But the rules being violated are many:

■ **The Gertrude Stein rule.** A gene is a gene is a gene, says Mendelian genetics. But that was before researchers stumbled over "imprinted" genes a couple of years ago. It seems that some bits of DNA—genes strung along the chromosomes like beads on a string—can be marked, with the molecular equivalent of a pink or blue ribbon, as having come from a particular parent (diagram). For these genes, says Hall, "it makes a difference whether they are inherited from the mother or the father." (New molecular techniques can trace any gene in an individual to one or the other parent.) If the father's chromosome 15 is missing some DNA, for instance, his child will have the rare Prader-Willi syndrome, which is marked by mental retardation and growth abnormalities; if the mother is missing the same bit, the child will have Angelman syndrome, marked by more severe retardation, excess laughing and unusual movement. In other cases a paternal gene leaves the child healthy, but the identical maternal gene produces a birth defect. Psoriasis, diabetes and some forms of mental retardation all manifest themselves differently depending which parent they are inherited from. "It isn't nice and clean like it used to be," says Hall.

Even cancer may have a "parent of origin" effect. In some cases of a neck tumor called paraganglioma, patients inherited a bit of DNA on the chromosome 11 inherited from the father. Inheriting the identical bit from the mother doesn't cause tumors. Say a boy and girl, call them Dick and Jane, inherit the defective gene on chromosome 11 from their father; both develop the neck tumor. Jane passes the same gene she inherited from her father to her own children, but they don't develop the tumor: the gene came from a mother. But when Dick passes the DNA to his daughters, they do develop the tumor—the gene came from Dad. His daughters' children don't get the tumor.

How the sperm or egg gets tagged with these pink or blue bows remains a mystery. For eggs, at least, it happens when the child's mother is in the womb. That's when eggs form. A grandmother's exposure to chemicals, radiation or disease during her pregnancy, which affects her fetus's eggs, can affect her grandchildren's health.

■ **The stability rule.** Genes can mutate. But mutations are not supposed to grow like a loaf of bread with too much yeast. Yet consider Martha (not her real name), who has 50 copies of a particular snippet of DNA on her X chromosome (two X's make a girl a girl). Her daughter, Zoe, has 100 copies but is still healthy. Zoe's child has 1,000 copies—and is mentally retarded. Somehow, when the X was passing down through the generations, the dangerous bit grew like Topsy. In growing, it knocked out healthy genes; the more it grew the more healthy genes it toppled. "The same mutation, depending what gene it knocks out, can cause very different problems," says Dr. Haig Kazazian of Johns Hopkins medical school. "They could include manic depression, schizophrenia, coronary-artery disease and learning disabilities." So much for the conclusion of classical genetics that one mutation causes one specific defect.

■ **Federalism.** A cell supposedly has a strong central government. Its seat is the cell nucleus, and the laws are writ in the chromosomes within. But now geneticists find a rogue government in the hinterlands. The rebels are mitochondria, little bodies inside cells that generate energy to make muscles move, heart tissue contract, lungs expand. Each cell has hundreds of mitochondria. Each mitochondrion contains its own genes, which sometimes mutate. Mitochondria with mutant genes do not generate as much energy as normal mitochondria.

The trouble starts when the mutation hits a cell that is dividing to form, say, eggs. By chance, one egg may get the lion's share of mutant mitochondria. If it goes on to develop into a fetus, the child could grow up to have a disease of the heart, brain, muscle or other energy-guzzling organ. But that baby's sister, if born of an egg that happened to get very few mutant mitochondria, would be perfectly healthy. "Mendel's rules say that a single mutation should cause a single change and thus a single medical effect," says Douglas Wallace of Emory University. "But a mutation in mitochondria can have many different clinical effects, depending on what [percentage] of mutant mitochondria an individual inherits."

The effect also depends on what organs the mutants wind up in. When a fertilized egg divides and multiplies, the mutant mitochondria randomly go into one or another embryonic organ-to-be. If the nascent heart cells get a lot of mutants, for instance, the child will get heart disease. But if, in that child's brother, the mutants happen to go to the brain, the brother would have epilepsy. "Mitochondrial genetics defies everything you've ever learned about genetics," says Wallace. Among the diseases traced to mitochondrial mutations: adult-onset diabetes and blindness.

■ **Sexual equality.** According to the rules, children get their 23 pairs of chromosomes equally from Mom and Dad: one of each pair comes from Mom, the other from Dad. Now it turns out that both chromosomes of a pair

Mendel's Mistakes

The Sexual Equality Rule: Textbooks say each parent gives us one of each member of a pair of chromosomes. Turns out you can get two from mom and none from dad, and thus inherit a recessive disease like cystic fibrosis.

The Gertrude Stein Rule: A gene is a gene is a gene, goes dogma. But for some genes, which parent it came from makes a big difference. Inheriting the gene from father causes a rare disorder; inheriting the identical gene from mother doesn't.

ROHR—NEWSWEEK

can come from the same parent (diagram). Eggs and sperm are supposed to have just half of a human's requisite DNA per cell; when they fuse, the fetus has the right allotment. But sometimes an egg, or a sperm, has all the needed DNA; when it meets its mate, the embryo has too much DNA. Usually such an embryo aborts. But sometimes it survives, by shedding the extra DNA. If it's the DNA from the sperm that gets jettisoned, then the fetus grows with a double dose of maternal DNA.

And that can make genetic counselors look no wiser than palm readers. Say a couple is tested for cystic fibrosis. Joe doesn't have the gene; Carol has one CF gene and one normal gene. Since the normal gene masks the CF gene, she doesn't have CF. (As Mendel found, someone can show a recessive trait only if she has two of the recessive genes.) The counselor tells the couple that their child cannot inherit CF. But say the child inherits both chromosomes from Carol and, by chance, two copies of her disease gene. There is no healthy gene from Joe to defeat the CF gene. The child will have cystic fibrosis. At least five babies who "couldn't" inherit CF have recently been born with it.

Exceptions to Mendel's rules, and the heartbreak they cause, are probably rare. But then it took scientists more than a century after Mendel harvested his bumper crop of genetic laws to see that people are more complicated than peas. So far this genetics revolution has hit the lab more than the doctor's or counselor's office; researchers say practitioners hardly know what to make of it all. They should figure it out quickly.

CLONING:
Where Do We Draw the Line?

Researchers duplicate a human embryo,
provoking cries that technology has gone too far

PHILIP ELMER-DEWITT

WHEN IT FINALLY HAP-pened—after years of ethical hand wringing and science-fiction fantasy—it was done in such a low-key way by researchers so quiet and self-effacing that the world nearly missed it. The landmark experiment was reported by Jerry Hall at a meeting of the American Fertility Society in Montreal three weeks ago. Afterward, colleagues came up to congratulate him and say "Nice job." Others voted to give his paper, written with his supervisor, Dr. Robert Stillman, the conference's first prize. But nobody seemed to want to pursue the one fact that made his little experiment—in which he started with 17 microscopic embryos and multiplied them like the Bible's loaves and fishes into 48— different from anything that had preceded it. Hall flew back to George Washington University, where he is director of the in-vitro lab and where Stillman heads the entire in-vitro fertilization program, reassured that people would view his work as he saw it: a modest scientific advance that might someday prove useful for treating certain types of infertility.

How wrong he was. When the story broke last week—on the front page of the New York *Times* under the headline SCIEN-

Do you think human cloning is a good thing?

Yes	14%
No	75%

Would you like to have been a clone?

Yes	6%
No	86%

From a telephone poll of 500 adult Americans, taken for TIME/CNN on Oct. 28 by Yankelovich Partners Inc. Sampling error is + 4.5%.

TIST CLONES HUMAN EMBRYOS, AND CRE-ATES AN ETHICAL CHALLENGE—everybody focused on the one thing the scientists seemed willing to overlook: the cells Hall had manipulated came not from plants or pigs or rabbits or cows, but from human beings.

Once it was out, the news that human embryos had been cloned flew around the world with the speed of sound bites bouncing off satellites. That afternoon the switch-board at George Washington logged 250 calls from the press. By the next day more calls and faxes were flooding in from as far away as Spain, Sweden, South Africa

and Australia. A spokesman for the Japan Medical Association found the experiment "unthinkable." French President François Mitterrand pronounced himself "horrified." The Vatican's *L'Osservatore Romano* warned in a front-page editorial that such procedures could lead humanity down "a tunnel of madness."

It was the start of the fiercest scientific debate about medical ethics since the birth of the first test-tube baby 15 years ago. A line had been crossed. A taboo broken. A Brave New World of cookie-cutter humans, baked and bred to order, seemed, if not just around the corner, then just over the horizon. Ethicists called up nightmare visions of baby farming, of clones cannibalized for spare parts. Policymakers pointed to the vacuum in U.S. bioethical leadership. Critics decried the commercialization of fertility technology, and protesters took to the streets, calling for an immediate ban on human-embryo cloning. Scientists steeled themselves against a backlash they feared would obstruct a promising field of research—and close off options to the infertile couples the original experiment had intended to serve.

Indeed, the results of a TIME/CNN poll taken last week suggest that Americans find the idea of human cloning deeply troubling: 3 out of 4 disapprove. A substantial

40% would put a temporary halt on research, and 46% would favor a law making it a crime to clone a human being.

THE EXPERIMENT AT THE center of the controversy seems, in many ways, unworthy of the hoopla. It is not the *Jurassic Park*-type cloning most people think of, in which genetic material from a mature individual—or DNA from an extinct dinosaur—is nurtured and grown into a living replica of the original. This is far beyond the reach of today's science. There is a vast difference between cloning an embryo that is made up of immature, undifferentiated cells and cloning adult cells that have already committed themselves to becoming skin or bone or blood. All cells contain within their DNA the information required to reproduce the entire organism, but in adult cells ac-

---

If you conceived a child, might you be interested in cloning the embryo?

Yes	7%
No	90%

---

cess to parts of that information has somehow been switched off. Scientists do not yet know how to switch it back on.

Nor does the Hall-Stillman experiment involve genetic engineering—the cutting and splicing procedures by which DNA strands within the nuclei of cells are mixed and matched. In one kind of genetic engineering, scientists have inserted human genes into the DNA of bacteria in order to mass-produce insulin and other human proteins. They have also experimented with therapies that involve replacing genes in human patients who either lack those genes or whose genes are defective. The George Washington research required none of that. The cells were just copied with their genes intact—a far simpler process. Simple enough, in fact, that agricultural researchers have used it to clone embryos from cattle, pigs and other animals for more than a decade.

What brought the research into the human arena was the rapidly developing field of in-vitro fertilization. In clinics popping up around the world, couples who have trouble conceiving can have their sperm and eggs mixed in a Petri dish—and the resulting embryos transferred to the mother's womb. The process is distressingly hit-or-miss, though, and the odds of a successful pregnancy go up with the number of embryos used. In a typical in-vitro procedure, doctors will

insert three to five embryos in hopes that, at most, one or two will implant.

But some couples cannot produce more than one embryo, perhaps because the man's semen is in short supply or the woman's ovaries are running out of eggs or do not respond well to hormone treatments designed to stimulate them into superovulating (producing large numbers of eggs on demand). A woman with only one embryo has about a 10% to 20% chance of getting pregnant through in-vitro fertilization. If that embryo could be cloned and turned into three or four, the chances of a successful pregnancy would increase significantly.

This is the reason Hall and Stillman began experimenting with cloning. But they weren't trying, in their initial effort, to produce clones that would actually be implanted in their mothers and later born. The scientists said they just wanted to take the first step toward determining if cloning is as feasible in humans as it is in cattle. Working in George Washington's in-vitro fertilization clinic, they selected embryos that were abnormal because they came from eggs that had been fertilized by more than one sperm; these flawed embryos were destined for an early death whether or not they were implanted. Thus Hall and Stillman saw nothing unethical about experimenting with them, and they got permission to do so from the university.

When one of those single-celled embryos divided into two cells, the first step in development, the scientists quickly separated the cells, creating two different embryos with the same genetic information. (This sometimes happens naturally inside a mother, and the result is identical twins.) In the process, though, the researchers had to strip away an outer coating, called the zona pellucida, that is essential to development. Then came the trickiest part of the procedure. Over the years, Hall had been working with a gel derived from seaweed that could serve as a substitute for the zona pellucida. When Hall put the artificial coating around the cloned embryos, they began to grow and develop. The experiment was a success.

Do you think medical research on cloning should be allowed to continue?

Allowed to continue	19%
Temporary halt	40%
Banned	37%

The scientists replicated their procedure many times, producing 48 clones in all. That was the entire experiment. None of the clones grew for more than six days. The scientists had no intention of starting an embryo factory, selling babies or doing anything else that ethicists worry about.

In fact, Hall and Stillman were totally taken aback by the furor they created. TIME correspondent Ann Blackman asked Hall if he feared that his work would create a backlash against this kind of research. "I revere human life," said Hall, his voice choking with emotion. "I respect people's concerns and feelings. But we have not created human life or destroyed human life in this experiment." To Hall and Stillman, human cloning is simply the next step in the logical progression that started with in-vitro fertilization and is driven by a desire to relieve human suffering—in this case, the suffering of infertile couples.

That is certainly the least controversial of the technology's potential applications. In the TIME/CNN poll, Americans were evenly split on whether they approved or disapproved of cloning for this purpose. If it works—and that is still a big if—it could probably find a market among infertility patients who have tried everything else. "It's pretty scary," said Barbara Tilden, a 39-year-old Illinois woman who has gone through eight different infertility treatments in the past 10 years. "But I'd probably consider it as a desperate last attempt."

Arthur Caplan, director of the Center for Bioethics at the University of Minnesota, could conjure up several equally defensible ways in which cloning human embryos might be medically appropriate. Suppose, for example, a woman knew she was about to become sterile, either because of chemotherapy or through exposure to toxic substances. She might consider having an embryo cloned for future use. Or suppose a couple knew that their children had a chance of inheriting hemophilia or cystic fibrosis. Researchers have developed DNA-analysis techniques to screen embryos for such disorders, but the procedures require snipping cells off embryos, a process that sometimes kills them. In such situations, having a couple of extra clones around could mean the difference between passing on a defective gene or giving birth to a perfectly healthy child.

Even these uses of cloning are fraught with ethical difficulties—not the least of which is the assumption that a defective embryo will be discarded, an action that most right-to-life advocates equate with murder. Medical ethicists have worried for some time that advances in reproductive technology in the U.S. are proceeding in an ethical vacuum, one created not by the technology but by the politics of abortion. "Congress and our state legislatures

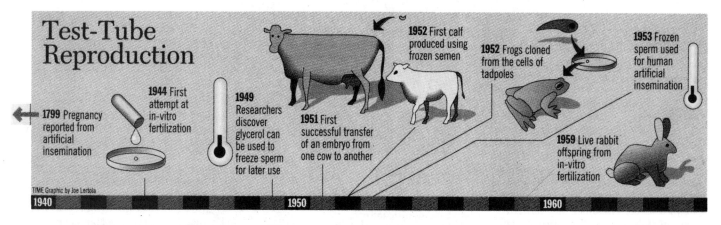

Test-Tube Reproduction

1799 Pregnancy reported from artificial insemination

1944 First attempt at in-vitro fertilization

1949 Researchers discover glycerol can be used to freeze sperm for later use

1951 First successful transfer of an embryo from one cow to another

1952 First calf produced using frozen semen

1952 Frogs cloned from the cells of tadpoles

1953 Frozen sperm used for human artificial insemination

1959 Live rabbit offspring from in-vitro fertilization

TIME Graphic by Joe Lertola

1940   1950   1960

are fearful of anything that gets them near the abortion debate," complained Caplan. "As a result, we have had no systematic discussion of surrogacy, of what to do with frozen embryos when parents die, of who can operate a fertility clinic. And we have had no systematic discussion of cloning."

As soon as Caplan heard the news from the American Fertility Society meeting, he phoned Gina Kolata, the reporter at the New York *Times* who broke the story. As a result, Caplan helped shape the discussion that followed. For example, although Hall's technique cannot produce more than two or three clones of any embryo, several stories written about his experiment included the scenario, put forward by Caplan and other ethicists, in which an infertility clinic offers prospective parents a catalog filled with children's photographs. Below each

the child could be replaced with a genetic equivalent. If another required a bone marrow or kidney transplant, a donor could be thawed and raised with tissues that are guaranteed to be 100% compatible. Or what if the couple just feels like having a third child that is more like their daughter than their son? By thawing out the corresponding embryo they could have a second daughter who would be a twin of the first, only several years younger. A couple for whom money was no object could give birth to the same child every few years. A woman could even give birth to her *own* twin, provided her parents had the foresight to preserve a clone of the embryo that produced her.

ONE DOESN'T HAVE TO BE AN ethicist to see the difficulties these situations could create. All parents know how hard it is to separate what they think a child ought to be from what he or she actually is. That difficulty would be compounded—for both the parent and the child—if an exact template for what that child could become in 10 or 20 years were before them in the form of an older sibling. "I think we have a right to our own individual genetic identity," said Daniel Callahan, director of the Hastings Center, an ethics-research organization in Briarcliff Manor, New York. "I think this could well violate that right."

Do you think human cloning is morally wrong?

Yes	58%
No	31%

Do you think it is against God's will?

Yes	63%
No	26%

picture is a report on the child's academic and social achievement. Couples could choose from among the pictures, receive a frozen embryo, and then raise that child—not a sibling or near relative—but an exact genetic duplicate.

Or what about the couple that sets aside, as a matter of course, a clone of each of their children? If one of them died,

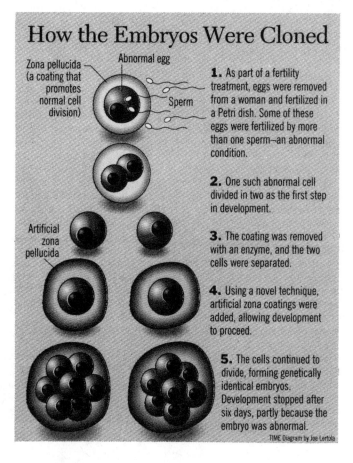

How the Embryos Were Cloned

Zona pellucida (a coating that promotes normal cell division)

Abnormal egg

Sperm

Artificial zona pellucida

1. As part of a fertility treatment, eggs were removed from a woman and fertilized in a Petri dish. Some of these eggs were fertilized by more than one sperm—an abnormal condition.

2. One such abnormal cell divided in two as the first step in development.

3. The coating was removed with an enzyme, and the two cells were separated.

4. Using a novel technique, artificial zona coatings were added, allowing development to proceed.

5. The cells continued to divide, forming genetically identical embryos. Development stopped after six days, partly because the embryo was abnormal.

TIME Diagram by Joe Lertola

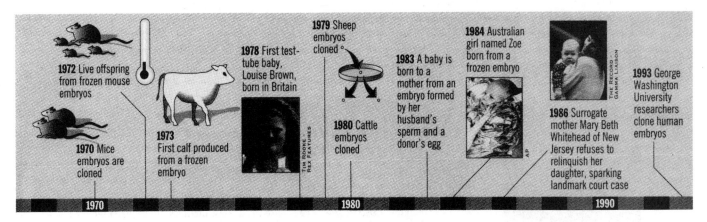

1972 Live offspring from frozen mouse embryos

1970 Mice embryos are cloned

1973 First calf produced from a frozen embryo

1978 First test-tube baby, Louise Brown, born in Britain

TIM ROOKE - REX FEATURES

1979 Sheep embryos cloned

1980 Cattle embryos cloned

1983 A baby is born to a mother from an embryo formed by her husband's sperm and a donor's egg

1984 Australian girl named Zoe born from a frozen embryo

AP

1986 Surrogate mother Mary Beth Whitehead of New Jersey refuses to relinquish her daughter, sparking landmark court case

THE RECORD - GAMMA LIAISON

1993 George Washington University researchers clone human embryos

1970   1980   1990

Many of the uses envisioned for cloning are not particularly farfetched compared with things that are already happening. A few years ago, a California couple made a remarkable decision when faced with the news that their daughter was dying of leukemia. The father braved a vasectomy reversal and the mother a pregnancy at 43 to have a new child born for the express purpose of providing the bone-marrow transplant that saved the older child's life.

Husband and wives who have been through in-vitro fertilization with some embryos left over have had to wrestle with the fact that they have a potential human being stored on ice. There are already 10,000 frozen embryos floating around in liquid-nitrogen baths in the U.S., stuck in a kind of icy limbo as their would-be parents sort out the options. Do they let the embryos thaw out and die? Do they give them away? Do they have the right to sell embryos to the highest bidder? And who gets custody—or the cash—in a divorce?

When the profit motive enters into the equation, ethical considerations tend to be forgotten. And private profit drives the infertility business in the U.S. "We are one of the few countries in the world where you can sell sperm and eggs," said George Annas, a medical ethicist at Boston University. There are already catalogs that list the characteristics of sperm donors—including one made up of Nobel prizewinners. Without regulation, it will only be a matter of time, said Annas, before some entrepreneur tries to market embryos derived from Michael Jordan or Cindy Crawford.

"This is the dawn of the eugenics era," declared Jeremy Rifkin, founder of the Foundation on Economic Trends, a biotechnology-watchdog group in Washington. Painting a dark picture of "standardized human beings produced in whatever quantity you want, in an assembly-line procedure," Rifkin organized protests last week outside George Washington University and other reproductive-research institutions.

They Clone Cattle, Don't They?

Want to peek into a crystal ball and glimpse at the future of cloning? One way might be to look at the livestock industry, the proving ground for reproductive technology. More than a decade has passed since the first calves, lambs and piglets were cloned, and yet there are no dairy herds composed of carbon-copy cows, no pigpens filled with identical sows. While copying particular strains of valuable plants such as corn and canola has become an indispensable tool of modern agriculture, cloning farm animals, feasible as it may be, has never become widespread. Even simple embryo splitting, the technique used by the George Washington University researchers on human cells, is too expensive and complicated to take off commercially. "Cloning," says George Seidel, an animal physiologist at Colorado State University, "remains very much a niche technology."

But people have certainly tried to turn livestock cloning into a booming branch of agribusiness, and they're still trying. Wisconsin-American Breeders Service, a subsidiary of W. R. Grace & Co., now owns the rights to cattle-cloning technology developed by Granada Biosciences, a once high-flying biotech firm that went out of business in 1992. The process calls for single cells to be separated from a growing calf embryo. Each cell is then injected into an unfertilized egg and implanted in the womb of a surrogate cow. Because the nucleus of the unfertilized egg is removed beforehand, it contains no genetic material that might interfere with the development of the embryo. In theory, then, it ought to be possible to extract a 32-cell embryo from a prize dairy cow and use it to produce 32 identical calves, each brought to term by a less valuable member of the herd. In practice, however, only 20% of the cloned embryos survive, meaning that instead of 32 calves, researchers generally end up with only five or six.

While the success rate may improve, at present this method of cloning does not seem much better than embryo splitting, which typically produces twins and sometimes triplets. There have been other problems as well. Some of the calves produced have weighed so much at birth that they have had to be delivered through caesarean section. Scientists aren't sure what causes this phenomenon, but they know that ranchers wouldn't appreciate the expense of having to deliver some calves with surgery. Says Carol Keefer, an embryologist at American Breeders Service: "There is so much to learn about cattle yet."

When cattle cloning is perfected, it may not be welcomed down on the farm. Idaho dairyman Kurt Alberti, for instance, isn't so sure he wants to clone the offspring of prizewinning cows like his Twinkie, even though she was the American Jersey Cattle Club's top milk producer last year and her calves fetch handsome prices on the auction block. Using cloning to create large numbers of identical calves runs counter to what breeders strive to do. Alberti wants to create cows even better than Twinkie, and the only way to do that is by constantly reshuffling the genetic deck with a fresh supply of genes. Indeed, rather than a major advance in livestock breeding, cloning taken to extremes could prove to be the exact opposite—a big step, all right, but in the wrong direction.

—By J. Madeleine Nash/Chicago

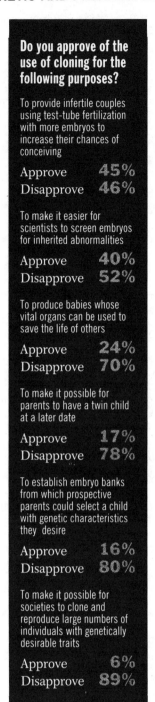

Do you approve of the use of cloning for the following purposes?

To provide infertile couples using test-tube fertilization with more embryos to increase their chances of conceiving

Approve 45%
Disapprove 46%

To make it easier for scientists to screen embryos for inherited abnormalities

Approve 40%
Disapprove 52%

To produce babies whose vital organs can be used to save the life of others

Approve 24%
Disapprove 70%

To make it possible for parents to have a twin child at a later date

Approve 17%
Disapprove 78%

To establish embryo banks from which prospective parents could select a child with genetic characteristics they desire

Approve 16%
Disapprove 80%

To make it possible for societies to clone and reproduce large numbers of individuals with genetically desirable traits

Approve 6%
Disapprove 89%

Cloning Classics

When it comes to dealing with cloning, ethicists and science-fiction writers have almost indistinguishable job descriptions. Both groups propose hypothetical situations in which cloning might happen, then examine the likely implications. The only real difference is that ethicists respect the laws of plausibility and won't waste much time on scenarios that probably won't ever come to pass. Science-fiction writers trash those same laws with creative gusto.

The result has been a relentless stream of outrageous books, movies and television shows, beginning with Aldous Huxley's *Brave New World,* published 61 years ago, and continuing through the summer's box-office behemoth, *Jurassic park.* There are mysteries, thrillers, love stories—even a sci-fi parody of an old pop song ("Weird Al" Yankovic's *I Think I'm a Clone Now,* sung to the tune of Tommy James and the Shondell's *I Think We're Alone Now*). Cloning, in fact, has been a fertile enough subject to earn its own lengthy entry in the *Encyclopedia of Science Fiction.*

Freed from the anchor of realism, fiction writers have drifted off in all sorts of strange directions. Huxley's idea was that cloning based on embryo splitting (he called it "bokanovskification") would be used to mass-produce drones for performing menial labor. Huxley's Gammas, Deltas and Epsilons were separated from the higher-class Alphas and Betas not just by economic status but also by biologically engineered physical and intellectual traits.

A different vision of cloning, involving not just the splitting of embryos but the generation of an entire human from a bit of tissue, leads down another fanciful path: re-creating a specific person. In Ben Bova's novel *Multiple Man* (1976), several exact copies of the U.S. President are found dead and no one is certain whether a clone or the real McCoy sits in the Oval Office. In Nancy Freedman's 1973 book *Joshua, Son of None,* the clone is a real President, John F. Kennedy. And Ira Levin's 1976 novel (later a movie), *The Boys from Brazil,* imagines neo-Nazis cloning a batch of Hitlers; luckily the conspirators' failure to duplicate precisely the real Hitler's upbringing leaves the ersatz Führers imperfectly evil.

If cloning became common, then sex—along with male and female genders—would be unnecessary. That's the conceit of books such as Charles Eric Maine's *World Without Men* (1958) and Poul Anderson's *Virgin Planet* (1959). Conversely, cloning might be a device for preserving love. The 1991 British TV miniseries *The Cloning of Joanna May,* based on a Fay Weldon novel, is about a man who dumps his unfaithful wife—but only after cloning her so he can replace her with her twin a few years down the line.

There is one aspect of cloning, though, that writers have largely overlooked: its potential for laughs. The most obvious exception to that rule is Woody Allen in *Sleeper.* The high point of the film comes when Allen's character kidnaps the severed nose of a Big Brother–like dictator before it can be cloned to oppress the world once more, and holds it hostage at gunpoint. It's hard, though intriguing, to imagine what ethicists would do with that one.

—By Michael D. Lemonick.
Reported by David Bjerklie/New York

Rifkin, however, was the exception. Few people seemed to be thinking of the *Brave New World* visions in which a totalitarian government creates whole subclasses of clones designed expressly for particular tasks. As Annas pointed out, there are better ways to create a crack Navy SEAL team or an astronaut corps than to clone the appropriate mix of sperm and egg and wait 20 years. "Maybe if this were Nazi Germany, we would worry more about the government," said Annas. "But we're in America, where we have the private market. We don't need government to make the nightmare scenario come true."

Most people seemed to respond to the idea of human cloning at a more fundamental level. In the TIME/CNN poll, 58% said they thought cloning was morally wrong, while 63% said they believed it was against God's will. "It's not that anyone thinks there is a commandment 'Thou shalt not clone,'" said Margaret O'Brien Steinfels of *Commonweal* magazine. "But there are limits to what humans ought to be thinking about doing." For many, the basic sanctity of human life seemed to be under attack, and it made them angry. "The people doing this ought to contemplate splitting themselves in half and see how they like it," said Germain Grisez, a professor of Christian ethics in Mount Saint Mary's College in Emmitsburg, Maryland.

The reaction from around the world was, in many ways, even more heated. "This is not research," snapped Dr. Jean-François Mattei of Timone Hospital in Marseilles, France. "It's aberrant, showing a lack of a sense of reality and respect for people." In Germany, Professor Hans-

Bernhard Wuermeling, a medical ethicist at the University of Erlangen, was equally repelled by the notion of producing clones for spare parts, calling it "a modern form of slavery."

German officials were quick to point out that the experiment Hall and Stillman conducted—cloning a human embryo—would be considered a federal offense in Germany, punishable by up to five years in prison. "The Americans do not even have our scruples," complained Rudolf Dressler, deputy whip of the Social Democratic opposition in the Bundestag. "They simply go ahead with research, cost what it may." More than 25 countries have commissions that set policy on reproductive technology. In Britain, cloning human cells requires a license the governing body refuses to grant. Violators face up to 10 years in prison. In Japan all research on human cloning is prohibited by guidelines that in the country's highly conformist society have the force of law.

Should the U.S. adopt similar restrictions? That may be difficult at this point. Such research is usually controlled indirectly through the federal purse strings: the government simply cuts off funding to projects Congress finds offensive. But that wouldn't work in this case since there is no federal funding for embryo research; experiments are financed largely by private money, much of it derived from the booming business of in-vitro fertilization.

MAKING MATTERS EVEN more complicated, there is no federal body charged with setting artificial-fertilization policy in the U.S. The last congressional commission empowered to debate the new technology was disbanded in 1990. Instead, policy is set by a patchwork of state laws, professional societies and local review boards, like the one at George Washington that gave the go-ahead to Hall and Stillman.

Two weeks ago, a report by the congressional Office of Technology Assessment presciently recommended that the government step in. In the past, bioethical policy could have been addressed by any one of a series of federal boards. Perhaps the best was a presidential commission established under President Carter that developed broad policy guidelines on some of the most controversial issues in medicine, such as deciding when brain death has occurred or when it is ethically correct for a doctor to withhold treatment. The commission was disbanded in 1983. Last week's debate made it likely that some kind of national board will be established during President Clinton's watch. It had better be done quickly. Hall told TIME that his technique could produce human clones within "a minimum of a couple of years."

Sensing a shift in the regulatory wind, many reproductive scientists wished aloud that the cloning issue had never been raised—or at least not in this way. "[Hall and Stillman] haven't done science or medicine any favors," said Dr. Marilyn Monk, a researcher at London's Institute of Child Health. Dr. Leeanda Wilton, director of embryology at Australia's Monash IVF Center, where much of the in-vitro fertilization technology was developed, said there were hundreds of scientists who could have split an embryo in half, just the way Hall and Stillman did. "They haven't done so because it opens a can of worms," she said.

Hall and Stillman discovered this, to their dismay, in the glare of publicity. At an impromptu press conference the evening the story broke, and in subsequent appearances on *Nightline, Good Morning America* and *Larry King Live,* the bewildered scientists tried to keep the discussion focused on the facts of their experiment: that the embryos were defective, that they were never implanted, and that they could never have grown into living humans. Instead they had to field questions from callers like the one who wondered if their technique could be used to put a lion's head on a horse's body.

Having set the terms of the debate—which focused not on what had actually happened but on the frightening scenarios that could arise sometime in the future—the ethicists clearly carried the day. Hall and Stillman retreated to the last refuge of the research scientist. "We have set out to provide some basic information," said an exasperated Hall on *Larry King.* "It's up to the ethicists and the medical community, with input from the general public, to decide what kind of guidelines will lead us in the future."

But that stance may not be adequate in the years to come, as genetic engineering and cloning begin to converge. It is becoming increasingly apparent to the researchers exploring these frontiers that they have to become ethicists as well as scientists. Technology tends to develop a momentum of its own. The time to discuss whether it is right or wrong is before it has been put to use, not after.

—Reported by David Bjerklie/ New York, Ann Blackman/Washington, Jeanne McDowell/Los Angeles and J. Madeleine Nash/ Chicago

Choosing a Perfect Child

Brave new technology is allowing us to look at tiny preembryonic 8-cell clusters and decide which ones are healthy enough to be allowed to develop into babies.

Ricki Lewis

Ricki Lewis is the author of Life, *a college biology text, and has just written a human genetics text. She is a genetic counselor and an adjunct assistant professor at SUNY Albany and Miami University, where she has taught human genetics and bioethics courses. She has published hundreds of articles for both laymen and scientists.*

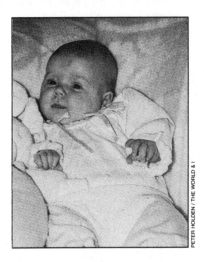

PETER HOLDEN / THE WORLD & I

Chloe O'Brien, who celebrates her first birthday this month, is a very wanted child, perhaps more so than most. When she was a mere ball of cells, smaller than the smallest speck of sand, a test determined that she would be free of the cystic fibrosis genes that each of her parents carries. Chloe-to-be, along with another ball of cells (a potential twin), was implanted into her mother's uterus. Only one of the two balls of cells, Chloe-to-be, survived the rigors of prenatal development, and Chloe today is a healthy little girl.

The O'Briens had already had a child who suffered from the stiflingly thick mucus clogging the lungs that is a hallmark of cystic fibrosis, the most common genetic disease among Caucasians. They wanted to spare their future children this fate—but they also wanted to avoid having to end a pregnancy that would yield an affected child.

"Previously, couples had to wait from 9 to 15 weeks [after conception] to find out if their developing baby was affected by a known genetic disease. Now, we can diagnose these inherited diseases within three days after an egg is fertilized in the laboratory, before it is transferred back to the woman," says Mark Hughes of the Baylor College of Medicine in Houston. Hughes, along with John Lesko, also of Baylor, and Alan Handyside, Robert Winston, and Juan Tarin, of Hammersmith Hospital in London, reported the preimplantation diagnosis of cystic fibrosis in September 1992 in the *New England Journal of Medicine.*

The preimplantation genetic diagnosis that confirmed Chloe to be free of the cystic fibrosis gene is built primarily on three existing technologies: in vitro fertil-ization (IVF); gene amplification, a way to rapidly copy a single gene from a single cell; and gene probing, which detects the gene responsible for the disorder. The latter two interventions are performed on the 8-cell "preembryo."

Few couples have so far had their preembryos examined for genetic problems, and the high costs of the procedure will likely keep the numbers down. However, with the rapid progress being made by the Human Genome Project in identifying genes associated with specific genetic disorders, preembryos in the future may be scrutinized for a wider range of diseases, from rare inherited ailments to the more common heart disease and cancer.

Is a brave new world of mechanized reproduction upon us? To understand how we may someday pick and choose the traits of our children, we must understand the procedures that serve as a backdrop to preimplantation genetic diagnosis.

Prenatal diagnosis—the state of the art

A generation ago, pregnancy was shrouded in secrecy. A woman would discover her expectant state in the second or third month and announce it in the fourth month, when most risk of miscarriage was past. Today, pregnancy is marked by a series of medical tests providing prenatal peeks into the health of the child-to-be.

The most familiar prenatal test is amniocentesis, a procedure in which a needle is inserted into the amniotic sac cushioning a fetus and a small amount of fluid is withdrawn. The fluid contains a few fetal cells, whose nuclei contain the rod-shaped chromosomes, which consist of the genes. If examination reveals missing or extra chromosomes, the fetus is likely to develop into a baby with a serious syndrome.

Today, amniocentesis is a rite of passage for pregnant women over age 35, because at that age the chance of the fetus having a chromosomal problem about equals the risk of amniocentesis causing miscarriage (1 in 200). (The risk of abnormal fetal chromosomes increases with maternal age.)

The major limitation of amniocentesis is that it is performed in the 16th week of pregnancy. By then the fetus is quite well developed. If a chromosome abnormality is detected, the parents are faced with an agonizing choice: either terminate the pregnancy or prepare for the birth of a physically or mentally challenged child.

An alternative to amniocentesis is chorionic villus sampling (CVS), which also examines fetal chromosomes. This procedure can be performed earlier, usually between weeks 8 and 10. The fetus is far smaller and less well developed, about the size and weight of a paper clip, making the decision to end the pregnancy somewhat easier.

CVS was pioneered in China in the 1970s and became available in the United States only in the mid-1980s. Though the World Health Organization endorsed CVS in 1984, it also suggested

The biological basis of preimplantation genetic diagnosis is that all the cells of an individual have the same genes.

that ways be found to diagnose genetic disease earlier, perhaps before the preembryo implants in the uterus. This occurs on the 6th day after sperm meets egg.

The biological basis of preimplantation genetic diagnosis is that all the cells of an individual have the same genes no matter what the stage of development. In principle, the techniques used to examine the genetic material of cells obtained through amniocentesis or CVS should work for cells obtained at other stages of prenatal development, even at the preembryonic stage.

Screening genes

An individual gene in a preembryo's cell can be identified through a technique invented in 1985, the polymerase chain reaction (PCR).

In PCR an enzyme, DNA polymerase, that is essential to the multiplication of DNA in every cell in the body, selectively multiplies only the DNA from the gene of interest. If that gene is present in the original genetic sample being tested it will be rapidly mass-produced in a test tube. If the gene of interest is not present, then it won't be multiplied by the PCR.

If PCR of a single cell from the 8-cell preembryo results in many copies of the target DNA sequence, then the disease-causing gene is there—as happened to a few of Chloe's potential siblings who were not implanted. If the DNA is not amplified, then the sequence of interest is not there. When the cell from 8-cell Chloe-to-be failed its PCR test, it meant that the 7-cell preembryo could develop into a cystic fibrosis-free baby.

The first experiments using PCR to identify preembryos free of a genetic disease took place in 1989 and 1990 in Hammersmith Hospital. Handyside and his team screened preembryos from couples in which the mothers carried a variety of conditions, called X-linked conditions, that occur mostly in males. X-linked conditions are caused by genes on the X chromosome. Since females have two X chromosomes, and males have one X and one Y chromosome, a male preembryo with a Y chromosome and an X chromosome bearing a disease-causing gene would be destined to have the X-linked condition. By using PCR to amplify a DNA sequence unique to the Y chromosome, Handyside's team could choose a female preembryo that could not inherit the disease carried by the mother. The disorders avoided thanks to early attempts at preimplantation genetic diagnosis include adrenoleukodystrophy, a nervous system degeneration that is lethal in early childhood; Lesch-Nyhan syndrome, in which the profoundly retarded child mutilates himself; and other forms of mental retardation.

In August 1992 Jamie Grifo and colleagues at New York Hospital–Cornell Medical Center reported the first child born in the United States after successful blastomere biopsy and genetic testing to avoid X-linked hemophilia.

Candidates for preimplantation genetic diagnosis

Preimplantation genetic diagnosis is a promising option for couples who know that their children are at a high risk for inheriting a certain disease.

According to the laws of inheritance, parents who both carry the same disorder not on the X chromosome, but on one of the other 22 chromosomes, can conceive children who inherit either two normal genes, or two abnormal genes, or, like the parents, one normal and one abnormal gene. The probability of inheriting two of the same gene, either normal or abnormal, is 1 in 4. The probability of being a carrier like the parents with one normal and one abnormal gene is 1 in 2.

Chloe's parents, for example, each have one disease-causing copy of the cystic fibrosis gene, and one normal copy. Thus there

is a 1 in 4 chance that a child conceived by them will suffer with cystic fibrosis.

The mechanics of preimplantation diagnosis

A human preembryo can be obtained in two ways—it can be flushed out of the uterus after being conceived in the normal manner, in which case it is more than 8 cells, or it can be nurtured from an egg fertilized by a sperm in a laboratory dish, the technique of in vitro fertilization (IVF). The first IVF or "test tube baby," Louise Joy Brown, was born in England in 1978, and has since been followed by thousands of other such children.

IVF is now a fairly routine, if difficult and costly, procedure, with hundreds of facilities providing it in the United States alone, and hundreds of others elsewhere. For the IVF procedure, the woman is given pergonal, a drug that causes the ovary to ripen more than one egg at a

time. Eggs, which **appear as** small bulges in the ovarian lining, are harvested by inserting a laparoscope, a tiny, illuminated telescopelike device, through an incision made near the woman's navel.

The eggs are placed with sperm donated by the man into a laboratory dish, along with other chemicals that simulate the environment in the woman's body. If all goes well, sperm and egg meet and merge. Extra fertilized eggs are frozen and saved in case they are needed later.

On the third day after fertilization comes the blastomere biopsy. The 8-cell, or 8-blastomere, preembryo is immobilized with a holding pipette (a narrow glass tube). Then a single blastomere is removed from the preembryo by exposing the target cell to a stream of acid and gently prodding it with a second, smaller pipette.

The next step is to thoroughly clean the blastomere, because PCR, the gene amplification part

■ In blastomere biopsy, as shown left to right in the sequence below, the 8-cell preembryo is held by one pipette while another narrower one is used to capture a single blastomere, which is used for genetic testing; the remaining seven cells can continue to develop normally. (Magnification 330x)

COURTESY JUAN COTA / BAYLOR COLLEGE OF MEDICINE

Genetic Disease Diagnosis Before Fertilization

The time when we can probe a prenatal human's genes is creeping ever earlier, from the 16-week peek permitted with amniocentesis, to the 8–10-week scrutiny of chorionic villus sampling, to preimplantation genetic diagnosis of an 8-celled, 2–3-day-old preembryo. Yet another technique on the horizon, called polar body removal, may reveal the genetic makeup of an egg before it is fertilized.

In the first step of a two-step cell division that produces an egg with 23 chromosomes, division of the 46-chromosome progenitor germ cell distributes 23 chromosomes to each of the two daughter cells. But one cell, destined to develop into the egg, receives the lion's share of nutrients and other cell components, while the other, called the first polar body, is deprived and scrawny by comparison. The egg and its first polar body are stuck together in the ovary.

If the woman is a carrier for a genetic disease, when the chromosomes are divvied up

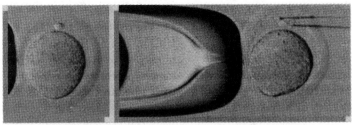

REPRINTED FROM *PREIMPLANTATION DIAGNOSIS OF GENETIC DISEASES*, EDITED BY Y. VERLINSKY AND A.M. KULIEV, COPYRIGHT © 1992, BY PERMISSION OF WILEY-LISS, A DIVISION OF JOHN WILEY AND SONS, INC.

■ *Left:* **Diagnosing a genetic disease before fertilization relies on the fact that each egg shares the mother's divided genetic material with a much smaller companion, called the polar body.** *Right:* **In polar body biopsy, as shown here, the egg is held by the large pipette while the polar body is captured by drawing it into the smaller pipette. (Magnification 188x)**

between the polar body and the egg, one normal gene goes to one, and the disease-causing gene to the other. So, if the polar body is examined and found to have the disease-causing gene, then it can be inferred that the corresponding egg does not. That egg can then be fertilized in the lab.

Polar body removal has been tested for more than three years at the Reproductive Genetics Institute of the Illinois Masonic Center in Chicago, yielding one pregnancy that spontaneously aborted due to

incidental chromosomal abnormality. So far a dozen couples have undergone the procedure, for such conditions as cystic fibrosis, hemophilia A, and Duchenne muscular dystrophy, but none has delivered a child.

Researchers are not sure why PBR's track record has so far been so poor. Perhaps the intervention is harming the egg, or perhaps it is just allowing us to see previously unknown ways that development can go awry.

—R.L.

of the process, can give a false genetic diagnosis if even one stray sperm happens to be clinging to the blastomere. When the blastomere is clean, it is broken open by a series of temperature changes to expose and disentangle the DNA. The PCR evaluation is then used to determine if the disease-causing gene is present.

After the blastomere biopsy and PCR, one or two preembryos that have passed the genetic test are implanted into the woman. If pregnancy occurs, human chorionic gonadotropin (hCG), the "pregnancy hormone," appears in the woman's blood and urine by the 14th day. By the fourth week,

an ultrasound exam will show a small, oval area in the uterus. This is the sac containing the embryo.

What we can do versus what we should do

At this time, the two biggest drawbacks to preimplantation genetic diagnosis are the low efficiency and high cost of IVF. In 1990, the American Fertility Society surveyed IVF clinics and found a 14 percent "take-home baby rate." However, Yury Verlinsky, director of the Reproductive Genetics Institute of the Illinois Masonic Medical Center in

Chicago, and Anver Kuliev, director of the research/cell bank at the same facility, point out that the typical couple seeking IVF has fertility problems and tends to be older, whereas couples seeking IVF as a prelude to preimplantation genetic diagnosis would be younger and more fertile.

The cost is out of reach for many. "The average cost of IVF is $7,000-8,000," says James Douglas of the Trinity Medical Center in Carrollton, Texas. Blastomere biopsy plus PCR can add another $2,000—all for a procedure that may have to be repeated.

Although physicians who perform IVF are excited about the value of preimplantation diagnosis for couples whose offspring are at high risk for genetic disease, they are nevertheless pessimistic about the technology's general utility. This is because once the procedure grows beyond its research stage, it will be prohibitively expensive. And even though there are expectations that automating some of the steps could bring the price down, these developments are on the far horizon.

Also, as Margaret Wallace, assistant professor in the genetics division at the University of Florida in Gainesville, points out, there is the problem of the "slippery slope"—who decides that a disorder is awful enough to intervene to prevent a birth? In 1990, she discovered the gene behind neurofibromatosis (NF1), another common inherited illness. NF1 presents a sticky problem—finding the responsible gene does not indicate how severely an individual may be affected. Manifestations of NF1 can range from a few brown spots on the body to thousands of tumors just beneath the skin.

"Blastomere biopsy is being performed only at a few IVF centers that are associated with a major medical teaching facility."

So far, the diseases detected by preimplantation genetic diagnosis cause extreme suffering to very young children, and the goal is prevention. "But for preimplantation diagnosis of some less devastating disorders, some physicians and insurers might not think it is ethical" to choose against implanting a diagnosed preembryo, says Wallace.

Another factor that may stifle development of preimplantation genetic diagnosis is that treatments for some genetic disorders are being developed so rapidly that selecting out affected preembryos may become obsolete before the technology can be perfected. "Cystic fibrosis research is moving so quickly that some may say, who cares who is born with it? We can treat them," says Wallace.

For now, preimplantation genetic diagnosis remains highly experimental. "Blastomere biopsy is being performed only at a few IVF centers that are associated with a major medical teaching facility," says Douglas.

However, Verlinsky and Kuliev predict that, once the success stories accumulate and the price drops, preimplantation genetic diagnosis will be offered at a few fetal medicine centers, where teams of embryo experts, molecular biologists, geneticists, and obstetricians will perform genetic tests that will grow ever more numerous as the trek through the human genome nears completion.

Although clearly not yet suitable for the general public, preimplantation genetic diagnosis will allow certain couples to avoid what was once their genetic fate—passing on a disease. And so Chloe O'Brien is today what Louise Joy Brown was to the world 15 years ago—a medical pioneer, after whom many will follow.

TRENDS IN BEHAVIORAL GENETICS

EUGENICS REVISITED

Scientists are linking genes to a host of complex human disorders and traits, but just how valid—and useful—are these findings?

John Horgan, *senior writer*

"How to Tell If Your Child's a Serial Killer!" That was the sound bite with which the television show *Donahue* sought to entice listeners February 25. On the program, a psychiatrist from the Rochester, N.Y., area noted that some men are born with not one Y chromosome but two. Double-Y men, the psychiatrist said, are "at special risk for antisocial, violent behavior." In fact, the psychiatrist had recently studied such a man. Although he had grown up in a "Norman Rockwell" setting, as an adult he had strangled at least 11 women and two children.

"It is not hysterical or overstating it," Phil Donahue told his horrified audience, "to say that we are moving toward the time when, quite literally, just as we can anticipate . . . genetic predispositions toward various physical diseases, we will also be able to pinpoint mental disorders which include aggression, antisocial behavior and the possibility of very serious criminal activity later on."

Eugenics is back in fashion. The message that genetics can explain, predict and even modify human behavior for the betterment of society is promulgated not just on sensationalistic talk shows but by our most prominent scientists. James D. Watson, co-discoverer of the double-helix structure of DNA and former head of the Human Genome Project, the massive effort to map our entire genetic endowment, said recently, "We used to think that our fate was in our stars. Now we know, in large part, that our fate is in our genes."

Daniel E. Koshland, Jr., a biologist at the University of California at Berkeley and editor of *Science*, the most influential peer-reviewed journal in the U.S., has declared in an editorial that the nature/nurture debate is "basically over," since scientists have shown that genes influence many aspects of human behavior. He has also contended that genetic research may help eliminate society's most intractable problems, including drug abuse, homelessness and, yes, violent crime.

Some studies cited to back this claim are remarkably similar to those conducted over a century ago by scientists such as Francis Galton, known as the father of eugenics. Just as the British polymath studied identical twins in order to show that "nature prevails enormously over nurture," so do modern researchers. But the primary reason behind the revival of eugenics is the astonishing successes of biologists in mapping and manipulating the human genome. Over the past decade, investigators have identified genes underlying such crippling diseases as cystic fibrosis, muscular dystrophy and, this past spring, Huntington's disease. Given these advances, researchers say, it is only a matter of time before they can lay bare the genetic foundation of much more complex traits and disorders.

The political base for eugenics has also become considerably broader in recent years. Spokespersons for the mentally ill believe demonstrating the genetic basis of disorders such as schizophrenia and manic depression—and even alcoholism and drug addiction—will lead not only to better diagnoses and

treatments but also to more compassion toward sufferers and their families. Some homosexuals believe society will become more tolerant toward them if it can be shown that sexual orientation is an innate, biological condition and not a matter of choice.

But critics contend that no good can come of bad science. Far from moving inexorably closer to its goals, they point out, the field of behavioral genetics is mired in the same problems that have always plagued it. Behavioral traits are extraordinarily difficult to define, and practically every claim of a genetic basis can also be explained as an environmental effect. "This has been a huge enterprise, and for the most part the work has been done shoddily. Even careful people get sucked into misinterpreting data," says Jonathan Beckwith, a geneticist at Harvard University. He adds, "There are social consequences to this."

The skeptics also accuse the media of having created an unrealistically optimistic view of the field. Richard C. Lewontin, a biologist at Harvard and a prominent critic of behavioral genetics, contends that the media generally give much more prominent coverage to dramatic reports—such as the discovery of an "alcoholism gene"—than to contradictory results or retractions. "Skepticism doesn't make the news," Lewontin says. "It only makes the news when you find a gene." The result is that spurious findings often become accepted by the public and even by so-called experts.

The claim that men with an extra Y chromosome are predisposed toward violence is a case in point. It stems from a survey in the 1960s that found more extra-Y men in prison than in the general population. Some researchers hypothesized that since the Y chromo-

"EERIE" PARALLELS between identical twins raised apart—such as Jerry Levey (*left*) and Mark Newman, who both became firefighters—are said to support genetic models of human behavior. Yet skeptics say the significance of such coincidences has been exaggerated.

some confers male attributes, men with an extra Y become hyperaggressive "supermales." Follow-up studies indicated that while extra-Y men tend to be taller than other men and score slightly lower on intelligence tests, they are otherwise normal. The National Academy of Sciences concluded in a report published this year that there is no evidence to support the link between the extra Y chromosome and violent behavior.

Minnesota Twins

No research in behavioral genetics has been more eagerly embraced by the press than the identical-twin studies done at the University of Minnesota. Thomas J. Bouchard, Jr., a psychologist, initiated them in the late 1970s, and since then they have been featured in the *Washington Post, Newsweek,* the *New York Times* and other publications worldwide as well as on television. *Science* has favorably described the Minnesota team's work in several news stories and in 1990 published a major article by the group.

The workers have studied more than 50 pairs of identical twins who were separated shortly after birth and raised in different households. The assump-

tion is that any differences between identical twins, who share all each other's genes, are caused by the environment; similarities are attributed to their shared genes. The group estimates the relative contribution of genes to a given trait in a term called "heritability." A trait that stems entirely from genes, such as eye color, is defined as 100 percent heritable. Height is 90 percent heritable; that is, 90 percent of the variation in height is accounted for by genetic variation, and the other 10 percent is accounted for by diet and other environmental factors.

The Minnesota group has reported finding a strong genetic contribution to practically all the traits it has examined. Whereas most previous studies have estimated the heritability of intelligence (as defined by performance on intelligence tests) as roughly 50 percent, Bouchard and his colleagues arrived at a figure of 70 percent. They have also found a genetic component underlying such culturally defined traits as religiosity, political orientation (conservative versus liberal), job satisfaction, leisure-time interests and proneness to divorce. In fact, the group concluded in *Science,* "On multiple measures of personality and temperament...monozy-

gotic twins reared apart are about as similar as are monozygotic twins reared together." (Identical twins are called monozygotic because they stem from a single fertilized egg, or zygote.)

The researchers have buttressed their statistical findings with anecdotes about "eerie," "bewitching" and "remarkable" parallels between reunited twins. One case involved Oskar, who was raised as a Nazi in Czechoslovakia, and Jack, who was raised as a Jew in Trinidad. Both were reportedly wearing shirts with epaulets when they were reunited by the Minnesota group in 1979. They also both flushed the toilet before as well as after using it and enjoyed deliberately sneezing to startle people in elevators.

Some other celebrated cases involved two British women who wore seven rings and named their firstborn sons Richard Andrew and Andrew Richard; two men who both had been named Jim, named their pet dogs Toy, married women named Linda, divorced them and remarried women named Betty; and two men who had become firefighters and drank Budweiser beer.

Other twin researchers say the significance of these coincidences has been greatly exaggerated. Richard J. Rose of Indiana University, who is collaborating on a study of 16,000 pairs of twins in Finland, points out that "if you bring together strangers who were born on the same day in the same country and ask them to find similarities between them, you may find a lot of seemingly astounding coincidences."

Rose's collaborator, Jaakko Kaprio of the University of Helsinki, notes that the Minnesota twin studies may also be biased by their selection method. Whereas he and Rose gather data by combing birth registries and sending questionnaires to those identified as twins, the Minnesota group relies heavily on media coverage to recruit new twins. The twins then come to Minnesota for a week of study—and, often, further publicity. Twins who are "interested in publicity and willing to support it," Kaprio says, may be atypical. This self-selection effect, he adds, may explain why the Bouchard group's estimates of heritability tend to be higher than those of other studies.

One of the most outspoken critics of

the Minnesota twin studies—and indeed all twin studies indicating high heritability of behavioral traits—is Leon J. Kamin, a psychologist at Northeastern University. In the 1970s Kamin helped to expose inconsistencies and possible fraud in studies of separated identical twins conducted by the British psychologist Cyril Burt during the previous two decades. Burt's conclusion that intelligence was mostly inherited had inspired various observers, notably Arthur R. Jensen, a psychologist at the University of California at Berkeley, to argue that socioeconomic stratification in the U.S. is largely a genetic phenomenon.

In his investigations of other twin studies, Kamin has shown that identical twins supposedly raised apart are often raised by members of their family or by unrelated families in the same neighborhood; some twins had extensive contact with each other while growing up. Kamin suspects the same may be true of some Minnesota twins. He notes, for example, that some news accounts suggested Oskar and Jack (the Nazi and the Jew) and the two British women wearing seven rings were reunited for the first time when they arrived in Minnesota to be studied by Bouchard. Actually, both pairs of twins had met previously. Kamin has repeatedly asked the Minnesota group for detailed case histories of its twins to determine whether it has underestimated contact and similarities in upbringing. "They've never responded," he says.

Kamin proposes that the Minnesota twins have particularly strong motives to downplay previous contacts and to exaggerate their similarities. They might want to please researchers, to attract more attention from the media or even to make money. In fact, some twins acquired agents and were paid for appearances on television. Jack and Oskar recently sold their life story to a film producer in Los Angeles (who says Robert Duvall is interested in the roles).

Even the Minnesota researchers caution against overinterpretation of their work. They agree with their critics that high heritability should not be equated with inevitability, since the environment can still drastically affect the expression of a gene. For example, the genetic disease phenylketonuria, which causes profound retardation, has a heritability of 100 percent. Yet eliminating the amino acid phenylalanine from the diet of affected persons prevents retardation from occurring.

Such warnings tend to be minimized in media coverage, however. Writers often make the same inference that Koshland did in an editorial in *Science:* "Bet-

ter schools, a better environment, better counseling and better rehabilitation will help some individuals but not all." The prime minister of Singapore apparently reached the same conclusion. A decade ago he cited popular accounts of the Minnesota research in defending policies that encouraged middle-class Singaporeans to bear children and discouraged childbearing by the poor.

Smart Genes

Twin studies, of course, do not indicate which specific genes contribute to a trait. Early in the 1980s scientists began developing powerful ways to unearth that information. The techniques stem from the fact that certain stretches of human DNA, called polymorphisms, vary in a predictable way. If a polymorphism is consistently inherited together with a given trait—blue eyes, for example—then geneticists assume it either lies near a gene for that trait or actually is the gene. A polymorphism that merely lies near a gene is known as a marker.

In so-called linkage studies, investigators search for polymorphisms co-inherited with a trait in families unusually prone to the trait. In 1983 researchers used this method to find a marker linked to Huntington's disease, a crippling neurological disorder that usually strikes carriers in middle age and kills them within 10 years. Since then, the same technique has pinpointed genes for cystic fibrosis, muscular dystrophy and other diseases. In association studies, researchers compare the relative frequency of polymorphisms in two unrelated populations, one with the trait and one lacking it.

Workers are already using both methods to search for polymorphisms associated with intelligence, defined as the ability to score well on standardized intelligence tests. In 1991 Shelley D. Smith of the Boys Town National Institute for Communication Disorders in Children, in Omaha, and David W. Fulker of the University of Colorado identified polymorphisms associated with dyslexia in a linkage study of 19 families exhibiting high incidence of the reading disorder.

Behavioral Genetics: A Lack-of-Progress Report

CRIME: Family, twin and adoption studies have suggested a heritability of 0 to more than 50 percent for predisposition to crime. (Heritability represents the degree to which a trait stems from genetic factors.) In the 1960s researchers reported an association between an extra Y chromosome and violent crime in males. Follow-up studies found that association to be spurious.

MANIC DEPRESSION: Twin and family studies indicate heritability of 60 to 80 percent for susceptibility to manic depression. In 1987 two groups reported locating different genes linked to manic depression, one in Amish families and the other in Israeli families. Both reports have been retracted.

SCHIZOPHRENIA: Twin studies show heritability of 40 to 90 percent. In 1988 a group reported finding a gene linked to schizophrenia in British and Icelandic families. Other studies documented no linkage, and the initial claim has now been retracted.

ALCOHOLISM: Twin and adoption studies suggest heritability ranging from 0 to 60 percent. In 1990 a group claimed to link a gene—one that produces a receptor for the neurotransmitter dopamine—with alcoholism. A recent review of the evidence concluded it does not support a link.

INTELLIGENCE: Twin and adoption studies show a heritability of performance on intelligence tests of 20 to 80 percent. One group recently unveiled preliminary evidence for genetic markers for high intelligence (an IQ of 130 or higher). The study is unpublished.

HOMOSEXUALITY: In 1991 a researcher cited anatomic differences between the brains of heterosexual and homosexual males. Two recent twin studies have found a heritability of roughly 50 percent for predisposition to male or female homosexuality. These reports have been disputed. Another group claims to have preliminary evidence of genes linked to male homosexuality. The data have not been published.

Two years ago Robert Plomin, a psychologist at Pennsylvania State University who has long been active in behavioral genetics, received a $600,000 grant from the National Institute of Child Health and Human Development to search for genes linked to high intelligence. Plomin is using the association method, which he says is more suited than the linkage technique to identifying genes whose contribution to a trait is relatively small. Plomin is studying a group of 64 schoolchildren 12 to 13 years old who fall into three groups: those who score approximately 130, 100 and 80 on intelligence tests.

Plomin has examined some 25 polymorphisms in each of these three groups, trying to determine whether any occur with greater frequency in the "bright" children. The polymorphisms have been linked to genes thought to have neurological effects. He has uncovered several markers that seem to occur more often in the highest-scoring children. He is now seeking to replicate his results in another group of 60 children; half score above 142 on intelligence tests, and half score less than 74 (yet have no obvious organic deficiencies). Plomin presented his preliminary findings at a meeting, titled "Origins and Development of High Ability," held in London in January.

At the same meeting, however, other workers offered evidence that intelligence tests are actually poor predictors of success in business, the arts or even advanced academic programs. Indeed, even Plomin seems ambivalent about the value of his research. He suggests that someday genetic information on the cognitive abilities of children might help teachers design lessons that are more suited to students' innate strengths and weaknesses.

But he also calls his approach "a fishing expedition," given that a large number of genes may contribute to intelligence. He thinks the heritability of intelligence is not 70 percent, as the Minnesota twin researchers have claimed, but 50 percent, which is the average finding of other studies, and at best he can only find a gene that accounts for a tiny part of variance in intelligence. "If you wanted to select on the basis of this, it would be of no use whatsoever," he remarks. These cautions did not prevent the *Sunday Telegraph*, a London newspaper, from announcing that Plomin had found "evidence that geniuses are born not made."

Evan S. Balaban, a biologist at Harvard, thinks Plomin's fishing expedition is doomed to fail. He grants that there may well be a significant genetic compo-

The Huntington's Disease Saga: A Cautionary Tale

The identification of the gene for Huntington's disease, which was announced in March, was hailed as one of the great success stories of modern genetics. Yet it provides some rather sobering lessons for researchers seeking genes linked to more complex human disorders and traits.

The story begins in the late 1970s, when workers developed novel techniques for identifying polymorphisms, sections of the human genome that come in two or more forms. Investigators realized that by finding polymorphisms linked—always and exclusively—to diseases, they could determine which chromosome the gene resides in. Researchers decided to test the polymorphism technique on Huntington's disease, a devastating neurological disorder that affects roughly one in 10,000 people. Scientists had known for more than a century that Huntington's was caused by a mutant, dominant gene. If one parent has the disease, his or her offspring have a 50 percent chance of inheriting it.

One of the leaders of the Huntington's effort was Nancy Wexler, a neuropsychologist at Columbia University whose mother had died of the disease and who therefore has a 50 percent chance of developing it herself. She and other researchers focused on a poor Venezuelan village whose inhabitants had an unusually high incidence of the disease. In 1983, through what has now become a legendary stroke of good fortune, they found a linkage with one of the first polymorphisms they tested. The linkage indicated that the gene for Huntington's disease was somewhere on chromosome 4.

The finding led quickly to a test for determining whether offspring of carriers—either in utero or already born—have inherited the gene itself. The test requires an analysis of blood samples from several members of a family known to carry the disease. Wexler herself has declined to say whether she has taken the test.

Researchers assumed that they would quickly identify the actual gene in chromosome 4 that causes Huntington's disease. Yet it took 10 years for six teams of workers from 10 institutions to find the gene. It is a so-called expanding gene, which for unknown reasons gains base pairs (the chemical "rungs" binding two strands of DNA) every time it is transmitted. The greater the expansion of the gene, researchers say, the earlier the onset of the disease. The search was complicated by the fact that workers had no physical clues about the course of the disease to guide them. Indeed, Wexler and others emphasize that they still have no idea how the gene actually causes the disease; treatments or cures may be years or decades away.

The most immediate impact of the new discovery will be the development of a better test for Huntington's, one that requires blood only from the person at risk

nent to intelligence (while insisting that studies by Bouchard and others have not demonstrated one). But he doubts whether investigators will ever uncover any specific genes related to high intelligence or "genius." "It is very rare to find genes that have a specific effect," he says. "For evolutionary reasons, this just doesn't happen very often."

The history of the search for markers associated with mental illness supports Balaban's view. Over the past few decades, studies of twins, families and adoptees have convinced most investigators that schizophrenia and manic depression are not caused by psychosocial factors—such as the notorious "schizophrenogenic mother" postulated by some Freudian psychiatrists—but by biological and genetic factors. After observing the dramatic success of linkage studies in the early 1980s, researchers immediately began using the technique to isolate polymorphic markers for mental illness. The potential value

of such research was enormous, given that schizophrenia and manic depression each affect roughly one percent of the global population.

They seemed to have achieved their first great success in 1987. A group led by Janice A. Egeland of the University of Miami School of Medicine claimed it had linked a genetic marker on chromosome 11 to manic depression in an Amish population. That same year another team, led by Miron Baron of Columbia University, linked a marker on the X chromosome to manic depression in three Israeli families.

The media hailed these announcements as major breakthroughs. Far less attention was paid to the retractions that followed. A more extensive analysis of the Amish in 1989 by a group from the National Institute of Mental Health turned up no link between chromosome 11 and manic depression. This year Baron's team retracted its claim of linkage with the X chromosome after

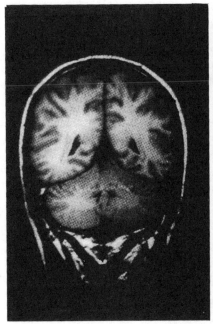
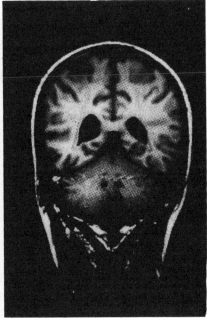

NANCY WEXLER helped to find the gene responsible for Huntington's disease by studying a population in Venezuela that has been ravaged by the disorder.

and not other family members. By measuring the length of the mutant gene, the test might also predict more accurately when carriers will show symptoms.

As difficult as it was to pinpoint the gene for Huntington's, it will be almost infinitely harder to discover genes for behavioral disorders, says Evan S. Balaban, a biologist at Harvard University. Unlike Huntington's disease, he notes, disorders such as schizophrenia and alcoholism cannot be unambiguously diagnosed. Furthermore, they stem not from a single dominant gene but from many genes acting in concert with environmental effects. If researchers do find a statistical association between certain genes and a trait, Balaban says, that knowledge may never be translated into useful therapies or tests. "What does it mean to have a 10 percent increased risk of alcoholism?" he asks.

doing a new study of its Israeli families with more sophisticated markers and more extensive diagnoses.

Schizophrenic Results

Studies of schizophrenia have followed a remarkably similar course. In 1988 a group headed by Hugh M. D. Gurling of the University College, London, Medical School announced in *Nature* that it had found linkage in Icelandic and British families between genetic markers on chromosome 5 and schizophrenia. In the same issue, however, researchers led by Kenneth K. Kidd of Yale University reported seeing no such linkage in a Swedish family. Although

BRAIN OF SCHIZOPHRENIC (*right*) appears different from the brain of his identical twin in these magnetic resonance images. Such findings suggest that factors that are biological but not genetic—such as viruses—may play a significant role in mental illness.

Gurling defended his result as legitimate for several years, additional research has convinced him that it was probably a false positive. "The new families showed no linkage at all," he says.

These disappointments have highlighted the problems involved in using linkage to study mental illness. Neil Risch, a geneticist at Yale, points out that linkage analysis is ideal for studying diseases, such as Huntington's, that have distinct symptoms and are caused by a single dominant gene. Some researchers had hoped that at least certain subtypes of schizophrenia or manic depression might be single-gene disorders. Single-gene mutations are thought to cause variants of breast cancer and of Alzheimer's disease that run in families and are manifested much earlier than usual. But such diseases are rare, Risch says, because natural selection quickly winnows them out of the population, and no evidence exists for distinct subtypes of manic depression or schizophrenia.

Indeed, all the available evidence suggests that schizophrenia and manic depression are caused by at least several genes—each of which may exert only a tiny influence—acting in concert with environmental influences. Finding such genes with linkage analysis may not be impossible, Risch says, but it will be considerably more difficult than identifying genes that have a one-to-one correspondence to a trait. The difficulty is compounded by the fact that the diagnosis of mental illness is often subjective—all the more so when researchers are relying on family records or recollections.

Some experts now question whether genes play a significant role in mental illness. "Personally, I think we have overestimated the genetic component of schizophrenia," says E. Fuller Torrey, a psychiatrist at St. Elizabeth's Hospital in Washington, D.C. He argues that the evidence supporting genetic models can be explained by other biological factors, such as a virus that strikes in utero. The pattern of incidence of schizophrenia in families often resembles that of other viral diseases, such as polio. "Genes may just create a susceptibility to the virus," Torrey explains.

The Drink Link

Even Kidd, the Yale geneticist who has devoted his career to searching for genes linked to mental illness, acknowledges that "in a rigorous, technical, scientific sense, there is very little proof that schizophrenia, manic depression" and other psychiatric disorders have a genetic origin. "Virtually all the evidence supports a genetic explanation, but there are always other explanations, even if they are convoluted."

The evidence for a genetic basis for alcoholism is even more tentative than that for manic depression and schizophrenia. Although some studies discern a genetic component, especially in males, others have reached the opposite conclusion. Gurling, the University College investigator, found a decade ago that identical twins were slightly *more* likely to be discordant for alcoholism than fraternal twins. The drinking habits of some identical twins were strikingly different. "In some cases, one drank a few bottles a day, and the other didn't drink at all," Gurling says.

Nevertheless, in 1990 a group led by Kenneth Blum of the University of Texas Health Science Center at San Antonio announced it had discovered a genetic marker for alcoholism in an association study comparing 35 alcoholics with a control group of 35 nonalcoholics. A page-one story in the *New York Times* portrayed the research as a potential watershed in the diagnosis and treatment of alcoholism without mentioning the considerable skepticism aroused among other researchers.

The Blum group claimed that its marker, called the A1 allele, was associated with a gene, called the D2 gene, that codes for a receptor for the neurotransmitter dopamine. Skeptics noted that the A1 allele was actually some 10,000 base pairs from the dopamine-receptor gene and was not linked to any detectable variation in its expression.

Since the initial announcement by Blum, three papers, including an addi-

tional one by Blum's group, have presented more evidence of an association between the A1 allele and alcoholism. Six groups have found no such evidence (and received virtually no mention in the popular media).

In April, Risch and Joel Gelernter of Yale and David Goldman of the National Institute on Alcohol Abuse and Alcoholism analyzed all these studies on the A1 allele in a paper in the *Journal of the American Medical Association*. They noted that if Blum's two studies are cast aside, the balance of the results shows no association between the D2 receptor and alcoholism, either in the disorder's milder or most severe forms. "We therefore conclude that no physiologically significant association" between the A1 allele and alcoholism has been proved, the group stated. "It's a dead issue," Risch says.

Gelernter and his colleagues point out that association studies are prone to spurious results if not properly controlled. They suggest that the positive findings of Blum and his colleagues may have derived from a failure to control for ethnic variation. The limited surveys done so far have shown that the incidence of the A1 allele varies wildly in different ethnic groups, ranging from 10 percent in certain Jewish groups to about 50 percent in Japanese.

Blum insists that the ethnic data, far from undermining his case, support it, since those groups with the highest prevalence of the A1 allele also exhibit the highest rates of "addictive behavior." He contends that the only reason the Japanese do not display higher rates of alcoholism is that many also carry a gene that prevents them from metabolizing alcohol. "They're pretty compulsive," explains Blum, who recently obtained a patent for a genetic test for alcoholism.

These arguments have been rejected even by Irving I. Gottesman of the University of Virginia, who is a strong defender of genetic models of human behavior. He considers the papers cited by Blum to support his case to be ambiguous and even contradictory. Some see an association only with alcoholism that leads to medical complications or even death; others discern no association with alcoholism but only with "polysubstance abuse," including cigarette smoking. "I think it is by and large garbage," Gottesman says of the alleged A1-alcoholism link.

By far the most controversial area of behavioral genetics is research on crime. Last fall complaints by civil-rights leaders and others led the National Institutes of Health to withdraw its funding

from a meeting entitled "Genetic Factors in Crime: Findings, Uses and Implications." The conference brochure had noted the "apparent failure of environmental approaches to crime" and suggested that genetic research might yield methods for identifying and treating potential criminals—and particularly those prone to violence—at an early age.

Critics contend that such investigations inevitably suggest that blacks are predisposed to crime, given that blacks in the U.S. are six times more likely than whites to be arrested for a violent crime. In fact, some prominent scientists, notably Richard J. Herrnstein, a psychologist at Harvard, have made this assertion. Others reject this view but insist biological research on attributes linked to violent crime, such as aggression, may still have some value. "People who are unwilling to address genetic and biochemical factors are just putting their heads in the sand," says Goldman, the alcoholism expert. "It is not fair to say that just because there have been geneticists who have had a very narrow view of this in the past, we shouldn't explore this now."

In fact, investigations of the biology of violent crime continue, albeit quietly. Workers at City of Hope Hospital in Duarte, Calif., claim to have found an association between the A1 allele—the alleged alcoholism marker—and "criminal aggression." Last year a group led by Markus J. P. Kruesi of the University of Illinois at Chicago presented evidence of an association between low levels of the neurotransmitter serotonin and disruptive-behavior disorders in children. Kruesi concedes there is no way to determine whether the serotonin levels are genetically influenced. In fact, the serotonin levels might be an effect—a reaction to an environmental trauma—rather than a cause. "This might be a scar marker," he says.

One reason such research persists is that studies of families, twins and adoptees have suggested a genetic component to crime. Glenn D. Walters, a psychologist at the Federal Correctional Institution in Schuylkill, Pa., recently reviewed 38 of these studies, conducted from the 1930s to the present, in the journal *Criminology*. His meta-analysis turned up a small genetic effect, "but nothing to get excited about." He observes that "a lot of the research has not been very good" and that the more recent, better-designed studies tended to turn up less evidence. "I don't think we will find any biological markers for crime," he says. "We should put our resources elsewhere."

"Better Breeding"

Fairly or not, modern genetics research is still haunted by the history of eugenics. "It offers a lot of cautionary lessons," says Daniel J. Kevles, a historian at the California Institute of Technology, who wrote the 1985 book *In the Name of Eugenics*. The British scientist Francis Galton, cousin to Charles Darwin, first proposed that human society could be improved "through better breeding" in 1865 in an article entitled "Hereditary Talent and Character." He coined the term "eugenics," from the Greek for "good birth," in 1883.

Galton's proposal had broad appeal. The American sexual libertarian John Humphrey Noyes bent eugenics into an ingenious argument for polygamy. "While the good man will be limited by his conscience to what the law allows," Noyes said, "the bad man, free from moral check, will distribute his seed beyond the legal limit."

A more serious advocate was the biologist Charles B. Davenport, founder of Cold Spring Harbor Laboratory and of the Eugenics Record Office, which gathered information on thousands of American families for genetic research. After demonstrating the heritability of eye, skin and hair color, Davenport went on to "prove" the heritability of traits such as "pauperism," criminality and "feeble-mindedness." In one monograph, published in 1919, he asserted that the ability to be a naval officer is an inherited trait, composed of subtraits for thalassophilia, or love of the sea, and hyperkineticism, or wanderlust. Noting the paucity of female naval officers, Davenport concluded that the trait is unique to males.

Beginning in the 1920s the American Eugenics Society, founded by Davenport and others, sponsored "Fitter Families Contests" at state fairs around the U.S. Just as cows and sheep were appraised by judges at the fairs, so were human entrants (such as the family shown above at the 1925 Texas State Fair). Less amusingly, eugenicists helped to persuade more than 20 U.S. states to authorize sterilization of men and women in prisons and mental hospitals, and they urged the federal government to restrict the immigration of "undesirable" races.

No nation, of course, practiced eugenics as enthusiastically as Nazi Germany, whose program culminated in "euthanasia" ("good death") of the mentally and physically disabled as well as Jews, Gypsies, Catholics and others. As revelations of these atrocities spread after World War II, popular support for eugenics programs waned in the U.S. and elsewhere.

Gay Genes

The ostensible purpose of investigations of mental illness, alcoholism and even crime is to reduce their incidence. Scientists studying homosexuality have a different goal: simply to test whether homosexuality is innate, as many homosexuals have long professed. That claim was advanced by a report in *Science* in 1991 by Simon LeVay of the Salk Institute for Biological Studies in San Diego. LeVay has acknowledged both that he is gay and that he believes evidence of biological differences between homosexuals and heterosexuals will encourage tolerance toward gays.

LeVay, who recently left the Salk Institute to found the Institute of Gay and Lesbian Education, focused on a tiny neural structure in the hypothalamus, a region of the brain known to control sexual response. He measured this structure, called the interstitial nucleus, in autopsies of the brains of 19 homosexual males, 16 heterosexual males and six heterosexual women. LeVay found that the interstitial nucleus was almost twice as large in the heterosexual males as in the homosexual males or in the women. He postulated that the interstitial nucleus "is large in individuals oriented toward women"—whether male or female.

Of course, LeVay's finding only addresses anatomic differences, not necessarily genetic ones. Various other researchers have tried to establish that homosexuality is not just biological in its origin—caused, perhaps, by hormonal influences in utero—but also genetic. Some have sought evidence in experiments with rats and other animals. A group headed by Angela Pattatucci of the National Cancer Institute is studying a strain of male fruit flies—which wags have dubbed either "fruity" or "fruitless"—that court other males.

In December 1991 J. Michael Bailey of Northwestern University and Richard C. Pillard of Boston University announced they had uncovered evidence of a genetic basis for male homosexuality in humans. They studied 161 gay men, each of whom had at least one identical or fraternal twin or adopted brother. The researchers determined that 52 percent of the identical twins were both homosexual, as compared with 22 percent of the fraternal twins and 11 percent of the adopted brothers.

Bailey and Pillard derived similar results in a study of lesbians published this year in the *Archives of General Psychiatry*. They compared 147 gay women with identical or fraternal twins or adopted sisters: 48 percent of the identical twins were both gay, versus 16 percent of the fraternal twins (who share only half each other's genes) and 6 percent of the adopted sisters. "Both male and female sexual orientation appeared to be influenced by genetic factors," Bailey and Pillard concluded.

This conclusion has disturbed some of Bailey and Pillard's own subjects. "I have major questions about the validity of some of the assumptions they are making," says Nina Sossen, a gay woman living in Madison, Wis., whose identical twin is heterosexual. Her doubts are shared by William Byne, a psychiatrist at Columbia University. He notes that in their study of male homosexuality Bailey and Pillard found more concordance between unrelated, adopted brothers than related (but non-twin) brothers. The high concordance of the male and female identical twins, moreover, may stem from the fact that such twins are often dressed alike and treated alike—indeed, they are often mistaken for each other—by family members as well as by others.

"The increased concordance for homosexuality among the identical twins could be entirely accounted for by the increased similarity of their developmental experiences," Byne says. "In my opinion, the major finding of that study is that 48 percent of identical twins who were reared together were discordant for sexual orientation."

Byne also criticizes LeVay's conclusion that homosexuality must be biological—although not necessarily genetic—because the brains of male homosexuals resemble the brains of women. That assumption, Byne points out, rests on still another assumption, that there are significant anatomic differences between heterosexual male and female brains. But to date, there have been no replicable studies showing such sexual dimorphism.

Byne notes that he has been suspected of having an antigay motive. Two reviewers of an article he recently wrote criticizing homosexuality research accused him of having a "right-wing agenda," he says. He has also been contacted by conservative groups hoping he will speak out against the admittance of homosexuals to the military. He emphasizes that he supports gay rights and thinks homosexuality, whatever its cause, is not a "choice." He adds that genetic models of behavior are just as likely to foment bigotry as to quell it.

"Hierarchy of Worthlessness"

Despite the skepticism of Byne and others, at least one group, led by Dean Hamer of the National Cancer Institute, is searching not merely for anatomic or biochemical differences in homosexuals but for genetic markers. Hamer has done a linkage study of numerous small families, each of which has at least two gay brothers. He says his study has turned up some tentative findings, and he plans to submit his results soon. Hamer's colleague Pattatucci is planning a similar study of lesbians.

What purpose will be served by pinpointing genes linked to homosexuality? In an information sheet for prospective participants in his study, Hamer expresses the hope that his research may "improve understanding between people with different sexual orientations." He adds, "This study is not aimed at developing methods to alter either heterosexual or homosexual orientation, and the results of the study will not allow sexual orientation to be determined by a blood test or amniocentesis."

Yet even Pillard, who is gay and applauds Hamer's work, admits to some concern over the potential uses of a genetic marker for homosexuality. He notes that some parents might choose to abort embryos carrying such a marker. Male and female homosexuals might then retaliate, he says, by conceiving children and aborting fetuses that lacked such a gene.

Balaban, the Harvard biologist, thinks the possible dangers of such research—assuming it is successful—outweigh any benefits. Indeed, he sees behavioral genetics as a "hierarchy of worthlessness," with twin studies at the bottom and linkage studies of mental illness at the top. The best researchers can hope for is to find, say, a gene associated with a slightly elevated risk of schizophrenia. Such information is more likely to lead

to discrimination by insurance companies and employers than to therapeutic benefits, Balaban warns.

His colleague Lewontin agrees. In the 1970s, he recalls, insurance companies began requiring black customers to take tests for sickle cell anemia, a genetic disease that primarily affects blacks. Those who refused to take the test or who tested positive were denied coverage. "I feel that this research is a substitute for what is really hard—finding out how to change social conditions," Lewontin remarks. "I think it's the wrong direction for research, given that we have a finite amount of resources."

Paul R. Billings, a geneticist at the California Pacific Medical Center, shares some of these concerns. He agrees that twin studies seem to be inherently ambiguous, and he urges researchers seeking markers for homosexuality to consider what a conservative government—led by Patrick Buchanan, for example—might allow to be done with such information. But he believes some aspects of behavioral genetics, particularly searches for genes underlying mental illness, are worth pursuing.

In an article published in the British journal *Social Science and Medicine* last year, Billings and two other scientists offered some constructive criticism for the field. Researchers engaged in association and linkage studies should establish "strict criteria as to what would constitute meaningful data." Both scientists and the press should emphasize the limitations of such studies, "especially when the mechanism of how a gene acts on a behavior is not known." Billings and his colleagues strive to end their article on a positive note. "Despite the shortcomings of other studies," they say, "there is relatively good evidence for a site on the X chromosome which is associated with [manic depression] in some families." This finding was retracted earlier this year.

WHAT CRACK DOES TO BABIES

JANICE HUTCHINSON

Janice Hutchinson is a pediatrician and former senior scientist for the American Medical Association. She is now the medical director of the Child and Youth Services Administration of the District of Columbia Department of Mental Health.

INQUIRING TEACHERS want to know: Who are these kids and how did they get this way? The question refers to the unprecedented numbers of children—estimates range as high as one-half to one million—who are entering the classroom having suffered inutero exposure to cocaine.

Crack, the cooked form of cocaine, became widely available in 1985; the children of the first crack addicts are now in school. Teachers have described them as a new breed, unlike other children with histories of drug exposure. They are often in constant motion, disorganized, and very sensitive to stimuli. Crawling, standing, and walking take longer to develop. They are irritable and hard to please. It is hard for them to make friends. They respond less to the environment. Internal stability is poor. Learning is more difficult. Smiling and eye contact are infrequent. They do not seem to know how to play with toys or with others. And nothing you do for them seems to matter or help.

If teachers are to meet the challenges that these children bring, they may find it helpful to understand the bio-neuro-physiological effects of cocaine on the developing fetus. Scientists are just beginning to understand these effects; research in the area is incomplete and at times conflicting. Thus what we know and what we can speculate about, some of which is summarized below, is just the tip of a rather unknown iceberg. There are surely many more effects—and more complicated avenues of effect—than those so far identified. Nonetheless, there are findings—mainly from research sponsored by the National Institutes of Health and the National Institute on Drug Abuse—that allow us to begin to make some sense of what is happening to the behaviors and learning styles of these children.

IMAGINE THAT a crack molecule has entered the body. It enters into the mucous membranes of the mouth. From there it enters the lungs, where it is absorbed into the bloodstream, and through which it then passes to the heart and, very quickly, to the brain. The immediate effect is an increase in breathing, blood pressure, and heart rate.

Upon arriving in the brain, crack acts at several sites along what is known as the brain's "pleasure pathway"—a collection of sites in the brain that seem in some ways to relate and affect each other. At one point on the pleasure pathway is the limbic system, which is the seat of strong emotional responses, including the very primitive urges to feed, flee, fight, and reproduce. At another point along the pathway is the motor cortex of the brain, which directs the body's movement. Between the limbic system and the motor cortex lies the nucleus accumbens. This is the "attraction center" of the brain; it is what pulls you toward pleasurable activity.

Indications are that crack acts on the fetus precisely the same way it acts on the mother.

The crack is very active here in the nucleus accumbens; a ripple effect then seems to carry the destruction around to other points along the pleasure pathway. With-

From *American Educator,* Spring 1991, pp. 31-32. Reprinted with permission from *American Educator,* the quarterly journal of the American Federation of Teachers.

in the nucleus accumbens, as elsewhere in the brain, are numerous nerve cells; the space between each nerve cell ending is known as the synaptic space. Each of these nerve cells communicates with the others across the synaptic space by sending a variety of neurotransmitters back and forth.

One such neurotransmitter is dopamine. Under normal biological conditions, dopamine, like other neurotransmitters, is continually moving across the synaptic space. In a constantly recurring pattern, the dopamine leaves its home cell, crosses the synaptic space, and reaches receptors on the receiving cell, an action that sends an electrical signal through the receiver cell. The dopamine then disattaches from the receptor cell and returns to its cell of origin where it will be recycled.

But if crack has been ingested, this normal cycle will be disrupted. Crack, upon entering the brain and then the pleasure pathway, seems to settle into the synaptic space between the neurotransmitters. It then acts to prevent the dopamine from returning to its home cell. Unable to return home, the dopamine continues to stimulate the receiver cell until the crack has spent itself and dissipated. It is probably this constant stimulation of the receiver cell that causes the euphoric feeling associated with the first few minutes of cocaine ingestion. But the crack high lasts only a few minutes, after which the user will either replenish his intake or experience an often devastating "low." The constant resupply soon leads to a physical addiction, the breaking of which is accompanied by extremely painful withdrawal symptoms.

WHILE THE crack is acting on the mother's brain, what is happening to the fetus? The crack crosses the placental barrier and heads for the inutero brain. The exact effect of the crack on the fetus will depend on the age of the fetus, the dosage of the crack, and probably on other variables that we have not yet identified. But it seems likely that in general a number of things happen. First, the crack probably acts on the fetal nucleus accumbens in the same way that it acts on the user's, leading the fetus to become highly stimulated and, often, addicted. As it stimulates the nucleus accumbens, and surely in other ways as well, the crack damages fetal brain cells and thus causes neurological damage all along the pleasure pathway and in other nearby parts of the brain.

Damage to brain cells in the limbic system, the nucleus accumbens, and elsewhere along the pleasure pathway would likely impair or alter a wide range of the child's normal emotional responses, including, for example, the ability to respond to pleasurable experiences, to form emotional attachments, or to make certain kinds of judgments. Perhaps this explains in part why the crack baby is often unable to proceed through the normal phases of separation-individuation described by child psychiatrist Margaret Mahler; crack babies appear to experience much greater anxiety and difficulty in leaving their mothers when it is time for school.

In addition, the brain's motor cortex may be damaged, which might explain such effects as the slow development of crawling, standing, and walking. The brain location for speech is also nearby, and damage to it may account for the speech impairments suffered by many crack babies. In turn, the speech impairment inhibits the child's ability to communicate, which may, in turn, account for some of the difficulty these children have in forming relationships.

Children who have been exposed to crack in their prenatal stage require an emotionally supportive and structured atmosphere.

In addition, crack, like nicotine, constricts the adult and fetal arteries, thus slowing the blood—and therefore the oxygen flow—to the fetus and around it. This condition of low oxygenation—known as hypoxia—can also produce brain damage, and it can bring on low birthweight. Low birthweight is, in turn, associated with a wide range of disabling symptoms, including intellectual disabilities.

Reading, mathematics, spelling, handwriting, and the arts are often difficult tasks for low-birthweight babies. Speech and language problems are prominent. Temperamental problems, such as low adaptability, low persistence, and arrhythmicity (for example, the failure to sleep and wake at normal, regular times) may be part of their behavioral style. They typically cry when separated from the mother, have trouble expressing themselves, speak only in short phrases, are very active, and clumsy. Findings to date suggest that temperament influences both behavior and cognition.

These low birthweight children tend to perform poorly on the Mullen Scale of Early Learning. This test, which consists of four scales, suggests the range of learning abilities that seem to be impaired in the children exposed inutero to crack. The Visual Receptive Organization (VRO) scale assesses visual discrimination, short-term memory, visual organization and sequencing, and visual spatial awareness, including position, size, shape, left/right, and detail. The Visual Expressive Organization (VEO) assesses bilateral and unilateral manipulation, writing, visual discrimination, and visual-motor plan and control. The language receptive organization (LRO) scale assesses auditory comprehension, short- and long-term auditory memory, integration of ideas and visual spatial cues, auditory sequencing, and verbal spatial concepts. The language expressive organization (LEO) scale assesses spontaneous and formal verbal ability, language formulation, auditory comprehension, and short- and long-term memory.

What all of this means ultimately is that these low-birthweight crack children experience the world around them in a very different way from other children. Adults, including teachers, are often unaware that these children see and hear their environment in a completely different manner from adults or even other children. What the teacher often does not realize is that this difficult-to-teach, hard-to manage child is processing information in an unusual way that the child does not determine. Hence, conflict and frustration can arise between teacher and student (and also at home between parent and child).

The combined effects of prenatal drug exposure with a home environment that provides little or no nurturance, understanding, or support for the child create a terrible challenge to teachers. But initial experimental programs suggest that these children can benefit greatly from placement in highly structured, highly tailored educational day care settings beginning in early infancy. In four Washington, D.C.-area therapeutic nurseries that provide such care, two-thirds of the children seem so far to have been successfully mainstreamed into first grade.

Among the characteristics that seem to make such programs successful are early identification of the infants and very low student-teacher ratios. The establishment of an emotionally supportive atmosphere and structure is necessary. Teaching must be intense and focal. Tasks should initially be simple and singular. Too many tasks or activities overstimulate these children, and they cannot respond. Teachers must also provide emotional support and form bonds with the children. Success also depends on aggressively approaching and engaging parents in the psychotherapeutic progress. Consultation with mental health professionals may assist teachers, parents, and students. Intellectually limited students may still require individual tutoring; some students will eventually require special education; and very emotionally disturbed students may require a mental health-based psychotherapy program.

But it does seem clear that with early, appropriate interventions many of these children can improve their behavior and academic performance. Like most childhood problems, the time to act is now; later is too late.

WAR BABIES

What happens when mothers-to-be become the victims of starvation? Now three generations after World War II, we are still learning the disturbing answers.

Jared Diamond

Contributing editor Jared Diamond is a professor of physiology at the UCLA School of Medicine. In June he wrote about the search for eternal youth [for Discover*].*

It is easy to write now that each person got 400 calories a day. In practice it was quite another thing. . . . People sought food everywhere in the streets and the surrounding countryside. Anything edible was picked up in this way, and they were lucky who found a potato or two or a handful of greens. . . . People dropped from exhaustion in the streets and many died there. Often people were so fatigued that they were unable to return home, before curfew; so they hid in barns or elsewhere to sleep and there died. . . . Older people, who lacked the strength to go searching for food, stayed at home in bed and died.
—Famine and Human Development: The Dutch Hunger
Winter of 1944–1945

Among the homey images I recall from my wife's pregnancy are the bigger-than-usual milk cartons in the refrigerator and her vitamin bottles on the kitchen counter. To our generation the value of good nutrition for pregnant women seems obvious. But what makes us so sure? After all, we can't run experiments on people to prove it. Starving hundreds of pregnant women and then comparing their kids with well-nourished cousins would be absolutely unthinkable.

Yet such an inhuman experiment was indeed once conducted. By imposing a famine on part of the population of the Netherlands during the last seven months of World War II, the Nazis effectively reduced 40,000 pregnant women to starvation. These cruel circumstances resulted in a study of the effects of prenatal nutrition that was grimly well-designed, complete with a control group: while these women were starving, other mothers-to-be in the same society were eating comparatively healthy rations.

Years later, when the babies who survived had grown into adults, epidemiologists could distinguish the different effects of prenatal and postnatal nutrition; they could even discern the effects of malnutrition at different stages of pregnancy, for at the time the famine took hold, some women were further along in their pregnancy than others. Even now we are still learning what toll was exacted by the events of 45 years ago. Only recently have researchers learned that the famine's effects reached far beyond its immediate victims: now that girls born to the starved Dutch women have grown up and had children of their own, it's become apparent that some of these children too are marked by the deprivations suffered years earlier by their grandmothers!

Today we accept without question that proper nutrition is important for maintaining our health as adults and even more important for the development of our children. The evidence seems most persuasive when we look at the malnourished Third World and see shorter life spans, lowered resistance to disease, and high infant mortalities. But even in the industrialized world we can readily see the positive effects of a good diet. For one thing, today's adults tend to be taller than their parents; the difference approaches six inches in Japan. On average, too, people who are poor, with comparatively limited access to food, are shorter and less healthy than their wealthier countrymen. Moreover, it is not just physical health that seems to be at risk. Many tests of mental function suggest that poor nutrition in childhood may affect learning ability throughout life.

One might speculate that if we are so susceptible to the effects of poor nutrition as children, we must be especially sensitive to those effects while we're still in the womb, when our brain and body are forming. And, indeed, many studies have shown an association between poor nutrition, low weight at birth, and poor physical and mental performance later on. Yet it's not easy to prove that inadequate prenatal nutrition itself is the culprit. Sadly, babies poorly nourished in the womb are likely to be poorly nourished after birth as well. Furthermore, diet may not be the only thing influencing their health. Access to medical care, schooling, and stimulation outside school may play a part.

Figuring out just how big a role prenatal malnutrition plays in this miserable chain of events, then, is difficult at best. But the starvation in the Nazi-occupied Netherlands nearly half a century ago offers some thought-provoking answers.

The Dutch tragedy was the result of one of the most controversial decisions of World War II. After the Allied forces invaded Normandy and liberated France in the summer of 1944, our generals debated two strategies for completing Germany's defeat: to advance northeastward from France into Germany's Ruhr industrial region or to push eastward into the Saar. Had all our resources been concentrated on a single strategy, either might have succeeded. In fact both advances were attempted at once, and both ground to a standstill.

The northern advance hinged on the famous Battle of Arnhem, which inspired the film *A Bridge Too Far*. On September 17, 1944, British paratroops were dropped on the Dutch city of Arnhem to take command of a crucial bridge over the Rhine; other Allied forces, meanwhile, tried to join them from the south. Dutch railroad workers courageously called a general strike to impede the Nazis' efforts to bring up reinforcements. But stiff Nazi resistance forced the Allies to retreat, on September 25, after

heavy losses. The Allies then shifted their military effort away from the Netherlands, most of which remained under German occupation until May 1945.

In retaliation for the Dutch strike an embargo on transport in the Netherlands, including transport of food, was ordered by the notorious Nazi Reichskommissar Seyss-Inquart, later tried and hanged at Nuremberg. The predictable result of the embargo, which began in October 1944, was a famine that became progressively worse as stored food supplies were exhausted and that was not lifted until the Netherlands was liberated the following spring. Because an unusually severe winter hampered relief efforts, the famine became known as the Dutch Hunger Winter.

Intake dropped as low as 400 calories a day, down from an already-reduced daily ration of 1,500 calories. Still, some people were better off than others. The hunger was milder in the farming regions of the north and south; it was most severe in the large industrial cities of the west, such as Amsterdam, Rotterdam, and The Hague. Those people with enough strength went to the countryside to seek food, including tulip bulbs, in the fields. The hunger was also somewhat selective by social class: people of higher socioeconomic status were able to use money, property, and influence to obtain additional food.

Altogether 10,000 people starved to death, and malnutrition contributed to the deaths of countless others. Adults in the famine cities who survived lost, on average, 15 to 20 percent of their body weight. Some women weighed less at the end of their pregnancy than at its inception.

When the Allies finally liberated the Netherlands in early May 1945, they rushed in food, and conditions quickly improved. But by then 40,000 fetuses had been subjected to the hardships of famine. Depending on their date of conception, these babies were exposed at various stages of gestation, for periods as long as seven months. For example, babies conceived in April 1944 and born in early January 1945 were exposed to the starvation just in the last trimester of pregnancy; those conceived in February 1945 and born in November 1945 were exposed only in the first trimester. Babies unlucky enough to be conceived in August 1944 and born in May 1945 spent their entire second and third trimesters inside increasingly malnourished mothers.

In the late 1960s four researchers at Columbia University School of Public Health—Zena Stein, Mervyn Susser, Gerhart Saenger, and Francis Marolla, all of whom had studied malnutrition in urban ghettos—realized that much might be learned from the now-grown babies of the Dutch Hunger Winter. The outcomes of pregnancies in the stricken cities of the west could be compared with those in towns to the north or south, outside the worst-hit area. In addition, the results of pregnancies during the famine could be compared with those that occurred before and after it.

Hospital records and birth registries yielded statistics

on the health of the wartime mothers and their new-borns. And at least for the boys, follow-up information on those same children as young adults could be extracted from the records of the Dutch military draft system. Virtually all boys at age 19 were called up for an exam that recorded their height and weight, medical history, results of mental-performance tests, level of schooling completed, and father's occupation; the latter served as a rough indicator of socioeconomic status.

A starving mother was forced to unconsciously "choose" whether to devote the few available calories to her own body or to her fetus.

These studies provided some important insights, the first of which concerned the famine's effect on fertility. During the winter of 1944 conceptions quickly declined to one-third the normal level. This suggests that the women's fertility became impaired as their fat reserves, already depleted due to reduced wartime rations, were rapidly used up. The decline was more pronounced for wives of manual workers than of nonmanual workers, presumably because the former had less means to buy their way out of starvation.

The Dutch results agree with other evidence that body weight affects our reproductive physiology. Women in German concentration camps often ceased to menstruate (while low sperm counts and impotence were common among male inmates). Moreover, studies have shown that girls begin menstruating earlier in well-fed indus-trialized nations than in underfed Third World countries. The same trend applies to the present generation of American women compared with their less well nourished grandmothers. All these pieces of evidence suggest that a woman's fertility is dependent on having sufficient body weight to support conception.

Among the famine babies themselves, the most obvious effects were seen in those who were exposed during the last trimester, which is normally the period when a fetus undergoes its most rapid weight gain: these babies had markedly lower average birth weights (6 pounds 10 ounces) than those born before the famine began (7 pounds 6 ounces). Starvation during the third trimester also resulted in babies who were born slightly shorter and with smaller head circumferences, indicating slightly slower than normal growth of the bones and brain. But the main impact was to retard the growth of muscle and fat.

The prefamine pregnancies had taken place while war-time rations still hovered around 1,500 daily calories—meager for a pregnant woman, who normally requires 2,500 calories a day. Medical records showed that these expectant mothers lost weight themselves but were able to maintain a normal birth weight for their babies. Once rations dropped below 1,500 calories, however, babies began to share the impact. And eventually, as the famine wore on and severe starvation struck, all further weight loss was suffered by the baby rather than the mother. Birth weight recovered quickly when food supplies improved, though: babies born three months after the famine's end had normal weights.

Both during and right after the Hunger Winter there was a sharp rise in infant deaths in the Netherlands' hard-hit cities. For babies exposed to famine only in the first trimester, the rate of stillbirth nearly doubled. Those babies had been conceived just three months before the famine's end, and so they in fact completed most of their gestation inside mothers who were relatively well nourished. Yet malnutrition during those first three months had evidently planted a slow-fuse time bomb that went off at birth.

Still greater, however, was the effect on babies exposed during the second, and especially the third, trimesters. Those babies had a higher-than-normal death rate in their first week of life, and the rate continued to climb until they were at least three months old. Some of these babies died of malnutrition itself, others succumbed to normal childhood infections to which they had lowered resistance. Fortunately, once the famine babies reached the age of one year, their increased risk of death disappeared.

Let's now see how the babies who survived the perils of birth and early infancy were faring 19 years later, when the boys were called up for the draft. In many respects these young men were similar to any others their age. Their height, for example, showed all the usual effects of socioeconomic factors, including family size and diet: sons of manual workers averaged nearly an inch shorter than sons of wealthier fathers, children from families with many mouths to feed were shorter than only children, and later-born sons were shorter than first-born sons. The common thread is that children who have access to less food end up shorter. But postnatal, rather than prenatal, nutrition was the culprit here. If you picked any given group—say, sons of manual workers—the young men whose mothers were starved during pregnancy were no shorter than their peers.

Records from the Dutch draft exams also allowed the Columbia researchers to see if poor nutrition in pregnancy might cause lasting mental deficits as well as physical ones. Experiments with rats had shown that offspring of mothers that are starved in pregnancy end up with fewer-than-normal brain cells and learning disabilities. So when the researchers compared the grown-up famine babies' performance on tests of mental proficiency with the performance of those who had received better prenatal nourishment, they expected to find poorer scores for those who had been starved during gestation.

No such result was forthcoming. The draft exam,

which included tests of verbal, arithmetic, clerical, and mechanical skills, clearly showed the effects of social environment, which were parallel to the physical effects already mentioned—thus, sons of manual laborers, sons from large families, and sons born late into a family of several children tended to score below other young men. But no effect whatsoever could be attributed to prenatal starvation. One possible explanation is that our brain has enough extra cells to preserve mental function even if some of our cells are lost. At any rate, whatever effects can be attributed to nutrition must be due to nutrition after birth, not before it.

The genetic interests of the fetus are served by saving itself. Hence we evolve as fetuses to be parasites commandeering our mother's nutrients.

This, then, was the good news, such as it was. Those starved children who made it to adulthood were no worse off than their better-nourished counterparts. However, the medical records of the male famine babies who never made it to a draft physical did reveal one consequence of prenatal starvation—and it was sobering. Fetuses exposed to famine during their first three months in the womb were twice as likely as others to have defects of the central nervous system, such as spina bifida (in which the spine fails to close properly) and hydrocephalus (a related condition, characterized by fluid accumulating in the brain). The birth defects, it now appears, almost certainly arose from starvation during the first trimester, when the nervous system was being laid down.

Just how did a lack of food have such a dire result? Animal experiments have raised the suspicion that such defects can arise from a deficiency of the B vitamin folic acid early in pregnancy. A year ago this finding was confirmed for humans in a study of 22,776 pregnant women in Boston. Babies born to mothers who took multivitamins including folic acid during the first six weeks of pregnancy had a nearly fourfold lower frequency of central nervous system defects than did babies born to women who did not take such supplements. Brands of multivitamins that lacked folic acid, or multivitamins taken only after the seventh week of pregnancy, offered no protection.

All the results from the Dutch famine studies that I've discussed so far describe the effects of starvation on mothers and their children. But recent findings have raised disturbing questions about the famine's effect on a third generation. By now the famine babies are 45 or 46, and most of the girls have long since had children of their own; the "girls" themselves are women at the end of their reproductive careers. More than 100 of these women happened to have had their babies in the same Amster-

dam hospital in which they themselves were born, which makes for an easy comparison of birth records. An examination of those records has revealed something very odd: it turns out that those women who were themselves fetuses in their first and second trimester during the Dutch Hunger Winter gave birth to underweight babies. That is, the babies were somehow affected by the starvation of their grandmothers many decades earlier.

This result might have been easier to understand if the mothers themselves had been underweight at birth or were small as adults. Neither was true. Recall that starvation in the first or second trimester produced babies with normal birth weights. Only third-trimester starvation led to small babies. Yet, paradoxically, when these small babies later became mothers, they gave birth to normal-size babies. It was the women who were themselves normal size at birth who became mothers of underweight infants.

Somehow the grandmothers' suffering programmed their children in utero so that the grandchildren would be affected. This astonishing result will undoubtedly inspire experiments aimed at identifying the still-unknown cellular mechanism. But what is indisputable is that the Dutch famine left its harsh imprint on at least three generations.

From the perspective of evolutionary biology, the famine posed to the bodies of pregnant mothers an agonizing dilemma. What would you do in a situation threatening both your life and your child's life if anything you did to help one would hurt the other? Think quickly: If you see a car about to crash head-on into your car, do you throw yourself in front of your child sitting strapped in the seat beside you or do you try to protect yourself instead? Now let's make the choice more agonizing: What if your child's subsequent survival hinges on your own? You've all heard the airlines' standard safety announcement that in the event of a loss of cabin pressure, place the oxygen mask on yourself first, *then* place the mask on your child. In that situation, you have to help yourself first, because you'll be in no state to help your child if you are unconscious.

Similarly a mother starving in the Netherlands in 1944 was forced to unconsciously "choose" whether to devote the few available calories to her own body or to her fetus. This is a classic example of a conflict between two genetically related individuals. Natural selection favors the individual who passes on his or her genes to the most descendants. The genetic interests of the fetus are served by saving itself, and hence we evolve as fetuses to be parasites on our mother, commandeering her nutrients as efficiently as possible. But the mother's genetic interests are served by passing her genes to offspring. She gains nothing if her nutritional sacrifices kill not only herself but her child. Perhaps she would be best off, from an evolutionary point of view, if she sacrificed that fetus and tried again later. Yet there is no certainty that she will have another chance later.

The outcome of the Dutch famine indicates that natural selection struck a compromise. When the famine began, a mother's body at first accepted the full brunt, losing weight while preserving the weight of the fetus. In the next stage of famine both the fetus and the mother shared the hardship. In the last stage all weight loss came at the expense of the fetus, because any more weight loss by the mother would have threatened the mother's survival and thereby the survival of her child.

These pregnant women had no say in how their body allocated its precious resources, of course. Natural selection proceeded along its inexorable journey oblivious to any human agony or ethical dilemma. To ask whether the decisions it made were wise, whether they were some-how the "right" decisions, is irrelevant. The choices were arrived at in accordance with the cold logic of evolution and nothing more.

But what about the decisions that created such cruel conditions in the first place? What about the reasoning that even today, in the guise of wartime expediency, can compel one group of people to consciously impose starvation on another and thus scar the lives of unborn generations? For that matter, what about the reduction of social programs in our own society that might subject untold numbers of children, both before and after birth, to the dangers of malnutrition simply by failing to ensure proper nourishment for them and their mothers? The lessons of the Dutch Hunger Winter are there for the learning. We can ignore them only at our children's, and our grandchildren's, expense.

WHEN A PREGNANT WOMAN DRINKS

**ELISABETH
ROSENTHAL**

Elisabeth Rosenthal is an emergency-room physician in New York City.

At the human and behavior genetics Laboratory at Emory University, in Atlanta, a videotape recording shows a smiling 8-year-old girl peering from behind thick glasses at two clear plastic boxes topped by red bows, each containing a chocolate-chip cookie. The game, a psychologist explains, is to open both boxes and remove the cookies—and no eating until both cookies are out. The girl's 35-year-old mother observes.

The child seems to understand and, with the eagerness of a race horse at the gate, lunges at the boxes. For an endless few minutes, she pulls intently at the ribbons and tugs doggedly at the bows, clearly not up to this most elementary task. Fi-

nally, the mother comes to the rescue by untying one box and, with the second still sealed, the grinning child pops a cookie in her mouth.

"Ugh. This is too painful to watch," exclaims Dr. Claire D. Coles, the center's director of Clinical and Developmental Research, as she puts the tape on pause. "Look at that nice little girl. Her face is dysmorphic. She's too small for her age. And her fine motor coordination is awful.

"What's worse, look at the mother. She's also mildly dysmorphic. She spent her childhood in special-ed classes. The whole family suffers from prenatal alcohol exposure. All three kids, the mother, her brother."

In the last decade it has become unquestionably clear that alcohol is a potent teratogen,

which can cause irreversible damage to the body and brain of the developing fetus. Experts like Dr. Coles now believe that women who are pregnant or contemplating pregnancy should not drink—at all.

Fetal alcohol syndrome and its more subtle variant, fetal alcohol effect, are umbrella terms used to describe the condition affecting the scarred offspring of drinking mothers. Victims with the full-blown syndrome, whose mothers generally drank heavily throughout pregnancy, often suffer physical malformations and mental retardation. Even those less fully affected, sometimes the progeny of women who drank only intermittently, may end up with lifelong learning disabilities and behavioral problems.

No one knows exactly how many individuals are afflicted

with fetal alcohol damage, but the estimates are staggering. The Centers for Disease Control estimate that more than 8,000 alcohol-damaged babies are born each year, or 2.7 babies for every 1,000 live births. Others feel that these figures are low. On some Indian reservations, 25 percent of all children are reportedly afflicted.

Although the syndrome was first described in 1973, the broad impact of alcohol-related fetal injury has only recently become apparent to scientists. "The Broken Cord," Michael Dorris's moving memoir about raising a severely alcohol-affected child, brought the syndrome to wider public attention when it was published last summer.

Some experts believe fetal-alcohol exposure is the most

common-known cause of mental retardation in this country. Dr. Robert J. Sokol, dean of the School of Medicine at Wayne State University in Detroit and director of Wayne State's Alcohol Research Center, estimates that 1 out of 10 retarded adults in residential care has fetal alcohol syndrome.

Experts in birth defects see the survivors of drinking pregnancies everywhere. When Dr. Coles recently lectured at a reform school, she recalls, she thought, "My God, half these kids look alcohol affected." And as the syndrome becomes better known, others are beginning to recognize it as well.

"I get a lot of calls saying, 'I've just figured out what's wrong with our 18-year-old adopted son. He's dropped out of school; he's always had learning problems; he's never fit in,' " says Dr. Ann Streissguth of the University of Washington, who has followed a group of children with alcohol-related disabilities for 14 years.

Still, as Dr. Coles says, "the vast majority of kids like this have never been identified or followed. People probably just assumed they were a little stupid or a little funny looking."

As she speaks, I stare sheepishly at the faces of the Atlanta girl and her mother still frozen on the screen: their eyes just slightly too far apart, their thin upper lips, their smallish heads. Although I received my medical training within the last 10 years, without Dr. Cole's coaching I would have missed this diagnosis.

IN SCREENING FOR ALCOhol-related injuries, an expert in birth defects, or dysmorphologist, examines the suspect child for the unusual facial characteristics, small head and body size, poor mental capabilities and abnormal behavior patterns that typify alcohol-related birth defects. In infancy, the evaluation is usually prompted by knowledge of a mother's drinking, or because a newborn develops the shakes or seizures typical of alcohol withdrawal. But at this stage the symptoms are easily overlooked. Only 20 percent of those with the full

syndrome have marked facial abnormalities, and those with the effect look fine.

"Except when a child is grossly dysmorphic," the syndrome is not diagnosed, says Dr. Sterling K. Claren, Aldrich Professor of Pediatrics at the University of Washington School of Medicine in Seattle. As for fetal alcohol effect, he adds, it "really cannot be diagnosed in newborns."

Many children with the full syndrome come to expert attention only after they fail to gain weight and meet developmental landmarks. Sometimes a physician notices an abundance of physical complaints—crossed eyes, heart murmurs or recurrent ear infections—that suggest congenital malformation. Some are not recognized until years later, when they begin having trouble at school. Some are not recognized at all. Dr. José F. Cordero of the Center for Disease Control's Division of Birth Defects and Developmental Disabilities believes that as many as two-thirds of cases of the full syndrome remain undiagnosed, with the figure for those less severely affected even higher.

Dr. Coles and her staff, as part of their study, crisscross Atlanta, turning their trained eyes on the progeny of alcoholic pregnancies to look for signs of damage. On a day in November, she visited a ramshackle housing project to examine a one-month-old boy whose mother is an alcohol and cocaine abuser. She put the baby through a series of tests: shaking rattles near his ear, tweaking a toe with a rubber band, recording his cry.

The boy has no physical signs of fetal alcohol syndrome, she later explains, but his behavior is worrisome. "He is too irritable, too distractable," she said. "Kids at 30 days should be calm and able to focus on a rattle." But, she added, "If you weren't trained you might not recognize this as a substance-abuse baby."

Anne Cutcliffe's adopted daughter had seen various doctors before she was referred to Dr. Coles for an evaluation at age 2. "I guess I recall when I got her at 9 months, she was not

an attractive child," said Mrs. Cutcliffe, who lives in Atlanta and has five older children. "She only weighed 10½ pounds and her eyes were crossed. All she could do was turn from her stomach to her back. I guess it proves love is blind, because I never did see all those things that other people saw." The girl's biological mother was an alcoholic.

AS MANY AS 86 PERCENT of women drink at least once during pregnancy, according to the Public Health Service, and experts estimate that between 20 and 35 percent of pregnant women drink regularly. In a 1989 study of 2,278 highly educated women (39 percent had postgraduate degrees), 30 percent consumed more than one drink a week during pregnancy; only 11 percent smoked.

Alcohol freely crosses the placenta, and the fetus's blood-alcohol level will equal that of the mother's. A recent study in The New England Journal of Medicine showed that women have lower levels than men of the stomach enzyme that neutralizes alcohol, leaving them particularly vulnerable to high levels of alcohol in the bloodstream. The mother's blood alcohol must reach a certain level—the toxic threshold—before the fetus is at risk. Binge drinking seems to be particularly risky. While a drink each night might never push a mother's blood level above the danger threshold, a night of drinking in honor of a birthday might well raise the level enough to endanger the fetus.

The type of damage produced by drinking depends on the fetus's stage of development. The first trimester of pregnancy is devoted to the organization of the fetus's bones and organs, while the second and third trimesters center on growth and maturation. The brain develops throughout the nine-month period. "So we'd predict physical malformations from heavy drinking in the first trimester and growth retardation from drinking in the third," says Dr. Claren. "But brain damage can occur at any time." In addition, the toxic

threshold for brain damage seems to be much lower than for damage to other organs.

There is a rough correlation between the amount a mother imbibes during pregnancy and the severity of the baby's defects, but scientists are struggling to understand the many other factors that come into play. One major mystery is why so many drinking women frequently have apparently normal babies. Even in hopeless alcoholics, the chance of having a baby with the full-blown syndrome is only 35 percent.

The fetus may be more vulnerable on certain days of pregnancy. "Two drinks may be above the threshold on day 33 and on day 39, below," Dr. Claren said.

Women may also differ in their genetic susceptibility to having children with the syndrome, a tendency which some believe may follow ethnic and racial lines. Dr. Sokol has found that black women are seven times more likely to have fetal-alcohol affected children than white women with similar drinking habits. (Pregnant or not, studies have found that black and Hispanic women are more likely to be abstinent than white women. And a woman's alcohol consumption tends to rise with her level of education and income.) The Centers for Disease Control data show that the syndrome is 30 times more commonly reported in Native Americans than it is in whites, and six times more common in blacks.

Dr. Coles believes these figures may be "partly an artifact of reporting. Researchers don't go into nice private hospitals and start looking for alcohol-damaged babies." At least one study found that women of lower socioeconomic status are diagnosed correctly more often.

Although experts stress that there is no evidence in human beings that a rare single drink does damage, most say that with so much still unknown the only prudent course for the pregnant mother is abstinence. "Pregnancy is a time when women should be conservative with their bodies," says Dr. Claren. "Women think three or four times before they take an aspirin. They quit smoking. Then they turn around and have a drink? Some obstetricians advise women not to drink. Many others make up some dose of liquor which they think is O.K. To me that's crazy." Experts recommend that women who are breast-feeding also abstain, because brain maturation continues after birth.

The good news is that those who stop drinking at any time during pregnancy can increase their chances of having a healthy child. In a study conducted by the Boston University Fetal Alcohol Education Program, 85 women who drank heavily stayed with the program until they gave birth. Thirty-three of the women gave up or reduced their drinking before the seventh month of pregnancy; among these women, there was not one baby born with a growth abnormality, according to Dr. Barbara A. Morse, the program's director. Of the 52 women who continued to drink heavily, 21 gave birth to babies with growth retardation, and 5 of these babies had identifiable fetal alcohol syndrome. Moderate drinkers during early pregnancy are advised to quit while they're ahead: "If a woman comes to me three months pregnant and says 'I'm a regular drinker,' " says Dr. Claren, 'I say, 'Whatever you did is probably safe but stop now.' "

The Boston University group has led the way in calling for better counseling and improved drug-treatment opportunities for pregnant women. "Pregnancy is a time of incredible motivation for women," says Dr. Morse, noting that of those heavy-drinking women in the program who received counseling two-thirds were able to cut down considerably or stop altogether. Unfortunately, many in-patient alcohol rehabilitation programs exclude pregnant women, she said. Massachusetts recently opened four residential programs (or 35 beds) to treat pregnant alcoholics and other substance abusers, making that state the leader nationwide.

RESEARCHERS ARE NOW focusing on moderate drinking during pregnancy in the hopes of learning more about alcohol's most subtle effects. Dr. Nancy Day of the University of Pittsburgh has studied the offspring of close to 700 women since 1988, most of whom reported consuming less than one drink a day during pregnancy. There were no babies with the full syndrome in the group, but there was a correlation between mothers who drank prenatally and the size of the child's head. Many also had an unusual number of "minor physical anomalies"—like crooked toes and funny ears. Most worrisome, the newborns had unusual brainwave patterns, of EEG's, potentially indicative of immature development of the brain.

Animal studies suggest that relatively low-level drinking can lead to damage. Dr. Claren's group at the University of Washington gave monkeys binges of alcohol once a week during pregnancy. The babies were unusually irritable, impulsive and distractable—a familiar triad of symptoms. "The good news is that the mothers had to get enough alcohol to get intoxicated to produce the defects," says Dr. Claren. "The bad news is that even if they only binged during the first three weeks of pregnancy"—equivalent to the first four to six weeks of the human term—"the babies still ended up with behavioral abnormalities."

There were physiological abnormalities as well. Though their brains were the right size and CT scans were totally normal, examination of their brain cells showed abnormal levels of dopamine, an important neurotransmitter. Dr. Claren sees these findings as a strong physiological correlate of fetal alcohol effect. He hopes PET scans, which can sense chemical abnormalities in the brain, may be helpful in nailing down the often elusive diagnosis.

TWO RESEARCH groups, Dr. Coles's in Atlanta and Dr. Streissguth's in Seattle, have followed alcohol-affected children for 6 and 14 years respectively. They find that some of the traits that are only hinted at in newborns blossom in early childhood, creating potentially disastrous school experiences. In Dr. Coles's group, children at age 6 showed poorer memory, shorter attention spans, lower I.Q.'s, diminished achievement levels and other learning disabilities when compared to normal children. Dr. Streissguth's group also reported attention deficits and other behavior problems at this age.

These shortcomings may add up to a limited ability to learn and to learn from experience. These kids "have a unique flavor among the learning disabled," observes Dr. Claren. "They seem to be really untrainable." Anne Cutcliffe remembers her daughter, at 6, making such slow progress in reading that her teachers decided she should repeat the first grade. When she started first grade a second time, after the four-month summer vacation, she had lost even the small progress she'd made the year before and had to start again at the most basic level.

Most children with the full syndrome will be found, with formal psychological testing, to be "developmentally delayed" and will qualify for special education. But some will limp along in regular classes. Even those who qualify for special education are often put into classes that don't meet their needs.

Most treatment programs for the mildly mentally handicapped were designed for patients like those with Down's syndrome, who are quiet, good workers and enjoy repetitive tasks. Parents and health professionals describe the alcohol-affected in very different terms: impulsive, unable to learn from mistakes, undisciplined, showing poor judgment, distractable, uninhibited. "We have to shift gears" to meet the needs of alcohol-affected kids, says Dr. Streissguth. He has applied for Federal funding to develop special therapeutic programs designed for them.

The flip side of the alcohol-affected personality is a winning one: outgoing, loving, physical, trusting. But together they lead to trouble. "She'll walk up to anyone on the street and stare at them and make conversation," says Anne Cutcliffe of her daughter. "Immediately she's buddies. It doesn't matter who." And Dr. Streissguth agrees that as young adults those with the syndrome often take sociability and physicality to unwelcome extremes: "They talk too loud and they stand too close. They seem not to pick up on normal social cues."

Paradoxically, researchers in the field say, alcohol-affected children who perform best on standardized tests end up with the toughest existence. Those who are obviously dysmorphic and mentally retarded receive social-service assistance and often end up in group homes. The others "fall into a pit," says Dr. Coles. Many drop out of school in frustration and their disabilities consign them to the margins of society, sometimes involved in prostitution and petty crime. "These are outgoing, trusting, fun-loving people, who are not able to evaluate the risks out there," said Dr. Streissguth.

SPERM UNDER SIEGE

MORE THAN WE EVER GUESSED, HAVING A HEALTHY BABY MAY DEPEND ON DAD

Anne Merewood

IT DIDN'T MAKE SENSE. Kate Malone's* first pregnancy had gone so smoothly. Yet when she and her husband Paul* tried to have a second child, their efforts were plagued by disaster. For two years, Kate couldn't become pregnant. Then she suffered an ectopic pregnancy, in which the embryo began to grow in one of her fallopian tubes and had to be surgically removed. Her next pregnancy heralded more heartache—it ended in miscarriage at four months and tests revealed that the fetus was genetically abnormal. Within months, she became pregnant and miscarried yet again. By this point, some four years after their troubles began, the couple had adopted a son; baffled and demoralized by the string of apparent bad luck, they gave up trying to have another child. "We had been to the top doctors in the country and no one could find a reason for the infertility or the miscarriages," says Kate.

Soon, however, thanks to a newspaper article she read, Kate uncovered what she now considers the likely cause of the couple's reproductive woes. When it all started, Paul had just been hired by a manufacturing company that used a chemical called paradichlorobenzene, which derives from benzene, a known carcinogen. The article discussed the potential effects of exposure to chemicals, including benzene, on a man's sperm. Kate remembered hearing that two other men in Paul's small office were also suffering from inexplicable infertility. Both of their wives had gone through three miscarriages as well. Kate had always considered their similar misfortunes to be a tragic coincidence. Now she became convinced that the chemical (which has not yet been studied for its effects on reproduction) had blighted the three men's sperm.

Paul had found a new job in a chemical-free workplace, so the couple decided to try once more to have a baby. Kate conceived immediately—and last August gave birth to a healthy boy. The Malones are now arranging for the National Institute for Occupational Safety and Health (NIOSH), the

*These names have been changed.

federal agency that assesses work-related health hazards for the public, to inspect Paul's former job site. "Our aim isn't to sue the company, but to help people who are still there," says Kate.

The Malones' suspicions about sperm damage echo the concerns of an increasing number of researchers. These scientists are challenging the double standard that leads women to overhaul their lives before a pregnancy—avoiding stress, cigarettes and champagne—while men are left confident that their lifestyle has little bearing on their fertility or their future child's health. Growing evidence suggests that sperm is both more fragile and potentially more dangerous than previously thought. "There seems to have been both a scientific resistance, and a resistance based on cultural preconceptions, to accepting these new ideas," says Gladys Friedler, Ph.D, an associate professor of psychiatry and pharmacology at Boston University School of Medicine.

But as more and more research is completed, sperm may finally be stripped of its macho image. For example, in one startling review of data on nearly 15,000 newborns, scientists at the University of North Carolina in Chapel Hill concluded that a father's drinking and smoking habits, and even his age, can increase his child's risk of birth defects— ranging from cleft palates to *hydrocephalus,* an abnormal accumulation of spinal fluid in the brain. Other new and equally worrisome studies have linked higher-than-normal rates of stillbirth, premature delivery and low birthweight (which predisposes a baby to medical and developmental problems) to fathers who faced on-the-job exposure to certain chemicals. In fact, one study found that a baby was more likely to be harmed if the father rather than the mother worked in an unsafe environment in the months before conception.

The surprising news of sperm's delicate nature may shift the balance of responsibility for a newborn's wellbeing. The research may also have social and economic implications far beyond the concerns of couples planning a family. In recent years a growing number of companies have sought

From *Health*, April 1991, pp. 53-57, 76-77. © 1991 by Anne Merewood. Reprinted by permission.

to ban women of childbearing age from jobs that entail exposure to hazardous substances. The idea is to protect the women's future children from defects—and the companies themselves from lawsuits. Already, the "fetal protection policy" of one Milwaukee-based company has prompted female employees to file a sex discrimination suit that is now before the U.S. Supreme Court. Conversely, if the new research on sperm is borne out, men whose future plans include fatherhood may go to court to *insist* on protection from hazards. Faced with potential lawsuits from so many individuals, companies may be forced to ensure that workplaces are safe for *all* employees.

SPERM UND DRANG

At the center of all this controversy are the microscopic products of the male reproductive system. Sperm (officially, spermatozoa) are manufactured by *spermatagonia,* special cells in the testes that are constantly stimulated by the male hormone testosterone. Once formed, a sperm continues to mature as it travels for some 80 days through the *epididymis* (a microscopic network of tubes behind the testicle) to the "waiting area" around the prostate gland, where it is expelled in the next ejaculation.

A normal sperm contains 23 chromosomes—the threadlike strands that house DNA, the molecular foundation of genetic material. While a woman is born with all the eggs she will ever produce, a man creates millions of sperm every day from puberty onwards. This awesome productivity is also what makes sperm so fragile. If a single sperm's DNA is damaged, the result may be a mutation that distorts the genetic information it carries. "Because of the constant turnover of sperm, mutations caused by the environment can arise more frequently in men than in women," says David A. Savitz, Ph.D., an associate professor of epidemiology and chief researcher of the North Carolina review.

If a damaged sperm fertilizes the egg, the consequences can be devastating. "Such sperm can lead to spontaneous abortions, malformations, and functional or behavioral abnormalities," says Marvin Legator, Ph.D., director of environmental toxicology at the department of preventative medicine at the University of Texas in Galveston. And in some cases, sperm may be too badly harmed even to penetrate an egg, leading to mysterious infertility.

Though the findings on sperm's vulnerability are certainly dramatic, researchers emphasize that they are also preliminary. "We have only a very vague notion of how exposure might affect fetal development, and the whole area of research is at a very early stage of investigation," says Savitz. Indeed, questions still far outnumber answers. For starters, there is no hard evidence that a chemical damages an infant by adversely affecting the father's sperm. A man who comes in contact with dangerous substances might harm the baby by exposing his partner indirectly—for example, through contaminated clothing. Another theory holds that the harmful pollutants may be carried in the seminal fluid that buoys sperm. But more researchers are becoming convinced that chemicals can inflict their silent damage directly on the sperm itself.

THE CHEMICAL CONNECTION

The most well-known—and most controversial—evidence that chemicals can harm sperm comes from research on U.S. veterans of the Vietnam war who were exposed to the herbicide Agent Orange (dioxin), used by the U.S. military to destroy foliage that hid enemy forces. A number of veterans believe the chemical is responsible for birth defects in their children. The latest study on the issue, published last year by the Harvard School of Public Health, found that Vietnam vets had almost twice the risk of other men of fathering infants with one or more major malformations. But a number of previous studies found conflicting results, and because so little is known about how paternal exposure could translate into birth defects, the veterans have been unsuccessful in their lawsuits against the government.

Scientific uncertainty also dogs investigations into other potentially hazardous chemicals and contaminants. "There seem to be windows of vulnerability for sperm: Certain chemicals may be harmful only at a certain period during sperm production," explains Donald Mattison, M.D., dean of the School of Public Health at the University of Pittsburgh. There isn't enough specific data to make definitive lists of "danger chemicals." Still, a quick scan of the research shows that particular substances often crop up as likely troublemakers. Chief among them: lead, benzene, paint solvents, vinyl chloride, carbon disulphide, the pesticide DBCP, anesthetic gases and radiation. Not surprisingly, occupations that involve contact with these substances also figure heavily in studies of sperm damage. For example, men employed in the paper, wood, chemical, drug and paint industries may have a greater chance of siring stillborn children. And increased leukemia rates have been detected among children whose fathers are medical workers, aircraft or auto mechanics, or who are exposed regularly to paint or radiation. In fact, a study of workers at Britain's Sellafield nuclear power plant in West Cambria found a sixfold leukemia risk among children whose fathers were exposed to the plant's highest radiation levels (about 9 percent of all employees).

Workers in "high-risk" industries should not panic, says Savitz. "The credibility of the studies is limited because we have no firm evidence that certain exposures cause certain birth defects." Yet it makes sense to be watchful for warning signs. For example, if pollution levels are high enough to cause skin irritations, thyroid trouble, or breathing problems, the reproductive system might also be at risk. Another danger signal is a clustered outbreak of male infertility or of a particular disease: It was local concern about high levels of childhood leukemia, for instance, that sparked the investigation at the Sellafield nuclear plant.

The rise in industrial "fetal protection policies" is

adding even more controversy to the issue of occupational hazards to sperm. In 1984, employees brought a class-action suit against Milwaukee-based Johnson Controls, the nation's largest manufacturer of car batteries, after the company restricted women "capable of bearing children" from holding jobs in factory areas where lead exceeded a specific level. The suit—which the Supreme Court is scheduled to rule on this spring—focuses on the obstacles the policy creates for women's career advancement. Johnson Controls defends its regulation by pointing to "overwhelming" evidence that a mother's exposure to lead can harm the fetus.

In effect, the company's rule may be a case of reverse discrimination against men. Males continue to work in areas banned to women despite growing evidence that lead may not be safe for sperm either. In several studies over the past 10 years, paternal exposure to lead (and radiation) has been connected to Wilms' tumor, a type of kidney cancer in children. In another recent study, University of Maryland toxicologist Ellen Silbergeld, Ph.D., exposed male rats to lead amounts equivalent to levels below the current occupational safety standards for humans. The rats were then mated with females who had not been exposed at all. Result: The offspring showed clear defects in brain development.

Johnson Controls claims that evidence linking fetal problems to a father's contact with lead is insufficient. But further research into chemicals' effects on sperm may eventually force companies to reduce pollution levels, since *both* sexes can hardly be banned from the factory floor. Says Mattison: "The workplace should be safe for everyone who wants to work there, men and women alike!"

FATHER TIME

Whatever his occupation, a man's age may play an unexpected role in his reproductive health. When researchers at the University of Calgary and the Alberta Children's Hospital in Canada examined sperm samples taken from 30 healthy men aged 20 to 52, they found that the older men had a higher percentage of sperm with structurally abnormal chromosomes. Specifically, only 2 to 3 percent of the sperm from men between ages 20 and 34 were genetically abnormal, while the figure jumped to 7 percent in men 35 to 44 and to almost 14 percent in those 45 and over. "The findings are logical," says Renée Martin, Ph.D., the professor of pediatrics who led the study. "The cells that create sperm are constantly dividing from puberty onwards, and every time they divide they are subject to error."

Such mistakes are more likely to result in miscarriages than in unhealthy babies. "When part of a chromosome is missing or broken, the embryo is more likely to abort as a miscarriage [than to carry to term]," Martin says. Yet her findings may help explain why Savitz's North Carolina study noted a doubled rate of birth defects like cleft palate and hydrocephalus in children whose fathers were over 35 at the time of conception, no matter what the mothers' age.

Currently, there are no tests available to pre-identify sperm likely to cause genetic defects. "Unfortunately there's nothing offered, because [the research] is all so new," says Martin. But tests such as amniocentesis, alpha fetoprotein (AFP) and chorionic villi sampling (CVS) can ferret out some fetal genetic defects that are linked to Mom *or* Dad. Amniocentesis, for example, is routinely recommended for all pregnant women over 35 because with age a woman increases her risk of producing a Down's syndrome baby, characterized by mental retardation and physical abnormalities.

With respect to Down's syndrome, Martin's study provided some good news for older men: It confirmed previous findings that a man's risk of fathering a child afflicted with the syndrome actually drops with age. Some popular textbooks still warn that men over 55 have a high chance of fathering Down's syndrome babies. "That information is outdated," Martin insists. "We now know that for certain."

THE SINS OF THE FATHERS?

For all the hidden dangers facing a man's reproductive system, the most common hazards may be the ones most under his control.

Smoking. Tobacco addicts take note: Smoke gets in your sperm. Cigarettes can reduce fertility by lowering sperm count—the number of individual sperm released in a single ejaculation. "More than half a pack a day can cause sperm density to drop by 20 percent," says Machelle Seibel, M.D., director of the Faulkner Centre for Reproductive Medicine in Boston. One Danish study found that for each pack of cigarettes a father tended to smoke daily (assuming the mother didn't smoke at all), his infant's birthweight fell 4.2 ounces below average. Savitz has found that male smokers double their chances of fathering infants with abnormalities like hydrocephalus, *Bell's palsy* (paralysis of the facial nerve), and mouth cysts. In Savitz's most recent study, children whose fathers smoked around the time of conception were 20 percent more likely to develop brain cancer, lymphoma and leukemia than were children whose fathers did not smoke (the results still held regardless of whether the mother had a tobacco habit).

This is scary news—and not particularly helpful: Savitz's studies didn't record how frequently the fathers lit up, and no research at all suggests why the links appeared. Researchers can't even say for sure that defective sperm was to blame. The babies may instead have been victims of passive smoking—affected by Dad's tobacco while in the womb or shortly after birth.

Drinking. Mothers-to-be are routinely cautioned against sipping any alcohol while pregnant. Now studies suggest that the father's drinking habits just before conception may also pose a danger. So far, research hasn't discovered why alcohol has an adverse effect on sperm, but it does suggest that further investigation is needed. For starters, one study of laboratory rats linked heavy alcohol use with infertility because the liquor lowered testosterone levels. Another study, from the University of Washington in Seattle, discovered that newborn babies whose fathers drank at least two glasses of wine or two bottles of beer per day weighed an average of 3 ounces less than babies whose fathers were only occasional sippers—even when all other factors were considered.

Illicit Drugs. Many experts believe that a man's frequent use of substances such as marijuana and cocaine may also result in an unhealthy fetus, but studies that could document such findings have yet to be conducted. However, preliminary research has linked marijuana to infertility. And recent tests at the Yale Infertility Clinic found that long-term cocaine use led to both very low sperm counts and a greater number of sperm with motion problems.

WHAT A DAD CAN DO

The best news about sperm troubles is that many of the risk factors can be easily prevented. Because the body overhauls sperm supplies every 90 days, it only takes a season to get a fresh start on creating a healthy baby. Most experts advise that men wait for three months after quitting smoking, cutting out drug use or abstaining from alcohol before trying to sire a child.

Men who fear they are exposed to work chemicals that may compromise the health of future children can contact NIOSH. (Write to the Division of Standards Development and Technology Transfer, Technical Information Branch, 4676 Columbia Parkway, Mailstop C-19, Cincinnati, OH 45226. Or call [800] 356-4674.) NIOSH keeps files on hazardous chemicals and their effects, and can arrange for a local inspection of the workplace. Because it is primarily a research institution, NIOSH is most useful for investigating chemicals that haven't been studied previously for sperm effects (which is why

the Malones approached NIOSH with their concerns about paradichlorobenzene). For better-known pollutants, it's best to ask the federal Occupational Safety and Health Administration (OSHA) to inspect the job site (OSHA has regional offices in most U.S. cities).

There is also advice for men who are concerned over exposure to radiation during medical treatment. Direct radiation to the area around the testes can spur infertility by halting sperm production for more than three years. According to a recent study, it can also triple the number of abnormal sperm the testes produce. Men who know they will be exposed to testicular radiation for medical reasons should consider "banking" sperm before the treatment, for later use in artificial insemination. Most hospitals use lead shields during radiation therapy, but for routine X-rays, even dental X-rays, protection might not be offered automatically. If it's not offered, patients should be sure to request it. "The risks are really, really low, but to be absolutely safe, patients—male or female—should *always* ask for a lead apron to protect their reproductive organs," stresses Martin.

Though the study of sperm health is still in its infancy, it is already clear that a man's reproductive system needs to be treated with respect and caution. Women do not carry the full responsibility for bearing a healthy infant. "The focus should be on both parents—not on 'blaming' either the mother or the father, but on accepting that each plays a role," says Friedler.

Mattison agrees: "Until recently, when a woman had a miscarriage, she would be told it was because she had a 'blighted ovum' [egg]. We never heard anything about a 'blighted sperm.' This new data suggests that both may be responsible. That is not unreasonable," he concludes, "given that it takes both an egg and a sperm to create a baby!"

■ MEDICINE

Moms, Kids and AIDS

Can testing and treatment before and after birth
help thousands of youngsters threatened by HIV?

CHRISTINE GORMAN

IT IS A SIMPLE TEST IN WHICH A DOLlop of blood is drawn from a baby's tiny heel and taken to a lab for analysis. The result could provide reassurance—or a death sentence. In most states all newborns are screened to see if they have antibodies to HIV, the virus that causes AIDS. In about 7,000 U.S. cases a year, the test is positive, which merely indicates that antibodies produced in the mother's blood have moved to the child during pregnancy. But the implications are grim: the mother is infected with the virus for sure, and there is a 25% chance that the child picked up not just antibodies but the virus itself while in the womb or during delivery.

Incredibly, this momentous news is not ordinarily passed along to the mother. In fact, the testing is generally done on a blind basis; the blood samples are identified by number, and not even the hospital staff knows which babies tested positive. Unless the mother requests HIV screening ahead of time and signals her consent, she won't be told the results of the test. She may go home from the hospital not knowing that AIDS stalks her and her child.

How can this be? The secrecy surrounding HIV screening in newborns grew out of a reasonable effort to balance the need for information about the extent of the epidemic with the need to protect the privacy of patients, who may be discriminated against by employers and insurance companies. But serious questions are being raised about HIV testing. Does protecting the privacy of mothers endanger the rights of babies, who cannot make decisions for themselves? Should test results be disclosed so that all HIV-infected babies can be given immediate treatment? Then there is a separate matter: Should women be tested for HIV early in pregnancy, since

it is now sometimes possible to use the drug AZT to block the transmission of the virus from mother to child?

These questions have no simple answers, and most people are still unfamiliar with the issues involved. But a few state legislatures, led by lawmakers in New York, are starting to consider bills to resolve some of the controversies swirling around HIV testing. The outcome of the debates will be of vital importance to the youngest generation of AIDS sufferers.

She may go home from
the hospital not knowing
that AIDS stalks her
and her child.

After the HIV test became available in 1985, the U.S. Centers for Disease Control and Prevention began planning screening programs. Federal officials needed to know how fast the virus was spreading, and they were particularly concerned about the vulnerability of childbearing women. But AIDS activists were fiercely opposed to mandatory screening, since identification of HIV-positive mothers could mark them for discrimination. Since there was no cure or even a good treatment for AIDS, knowing the results of the test would not help the mother and child much anyway. The CDC ultimately decided to set up blind screening, and 44 states eventually agreed to be part of the program.

The strategy made sense at first, but advances in treatment have changed the ethical equation. While a cure is still elusive, doctors have learned how to use antibiotics and other drugs to ward off some of the most devastating complications of AIDS. For babies, timing is the key to effective treatment. They have such immature immune systems that HIV makes them much sicker, much more quickly than it does adults. So doctors must start treatment as soon after birth as possible.

Recognizing the need to protect babies, many hospitals have set up counseling programs in which pregnant women are advised about the benefits of knowing their own as well as their child's HIV status. But it's not always easy to convince them. In New York, for example, mothers must sign a lengthy consent form warning, among other things, that society may treat them unfairly if they are identified as being infected with HIV. That's one reason why so many women refuse to volunteer for the test. Most of them never realize that their children are being screened anyway.

That situation has infuriated Nettie Mayersohn, a New York state legislator from Queens. She considers it a "horror story" that new mothers are not routinely given the good or bad news on HIV. "Those babies' rights are being violated by sending them home without telling anyone," Mayersohn says. "It's insane." She has introduced a bill in the New York legislature that would require identification of HIV-positive babies so that they can be treated, as are newborn victims of syphilis, for example. But the Mayersohn bill faces stiff opposition. Says Elizabeth Cooper of the New York Task Force on Women and AIDS: "As long as the stigma and discrimination exist around AIDS out there, we're going to have to treat it differently" from other diseases. A competing measure sponsored by state assemblyman Richard Gottfried merely mandates counseling of new mothers about HIV testing.

Many medical experts think forced screening would be counterproductive. "I strongly believe testing should not be mandatory," says Dr. Jean Anderson at Johns Hopkins Hospital in Baltimore, Maryland. Instead, she argues, "every woman who is pregnant should receive counseling about HIV and be offered testing. If it's presented in a reasonable way, people are going to accept screening; to force them into it is only going to drive them away and alienate them." Thanks to Anderson's approach, more than 90% of women who go to the obstetrical clinic at Hopkins voluntarily agree to be tested for HIV.

The issue took on a new dimension in February, when the National Institutes of Health reported preliminary evidence that AZT could in many cases keep a mother from passing HIV to her unborn child. In a study of HIV-positive pregnant women, three times as many HIV-infected babies were born to untreated mothers as were born to mothers given AZT. Some obstetricians have started to offer the treatment to their HIV-positive patients. "This is the most exciting finding in the 10 years I've been doing this," says Dr. Elaine Abrams, head of the pediatric AIDS program at Harlem Hospital. Now mothers have a greater incentive to be tested.

Other than temporary anemia, physicians have identified no short-term side effects of AZT on fetal development. However, no one knows what the long-term side effects of AZT might be. As a result, states have not rushed to get pregnant women tested for HIV. Michigan is considering requiring doctors to offer such screening, but North Carolina has abandoned the idea of mandatory testing. "If we identify the female, do we then mandate that she be treated with AZT?" asks Theresa Klimko, an epidemiologist who works for the state. "We have no reason to mandate testing [of mothers] unless we mandate treatment."

The debate is just beginning. "It is a very deep ethical and social dilemma," says Dr. Harvey Fineberg, dean of the Harvard School of Public Health, "and fraught with all manner of emotional responses." One thing is certain: each year about 1,800 newborns in the U.S. are infected with HIV. If AZT can safely reduce that number, the pressure for routine testing will only rise. —*Reported by Sam Allis/ New York, with other bureaus*

Development during Infancy and Early Childhood

- **Infancy (Articles 11–14)**
- **Early Childhood (Articles 15–18)**

Many new parents are surprised by the sight of their newborn baby. With curled up arms and legs, the infant looks very top heavy. In fact, the head is very large relative to its adult proportions: about 25 percent of the length. The head sits on the body with virtually no neck. This wobbly head is of vital importance to the infant's development. The lower brain is already equipped to control and direct the organ systems and maintain life. The higher brain (the cerebrum) must grow and develop rapidly after birth to equip the baby for thought. One of the most important lessons all new parents are taught is to "support the head."

All the neurons the baby will ever have are present at birth. Neurons are not replaced once they are lost. Another very important lesson all new parents are taught is, "let the baby eat and sleep." Breast milk or infant formula provides the proteins and sugars necessary for brain maturation. Brain growth takes place more rapidly during sleep. While all neurons are already formed, they must still grow bigger, develop their cell processes (axons and dendrites), develop myelin sheathing, form interconnections with other neurons, and communicate with each other through synapses. Failure to provide an adequate milk supply, or a safe, secure environment conducive to sleep, may leave infants with disabilities in all areas: physical growth, sensory and perceptual development, brain maturation, acquisition of motor skills, acquisition of cognitive skills and language, and acquisition of personal and social skills.

Jean Piaget proposed that cognitive development in infancy proceeds through six substages marked predominantly by the acquisition of new sensory and motor skills (sensorimotor development). The cognitive schemas (units of action or thought) of infants move from reflex activities to simple schemas to combinations of schemas and finally to mental representations. Language is a form of a mental schema or a mental representation. When an infant begins to master language, he or she moves to a new stage of cognitive development, the preoperational stage. Piaget's theory of cognition proposed that development during infancy and early childhood is qualitatively different from the cognition of older children and adults. Not only do infants, toddlers, and preschoolers know less, but they also know the world in different ways (through sensorimotor and preoperational schemas).

Language develops in a similar fashion in babies from every culture and language group. It proceeds through a series of cries, coos, babbles, holophrases, and telegraphic phrases to simple, then increasingly more complex sentences. Some theorists (notably Noam Chomsky) believe that human beings are preprogrammed to learn language. Other theorists (notably the behaviorists) believe that language is learned through progressive reinforcements of correct speech. Certainly the stimulation and reinforcement of infant speech does accelerate language development. However, nature and nurture cannot be separated. A biological readiness and cerebral brain organization is also necessary to learn language.

Infants arrive in the world with some ready-made personal and social skills. They show rudimentary emotional reactions through crying (distress) and cooing (delight). Researchers have noted three basic temperamental styles that are the forerunners of later personality development. These temperamental styles (difficult, slow to warm up, and easy) are broad categories. Each unique baby differs in some personal-social way from every other individual infant. However, there is some stability of inborn temperament in humans as they develop from infancy through early childhood and even into adulthood.

Personality and socialization patterns are very susceptible to environmental influences. Much of the personal-social research has focused on mother-infant, mother-toddler, and mother-preschooler interactions to determine the effect of the caregiver on development during infancy and early childhood. As more and more mothers have been returning to work after the birth of each child, more research has been focusing on other caregivers, such as fathers, babysitters, siblings, and day care staff. In the last several years, researchers have also been aware of each unique infant's effect on his or her caregivers. Personal and social development is multifactorial with many persons affecting its outcome. Personal and social development is also affected by nutrition, sleep, health, and many inanimate environmental factors.

Erik Erikson proposed that psychosocial development in infancy and early childhood followed the psychosexual stages of development proposed by Sigmund Freud earlier in the century. Freud felt that libidinous (sexual) urges led young children through oral, anal, and phallic stages of development. Erikson tied social conflicts into the Freudian sexual conflicts. Thus, while infants are going through the oral stage, their nuclear (central) conflict is learning trust vs. mistrust. Caregivers who support the child with a tender loving hold and provide ample opportunities for nursing and sleeping contribute to a sense of trust. Likewise, while toddlers are going through the anal stage, their nuclear conflict is learning autonomy vs. shame and doubt. Caregivers who encourage the child to walk, talk, use the toilet, and do other simple self-help activities contribute to a sense of autonomy. While preschoolers struggle through the Freudian phallic stage, Erikson believed their nuclear conflict is learning initiative vs. guilt. Caregivers who provide opportunities for children to plan and carry out activities of their own choosing contribute to a sense of initiative.

Martha Ainsworth and many other researchers have focused on attachment as a measure of personal and social development in recent years. Most babies become securely attached to their primary caregivers. Securely attached babies become independent, autonomous, initiating toddlers and preschoolers. Some babies, however, develop insecure attachments to their mothers or other primary caregivers. Insecurely attached babies may show an avoidant pattern or an ambivalent (uncertain) pattern of attachment. Efforts to demonstrate that infant day care by itself prevents secure attachment have not been successful. Most infants in good quality day care programs are securely attached to one or more of their primary caregivers.

The articles selected for this unit focus on recent concerns about physical development in infants and young children, cognitive and language development, and personal social development. Each article looks at the whole child so that the reader sees that physical, cognitive, and social changes affect all of the other areas of development.

Looking Ahead: Challenge Questions

Can infants "think" in the sensorimotor stage of cognition?

What are the mental competencies of infants?

How does "at-risk" status at birth affect infant and early childhood development?

How is infant and early childhood development changed by day care?

What does a home visiting program entail?

How can we help young children retrieve forgotten memories?

How can we help young children learn language?

What sex differences exist in young children and why?

A New Perspective on Cognitive Development in Infancy

Jean M. Mandler

Jean Mandler received her Ph.D. from Harvard in 1956. She is currently professor of psychology and cognitive science at the University of California, San Diego. Her interests are cognition and cognitive development, with emphasis on the representation of knowledge. She has done research on how our knowledge of stories, events, and scenes is organized and the way in which such organization affects remembering. In recent years her research has concentrated on conceptual development in infancy and early childhood. Preparation of this article was supported by an NSF grant. Address: Department of Cognitive Science D-015, University of California, San Diego, La Jolla, CA 92093.

Over the past decade something of a revolution has been taking place in our understanding of cognitive development during infancy. For many years one theory dominated the field—that of the Swiss psychologist Jean Piaget. Piaget's views on infancy were so widely known and respected that to many psychologists at least one aspect of development seemed certain: human infants go through a protracted period during which they cannot yet think. They can learn to recognize things and to smile at them, to crawl and to manipulate objects, but they do not yet have concepts or ideas. This period, which Piaget called the sensorimotor stage of development, was said to last until one-and-a-half to two years of age. Only near the end of this stage do infants learn how to represent the world in a symbolic, conceptual manner, and thus advance from infancy into early childhood.

Piaget formulated this view of infancy primarily by observing the development of his own three children—few laboratory techniques were available at the time. More recently, experimental methods have been devised to study infants, and a large body of research has been accumulating. Much of the new work suggests that the theory of a sensori-motor stage of development will have to be substantially modified or perhaps even abandoned (Fig. 1). The present article provides a brief overview of Piaget's theory of sensorimotor development, a summary of recent data that are difficult to reconcile with that theory, and an outline of an alternative view of early mental development.

In Piaget's (1951, 1952, 1954) theory, the first stage of development is said to consist of sensorimotor (perceptual and motor) functioning in an

Recent research suggests that infants have the ability to conceptualize much earlier than we thought

organism that has not yet acquired a representational (conceptual) capacity. The only knowledge infants have is what things look and sound like and how to move themselves around and manipulate objects. This kind of sensorimotor knowledge is often termed procedural or implicit knowledge, and is contrasted with explicit, factual (conceptual) knowledge (e.g., Cohen and Squire 1980; Schacter 1987; Mandler 1988). Factual knowledge is the kind of knowledge one can think about or recall; it is usually considered to be symbolic and propositional. Some factual information may be stored in the form of images, but these are also symbolic, in the sense that they are constructed from both propositional and spatial knowledge. Sensorimotor knowledge, on the other hand, is subsymbolic knowledge; it is knowing *how* to recognize something or use a motor skill, but it does not require explicitly knowing *that* something is the case. It is the

kind of knowledge we build into robots in order to make them recognize and manipulate objects in their environment, and it is also the kind of knowledge we ascribe to lower organisms, which function quite well without the ability to conceptualize facts. It is the kind of knowledge that tends to remain undisturbed in amnesic patients, even when their memory for facts and their personal past is severely impaired.

In the case of babies, the restriction of functioning to sensorimotor processing implies that they can neither think about absent objects nor recall the past. According to Piaget, they lack the capacity even to form an image of things they have seen before; a fortiori, they have no capacity to imagine what will happen tomorrow. Thus, the absence of a symbolic capacity does not mean just that infants cannot understand language or reason; it means that they cannot remember what they did this morning or imagine their mother if she is not present. It is, in short, a most un-Proustian life, not thought about, only lived (Mandler 1983).

According to Piaget, to be able to think about the world requires first that perceptual-motor schemas of objects and relations among them be formed. Then, symbols must be created to stand for these schemas. Several aspects of Piaget's formulation account for the slow course of both these developments. First, on the basis of his observations Piaget assumed that the sensory modalities are unconnected at birth, each delivering separate types of information. Thus, he thought that one of the major tasks of the first half of the sensorimotor stage is to construct schemas integrating the information from initially disconnected sights, sounds, and touches. Until this integration is

From *American Scientist*, Vol. 78, No. 3, May/June 1990, pp. 236-243. Reprinted by permission of *American Scientist*, journal of Sigma Xi, the Scientific Research Society.

accomplished, stable sensorimotor schemas of three-dimensional, solid, sound-producing, textured objects cannot be formed and hence cannot be thought about.

In addition, babies must learn about the causal interrelatedness of objects and the fact that objects continue to exist when not being perceived. Piaget thought that these notions were among the major accomplishments of the second half of the sensorimotor stage. He suggested that they derive from manual activity—for example, repeated covering and uncovering, poking, pushing, and dropping objects while observ-

represent bottles in their absence.

All the anticipatory behavior that Piaget observed throughout the first 18 months was accounted for in similar terms. Signs of anticipation of future events became more wideranging and complex but did not seem to require the use of images or other symbols to represent what was about to happen. Rather, Piaget assumed that an established sensorimotor schema set up a kind of imageless expectation of the next event, followed by recognition when the event took place. He used strict criteria for the presence of imagery—for example, verbal recall of the past

---

William James described the perceptual world of the infant as a "blooming, buzzing confusion"

---

ing the results. Handling objects leads to understanding them; it allows the integration of perceptual and motor information that gives objects substantiality, permanence, and unique identities separate from the self. Since motor control over the hands is slow to develop, to the extent that conceptual understanding requires physical interaction with objects, it is necessarily a late development. Much of the first year of life, then, is spent accomplishing the coordination of the various sources of perceptual and motor information required to form the sensorimotor object schemas that will then be available to be conceptualized.

According to Piaget, the development of the symbolic function is itself a protracted process. In addition to constructing sensorimotor schemas of objects and relations, which form the basic content or meaning of what is to be thought about, symbols to refer to these meanings must be formed. Piaget assumed that the latter development has its precursors in the expectancies involved in conditioning. For example, the sight of a bottle can serve as a signal that milk will follow, and babies soon learn to make anticipatory sucking movements. This process, essentially the same as that involved in Pavlovian conditioning, does not imply a symbolic function; there is no indication that the baby can use such signals to

(which implies the ability to represent absent events to oneself) or rapid problem-solving without trial and error. Neither of these can be ascribed merely to running off a practiced sensorimotor schema, but they require instead some representation of information not perceptually present.

Piaget did not observe recall or covert problem-solving until the end of the sensorimotor period. One might think that the fact that infants begin to acquire language during the latter part of the first year would be difficult to reconcile with a lack of symbolic capacity. However, Piaget characterized early words as imitative schemas, no different in kind from other motor schemas displayed in the presence of familiar situations.

Imitation, in fact, plays an important role in this account, because it provides the source of the development of imagery. Piaget assumed that images are not formed merely from looking at or hearing something, but arise only when what is being perceived is also analyzed. The attempt to imitate the actions of others provides the stimulus for such analysis to take place. Although infants begin to imitate early, it was not until near the end of the first year or beyond that Piaget found his children able to imitate novel actions or actions involving parts of their bodies they could not see themselves, such as blinking or sticking out their

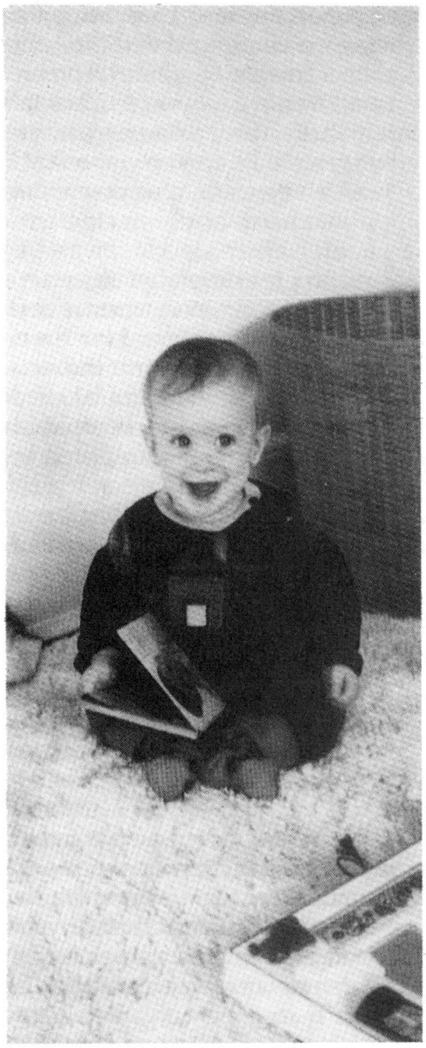

Figure 1. According to the Swiss psychologist Jean Piaget, babies like the author's 8-month-old grandson shown here have learned to recognize people, and their smile is a sign of that recognition. However, Piaget believed that babies have not yet learned to think at such an early age and thus cannot recall even the most familiar people in their lives when those people are not present. Recent research suggests that this view may be mistaken and that babies such as this one are already forming concepts about people and things in their environment.

tongues. He took this difficulty as evidence that they could not form an image of something complex or unobserved until detailed analysis of it had taken place; it is presumably during this analysis that imagery is constructed. Piaget's study of imitation suggested that such analysis, and therefore the formation of imagery, was a late development in infancy. To complete the process of symbol formation, then, the anticipatory mechanisms of sensorimotor schemas become speeded up and appear as images of what will occur, thus allowing genuine representation. Finally, by some mechanism left unspecified, these newly created images can be used to represent the world independent of ongoing sensorimotor activity.

All these developments—constructing sensorimotor schemas, establishing a coherent world of objects and events suitable to form the content of ideas, learning to imitate and to form images that can be used to stand for things—are completed in the second half of the second year, and result in the child's at last being able to develop a conceptual system of ideas. Images can now be used to recall the past and to imagine the future, and even perceptually present objects can begin to be interpreted conceptually as well as by means of motor interactions with them. With the onset of thought, an infant is well on the way to becoming fully human.

This theory of the sensorimotor foundations of thought has come under attack from two sources. One is experimental work suggesting that a stable and differentiated perceptual world is established much earlier in infancy than Piaget realized. The other is recent work suggesting that recall and other forms of symbolic activity (presumably mediated by imagery) occur by at least the second half of the first year. I will discuss each of these findings in turn.

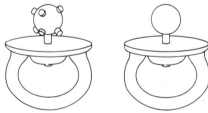

Figure 2. The old idea that the senses are unconnected at birth and are gradually integrated through experience is contradicted by an experiment using bumpy and smooth pacifiers to study the visual recognition of an object that has been experienced only tactilely. A one-month-old infant is habituated to one of the two kinds of pacifiers in its mouth without being allowed to see it. The pacifier is then removed, and the infant is shown both kinds of pacifiers. Infants look longer at the nipple they felt in their mouth. (After Meltzoff and Borton 1979.)

Perceptual development

The notion that the senses are unconnected at birth and that they become integrated only through experience is an old idea that was popularized by William James's (1890) description of the perceptual world of the infant as a "blooming, buzzing confusion." Recent work, however, suggests that either the senses are interrelated at birth or the learning involved in their integration is extremely rapid. There is evidence for integration of auditory and visual information as well as of vision and touch in the first months of life. What follows is a small sample of the research findings.

From birth, infants turn their heads to look at the source of a sound (Wertheimer 1961; Mendelson and Haith 1976). This does not mean that they have any particular expectations of what they will see when they hear a given sound, but it does indicate a mechanism that would enable rapid learning. By four months, if one presents two films of complex events not seen before and accompanied by a single sound track, infants prefer to look at the film that matches the sound (Spelke 1979). Perhaps even more surprising, when infants are presented with two films, each showing only a speaker's face, they will choose the correct film, even when the synchrony between both films and the soundtrack is identical (Kuhl and Meltzoff 1988). In addition, one-month-olds can recognize visually presented objects that they have only felt in their mouths (Fig. 2; Meltzoff and Borton 1979; Walker-Andrews and Gibson 1986). Such data suggest either that the output of each sensory transducer consists in part of the same amodal pattern of information or that some central processing of two similar patterns of information is accomplished. In either case, the data strongly support the view that there is more order and coherence in early perceptual experience than Piaget or James realized.

In addition to sensory coordination, a good deal of information about the nature of objects is provided by the visual system alone, information to which young infants have been shown to be sensitive. For example, it used to be thought that infants have difficulty separating objects from a background, but it ap-

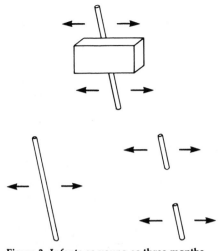

Figure 3. Infants as young as three months can use the perception of relative movement to determine object boundaries. They are habituated to the display shown at the top, which represents a rod moving back and forth behind a block of wood. Then they are tested with the two displays on the bottom: the rod moving as it did before, but with no block in front, or the two pieces of the rod that were visible behind the block, also moving as they did before. Infants tend to continue to habituate to the whole moving rod—that is, they cease to look at it, indicating that it is familiar to them. They prefer to look at the broken rod, indicating that they consider it something new. If the same experiment is done with a stationary rod behind a block, infants exhibit no preference when presented with a whole stationary rod or a broken stationary rod. (After Kellman and Spelke 1983.)

pears that such confusion is a rare event, not the norm. Infants may not "see" that a cup is separable from a saucer without picking it up, but in general they do not have difficulty determining the boundaries of objects. They use information from motion to parse objects from the perceptual surround long before they are able to manipulate them manually. At an age as young as three months, they can use the relative motion of objects against both stationary and moving backgrounds to determine the objects' boundaries (Fig. 3; Kellman and Spelke 1983; Spelke 1988). Even stationary objects are seen as separate if they are spatially separated, whether in a plane or in depth. Infants also use motion to determine object identity, treating an object that moves behind a screen and then reappears as one object rather than two (Spelke and Kestenbaum 1986).

Other work by Spelke and by

Baillargeon (Baillargeon et al. 1985; Baillargeon 1987a; Spelke 1988) shows that infants as young as four months expect objects to be substantial, in the sense that the objects cannot move through other objects nor other objects through them (Fig. 4), and permanent, in the sense that the objects are assumed to continue to exist when hidden. Finally, there is evidence that by six months infants perceive causal relations among moving objects (Leslie 1988) in a fashion that seems to be qualitatively the same as that of adults (Michotte 1963).

From this extensive research program, we can conclude that objects are seen as bounded, unitary, solid, and separate from the background, perhaps from birth but certainly by three to four months of age. Such young infants obviously still have a great deal to learn about objects, but the world must appear both stable and orderly to them, and thus capable of being conceptualized.

Conceptual development

It is easier to study what infants see than what they are thinking about. Nevertheless, there are a few ways to assess whether or not infants are thinking. One way is to look for symbolic activity, such as using a gesture to refer to something else. Piaget (1952) himself called attention to a phenomenon he called motor recognition. For example, he observed his six-month-old daughter make a gesture on catching sight of a familiar toy in a new location. She was accustomed to kicking at the toy in her crib, and when she saw it across the room she made a brief, abbreviated kicking motion. Piaget did not consider this true symbolic activity, because it was a motor movement, not a purely mental act; nevertheless, he suggested that his daughter was referring to, or classifying, the toy by means of her action. In a similar vein, infants whose parents use sign language have been observed to begin to use conventional signs at around six to seven months (Prinz and Prinz 1979; Bonvillian et al. 1983; see Mandler 1988 for discussion).

Another type of evidence of conceptual functioning is recall of absent objects or events. Indeed, Piaget accepted recall as irrefutable evidence of conceptual representation, since there is no way to account for recreating information that is not perceptually present by means of sensorimotor schemas alone; imagery or other symbolic means of representation must be involved. Typically we associate recall with verbal recreation of the past, and this, as Piaget observed, is not usually found until 18 months or older. But recall need not be verbal—and indeed is usually not when we think about past events—so that in principle it is possible in preverbal infants.

One needs to see a baby do something like find a hidden object after a delay or imitate a previously observed event. Until recently, only diary studies provided evidence of recall in the second half of the first year—for example, finding an object hidden in an unfamiliar location after

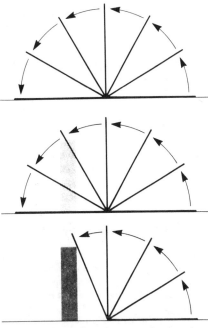

Figure 4. Shown here is a procedure used to demonstrate four- and five-month-olds' memory for the location of a hidden object. At the top is a screen moving through a 180° rotation, to which infants viewing from the right are habituated by repetition. Following habituation, a box is placed behind the screen, and the infants see two test events: an impossible (*middle*) and a possible event (*bottom*). In the impossible event, the screen continues to rotate 180°, moving "magically" through the hidden box (which the experimenter has surreptitiously removed). In the possible event, the screen rotates only to the point where it would hit the box. The infants' surprise at the impossible event demonstrates that they remember an object they cannot see. (After Baillargeon 1987a.)

a 24-hour delay (Ashmead and Perlmutter 1980). Now, however, similar phenomena are beginning to be demonstrated in the laboratory. Meltzoff (1988) showed that nine-month-olds could imitate actions that they had seen performed 24 hours earlier. Each action consisted of an unusual gesture with a novel object—for example, pushing a recessed button in a box (which produced a beeping sound)—and the infants were limited to watching the experimenter carry it out; thus, when they later imitated the action, they could not be merely running off a practiced motor schema in response to seeing the object again. Control subjects, who had been shown the objects but not the actions performed on them, made the correct responses much less frequently. We have replicated this phenomenon with 11-month-olds (McDonough and Mandler 1989).

Because of the difficulties that young infants have manipulating objects, it is not obvious that this technique can be used with infants younger than about eight months. One suspects, however, that if nine-month-olds can recall several novel events after a 24-hour delay, somewhat younger infants can probably recall similar events after shorter delays.

There is a small amount of data from a procedure that does not require a motor response and that, although using quite short delays, suggests recall-like processes. Baillargeon's experiments on object permanence, mentioned earlier, use a technique that requires infants to remember that an object is hidden behind a screen. For example, she has shown that infants are surprised when a screen appears to move backward through an object they have just seen hidden behind it (see Fig. 4). In her experiments with four- and five-month-olds, the infants had to remember for only about 8 to 12 seconds that there was an object behind the screen (Baillargeon et al. 1985; Baillargeon 1987a). However, in more recent work with eight-month-olds, Baillargeon and her colleagues have been successful with a delay of 70 seconds (Fig. 5; Baillargeon et al. 1989). This kind of performance seems to require a representational capacity not attributable to sensorimotor schemas. Not only is an absent

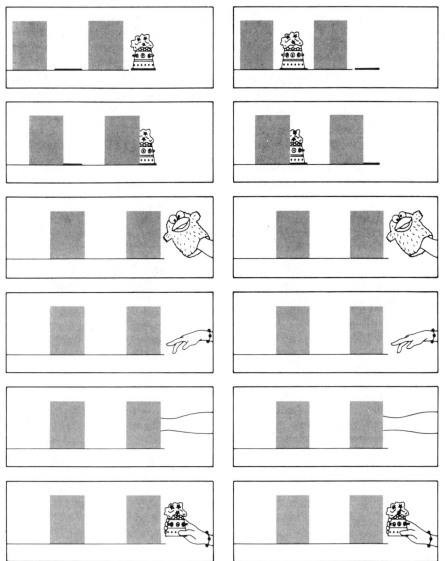

Figure 5. Another procedure involving possible *(left)* and impossible events *(right)* elicits meaningful responses from eight-month-old infants after a delay of 70 seconds. Moving from top to bottom, an object is hidden respectively behind the right or left of two screens; puppets and hand tiptoes are used to keep infants attentive during the delay period; the experimenter reaches behind the right screen and brings the hidden object into view from behind it. (The object was placed there surreptitiously as part of the impossible event.) Surprise at the impossible event indicates memory of the place where the object was hidden. The apparent recall suggests a kind of conceptual functioning that goes beyond the sensorimotor functioning described by Piaget. (After Baillargeon et al. 1989.)

object being represented, but the information is rather precise—for example, Baillargeon (1987b) found that infants remembered not only that an object was hidden but where it was located and how tall it was.

Where do concepts come from?

The data described above indicate that the theory of an exclusively sensorimotor stage of development, in which babies cannot yet represent the world conceptually, is in need of considerable revision. There does not

appear to be a protracted period during which infants have no conception of objects or events and cannot represent them in their absence. A great deal of information is available to and used by infants from an early age, even before they have developed the motor coordination enabling manual exploration that Piaget thought was crucial to conceptual development.

Indeed, a good deal of evidence suggests that we have tended to confuse infants' motor incompetence with conceptual incompetence. Piaget was particularly influenced in his theorizing by the difficulties that

children as old as a year have finding a hidden object, especially when it is hidden in more than one location a number of times in succession. The phenomena he demonstrated have been replicated many times, but it now appears that much of the difficulty infants have in such situations is due not to a lack of understanding of object permanence but to other factors. For example, repeatedly hiding an object in different locations can be confusing and leads to perseverative responding to the same place (see Diamond 1985; Mandler 1988, in press).

If a conceptual system of knowledge has begun to be formed by at least six months and perhaps earlier, where does it come from? Piaget's theory of a transformation of well-developed action schemas into conceptual thought cannot account for conceptual knowledge occurring before the action schemas themselves have developed. On the other hand, perceptual schemas about objects and events develop early. What is needed, then, is some mechanism for transforming these schemas into concepts, or ideas, about what is being perceived, preferably a mechanism that can operate as soon as perceptual schemas are formed.

Little has been written about this problem. One approach is to assume that even young infants are capable of redescribing perceptual information in a conceptual format. I have suggested a mechanism that might accomplish this (Mandler 1988): perceptual analysis, a process by which one perception is actively compared to another and similarities or differences between them are noted. (Such analysis, like other sorts of concept formation, requires some kind of vocabulary; this aspect, still little understood, is discussed below.) The simplest case of perceptual analysis occurs when two simultaneously presented objects are compared, or a single object is compared to an already established representation (i.e., one notes similarities or differences between what one is looking at and what one recalls about it). It is the process by which we discover that sugar bowls have two handles and teacups only one, or that a friend wears glasses. Unless we have engaged in this kind of analysis (or someone has told us), the information will not be accessible for us to think about. Much of the time, of course, we do not make such comparisons, which is why we often can recall few details of even recent experiences.

Although it is analytic, perceptual analysis consists primarily of simplification. Our perceptual system regularly processes vast amounts of information that never become accessible to thought. For example, we make use of a great deal of complex information every time we recognize a face: proportions, contours, subtle shading, relationships among various facial features, and so on. Yet little of this information is available to our thought processes. Few people are aware of the proportions of the human face—it is not something they have ever conceptualized. Even fewer know how they determine whether a face is male or female (this categorization depends on subtle differences in proportions). For the most part we do not even have words to describe the nuances that our perceptual apparatus uses instantly and effortlessly to make such a perceptual categorization.

For us to be able to think about such matters, the information must be reduced and simplified into a conceptual format. One way this redescription is done is via language; someone (perhaps an artist who has already carried out the relevant analytic process) conceptualizes aspects of a face for us. The other way is to look at a face and analyze it ourselves, such as noting that the ears are at the same level as the eyes. The analysis is often couched in linguistic form, but it need not be. Images can be used, but these, in spite of having spatial properties, have a major conceptual component (e.g., Kosslyn 1983).

An infant, of course, does not have the benefit of language, the means by which older people acquire much of their factual knowledge. So if infants are to transform perceptual schemas into thoughts, they must be able to analyze the perceptual information they receive. The perceptual system itself cannot decide that only animate creatures move by themselves or that containers must have bottoms if they are to hold things, and so forth. These are facts visually observed, but they are highly simpli-

Infants whose parents use sign language have been observed to begin to use conventional signs at around six to seven months

fied versions of the information available to be conceptualized.

The notion of perceptual analysis is similar to the process that Piaget theorized as being responsible for the creation of images. He thought that this kind of analysis does not even begin until around eight or nine months and does not result in imagery until later still. However, he had no evidence that image formation is such a late-developing process, and his own description of his children's imitative performance as early as three or four months strongly suggests that the process of perceptual analysis had begun. For example, he observed imitation of clapping hands at that time, a performance that would seem to require a good deal of analysis, considering the difference between what infants see and what they must do. In many places in his account of early imitation, Piaget

noted that the infants watched him carefully, studying both their own and his actions. Other developmental psychologists have commented on the same phenomenon. For example, Werner and Kaplan (1963) noted that infants begin "contemplating" objects at between three and five months. Ruff (1986) has documented intense examination of objects at six months (the earliest age she studied).

To investigate contemplation or analysis of objects experimentally is not easy. A possible measure is the number of times an infant looks back and forth between two objects that are presented simultaneously. Janowsky (1985), for example, showed that this measure increased significantly between four and eight months. At four months infants tend to look first at one object and then the other; at eight months they switch back and forth between the two a

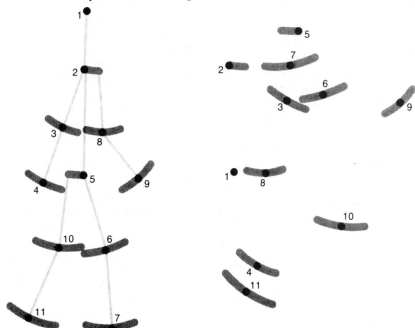

Figure 6. An equally subtle ability is involved in this demonstration of three-month-olds' responses to biological as opposed to nonbiological motion. The infants watch videotapes of computer-generated displays. On the left is a display of 11 point-lights moving as if attached to the head and major joints of a person walking. The motion vectors drawn through each point represent the perceived motions of the display; the lines connecting points, like the numbers and vectors, are not visible to the infants. The display on the right is identical to the normal walker except that the relative locations of the point-lights are scrambled. Correspondingly numbered points in the two displays undergo identical motions. Infants show greater interest in the scrambled display, indicating that they consider it novel. (After Bertenthal et al. 1987.)

good many times. Fox and his colleagues (1979) have reported a similar phenomenon. Interestingly, Janowsky found that the differences in looking back and forth are not associated with differences in total looking time, the rate at which infants habituate to objects (cease to look at them), or accuracy of recognition. So the looking back and forth must serve some other function. I would suggest that it is a comparison process, by which one object is being contrasted with the other.

A vocabulary for concepts

Assuming that perceptual analysis can lead to concept formation, it is still necessary to formulate the vocabulary in which the resulting concepts are couched. But here we face one of the major stumbling blocks in psychological theory: the problem of specifying conceptual primitives (see Smith and Medin 1981). Perhaps because of its difficulty, it has been largely ignored by developmental psychologists, in spite of the fact that any theory of conceptual development must resolve the issue of what the earliest concepts are like, no matter when they may first be formed. Leslie (1988) has offered an analysis of the primitives involved in early causal concepts, and people working on language acquisition have speculated about semantic primitives. For example, Slobin (1985) points out that children must already have concepts of objects and events, as well as relational notions about them, in order for language to be acquired. Since language comprehension begins at around nine to ten months (and perhaps earlier for sign language), some kind of conceptual system must be well established by that time. But we have almost no information as to its character.

Help may come from recent studies by cognitive linguists (e.g., Fauconnier 1985; Johnson 1987; Lakoff 1987). Although the primary goal of these theorists is to understand how language works, their analyses of the root concepts expressed in language may be of use in our search for babies' earliest concepts. For example, Lakoff and Johnson have proposed that image schemas—notions derived from spatial structure, such as trajectory, up-down, container, part-whole, end-of-path, and link—form the foundation of the conceptualizing capacity. These authors suggest that image schemas are derived from preconceptual perceptual structures, forming the core of many of our concepts of objects and events and of their metaphorical extensions to abstract realms. They demonstrate in great detail how many of our most complex concepts are grounded in such primitive notions. I would characterize image schemas as simplified redescriptions of sensorimotor schemas, noting that they seem to be reasonably within the capacity of infant conceptualization.

The potential usefulness of image schemas as conceptual primitives can be illustrated by the example of the container schema. According to Johnson and Lakoff, the structural elements of this image schema are "interior," "boundary," and "exterior." It has a bodily basis likely to be appreciated by quite young infants, and a perceptual basis that seems to require minimal redescription of the object schemas described earlier. It also has a simple binary logic—either in or not-in; if A is in B and B is in C, then A is in C—that may or may not be the sensorimotor basis of the Boolean logic of classes, as Lakoff suggests, but is certainly a characteristic of concepts as opposed to percepts. (The conceptual system tends to reduce the continuous information delivered by the perceptual system to a small number of discrete values.)

The use of such an image schema might be responsible for the better performance nine-month-old infants show on hiding tasks when a container is used rather than cloths or screens (Freeman et al. 1980). Current work by Baillargeon (pers. com.) suggests that at approximately the same age infants are surprised when containers without bottoms appear to hold things. Of course, these are only fragments of the kind of information needed to document the development of the idea of a container, but they indicate how we might go about tracking the early establishment of simple concepts.

A more complex concept that may also be acquired relatively early in infancy is that of animacy. Consider some possible sources for such a concept. We know that infants differentiate biological from nonbiological motion as early as three months (Fig. 6; Bertenthal et al. 1987). This perceptual differentiation, although an excellent source of information, does not constitute a concept by itself; it is an accomplishment similar to categorizing male and female faces, which infants have learned to do by six months (Fagan and Singer 1979). As discussed earlier, such perceptual categorization is not accessible for purposes of conceptual thought unless it has been redescribed in conceptual terms. An infant needs to conceptualize some differences between categories of moving objects, such as noting that one type starts up on its own and (sometimes) responds to the infant's signals, whereas the other type does not. An image schema of a notion such as beginning-of-path could be used to redescribe the perceptual information involved in initiation of motion. A link schema (whose elements are two entities and some kind of path between them) could be used to describe the observation of responsivity to self. From such simple foundations might arise a primitive concept of animal, a concept that we have reason to believe is present in some form by at least the end of the first year of life (Golinkoff and Halperin 1983; Mandler and Bauer 1988).

These are some examples of how a conceptual system might emerge from a combination of perceptual input and some relatively simple redescriptions of that input. I have suggested that a mechanism of perceptual analysis could enable such redescription, with the terms of the redescription being derived from spatial structure. The mechanism would not require an extended period of

---

A good deal of evidence suggests that we have tended to confuse infants' motor incompetence with conceptual incompetence

---

exclusively sensorimotor functioning but would allow conceptualization of the world to begin early in infancy. The data I have summarized indicate that babies do indeed begin to think earlier than we thought. Therefore, it seems safe to assume that they either are born with or acquire early in life the capacity to form concepts, rather than to assume that conceptual functioning can occur only as an outcome of a lengthy sensorimotor stage.

References

Ashmead, D. H., and M. Perlmutter. 1980. Infant memory in everyday life. In *New Directions for Child Development: Children's Memory*, vol. 10, ed. M. Perlmutter, pp. 1–16. Jossey-Bass.

Baillargeon, R. 1987a. Object permanence in 3.5- and 4.5-month-old infants. *Devel. Psychol.* 23:655–64.

———. 1987b. Young infants' reasoning about the physical and spatial properties of a hidden object. *Cognitive Devel.* 2:179–200.

Baillargeon, R., J. De Vos, and M. Graber. 1989. Location memory in 8-month-old infants in a nonsearch AB task: Further evidence. *Cognitive Devel.* 4:345–67.

Baillargeon, R., E. S. Spelke, and S. Wasserman. 1985. Object permanence in five-month-old infants. *Cognition* 20:191–208.

Bertenthal, B. I., D. R. Proffitt, S. J. Kramer, and N. B. Spetner. 1987. Infants' encoding of kinetic displays varying in relative coherence. *Devel. Psychol.* 23:171–78.

Bonvillian, J. D., M. D. Orlansky, and L. L. Novack. 1983. Developmental milestones: Sign language and motor development. *Child Devel.* 54:1435–45.

Cohen, N. J., and L. R. Squire. 1980. Preserved learning and retention of pattern-analyzing skills in amnesia: Dissociation of knowing how and knowing that. *Science* 210:207–10.

Diamond, A. 1985. The development of the ability to use recall to guide action, as indicated by infants' performance on AB. *Child Devel.* 56:868–83.

Fagan, J. F., III, and L. T. Singer. 1979. The role of simple feature differences in infant recognition of faces. *Infant Behav. Devel.* 2:39–46.

Fauconnier, G. 1985. *Mental Spaces.* MIT Press.

Fox, N., J. Kagan, and S. Weiskopf. 1979. The growth of memory during infancy. *Genetic Psychol. Mono.* 99:91–130.

Freeman, N. H., S. Lloyd, and C. G. Sinha. 1980. Infant search tasks reveal early concepts of containment and canonical usage of objects. *Cognition* 8:243–62.

Golinkoff, R. M., and M. S. Halperin. 1983. The concept of animal: One infant's view. *Infant Behav. Devel.* 6:229–33.

James, W. 1890. *The Principles of Psychology.* Holt.

Janowsky, J. S. 1985. Cognitive development and reorganization after early brain injury. Ph.D. diss., Cornell Univ.

Johnson, M. 1987. *The Body in the Mind: The Bodily Basis of Meaning, Imagination, and Reason.* Univ. of Chicago Press.

Kellman, P. J., and E. S. Spelke. 1983. Perception of partly occluded objects in infancy. *Cognitive Psychol.* 15:483–524.

Kosslyn, S. M. 1983. *Ghosts in the Mind's Machine: Creating and Using Images in the Brain.* Norton.

Kuhl, P. K., and A. N. Meltzoff. 1988. Speech as an intermodal object of perception. In *Perceptual Development in Infancy: The Minnesota Symposia on Child Psychology*, vol. 20, ed. A. Yonas, pp. 235–66. Erlbaum.

Lakoff, G. 1987. *Women, Fire, and Dangerous Things: What Categories Reveal about the Mind.* Univ. of Chicago Press.

Leslie, A. 1988. The necessity of illusion: Perception and thought in infancy. In *Thought without Language*, ed. L. Weiskrantz, pp. 185–210. Clarendon Press.

Mandler, J. M. 1983. Representation. In *Cognitive Development*, ed. J. H. Flavell and E. M. Markman, pp. 420–94. Vol. 3 of *Manual of Child Psychology*, ed. P. Mussen. Wiley.

———. 1988. How to build a baby: On the development of an accessible representational system. *Cognitive Devel.* 3:113–36.

———. In press. Recall of events by preverbal children. In *The Development and Neural Bases of Higher Cognitive Functions*, ed. A. Diamond. New York Academy of Sciences Press.

Mandler, J. M., and P. J. Bauer. 1988. The cradle of categorization: Is the basic level basic? *Cognitive Devel.* 3:247–64.

McDonough, L., and J. M. Mandler. 1989. Immediate and deferred imitation with 11-month-olds: A comparison between familiar and novel actions. Poster presented at meeting of the Society for Research in Child Development, Kansas City.

Meltzoff, A. N. 1988. Infant imitation and memory: Nine-month-olds in immediate and deferred tests. *Child Devel.* 59:217–25.

Meltzoff, A. N., and R. W. Borton. 1979. Intermodal matching by human neonates. *Nature* 282:403–04.

Mendelson, M. J., and M. M. Haith. 1976. The relation between audition and vision in the newborn. *Monographs of the Society for Research in Child Development*, no. 41, serial no. 167.

Michotte, A. 1963. *The Perception of Causality.* Methuen.

Piaget, J. 1951. *Play, Dreams and Imitation in Childhood*, trans. C. Gattegno and F. M. Hodgson. Norton.

———. 1952. *The Origins of Intelligence in Children*, trans. M. Cook. International Universities Press.

———. 1954. *The Construction of Reality in the Child*, trans. M. Cook. Basic Books.

Prinz, P. M., and E. A. Prinz. 1979. Simultaneous acquisition of ASL and spoken English (in a hearing child of a deaf mother and hearing father). Phase I: Early lexical development. *Sign Lang. Stud.* 25:283–96.

Ruff, H. A. 1986. Components of attention during infants' manipulative exploration. *Child Devel.* 57:105–14.

Schacter, D. L. 1987. Implicit memory: History and current status. *J. Exper. Psychol.: Learning, Memory, Cognition* 13:501–18.

Slobin, D. I. 1985. Crosslinguistic evidence for the language-making capacity. In *The Crosslinguistic Study of Language Acquisition*, vol. 2, ed. D. I. Slobin, pp. 1157–1256. Erlbaum.

Smith, E. E., and D. L. Medin. 1981. *Categories and Concepts.* Harvard Univ. Press.

Spelke, E. S. 1979. Perceiving bimodally specified events in infancy. *Devel. Psychol.* 15:626–36.

———. 1988. The origins of physical knowledge. In *Thought without Language*, ed. L. Weiskrantz, pp. 168–84. Clarendon Press.

Spelke, E. S., and R. Kestenbaum. 1986. Les origines du concept d'objet. *Psychologie française* 31:67–72.

Walker-Andrews, A. S., and E. J. Gibson. 1986. What develops in bimodal perception? In *Advances in Infancy Research*, vol. 4, ed. L. P. Lipsitt and C. Rovee-Collier, pp. 171–81. Ablex.

Werner, H., and B. Kaplan. 1963. *Symbol Formation.* Wiley.

Wertheimer, M. 1961. Psychomotor coordination of auditory and visual space at birth. *Science* 134:1692.

The Amazing Minds of Infants

Looking here, looking there, babies are like little scientists, constantly exploring the world around them, with innate abilities we're just beginning to understand.

Text by **Lisa Grunwald**
Reporting by **Jeff Goldberg**

Additional reporting: **Stacey Bernstein, Anne Hollister**

A light comes on. Shapes and colors appear. Some of the colors and shapes start moving. Some of the colors and shapes make noise. Some of the noises are voices. One is a mother's. Sometimes she sings. Sometimes she says things. Sometimes she leaves. What can an infant make of the world? In the blur of perception and chaos of feeling, what does a baby know?

Most parents, observing infancy, are like travelers searching for famous sites: first tooth, first step, first word, first illness, first shoes, first full night of sleep. Most subtle, and most profound of all, is the first time the clouds of infancy part to reveal the little light of a human intelligence.

For many parents, that revelation may be the moment when they see their baby's first smile. For others, it may be the moment when they watch their child show an actual

---

At three months, babies can learn—and remember for weeks—visual sequences and simple mechanical tasks.

---

preference—for a lullaby, perhaps, or a stuffed animal. But new evidence is emerging to show that even before those moments, babies already have wonderfully active minds.

Of course, they're not exactly chatty in their first year of life, so what—and how—babies truly think may always remain a mystery. But using a variety of ingenious techniques that interpret how infants watch and move, students of child development are discovering a host of unsuspected skills. From a rudimentary understanding of math to a

sense of the past and the future, from precocious language ability to an innate understanding of physical laws, children one year and younger know a lot more than they're saying.

MEMORY

Does an infant remember anything? Penelope Leach, that slightly scolding doyenne of the child development field, warns in *Babyhood* that a six- to eight-month-old "cannot hold in his mind a picture of his mother, nor of where she is." And traditionally psychologists have assumed that infants cannot store memories until, like adults, they have the language skills needed to form and retrieve them. But new research suggests that babies as young as three months may be taking quite accurate mental notes.

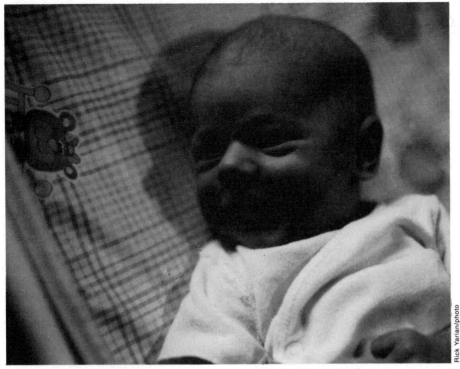

Babies show an unexpected ability to remember surprisingly intricate details.

Rick Yarian/photo

In his lab at the University of Denver, psychologist Marshall Haith has spent much of the past four years putting infants into large black boxes where they lie and look up at TV screens. The program they see is a Haith invention: a sequence of colorful objects appearing on different sides of the monitor. Using an infrared camera linked to a computer, Haith follows the babies' eye movements and has found that after only five tries the babies can anticipate where the next object will appear. With a little more practice, they can foresee a four-step sequence. And up to two weeks later, most can still predict it. Says Haith: "The babies are not just looking. They're analyzing, creating little hypotheses."

Similar findings by Carolyn Rovee-Collier, a psychologist at Rutgers University, suggest that infants can remember surprisingly intricate details. In a typical experiment, she places a baby in a crib beneath an elaborate mobile, ties

one of the baby's ankles to it with a satin ribbon, then observes as the baby kicks and—often gleefully—makes it move. When, weeks later, the baby's feet are left untied and the mobile is returned to the crib, the baby will try to kick again, presumably recalling the palmy days of kicking the last time. But if the mobile's elements are changed even slightly, the baby will remain unmoved—and unmoving. "When we change things," explains Rovee-Collier, "it wipes out the memory. But as soon as we bring back what had become familiar and expected, the memory comes right back. What we've learned from this is that even at two and a half months, an infant's memory is very developed, very specific and incredibly detailed."

Rachel Clifton, a psychologist at the University of Massachusetts, says that an infant's experience at six months can be remembered a full two years later. Clifton stumbled upon her findings while researching motor and hearing

skills. Three years ago she placed 16 six-month-olds in a pitch-dark room with objects that made different sounds. Using infrared cameras like Haith's, she observed how and when the infants reached for the objects. Later, realizing she had created a unique situation that couldn't have been duplicated in real life, she wondered if the babies would remember their experience. Two years after the original experiment, collaborating with psychologist Nancy Myers, she brought the same 16 children back to the lab, along with a control group of 16 other two-and-a-half-year-olds. Amazingly, the experimental group showed the behavior they had at six months, reaching for objects and showing no fear. Fewer control-group toddlers reached for the objects, and many of them cried.

Says Myers: "For so long, we didn't think that infants could rep-

At five months, babies have the raw ability to add.

resent in their memories the events that were going on around them, but put them back in a similar situation, as we did, and you can make the memory accessible."

MATH

At least a few parental eyebrows—and undoubtedly some expectations—were raised by this recent headline in *The New York Times:* "Study Finds Babies at 5 Months Grasp Simple Mathematics." The story, which reported on the findings of Karen Wynn, a psychologist at the University of Arizona, explained that infants as young as five months had been found to exhibit "a rudimentary ability to add and subtract."

Wynn, who published her research in the renowned scientific journal *Nature,* had based her experiments on a widely observed phenomenon: Infants look longer at things that are unexpected to them, thereby revealing what they do expect, or know. Wynn enacted addition and subtraction equations for babies using Mickey Mouse dolls. In a typical example, she had the babies watch as she placed a doll on a puppet stage, hid it behind a screen, then placed a second doll behind the screen (to represent one plus one). When she removed the screen to reveal three, not two, Mickey Mouse dolls, the infants stared longer at such incorrect outcomes than they had at correct ones. Wynn believes that babies' numerical understanding is "an innate mechanism, somehow built into the biological structure."

Her findings have been met with enthusiasm in the field—not least from Mark Strauss at the University of Pittsburgh, who a decade ago found that somewhat older babies could distinguish at a glance the difference between one, two, three and four balls—nearly as many objects as adults can decipher without counting. Says Strauss: "Five-month-olds are clearly thinking about quantities and applying numerical concepts to their world."

Wynn's conclusions have also inspired skepticism among some researchers who believe her results may reflect infants' ability to perceive things but not necessarily an ability to know what they're perceiving. Wynn herself warns parents not to leap to any conclu-

sions, and certainly not to start tossing algebra texts into their children's cribs. Still, she insists: "A lot more is happening in infants' minds than we've tended to give them credit for."

LANGUAGE

In an old stand-up routine, Robin Williams used to describe his son's dawning ability as a mimic of words—particularly those of the deeply embarrassing four-letter variety. Most parents decide they can no longer speak with complete freedom when their children start talking. Yet current research on language might prompt some to start censoring themselves even earlier.

At six months, babies recognize their native tongue.

At Seattle's University of Washington, psychologist Patricia Kuhl has shown that long before infants actually begin to learn words, they can sort through a jumble of spoken sounds in search of the ones that have meaning. From birth to four months, according to Kuhl, babies are "universal linguists" capable of distinguishing each of the 150 sounds that make up all human speech. But by just six months, they have begun the metamorphosis into specialists who recognize the speech sounds of their native tongue.

In Kuhl's experiment babies listened as a tape-recorded voice repeated vowel and consonant combinations. Each time the sounds changed—from "ah" to "oooh," for example—a toy bear in a box

was lit up and danced. The babies quickly learned to look at the bear when they heard sounds that were new to them. Studying Swedish and American six-month-olds, Kuhl found they ignored subtle variations in pronunciation of their own language's sounds—for instance, the different ways two people might pronounce "ee"—but they heard similar variations in a foreign language as separate sounds. The implication? Six-month-olds can already discern the sounds they will later need for speech. Says Kuhl: "There's nothing external in these six-month-olds that would provide you with a clue that something like this is going on."

By eight to nine months, comprehension is more visible, with babies looking at a ball when their mothers say "ball," for example. According to psychologist Donna Thal at the University of California, San Diego, it is still impossible to gauge just how many words babies understand at this point, but her recent studies of slightly older children indicate that comprehension may exceed expression by a factor as high as a hundred to one. Thal's studies show that although some babies are slow in starting to talk, comprehension appears to be equal between the late talkers and early ones.

PHYSICS

No, no one is claiming that an eight-month-old can compute the trajectory of a moon around a planet. But at Cornell University, psychologist Elizabeth Spelke is finding that babies as young as four months have a rudimentary knowledge of the way the world works—or should work.

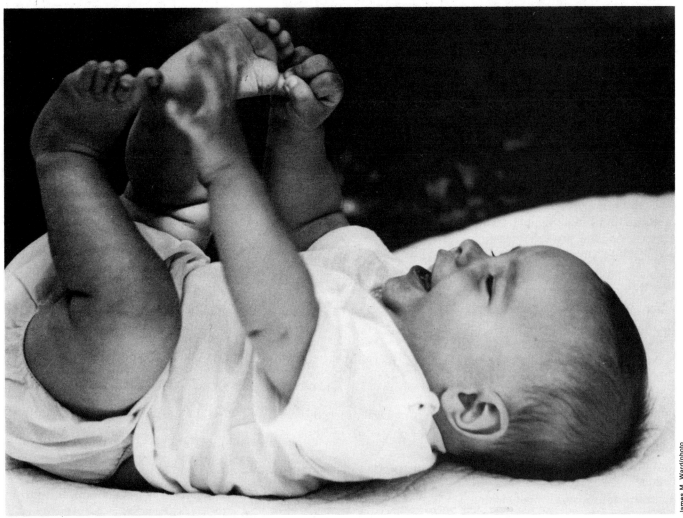

Babies learn how physical objects behave by moving their body parts.

Babies have a built-in sense of how objects behave.

Spelke sets her young subjects up before a puppet stage, where she shows them a series of unexpected actions: a ball seems to roll through a solid barrier, another seems to leap between two platforms, a third seems to hang in midair. Like Karen Wynn with her math experiments, Spelke measures the babies' looking time and has recorded longer intervals for unexpected actions than for expected ones. Again like Wynn, Spelke believes that babies must have some "core" knowledge—in this case, about the way physical objects behave. Says Spelke: "At an age when infants are not able to talk about objects, move around objects, reach for and manipulate objects, or even see objects with high resolution, they appear to recognize where a moving object is when it has left their view and make inferences about where it should be when it comes into sight again."

The notion of an infant's possessing any innate mechanism—other than reflexes like sucking that fade with time—would have shocked the shoes off the pioneers of child development research, who believed, as some still do, that what we know can be learned only through experience. But the belief in biologically programmed core knowledge lies at the heart of the current research—not only with math and physics but with other cognitive skills as well. Indeed, Carnegie Mellon's Mark Johnson believes that the ability of infants to recognize the human face is not learned, as previously thought, but is present at birth. Studying infants, some only 10 minutes old, Johnson has observed a marked preference for pictures of faces to pictures of blank ovals or faces with scrambled features. He believes that we are born with a "template" of the human face that aids our survival by helping us recognize our meal ticket.

EMOTIONS: THE SHY AND THE LIVELY

A growing number of researchers believe early temperament may indicate later troubles.

One thing that infants are *not* good at is hiding what they feel. Fear, glee, rage, affection: Long before babies start talking, emotions tumble out of them in gestures, tears and belly laughs. But measuring infant temperament—finding a way to quantify its traits—has always been harder than measuring skills.

Around the country, researchers are now combining questionnaires filled in by parents, home visits by trained observers, and newly devised lab tests to explore the mystery of temperamenat. Concentrating on babies older than eight months (the age at which the full range of infant emotions has emerged), investigators have designed more than 50 experimental situations to provoke emotions from fear to sadness, from interest to pleasure. Most children's reactions fall within an average range on such tests. But there are babies on either extreme, and psychologist Nathan Fox at the University of Maryland has begun to explore their responses. Putting his babies in electroencephalogram (EEG) helmets, he has found that particularly inhibited babies show a distinctive brain-wave pattern, which others believe may predict later emotional problems, including depression. Although some scientists agree that early behavior can predict later temperament, other researchers argue that enduring character traits are the exception, not the rule. For psychiatrist Stanley Greenspan of Bethesda, Md., the ability of infants to change is an article of faith. Specializing in babies as young as three months, Greenspan says he can treat what he calls the garden-variety problems of sleep disorders, tan-

Long before babies begin talking, emotions are graphically expressed in their gestures and facial expressions.

trums and anger in a few sessions. (Don't imagine tiny couches for infant patients; although the babies are closely observed, it's the parents who often get treatment.) For more severe problems, such as suspected learning disorders, he recommends more intensive early intervention—often involving a team of therapists—and has found that this can make a huge difference: "Babies who were very scared, shy and inhibited can completely change and become very assertive, outgoing and confident over a number of months."

The University of Washington's Mary Rothbart has compared infants in Japan, the Netherlands and the U.S. and notes that northern European mothers are most prone to ignore their babies' fussiness with a stiff-upper-lip approach. When tested at one year by having their mothers leave a room, the Dutch babies are the most distressed and ignore their mothers upon their return. Psychologists call this response an "insecure attachment relationship," and some regard it as an early warning of later anxiety disorders. Says Rothbart: "In the process of soothing a baby, you're helping to teach it to shift its attention away from negative sensations. Adults with anxiety disorders may never have learned to do this." Tellingly, when Dutch mothers were instructed to soothe and play with their fussy babies, the follow-up sessions showed positive results. "With intervention," concludes Rothbart, "you can turn things around."

TAKING INFANTS SERIOUSLY

The ultimate question becomes, should education begin at three months?

One question that might leap to the minds of parents newly informed of their infants' skills is a simple one: So what? What does it mean if children really have these unexpected abilities?

Pointing to the findings on memory that she has published with partner Rachel Clifton, Nancy Myers suggests that if memories of the babies' experience allowed them to be unafraid in the pitch-black room, then exposing children to a wide variety of events and places may make them more accepting of similar situations later on. "I don't want to say that mothers should make an extreme effort to stimulate their babies," Myers says, "but taking a baby to different places, allowing him to see and smell different things, is an important means of establishing familiarity. It will allow the baby to feel freer in the future."

But what about other kinds of skills: Should infants' innate abilities with language or math be consciously nurtured and pushed along?

In Philadelphia, instructors at the Institutes for the Achievement of Human Potential have been coaching parents since 1963 to teach their babies to read from birth. Touting "genetic potential," their program recommends that parents write out on cards everything from "nose" to "kiss" to "Mommy." The new findings about infants' skills have hardly gone unnoticed at the Institutes, where director Janet Doman says: "For the past thirty years, we've been saying that children can learn at very early ages. It's nice to know that science is finally validating what we've known all along."

Yet many of the scientists performing the experiments question the value of such intensive efforts. Says Rutgers's Carolyn Rovee-Collier: "Most of us agree that an infant could be taught to recognize letters and numbers. But the problem is that parents who do these kinds of programs start investing a lot in their infants and become very bound up in their success. It puts great strain on the infants and the parents."

University of Denver psychologist Marshall Haith agrees: "Babies are born prepared to take on the world. We've got to get away from the feeling that we've got this wonderful brain sitting there and we've got to keep pumping information into it. Nature wouldn't have done anything so stupid."

To most researchers, the moral of the story seems to be: Respect your baby, but don't go nuts. "Don't waste your child's fun months," says Karen Wynn, who says her findings about math "should be viewed as no more than a new insight for parents who have young children." Says the University of Pittsburgh's Mark Strauss: "Ideally, we can tell parents a lot more about subtle things they can watch happening in their infants, and that will make watching and getting involved more fun."

CLIPPED WINGS

The Fullest Look Yet at How
Prenatal Exposure to Drugs, Alcohol, and Nicotine
Hobbles Children's Learning

LUCILE F. NEWMAN AND STEPHEN L. BUKA

Lucile F. Newman is a professor of community health and anthropology at Brown University and the director of the Preventable Causes of Learning Impairment Project. Stephen L. Buka is an epidemiologist and instructor at the Harvard Medical School and School of Public Health.

SOME FORTY thousand children a year are born with learning impairments related to their mother's alcohol use. Drug abuse during pregnancy affects 11 percent of newborns each year—more than 425,000 infants in 1988. Some 260,000 children each year are born at below normal weights—often because they were prenatally exposed to nicotine, alcohol, or illegal drugs.

What learning problems are being visited upon these children? The existing evidence has heretofore been scattered in many different fields of research—in pediatric medicine, epidemiology, public health, child development, and drug and alcohol abuse. Neither educators, health professionals, nor policy makers could go to one single place to receive a full picture of how widespread or severe were these preventable causes of learning impairment.

In our report for the Education Commission of the States, excerpts of which follow, we combed these various fields to collect and synthesize the major studies that relate prenatal exposure to nicotine, alcohol, and illegal drugs* with various indexes of students' school performance.

The state of current research in this area is not always as full and satisfying as we would wish. Most of what

*The full report for the ECS also addressed the effect on children's learning of fetal malnutrition, pre- and postnatal exposure to lead, and child abuse and neglect.

exists is statistical and epidemiological data, which document the frequency of certain high-risk behaviors and correlate those behaviors to student performance. Such data are very interesting and useful, as they allow teachers and policy makers to calculate the probability that a student with a certain family history will experience school failure. But such data often cannot control for the effects of other risk factors, many of which tend to cluster in similar populations. In other words, the same mother who drinks during her pregnancy may also use drugs, suffer from malnutrition, be uneducated, a teenager, or poor—all factors that might ultimately affect her child's school performance. An epidemiological study generally can't tell you how much of a child's poor school performance is due exclusively to a single risk factor.

Moreover, the cumulative damage wrought by several different postnatal exposures may be greater than the damage caused by a single one operating in isolation. And many of the learning problems that are caused by prenatal exposure to drugs can be compounded by such social factors as poverty and parental disinterest and, conversely, overcome if the child lives in a high-quality postnatal environment.

All of these facts make it difficult to isolate and interpret the level and character of the damage that is caused by a single factor. Further, until recently, there was little interest among researchers in the effects of prenatal alcohol exposure because there was little awareness that it was affecting a substantial number of children. The large cohort of children affected by crack is just now entering the schools, so research on their school performance hasn't been extensive.

What does clearly emerge from the collected data is that our classrooms now include many students whose ability to pay attention, sit still, or fully develop their visual, auditory, and language skills was impaired even before they walked through our schoolhouse doors. On the

From *American Educator,* Spring 1991, pp. 27-33, 42. Adapted from *Every Child a Learner: Reducing Risks of Learning Impairment During Pregnancy and Infancy,* supported by the Exxon Educational Foundation, published by the Education Commission of the States. Reprinted with permission from *American Educator,* the quarterly journal of the American Federation of Teachers.

brighter side, the evidence that many of these impairments can be overcome by improved environmental conditions suggests that postnatal treatment is possible; promising experiments in treatment are, in fact, under way and are outlined at the end of this article.

1. Low Birthweight

The collection of graphs begins with a set on low birthweight, which is strongly associated with lowered I.Q. and poor school performance. While low birthweight can be brought on by other factors, including maternal malnutrition and teenage pregnancy, significant causes are maternal smoking, drinking, and drug use.

Around 6.9 percent of babies born in the United States weigh less than 5.5 pounds (2,500 grams) at birth and are considered "low-birthweight" babies. In 1987, this accounted for some 259,100 infants. Low birthweight may result when babies are born prematurely (born too early) or from intrauterine growth retardation (born too small) as a result of maternal malnutrition or actions that restrict blood flow to the fetus, such as smoking or drug use.

In 1987, about 48,750 babies were born at very low birthweights (under 3.25 lbs. or 1,500 grams). Research estimates that 6 to 8 percent of these babies experience major handicaps such as severe mental retardation or cerebral palsy (Eilers et al., 1986; Hack and Breslau, 1986). Another 25 to 26 percent have borderline I.Q. scores, problems in understanding and expressing language, or other deficits (Hack and Breslau, 1986; Lefebvre et al., 1988; Nickel et al., 1982; Vohr et al., 1988). Although these children may enter the public school system, many of them show intellectual disabilities and require special educational assistance. Reading, spelling, handwriting, arts, crafts, and mathematics are difficult school subjects for them. Many are late in developing

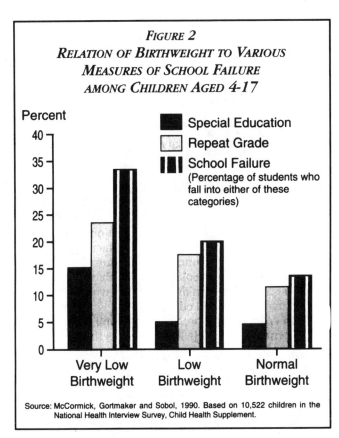

FIGURE 2

RELATION OF BIRTHWEIGHT TO VARIOUS MEASURES OF SCHOOL FAILURE AMONG CHILDREN AGED 4-17

Source: McCormick, Gortmaker and Sobol, 1990. Based on 10,522 children in the National Health Interview Survey, Child Health Supplement.

their speech and language. Children born at very low birthweights are more likely than those born at normal weights to be inattentive, hyperactive, depressed, socially withdrawn, or aggressive (Breslau et al., 1988).

New technologies and the spread of neonatal intensive care over the past decade have improved survival rates of babies born at weights ranging from 3.25 pounds to 5.5 pounds. But, as Figures 2 and 3 show, those born at low birthweight still are at increased risk of school failure. The increased risk, however, is very much tied to the child's postnatal environment. When the data on which Figure 2 is based are controlled to account for socioeconomic circumstances, very low-birthweight babies are approximately twice, not three times, as likely to repeat a grade.

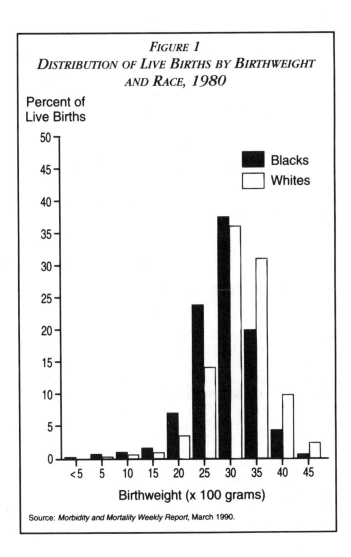

FIGURE 1

DISTRIBUTION OF LIVE BIRTHS BY BIRTHWEIGHT AND RACE, 1980

Source: *Morbidity and Mortality Weekly Report*, March 1990.

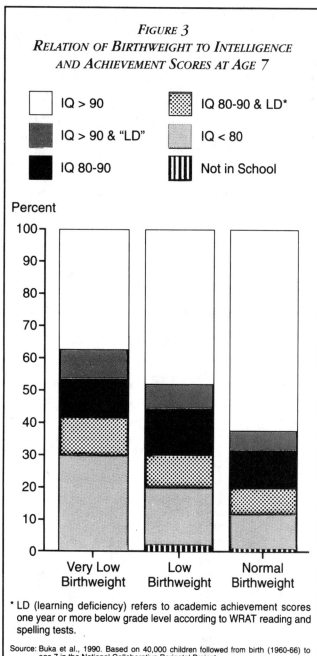

FIGURE 3
RELATION OF BIRTHWEIGHT TO INTELLIGENCE
AND ACHIEVEMENT SCORES AT AGE 7

☐ IQ > 90   ▒ IQ 80-90 & LD*

■ IQ > 90 & "LD"   ▒ IQ < 80

■ IQ 80-90   ⫴ Not in School

Percent

* LD (learning deficiency) refers to academic achievement scores one year or more below grade level according to WRAT reading and spelling tests.

Source: Buka et al., 1990. Based on 40,000 children followed from birth (1960-66) to age 7 in the National Collaborative Perinatal Project.

to, among other problems, frequent hospitalization and school absence (Streissguth, 1986). A growing number of new studies has shown that children of smokers are smaller in stature and lag behind other children in cognitive development and educational achievement. These children are particularly subject to hyperactivity and inattention (Rush and Callahan, 1989).

Data from the National Collaborative Perinatal Project on births from 1960 to 1966 measured, among other things, the amount pregnant women smoked at each prenatal visit and how their children functioned in school at age seven. Compared to offspring of nonsmokers, children of heavy smokers (more than two packs per day) were nearly twice as likely to experience school failure by age seven (see Figure 4). The impact of heavy smoking is apparently greater the earlier it occurs during pregnancy. Children of women who smoked heavily during the first trimester of pregnancy were more than twice as likely to fail than children whose mothers did not smoke during the first trimester. During the second and third trimesters, these risks decreased. In all of these analyses, it is difficult to differentiate the effects of exposure to smoking before birth and from either parent after birth; to distinguish between learning problems caused by low birthweight and those caused by other damaging effects of smoking; or, to disentangle the effects of smoke from the socioeconomic setting of the smoker. But it is worth noting that Figure 4 is based on children born in the early sixties, an era when smoking mothers were fairly well distributed across socioeconomic groups.

One study that attempted to divorce the effects of smoking from those of poverty examined middle-class children whose mothers smoked during pregnancy (Fried and Watkinson, 1990) and found that the infants showed differences in responsiveness beginning at one week of age. Later tests at 1, 2, 3, and 4 years of age showed that on verbal tests "the children of the heavy smokers had mean test scores that were lower than those born to lighter smokers, who in turn did not perform as well as those born to nonsmokers." The study also indicated that the effects of smoke exposure, whether in the womb or after birth, may not be identifiable until later ages when a child needs to perform complex cognitive functions, such as problem solving or reading and interpretation.

3. Prenatal Alcohol Exposure

Around forty thousand babies per year are born with fetal alcohol effect resulting from alcohol abuse during pregnancy (Fitzgerald, 1988). In 1984, an estimated 7,024 of these infants were diagnosed with fetal alcohol syndrome (FAS), an incidence of 2.2 per 1,000 births (Abel and Sokol, 1987). The three main features of FAS in its extreme form are facial malformation, intrauterine growth retardation, and dysfunctions of the central nervous system, including mental retardation.

There are, in addition, about 33,000 children each year who suffer from less-severe effects of maternal alcohol use. The more prominent among these learning impairments are problems in attention (attention-deficit disorders), speech and language, and hyperactivity. General

Indeed, follow-up studies of low-birthweight infants at school age have concluded that "the influence of the environment far outweighs most effects of nonoptimal prenatal or perinatal factors on outcome" (Aylward et al., 1989). This finding suggests that early assistance can improve the intellectual functioning of children at risk for learning delay or impairment (Richmond, 1990).

2. Maternal Smoking

Maternal smoking during pregnancy has long been known to be related to low birthweight (Abel, 1980), an increased risk for cancer in the offspring (Stjernfeldt et al., 1986), and early and persistent asthma, which leads

school failure also is connected to a history of fetal alcohol exposure (Abel and Sokol, 1987; Ernhart et al., 1985). Figure 5 shows the drinking habits of women of childbearing age by race and education.

When consumed in pregnancy, alcohol easily crosses the placenta, but exactly how it affects the fetus is not well known. The effects of alcohol vary according to how far along in the pregnancy the drinking occurs. The first trimester of pregnancy is a period of brain growth and organ and limb formation. The embryo is most susceptible to alcohol from week two to week eight of development, a point at which a woman may not even know she is pregnant (Hoyseth and Jones, 1989). Researchers have yet to determine how much alcohol it takes to cause problems in development and how alcohol affects each critical gestational period. It appears that the more alcohol consumed during pregnancy, the worse the effect.

And many of the effects do not appear until ages four to seven, when children enter school.

Nearly one in four (23 percent) white women, eighteen to twenty-nine, reported "binge" drinking (five

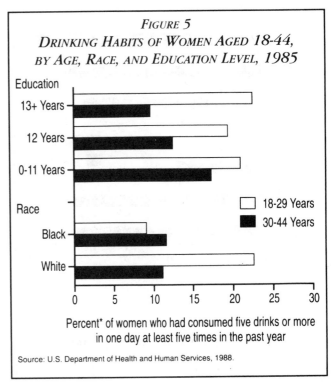

FIGURE 5
DRINKING HABITS OF WOMEN AGED 18-44,
BY AGE, RACE, AND EDUCATION LEVEL, 1985

Percent* of women who had consumed five drinks or more
in one day at least five times in the past year

Source: U.S. Department of Health and Human Services, 1988.

drinks or more a day at least five times in the past year). This was nearly three times the rate for black women of that age (about 8 percent). Fewer women (around 3 percent for both black and white) reported steady alcohol use (two drinks or more per day in the past two weeks).

4. Fetal Drug Exposure

The abuse of drugs of all kinds—marijuana, cocaine, crack, heroin, or amphetamines—by pregnant women affected about 11 percent of newborns in 1988—about 425,000 babies (Weston et al., 1989).

Cocaine and crack use during pregnancy are consistently associated with lower birthweight, premature birth, and smaller head circumference in comparison with babies whose mothers were free of these drugs (Chasnoff et al., 1989; Cherukuri et al., 1988; Doberczak et al., 1987; Keith et al., 1989; Zuckerman et al., 1989). In a study of 1,226 women attending a prenatal clinic, 27 percent tested positive for marijuana and 18 percent for cocaine. Infants of those who had used marijuana weighed an average of 2.8 ounces (79 grams) less at birth and were half a centimeter shorter in length. Infants of mothers who had used cocaine averaged 3.3 ounces (93 grams) less in weight and .7 of a centimeter less in length and also had a smaller head circumference than babies of nonusers (Zuckerman et al., 1989). The study concluded that "marijuana use and cocaine use during pregnancy are each independently associated with impaired fetal growth" (Zuckerman et al., 1989).

In addition, women who use these substances are like-

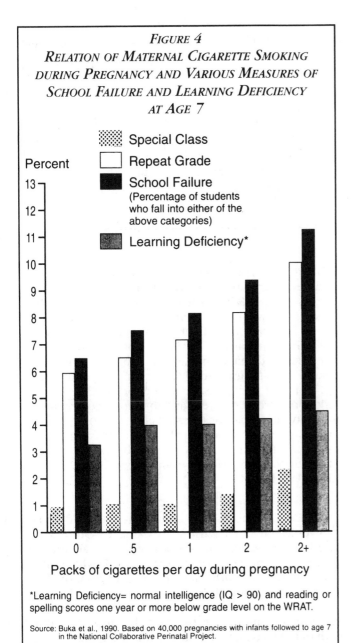

FIGURE 4
RELATION OF MATERNAL CIGARETTE SMOKING
DURING PREGNANCY AND VARIOUS MEASURES OF
SCHOOL FAILURE AND LEARNING DEFICIENCY
AT AGE 7

Special Class
Repeat Grade
School Failure
(Percentage of students who fall into either of the above categories)
Learning Deficiency*

Packs of cigarettes per day during pregnancy

*Learning Deficiency= normal intelligence (IQ > 90) and reading or spelling scores one year or more below grade level on the WRAT.

Source: Buka et al., 1990. Based on 40,000 pregnancies with infants followed to age 7 in the National Collaborative Perinatal Project.

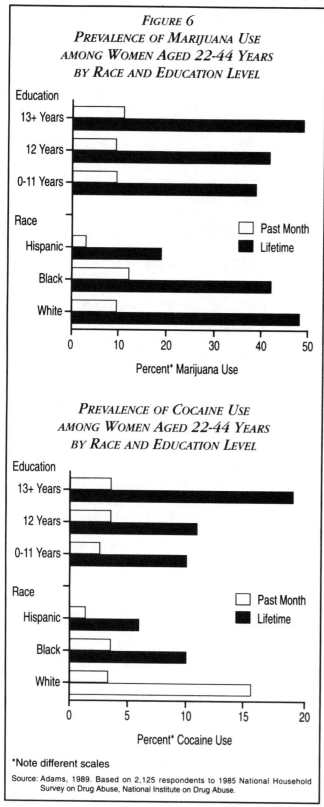

FIGURE 6
PREVALENCE OF MARIJUANA USE
AMONG WOMEN AGED 22-44 YEARS
BY RACE AND EDUCATION LEVEL

PREVALENCE OF COCAINE USE
AMONG WOMEN AGED 22-44 YEARS
BY RACE AND EDUCATION LEVEL

*Note different scales

Source: Adams, 1989. Based on 2,125 respondents to 1985 National Household Survey on Drug Abuse, National Institute on Drug Abuse.

aged nearly a pound (14.6 ounces or 416 grams) smaller than those born to women who had normal weight gain and did not use cigarettes, marijuana, and cocaine (see Table 1). The effect of these substances on size is more than the sum of the risk factors combined.

Like alcohol use, drug use has different effects at different points in fetal development. Use in very early pregnancy is more likely to cause birth defects affecting organ formation and the central nervous systems. Later use may

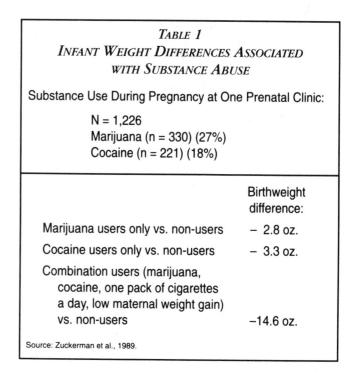

TABLE 1
INFANT WEIGHT DIFFERENCES ASSOCIATED
WITH SUBSTANCE ABUSE

Substance Use During Pregnancy at One Prenatal Clinic:

N = 1,226
Marijuana (n = 330) (27%)
Cocaine (n = 221) (18%)

	Birthweight difference:
Marijuana users only vs. non-users	− 2.8 oz.
Cocaine users only vs. non-users	− 3.3 oz.
Combination users (marijuana, cocaine, one pack of cigarettes a day, low maternal weight gain) vs. non-users	−14.6 oz.

Source: Zuckerman et al., 1989.

result in low birthweight due to either preterm birth or intrauterine growth retardation (Kaye et al., 1989; MacGregor et al., 1987; Petitti and Coleman, 1990). While some symptoms may be immediately visible, others may not be apparent until later childhood (Weston et al., 1989; Gray and Yaffe, 1986; Frank et al., 1988).

In infancy, damaged babies can experience problems in such taken-for-granted functions as sleeping and waking, resulting in exhaustion and poor development. In childhood, problems are found in vision, motor control, and in social interaction (Weston et al., 1989). Such problems may be caused not only by fetal drug exposure but also by insufficient prenatal care for the mother or by an unstimulating or difficult home environment for the infant (Lifschitz et al., 1985).

WHAT CAN be done to ameliorate the condition of children born with such damage? Quite a bit, based on the success of supportive prenatal care and the results of model projects that have provided intensive assistance to both baby and mother from the time of birth. These projects have successfully raised the I.Q. of low- and very-low birthweight babies an average of ten points or more—an increase that may lift a child with below-average intelligence into a higher I.Q. cate-

ly to smoke and to gain less weight during pregnancy, two factors associated with low birthweight. The cumulative effect of these risk factors is demonstrated by the finding that infants born to women who gained little weight, who had smoked one pack of cigarettes a day, and who tested positive for marijuana and cocaine aver-

gory (i.e., from retarded to low average or from low average to average). Generally known as either educational day care or infant day care, these programs provide a developmentally stimulating environment to high-risk babies and/or intensive parent support to prepare the parent to help her child.

In one such program based at the University of California/Los Angeles, weekly meetings were held among staff, parents, and infants over a period of four years. By the project's end, the low-birthweight babies had caught up in mental function to the control group of normal birthweight children (Rauh et al., 1988). The Infant Health and Development Project, which was conducted in eight cities and provided low-birthweight babies with pediatric follow-up and an educational curriculum with family support, on average increased their I.Q. scores by thirteen points and the scores of very-low birthweight children by more than six points. Another project targeted poor single teenage mothers whose infants were at high risk for intellectual impairment (Martin, Ramey and Ramey, 1990). One group of children was enrolled in educational day care from six and one-half weeks of age to four and one-half years for five days a week, fifty weeks a year. By four and one-half years, the children's I.Q. scores were in the normal range and ten points higher than a control group. In addition, by the time their children were four and one-half, mothers in the experimental group were more likely to have graduated from high school and be self-supporting than were mothers in the control group.

These studies indicate that some disadvantages of poverty and low birthweight can be mitigated and intellectual impairment avoided. The key is attention to the cognitive development of young children, in conjunction with social support of their families.

Mental Health for Babies: What Do Theory and Research Teach Us?

Alice Sterling Honig

Alice Sterling Honig, Ph.D., conducts a national infant/ toddler training workshop every June; is a former Research in Review editor for Young Children; *edited* Risk Factors in Infancy; *coauthored (with J.R. Lally)* Infant Caregiving: A Design for Training; *and wrote* Parent Involvement in Early Childhood Education, *which is published by NAEYC.*

As families seek child care for even younger children, more and more infants and toddlers enter nonparental care. Because many early childhood specialists have been prepared predominantly to serve preschool children, there is great urgency for further understanding of the insights of theorists, clinicians, and researchers for providers who wish to extend their competencies to promote the mental health of infants and toddlers.

In the cognitive domain infants and toddlers mostly function in Piaget's sensorimotor and early preoperational period. They are learning about causality (turn the handle and the jack-in-the-box pops up), the permanence and spatial arrangements of objects, and how to use a special activity (such as pulling a string) as a means

Some parents have never thought of how the threats they use in anger might make a baby feel unloved or unlovable. Aside from interaction styles and words, some employed parents need to rethink how they are spending those precious hours between pick-up time and bedtime for the baby. Offer parents specific ideas about how to provide more special attention through activities such as leisurely bath time, picture-book reading with the baby on the parent's lap, dancing to slow music with the baby closely snuggled in the parent's arms, cheek-to-cheek, to encourage infant confidence in adult caring.

toward a goal (such as making a pull toy move along). Of course caregivers need to know all about the sensorimotor accomplishments of infants who are learning such a variety of skills, for example, adorning oneself with a pop-it-bead necklace, pretending to walk a toy dog, listening to a music box, learning spatially how to crawl around a detour, or learning to use two hands differentially in play—one to hold a toy and the other to make it work by winding it up.

More serious problems for infants lie in the domain of emotional/social functioning, however. Some caregivers provide the right toys for sensorimotor learning, but they handle infant bodies as objects and focus predominantly on housekeeping chores. They check on wet diapers but forget the *personhood* of each baby. Those who care for infants need, above all, to have as their goal *insuring good infant mental health.*

The earliest research into the outcomes of high-quality university-based infant care found no detrimental emotional effects (Caldwell, Wright, Honig, & Tannenbaum, 1970) and some cognitive advantages, particularly for disadvantaged babies. Yet some recent researchers looking at community infant care have found a disconcerting possibility that full-time infant care begun in the first year of life may be associated with increased cognitive ability but also with increased aggression and noncompliance (Belsky, 1986; Belsky & Rovine, 1988; Egeland, 1991; Park & Honig, 1991); thus, it becomes particularly urgent that caregivers learn as much as possible about the *emotional* dimensions of infant development.

Who are the major theorists clarifying infant/toddler emotional development? Which behavioral warning signals alert and galvanize caregivers toward more specialized efforts to nourish babies' emotional well-being? What specific childrearing practices can boost infant mental health?

Theorists whose ideas help us understand infant mental health

Eric Erikson

In their first year infants struggle with the Eriksonian dialectical problems of acquiring more basic trust (than mistrust) in their own goodness and in their caregivers' benevolence. During their second and third years, toddlers struggle to acquire a secure sense of autonomy and ability to exercise choice. If the sense of will is damaged through adult harshness, emotional indifference, and ridicule/shaming, infants inherit a disturbing legacy. Children may permanently doubt their right to have their own wishes and make their own choices. They may develop a sense of shame or defiance about asserting their will and may express frustration, anger, and rage at being frequently thwarted, misunderstood, and punished for their budding attempts to assert themselves (Erikson, 1963).

Caregivers need to accept with patience rather than exasperation the seesawing, often contradictory behaviors of toddlers. A toddler runs away in defiant and delighted independence when called to lunch or to clean up, but he clings to you and needs to cuddle if he is tired or frightened (Honig, 1990; 1993a). Provide continuity of trust for toddlers. They struggle to assert their wills, but they still need leisurely lap times and reassurance that their tantrums or negativism don't lose them the caregiver's support and nurturance. Perceptive, caring adults bring firmness, clarity of rules, and unconditional commitment, rather than rejection or anger, to confrontations with toddlers. Always be alert. Be especially sure not to get carried away into returning hurt for hurt. Sometimes adults get trapped into *re-creating* negative struggles for power that may be going on in the home (Wittmer & Honig, 1990). A toddler may be acting with increased stubbornness to family anger and disapproval that he or she does not cooperate yet with demands for more mature behaviors in toileting or neat eating, and that stubbornness—when acted out in child care—can puzzle or upset the unwary caregiver.

Margaret Mahler

Mahlerian theory details stages in infant emotional growth and development in relation to modes of maternal care. Infants move from a close body relationship, during which their inner needs for nursing and bodily contact are paramount; through a "hatching" period, during which they begin to tune in with bright eyes, postural alertness, and genuine interest in the outside world; through a "practicing" subphase, during which they count on the primary loved caregiver as a secure base from which to venture away, using newly developed locomotor skills to explore the environment. From about one and one-half to three years, babies' dawning cognitive abilities permit them to think about and struggle to make sense of separation problems. Baby longs for a return to the closeness originally enjoyed with the primary caregiver; yet, in awesome contradiction, powerful new urges impel the baby in this "rapprochement" period toward new freedom to be a special individual with *separate* wishes and desires (Kaplan, 1978). During this gray, crashing-down, crabby period (Honig, 1991), babies sometimes behave in ways that bewilder and exasperate caregivers. Understanding these emotional struggles of toddlerhood helps. A wise caregiver tunes into the needs of babies to support their growing autonomy while still providing the nurturing responsivity and body-loving care that permit toddlers to develop beyond the rapprochement period into Mahlerian "constancy." The beginning of achieving constancy occurs when the toddler can hold *opposing* emotional feelings (such as loving and yet sometimes feeling angry with the caregiver) in dialectical balance. Constancy helps a child to support lengthy daily separations from parents who are both resented *and* loved. Constancy helps toddlers come to terms with strong differences between their own and adult wishes and preferences. Babies learn to integrate and accept dualities of feeling and still retain clear sense of a loving relationship.

John Bowlby and Mary Ainsworth

Attachment theory is possibly the most powerful new tool that ethological theorists have provided us with in recent decades. Bowlby proposed that infants build nonverbal, internal working models of early relationships with each caregiver (Bretherton & Waters, 1985). These models are unconscious, yet they serve as tenacious templates for expecting other close relationships later in life to be similarly depressed or happy, kind or cruel, orderly or chaotic. Sadly, an abused toddler will often behave in inappropriate ways in child care that can ensnare an unwary caregiver into the punitive, unhappy interactions that the child has already so well internalized and construed as the model for intimate relationships!

Some caregivers provide the right toys for sensorimotor learning, but they handle infant bodies as objects and focus predominantly on housekeeping chores. They check on wet diapers but forget the *personhood* of each baby. Those who care for infants need, above all, to have as their goal *insuring good infant mental health*.

Ethological theory suggests that to ensure survival, nature has equipped babies with the ability to cry loud, cling to the caregiver, call, smile dazzlingly, lift arms to be picked up, creep, and follow after a departing adult. With these fundamental postures and vocalizations, babies enhance their chances of survival through entraining their caregiver into a more caring, close relationship; yet needs for felt security are always in balance with growing needs to explore. When the baby's special person is there emotionally for her, she can explore freely, and the quality of her play will be more focused and creative. When the attachment figure disappears or is rejecting, the quality of play suffers. A baby acts independent in play with peers and toys when he is feeling deeply sure that his special person is readily available to comfort and protect him if fear or tiredness upsets him.

During the last half of the first year of life, infants show a particular strength of *differential* smiling, body molding, approaching, and greeting their special person—usually the parent who has provided most of the intimate bodily care and attention (Honig, 1992); however, babies can and do adopt several different attachment figures. The quality of security or insecurity in the baby's relationship will depend in each case on the *unique* interactions between the baby and that adult (Honig, 1982b). That is why assigning babies to a special caregiver in child care is important. As infants begin to trust the familiar, tender care received daily, they begin to show differential signs of that caregiver becoming a special attachment figure. This is why *stability of provider* and *continuity of care* are so very important. Babies should not be moved like chess pawns to a "younger toddler group" or other such groups! Babies need to feel that they can make sense of and trust sameness in responsive cherishing in their child care facility.

Assessment of security. How is security of attachment assessed? Ainsworth's Strange Situation technique has become the major measure by which infant attachment is determined at 12 and 18 months. A mother and infant enter a toy play room, and during three-minute time periods the baby is first with mother, then with a stranger, then reunited with mother, then alone, then with a stranger, and finally again reunited with mother. From careful analysis of the *reunion* behaviors of the infant when mother enters the room, four kinds of attachment patterns have been noted. *Securely attached* (B) babies actively seek reunion; they sink into and mold onto the body of caregiver. Having "touched base" and relaxed deeply, these babies are then ready to leave the security of the lap to go back to interested play with toys. Their

parents have been identified as promptly responsive to signals of distress and tenderly careful in their holding. The parents of secure babies are sensitive, reciprocal partners rather than intrusive, pushy, resentful, or chaotic in their ministrations.

Babies who begin to seek comfort but then turn away in anger/irritability or struggle to get down from the caregiver's arms are identified as insecure/ambivalent/resistive (C) babies. The parent has shown insensitivity to the C baby's tempos, rhythms, and distress signals. The baby is picked up or attended to more at the parent's convenience or whim rather than when she or he expresses a need.

Two other categories of insecure attachment have been identified. Some babies do not seek the parent upon re-entry. They ignore the adult and continue to play with toys. These avoidant/insecure (A) babies, who look as if they are "mature" in accepting separations, often turn out to be angry at home and hostile and unfeeling with preschool peers. Ainsworth (1982) has reported that mothers of A babies dislike or are impatient with physical caressing. Other babies seem to show intense desires to go to the parent at reunion and equally intense sudden blank looks, anger, or turning away. Main, Kaplan, and Cassidy (1985) label this response "D" for dazed/disorganized/disoriented and report that the mother of a D baby often has a history of early trauma and loss in her own life. Even at six years of age, D children responded to pictured stories of separation between parents and children in ways that reflected extreme discomfort or almost bizarre denial of upset feelings. They were unable to think of ways to cope with separations, such as going to stay with a grandmother. Secure children, in contrast, when presented with separation pictures (such as parents leaving for a night out or for an extended trip), even thought up ingenious solutions such as hiding in the parents' car before they drove off on a two-week vacation!

Attachment research thus has given us subtle tools for discerning from infant responses in daily innumerable,

In their first year infants struggle with problems of acquiring more basic trust (than mistrust) in their own goodness and in their caregivers' benevolence.

small interactions (Stern, 1985) what emotional troubles may be brewing. If a baby is irritable or avoidant, the child care worker may not find this infant pleasurable to play with, to croon to, or to caress. When caregivers are alert to such relationship pitfalls, they are more likely to provide healing opportunities for such infants to become attached securely to their precious person—the caregiver.

Caregivers who wish to meet the needs of under-threes for emotionally supportive care will find perceptive and helpful guidelines in clinicians' unfolding story of the stages of normal emotional/social growth.

Body cues for judging infant mental health

Despite staff attentiveness to prevention of emotional distress, some babies still may not be thriving emotionally in nonparental care or in group care. In such cases perceptive awareness and monitoring of baby behaviors is a caregiver's first line of defense. *Body cues* that the infant or toddler provides to the caregiver are early indicators that mental health may be in jeopardy.

Research and clinical findings specify the following telltale signs that indicate emotional distress and mental health troubles in infants and toddlers:

- dull eyes without sparkle
- back arching and body stiffening as a regular response
- eye gaze avoidance
- pushing away rather than relaxed molding onto the adult
- limp, floppy, listless body (without illness)
- rare smiles despite tender adult elicitation
- diarrhea or very hard stools, without infection present
- difficulties in sinking into deep, refreshing sleep
- compulsive body rocking back and forth
- inconsolable crying for hours
- scattered attention rather than attention flowing freely between caregiver and baby during intimate exchanges
- dysfluency in the older toddler who is already verbal
- head banging against crib persistently
- grimaces of despair
- frozen affect (apathetic look)
- reverse emotions (e.g., giggling hysterically when frightened)

- impassiveness or anger when a peer becomes hurt or distressed
- lack of friendliness to loving adult overtures
- echoic verbalizations (e.g., repeating ends of adult phrases)
- wild, despairing, thrashing tantrums
- constant masturbation daily even when not tired or at naptime
- fearful withdrawal/flinching when caregiver tries to caress
- regular avoidance of/indifference to parent at pick-up time
- anxious "shadowing" of caregiver without letup
- continuous biting/hitting of others with no prior aggressive provocation; strong aversion to "victim-centered discipline" explanations of caregiver
- little if any interest in peers or persons
- banging headlong into furniture or hurting self a lot, without turning to caregiver for comfort
- allowed by other children to aggress strongly, in deference to his "disabled" status, but then mostly avoided by other children in play

Mental health prescriptions

If any of the previously mentioned danger signs appears consistently, then parents and caregivers must mobilize urgently for alleviation of the infant's stress and enhancement of her coping skills (Honig, 1986). Sometimes a family feels isolated and stressed and has little energy left for the baby-holding and attunement that are so necessary to build secure attachment. If a baby does not have at least one secure attachment figure in the family, she or he will be vulnerable to the stress of daily separation from familiar family members. In the child care facility, watch for specific signs of vulnerability. Especially if you observe clusters of such signs, mobilize community and child care resources *and* family members to support the emotionally distressed baby.

Help parents reframe

Some parents have never thought of how the threats they use in anger might make a baby feel unloved or unlovable. Aside from interaction styles and words, some employed parents need to rethink how they are spending

---

During their second and third years, toddlers struggle to acquire a secure sense of autonomy and ability to exercise choice. If the sense of will is damaged through adult harshness, emotional indifference, and ridicule/shaming, infants inherit a disturbing legacy. Children may permanently doubt their right to have their own wishes and make their own choices. They may develop a sense of shame or defiance about asserting their will and may express frustration, anger, and rage at being frequently thwarted, misunderstood, and punished for their budding attempts to assert themselves.

those precious hours between pick-up time and bedtime for the baby. Offer parents specific ideas about how to provide more special attention through activities such as leisurely bath time, picture-book reading with the baby on the parent's lap, dancing to slow music with the baby closely snuggled in the parent's arms, cheek-to-cheek, to encourage infant confidence in adult caring (Honig, 1990, 1991).

Professional resources

Professional community mental health resources, especially parent-infant specialists, offer in-center or "kitchen therapy" counseling for parents (Fraiberg, Shapiro, & Adelson, 1984). A staff social worker can alleviate some stresses, such as finding better housing or transportation to medical clinics. A local mental health agency may provide weekly home visitors or trained resource mothers. The Homebuilders model (Kinney, Haapala, & Booth, 1991) provides intensive, daily, in-home casework efforts. Some therapeutic groups specialize in work with parents of very young children with emotional difficulties (Koplow, 1992). Mobilize community network resources to support parents.

Cultural sensitivity

When reaching out therapeutically on behalf of emotionally distressed infants and toddlers, staff will need to be sensitive to *cultural* issues in how families react to child disability or dysfunction. This may entail learning about considerations of shame, of cultural healing practices, or even of family hierarchical status that necessitates talking only with the oldest male, for example, rather than with the mother. Lieberman (1989) advises that the culturally sensitive worker must know about the content of different cultural perceptions and maintain an attitude of openness to find out more about the "values and preconceptions of the other" (p. 197).

Stress prevention: Organizational considerations

Staffing patterns

Caregivers can make changes in the environment and in routines to decrease risk factors that negatively affect optimal infant development. Day care research reveals that variables such as "high caregiver to infant ratios, small group size, stability of caregiving arrangements and adequate staff training" optimize child outcomes (Berger, 1990, p. 371).

Physical health

Child care facilities must ensure the best possible chances for good *physical* health for babies as a basic foundation for mental health. Establish clear, strong guidelines and rules, such as frequent caregiver hand washing and diaper changing.

Space and time arrangements

Caregivers should arrange living spaces thoughtfully to decrease stress, including quiet places that support deep and peaceful sleep times, as well as cubbies and snuggly, soft pillows where a baby can creep for privacy and comfort when group care seems overwhelming. Adults need to plan daily outdoor time with fresh air and safe spaces for toddlers to gallop about. Sometimes stress is reduced by decreasing overstimulation. Conversely, enriching the environment provides grist for exuberant toddlers' safe explorations.

The assigned caregiver will need to provide more one-on-one time for emotionally vulnerable babies. The youngest babies may need to be carried in bodyslings. A caregiver's increasingly sensitive attunement to the infant's needs and more prompt, nurturant responsiveness to distress build basic trust and reassurance. Particularly when such infants are in full-time care early in the first year, well-trained caregivers must develop *personalized,* cherishing relationships and thus try to prevent many of the insecure attachment sequelae—such as increased aggression—that have been reported in the literature. Differences between the parent and the caregiver should be minimized when infant mental health is at stake. Babies need loving and will thrive if they are well "mothered" regardless of the age or sex of the caregiver. The director's role in this special effort is crucial. Some caregivers might begin to feel like possessive "rescuers" of this infant; some may be very upset when the infant graduates from the facility. A director's sensitivity to staff problems is an important consideration as caregivers work hard to build secure mental health for babies who are at risk for emotional distress.

© Subjects & Predicates

Holding infants and toddlers a lot while pleasantly talking, walking, playing, and reading with them strengthens mental health.

Caregiver behaviors that promote infant mental health

In addition to theoretical understanding of infant/toddler development and awareness of stress signs in babies, and in addition to logistical and environmental policies that support infant mental health, the caregiver of under-threes needs practical suggestions for enhancing personal interactions (Honig, 1989). Research findings provide good ideas (1) for positive discipline techniques (Honig & Wittmer, 1990); (2) for ways to ease the adjustment of infants into nonparental care; and (3) for ideas that help caregivers forge a partnership with stressed parents, who occasionally may feel jealous or inadequate and in some cases even resent the trained professional caregiver.

Below are some of the specific *personal interaction patterns* culled from attachment researchers, clinicians, and expert practitioners (Greenberg,1991)—that caregivers can use to promote infant mental health:

• Hold the baby tenderly and cuddle extensively.

• Express verbal joy and bodily pleasure at the baby's being.

• Tempt babies with rich toy variety that permits them to find out how to work toys at their own pace and interest.

• Remember that temperament styles differ—easy, slow-to-warm-up, and triggery/irritable babies need different adult approaches (California State Department of Education, 1990).

• Sensitively interpret infant cues and signals of distress.

• Provide prompt, tuned-in responsiveness to infant cues.

• Be perceptive about a toddler's seesawing needs.

• Reassure with caresses and calm words.

• Offer your body and lap generously for needy babies.

• Send admiring glances baby's way.

• Give babies leisurely chances to explore toys as they wish and at their own tempo without intrusiveness.

• Wait until a toddler shows signs of readiness before insisting on potty training or neat eating.

• Gently rub backs to soothe tired, tense, crabby babies.

• Croon and sing softly, especially in a mode to "speak for the body of the baby" in interpreting his or her needs, as in the following example:

Shoshannah wanted to go home. She could not nap easily and was disconsolate. Her caregiver patted her back soothingly and started a low chanting song to the tune of "The Farmer in the Dell." She sang, "You want your mama to come back. You want your mama to come back. You want your mama to come back soon. You want your mama to come back." Over and over the caregiver slowly sang the simple melody reassuringly, with firm conviction. After about 20 repetitions, during which Shoshannah had quieted and breathed more easily on her cot, the caregiver stopped singing. The toddler stirred restlessly. "Sing more," she asked simply. So Miss Alice sang the song softly several more times until the toddler fell peacefully asleep. Next day at naptime the toddler specifi-cally asked her caregiver, "Sing me the 'I want my mama to come back' song." Satisfied with the simple song sung soothingly several times over, Shoshannah dozed off comfortably. (Honig, 1993b, p. 42)

• Feed babies leisurely and in your arms while regarding them.

• Accept infant attempts to manage self-feeding despite their messiness.

• Massage babies to increase body relaxation and pleasure (Evans, 1990).

• Engage in interactive games like pat-a-cake with baby to further a sense of partnering and intimacy.

• Increase shared meanings by following a baby's pointing finger and commenting on objects pointed to; retrieve an object that the baby asks for; create cognitive "scaffolding" and expand shared meaning through empathetic interpretations (Emde, 1990).

• Use diapering time to enhance a sense of body goodness; caress the rounded tummy; stroke cheeks and hair; tell the baby in delighted tones how delicious and beautiful he or she is.

• Play reciprocal, turn-taking games, such as rolling a ball back and forth while seated on the ground with wide-apart legs, facing each other. Place the seated baby on your knees facing yourself and play a rocking-horse game with slower and then faster motions and rhythms (Honig & Lally, 1981, p. 52).

• Make everyday experiences and routines predictable and reassuring (although not rigidly because special outings or events must become part of a baby's world experiences too) so that the baby gets a secure sense of what to expect and in what sequence.

• Explain your actions even to very young babies. If you are leaving a room to get a supply of new diapers, tell the babies what you are doing, where you are going, and that you will be back soon. Give your babies a sense, not of the absurdity and disconnectedness of life experiences, but of the orderliness and meaningfulness of daily activities. Convince babies that they are important, precious members of the cooperative enterprise called *child care.*

• Be a model of generous and genuine empathetic, but not anxious, comfort when a baby is scared or upset (Honig, 1989).

• Serve as a beacon of security and safety for your babies. Let them know that you are there for them when they need to return for a hug, a pat, a cuddle, or a bodily reassurance.

• Arrange ample floor freedom for play and peer acquaintance.

• Choose the active/calm alert state as the optimal state for engaging tiny babies in cooing turn-taking and other interaction games.

• Send *long-distance* cues to cruising babies that you are their *refueling station* par excellence. Your cheerful words called out, your grin of encouragement from a distance, your smile of pride, and your postures of appreciation confirm for newly creeping-away babies that you are **present** for them and affirming them.

From about one and one-half to three years, babies' dawning cognitive abilities permit them to think about and struggle to make sense of separation problems. Baby longs for a return to the closeness originally enjoyed with the primary caregiver; yet, in awesome contradiction, powerful new urges impel the baby in this "rapprochement" period toward new freedom to be a special individual with *separate* wishes and desires. During this gray, crashing-down, crabby period, babies sometimes behave in ways that bewilder and exasperate caregivers. Understanding these emotional struggles of toddlerhood helps.

- Focus your genuine attention to send each child powerful messages of deeply acceptable selfhood (Briggs, 1975).
- Lure disengaged toddlers who wander and cannot connect with materials or peers into intimate interactions using the Magic Triangle technique of interesting baby in the activity rather than in personal interaction or confrontation (Honig, 1982a).

Caregiver interest and pleasuring engagement teach babies their first lessons of learning *intimacy* (rather than isolation and loneliness) and shared human feelings (rather than callous disregard for others). One of the chilling signs that a toddler has been abused is his indifference or anger, even hitting another toddler who is crying and acting upset. If, by 18 months, a toddler is beginning to show expressions of concern and empathetic attempts to soothe a crying baby or to retrieve for that baby a fallen cracker or toy, then a caregiver knows that baby altruism is emerging positively—a good sign of infant mental health.

The best way for a baby to learn to be a kind and caring person early in life (the critical period for this is before age two) is to have a caregiver who (1) models empathetic nurturance when a baby is distressed, and (2) firmly forbids a baby to hurt another person (Pines, 1979).

Conclusions

Let us work together with families toward more positive practices to prevent any possible disturbing emotional effects of nonparental full-time care early in infancy. Nurturant, body-generous caregivers who talk sincerely and interestedly with babies promote feelings of personal competence. Individualized attention and caresses energize babies to cope well with the world of child care. The challenge is to provide enough supports, education, and respect for child care workers so that they can become skilled new baby-therapists of the future through their attunement with babies and sensitivity to families.

Competent, wise supervisors are invaluable assets for programs that train infant caregivers and infant/parent facilitators. Fenichel (1991) introduces this theme in a special issue of *Zero to Three*. Political, educational, and therapeutic efforts will all be needed to increase training efficacy to achieve the desired goal: tender, tuned-in, responsive caregivers and parents who give the gifts of joy, of intimacy, of courage, and of good mental health to babies.

References

Ainsworth, M.D.S. (1982). Early caregiving and later patterns of attachment. In J.H. Kennell & M.H. Klaus (Eds.), *Birth, interaction and attachment* (pp. 35–43). Skillman, NJ: Johnson & Johnson.

Belsky, J. (1986). Infant day care: A cause for concern? *Zero to Three, 6*(5), 1–7.

Belsky, J., & Rovine, M. (1988). Nonmaternal care in the first year of life and the security of infant/parent attachment. *Child Development, 59,* 157–167.

Berger, S.P. (1990). Infant day care, parent-child attachment, and developmental risk: A reply to Caruso. *Infant Mental Health Journal, 11*(4), 365–373.

Bretherton, I., & Waters, E. (Eds.). (1985). Growing points of attachment theory and research. *Monographs of the Society for Research in Child Development, 50* (1–2, Serial No. 209).

Briggs, D. (1975). *Your child's self esteem.* Garden City, NY: Doubleday.

Caldwell, B.M., Wright, C.M., Honig, A.S., & Tannenbaum, J. (1970). Infant day care and attachment. *American Journal of Orthopsychiatry, 40,* 397–412.

California State Department of Education. (1990). *Flexible, fearful, or feisty: The different temperaments of infants and toddlers* [Video]. Sacramento, CA: Program for Infant/Toddler Caregivers.

Egeland, B. (1991, August). The relation between day care in infancy and outcomes in preschool and the school years. In A. Clarke-Stewart (Chair), *Early child care patterns and later child behavior.* Symposium conducted at the meeting of the American Psychological Association, San Francisco, CA.

Emde, R. (1990). Lessons from infancy: New beginnings in a changing world and a morality for health. *Infant Mental Health Journal, 11*(3), 196–212.

Erikson, E. (1963). *Childhood and society.* New York: Norton.

Evans, L. (1990). Impact of infant massage on the neonate and the parent-infant relationship. In N. Gunzenhauser (Ed.), *Advances in touch: New implications in human development* (pp. 71–79). Skillman, NJ: Johnson & Johnson.

Fenichel, E. (1991). Learning through supervision and mentorship to support the development of infant, toddler and their families. *Zero to Three, 12*(2), 1–9.

Fraiberg, S., Shapiro, V., & Adelson, E. (1984). Ghosts in the nursery: A psychoanalytic approach to the problems of impaired infant-mother relationships. In L. Fraiberg (Ed.), *Clinical studies in infant mental health* (pp. 100–136). Columbus, OH: Ohio University Press.

Greenberg, P. (1991). *Character development: Encouraging self-esteem & self-discipline in infants, toddlers, & two-year-olds*. Washington, DC: NAEYC.

Honig, A.S. (1982a). *Playtime learning games for young children*. Syracuse, NY: Syracuse University Press.

Honig, A.S. (1982b). Research in review. Infant-mother communication. *Young Children, 37*(3), 52–62.

Honig, A.S. (1986). Research in review. Stress and coping in children. In J.B. McCracken (Ed.), *Reducing stress in young children's lives* (pp. 142–167). Washington, DC: NAEYC.

Honig, A.S. (1989). Quality infant/toddler caregiving: Are there magic recipes? *Young Children, 44*(4), 4–10.

Honig, A.S. (1990). Infant-toddler education: Principles, practices, and promises. In C. Seefeldt (Ed.), *Continuing issues in early childhood education* (pp. 61–105). Columbus, OH: Merrill/Macmillan.

Honig, A.S. (1991). For babies to flourish. *Montessori Life, 3*(2), 7–10.

Honig, A.S. (1992). Dancing with your baby means sometimes leading, sometimes following. *Dimensions, 20*(3), 10–13.

Honig, A.S. (1993a). The Eriksonian approach. In J.L. Roopnarine & J.E. Johnson (Eds.), *Approaches to early childhood education* (2nd ed.) (pp. 47–70). New York: Macmillan.

Honig, A.S. (1993b). The power of song. *Pre-K Today, 7*(4), 42–43.

Honig, A.S., & Lally, J.R. (1981). *Infant caregiving: A design for training*. Syracuse, NY: Syracuse University Press.

Honig, A.S., & Wittmer, D.S. (1990). Infants, toddlers and socialization. In R.J. Lally (Ed.), *A caregiver's guide to social emotional growth and socialization* (pp. 62–80). Sacramento, CA: California State Department of Education.

Kaplan, L. (1978). *Oneness and separateness*. New York: Washington Square Press (Simon & Schuster).

Kinney, J., Haapala, D., & Booth, C. (1991). *Keeping families together: The Homebuilders model*. Hawthorne, NY: Aldine De Gruyter.

Koplow, L. (1992). Finding common ground: Facilitating a therapeutic group for diverse parents of young disturbed children. *Zero to Three, 12*(3), 22–26.

Lieberman, A. (1989). What is culturally sensitive intervention? In A.S. Honig (Ed.), Cross-cultural aspects of parenting normal and at-risk children [Special issue]. *Early Child Development and Care, 50,* 197–204.

Main, M., Kaplan, N., & Cassidy, J. (1985). Security in infancy, childhood, and adulthood: A move to the level of representation. In I. Bretherton & E. Waters (Eds.), Growing points of attachment theory and research (pp. 66–104). *Monographs of the Society for Research in Child Development, 50*(1–2, Serial No. 209).

Park, K., & Honig, A.S. (1991). Infant care and later teacher ratings of preschool behaviors. *Early Child Development and Care, 68,* 89–96.

Pines, M. (1979). Good samaritans at age two? *Psychology Today, 13*(1), 66–77.

Stern, D. (1985). *The interpersonal world of the infant: A view from psychoanalysis and developmental psychology*. New York: Basic Books.

Wittmer, D.S., & Honig, A.S. (1990). Teacher re-creation of negative interactions with toddlers. In A.S. Honig (Ed.), *Optimizing early child care and education* (pp. 77–88). London: Gordon & Breach.

Home Visiting Programs and the Health and Development of Young Children

Craig T. Ramey
Sharon Landesman Ramey

Craig T. Ramey, Ph.D., is director of the Civitan International Research Center and professor of psychology, pediatrics, public health science, and sociology at the University of Alabama at Birmingham. He was founder and investigator for a number of prominent early intervention programs, including the Abecedarian Project, Project CARE, and the Infant Health and Development Program.

Sharon Landesman Ramey, Ph.D., is director of the Civitan International Research Center and professor of psychiatry, psychology, public health science, and sociology at the University of Alabama at Birmingham. She is currently co-directing the research and evaluation of the Head Start/Public School Transition Demonstration Project, a randomized trial of early intervention programs.

Abstract

This article presents a conceptual framework for thinking about the health and development of young children. The discussion of theory is followed by a description of how home visiting, as a process, can be used to improve the health and development of young children within their many domains of functioning. The authors . . . conclude that home visiting programs which address only one or a few domains of a child's functioning are not likely to have a robust or lasting effect. Accordingly, to be successful, home visiting programs must be comprehensive in their approach to addressing children's and families' needs in multiple domains of functioning. Finally, an analytical grid is presented to assist in describing and clarifying the relationships among the characteristics of home visiting programs and their desired consequences. The Appendix to this article illustrates application of this grid to describe the Infant Health and Development project.

The preparation of this paper was supported by the David and Lucile Packard Foundation, the Administration for Developmental Disabilities, the Maternal and Child Health Bureau of the Public Health Service, and the Administration for Children, Youth, and Families.

Home visiting appears to be one of the most frequently used early intervention strategies or family support programs in the United States to improve the health and development of children. Although some home visiting programs are conceptualized merely as an efficient or economical means of service delivery, these programs are most often construed as a treatment strategy that contains unique and powerful characteristics relative to improving children's health and development. As one recent review of home visiting programs concluded, however, the diversity among programs providing home visiting and the "incomplete but suggestive empirical support for its usefulness, creates an imperative for a more systematic approach to demonstration and evaluation efforts in this area."[1]

This article outlines one of the next steps in developing such an approach. It offers a conceptual framework for understanding and describing more precisely the modes of operation of home visiting programs and the specific domains of early childhood health and development they intend to address. Thus, the article begins with a discussion of health and development in the first three years of life. Then, the implications of this knowledge for the design of home visiting programs are considered. Finally, an analytical grid is presented as a tool for both describing and evaluating home visiting programs. Although this article focuses on children, programs that improve their health and development are likely also to bring about beneficial changes in their parents and the family as a whole.

Health and Development in the First Three Years of Life

Both health and development involve complex and sophisticated ideas about the human condition. These two terms have many definitions and implications for intervention strategies. For the purpose of conceptualizing home visiting programs and their possible positive effects on children's health and development, definitions should emphasize the multidimensionality of each concept. For example, the World Health Organization has advocated that health be defined as a state of physical, mental, and social well-being.[2] Similarly, we believe that development should be seen as a multidimensional process of simultaneously achieving progressive states of (1) increased differentiation (the ability to make distinctions or to perceive differences in closely related items or ideas), (2) increased ability for self-initiation and self-control, (3) increased interpersonal awareness, and (4) increased social responsibility. The central premise of this article is that, because both health and development are multidimensional and dynamic with each dimension affecting the other, home visiting programs and other early intervention efforts must consider the full range of needs for young children in developing their goals and the strategies to achieve them.

The first three years of life represent the period of most rapid growth and development, especially in terms of central nervous system development and associated

Children's health and development are multidimensional and comprised of distinct, but interdependent, domains of functioning.

physical development and social behavior.[3] It is during the first three years that infants and young children are the most dependent on others for their basic care, including health care, intellectual stimulation, social guidance, and love. Failure to provide for young children's basic needs during this period is likely to result in serious consequences, including impaired health, poor sensory-motor functioning, below average intellectual capacity, and compromised abilities to form positive and lasting social relationships.[4] Therefore, home visiting programs in the first three years of life can and often do have goals of both enrichment and prevention, that is, to enhance health and development by providing services and to prevent the negative consequences of suboptimal care or inadequate family support.

Young children's health and development must be viewed within a conceptual framework that explicitly recognizes that their worlds are fundamentally embedded in and influenced by the specific developmental and ecological contexts of their families and communities.[5] Congruent with the theories of authors such as Bronfenbrenner[6] and Sameroff and Fiese,[7] this perspective emphasizes that the forces which affect young children are dynamic and often are the same ones which directly affect the development and functioning of their families and their communities. Accordingly, to alter the course of children's development, early intervention programs—including those that use home visiting—need to take into account the needs and resources of families and communities, as well as the basic needs of children themselves. . . .

Furthermore, even when focusing only on the children, it is clear that their development is complex. Children's health and development are multidimensional and comprised of distinct, but interdependent, domains of functioning. The eight key developmental domains, based on a content analysis of the developmental literature, are (1) survival, (2) values and goals, (3) a

Figure 1

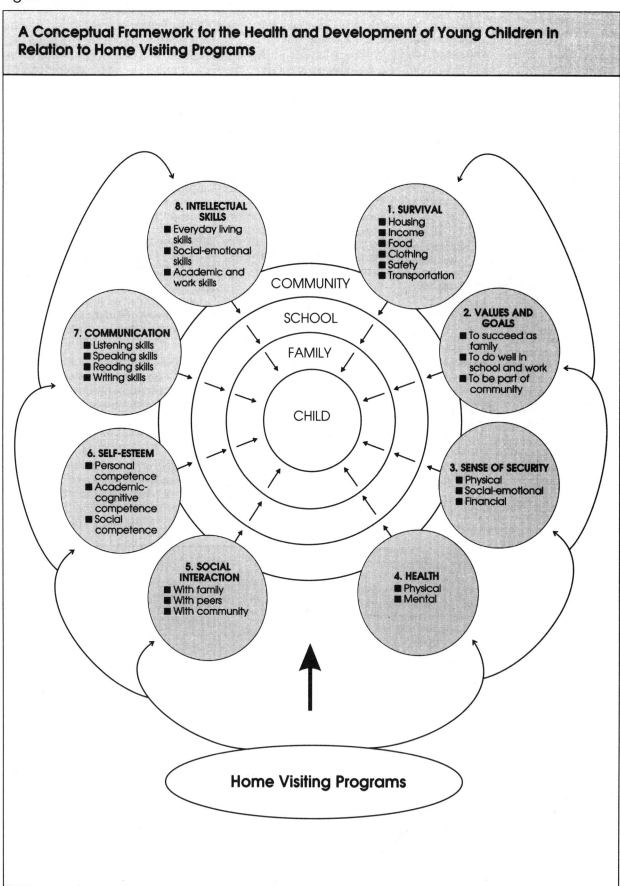

A Conceptual Framework for the Health and Development of Young Children in Relation to Home Visiting Programs

sense of security, (4) health, (5) social interaction, (6) self-esteem, (7) communication, and (8) basic intellectual skills. Figure 1 provides examples of functioning within each of these domains.

Within this conceptual framework, the eight domains of functioning comprise the substance of health and development. These domains are intertwined with each other and with the child and family's whole environment. These domains are influenced by the everyday family supports (for example, kinship and friendship networks) and by the community resources (for example, social welfare and health care networks) that form the context within which the young child develops. A central premise of most home visiting programs is that the ecological context of the family can be significantly and positively altered through specific program elements associated with individual home visiting programs. In turn, most programs assume changes in the family environment will mediate changes in the child's everyday experiences. Figure 1 not only presents the eight domains of functioning, but also illustrates the fact that home visiting programs may affect children and families by altering some or all of the major domains of function through strategies directed toward the child, family, school, and/or community.

Implications for Home Visiting Programs

In practice, most home visiting programs place differential and selective emphasis on one or more of the identified eight domains of functioning. Often home visiting programs address first, and with greatest intensity of effort, those needs that appear to home visitors and/or to family members to be the most pressing. For instance, some home visiting programs invest substantial time and resources in helping families to meet needs in the domains of survival (for example, by providing assistance with housing, food, clothing, and transportation) and health (for example, by providing routine checkups and monitoring, encouraging positive health habits, and taking family members to medical appointments). Other home visiting programs emphasize the domains of social interaction and social support for the mother, or systematically seek to change the domains of communication and basic intellectual skills by providing educational programs and direct instruction to mothers and/or their children.

The reasons that programs emphasize different domains of functioning, and may even fail to consider some domains, include the following: (1) the anticipated and most pressing needs of the population with which the program is working, (2) the professional orientation and expertise of the individuals designing and implementing the program, (3) the resources available to the program, and (4) the philosophical orientation of the program (such as whether some domains of functioning are judged to be more or less important or whether home visitors are encouraged not to become involved in some domains for reasons of professional competence or safety). Often, the implicit assumption or hope is that, once the most urgent family issues have been resolved satisfactorily, then there will be time and energy to address other less pressing but important aspects of young children's health and development.

Limiting the focus in home visiting programs to supporting the family first, without special efforts to target the child's early development as well, may be self-defeating. The article by Olds and Kitzman [see *The Future of Children*, Winter 1993, pp. 53–92] reviews the effectiveness of diverse home visiting programs. What is clear from their excellent review of the empirical studies is that there is little evidence that programs which are not intensive and comprehensive, but instead target for change one or a few domains of functioning, are likely to have a lasting beneficial effect, even on the targeted aspects of the lives of children. Those areas may show some improvement; however, in the absence of continuing resource allocation, such changes are unlikely to occur in a robust or lasting manner. In addition, short-term change in one or a few domains will not have a domino, or spillover, effect to other equally important domains of children's functioning. Unfortunately, the nature of developmental processes in young children is such that not one of their needs can wait until other needs are met; children's development does not go on hold while family problems are being solved.

This does not imply that attending to survival and health is less important than focusing on a child's social or intellectual development (or vice versa), but rather that there is a pressing need in the first few years of life to consider simultaneously and to coordinate all of the important needs of a young child. Meeting this need challenges many home visiting programs, especially those in which the amount of time allotted to each home visit is constrained and the frequency of home visits is not sufficient to provide effective assistance in multiple domains. Although a given home visiting program may appear initially to do better at achieving its goals if the scope is narrow and clearly focused, this does not necessarily ensure that the families—and especially the infants and young children—will directly benefit in a lasting way from a narrowly focused program.

A home visiting program does not have to be comprehensive in and of itself. The home visits can be an integral part of a broader early intervention and family support program. . . . In this situation, the issue of coordination across different program components, as well as across the domains of functioning, is highly significant. It is an important challenge in such efforts to minimize fragmentation and duplication.

An Analytical Grid for Describing Home Visiting Programs

The multidimensional and dynamic developmental framework illustrated in Figure 1 and the research suggesting that effectiveness of early intervention similarly requires a multidimensional approach highlight the importance of understanding in detail the goals and scope of home visiting programs when planning or evaluating them. Home visiting programs need to be described in terms of which specific domains of health

There is little evidence that programs which are not intensive and comprehensive, but instead target for change one or a few domains of functioning, are likely to have a lasting beneficial effect.

and development they address directly. In Figure 1, these potential interventions are represented by solid arrows. In essence, this greater specificity can lead to a much

needed and more refined typology of early intervention and home visiting programs based on explicit domains of intended impact and associated strategies and resources.

In addition to considering which domains a given intervention program directly addresses and why (the program's philosophy and strategy), other important dimensions to specify include the timing of the program (including when the home visiting begins in the family's life cycle and its duration), the intensity of the program, (for example, the number of visits per month and the length of each visit), and the coordination of the home visit activities across the various domains of functioning (for example, whether activities for diverse domains are discrete or embedded in larger activities, and whether home visitors and other support personnel communicate with one another frequently and effectively).[5,8] Two additional program features to consider, although difficult to measure well, are (1) cultural sensitivity and adaptation of a program to diverse family ecologies and (2) the quality and degree of implementation of the intended program. These might be determined by the extent to which there is specific documentation verifying program delivery to individual families and children, as well as responses of participants to particular aspects of the program. . . .

Figure 2 summarizes the critical program characteristics that warrant consideration in seeking to better understand home visiting programs and their differential effects. To fully use this model, a home visiting program would be described in detail so that the program's philosophy, implementation strategy, and content would be specified for each domain the program seeks to change.

Appendix Box A1 to this article illustrates use of this grid to describe the Infant Health and Development Program. This analytical grid fosters a comparative analysis of different home visiting programs, recognizing that not all home visiting programs have the same resources or breadth of focus and that they differ in the populations with which they work. For instance, some programs are conceptualized as universal home visiting programs (for example, regularly scheduled home visits to all mothers and newborns within a specific geographic catchment area), whereas many others are targeted for high-risk sub-

Figure 2

An Analytical Grid for Describing Home Visiting Programs

Domains of Functioning

	Survival	Values and Goals	Security	Health	Social Interaction	Self-esteem	Communication	Intellectual Skills
Philosophy								
Strategy								
Timing								
Intensity								
Coordination across domains								
Sensitivity to cultural and family context								
Quality and degree of implementation								

Program Characteristics

---

populations (for example, substance-abusing women, low birth weight and premature infants, families with multiple preidentified risk factors). On the analytical grid, this would be noted as features of both the program's philosophy and strategy.

This analytical grid is one that is admittedly detailed and potentially quite complex. Yet, all home visiting programs make choices and decisions about each element in this grid, even if sometimes those choices are by default. For instance, when certain functional domains are left out of the planning and conceptualization of a home visiting program or when issues such as timing and intensity are not systematically specified or monitored, these characteristics of the intervention program nonetheless may directly affect its success. Equally important, what is excluded or not addressed in a given home visiting program often reflects unrecognized biases or assumptions that guide the program and its philosophy.

Use of this analytical framework can make both description and evaluation of home visiting programs more precise. Home visiting programs are not monolithic entities, and this grid can help make that clear. In addition, to the extent that future empirical work about home visiting programs can yield more precise information about the nature and format of the programs themselves, as well as a valid and comprehensive description of program participants and their initial and ongoing needs, the conclusions about the effects of home visiting programs will become more useful. A fuller understanding of effectiveness will assist in modifying and replicating promising programs, as well as in guiding public policy about the role of home visiting in improving the health and development of young children.

Conclusion

Home visiting programs are an increasingly important and prominent part of the human service delivery system in the United States to improve the health and development of young children and their families. There is a need to specify in greater detail which aspects of health and development are within the purview of individual home visiting programs. This article offers a conceptual framework and an analytic tool to facilitate the systematic description and evaluation of various home visiting programs. By systematically assessing our expanding knowledge about home visiting, we can direct the use of scarce public resources more precisely and, overall, make home visiting programs more cost-effective.

We gratefully acknowledge the support and the assistance of Zee Hildreth and Leslie Franklin in the preparation of the manuscript.

1. Roberts, R., Casto, G., Wasik, B., and Ramey, C. T. Family support in the home: Programs, policy and social change. *American Psychologist* (1991) 46,2:131–37.

2. World Health Organization. *International classification of impairments, disabilities, and handicaps: A manual of classification relating to the consequences of disease.* Geneva, Switzerland: World Health Organization, 1980.

3. Purpura, D. P. Normal and abnormal development of cerebral cortex in man. *Neuroscience Research Program Bulletin* (1982) 20,4:569–77.

4. Landesman, S. Institutionalization revisited: Expanding views on early and cumulative life experiences. In *Handbook of developmental psychopathology.* M. Lewis and S. Miller, eds. New York: Plenum Press, 1982, pp. 455–62.

5. Ramey, S. L., and Ramey, C. T. Early educational intervention with disadvantaged children—To what effect? *Applied and Preventive Psychology* (1992) 1,3:131–40.

6. Bronfenbrenner, U. *The ecology of human development.* Cambridge, MA: Harvard University Press, 1979.

7. Sameroff, A., and Fiese, B. Family representations of development. In *Parental belief system: The psychological consequences for children* I. Sigel, A. McGillicutty-Delsi, and J. Goodman, eds. Rev. ed. Hillsdale, NJ: Lawrence Erlbaum Associates, Inc., 1992, pp. 347–69.

8. Ramey, C. T., and Ramey, S. L. Effective early intervention. *Mental Retardation* (1992) 30,5:1–9.

9. The Infant Health and Development Program. Enhancing the outcomes of low-birth-weight, premature infants: A multisite randomized trial. *Journal of the American Medical Association* (1990) 263,22:3035–42.

10. Ramey, C. T., Bryant, D. M., Wasik, B. H. et al. The Infant Health and Development Program for low birth weight, premature infants: Program elements, family participation, and child intelligence. *Pediatrics* (1992) 89,3:454–65.

11. Sparling, J., Lewis, I., Ramey, C. T., et al. Partners, a curriculum to help premature, low-birth-weight infants to get off to a good start. *Topics in Early Childhood Special Education* (1991) 11,1:36–55.

(Appendix Box A1 begins on next page.)

The Analytical Home Visiting Grid Applied to the Infant Health and Development Program

The Infant Health and Development Program (IHDP) was an eight-site controlled, randomized trial to test the effectiveness of a multipronged early intervention effort to facilitate the health outcomes and social and intellectual development of the targeted population of low birth weight, premature infants. Many aspects of the program reflect the fact that it was simultaneously a demonstration and research endeavor. The description below refers only to the children and families who received the multipronged intervention of medical services, a center-based child development program, and home visiting services.[9,10,11]

The following narrative illustrates how the analytical home visiting grid would be used to describe this program in greater detail.

Targeted Population

Low birth weight (2,500 g), premature (<37 weeks) infants born in Level III hospitals, with no major congenital anomalies.

Philosophy and Priority for Each Domain

IHDP identified three domains as being of high priority. Home visiting was viewed as one of several methods or strategies for delivering needed supports to families and children. The three targeted domains were: children's health, children's intellectual skills, and children's social interaction. These priorities were selected based on the empirical evidence that this target population is at especially high risk in these three areas during the early years of life. Because the families were expected to be diverse with regard to socioeconomic status as well as cultural and ethnic identity, systematic interventions were not designed in advance regarding many other aspects of family life. Rather, the IHDP's philosophy was to individualize each family intervention largely through the home visiting component of the program. That is, the home visitor was a regularly assigned person who was expected to develop a close working relationship with the families. The home visitors were all college graduates with additional specialized training that focused mostly on the three targeted domains, supplemented by training in how to promote problem-solving skills in parents, so that other family and child needs could be addressed and resolved in a timely and effective manner.

In the three targeted health and developmental domains, the underlying philosophy was as described below.

- **Health.** IHDP's philosophy about health emphasized preventive techniques and regular professional surveillance, consistent with the guidelines recommended by the American Academy of Pediatrics. Because it was assumed that home visiting alone could not ensure adequate health care, this was provided to all participants in either university-based clinics or through private providers. Home visitors facilitated the delivery of health care by explaining the importance of specific procedures, arranging for transportation to offices and clinics, accompanying parents (when useful), and observing the hygiene and health care behaviors in the home. Thus, home visitors were viewed as liaisons in the health domain, but not as the primary providers of health care.

- **Intellectual Skills and Social Interaction.** In contrast, in the area of intellectual skills, the home visitors concentrated on enhancing the parents' decision-making abilities and provided a home education program to promote the children's intellectual development. In the second year of life, the children's home education program closely paralleled that provided to the children in the Child Development Center (on a five-day-a-week, year-round basis). Social interaction was addressed by providing a curriculum that integrated the intellectual and social domains for children. Parents' own interactions with children were observed and discussed during each home visit, problems the parents identified were addressed, and new ideas and materials appropriate to the children's changing developmental needs were introduced on a regular basis (e.g., toys, books, observation sheets).

   Because working with biologically at-risk children, many of whom came from economically and educationally low-resource families, is recognized to be highly demanding, psychological and educational supports were provided to all home visitors on a frequent and regular basis. Home visitors had opportunities for weekly supervision and weekly (or more frequent) contact with other home visitors engaged in similar activities. Excellent benefits were provided to home visitors for health coverage, vacation, and sick leave. If desired, additional psychological counseling was available to home visitors to help with their personal reactions to a potentially highly stressful set of responsibilities.

- **Other Domains.** The IHDP did not specifically intervene in the areas of the family's values and goals for their children (such as the priority the family placed on the child's subsequent school achievement), in large part because of the very young age of the children (infancy to three years) and the more pressing concerns of the children's physical, intellectual, and social well-being based on their premature, low birth weight status.

➡

Box A1 (continued)

Survival needs did arise for many low-income, inner-city families, and these were addressed on an individual family basis, often involving referrals to appropriate agencies and the use of the specially developed family problem-solving curriculum. Of necessity, an unanticipated component of some home visiting activities included seeking help for substance abuse and family violence.

- **Overall Philosophy.** The home visiting activities were conceptualized as an important and integral component of an effective early intervention but were not considered sufficient to create the desired positive changes without the other health care and educational components of IHDP. Philosophically, the IHDP endorsed the view that parents are the single most influential people in their children's lives; accordingly, parents must be well supported in this role and must understand and participate (as appropriate) in any supplemental services to enhance their children's developmental outcomes. At the same time, children's early intellectual and social development was considered to be highly important and to depend on the provision of regular and developmentally appropriate stimulation, embedded within the types of everyday activities in which children engage. To ensure this availability to all high-risk children, external supports in the form of the Child Development Centers complemented the home visiting program.

Strategies

The strategies used in the three targeted health and developmental domains are described in the paragraphs that follow.

- **Health.** The strategy for addressing health of the children included (1) regular high-quality health surveillance (following the schedule recommended by the American Academy of Pediatrics for visits and procedures during the first three years of life), including home visitor assistance with scheduling, transportation, referral, and additional care as needed; (2) parent education through home visiting regarding basic nutrition, hygiene, and the need for specialized care of premature and low birth weight children (adapted for each child); (3) in the Child Development Centers, when children were between 12 and 36 months of corrected age (determined as chronological age minus weeks of prematurity), all employees were trained in health care behaviors to meet standards set by the American Academy of Pediatrics and the Centers for Disease Control. Because of the potential vulnerability of these at-risk children, the maintenance of these standards was monitored weekly by project staff, including written documentation, and supplemented by outside professional monitoring. In the domain of health, some children were judged to need specialized therapies, such as physical therapy and speech therapy, and these were provided to all children for whom it was recommended by the primary physician. Transportation and other assistance in receiving these supplemental therapies were facilitated by home visitors and other project staff.

- **Intellectual Skills.** Strategies for promoting intellectual skills included four primary sets of activities:

1. Enhancing the parents' own intellectual competence, particularly related to everyday problems and decision making, by a specially developed Problem Solving Curriculum. This curriculum was taught by the home visitors and, during each home visit, was implemented and applied to the family's dynamic situation. Data were maintained on parents' progress and use of the problem-solving strategies was promoted.

2. Enhancing the parents' intellectual skills and their social interactional skills in the service of promoting their child's intellectual development. A home version of the Child Development Center curriculum, known as Partners for Learning,[10] was provided to parents in developmental levels appropriate to their own child's progress. The home visitor helped explain these materials and often demonstrated their use during the home visit.

3. Promoting children's intellectual development directly, via provision of a high-quality, five-days-a-week, year-round Child Development Center. High standards for the centers were met through the following strategies: the directors hired had advanced degrees in early childhood education or child development; training was provided to the center directors by experienced educators and psychologists (who had previously enacted the curriculum and established other child development centers); teachers had bachelor's degrees or higher and also received in-service orientation, ongoing training, and weekly supervision and feedback on their performance. Teachers and directors, as well as home visitors, maintained daily logs of their activities, including documentation of child-specific encounters and progress. When necessary, staff received supplemental training or were terminated. Full supplies for enacting the curriculum were provided to all centers and home visitors, with adequate budgets for replacing supplies and equipment. Program implementation technical assistance was available from a national center by request from each site. A multidisciplinary team supervising the IHDP program visited external sites at least once a year.

➤

Box A1 (continued)

The Analytical Home Visiting Grid Applied to the Infant Health and Development Program

Social Development

This domain was addressed within the same curriculum used by parents and by teachers in the Child Development Center. Monthly parent meetings provided another strategy for sharing information with parents which may have helped to promote both social and intellectual development as well as good health care and health outcomes for these children. Monthly parent meetings varied in response to what parents said they were interested in.

Timing

The IHDP home visiting component began at the infant's discharge from the hospital and continued until all infants in the program at a given site reached 36 months corrected age. At 12 months corrected age, each infant entered a specially constructed and staffed Child Development Center. Children attended the center each weekday until all children in the yearly cohort were 36 months corrected age. At that point the children and their families were supported in their transition to other community services as appropriate and available, and the centers were closed and the program terminated or continued under new auspices.

Intensity

Until 12 months of age, home visits were scheduled weekly (although documentation indicates that they were less frequent for some families for a variety of reasons). Between 12 months of age and program termination at 36 months, home visits were scheduled every two weeks. Attempted and completed visits were documented on special forms and entered weekly into a national computer data base as was the specific content of each visit, including both the occurrence of precoded events and extensive clinical notes about particularly noteworthy special conditions or circumstances. Similar documentation occurred for the pediatric and Child Development Center components of the IHDP. These data were summarized monthly by the national program center and shared with project staff at the eight sites. Technical assistance was provided as necessary to increase the likelihood of consistency of program implementation and, therefore, to maximize the probability of close cross-site comparisons.

Coordination Across Domains

The Partners for Learning curriculum[10] that was used in both the home visiting and Child Development Center components contains procedures for internal guidance and documentation and associated forms and charts to coordinate developmental activities for children in the domains of social interaction and intellectual skills. These forms were shared and supplemented by weekly, biweekly, monthly, or as-needed conferences between home visitors and parents; home visitors and teachers at the Child Development Center; and home visitors, parents, pediatricians, and nurses. Each of these conferences was summarized and documented.

Sensitivity to Cultural and Family Context

The IHDP was restricted to families who could receive the program in the English language because of its development and previous experimental testing in that language only. No special programmatic features were designed to tailor the program to particular cultural or linguistic groups. Program personnel were encouraged to consider individual families' preferences. The importance of tailoring services according to individual needs was explicitly recognized in the design and implementation of IHDP.

Quality and Degree of Documentation

Especially because IHDP was a controlled randomized trial to test the effectiveness of a multipronged early intervention program for low birth weight, premature infants, documentation of all program aspects was extensive. Specifically, all contacts with each family were documented in prespecified ways, and all personnel were trained in documentation procedures. To ensure that documentation was maintained with rigor throughout the three years of program implementation, it was reviewed regularly and frequently, and appropriate feedback was provided to program staff so that they knew their notes and forms had been studied by their supervisors. The specificity of documentation for individual families permitted the construction of an individual Family Participation Index, which subsequently was demonstrated to relate clearly to how much benefit the children showed in terms of their intellectual development by ages two and three. Quality was addressed by site visits of professionals not involved in ongoing service delivery at the site at least annually by frequent and systematic review of documentation and phone calls, and by meetings with local site staff. Regular feedback was provided from national program implementation support staff to each local site regarding their performance. ◆

"I Forget"

Kids remember a lot more than they know—or tell us. What are the keys that unlock those precious memories?

David F. Bjorklund, Ph.D., and Barbara R. Bjorklund

David F. Bjorklund, Ph.D., and **Barbara R. Bjorklund** are the authors of the *Parents Book of Discipline* (Ballantine) and *Looking at Children* (Brooks/Cole).

Our friend Marie laughed when we told her that we were doing a research project on preschoolers' memory abilities. "Preschoolers' memory?" she said with a quizzical look on her face. "Well, if Jonathan is any example, it'll be a very short project."

Marie went on to tell us about her four-year-old son's recent school trip to a fire station. "How was your day?" she asked after school.

"Okay," Jonathan answered.

She tried again: "What did you do at school today?"

"Nothing much," he said.

Thinking she might have been mistaken about the date of the trip, Marie asked, "Wasn't this the day you were going to the fire station?"

"Yeah, we did," Jonathan replied.

"Well, tell me about it!" she prompted.

"We went on a bus and we saw the fire engine and we ate lunch at the park. Lisa gave me her cookies."

For all parents, this exchange has a familiar ring to it. Surely Jonathan remembers more about his field trip to the fire station than the bus ride and lunch in the park. For example, he probably learned a lot of new things and has many details of the morning tucked away in his memory. But deciding which tidbits to tell his mother first and which words to use to tell them is a difficult task.

How memory works.

There are many aspects of memory that a young child needs to master. First the event must be attended and perceived. Then the child must make some sense of that event so that it can be represented in his mind and recalled later on. If a child doesn't tune in to the important aspects of an event or cannot make sense of what he experienced, there is really nothing for the child to draw on.

Once the youngster has managed to accomplish all of this, the trick is to retrieve the memory, translate the mental picture he has in his head, and bring it to consciousness. The child must then find a way to explain that experience to another person. Broken down into its components, the process of remembering is quite complicated. It is understandable that young children, like Jonathan, often have a hard time doing it.

"Give me a hint!"

One thing that helps jog the memory is a cue. If someone asked you the name of Walter Mondale's running mate in the 1984 election, you might not be able to recall the name immediately. But if that person then told you that the first name of Mondale's running mate was Geraldine, you would no doubt snap your fingers and say, "Ferraro! I knew that all the time."

Children need cues too. According to Wolfgang Schneider, Ph.D.—professor of educational psychology at the University of Wuerzburg, in Germany, and coauthor, with Michael Pressley, of *Memory Development Between Two and Twenty* (Springer-Verlag)—young children have more difficulty retrieving information from their memory than they do storing it. To help them out, we need to use careful questioning techniques, involving a large dose of hints or cues. According to Schneider, the younger children are, the more hints they need to recall information. Robyn Fivush, Ph.D.—associate professor of psychology at Emory University, in Atlanta—and Nina R. Hamond, Ph.D., explain in *Knowing and Remembering in Young Children* (Cambridge University Press) that "younger children recall as much information as older children do, but they need more memory questions in order to do so." In other words, if Marie had asked Jonathan more specific questions when she picked him up, she might have gotten better answers. "Tell me about your trip to the fire station" would have been a good opener. "Did you see the fire fighters' clothes and boots? Did they have a spotted dog like the one we saw on TV? Did you get to see the fire engine? Did the fire chief talk to you?" Any of these questions, with the appropriate follow-up, would have had a better chance of winning detailed answers from a four-year-old than "How was your day?"

What to remember?

Preschoolers also have trouble selecting what to remember. Most adults know to watch the players on the field play ball at a baseball game. We automatically pay less attention to the field-maintenance staff, the players on the bench, and most of the other spectators. Young children do not always tune in to what adults view as the main point of the event. At a baseball game, they may spend more time watching the hot-dog vendors, the bat boys, and the second-base umpire.

We discovered this when we took our five-year-old grandson, Nicholas, to his first play—a community production of *Little Shop of Horrors*. He reported to his mother that the highlight of the afternoon was the punch and cookies that they served at "halftime." After some pointed questioning, she found that he remembered a lot about the play. But the punch and cookies were clearly his strongest recollection.

This reminded us of the family trip we took many years ago to the west coast of Florida, which included a tour of the Ringling Art Museum, in Sarasota. Our son, Derek, a typical five-year-old, wasn't interested in the paintings and sculpture that were featured in the building and gardens. The "art" that captured *his* attention was the pattern on the wood parquet floors. Years later we were amazed that he remembered details of the trip to Sarasota, specifically the patterned floor at "some museum."

Children's perspective of the world is unique, and we respect their sense of wonder at parquet floors and punch and cookies. Life's little details are important to young children. But we need to help them pay attention also to the salient features of events so that their memories of an experience don't exclude the baseball players, the actors on stage, and the art at a museum.

To prepare for an outing, try giving your youngster a child's-eye view of what you expect to happen. Keep it short and simple. Before a recent trip to the Boston Aquarium with our three-year-old grandson, Jeffrey, we told him that we were going to visit a big tank where a lot of fish lived. We told him we would also see some penguins and some other water animals. He would be able to touch some of the water animals if he wanted to, but he didn't have to. This simple summary of the events told him that the fish and water animals were the main topics of interest. No doubt he would also be interested in other children, the vending machines, and so on—which was okay—but the special thing about the trip was the fish and other water animals. A stop at the gift shop for postcards gave us a few more memory aides so that Jeffrey could tell his big brother all about his trip, which he did with reasonable accuracy after a few hints.

Total recall . . . sort of.

One thing that children tend to remember well is recurring events—what typically happens on a day-to-day basis. For example, research by Katherine Nelson, Ph.D.—professor of developmental psychology at the Graduate Center of the City University of New York, in New York City—and her colleagues has shown that preschool children remember novel information in the context of familiar events, such as a special clown cake served at a birthday party. Similarly, in a study by Robyn Fivush and Nina Hamond, two-and-a-half-year-olds—even when questioned about special events, such as a trip to the beach, a camping trip, and a ride on an airplane—tended to recall what adults would consider to be routine information. Take, for instance, the following conversation between an adult and a child about a camping trip, reported by Fivush and Hamond. The child first recalled sleeping outside, which is unusual, but then remembered very routine things:

Interviewer: You slept outside in a tent? Wow, that sounds like fun.

Child: And then we waked up and eat dinner. First we eat dinner, then go to bed, and then wake up and eat breakfast.

Interviewer: What else did you do when you went camping? What did you do . . . after breakfast?

Child: Umm, in the night, and went to sleep.

It seems strange that a child would talk about such routine tasks as waking up, eating, and going to bed when so many new and exciting things must have happened on the trip. But the younger the child, the more she may need to embed novel events in familiar routines. According to Fivush and Hamond's study, everything is new to two-year-olds, and they are constantly learning about their surroundings "so that they can anticipate and predict the world around them. In order to understand novel experience, young children may need to focus on what is familiar about this event, what makes [it] similar to events already known about, rather than what is distinctive or unusual about this event."

Just as strange—or at least surprising—is the accuracy with which children recall long-ago events. For example, two-and-a-half-year-old Katherine, upon seeing an ice cube wrapped in a washcloth, began a detailed account of a bee sting that she had received well over six months earlier, complete with time of day, where she had been when the incident occurred, and what her mother had done to soothe the pain.

This is all the more remarkable because Katherine had begun to talk only six months before, and the accurate account that she was now giving was far more detailed than she could have given at the time of the sting. But this and other impressive acts of long-term memory by young children are always prompted by a very specific cue, in this case the wrapped ice cube. Rarely will a three-year-old who is sitting pensively recount, out of the blue, an event that happened long ago. But with the proper prompt, a flood of information may gush forth.

We're amazed at young children's feats of long-term memory because they're clearly not able to learn as much or as quickly as older children. But learning and remembering are different. According to Charles Brainerd, Ph.D., professor of educational psychology at the University of Arizona, in Tucson, "Despite what our common sense tells us, research shows that learning does not have much to do with what we later remember or forget. A child who can't learn a four-line poem on Tuesday may have a very firm memory of what she had for dinner at Grandma's last month."

Teaching kids to remember.

The ability to remember is not usually thought of as a skill that we need to teach our children. Most of us think that it will simply develop with age: Children grow taller, run faster, and remember more with every birthday. It is true, to a certain extent, that a two-year-old cannot hold in her mind the number of things that a five-year-old can. And much of the trouble that preschoolers get into can be attributed to their forgetting. Young children really do forget to put away their toys, to wash their hands and face, and to return the pretty bracelet to Mommy's bedroom. The best thing that parents can do is to have realistic expectations of what their child can remember, and to be patient. When you're giving instructions, a handy rule of thumb is not to give your child more things to remember than her age. "Go get your shoes and your gloves" is enough for a two-year-old. Three-year-olds can handle three items ("Remember to brush your teeth, comb your hair, and put on your shirt"); most four-year-olds, four related items ("Call your brother for dinner, put away your tricycle, and bring in your jump rope and doll"). In fact, giving children one item less than their age increases the chances that the instructions will be followed.

Parents can play an important role in improving their child's memory. Judith Hudson, Ph.D., an associate professor of psychology at Rutgers University, in New Brunswick, New Jersey, and coeditor of *Knowing and Remembering in Young Children*, believes that children learn how to remember by interacting with their parents. She writes that "remembering can be viewed as an activity that is at first jointly carried out by parent and child and then later performed by the child alone."

In most families, Hudson explains, parents begin talking with young children about things that happened in the past. They ask questions such as, "Where did we go this morning?" "What did we see at the zoo?" "Who

went with us?" and "What else did we see?" From these exchanges, children learn that the important facts to remember about events are who, what, when, and where. These conversations help children learn to notice the important details of their experiences and to store their memories in an organized way so that they can easily be recalled.

In studying these exchanges between parents and preschoolers, Hudson found that parents do more than just ask the right questions; they also give the right answers when the child cannot remember. By providing the missing information, Hudson explains, parents help their child learn that if she is having difficulty recalling information, they will help her retrieve it.

A good example of this is a conversation that we overheard while riding on the Metro in Washington, D.C. A young mother and her daughter, who appeared to be around two, were returning home after a trip to the zoo.

Mother: Brittany, what did we see at the zoo?

Brittany: Elephunts.

Mother: That's right! We saw elephants. What else?

Brittany: *(Shrugs and looks at her mother.)*

Mother: Panda bear? Did we see a panda bear?

Brittany: *(Smiles and nods.)*

Mother: Can you say "panda bear"?

Brittany: Panda bear.

Mother: Good! Elephants and panda bears. What else?

Brittany: Elephunts.

Mother: That's right, elephants. And also a gorilla.

Brittany: Gorilla!

The importance of these hand-holding conversations has been shown in research by Hilary Horn Ratner, Ph.D., professor of psychology at Wayne State University, in Detroit. She observed two- and three-year-olds interacting with their mothers at home and recorded the number of times that the mother asked the child about past events. Ratner then tested the children's memories; those whose mothers had asked them many questions about past events showed better memory abilities both at that time and a year later.

Thinking about thinking.

The fact is that preschoolers simply don't think much about their thinking—if at all. They are still in that nice stage of mental life when remembering and learning "just happen." It will be many years before they are able to evaluate their memory ability and to think of how to make it work better.

When parents tell their preschoolers to "think harder" or "remember better," they are wasting their words. But through daily interactions—by not only asking their preschoolers questions that involve memory but also showing them how to answer—parents serve as memory teachers. Their children are then able to use these memory questions later on as they try to recall the details of specific events. Subtly, and almost effortlessly, parents help their children develop the memory, thinking, and learning skills that will be so useful to them throughout their lives.

Toddler Talk

New research shows that when you stimulate your child's language development, you stimulate her mind.

Chris Ravashiere Medvescek

Chris Ravashiere Medvescek is a mediator and freelance writer living in Tucson, Arizona. She has two children.

"I'll cry to the moon!"

Four-year-old Jason meant it, too. Language, in all its poetic possibilities, sprang forth to keep Mom from turning off the light at bedtime.

Where did Jason learn to say this? His mom and dad had never used such a phrase (although they certainly enjoyed hearing it). And who had taught him that words could be useful substitutes for wails?

Jason didn't really "learn" this. Nobody deliberately "taught" him. He simply had acquired one of the most complex and highly abstract systems in all of life: language.

"You don't have to learn to use language. You can't prevent it from happening," says Susan Curtiss, Ph.D., a linguist studying language and brain function at the University of California at Los Angeles Medical Center. "It's part of the biological phenomenon of growing as a human being, like 'learning' to walk."

Language acquisition—what most of us call learning to talk—is really a lifelong process. But by far the most intense advancement occurs during the "toddler talk" years, roughly between the ages of two and five. It is a time of poetic phrases, charming mispronunciations, and garbled syntax. By the end, a child will have moved from silly statements ("Ducks eat me!") to complete sentences ("The ducks are eating my bread").

"They will have reached their goal," says Naomi Baron, Ph.D., linguist and author of several books on children's language, including *Growing Up With Language* (Addison-Wesley). "They now can form complex abstract sentences.

How does this happen? If language is acquired instinctively, what is the parents' role? And what does toddler talk reveal about the complex communication system children are gaining as they move from being burbling babies to fluent speakers?

Parents who take the time to answer these questions will be repaid many times over. Toddler talk, shared with a caring, attentive adult, builds bonds of trust and love. And ultimately, parents will have helped their children academically as well. Because language is expressed thought, stimulating language means stimulating the mind. And the beauty of it is, you probably already know how to do it.

How parents help.

Because language acquisition is too important to leave to chance, nature has programmed parents into the process. "Helping children learn to talk is not something we do consciously, even if we sometimes consciously try," says Judith Creighton, Ph.D., a child-development specialist and coauthor of *Learning to Talk Is Child's Play* (Communication Skill Builders). "We instinctively go along with their budding ability."

For example, parents routinely name things for their children, obligingly providing them with the vocabulary necessary to build sentences. Naming objects actually helps establish a core concept: Words represent reality. It is the first abstract step toward mastering language.

"Simplification" is another language aid that comes easily even to those who aren't parents. The use of short sentences that generally match the child's verbal skills ("Want a drink? Here you go!") stimulates "the child's comfortable and timely development of language," says Creighton.

By "repeating" and "expanding," parents naturally facilitate their child's speech development. Their conversations often go something like this:

Child: Doggie.
Parent: Doggie bark.
Child: Doggie bark.
Parent: The doggie is barking.

As parents repeat what they hear and add a few words, they mold their child's language, explains Naomi Baron. In doing so, parents also are tacitly giving their child permission to practice talking, are building parent-child trust, and, most important, are saying, "I'm listening."

Through "parallel talk" and "snapshotting," parents act as language tour guides. In the first instance, parents describe their own actions: "I'm putting milk on your cereal right now." In the second, parents create a verbal snapshot of what their child is doing: "Oh, you're building a tall tower! You're using red and yellow blocks." Either tactic has the effect of "pouring language on top of experience," says Judith Creighton, which is the most effective way to learn language.

Pretty simple stuff, yet these unsophisticated, unconscious strategies are all basic to language acquisition. Applied conscientiously by interested parents, they lead to an invaluable activity for building language and thinking skills: conversation.

Studies show that even parent-infant conversation lays a foundation for creative and critical thought, reading, writing, decision making, and problem solving. A program for poverty-level toddlers that encouraged their mothers to talk to them resulted in an average eighteen-point increase in the children's IQ scores. In addition, the children became more cooperative and attentive, asked more questions, and demonstrated an increase in their vocabulary.

Talking *with*, not *at*, children is the key: asking questions, pausing for an answer (verbal or nonverbal), then responding. No matter how limited your child's vocabulary, your efforts invite her to stretch her language and, therefore, her mind.

The best avenue for conversation is play. "Language and play are very closely linked. Both are symbolic activities," says Jill Heerboth, a pediatric speech-language pathologist in Tucson, Arizona. "If parents want to help their children with language, they should play with them."

Play provides perfect opportunities for parents to use the tactics that encourage children to speak. There are many objects, actions, and concepts to name, as well as comments to repeat and expand upon. "You're making the car go fast," a parent watching his toddler roll a toy vehicle might say. Picking up some blocks nearby, the parent could add, "I'm building a big house."

Just like grown-ups, toddlers respond best when you talk about the things that interest them. "Pay attention to what your child thinks is important," advises Creighton. "Is she stacking blocks? Sorting by color or size? Watch and listen, then try out a

few neutral comments: 'I see you're using all the blue blocks.' If the reply comes back, 'It's getting tall,' change direction to focus on stacking.

"This leads naturally to true communication: 'I listen to you, you listen to me,'" adds Creighton. Insisting that children talk about your focus only shuts them down. Sometimes, though, kids are too busy to talk. By describing what they're doing and remaining attentive without demanding a reply, you can create a relaxed atmosphere that usually will lead to later exchanges.

Asking questions can provide lots of conversational fodder—provided that they are the right ones, observes Heerboth. Being asked, "What's this? What color is it? How many are there?" feels more like a test than a talk, and kids will tune out. But open and sincere questions, such as "What should we do next?" and "Why did that happen?" prolong discussion.

Parents can mix in questions with their repetitions and expansions. Linguists call this "scaffolding," or building a structure around your child's language to encourage further growth:

Child: *(Pointing to his drawing)* A looong line.

Parent: You made a looong line. Where is it going?

Encourage reasoning through "what," "why," and "what if" questions, especially when your child shows signs that he is ready mentally. "When children start using because or if clauses, such as, 'My teddy's crying because he's hungry,'" says Heerboth, "they're showing they now understand cause and effect and are ready to reason."

From nonsense to sense.

Okay—you're holding up your end of the conversation. What are your pint-size partners doing with theirs? Most likely they are valiantly throwing together everything they know about language in the hope of coming up with something that makes sense to you.

Imagine an American tourist in Mexico City desperately calling up every remembered bit of high school Spanish to order a meal in a restaurant. A few words, a little grammar, and a lot of pointing—coupled with a concrete topic (food) and a mutual desire to communicate—have fed more than one hungry tourist. Naomi Baron calls this process "managing on a linguistic shoestring."

Toddlers are out there on a shoestring, dangling at the limit of their abilities, bravely trying to bring that sentence in on a wing and a prayer. To do so, they all use basically the same strategies and acquire new skills in basically the same order.

Children first acquire a vast collection of single words, then begin using them in two-word phrases ("Mommy eat"); they then string them together in a telegraphic, "Cookie Monster" fashion: "Me so hungry!" From the age of about two and a half to five years, they acquire grammatical morphemes—words or parts of words that add meaning to their sentences. All English-speaking children—including those with hearing or language disorders—learn the same number of morphemes in the same general order, although at different rates.

The first one that children learn is "ing," as in walking or eating. This is followed by the prepositions "in" and "on," then "s" to form plurals. The last morphemes to be acquired are "is" and "were" and contractions ("*That's* Daddy"; "*We're* home").

Practice makes perfect.

Acquiring morphemes is one thing. Using them, and the rest of vocabulary and grammar, is another. Kids broadly rely on three basic grammatical strategies—"analogies," "scissors and paste," and "potshots"—when putting together what they know, explains Baron. These strategies would pass unnoticed but for the errors kids make in using them. Mistakes are your clue that your child is actively practicing the art of language.

When four-year-old Jason protested he wasn't sleepy, his mom replied, "Well, just rest, then."

"But I'm not resty, either," he moaned. Jason was creating a language "analogy." His strategy: If "sleep" can become "sleepy," then "rest" can become "resty."

As children learn grammatical structures and morphemes, they look for consistency among the rules. Hence, Ryan, at three and a half, yelled, "Go down in the hole. Even downer!" (low, lower; down, downer). Sometimes the analogy is correct but the context is wrong: "Can I listen in your ears?" asked Nick, three, doctor kit in hand (look, eyes; listen, ears).

"I can't get out!" wailed Rosie. Actually, she wasn't having trouble getting out of the wading pool—in fact, she didn't want to get out at all! But

When a Child Doesn't Say Much

According to experts, there may be several explanations as to why a child is slow to begin speaking, ranging from birth order to personal style to poor hearing. Children with older siblings tend to talk less (since their big brother or sister may communicate for them), as do naturally shy children.

For some kids (especially preemies), the coordination needed to vocalize speech sounds and syllables may be slow to develop. Poor hearing—sometimes caused by chronic ear infections—is a common culprit; if it's undetected, children miss out on a critical period of language development.

Check with your pediatrician.

As a rule of thumb, if your child hasn't started using two-word phrases by the time he is two to two and a half, or if you are simply worried, check with your pediatrician. He or she may recommend hearing- and language-assessment testing. If a hearing problem is ruled out, there are many ways to encourage your child to speak, according to child-development specialist Judith Creighton.

First, Creighton recommends, parents should accept body language, actions, and gestures as dialogue. (In this example a boy is working on a puzzle.)

Parent: You're putting it all together. (Child tries to force a piece into the wrong space.)

Parent: Oh, no, it won't fit. (Child throws the piece away.)

Parent: You don't want that piece. Good-bye! (Child fits another piece in the right space.) It fits! You did it! (Child smiles broadly.)

Often you will hear your child repeat what you have said earlier. (Child pulling on his shoe: "It fits!") Encourage him to use language that you've modeled. For instance, after showing your child how a toy works, you might suggest that he show someone else how to play with it. Also, ask rhetorical questions: "I wonder what that little kitty is thinking?" The child can consider the question without being put on the spot.

Empathize with your child.

Because children know more than they can convey, they often become frustrated and throw temper tantrums. In these cases, "Children won't hear reason, but they will hear the language of their own feelings," says Creighton. "You can say, 'I see that you're crying, and I guess you're feeling very frustrated.' This is another way to give children language to express and control the world around them." Empathy does not mean giving in or coddling, only acknowledging that you understand what your child is experiencing.

If your child is upset, try verbalizing his feelings or playing twenty questions: "Can you tell me with words?" "Show me with your hands?" "Take me to where it is?" Both tactics model language and encourage him to be a full, if nonverbal, partner. Knowing that in time your child will be able to articulate his thoughts and feelings will make his slow start easier to manage. —**C.R.M.**

---

to say, "I don't want to get out," required more linguistic dexterity than she possessed at age three. So she simply pasted a negative onto the front of her sentence and hoped for the best.

Preschoolers rely on the "scissors and paste" strategy when asking questions and expressing negatives, two very complicated undertakings in English. They just paste the question or negative at the beginning of the sentence ("Why you go home?" "No eat dinner"). As children progress, they put the words in a more grammatically correct order, but there may still be glitches: "That dog not go away," Sarah, three, noted apprehensively.

Locating the right word to paste onto a sentence is challenging, especially when kids try to use words that sound similar. Ever willing to try, preschoolers puzzle this out and go with their best guess: "What are we going?" "Where does it do?" Some thoughts just have to come out, no matter what they sound like. "Are you still have any of these candies before?" inquired a very excited recipient of a new kind of candy. Huh? That must be some candy! " 'Potshots' provide a lifeline for preschoolers who have important thoughts to express but who lack control over the plethora of grammatical detail," says Baron.

While grammatical oddities can last for months as preschoolers figure out the rules (for example, saying "goed" instead of "went"), a potshot is a one-time affair. The child grabs whatever language is handy and throws it out the door. "Then it won't be any more gooder," protested Susan when her mom cut her sandwich in half. "I gots both twos together," crowed Nick, his arms full of Daddy's shoes. Often a child cannot reconstruct the potshot even when asked to immediately afterward.

Because we seek meaning from language, Baron observes, parents often overlook their children's potshots. Like good conversational partners, parents listen to their children's thoughts, not their words.

The journey to fluency—part nature, part nurture—lasts, as Jason says, just "a couple little whiles." The charm of toddler talk soon is replaced with a first-grader's precision and reasoning, so take advantage of this time. When you slow down enough to become a conversational partner to a preschooler, your reward is a magical glimpse of the world through his eyes.

"Just step back, stop worrying, and enjoy the thrill of your child's discovering and developing his language skills," advises Susan Curtiss. "It's full of fascinating parts. To think that we can have this system that allows us to represent the world, that we can carry ideas and notions around in our head and communicate them to someone else—it's really pretty miraculous."

Sizing Up The Sexes

Scientists are discovering that gender differences have as much to do with the biology of the brain as with the way we are raised

CHRISTINE GORMAN

What are little boys made of?
What are little boys made of?
Frogs and snails
And puppy dogs' tails,
That's what little boys are made of.

What are little girls made of?
What are little girls made of?
Sugar and spice
And all that's nice,
That's what little girls are made of.
—Anonymous

Many scientists rely on elaborately complex and costly equipment to probe the mysteries confronting humankind. Not Melissa Hines. The UCLA behavioral scientist is hoping to solve one of life's oldest riddles with a toybox full of police cars, Lincoln Logs and Barbie dolls. For the past two years, Hines and her colleagues have tried to determine the origins of gender differences by capturing on videotape the squeals of delight, furrows of concentration and myriad decisions that children from 2 1/2 to 8 make while playing. Although both sexes play with all the toys available in Hines' laboratory, her work confirms what most parents (and more than a few aunts, uncles and nursery-school teachers) already know. As a group, the boys favor sports cars, fire trucks and Lincoln Logs, while the girls are drawn more often to dolls and kitchen toys.

But one batch of girls defies expectations and consistently prefers the boy toys. These youngsters have a rare genetic ab-

normality that caused them to produce elevated levels of testosterone, among other hormones, during their embryonic development. On average, they play with the same toys as the boys in the same ways and just as often. Could it be that the high levels of testosterone present in their bodies before birth have left a permanent imprint on their brains, affecting their later behavior? Or did their parents, knowing of their disorder, somehow subtly influence their choices? If the first explanation is true and

biology determines the choice, Hines wonders, "Why would you evolve to want to play with a truck?"

Not so long ago, any career-minded researcher would have hesitated to ask such questions. During the feminist revolution of the 1970s, talk of inborn differences in the behavior of men and women was distinctly unfashionable, even taboo. Men dominated fields like architecture and engineering, it was argued, because of social, not hormonal, pressures. Women did the vast majority

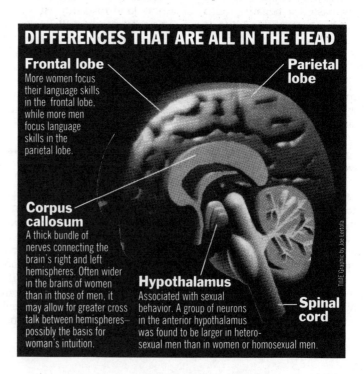

DIFFERENCES THAT ARE ALL IN THE HEAD

Frontal lobe
More women focus their language skills in the frontal lobe, while more men focus language skills in the parietal lobe.

Parietal lobe

Corpus callosum
A thick bundle of nerves connecting the brain's right and left hemispheres. Often wider in the brains of women than in those of men, it may allow for greater cross talk between hemispheres—possibly the basis for woman's intuition.

Hypothalamus
Associated with sexual behavior. A group of neurons in the anterior hypothalamus was found to be larger in heterosexual men than in women or homosexual men.

Spinal cord

TIME Graphic by Joe Lertola

of society's child rearing because few other options were available to them. Once sexism was abolished, so the argument ran, the world would become a perfectly equitable, androgynous place, aside from a few anatomical details.

But biology has a funny way of confounding expectations. Rather than disappear, the evidence for innate sexual differences only began to mount. In medicine, researchers documented that heart disease strikes men at a younger age than it does women and that women have a more moderate physiological response to stress. Researchers found subtle neurological differences between the sexes both in the brain's structure and in its functioning. In addition, another generation of parents discovered that, despite their best efforts to give baseballs to their daughters and sewing kits to their sons, girls still flocked to dollhouses while boys clambered into tree forts. Perhaps nature is more important than nurture after all.

Even professional skeptics have been converted. "When I was younger, I believed that 100% of sex differences were due to the environment," says Jerre Levy, professor of psychology at the University of Chicago. Her own toddler toppled that utopian notion. "My daughter was 15 months old, and I had just dressed her in her teeny little nightie. Some guests arrived, and she came into the room, knowing full well that she looked adorable. She came in with this saucy little walk, cocking her head, blinking her eyes, especially at the men. You never saw such flirtation in your life." After 20 years spent studying the brain, Levy is convinced: "I'm sure there are biologically based differences in our behavior."

Now that it is O.K. to admit the possibility, the search for sexual differences has expanded into nearly every branch of the life sciences. Anthropologists have debunked Margaret Mead's work on the extreme variability of gender roles in New Guinea. Psychologists are untangling the complex interplay between hormones and aggression. But the most provocative, if as yet inconclusive, discoveries of all stem from the pioneering exploration of a tiny 3-lb. universe: the human brain. In fact, some researchers predict that the confirmation of innate differences in behavior could lead to an unprecedented understanding of the mind.

Some of the findings seem merely curious. For example, more men than women are lefthanded, reflecting the dominance of the brain's right hemisphere. By contrast, more women listen equally with both ears while men favor the right one.

Other revelations are bound to provoke more controversy. Psychology tests, for instance, consistently support the notion that men and women perceive the world in subtly different ways. Males excel

EMOTIONS

FEMALE INTUITION: THERE MAY BE SOMETHING TO IT

Do women really possess an ability to read other people's hidden motives and meanings? To some degree, they do. When shown pictures of actors portraying various feelings, women outscore men in identifying the correct emotion. They also surpass men in determining the emotional content of taped conversation in which the words have been garbled. This ability may result from society's emphasis on raising girls to be sensitive. But some researchers speculate that it has arisen to give women greater skill in interpreting the cues of toddlers before they are able to speak.

MALE INSENSITIVITY: IT'S A CULTURAL RELIC

If men seem less adept at deciphering emotions, it is a "trained incompetence," says Harvard psychologist Ronald Levant. Young boys are told to ignore pain and not to cry. Some anthropologists argue that this psychic wound is inflicted to separate boys from their mothers and prepare them for warfare. Many men, says Levant, can recognize their emotions only as a physical buzz or tightness in the throat—a situation that can be reversed, he insists, with training.

at rotating three-dimensional objects in their head. Females prove better at reading emotions of people in photographs. A growing number of scientists believe the discrepancies reflect functional differences in the brains of men and women. If true, then some misunderstandings between the sexes may have more to do with crossed wiring than cross-purposes.

Most of the gender differences that have been uncovered so far are, statistically speaking, quite small. "Even the largest differences in cognitive function are not as large as the difference in male and female height," Hines notes. "You still see a lot of overlap." Otherwise, women could never read maps and men would always be lefthanded. That kind of flexibility within the sexes reveals just how complex a puzzle gender actually is, requiring pieces from biology, sociology and culture.

Ironically, researchers are not entirely sure how or even why humans produce two sexes in the first place. (Why not just one—or even three—as in some species?)

What is clear is that the two sexes originate with two distinct chromosomes. Women bear a double dose of the large X chromosome, while men usually possess a single X and a short, stumpy Y chromosome. In 1990 British scientists reported they had identified a single gene on the Y chromosome that determines maleness. Like some kind of biomolecular Paul Revere, this master gene rouses a host of its compatriots to the complex task of turning a fetus into a boy. Without such a signal, all human embryos would develop into girls. "I have all the genes for being male except this one, and my husband has all the genes for being female," marvels evolutionary psychologist Leda Cosmides, of the University of California at Santa Barbara. "The only difference is which genes got turned on."

Yet even this snippet of DNA is not enough to ensure a masculine result. An elevated level of the hormone testosterone is also required during the pregnancy. Where does it come from? The fetus' own undescended testes. In those rare cases in which the tiny body does not respond to the hormone, a genetically male fetus develops sex organs that look like a clitoris and vagina rather than a penis. Such people look and act female. The majority marry and adopt children.

The influence of the sex hormones extends into the nervous system. Both males and females produce androgens, such as testosterone, and estrogens—although in different amounts. (Men and women who make no testosterone generally lack a libido.) Researchers suspect that an excess of testosterone before birth enables the right hemisphere to dominate the brain, resulting in lefthandedness. Since testosterone levels are higher in boys than in girls, that would explain why more boys are southpaws.

Subtle sex-linked preferences have been detected as early as 52 hours after birth. In studies of 72 newborns, University of Chicago psychologist Martha McClintock and her students found that a toe-fanning reflex was stronger in the left foot for 60% of the males, while all the females favored their right. However, apart from such reflexes in the hands, legs and feet, the team could find no other differences in the babies' responses.

One obvious place to look for gender differences is in the hypothalamus, a lusty little organ perched over the brain stem that, when sufficiently provoked, consumes a person with rage, thirst, hunger or desire. In animals, a region at the front of the organ controls sexual function and is somewhat larger in males than in females. But its size need not remain constant. Studies of tropical fish by Stanford University neurobiologist Russell Fernald reveal that certain cells in this tiny region of the brain swell markedly in an individual male whenever he comes to dominate a school. Unfortunately for the piscine pasha, the cells will also shrink if he loses control of his harem to another male.

Many researchers suspect that, in humans too, sexual preferences are controlled by the hypothalamus. Based on a study of 41 autopsied brains, Simon LeVay of the Salk Institute for Biological Studies announced last summer that he had found a region in the hypothalamus that was on average twice as large in heterosexual men as in either women or homosexual men. LeVay's findings support the idea that varying hormone levels before birth may immutably stamp the developing brain in one erotic direction or another.

These prenatal fluctuations may also steer boys toward more rambunctious behavior than girls. June Reinisch, director of the Kinsey Institute for Research in Sex, Gender and Reproduction at Indiana University, in a pioneering study of eight pairs of brothers and 17 pairs of sisters ages 6 to 18 uncovered a complex interplay between hormones and aggression. As a group, the young males gave more belligerent answers than did the females on a multiple-choice test in which they had to imagine their response to stressful situations. But siblings who had been exposed in utero to synthetic antimiscarriage hormones that mimic testosterone were the most combative of all. The affected boys proved significantly more aggressive than their unaffected brothers, and the drug-exposed girls were much more contentious than their unexposed sisters. Reinisch could not determine, however, whether this childhood aggression would translate into greater ambition or competitiveness in the adult world.

PERCEPTION

HE CAN READ A MAP BLINDFOLDED, BUT CAN HE FIND HIS SOCKS?
It's a classic scene of marital discord on the road. Husband: "Do I turn right?" Wife, madly rotating the map: "I'm not sure where we are." Whether men read maps better is unclear, but they do excel at thinking in three dimensions. This may be due to ancient evolutionary pressures related to hunting, which requires orienting oneself while pursuing prey.

IF LOST IN A FOREST, WOMEN WILL NOTICE THE TREES
Such prehistoric pursuits may have conferred a comparable advantage on women. In experiments in mock offices, women proved 70% better than men at remembering the location of items found on a desktop—perhaps reflecting evolutionary pressure on generations of women who foraged for their food. Foragers must recall complex patterns formed of apparently unconnected items.

While most of the gender differences uncovered so far seem to fall under the purview of the hypothalamus, researchers have begun noting discrepancies in other parts of the brain as well. For the past nine years, neuroscientists have debated whether the corpus callosum, a thick bundle of nerves that allows the right half of the brain to communicate with the left, is

larger in women than in men. If it is, and if size corresponds to function, then the greater crosstalk between the hemispheres might explain enigmatic phenomena like female intuition, which is supposed to accord women greater ability to read emotional clues.

These conjectures about the corpus callosum have been hard to prove because the structure's girth varies dramatically with both age and health. Studies of autopsied material are of little use because brain tissue undergoes such dramatic changes in the hours after death. Neuroanatomist Laura Allen and neuroendocrinologist Roger Gorski of UCLA decided to try to circumvent some of these problems by obtaining brain scans from live, apparently healthy people. In their investigation of 146 subjects, published in April, they confirmed that parts of the corpus callosum were up to 23% wider in women than in men. They also measured thicker connections between the two hemispheres in other parts of women's brains.

Encouraged by the discovery of such structural differences, many researchers have begun looking for dichotomies of function as well. At the Bowman Gray Medical School in Winston-Salem, N.C., Cecile Naylor has determined that men and women enlist widely varying parts of their brain when asked to spell words. By monitoring increases in blood flow, the neuropsychologist found that women use both sides of their head when spelling while men use primarily their left side. Because the area activated on the right side is used in understanding emotions, the women apparently tap a wider range of experience for their task. Intriguingly, the effect

LANGUAGE

IN CHOOSING HER WORDS, A WOMAN REALLY USES HER HEAD
For both sexes, the principal language centers of the brain are usually concentrated in the left hemisphere. But preliminary neurological studies show that women make use of both sides of their brain during even the simplest verbal tasks, like spelling. As a result, a woman's appreciation of everyday speech appears to be enhanced by input from various cerebral regions, including those that control vision and feelings. This greater access to the brain's imagery and depth may help explain why girls often begin speaking earlier than boys, enunciate more clearly as tots and develop a larger vocabulary.

IF JOHNNY CAN'T READ, IS IT BECAUSE HE IS A BOY?
Visit a typical remedial-reading class, and you'll find that the boys outnumber the girls 3 to 1. Stuttering affects four times as many boys as girls. Many researchers have used these and other lopsided ratios to support the argument that males, on average, are less verbally fluent than females. However, the discrepancy could also reflect less effort by teachers or parents to find reading-impaired girls. Whatever the case, boys often catch up with their female peers in high school. In the past few years, boys have even begun outscoring girls on the verbal portion of the Scholastic Aptitude Test.

occurred only with spelling and not during a memory test.

Researchers speculate that the greater communication between the two sides of the brain could impair a woman's performance of certain highly specialized visual-spatial tasks. For example, the ability to tell directions on a map without physically having to rotate it appears stronger in those individuals whose brains restrict the process to the right hemisphere. Any crosstalk between the two sides apparently distracts the brain from its job. Sure enough, several studies have shown that this mental-rotation skill is indeed more tightly focused in men's brains than in women's.

But how did it get to be that way? So far, none of the gender scientists have figured out whether nature or nurture is more important. "Nothing is ever equal, even in the beginning," observes Janice Juraska, a biopsychologist at the University of Illinois at Urbana-Champaign. She points out, for instance, that mother rats lick their male offspring more frequently than they do their daughters. However, Juraska has demonstrated that it is possible to reverse some inequities by manipulating environmental factors. Female rats have fewer nerve connections than males into the hippocampus, a brain region associated with spatial relations and memory. But when Juraska "enriched" the cages of the females with stimulating toys, the females developed more of these neuronal connections. "Hormones do affect things—it's crazy to deny that," says the researcher. "But there's no telling which way sex differences might go if we completely changed the environment." For humans, educational enrichment could perhaps enhance a woman's ability to work in three dimensions and a man's ability to interpret emotions. Says Juraska: "There's nothing about human brains that is so stuck that a different way of doing things couldn't change it enormously."

Nowhere is this complex interaction between nature and nurture more apparent than in the unique human abilities of speaking, reading and writing. No one is born knowing French, for example; it must be learned, changing the brain forever. Even so, language skills are linked to specific cerebral centers. In a remarkable series of experiments, neurosurgeon George Ojemann of the University of Washington has produced scores of detailed maps of people's individual language centers.

First, Ojemann tested his patients' verbal intelligence using a written exam. Then, during neurosurgery—which was performed under a local anesthetic—he asked them to name aloud a series of objects found in a steady stream of black-and-white photos. Periodically, he touched different parts of the brain with an electrode that temporarily blocked the activity of that region. (This does not hurt because the brain has no sense of pain.) By noting when his patients made mistakes, the surgeon was able to determine which sites were essential to naming.

Several complex sexual differences emerged. Men with lower verbal IQs were more likely to have their language skills located toward the back of the brain. In a number of women, regardless of IQ, the naming ability was restricted to the frontal lobe. This disparity could help explain why strokes that affect the rear of the brain seem to be more devastating to men than to women.

Intriguingly, the sexual differences are far less significant in people with higher verbal IQs. Their language skills developed in a more intermediate part of the brain. And yet, no two patterns were ever identical. "That to me is the most important finding," Ojemann says. "Instead of these sites being laid down more or less the same in everyone, they're laid down in subtly different places." Language is scattered randomly across these cerebral centers, he hypothesizes, because the skills evolved so recently.

What no one knows for sure is just how hardwired the brain is. How far and at what stage can the brain's extraordinary flexibility be pushed? Several studies suggest that the junior high years are key. Girls show the same aptitudes for math as boys until about the seventh grade, when more and more girls develop math phobia. Coincidentally, that is the age at which boys start to shine and catch up to girls in reading.

By one account, the gap between men and women for at least some mental skills has actually started to shrink. By looking at 25 years' worth of data from academic tests, Janet Hyde, professor of psychology and women's studies at the University of Wisconsin at Madison, discovered that overall gender differences for verbal and mathematical skills dramatically decreased after 1974. One possible explanation, Hyde notes, is that "Americans have changed their socialization and educational patterns over the past few decades. They are treating males and females with greater similarity."

Even so, women still have not caught up with men on the mental-rotation test. Fascinated by the persistence of that gap, psychologists Irwin Silverman and Marion Eals of York University in Ontario wondered if there were any spatial tasks at which women outperformed men. Looking at it from the point of view of human evolution, Silverman and Eals reasoned that while men may have developed strong spatial skills in response to evolutionary pressures to be successful hunters, women would have needed other types of visual skills to excel as gatherers and foragers of food.

The psychologists therefore designed a test focused on the ability to discern and later recall the location of objects in a complex, random pattern. In series of tests, student volunteers were given a minute to study a drawing that contained such unrelated objects as an elephant, a guitar and a cat. Then Silverman and Eals presented their subjects with a second drawing containing additional objects and told them to cross out those items that had been added and circle any that had moved. Sure enough, the women consistently surpassed the men in giving correct answers.

What made the psychologists really sit up and take notice, however, was the fact that the women scored much better on the mental-rotation test while they were menstruating. Specifically, they improved their scores by 50% to 100% whenever their estrogen levels were at their lowest. It is not clear why this should be. However, Silverman and Eals are trying to find out if women exhibit a similar hormonal effect for any other visual tasks.

Oddly enough, men may possess a similar hormonal response, according to new research reported in November by Doreen Kimura, a psychologist at the University of Western Ontario. In her study of 138 adults, Kimura found that males perform better on mental-rotation tests in the spring, when their testosterone levels are low, rather than in the fall, when they are higher. Men are also subject to a daily cycle, with testosterone levels lowest around 8 p.m. and peaking around 4 a.m. Thus, says June Reinisch of the Kinsey Institute: "When people say women can't be trusted because they cycle every month, my response is that men cycle every day, so they should only be allowed to negotiate peace treaties in the evening."

Far from strengthening stereotypes about who women and men truly are or how they should behave, research into innate sexual differences only underscores humanity's awesome adaptability. "Gender is really a complex business," says Reinisch. "There's no question that hormones have an effect. But what does that have to do with the fact that I like to wear pink ribbons and you like to wear baseball gloves? Probably something, but we don't know what."

Even the concept of what an innate difference represents is changing. The physical and chemical differences between the brains of the two sexes may be malleable and subject to change by experience: certainly an event or act of learning can directly affect the brain's biochemistry and physiology. And so, in the final analysis, it may be impossible to say where nature ends and nurture begins because the two are so intimately linked.

—*Reported by*
J. Madeleine Nash/Los Angeles

Development during Childhood – Cognition and Schooling

- Cognition (Articles 19–22)
- Schooling (Articles 23–26)

Cognition and the study of cognitive development were jump-started by the Swiss biologist, turned epistemologist, Jean Piaget, during the twentieth century. As a young biologist struggling to find his niche in the 1920s, Piaget went to Paris. He took a job helping Alfred Binet and Thomas Simon develop the first standardized test of intelligence. He was much more intrigued by what children answered incorrectly than by what they knew. While in Paris, Piaget studied philosophy and logic at the Sorbonne. He combined his interests in biology, philosophy, and logic and went back to Switzerland to begin the now famous Center for Genetic Epistemology. Epistemology, a branch of philosophy concerned with how we know what we know, led to Piaget's theory of cognition.

Piaget believed that children know the world qualitatively differently than adults. This belief was in opposition to the commonly held assumption that children simply know less than adults. Explaining that biological maturation limited the memory and organizational abilities of children, Piaget suggested that there are four stages of

knowing. At first, infants only understand their world from a sensory and motoric perspective. After language develops, toddlers and preschoolers understand their world symbolically. However, since they cannot use any kind of logical operations to organize or classify their symbols and schemas, they have a preoperational form of intelligence. By school age, children understand their world in terms of concrete operations. They can number, seriate, classify, and conserve. They can think backwards and forwards and think about their own thinking (metacognition). They have reached "the age of reason." The thing most lacking in the cognitions of school-age children is the ability to think abstractly about things they cannot experience. This last stage of knowing abstractly emerges during puberty and is called formal operations.

Piaget's beliefs about cognitive development have been supported by numerous research studies. Contemporary researchers are, for the most part, refining rather than refuting Piaget's theory. As our techniques for examining children's cognitions and metacognitions improve,

we are discovering that Piaget may have underestimated the ages at which children acquire certain abilities. As our techniques for examining neuroanatomy and neurophysiology improve, we are discovering more answers to the questions of how memories are organized and stored.

The information-processing view of cognitive development, while not refuting Piaget's theory, compares human neuroanatomy and neurophysiology to computer models. Information-processing theorists are trying to discover how the amazingly complex human brain receives, attends to, selects, rehearses, encodes, organizes, stores, and finally retrieves memories.

Many parents, teachers, researchers, and other persons concerned with cognitive development during the school-age years have tried to use theoretical knowledge about cognition to speed up children's learning. While learning can be accelerated, many people question the wisdom of hurrying children. The slow cognitive maturation of humans, like their slow physical maturation, may be adaptive.

Many children have various types of learning disabilities. These learning disabilities are not symptomatic of mental retardation. In fact, many learning disabled children are intellectually gifted. Why do some children receive, attend to, select, rehearse, encode, organize, store, or retrieve information differently? Are their differences in information-processing really disabilities, or simply alternate ways of knowing about their worlds? There are still many unanswered questions about cognition.

Language expands exponentially as children enter school and begin reading and writing. Most children use language differently, or use different languages, depending on their audience. School-age children like to play with language. Thus, they may use dialects, coded languages, curse words, or other languages on occasion. Bilingual and multilingual children may speak English more slowly, or with a more limited vocabulary in primary school. However, there may be many cognitive and psycholinguistic advantages to being bilingual or multilingual, or even bidialectual. Many forms of nonstandard English follow grammatical rules and indicate great flexibility with syntactical structures.

American schools have been under attack from many sources for many years. Students from many other nations, notably Asian nations, achieve better than American students in academic subjects. Are academic subjects the only thing that teachers should emphasize? Who should teach ethics and morality? Do sex education, drug education, and AIDS education belong in American classrooms? American public schools tend to have overcrowded classrooms, underpaid teachers, and more problems with truancy and delinquency than the schools of other nations. American parents who can afford it often place their children in private schools. Are public schools serving the needs of America's children? Should schools test children for academic potential and then track them into different classrooms relative to their high, average, or low intelligence? Are intelligence tests valid? How would children with different cognitive styles or learning differences/disabilities be tracked?

The articles selected for this unit deal with many of the issues discussed in this overview. The first two readings examine the complexities of human cognition and recent refinements to the theories of Piaget and information-processing. The next two articles examine some of the differences in cognitive development and language development experienced by individual children. The last four articles are grouped into a subsection on schooling. The differences between Asian and American schools are clarified. The controversial practice of testing and tracking students is discussed. Finally, the issue of providing education concerned with nonacademic subjects—ethics, morality, sex, AIDS—is examined.

Looking Ahead: Challenge Questions

Is the human mind intangible? How much do we comprehend about our own cognitive skills?

Does a prolonged period of cognitive development contribute to greater intellectual plasticity?

What should we know about bilingual/bicultural children?

Are learning differences really disabilities or just alternate cognitive styles? Could attention deficit disorder have advantages in human cognition?

How do American schools compare to Asian schools? Should American schools change? Explain your answer.

Is educational tracking a form of discrimination? Who should be responsible for tracking, and on what should it be based?

Explain why schools should or should not give lessons on ethics and morality.

How can teachers explain AIDS to students?

The Human Mind
Touching the intangible

The human brain is the most complex object in the known universe. But out of that complexity emerges a stranger structure still—the human mind

ONLY connect. Forster's injunction is the crux of modern thinking on the mechanisms of the mind. As neurologists have taken the brain apart, they have been astonished at how bitty it is. Outwardly coherent behaviour, like talking and listening, is subcontracted all over the place. Nouns are stored here, adjectives there, syntax elsewhere. Verbs spelled with regular endings are learned using one sort of memory, those spelt with irregular endings are learnt by another; for memory, too, has been atomised into so many pieces that psychologists cannot agree on their number. And the senses, the brain's link with wider reality, do not simply imprint an image of the world upon it; they decompose that image, and shuttle the pieces around like the squares in a Chinese puzzle.

Yet that intangible organ, the conscious mind, seems oblivious to all this. The connections are perfect, the garment apparently seamless. The mental sewing-machine connects nerve cell to nerve cell, senses to memory, memory to language, and consciousness to them all. At every level, the mind is a connection machine.

To understand brains (the traditional task of neurologists), and therefore minds (which psychologists have laboured to do), first remember that they have evolved to do a specific job. Each is there to run a body, keep it out of trouble and see that it passes its genes on to the next generation. Abilities to do things irrelevant to these tasks are likely to get short shrift from natural selection. Computers, with which brains are often compared, can turn their circuits to almost anything—pop in a new program and your computerised accountant is transformed into a chess grandmaster. Brains are not like this. Flexibility, except in a few, limited areas, is not at a premium. Neural "programs" are wired in during development. Circuits which deal with vision cannot be switched over to hear-

ing or taste. And such changes as do occur— for instance, when a new word or face is learnt—take place by modifying the wiring.

The nerve cells, known as neurons, which make up this wiring are rather unusual affairs. Most living cells measure a few millionths of a metre across, but neurons have filamentous projections which often go on for centimetres and occasionally for metres. These projections—called axons if they transmit messages, and dendrites if

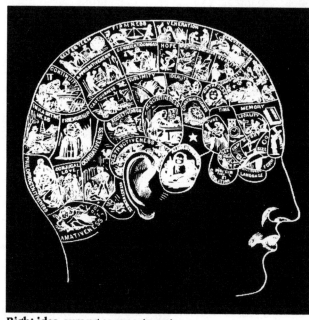

Right idea, wrong compartments

they receive them—enable neurons to talk to each other over long distances, to gather information, to pass it on, and to give and take orders.

The messages themselves are trains of electrical waves called action potentials. Unlike the current in a metal wire, which is caused by things (in this case electrons) moving along the wire, action potentials happen when electrically charged atoms (known as ions) of sodium and potassium move in and out of a filament. An action potential is like a bore in a river: the wave moves on even though the water merely

goes up and down.

Messages pass from neuron to neuron at junctions called synapses, where the tip of an axon touches the surface of a dendrite. Synapses act as the diodes of neurology, allowing the signal to go in only one direction. Action potentials cannot cross them; instead, a synapse passes the signal on via a chemical messenger known as a neurotransmitter. These neurotransmitters can leap the gap to the next cell, where special proteins are ready to greet them. Each sort of receptor protein fits hand-in-glove with a particular neurotransmitter (about 50 of which have been identified so far). If enough receptors are stimulated, one of two things may happen. The cell on the far side of the synapse may become excited and start firing pulses of its own, or it may be inhibited, damping down any pulse-firing that is already going on.

Neurons are thus devices that monitor the exciting and inhibiting signals arriving at their dendrites, weigh up the balance between them, and then decide whether or not to send out pulses of their own. This rather prosaic process is the basis for the activity of the brain. The magic lies in the way the neurons are wired together. But with around 100 billion neurons in a healthy human brain, and 60 trillion synapses, there is plenty of scope for sleight of hand.

Human conjurors have shown that the trick can work. Artificial neural networks, made by wiring lots of microprocessors together and programming them to behave like neurons, can do the same sorts of tricks as real ones. Give them senses, for example, and they can learn to recognise things. And the way they do so is instructive.

A common design for an artificial neural network is to arrange the "neurons" in a three-layered sandwich: an input layer connected to a sense organ such as a television camera; an output layer, which passes the result on to the human operator; and an intermediate, or "hidden" layer, connected to both. The network learns by changing the strengths (or "weights") of the connections between neurons in the three layers. With the correct pattern of weights, simple sensory data (such as handwritten numbers, or faces presented from different angles) can be distinguished and identified.

Real brains, of course, are much more

complicated. The main information-processing part of the brain, the cerebral cortex, has six layers of neurons, rather than three. It is, nevertheless, a layered structure. And the way an artificial network learns by varying the strength of the connections between its silicon neurons is, as will be seen later, reminiscent of the way neurologists think that learning happens in what their computing colleagues disparagingly refer to as "wetware".

Sense and sensibility

Look at the triangle below. Now look closely. There is no triangle. So why did you see it? This may sound a trivial question,

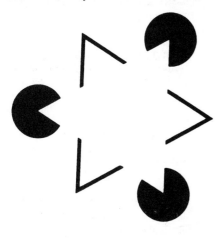

but it isn't. Imposing order on the world is not a two-stage process of first creating an image of outside events, and then interpreting it. The two things happen simultaneously as the sensory information is dismantled and re-assembled in ways which, given the coherence of the result, seem bizarre. Only occasionally, when a sensory illusion or a specific piece of damage to the brain produces some strange result, is it clear that sense and sensibility are inextricably linked.

Vision, the best-understood sense, illustrates the point. For visual information to be processed by the brain, it must first be converted into a form that neurons can deal with—action potentials. This is done by cells in the retina, the place where the image formed by the eye's lens ends up. Some retinal cells have catholic tastes, and respond to many wavelengths. Others are tuned in to specific parts of the spectrum. But each connects to a neuron, and via this to the optic nerves. These nerves carry the signals to the back of the brain, where they are processed.

The connections between the eyes and the primary visual cortex, as the receiving area is called, have been known about for decades. They are orderly. Adjacent parts of the retinal image seemed to end up next to each other. The primary visual cortex appeared, in effect, to be a map of the retina—the mind's eye. Whatever happened next—action, learning or thought—was assumed

to involve the whole image.

It all looked very neat. But it was wrong. The map is not passed around as a whole. It is broken up into different sorts of information—edges, movement, colour—which are then processed in different parts of the visual cortex. This can be seen by watching brains in action. Positron emission tomography (PET) enables researchers to watch people think. It uses a radioactive form of oxygen, mixed into the blood via a catheter in the wrist, to find out which parts of the brain are working hardest from moment to moment. Active areas need more oxygen, and the local blood supply increases to provide it. Positrons emitted by the oxygen annihilate nearby electrons—of which they are the anti-matter equivalent—producing detectable gamma rays.

PET, combined with studies of the electrical signals from single neurons in monkeys and the examination of people with localised brain damage, has revealed the true fate of the image. It does, indeed, pass first to the primary visual cortex (known to neurologists as V1). But this area is just a clearing-house. It contains two sorts of neuron. One sort, organised into columns which penetrate all six layers of the cortex, responds to colour. The other sort, between the columns, responds to form.

Area V1 is surrounded by area V2 (as medieval anatomists preferred Greek and Latin, so modern ones prefer letters and numbers). Here, instead of columns, there are stripes. Thin stripes respond to colour again, thick ones to motion. But the information in V1 and V2 is local: their cells get excited only about signals from their particular patch of the retina. From then on, the information is passed on to areas imaginatively named V3, V4 and V5. V3 and V4 both deal with shape, but V4 also deals with colour, while V3 is colourblind. V5 specialises in detecting motion. It is from these specialised areas, not from the more general-purpose image of V1, that visual information is passed on to the other areas of the brain that need it.

This parcelling-out of tasks explains some of the predicaments of people whose visual cortices have been damaged. Those who have lost V4 can no longer conceive of colour. Those with damage to V5 can see things only when they are stationary—the reverse of the case of Dr P, described in Oliver Sacks's book, "The Man Who Mistook His Wife For A Hat", who could not distinguish stationary objects, and was probably suffering from damage to area V2.

There is also a strange phenomenon called blindsight which, like the loss of the concept of colour in people with damaged V4, touches directly on the issue of consciousness. Lose area V1, and you will believe yourself blind. But you might not be. There are some direct connections from the retina to the other vision-processing areas.

People with V1 damage can often track the movement of objects through space, or tell you the colour of things they truly believe that they cannot see.

And the triangle? The illusion seems to be caused by a conflict between the cells of V1 and those of V2. V1 cells handle only smalls parts of the visual field. Some see bits of the design, some see space. V2 cells, which deal with larger areas, use the bites out of the circles and the ends of the arrows to infer a line, rather as rows of lights on an advertising hoarding are mentally connected into letters. The conflicting interpretations leave the viewer with the uncomfortable feeling of seeing a border where he knows that none exists. Neurology and a psychological test have combined to show specialisation in the brain.

Memory and learning

Another area where psychology and neurology have combined to demonstrate these specialisations is memory. On the face of it, memory seemed, like visual perception, to be a single entity. In fact, it is also highly compartmentalised, with different functions carried out in different parts of the brain.

The first evidence for this specialisation came from neuroanatomy. In the 1950s, surgeons found that, as a last resort, they could control severe epilepsy by destroying parts of the brain. One target for this surgery was the temporal lobe. Some patients suffered a strange form of amnesia after such surgery. They were able to recall things that had happened to them until a few weeks before the operation, and they were also able to remember the very recent past, a matter of a few minutes. But they could not form permanent memories any more—they could no longer learn. All these people had suffered damage to the hippocampus, a structure inside the temporal lobe. Since then, experiments done on monkeys have confirmed that the hippocampus and its neighbours in the limbic system are way-stations to the formation of permanent memories.

The actual information is stored in the cortex; but, for several weeks after it is first learnt, it is passed around via the hippocampus. If it is recalled and used, more direct connections develop in the cortex, and the hippocampus is gradually excluded. If not recalled, it may be forgotten. But if the hippocampal nexus is broken, it is always forgotten. Without a hippocampus, learning is impossible.

Or, rather, some sorts of learning are impossible. For, partly as a consequence of observations on patients with damaged hippocampuses, it has become clear that learning comes in two broad forms: the explicit, or "declarative", sort which remembers objects and events; and the implicit sort, which remembers how to do things.

Implicit learning is part of unconscious

behaviour, and is encapsulated in the phrase "practice makes perfect". It is the sort of incremental improvement which allows people to acquire skills almost incidentally and it does not require an intact hippocampus. One hippocampally damaged patient, for instance, learnt how to read mirror writing, an extraordinary feat for a man who could not remember the faces of his nurses.

Psychologists argue endlessly over how many types of implicit learning there are, and neurology has not yet come to their rescue. But another phenomenon exposed by hippocampal damage has been neatly dissected by psychology.

Patients with such damage are still able to hold the events of the very recent past in their heads, and to synthesise them with knowledge they already have. This enables them to do crosswords, for example. This short-term, or "working", memory is very amenable to psychological testing.

Such tests suggest that working memory has at least three subcomponents. They are known as the "central executive" (which controls attention), the "visuospatial sketchpad" (which manipulates visual information) and the "phonological loop" (which deals with speech). Teasing out these components was done by making people do more than one thing at a time and seeing how well they performed.

Broadly speaking, people can hold about seven pieces of information in their minds at once. But if some of that information is visual, and some linguistic, the total increases. And if an experimenter disrupts a verbal task, a parallel visual one is usually unaffected. The systems which deal with the data are independent of one another.

So how are memories actually stored? PET scanning shows that working memory is located in the pre-frontal cortex. When something is being "kept in mind", that is where it is. Working memories are retained by the continuous activity of particular neurons. These neurons stimulate themselves, either directly or via a loop involving others. When they stop firing, the memory is lost unless it has been passed on to the hippocampus for more permanent storage.

The process by which the hippocampus begins the laying down of permanent memories is different, and intriguingly like the one used to train artificial neural nets—the weights of the connections between nerve cells are altered. This process, called long-term potentiation (LTP), happens when a particular neurotransmitter called glutamate is released by the axon side of a synapse and picked up on the dendrite side by a particular sort of receptor, the N-methyl-D-aspartate (NMDA) receptor. The reaction between glutamate and NMDA stimulates two things. First, the production of proteins called kinases, which enhance the passage of action potentials by opening up passages

that pass ions through the cell membrane. Second, the manufacture in the dendrite of a messenger molecule (believed to be nitric oxide) which flows back to the axon and, in turn, stimulates more glutamate production, thus keeping the whole process going.

However, NMDA is receptive to glutamate only if enough action potentials are already passing along the dendrite it is in. This means that the strengthening of one synaptic connection depends on what is happening to generate action potentials at others. This is the key to neural networks, whether wet or dry, because it enables activity in one part of the net to affect another part indirectly. The pattern of input-signals acts in unison to produce a particular output.

LTP can preserve memories for hours or days. The final stage of the process, permanent storage, seems to involve the formation of new synapses in active areas, and the withering of those which remain unstimulated. Recent research suggests that this happens during sleep. In particular, it seems to happen during the type of sleep known as rapid eye movement (REM) sleep. During REM sleep, people dream, and one of the many explanations suggested for dreams is that they are like the film on a cutting-room floor—the bits left over when experiences that have been waiting in hippocampal limbo are edited into permanent memories. Now there is some evidence to back this up. It has been shown that disrupting REM sleep also disrupts the formation of long-term declarative memories.

Other recent work has shed some light on how memories become tinged with emotion. Fear, at least, seems to be injected by the hippocampus's limbic-system neighbour the amygdala. Drugs which block LTP (and therefore learning) if injected into the hippocampus merely block the learning of

fear if applied to the amygdala. Rats whose amygdalas have been treated in this way behave as if they do not know the meaning of fear. And it seems likely that at least some people who suffer from anxiety attacks have over-active amygdalas.

Speaking in tongues

Despite the claims made for chimpanzees, dolphins, sea-lions and even parrots, it is the use of language which distinguishes man from his fellow creatures. Language—which allows knowledge and ideas to be shared within a community and passed from generation to generation—is the basis of civilisation and of human dominion over the rest of nature. It is also bound up in consciousness; the "inner dialogue" that people often have with themselves is one example of conscious introspection.

Language, unlike memory and sensation, is not even-handed. It generally inhabits the left-hand side of the brain, a fact discovered over a century ago by studying people with localised brain-damage, and dramatically shown up in PET scans. The reason for this geographical imbalance is unclear, but it is associated with another uniquely human phenomenon: "handedness". Right-handed people almost always do their language-processing in their left cerebral hemispheres. Left-handers tend to favour the right hemisphere, although the distinction is not so clear. Indeed, there is evidence associating dyslexia with a failure of the asymmetry, an observation which helps explain why left-handers are more often dyslexic than right-handers.

Within whichever hemisphere commands the process, the component parts of language, like those of sensibility and memory, appear to be parcelled out over the cortex. Broca and Wernicke, two nineteenth-century neurologists who studied failures of

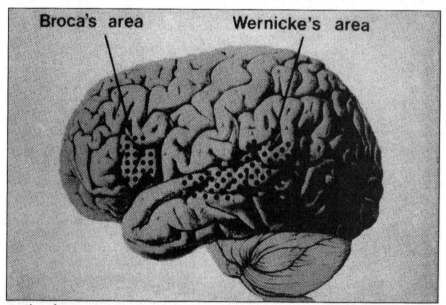

Getting closer

speech and comprehension, mapped areas of the brain where damage seemed to cause specific problems. PET shows up a broadly similar pattern. When words are heard, part of the temporal lobe lights up. Speaking provokes activity in the frontal lobe. There also seems to be a distinction between the handling of nouns (done in the temporal lobe) and verbs (where the frontal lobe seems to predominate).

The meaning of these distinctions is not clear. Some see a specific language function, separately evolved, which deals with all aspects of the phenomenon including the formation of abstract concepts. Others believe that speech developed merely because changes to the muscles of the mouth and throat (which came about when people began to walk upright) allowed it to. According to this view, speaking and listening are merely matters of training. The concepts are already there (which is why other animals can also be trained into language-like abilities); what has to be learnt is a way of attaching words to them, and this is done by the normal mechanisms of memory. Regular verbs, for instance, are learnt implicitly, but declarative memory kicks in for the irregular ones.

In any case, the concepts associated with words are also to be found in widely scattered parts of the brain, and not necessarily on its left-hand side. Colours, for instance, live in region v4 of the visual cortex. And some people with serious damage to the language-control areas can still swear like troopers. Other specific bits of damage can cause problems akin to losing colour-conception—an inability to remember the names of otherwise-familiar people, for instance. Though the connections are not so well understood as those in vision and learning (perhaps because they impinge on more mental functions), they are being thoroughly studied.

The elusive whole

Sensibility, working memory and language are all aspects of mind, but they are not the whole thing. What binds them together? What is the conscious mind? It is certainly not the be-all and end-all of complex behaviour. Anyone who has driven along a motorway and suddenly realised he cannot remember the past few miles will realise this. Nor does partial loss of faculty make a person mindless—although dementias which attack the pre-frontal cortex might.

Whatever the conscious mind is, though, it is no longer regarded by students of the brain as the proper province of philosophers and divines. The problem is under experimental attack.

Hypotheses of how the mind evolved are still vague and contradictory, but they fall into two groups. One interpretation is that consciousness is an epi-phenomenon—a side-effect of increased complexity in the brains of higher primates and particularly of people. Such side-effects, known as emergent properties, are just starting to be explored. Some theories of the origin of life see life itself as an emergent property. They think it suddenly "switched on" when a network of chemical reactions grew so big that each reaction was able to assist the progress of another. On this theory, brains, and particularly cerebral cortices, passed some threshold of size and complexity during their evolution which allowed the system to feed upon itself and generate the phenomenon now labelled consciousness.

Others believe that consciousness has evolved specifically. In their view consciousness is an evolutionary advantage which has dictated the brain's complexity rather than the other way round. One widely held theory is that consciousness is a way of dealing with the diplomatic niceties of group living. It is there mainly to answer the question, "what would I do if I were in the other person's shoes?" Armed with the answer, arrived at by conscious introspection, you can make a better guess at what the other person will actually do next, and modify your behaviour accordingly. Some evidence to support this idea comes from experiments on self-awareness. Among primates, at least, the ability to recognise oneself in a mirror is restricted to man and a few of the great apes. Even monkeys see the reflection as a stranger.

As to the question of mechanism, most neurologists agree that it is the continuity of the process—how the connections produce the stream of consciousness—that most needs to be explained. Occasionally this stream breaks down. Some people who suffer from schizophrenia report seeing the world in freeze-frame, a phenomenon which healthy people can also experience if they are very tired but are forced to concentrate on some task. Among schizophrenics, freeze-framing is associated with problems in the working memory, another piece of evidence that this structure has a key role in maintaining consciousness. But this does not explain how the information is co-ordinated.

One of the most promising lines of inquiry in the co-ordination problem is known as the 40 hertz binding frequency. Particular stimuli will set neurons all over a brain firing together at between 40 and 70 action potentials per second. Different stimuli excite different networks. This network of simultaneous firing serves to illuminate the fragmented information scattered around the brain. Change the input and, like a simple neural network switching from recognising one face to another, you change the output. Change fast enough and the result appears, like a cinema film, to be continuous. In nature, the change seems to come every tenth of a second.

Of course, there is no reason why such integration necessarily implies consciousness; but a refinement of the model looks promising. This is based on a hierarchy of the sort found in the visual system. Each level of the hierarchy is a "convergence zone", gathering information from lower levels and passing it on to a higher one if the processing task cannot be completed at that level. The system can oscillate because some axons from each level reach back into the lower ones, feeding information back to them. If the task is so difficult that it is necessary to recruit the central executive of the working memory, then it enters the stream of consciousness. Your executive normally has better things to do than drive your car, but if someone cuts you up, it connects.

The Adaptive Nature of Cognitive Immaturity

David F. Bjorklund and Brandi L. Green
Florida Atlantic University

The prolonged cognitive immaturity characteristic of human youth is described as adaptive in and of itself. The adaptive nature of cognitive immaturity is examined in developmental research in the areas of metacognition, egocentricity, plasticity and the speed of information processing, and language acquisition. Some of the consequences of viewing children's immature cognition as adaptive for cognitive development and education are discussed.

Humans are the intelligent species in that we, more than any other species, adapt ourselves and modify the environment to suit our needs. Our intelligence has permitted us to alter the typical course of evolution, making cultural changes more rapid and significant than biological changes. This intelligence, however, requires a long apprenticeship. Human development is noted for its extended period of youth (see Gould, 1977; Montagu, 1989), with delayed physical and sexual maturity being associated with delayed cognitive maturity, making the human child's dependency on adults all the greater.

But why must the cognitive abilities of humans stay immature as long as physical abilities? It would seem that if the human child has much to learn, it would be to the species's advantage to have the prolonged physical childhood be accompanied by a relatively mature cognitive system. Surely an intellectually mature organism can learn more and better than an intellectually immature one. This would result in a physically dependent being who is more capable of learning the complexities of the world. Yet, this is not the way nature has chosen to work.

One problem with this line of thinking is the tendency to equate *immaturity* with *inefficiency*—a poorly functioning system that must develop further if true advancement is to occur. An alternative perspective is that the prolonged cognitive immaturity of humans has a specific role in development. From this point of view, there may be many aspects of children's immature cognition that have adaptive functions and are more than mere deficits. For example, what contemporary or future benefits might be afforded children by slow information processing, egocentric thinking, or overly optimistic opinions about their mental abilities?

One of the most popular explanations for the adaptive function of prolonged immaturity is the extended period of time available for practicing adult roles and socialization (Bruner, 1972; Poirier & Smith, 1974; Washburn & Hamburg, 1965). Much of this practice and socialization is realized through play. Like the extended period of youth, and, in fact, correlated with it, play is most frequently found in species that are behaviorally flexible (Beckoff, 1972; Poirier & Smith, 1974; Vandenberg, 1981). Many writers believe that it is primarily through play that children's cognition develops (e.g., Dansky, 1980; Piaget, 1962). Although play itself cannot be regarded as immature cognition, it can be viewed as a vehicle through which an extended childhood affects cognitive development.

In this article we take a different perspective, arguing that aspects of children's immature thinking are adaptive in their own right. We propose, as have others (e.g., Lenneberg, 1967; Oppenheim, 1981), that some aspects of the young child's cognitive system are qualitatively different from those of the older child or adult and are well suited to attain important cognitive–social milestones such as attachment and language. In a similar vein, Oppenheim discussed the presence of neurobehavioral characteristics of immature animals that have a specific role in survival during infancy or youth but disappear when they are no longer necessary. These *ontogenetic adaptations* are not simply incomplete versions of adult characteristics but serve specific adaptive functions for the developing animal. Oppenheim went as far as to suggest that "even the absence of adult capabilities may be developmentally adaptive . . . [and] should be considered in any comprehensive theory of ontogeny" (p. 92). Similar arguments have been put forward by Turkewitz and Kenny (1982), who suggested that the limitations (or immaturity) of sensory and motor systems may play adaptive

Bernadette Gray-Little served as action editor for this article.

Portions of the article were written while David F. Bjorklund was supported by a grant from The Spencer Foundation. We would like to thank the following people for their helpful comments on earlier drafts of this article: Barbara Bjorklund, Katherine Kipp Harnishfeger, Jean-Louis Gariépy, Ingrid Johanson, Thomas Monson, Jacqueline Muir-Broaddus, and Robin Vallacher. We would also like to thank Robert Cairns, Gilbert Gottlieb, Robert McCall, and an anonymous reviewer for their constructive suggestions.

Correspondence concerning this article should be addressed to David F. Bjorklund, Department of Psychology, Florida Atlantic University, Boca Raton, FL 33431. Electronic mail may be sent to bjorkldf@fauvax.

roles in ontogeny. The limited motor capacities of juvenile animals serve to prevent their wandering from the mother, which thereby enhances their chances of survival. In an elegant review, these authors suggested that the sensory limitations of many newborn and juvenile animals are adaptive features that may help reduce the amount of information infants have to deal with and thus aid in constructing a simplified, comprehensible world. Like Oppenheim, Turkewitz and Kenny suggested that the lack of adult characteristics may be an adaptive feature of ontogenetic development.

Other aspects of young children's cognition, we propose, are qualitatively similar to those found in the adult but function poorly. Such low levels of functioning may provide some advantages for young children and do not represent imperfect stages that must be overcome. We propose that the advantages of immature cognition are found in many areas, four broad examples of which are metacognition, egocentricity, speed of cognitive processing, and language acquisition, each of which are discussed below. The belief that cognitive immaturity has a significant role in ontogeny has important implications for how we view cognitive development and education, and these are discussed briefly in a final section.

Adaptive Value of Cognitive Immaturity

Metacognition

Metacognition refers to a person's knowledge about his or her own cognitions and the factors that influence thinking. For every form of cognition, it is possible to think of a corresponding metacognition, and metacognition has been studied with respect to memory, communication, reading, and attention, among others (e.g., Flavell & Wellman, 1977; Garner, 1990; Miller, 1985; Whitehurst & Sonnenschein, 1985). A general finding of developmental metacognitive research is that there is a concomitant age-related improvement in cognitive and metacognitive abilities (see Bjorklund, 1989).

Studies of children's *metamemory* (see, e.g., Flavell, Friedrichs, & Hoyt, 1970; Yussen & Levy, 1975) have shown that young children are prone to overestimate their recall abilities, with the frequency and degree of overestimation declining with age (for reviews, see Cavanaugh & Perlmutter, 1982; Flavell & Wellman, 1977; Schneider, 1985; Schneider & Pressley, 1989). Yussen and Levy noted that preschool children's predictions of their memory abilities were minimally influenced by their previous performance. In their study, Yussen and Levy found that many four-year-old children continued to make unrealistically high predictions, even after being shown that they could not recall the number of items they had predicted. The authors noted that these children appeared to realize that they had failed, but persisted in believing that they could do it the next time.

Unrealistic optimism in performance expectations has also been reported frequently in the achievement motivation literature (see Stipek, 1984; Stipek & Mac Iver, 1989). A series of experiments by Stipek and her colleagues (Stipek, 1981; Stipek & Hoffman, 1980; Stipek, Roberts, & Sanborn, 1984), among others, has shown

that young children generally overestimate their skills on a wide variety of academic tasks and have more optimistic (and less realistic) expectations for their own future performance relative to that of other children. Similar results have been reported by Schneider (1988, 1991) for predictions of performance on a memory-span task. Although young children do not ignore past failures altogether, they do not use this information as efficiently as do older children when making predictions about their own future performances (Stipek, 1984).

Again, poor metacognition is usually viewed as a handicap, and in older children and adults it would certainly seem to be a handicap. But children who are out of touch with their own intellectual and motoric abilities may, in some situations, have an advantage. One benefit of poor metacognition, we believe, is motivational. Children's beliefs in their good track record foster feelings of self-efficacy. According to social cognitive theory (Bandura, 1982, 1989a, 1989b), judgments of self-efficacy are based on several sources of information, the most important of which is *perceived enactive mastery.* Children's self-perceptions of their efficacy, whether they are accurate or fanciful, serve to mediate action. Children's perceived self-efficacy influences which environments and activities they select, as well as the amount of time and effort they expend on those activities. When self-efficacy is poor, people tend to behave ineffectually regardless of their actual abilities (Bandura, 1989a, 1989b).

Unrealistic optimism about their own abilities and an equally unrealistic evaluation of their behaviors give young children the opportunity to practice skills in situations in which accurate metacognition might discourage them from doing so (Bjorklund, Gaultney, & Green, in press). As pointed out by Stipek (1984), learned helplessness, the belief that one has no control over a situation, is relatively rare among young children, who generally expect success in achievement situations and evaluate their competencies favorably. This optimistic attitude may encourage children to attempt behaviors they would not otherwise try if they had more realistic conceptions of their abilities. Ignorance of their limitations allows children to try more diverse and complex behaviors that may be out of their grasp at the present time. This allows them to practice skills to a greater degree and may foster long-term cognitive benefits.

Some recent research from our laboratory illustrates the potential usefulness of immaturity in perfecting the mechanisms by which imitation operates. In a series of studies, we investigated the development of *meta-imitation,* the knowledge of one's own imitative abilities, in children between three and five years of age (Bjorklund et al., in press). Our findings revealed that very young children consistently overestimated their imitative abilities and therefore attempted to imitate behaviors that were often well beyond their current grasp. Moreover, after attempting to mimic a modeled behavior (e.g., juggling one, two, or three balls or tossing a ball into a basket from one and one half, three, or seven feet away), young children were equally inept at evaluating how successful they had been. Both prediction (how well they thought they could imitate a modeled behavior) and *postdiction* (how well they thought they actually had imitated the behavior) were overestimated by preschool children, with the degree of overestimation being highest among three-year-olds and lowest among five-year-olds.[1]

Bjorklund et al. (in press) proposed that poorly developed meta-imitation encourages young children to attempt to imitate a diverse range of models and behaviors; this in turn permits them to practice and improve these behaviors. In support of this, Bjorklund et al. reported that there was a relationship between degree of overestimation of one's imitative abilities on the tossing and juggling tasks and intelligence, as judged by the vocabulary subscale of the Wechsler Preschool and Primary Scale of Intelligence (WPPSI), and that this relationship varied with age. In this study, a negative correlation between WPPSI and accuracy scores is an indication that children with better metacognition (i.e., more accurate estimations) have higher verbal intelligence. This pattern was found for the oldest preschool children in our sample (five-year-olds), a finding consistent with those of other researchers studying the relationship between metacognition and intelligence in school-age children (e.g., Schneider, Körkel, & Weinert, 1987). In contrast, for the three- and four-year-olds tested, positive (albeit low to moderate) correlations were found, reflecting that brighter children overestimated slightly more than less bright children. Correlations were significant only for the postdiction scores for the four-year-olds ($r = +0.46$) and the five-year-olds ($r = -0.39$), but differences in the magnitude of the correlations between the oldest and the younger groups of children were significant or approached significance in three out of four contrasts.

We do not mean to imply that young children with good metacognition will grow up to be older children with poor cognitive abilities, or vice versa. The correlations between WPPSI and meta-imitation scores for the three-year-olds were low and nonsignificant in our study ($rs = 0.19$ and 0.15 for prediction and postdiction, respectively). What is of significance is that the canonical relationship between metacognition and intelligence was not obtained on these tasks until the age of five. Young children, in general, overestimated their imitative abilities, with accurate children having no intellectual edge over inaccurate children, at least through the age of four. Whether the older children would show a similar positive relationship between overestimation and intelligence for more demanding tasks is speculative, although such a finding would be consistent with the data of Stipek and her colleagues (see Stipek, 1984; Stipek & Mac Iver, 1989).

The findings of the meta-imitation study and the hypothesis that poor metacognition is adaptive for young children mirrors the opinions of Oppenheim (1981) and Turkewitz and Kenny (1982) with regard to the adaptive benefits of the absence of adult capacities in early development. Rather than being an imperfect attempt at adult abilities, these limitations may serve the needs of the developing organism at its particular stage of ontogeny.

Egocentricity

Piaget (1955; Piaget & Inhelder, 1967) described preschool children as being *egocentric,* in that they cannot easily take a perspective other than their own. Piaget proposed that young children's cognition is centered around themselves, and they have a difficult time perceiving the world as someone else does. According to Piaget, this egocentricity permeates all areas of children's cognitive lives, influencing their perceptions, their language, and their social interactions. Research over the past two decades has indicated that young children are not as egocentric as Piaget had initially proposed (e.g., Borke, 1975; Gzesh & Surber, 1985; Flavell, Everett, Croft, & Flavell, 1981); yet their abilities to take the perspective of another certainly improve with age, *egocentric* accurately describing many of the cognitions of preschool children.

Although young children's egocentrism has generally been viewed as a cognitive liability, their tendencies to interpret events from their own perspective may have some unforeseen benefits. For example, in memory research with both children and adults, higher levels of recall are achieved when subjects relate the target information to themselves during either encoding or retrieval (see Kail & Levine, 1976; Lord, 1980; Nadelman, 1974; Pratkanis & Greenwald, 1985). If, during the presentation of stimuli, subjects are asked whether each item applies to them, subsequent recall is higher than under control conditions (Pratkanis & Greenwald, 1985). For example, in research by Lord (1980), adult subjects were asked to determine whether each adjective on a list was like themselves, their fathers, or Walter Cronkite. The subjects remembered items identified as related to themselves significantly more often than the other words. Lord concluded that when it comes to semantic processing, remembering is facilitated by self-reference more than other frames of reference.

The results of the self-referencing experiments suggest that young children's egocentric attitude may result in enhanced levels of cognitive performance in some situations, and thus may be adaptive. We do not mean to imply that young children's self-concepts are as well integrated as those of adults. However, because young children's initial bias is to interpret events in terms of their own perspectives, they may retain or comprehend some events better than if they were less self-centered. This was illustrated in a study by Mood (1979) of egocentrism in children's sentence comprehension. Mood reported that sentence content describing the children and their personal experiences facilitated their comprehension. In other words, following Piaget's terminology, enhancing the opportunity for children to bring their own perspectives to bear on the solution of a cognitive task increased their ability to assimilate the requirements of the task to their existing cognitive structures. This egocentric benefit allows the children to practice and refine comprehension skills that they would not have had the opportunity to do otherwise. Egocentrism, then, is not a cognitive deficit; rather, it provides some information-processing benefits to young children. As Mood stated, "Focusing on the nonadaptive aspects of preoperational egocentrism results

---

[1] Three-, four-, and five-year olds overestimated their performance comparably for both prediction and postdiction in an experiment in which children watched a model, stated how well they thought they could imitate the model, performed the task, and then evaluated their own performance (Bjorklund et al., in press, Study 3). Postdiction was more accurate than prediction, however, in a diary study (Study 1) in which parents observed and interviewed their children about their imitative attempts. In the diary study, children between the ages of 3 and 5 years still overestimated their performance approximately 40% of the time. Underestimation was rare in all studies reported by Bjorklund et al.

in an incomplete picture of children's development in that the potential adaptive function of egocentrism is minimized or overlooked" (p. 247).

Another aspect of young children's egocentrism is found in their play. Preschool children often engage in *parallel play;* this involves two (or more) children playing near one another, and possibly being involved in similar activities (e.g., building castles in a sandbox), but not truly being involved in mutual or cooperative play (Rubin, Watson, & Jambor, 1978). During parallel play, children may engage in *collective monologues,* in which they talk with one another, but not really to one another (Piaget, 1955). The children would not be so vocal if they were not playing beside one another, so the social situation influences their behavior. The situation can best be described as semisocial.

Some researchers have suggested that this semisocial parallel play may lead children into more cooperative and social play. For example, Bakeman and Brownlee (1980) showed that preschoolers often move from parallel play to group play during the course of a play session. They suggested that children may play beside one another as an unconscious strategy that leads them into group play. Thus, young children's egocentricity serves as a technique that gives them access to more socially oriented activities. Socially immature children who did not talk to themselves in group settings might be less apt to later find themselves in cooperative play situations.

Although highly speculative, the egocentricity that Inhelder and Piaget (1958) and others (e.g., Elkind, 1967; Elkind & Bowen, 1979; Gray & Hudson, 1984) observed in adolescents may also have some adaptive qualities. During adolescence, egocentricity is expressed in part by teenagers' belief that they are invincible and that bad things happen only to other people. Elkind (1967) has referred to this adolescent viewpoint as the *personal fable.* It is likely that such an attitude facilitates children taking risks and separating themselves from their parents. Such risk-taking behavior clearly can have negative consequences, but it also ensures that adolescents experiment with new ideas and new tasks and generally behave more independently. Many of these experiences will be adaptive for adult life and for making the transition to adulthood. Consistent with this argument and equally speculative is the proposal that hunting skills developed first in humans as a result of the risk-taking and exploratory dispositions of young male hominids (see Crook, 1980).

Plasticity and Speed of Cognitive Processing

A general truism of development is that plasticity is reduced with time (Jacobson, 1969; Lerner, 1984; McCall, 1981; Scott, 1968). Children have shown impressive reversibility of the effects of an intellectually deleterious early environment when conditions in their lives change for the better during their second and third years (e.g., E. A. Clark & Hanisee, 1982; Kagan & Klein, 1973; Skeels, 1966).

A major reason for this plasticity, we believe, is that children's cognitive systems are immature, particularly their ability to process information quickly and efficiently. One well-established fact in the cognitive developmental literature is that there are regular age-related changes throughout childhood in speed of processing (Case, 1985; Dempster, 1985; Hale, 1989; Kail, 1986, 1991). Speed of processing (e.g., in identifying pictures or words) is related to level of cognitive performance (Case, 1985; Case, Kurland, & Goldberg, 1982; Chi, 1977), with older (and quicker) children typically performing at higher levels on cognitive tasks than younger (and slower) children.

Processing speed has been hypothesized to be related to age differences in *myelinization* of associative areas of the brain and to experience (Bjorklund & Harnishfeger, 1990; Case, 1985; Dempster, 1985; Konner, 1991). According to Bjorklund and Harnishfeger, "the slower processing of poorly myelinated nerves affords younger children less time to process information" (p. 61). When one considers that processing resources are limited (Bjorklund, 1987; Case, 1985; Hasher & Zacks, 1979), more of a young child's "limited mental resources must be allocated to the activation of nerve bundles than for older children, who have more completely myelinated nerve bundles" (Bjorklund & Harnishfeger, 1990, p. 61). The overall slower speed of mental processing for younger children means that more of their processing is effortful in nature, in that it consumes substantial portions of their limited mental resources (Hasher & Zacks, 1979). In contrast, more of older children's and adults' cognitive processing is automatic, in that it can be done without conscious awareness and requires little or none of one's limited capacity.

Although processing speed varies with age (presumably as a function of myelinization; see Konner, 1991), it is also affected by experience, so that young children who are especially expert at a particular subject process information from that domain rapidly and perform well on tests related to their area of expertise (Roth, 1983). However, this rapid processing and high level of performance does not generalize, with expert children behaving in an age-appropriate manner when dealing with domains for which they have no special expertise (e.g., Chi, 1978; Opwis, Gold, Gruber, & Schneider, 1990).

Slow and inefficient processing through infancy and early childhood may be the factor most responsible for the intellectual plasticity observed in humans. Because mental operations are slow, less information is activated and processed automatically. This reduced automaticity makes processing more laborious and ineffective for the young child, but at the same times protects the child from acquiring cognitive patterns early in life that may not be advantageous later on. Because little in the way of cognitive processing can be automatized early, presumably because of children's incomplete myelinization, children are better prepared to adapt cognitively to later environments. If experiences early in life yielded automization, the child would lose the flexibility necessary for adult life. Processes automatized in response to the demands of early childhood may be useless and even detrimental for coping with the very different cognitive demands faced by adults. Cognitive flexibility in the species is maintained by an immature nervous system that gradually permits the automization of more mental operations, increasing the likelihood that lessons learned as a young child will not interfere with the qualitatively different tasks required of the adult.[2]

Language Acquisition

In each of the three topics discussed above, immature cognition was defined as cognition characterizing the young children that was less proficient than that characterizing the adult. Thus, adults have superior metacognitive abilities, are less egocentric, and process information faster than children. Despite these disadvantages, some benefits are associated with children's less-skilled cognition. The picture is different for language acquisition. Children are better at acquiring both first and second languages than are adults. The cognitive system of the child is seemingly not less efficient than the adults' when it comes to language learning; rather, it is well suited to the demands, making the immaturity of early cognition highly adaptive for the important human phenomenon of language acquisition. The arguments for a critical period of language acquisition are well known, and we will not belabor them here. We will only restate briefly some of those arguments in terms of our thesis and review some recent findings supportive of them.

Lenneberg (1967) is most associated with the critical period hypothesis for language acquisition. He proposed that language learning occurred exclusively or primarily in childhood. The nervous system loses its plasticity with age, so that by puberty the organization of the brain is fixed for all practical purposes, making language learning difficult. There has been much evidence consistent with this position, including differences between adults and children in recovery from aphasia (see Witelson, 1987), and behavioral studies examining language acquisition in older children who were severely deprived early in life (e.g., Curtiss, 1977).

More recent research by Johnson and Newport (1989) has examined second language learning as a function of age. They reported that proficiency in a person's second language was related to the age at which language training began, so that people who learned their second language early in childhood showed greater proficiency as adults than did people who learned their second language later. Similar results have recently been reported for deaf people learning American Sign Language (Newport, 1990) as their first language. These data require a modified interpretation of the critical period hypothesis for language development, indicating that there is a grad-

ual decline in a person's ability to acquire a second language through childhood, rather than a discontinuity at puberty.

It is clear that the cognitive system of the young child is especially suited for learning both a first and a second language. This ability is gradually lost over childhood, and although adults are able to acquire a second language, they rarely attain the same proficiency that is achieved when language is acquired in childhood. Slow neurological development affords children the cognitive flexibility to acquire a language. Johnson and Newport (1989) suggested an alternative and complementary hypothesis to describe their data on age of learning a second language. They proposed that "an increase in certain cognitive abilities may, paradoxically, make language learning more difficult" (p. 97). Newport (1990) speculated that young children's limitations in encoding complex stimuli may actually make some aspects of language learning easier. According to Newport, "If children perceive and store only component parts of the complex linguistic stimuli to which they are exposed, while adults more readily perceive and remember the whole complex stimulus, children may be in a better position to locate the components" (p. 24). Specifically, children should be aided in acquiring structures that require some type of componential analysis, such as morphology, whereas adults should have an advantage in acquiring aspects of language that require integration of complex wholes, such as whole word learning. Other researchers have suggested that the advent of formal operations in early adolescence interferes with implicit learning strategies, making language acquisition more difficult (Krashen, 1982; Rosansky, 1975).

These interpretations, as well as the critical period explanation for language learning, are consistent with our view that children's immature cognition is adaptive and plays an important role in cognitive development.

Our discussion of language acquisition to this point has dealt with *syntactic* development. There is some evidence that young children's cognitive immaturity may facilitate certain aspects of *semantic* development as well. For example, during the early stages of language acquisition, children tend to overextend the meaning of words. They use one word, such as "doggie," as a label not only for its proper referent but also for related objects, such as mammals in general (de Villiers & de Villiers, 1979). Yet, when given a selection of pictures from which to choose, children who overextend the meaning of words can usually select the proper picture, indicating that they know the correct meaning of the word (Thompson & Chapman, 1977). In most language cultures, such overextensions frequently result in parents correcting children (e.g., "That's not a doggie, that's a kitty"), which provides the children with information they might not have received had they remained silent. Children's overextensions, despite their knowledge of what a word actually refers to, suggests that they have a very low threshold for determining whether an object corresponds to a previously acquired label (cf. Siegler, 1988, 1990). This tendency not to inhibit erroneous responses is a youthful one (see Bjorklund & Harnishfeger, 1990; Dempster, in press; Harnishfeger & Bjorklund, in press) that, in this situation, results in children receiving more important

---

[2] Our colleague Ingrid Johanson suggested to us that the well-known phenomenon of infantile amnesia may be similarly explained. Few people can recall events from early childhood, and those events that are recalled are frequently reconstructions of events that occurred years later. Freud (1905/1953) proposed that the experiences of infancy are traumatic because of their sexual nature and that infantile memories are actively repressed. A more plausible interpretation is that events encoded in infancy cannot be retrieved by the qualitatively different cognitive system that resides in the mind of the older child or adult (e.g., Bjorklund, 1989). Although not wishing to give credence to Freud's repression hypothesis, the general inability of humans to recall details from childhood and infancy is probably adaptive. Many of the experiences of infancy and childhood are relevant only to that time in development. Having vivid memories of early experiences, although not necessarily resulting in traumatization, may interfere with and contradict the knowledge that is needed to function in later environments.

information than they would receive were they to use a more conservative (and mature) criterion. Given the state of young children's knowledge, the use of error-producing thresholds serves them well.

Conclusions and Implications for Education

In viewing the role of prolonged immaturity as simply providing more time for learning and socialization, researchers and educators often assume that acceleration of this learning would be beneficial and would provide more time to do even more learning. However, a closer look at the mechanisms of learning in youth suggests that immaturity, along with its limitations and imperfections, serves an adaptive purpose.

This view of the adaptive nature of cognitive immaturity has important implications for cognitive development and for education. For example, textbooks of developmental psychology have traditionally presented Piaget's account of preoperations by emphasizing what young children cannot do relative to concrete-operational children. Some authors and instructors have tried to rectify this by pointing out some of the cognitive skills that young children possess, stressing that young children are more accomplished than Piaget (and others) had given them credit for (e.g., Lefrancois, 1989; Shaffer, 1989). However, if immature cognition is seen as playing an adaptive role in children's development, the "deficiencies" of the preschool child need not be apologized for, but can be regarded as important and necessary components of a fully developed cognitive system.

Similarly, educators' attempts to enhance young children's intelligence through intense instruction, sometimes beginning in infancy (e.g., Doman, 1984; Eastman & Barr, 1985; Engelmann & Engelmann, 1981), must be seriously rethought. It has become clear over the years that infants and young children are capable of greater intellectual feats than had previously been believed, and some educators have argued that formal instruction should begin in the crib. Perhaps the most vocal proponent of this position is Glenn Doman (1984), who claimed that "It is easier to teach a one-year-old *any* set of *facts* than it is to teach a seven-year-old," and "You can teach a baby anything that you can present in an *honest* and *factual* way." (p. 59). This seems to be taking to the extreme Jerome Bruner's (1960) statement that "any subject can be taught effectively in some intellectually honest form to any child at any stage of development" (p. 33).

Others have argued with equal ardor that academically oriented instruction for low-risk infants and preschoolers has no educational merit (e.g., Ames & Chase, 1981; Elkind, 1987a, 1987b; Gallagher & Coche, 1987; Sigel, 1987; Winn, 1983; Zigler, 1987). David Elkind labeled the academic pressure placed on young children as *miseducation*. He argued that exposing young children to formal education puts them unnecessarily at both short-term and long-term risk. Short-term risks are associated with the stress formal education places on young children and are expressed as fatigue, loss of appetite, decreased efficiency, and eventual psychosomatic ailments. Long-term risks associated with early formal ed-

ucation include reduced motivation for learning, interference with self-directed learning and reflective abstraction (i.e., reflecting on the outcomes of one's own cognitions), and the potentially deleterious effects of social comparisons of intelligence.

Despite the claims by such educators as Doman (1984) and the counterclaims by such educators as Elkind (1987a, 1987b), there has been surprisingly little research assessing the long-term costs and benefits of infant and toddler instruction. A recent study by Hyson, Hirsh-Pasek, and Rescorla (1989) is a notable exception. In their study, four-year-old children attending academic or non-academic prekindergarten programs were assessed. The children were given tests of academic skills, creativity, social competence, and emotional well-being at the end of their prekindergarten program and again after kindergarten. Parents were also interviewed about their attitudes about education and their expectations for their children's academic achievement.

Hyson et al. (1989) reported some initial intellectual advantages for children in the academic programs. When tested at the conclusion of the prekindergarten program, children who attended academically oriented schools performed better on tests of academic skills (e.g., knowledge of letters, numbers, and shapes) than did children who did not. However, there was no difference between the groups on more general measures of intelligence, and even the advantage in the specific academic skills was not maintained by the end of kindergarten. Hyson et al. reported that there was no difference in social competence between children who attended the academic and nonacademic schools. Moreover, children in the academic programs showed greater signs of test anxiety and had a more negative attitude toward school at the end of kindergarten than did children from the nonacademic schools. Children who attended the academic preschools were also judged to be less creative. Hyson et al. suggested that creativity during the preschool years may be enhanced by environments that encourage playfulness and minimize adult control. For preschool children from middle- and upper-middle-class homes who receive an average amount of intellectual stimulation, Hyson et al.'s study indicates "that the effort spent on formal, teacher-directed academic learning in preschool may not be the best use of children's time at this point in their development" (p. 15).

It has long been recognized by some scholars that certain aspects of learning must await requisite levels of maturation (e.g., Gesell et al., 1940; Uphoff, Gilmore, & Huber, 1986). We concur with this position. However, we propose that the time spent developing this maturity is not merely a waiting period, but instead encompasses a diverse array of adaptive limitations that function ontogenetically to increase a child's learning potential throughout development. A consideration of the adaptive aspects of slow maturation cautions us to provide children with intellectual experiences tailored to their capabilities, rather than trying to endow them with skills ill suited for their biologically determined cognitive systems. What were once viewed as youthful liabilities (e.g., poor metacognition and egocentrism) may instead be exactly what are needed at a particular period of cognitive development. With this perspective in mind, we should rethink our efforts to hurry children through a childhood that has uses in and of itself.[3]

---

[3] It is worth mentioning that the most eminent scholar of this century, Albert Einstein, speculated about the advantages that immature cognition may have on adult thinking. Although we cannot claim Einstein's views as data for our arguments, it is interesting to note that he attributed some of his success to his slower-than-average intellectual development: "I sometimes ask myself how it came about that I was the one to develop the theory of relativity. The reason, I think, is that a normal adult never stops to think about problems of space and time. These are things which he has thought of as a child. But my intellectual development was retarded, as a result of which I began to wonder about space and time only when I had already grown up. Naturally, I could go deeper into the problem than a child with normal abilities" (cited in R. W. Clark, 1971, p. 10).

REFERENCES

Ames, L. B., & Chase, J. A. (1981). *Don't push your preschooler.* New York: Harper & Row.

Bakeman, R., & Brownlee, J. R. (1980). The strategic use of parallel play: A sequential analysis. *Child Development, 51,* 873–878.

Bandura, A. (1982). Self-efficacy mechanism in human agency. *American Psychologist, 37,* 122–147.

Bandura, A. (1989a). Human agency in social cognitive theory. *American Psychologist, 44,* 1175–1184.

Bandura, A. (1989b). Regulation of cognitive processes through perceived self-efficacy. *Developmental Psychology, 25,* 729–735.

Beckoff, M. (1972). The development of social interaction, play, and metacommunication in mammals: An ethological perspective. *Quarterly Review of Biology, 47,* 412–434.

Bjorklund, D. F. (1987). How age changes in knowledge base contribute to the development of children's memory: An interpretive review. *Developmental Review, 7,* 93–130.

Bjorklund, D. F. (1989). *Children's thinking: Developmental function and individual differences.* Pacific Grove, CA: Brooks/Cole.

Bjorklund, D. F., Gaultney, J. F., & Green, B. L. (in press). "I watch, therefore I can do:" The development of meta-imitation over the preschool years and the advantage of optimism in one's imitative skills. In M. L. Howe & R. Pasnak (Eds.), *Emerging themes in cognitive development* (Vol. 2). New York: Springer-Verlag.

Bjorklund, D. F., & Harnishfeger, K. K. (1990). The resources construct in cognitive development: Diverse sources of evidence and a theory of inefficient inhibition. *Developmental Review, 10,* 48–71.

Borke, H. (1975). Piaget's mountains revisited: Changes in the egocentric landscape. *Developmental Psychology, 11,* 240–243.

Bruner, J. S. (1960). *The process of education.* Cambridge, MA: Harvard University Press.

Bruner, J. S. (1972). The nature and uses of immaturity. *American Psychologist, 27,* 687–708.

Case, R. (1985). *Intellectual development: Birth to adulthood.* San Diego, CA: Academic Press.

Case, R., Kurland, M., & Goldberg, J. (1982). Operational efficiency and the growth of short-term memory span. *Journal of Experimental Child Psychology, 33,* 386–404.

Cavanaugh, J. C., & Perlmutter, M. (1982). Metamemory: A critical examination. *Child Development, 53,* 11–28.

Chi, M. T. H. (1977). Age differences in memory span. *Journal of Experimental Child Psychology, 23,* 266–281.

Chi, M. T. H. (1978). Knowledge structures and memory development. In R. S. Siegler (Ed.), *Children's thinking: What develops?* (pp. 73–96). Hillsdale, NJ: Erlbaum.

Clark, E. A., & Hanisee, J. (1982). Intellectual and adaptive performance of Asian children in adoptive American settings. *Developmental Psychology, 18,* 595–599.

Clark, R. W. (1971). *Einstein: The life and times.* New York: The World Publishing Co.

Crook, J. H. (1980). *The evolution of human consciousness.* Oxford, England: Clarendon Press.

Curtiss, S. (1977). *Genie: A psycholinguistic study of a modern day "wild child."* San Diego, CA: Academic Press.

Dansky, J. L. (1980). Make-believe: A mediator of the relationship between play and associative fluency. *Child Development, 51,* 576–579.

Dempster, F. N. (1985). Short-term memory development in childhood and adolescence. In C. J. Brainerd & M. Pressley (Eds.), *Basic processes in memory development: Progress in cognitive development research* (pp. 209–248). New York: Springer.

Dempster, F. N. (in press). Resistance to interference: Developmental changes in a basic information processing mechanism. In R. Pasnak & M. L. Howe (Eds.), *Emerging themes in cognitive development* (Vol. 1). New York: Springer-Verlag.

de Villiers, P. A., & de Villiers, J. G. (1979). *Early language.* Cambridge, MA: Harvard University Press.

Doman, G. (1984). *How to multiply your baby's intelligence.* Garden City, NY: Doubleday.

Eastman, O., & Barr, J. L. (1985). *Your child is smarter than you think.* New York: Morrow.

Elkind, D. (1967). Egocentrism in adolescence. *Child Development, 38,* 1025–1034.

Elkind, D. (1987a). Early childhood education on its own terms. In S. L. Kagan & E. F. Zigler (Eds.), *Early schooling: The national debate.* New Haven, CT: Yale University Press.

Elkind, D. (1987b). *The miseducation of children: Superkids at risk.* New York: Knopf.

Elkind, D., & Bowen, R. (1979). Imaginary audience behavior in children and adolescents. *Developmental Psychology, 15,* 38–44.

Engelmann, S., & Engelmann, T. (1981). *Give your child a superior mind.* New York: Cornerstone.

Flavell, J. H., Everett, B. A., Croft, K., & Flavell, E. (1981). Young children's knowledge about visual perception: Further evidence for level 1–level 2 distinction. *Developmental Psychology, 17,* 99–107.

Flavell, J., Friedrichs, A., & Hoyt, J. (1970). Developmental changes in memorization processes. *Cognitive Psychology, 1,* 324–340.

Flavell, J., & Wellman, H. (1977). Metamemory. In R. V. Kail, Jr. & J. W. Hagen (Eds.), *Perspectives on the development of memory and cognition* (pp. 3–33). Hillsdale, NJ: Erlbaum.

Freud, S. (1953). Three essays on the theory of sexuality. In J. Strachey (Ed. and Trans.), *The standard edition of the complete psychological works of Sigmund Freud* (Vol. 7, pp. 125–145). London: Hogarth Press. (Original work published 1905)

Gallagher, J. M., & Coche, J. (1987). Hothousing: The clinical and educational concerns over pressuring young children. *Early Childhood Research Quarterly, 2,* 203–210.

Garner, R. (1990). Children's use of strategies in reading. In D. F. Bjorklund (Ed.), *Children's strategies: Contemporary views of cognitive development* (pp. 245–268). Hillsdale, NJ: Erlbaum.

Gesell, A., Halverson, H. M., Thompson, H., Ilg, F. L., Castner, B. M., Ames, L. B., & Amatruda (1940). *The first five years of life: A guide to the study of the preschool child.* New York: Harper.

Gould, S. J. (1977). *Ontogeny and phylogeny.* Cambridge, MA: Harvard University Press.

Gray, W. M., & Hudson, L. M. (1984). Formal operations and the imaginary audience. *Developmental Psychology, 20,* 619–627.

Gzesh, S. M., & Surber, C. F. (1985). Visual perspective-taking skills in children. *Child Development, 56,* 1204–1213.

Hale, S. (1989, April). *A global trend in the development of information processing speed.* Paper presented at the meeting of the Society for Research in Child Development, Kansas City, MO.

Harnishfeger, K. K., & Bjorklund, D. F. (in press). The ontogeny of inhibition mechanisms: A renewed approach to cognitive development. In R. Pasnak & M. L. Howe (Eds.), *Emerging themes in cognitive development* (Vol. 1). New York: Springer-Verlag.

Hasher, L., & Zacks, R. T. (1979). Automatic and effortful processes in memory. *Journal of Experimental Psychology: General, 108,* 356–388.

Hyson, M. C., Hirsh-Pasek, K., & Rescorla, L. (1989). *Academic environments in early childhood: Challenge or pressure?* Summary report to The Spencer Foundation, Chicago, IL.

Inhelder, B., & Piaget, J. (1958). *The growth of logical thinking from childhood to adolescence.* New York: Basic Books.

Jacobson, M. (1969). Development of specific neuronal connections. *Science, 163,* 543–547.

Johnson, J. S., & Newport, E. L. (1989). Critical period effects in second language learning: The influence of instructional state on the acquisition of English as a second language. *Cognitive Psychology, 21,* 60–99.

Kagan, J., & Klein, R. E. (1973). Cross-cultural perspectives on early development. *American Psychologist, 28,* 947–961.

Kail, R. (1986). Sources of age differences in speed of processing. *Child Development, 57,* 969–987.

Kail, R. (1991). Processing time declines exponentially during childhood and adolescence. *Developmental Psychology, 27,* 259–266.

Kail, R. V., & Levine, L. E. (1976). Encoding processes and sex-role preferences. *Journal of Experimental Child Psychology, 21,* 256–263.

Konner, M. (1991). Universals of behavioral development in relation to brain myelinization. In K. R. Gibson & A. C. Petersen (Eds.), *Brain maturation and cognitive development: Comparative and cross-cultural perspectives* (pp. 181–223). New York: Aldine de Gruyter.

Krashen, S. (1982). Accounting for child–adult differences in second language rate and attainment. In S. Krashen, R. Scracella, & M. Long (Eds.), *Child–adult differences in second language acquisition* (202–226). Rowley, MA: Newbury House.

Lefrancois, G. R. (1989). *Of children: An introduction to child development.* Belmont, CA: Wadsworth.

Lenneberg, E. H. (1967). *Biological foundations of language.* New York: Wiley.

Lerner, R. M. (1984). *On the nature of human plasticity.* New York: Cambridge University Press.

Lord, C. G. (1980). Schemas and images as memory aids: Two modes of processing social information. *Journal of Personality and Social Psychology, 38,* 257–269.

McCall, R. B. (1981). Nature–nurture and the two realms of development: A proposed integration with respect to mental development. *Child Development, 52,* 1–12.

Miller, P. H. (1985). Metacognition and attention. In D. L. Forrest-Pressley, G. E. MacKinnon, & T. G. Waller (Eds.), *Metacognition, cognition, and human performance* (Vol. 2, pp. 181–221). San Diego, CA: Academic Press.

Montagu, A. (1989). *Growing young* (2nd Ed.). Grandy, MA: Bergin & Garvey.

Mood, D. W. (1979). Sentence comprehension in preschool children: Testing an adaptive egocentrism hypothesis. *Child Development, 50,* 247–250.

Nadelman, L. (1974). Sex identity in American children: Memory, knowledge, and preference tests. *Developmental Psychology, 10,* 413–417.

Newport, E. L. (1990). Maturational constraints on language learning. *Cognitive Science, 14,* 11–28.

Oppenheim, R. W. (1981). Ontogenetic adaptations and retrogressive processes in the development of the nervous system and behavior. In K. J. Connolly & H. F. R. Prechtl (Eds.), *Maturation and development: Biological and psychological perspectives* (pp. 73–108). Philadelphia: International Medical Publications.

Opwis, K., Gold, A., Gruber, H., & Schneider, W. (1990). Zum Einfluss von Expertise auf Gedachtnisleistungen und ihre Selsteinschätzung bei Kindern und Erwachsesen [The impact of expertise on memory performance and performance prediction in children and adults]. *Zeitschrift für Entwicklungspsychologie und Pädagogische Psychologie, 21,* 207–224.

Piaget, J. (1955). *The language and thought of the child.* New York: World.

Piaget, J. (1962). *Play, dreams, and imitation in childhood.* New York: Norton.

Piaget, J., & Inhelder, B. (1967). *The child's conception of space.* New York: Norton.

Poirier, F. E., & Smith, E. O. (1974). Socializing functions of primate play. *American Zoologist, 14,* 275–287.

Pratkanis, A. R., & Greenwald, A. B. (1985). How shall the self be conceived? *Journal for the Theory of Social Behavior, 15,* 311–328.

Rosansky, E. (1975). The critical period for the acquisition of language: Some cognitive developmental considerations. *Working Papers on Bilingualism, 6,* 10–23.

Roth, C. (1983). Factors affecting developmental changes in the speed of processing. *Journal of Experimental Child Psychology, 35,* 509–528.

Rubin, K. H., Watson, K. S., & Jambor, T. W. (1978). Free-play behaviors in preschool and kindergarten children. *Child Development, 49,* 534–536.

Schneider, W. (1985). Developmental trends in the metamemory–memory behavior relationship: An integrative review. In D. L. Forrest-Pressley, G. E. MacKinnon, & T. G. Waller (Eds.), *Cognition, metacognition, and human performance* (Vol. 1, pp. 57–109). San Diego, CA: Academic Press.

Schneider, W. (1988, March). *Conceptual and methodological problems in doing self-report research.* Paper presented at the annual meetings of the American Educational Research Association, New Orleans, LA.

Schneider, W. (1991, April). *Performance prediction in young children: Effects of skill, metacognition, and wishful thinking.* Paper presented at meeting of the Society for Research in Child Development, Seattle, WA.

Schneider, W., Körkel, J., & Weinert, F. E. (1987). The effects of intelligence, self-concept, and attributional style on metamemory and memory behaviour. *International Journal of Behavioral Development, 10,* 281–299.

Schneider, W., & Pressley, M. (1989). *Memory development between 2 and 20.* New York: Springer-Verlag.

Scott, J. P. (1968). *Early experience and the organization of behavior.* Monterey, CA: Brooks/Cole.

Shaffer, D. R. (1989). *Developmental psychology: Childhood and adolescence* (2nd ed.). Pacific Grove, CA: Brooks/Cole.

Siegler, R. S. (1988). Individual differences in strategy choices: Good students, not-so-good students, and perfectionists. *Child Development, 59,* 833–851.

Siegler, R. S. (1990). How content knowledge, strategies, and individual differences interact to produce strategy choice. In W. Schneider & F. E. Weinert (Eds.), *Interactions among aptitudes, strategies, and knowledge in cognitive performance* (pp. 74–89). New York: Springer-Verlag.

Sigel, I. E. (1987). Does hothousing rob children of their childhood? *Early Childhood Research Quarterly, 2,* 211–225.

Skeels, H. M. (1966). Adult status of children with contrasting early life experiences. *Monograph of the Society for Research in Child Development, 31* (Serial No. 105).

Stipek, D. (1981). Children's perceptions of their own and their classmates' ability. *Journal of Experimental Child Psychology, 73,* 404–410.

Stipek, D. (1984). Young children's performance expectations: Logical analysis or wishful thinking? In J. G. Nicholls (Ed.), *Advances in motivation and achievement: Vol. 3. The development of achievement motivation* (pp. 33–56). Greenwich, CT: JAI Press.

Stipek, D., & Hoffman, J. (1980). Development of children's performance-related judgments. *Child Development, 51,* 912–914.

Stipek, D., & Mac Iver, D. (1989). Developmental change in children's assessment of intellectual competence. *Child Development, 60,* 521–538.

Stipek, D., Roberts, T., & Sanborn, M. (1984). Preschool-age children's performance expectations for themselves and another child as a function of the incentive value of success and the salience of past performance. *Child Development, 55,* 1983–1989.

Thompson, J. R., & Chapman, R. S. (1977). Who is "Daddy" revisited? The status of two-year-olds' overextended words in use and comprehension. *Journal of Child Language, 4,* 359–375.

Turkewitz, G., & Kenny, P. (1982). Limitations on input as a basis for neural organization and perceptual development: A preliminary theoretical statement. *Developmental Psychobiology, 15,* 357–368.

Uphoff, J., Gilmore, J., & Huber, R. (1986). *Summer children: Ready or not for school.* Middletown, OH: J & J Publishing.

Vandenberg, B. (1981). Play: Dormant issues and new perspectives. *Human Development, 24,* 357–365.

Washburn, S., & Hamburg, D. (1965). The implications of primate research. In I. Devore (Ed.), *Primate behavior: Field studies of monkeys and apes* (pp. 607–623). New York: Hold, Rinehart & Winston.

Whitehurst, G. J., & Sonnenschein, S. (1985). The development of communication: A functional analysis. In G. J. Whitehurst (Ed.), *Annals of child development* (Vol. 2, pp. 1–48). Greenwich, CT: JAI Press.

Winn, M. (1983). *Children without childhood.* New York: Penguin.

Witelson, S. F. (1987). Neurobiological aspects of language in children. *Child Development, 58,* 653–688.

Yussen, S., & Levy, V. (1975). Developmental changes in predicting one's own span of short-term memory. *Journal of Experimental Child Psychology, 19,* 502–508.

Zigler, E. (1987). Formal schooling for 4-year-olds? No. In S. L. Kagan & E. Zigler (Eds.), *Early schooling: The national debate.* New Haven, CT: Yale University Press.

Understanding Bilingual/Bicultural Young Children

Lourdes Diaz Soto

Dr. Lourdes Diaz Soto is Assistant Professor of Early Childhood Education at The Pennsylvania State University. A former preschool teacher, she studies the learning environments of culturally and linguistically diverse young children.

E arly childhood educators have long created exciting and enriching environments for young children but may find an additional challenge when attempting to meet the needs of bilingual/bicultural learners. Teachers currently working with young linguistically and culturally diverse children have asked questions such as: "I feel confident with the art, music and movement activities I have implemented, but how can I best address the needs of speakers of other languages? Are there specific educational strategies that I should incorporate to enhance second language learning? What practical applications can I gain from the research evidence examining second language learning and successful instructional approaches in bilingual early childhood education?"

This review examines:

● demographic and educational trends pointing to the growing numbers of

More and more bilingual/bicultural children are appearing in early childhood classrooms across the country.

bilingual/bicultural young children in America today

● misconceptions about young children learning a second language

● successful educational approaches in early childhood bilingual education

● practical applications of existing research which can be readily implemented by early childhood educators.

Demographic and educational trends

Although the reliability of statistics over the past nine years describing the size and characteristics of the non-English language background (NELB) population has been questioned (Wong Fillmore, in press), it is clear from existing data and projections that language minority students comprise an increasing proportion of our youngest learners. The number of NELB children

aged birth to 4 years old rose steadily from 1.8 million (1976) to a projected 2.6 million in 1990, while the number of children aged 5 to 14 are projected to rise from 3.6 million to 5.1 million in the year 2000 (Oxford, 1984). Additional evidence points to "minority" enrollments, which include culturally diverse learners, ranging from 70 percent to 96 percent in the nation's 15 largest school districts (Hodgkinson, 1985).

Immigrant children from diverse, developing nations such as Haiti, Vietnam, Cambodia, El Salvador, Guatemala, Honduras, and Laos are entering classrooms which are usually unprepared to receive them. La Fontaine (1987) estimates that two-thirds of school-age, language-minority children may not be receiving the language assistance needed to succeed in school. This situation is bound to intensify with the projected increases in total school-age population of language-

From *Young Children,* January 1991, pp. 30-36. © 1991 by the National Association for the Education of Young Children. Reprinted by permission.

minority students, ranging from 35 percent to 40 percent by the year 2000 (Oxford, 1984). Existing demographic data provides evidence that meeting the educational needs of bilingual/bicultural young children is an important mandate for our schools.

The field of Bilingual Early Childhood Education has evolved from two educational domains, contributing to differing philosophies and practices. The elementary domain has, with some exceptions, largely emphasized formal language learning instruction; while the early childhood domain has emphasized a variety of approaches including natural language acquisition. Based upon existing bilingual research and what we know about how young children develop, a supportive, natural, language-rich environment, affording acceptance and meaningful interactions, appears optimal.

Early childhood educators are faced with a recurrent challenge, however, when programs earmarked for speakers of other languages are continually viewed as compensatory, or incorporate deficit philosophies. The practice of many instructional programs has been to develop English proficiency at the expense of the native language. The latter approach is called "subtractive" (Lambert, 1975) because the language learning process substitutes one language for another. This form of "bilingual education" may be a misnomer, since it continues to foster monolingualism (Snow & Hakuta, 1987).

Language learning and cultural enhancement need to be viewed as a resource, and not as a deficiency. Garcia (1986) has suggested that early childhood bilingualism includes the following characteristics:

• the child is able to comprehend and produce linguistic aspects of two languages
• the child is exposed naturally to two systems of language as used in the form of social interaction during early childhood
• both languages are developed at the same time.

Garcia (1983) notes that definitions of early childhood bilingualism must consider linguistic diversity, as well as social and cognitive parameters. Teachers of young children need a broad educational framework because a child's social, mental, and emotional worlds are an integral part of language learning.

Simplistic categorizations of bilin-

gual children are not appropriate, since a variety of dimensions and possibilities exist for individual learners. Both experienced and novice bilingual/bicultural educators have noted differing educational terminology, reflecting the political mood of the nation. The table on page 32 illustrates the variety of terms in use. For example, the term "limited English proficient" (LEP) often cited in the literature points to a child's limitation rather than strength. The definitions proposed by Snow (1987) provide both clarity and recency, and are presented in the table in an attempt to show the range of concepts related to second language education. Casanova (1990) introduced the term "speakers of other languages" (SOL), helping to portray a positive attribute. The addition of the term "speakers of other languages" seems especially useful because there is ample documentation of the existence of both bilingual and multilingual young children in our schools.

Educators need to think in terms of "additive" (Lambert, 1975) bilingualism by incorporating practices which will enhance, enrich, and optimize educational opportunities for second language learners. Minimum standards and compensatory approaches are likely to sustain the existing educational difficulties faced by second language learners, speakers of other languages (SOL), and monolingual (EO) learners currently being deprived of a second language.

Misconceptions about young learners

A variety of misconceptions about second language acquisition and young learners exists (McLaughlin, 1984). **One misconception is that young children acquire language more easily than adults.** This idea was borne of the assumption that children are biologically programmed to acquire languages.

Although we know that early, simultaneous bilingualism will not harm young children's language development, and that they are capable of acquiring a second language without explicit instructions, it is a myth to think that children find the process "painless" (Hakuta, 1986).

Experimental research comparing young children and adults in second language learning has consistently indicated poorer performance by young children, except in pronunciation. Factors leading to the impression that young children acquire languages more easily are that children have fewer inhibitions, and greater frequency of social interactions (McLaughlin, 1984).

A second, related misconception states that the younger the child, the more quickly a second language is acquired. There is no evidence of a critical period for second language learning with the possible exception of accent (Hakuta, 1986). Studies reported by Krashen, Long, and Scarcella (1979), which examine rate of second language acquisition, favor adults. In addition,

---

Table. **Explanation of Terms Used in Second Language Education**

Linguistic minority student	*speaks the language of a minority group, e.g., Vietnamese*
Linguistic majority student	*speaks language of the majority group, i.e., English in the U.S.*
Limited English proficient	*any language background (LEP) student who has limited speaking skills in English as a second language*
Non-English proficient (NEP)	*has no previous experience learning English; speaks only the home language*
English Only (EO)	*is monolingual English speaker*
Fluent English proficient	*speaks both English and another language at home. This student speaks English fluently, e.g., ethnically diverse student born in the U.S., who speaks a second language at home.*

(Adapted from Snow, 1987)

adolescent learners acquire a second language faster than younger learners. Young children who receive natural exposure to a second language, however, are likely to eventually achieve higher levels of second language proficiency than adults.

It may be that "threshold levels" (Cummins, 1977; Skutnabb-Kangas, 1977) of native language proficiency are needed by young language minority learners in order to reap the benefits of

It is not true that young children learn a new language more quickly and easily than adults.

becoming bilingual. Young children, as a rule, will eventually catch up to, and surpass, most adults, but we need to provide them with a necessary gift of time.

A third misconception is that there is a single path to acquiring a second language in childhood. Wong Fillmore's (1976, 1985, 1986) research emphasizes the complex relationship among individual differences in young second language learners. Wong Fillmore (1985) suggests that three interconnected processes, including the social, linguistic, and cognitive domains, are responsible for variability in language learning. Learner characteristics contribute substantially to differential second language learning in children, but the relationship between learner characteristics and outcomes is not simple. No one characteristic can determine language learning (e.g., gregariousness) because variables such as situations, input, and interactions are also important (Wong Fillmore, 1986).

The research viewing individual differences points to the fact that young learners' second language acquisition abilities vary a great deal and are dependent upon social situations. Teachers of young children need to be cognizant of these variabilities by becoming keen observers of existing knowledge and abilities (Genishi, 1989). The assessment of language is a complex endeavor, and informal observations and teacher documentation can be extremely valuable tools. Readers are referred to Genishi and Dyson (1984) for a practical and sensitive review of how to assess progress in second language acquisition.

The second language learning process cannot be isolated from the young child's cultural learning. Ethnographic studies examining linguistically and culturally diverse children have found that classroom patterns also need to be culturally responsive, since differing approaches may work well with diverse children. For instance, Phillips (1972) found that Native American children were more willing to participate in group speaking activities than non-Native American children. Also, Au and Jordan (1981) found that reading and test scores improved when teachers incorporated narrative speech patterns such as talk story and overlapping speech into classroom routines with native Hawaiian children. Young children need to develop a positive and confident sense of biculturalism.

A great deal of trial and error takes place when a young child acquires a second language (McLaughlin, 1984). Learning to walk may serve as an example of another skill where exploration and experimentation are necessary. Young children progress at their own rate and persist until the skill is mastered. An accepting attitude is necessary during the trial and error phases of language acquisition. Rigid instructional practices emphasizing grammar construction are not appropriate because they can confuse and interfere with the natural developmental progression of second language acquisition (Felix, 1978, Lightbrown, 1977). The developmentally appropriate instructional practices advocated by NAEYC (Bredekamp, 1987) apply to second language learners as well. Young bilingual/bicultural children experience the same developmental progressions, with additional challenges involving second language/cultural learning.

Successful instructional approaches

In the United States, bilingual education is typically defined as an educational program for language minority students, in which instruction is provided in the child's primary language while the child acquires sufficient English skills to function academically. As noted earlier, an *additive* approach focuses on enrichment by the addition of a second language while supporting the native language, and a *subtractive* approach teaches a second language as a replacement, often at the expense of the native language. Programs that offer no aid to students learning a second language are referred to as "sink or swim" or "submersion" efforts (Snow, 1987). While it is beyond the scope of this paper to examine the pervasive "English Only" attitudes in our nation today, it should be noted that bilingual instruction is controversial, and that the sociopolitical climate has often prompted the needs of young bilingual/bicultural children to be overlooked. It is also often the case that programs purporting to include bilingual approaches, in truth, emphasize English only, and a "sink or swim" approach.

Nevertheless, three bilingual education approaches are prevalent for preschoolers and early elementary school students (Ovando & Collier, 1985). The **transitional** approach is widespread and emphasizes the rapid development of English language skills, so the student can participate in the mainstreamed setting as soon as possible. Native language instruction is used initially but the major focus is generally to quickly transfer the learner to the mainstreamed setting. We need to look carefully at these programs in light of Cummins' (1979, 1984, 1985) research, emphasizing the need for learners to obtain optimal levels of native language proficiency.

The **maintenance/developmental** approach emphasizes the development of language skills in the home language, with an additional goal of English mastery. This strategy enhances the child's native language and allows learners to gain concepts in the native language while introducing English as a Second Language (ESL). Children are usually served by additional "pull out" English as a Second Language (ESL) instruction from teachers trained in ESL methods.

The **two-way** bilingual approach serves both the language majority and the language minority, expecting both groups of learners to become bilingual, and to experience academic success. An advantage of the two-way bilingual approach is that children are afforded an opportunity to participate in culturally and linguistically diverse intergroup relations. Recent research points to long-term attitudinal effects from this newly emerging bilingual approach (Collier, 1989).

The role of Head Start in Bilingual Early Childhood Education needs to be acknowledged in light of exemplary service for over 25 years (U.S. Department of Health and Human Services, 1990). Soledad Arenas (1980) describes a bilingual early childhood Head Start effort initiated by Administration for Children, Youth and Families (ACYF). Four contracts were awarded throughout the nation, including: Un Marco Abierto at the High/Scope Center in Ypsilanti, Michigan; Nuevas Fronteras de Aprendizaje at the University of California; Alerta at Columbia University; and Amanecer in San Antonio, Texas. Each program differed considerably, but was based upon an additive philosophy, and serviced Spanish-speaking Head Start children. The evaluation conducted by Juarez and Associates (1980), viewing the impact of the programs over a three-and-a-half year period, found the bilingual preschool curricula to be effective for both Spanish and English preferring young children. In addition, the evaluation concluded that parent and teacher attitudes were favorable, that models can be implemented in differing geographical locations, and that dual language strategies were most related to positive child outcomes.

An important and thorough review of bilingual education research involving 23 different programs found that preschool, elementary, and middle school children who were enrolled in the bilingual programs reviewed, outperformed children on a variety of standardized measures in nonbilingual programs, regardless of the language used for testing (Willig, 1985). Also, research examining bilingualism and cognitive competence favors the attainment of higher levels of bilingual proficiency (Barrik & Swain, 1974; Cummins & Gulutson, 1974; Cummins & Mulcahy, 1976; Duncan & De Avila, 1979; Lessler & Quinn, 1982; Peal & Lambert, 1962; Skutnabb-Kangas, 1977; Hakuta, 1986). Advanced bilingualism has been found to be associated with cognitive flexibility and divergent thinking (Hakuta, 1986). These are powerful findings in an era when the usefulness of bilingual approaches continues to be questioned.

It has been suggested that successful programs progress from native language instruction to initial second language learning, to a stage of enrichment and eventually a return to the native language instruction via the incorporation of literature and social studies, in order to incorporate a healthy sense of biculturalism (Krashen & Biber, 1988). The three components of successful programs serving limited English proficient children reviewed by Krashen and Biber include:

● high-quality subject matter instruction in the native language without concurrent translation

● development of literacy in the native language

● comprehensible input in English

The Carpinteria Preschool Program (Keatinge, 1984; Krashen & Biber, 1988) is particularly interesting because of the emphasis on native language instruction. The children in this program received instruction in Spanish, yet outperformed comparison learners on a test of conversational English (Bilingual Syntax Measure), and exceeded published norms on tests of school readiness (School Readiness Inventory), and academic achievement (California Achievement Test). This particular program supports Cummins' (1984) contention that learners need to obtain a "threshold level" or optimal level of native language proficiency. It appears that native language instruction actually gave students an advantage in their acquisition of a second language.

What can we conclude from this discussion? In an attempt to summarize selected research findings regarding second language acquisition and successful approaches to bilingual education, a list of practical classroom applications is proposed.

Practical applications for teachers of young children

As a caretaker in a decision-making capacity, the early childhood educator plays a critical role in the lives of linguistically and culturally diverse young children. The early childhood setting becomes a home away from home, the first contact with non-family members, the first contact with culturally different people, and the first experience with non-native speakers. A teacher's attitude and knowledge base is crucial in setting the educational goals of acceptance and appreciation of diversity (Ramsey, 1987). The possibilities are endless for teachers of young children who, as role models, are in a unique position to establish the tone, or "classroom climate," through decision making, collaboration, interactions, and activities.

Teachers of young children are currently implementing a variety of educationally sound strategies. In addition, based upon the recent research, and what we know about young children, we can:

1. Accept individual differences with regard to language-learning time frames. It's a myth to think that young children can learn a language quickly and easily. Avoid pressures to "rush" and "push out" children to join the mainstream classrooms. Young children need time to acquire, explore, and experience second language learning.

2. Accept children's attempts to communicate, because trial and error are a part of the second language learning process. Negotiating meaning, and collaboration in conversations, is important. Children should be given opportunities to practice both native and newly established language skills. Adults should not dominate the conversations; rather, children should be listened to. Plan and incorporate opportunities for conversation such as dramatic play, storytime, puppetry, peer interactions, social experiences, field trips, cooking and other enriching activities.

3. Maintain an additive philosophy by recognizing that children need to acquire new language skills instead of replacing existing linguistic skills. Afford young children an opportunity to retain their native language and culture. Allow young learners ample social opportunities.

4. Provide a stimulating, active, diverse linguistic environment with many opportunities for language use in meaningful social interactions. Avoid rigid or didactic grammatical approaches with young children. Children enjoy informal play experiences, dramatizations, puppetry, telephone conversations, participation in children's literature, and social interactions with peers.

5. Incorporate culturally responsive experiences for all children. Valuing each child's home culture and incorporating meaningful/active participation will enhance interpersonal skills, and contribute to academic and social success.

6. Use informal observations to guide the planning of activities, interactions, and conversations for speakers of other languages.

7. Provide an **accepting** classroom climate that values culturally and linguistically diverse young children. We know that young children are part of today's natural resources, capable of contributing to tomorrow's multicultural/multilingual society.

References

Arenas, S. (1980, May/June). Innovations in bilingual/multicultural curriculum development. *Children Today.* Washington, DC: U.S. Government Printing Office No. 80–31161.

Au, K., & Jordan, C. (1981). Teaching reading to Hawaiian children: Finding a culturally appropriate solution. In H. T. Trueba & G. P. Guthrie (Eds.), *Culture and the bilingual classroom: Studies in classroom ethnography.* Cambridge, MA: Newbury House.

Baker, C. (1988). *Key issues in bilingualism and bilingual education.* Clevedon, Avon, England: Multilingual Matters, Ltd.

Barrik, H., & Swain M. (1974). English-French bilingual education in the early grades: The Elgin study. *Modern Language Journal, 58,* 392–403.

Bredekamp, S. (1987). (Ed.). *Developmentally appropriate practice in early childhood programs serving children from birth through age 8.* Washington, DC: NAEYC.

Casanova, U. (1990). *Shifts in bilingual education policy and the knowledge base.* Tuscon, AZ: Research Symposia of the National Association of Bilingual Educators.

Dulay, H., & Burt, M. (1974). Natural sequences in child second language acquisition. *Language Learning, 24,* 37–53.

Duncan, S. E., & DeAvila, E. (1979). Bilingualism and cognition: Some recent findings. *NABE Journal, 4,* 15–50.

Escobedo, T. (1983). *Early childhood bilingual education. A Hispanic perspective.* New York: Teachers College Press, Columbia University.

Felix, S. W. (1978). Some differences between first and second language acquisition. In C. Waterson & C. Snow (Eds.), *The development of communication.* New York: Wiley.

Garcia, E. (1983). *Early childhood bilingualism.* Albuquerque: University of New Mexico.

Garcia, E. (1986). Bilingual development and the education of bilingual children during early childhood. *American Journal of Education, 11,* 96–121.

Collier, V. (1989). Academic achievement, attitudes, and occupation among graduates of two-way bilingual classes. Paper presented at the American Educational Research Association, San Francisco, California.

Contreras, R. (1988). *Bilingual education.* Bloomington, IN: Phi Delta Kappa.

Cook, V. J. (1973). The comparison of language development in native children and foreign adults. *International Review of Applied Linguistics in Language Teaching, 11,* 13–29.

Cummins, J. (1977). Cognitive factors associated with intermediate levels of bilingual skills. *Modern Language Journal, 61,* 3–12.

Cummins, J. (1979). Linguistic interdependence and the educational development of bilingual children. *Review of Educational Research, 49*(2), 222–251.

Cummins, J. (1984). *Bilingualism and special education: Issues in assessment and pedagogy.* Clevedon, Avon, England: Multilingual Matters, Ltd.

Cummins, J. (1985). The construct of language proficiency in bilingual education. In James Alatis & John Staczek (Eds.), *Perspectives on bilingualism and bilingual education* (pp. 209–231). Washington, DC: Georgetown University.

Cummins, J., & Gulutson, M. (1974). Some effects of bilingualism on cognitive functioning. In S. Carey (Ed.), *Bilingualism, biculturalism and education.* Edmonton: University of Alberta.

Cummins, J., & Mulcahy, R. (1978). Orientation to language in Ukrainian-English bilingual children. *Child Development, 49,* 1239–1242.

Genishi, C. (1984). *Language assessment in the early years.* Norwood, NJ: Ablex.

Genishi, C. (1989). Observing the second language learner: An example of teachers' learning. *Language Arts, 66*(5), 509–515.

Hakuta, K. (1986). *Mirror of language. The debate of bilingualism.* New York: Basic.

Hodgkinson, H. (1985). *All one system: Demographics of education, kindergarten through graduate school.* Washington, DC: Institute for Educational Leadership, Inc.

Juarez & Associates (1980). Final report of an evaluation of the Head Start bilingual/bicultural curriculum models. Washington, DC: U.S. Department of Health and Human Services. No. 105–77–1048.

Keatinge, R. H. (1984). An assessment of the pinteria preschool Spanish immersion program. *Teacher Education Quarterly, 11,* 80–94.

Kessler, C., & Quinn, M. (1982). Cognitive development on bilingual environments. In B. Hartford, A. Valdman, & C. Foster (Eds.), *Issues in international bilingual education.* New York: Plenum.

Krashen, S., & Biber, D. (1988). *On course: Bilingual education's success in California.* Sacramento: California Association for Bilingual Education.

La Fontaine, H. (1987). *At-risk children and youth—The extra educational challenges of limited English-proficient students.* Washington, DC: Summer Institute of the Council of Chief State School Officers.

Lightbron, P. (1977). French second language learners: What they're talking about. *Language Learning, 27,* 371–381.

McLaughlin, B. (1984). *Second-language acquisition on childhood: Volume 1: Preschool children.* Hillsdale, NJ: Erlbaum.

Ovando, C., & Collier, V. (1985). *Bilingual and ESL classrooms.* New York: McGraw-Hill.

Oxford, C., et al. (1984). Demographic projections of non-English background and limited English-proficient persons in the United States in the year 2000. Rosslyn, VA: InterAmerica Research Associates.

Peal, E., & Lambert, W. (1962). The revelations of bilingualism to intelligence. *Psychological Monographs, 76*(27), 1–23.

Phillips, S. (1972). Participation structures and communicative competence: Warm Springs children in community and classroom. In C. Cazden, V. John, & D. Hymes, (Eds.), *Functions of language in the classroom.* New York: Teachers College, Columbia University.

Ramsey, P. (1987). *Teaching and learning in a diverse world.* New York: Teachers College Press, Columbia University.

Skutnabb-Kangas, T. (1977). *Bilingualism or not: The education of minorities.* Clevedon, Avon, England: Multilingual Matters, Ltd.

Sleeter, C., & Grant, C. (1987). An analysis of multicultural education in the United States. *Harvard Educational Review, 57*(4), 421–444.

Snow, M. (1987). *Common terms in second language education: Center for Language Education and Research.* Los Angeles: University of California.

Snow, C., & Hakuta, K. (1987). *The costs of monolingualism.* Unpublished monograph, Cambridge, MA: Harvard University.

Soto, L. D. (in press). Alternate research paradigms in bilingual education research. In R. Padilla and A. Benavides (Eds.), *Critical perspectives on bilingual education research.* Phoenix: Bilingual Review/Press.

Soto, L. D. (in press). Success stories. In C. Grant (Ed.), *Research directions for multicultural education.* Bristol, PA: Falmer Press.

Swain, M. (1987). Bilingual education: Research and its implications. In M. Long and J. Richards (Eds.), *Methodology in TESOL.* Cambridge, MA: Newbury House.

U.S. Department of Health and Human Services. (1990). Head Start: A child development program. Washington, DC: Office of Human Development Services, Administration for Children, Youth and Families.

Willig, A. (1985). A meta-analysis of selected studies on the effectiveness of bilingual education. *Review of Educational Research, 55*(3), 269–317.

Wong Fillmore, L. (1976). *The second time around: Cognitive and social strategies.* Unpublished doctoral dissertation, Stanford University, Stanford, CA.

Wong Fillmore, L. (1985). *Second language learning in children: A proposed model.* Proceedings of a conference on issues in English language development, Arlington, VA. ERIC Document 273149.

Wong Fillmore, L. (in press). Language and cultural issues in early education. In S. Kagan (Ed.), *The care and education of America's young children: Obstacles and opportunities.* The 90th yearbook of the National Society for the Study of Education.

Wong Fillmore, L., & Valadez, C. (1986). **Teaching bilingual learners. In M. Wittrock (Ed.),** *Handbook of research on teaching.* New York: Macmillan.

LIFE IN OVERDRIVE

Doctors say huge numbers of kids and adults have attention deficit disorder. Is it for real?

CLAUDIA WALLIS

USTY NASH, AN ANGELIC-looking blond child of seven, awoke at 5 one recent morning in his Chicago home and proceeded to throw a fit. He wailed. He kicked. Every muscle in his 50-lb. body flew in furious motion. Finally, after about 30 minutes, Dusty pulled himself together sufficiently to head downstairs for breakfast. While his mother bustled about the kitchen, the hyperkinetic child pulled a box of Kix cereal from the cupboard and sat on a chair.

But sitting still was not in the cards this morning. After grabbing some cereal with his hands, he began kicking the box, scattering little round corn puffs across the room. Next he turned his attention to the TV set, or rather, the table supporting it. The table was covered with a checkerboard Con-Tact paper, and Dusty began peeling it off. Then he became intrigued with the spilled cereal and started stomping it to bits. At this point his mother interceded. In a firm but calm voice she told her son to get the stand-up dust pan and broom and clean up the mess. Dusty got out the dust pan but forgot the rest of the order. Within seconds he was dismantling the plastic dust pan, piece by piece. His next project: grabbing three rolls of toilet paper from the bathroom and unraveling them around the house.

It was only 7:30, and his mother Kyle Nash, who teaches a medical-school course on death and dying, was already feeling half dead from exhaustion. Dusty was to see his doctors that day at 4, and they had asked her not to give the boy the drug he usually takes to control his hyperactivity and attention problems, a condition known as attention deficit hyperactivity disorder (ADHD). It was going to be a very long day without help from Ritalin.

Karenne Bloomgarden remembers such days all too well. The peppy, 43-year-old entrepreneur and gym teacher was a disaster as a child growing up in New Jersey. "I did very poorly in school," she recalls. Her teachers and parents were constantly on her case for rowdy behavior. "They just felt I was being bad—too loud, too physical, too everything." A rebellious tomboy with few friends, she saw a psychologist at age 10, "but nobody came up with a diagnosis." As a teenager she began prescribing her own medication: marijuana, Valium and, later, cocaine.

The athletic Bloomgarden managed to get into college, but she admits that she cheated her way to a diploma. "I would study and study, and I wouldn't remember a thing. I really felt it was my fault." After graduating, she did fine in physically active jobs but was flustered with administrative work. Then, four years ago, a doctor put a label on her troubles: ADHD. "It's been such a weight off my shoulders," says Bloomgarden, who takes both the stimulant Ritalin and the antidepressant Zoloft to improve her concentration. "I had 38 years of thinking I was a bad person. Now I'm rewriting the tapes of who I thought I was to who I really am."

Fifteen years ago, no one had ever heard of attention deficit hyperactivity disorder. Today it is the most common behavioral disorder in American children, the subject of thousands of studies and symposiums and no small degree of controversy. Experts on ADHD say it afflicts as many as 3½ million American youngsters, or up to 5% of those under 18. It is two to three times as likely to be diagnosed in boys as in girls. The disorder has replaced what used to be popularly called "hyperactivity," and it includes a broader collection of symptoms. ADHD has three main hallmarks: extreme distractibility, an almost reckless impulsiveness and, in some but not all cases, a knee-jiggling, toe-tapping hyperactivity that makes sitting still all but impossible. (Without hyperactivity, the disorder is called attention deficit disorder, or ADD.)

For children with ADHD, a ticking clock or sounds and sights caught through a window can drown out a teacher's voice, although an intriguing project can absorb them for hours. Such children act before thinking; they blurt out answers in class. They enrage peers with an inability to wait their turn or play by the rules. These are the kids no one wants at a birthday party.

Ten years ago, doctors believed that the symptoms of ADHD faded with maturity. Now it is one of the fastest-growing diagnostic categories for adults. One-third to

Many adults respond to the diagnosis with relief—a sense that "at last my problem has a name and it's not my fault."

two-thirds of ADHD kids continue to have symptoms as adults, says psychiatrist Paul Wender, director of the adult ADHD clinic at the University of Utah School of Medicine. Many adults respond to the diagnosis with relief—a sense that "at last my problem has a name and it's not my fault." As more people are diagnosed, the use of Ritalin (or its generic equivalent, methylphenidate), the drug of choice for ADHD, has surged: prescriptions are up more than 390% in just four years.

As the numbers have grown, ADHD awareness has become an industry, a passion, an almost messianic movement. An advocacy and support group called CHADD (Children and Adults with Attention Deficit Disorders) has exploded from its founding in 1987 to 28,000 members in 48 states. Information bulletin boards and support groups for adults have sprung up on CompuServe, Prodigy and America Online. Numerous popular books have been published on the subject. There are summer camps designed to help ADHD kids, videos and children's books with titles like *Jumpin' Johnny Get Back to Work!* and, of course, therapists, tutors and workshops offering their services to the increasingly self-aware ADHD community.

I T IS A COMMUNITY THAT VIEWS ITSELF with some pride. Popular books and lectures about ADHD often point out positive aspects of the condition. Adults see themselves as creative; their impulsiveness can be viewed as spontaneity; hyperactivity gives them enormous energy and drive; even their distractibility has the virtue of making them alert to changes in the environment. "Kids with ADHD are wild, funny, effervescent. They have a love of life. The rest of us sometimes envy them," says psychologist Russell Barkley of the University of Massachusetts Medical Center. "ADHD adults," he notes, "can be incredibly successful. Sometimes being impulsive means being decisive." Many ADHD adults gravitate into creative fields or work that provides an outlet for emotions, says Barkley. "In our clinic we saw an adult poet who couldn't write poetry when she was on Ritalin. ADHD people make good salespeople. They're lousy at desk jobs."

In an attempt to promote the positive side of ADHD, some CHADD chapters circulate lists of illustrious figures who, they contend, probably suffered from the disorder: the messy and disorganized Ben Franklin, the wildly impulsive and distractible Winston Churchill. For reasons that are less clear, these lists also include folks like Socrates, Isaac Newton, Leonardo da Vinci—almost any genius of note. (At least two doctors interviewed for this story suggested that the sometimes scattered Bill Clinton belongs on the list.)

However creative they may be, people with ADHD don't function particularly well in standard schools and typical office jobs. Increasingly, parents and lobby groups are demanding that accommodations be made. About half the kids diagnosed with ADHD receive help from special-education teachers in their schools, in some cases because they also have other learning disabilities. Where schools have failed to provide services, parents have sometimes sued. In one notable case that went to the U.S. Supreme Court last year, parents argued—successfully—that since the public school denied their child special education, the district must pay for her to attend private school. Another accommodation requested with increasing frequency: permission to take college-entrance exams without a time limit. Part of what motivates parents to fight for special services is frightening research showing that without proper care, kids with ADHD have an extremely high risk not only of failing at school but also of becoming drug abusers, alcoholics and lawbreakers.

Adults with ADHD are beginning to seek special treatment. Under the 1990 Americans with Disabilities Act, they can insist upon help in the workplace. Usually the interventions are quite modest: an office door or white-noise machine to reduce distractions, or longer deadlines on assignments. Another legal trend that concerns even ADHD advocates: the disorder is being raised as a defense in criminal cases. Psychologist Barkley says he knows of 55 such instances in the U.S., all in the past 10 years. ADHD was cited as a mitigating factor by the attorney for Michael Fay, the 19-year-old American who was charged with vandalism and caned in Singapore.

Many of those who treat ADHD see the recognition of the problem as a humane breakthrough: finally we will stop blaming kids for behavior they cannot control. But some are worried that the disorder is being embraced with too much gusto. "A lot of people are jumping on the bandwagon," complains psychologist Mark Stein, director of a special ADHD clinic at the University of Chicago. "Parents are putting pressure on health professionals to make the diagnosis." The allure of ADHD is that it is "a label of forgiveness," says Robert Reid, an assistant professor in the department of special education at the University of Nebraska in Lincoln. "The kid's problems are not his parents' fault, not the teacher's fault, not the kid's fault. It's better to say this kid has ADHD than to say this kid drives everybody up the wall." For adults, the diagnosis may provide an excuse for personal or professional failures, observes Richard Bromfield, a psychologist at Harvard Medical School. "Some people like to say, 'The biological devil made me do it.'"

A DISORDER WITH A PAST Other than the name itself, there is nothing new about this suddenly ubiquitous disorder. The world has always had its share of obstreperous kids, and it has generally treated them as behavior problems rather than patients. Most of the world still does so: European nations like France and England report one-tenth the U.S. rate of ADHD. In Japan the disorder has barely been studied.

The medical record on ADHD is said to have begun in 1902, when British pediatrician George Still published an account of 20 children in his practice who were "passionate," defiant, spiteful and lacking "inhibitory volition." Still made the then radical suggestion that bad parenting was not to blame; instead he suspected a subtle brain injury. This theory gained greater credence in the years following the 1917-18 epidemic of viral encephalitis, when doctors observed that the infection left some children with impaired attention, memory and control over their impulses. In the 1940s and '50s, the same constellation of symptoms was called minimal brain damage and, later, minimal brain dysfunction. In 1937 a Rhode Island pediatrician reported that

giving stimulants called amphetamines to children with these symptoms had the unexpected effect of calming them down. By the mid-1970s, Ritalin had become the most prescribed drug for what was eventually termed, in 1987, attention deficit hyperactivity disorder.

Nobody fully understands how Ritalin and other stimulants work, nor do doctors have a very precise picture of the physiology of ADHD. Researchers generally suspect a defect in the frontal lobes of the brain, which regulate behavior. This region is rich in the neurotransmitters dopamine and norepinephrine, which are influenced by drugs like Ritalin. But the lack of a more specific explanation has led some psychologists to question whether ADHD is truly a disorder at all or merely a set of characteristics that tend to cluster together. Just because something responds to a drug doesn't mean it is a sickness.

ADHD researchers counter the skeptics by pointing to a growing body of biological clues. For instance, several studies have found that people with ADHD have decreased blood flow and lower levels of electrical activity in the frontal lobes than normal adults and children. In 1990 Dr. Alan Zametkin at the National Institute of Mental Health found that in PET scans, adults with ADD showed slightly lower rates of metabolism in areas of the brain's cortex known to be involved in the control of attention, impulses and motor activity.

Zametkin's study was hailed as the long-awaited proof of the biological basis of ADD, though Zametkin himself is quite cautious. A newer study used another tool—magnetic resonance imaging—to compare the brains of 18 ADHD boys with those of other children and found several "very subtle" but "striking" anatomical differences, says co-author Judith Rapoport, chief of the child psychiatry branch at NIMH. Says Zametkin: "I'm absolutely convinced that this disorder has a biological basis, but just what it is we cannot yet say."

W HAT RESEARCHERS DO say with great certainty is that the condition is inherited. External factors such as birth injuries and maternal alcohol or tobacco consumption may play a role in less than 10% of cases. Suspicions that a diet high in sugar might cause hyperactivity have been discounted. But the influence of genes is unmistakable. Barkley estimates that 40% of adhd kids have a parent who has the trait and 35% have a sibling with the problem; if the sibling is an identical twin, the chances rise to between 80% and 92%.

Interest in the genetics of ADHD is enormous. In Australia a vast trial involving

3,400 pairs of twins between the ages of 4 and 12 is examining the incidence of ADHD and other behavioral difficulties. At NIMH, Zametkin's group is recruiting 200 families who have at least two members with ADHD. The hope: to identify genes for the disorder. It is worth noting, though, that even if such genes are found, this may not settle the debate about ADHD. After all, it is just as likely that researchers will someday discover a gene for a hot temper, which also runs in families. But that doesn't mean that having a short fuse is a disease requiring medical intervention.

TRICKY DIAGNOSIS In the absence of any biological test, diagnosing ADHD is a rather inexact proposition. In most cases, it is a teacher who initiates the process by informing parents that their child is daydreaming in class, failing to complete assignments or driving everyone crazy with thoughtless behavior. "The problem is that the parent then goes to the family doctor, who writes a prescription for Ritalin and doesn't stop to think of the other possibilities," says child psychiatrist Larry Silver of

Is ADD truly a disorder? Just because something responds to a drug doesn't mean it is a sickness.

Georgetown University Medical Center. To make a careful diagnosis, Silver argues, one must eliminate other explanations for the symptoms.

The most common cause, he points out, is anxiety. A child who is worried about a problem at home or some other matter "can look hyperactive and distractible." Depression can also cause ADHD-like behavior. "A third cause is another form of neurological dysfunction, like a learning disorder," says Silver. "The child starts doodling because he didn't understand the teacher's instructions." All this is made more complicated by the fact that some kids—and adults—with ADHD also suffer from depression and other problems. To distinguish these symptoms from ADHD, doctors usually rely on interviews with parents and teachers, behavior-ratings scales and psychological tests, which can cost from $500 to $3,000, depending on the thoroughness of the testing. Insurance coverage is spotty.

Among the most important clues doctors look for is whether the child's problems can be linked to some specific experience or time or whether they have been present almost from birth. "You don't suddenly get ADD," says Wade Horn, a child psychologist and former executive director

of CHADD. Taking a careful history is therefore vital.

For kids who are hyperactive, the pattern is unmistakable, says Dr. Bruce Roseman, a pediatric neurologist with several offices in the New York City area, who has ADHD himself. "You say to the mother, 'What kind of personality did the child have as a baby? Was he active, alert? Was he colicky?' She'll say, 'He wouldn't stop—waaah, waaah, waaah!' You ask, 'When did he start to walk?' One mother said to me, 'Walk? My son didn't walk. He got his pilot's license at one year of age. His feet haven't touched the ground since.' You ask, 'Mrs. Smith, how about the terrible twos?' She'll start to cry, 'You mean the terrible twos, threes, fours, the awful fives, the horrendous sixes, the God-awful eights, the divorced nines, the I-want-to-die tens!' "

Diagnosing those with ADD without hyperactivity can be trickier. Such kids are often described as daydreamers, space cases. They are not disruptive or antsy. But, says Roseman, "they sit in front of a book and for 45 minutes, nothing happens." Many girls with ADD fit this model; they are often misunderstood or overlooked.

Christy Rade, who will be entering the ninth grade in West Des Moines, Iowa, is fairly typical. Before she was diagnosed with ADD in the third grade, Christy's teacher described her to her parents as a "dizzy blond and a space cadet." "Teachers used to get fed up with me," recalls Christy, who now takes Ritalin and gets some extra support from her teachers. "Everyone

thought I was purposely not paying attention." According to her mother Julie Doy, people at Christy's school were familiar with hyperactivity but not ADD. "She didn't have behavior problems. She was the kind of kid who could fall through the cracks, and did."

Most experts say ADHD is a lifelong condition but by late adolescence many people can compensate for their impulsiveness and disorganization. They may channel hyperactivity into sports. In other cases, the symptoms still wreak havoc, says UCLA psychiatrist Walid Shekim. "Patients cannot settle on a career. They cannot keep a job. They procrastinate a lot. They are the kind of people who would tell their boss to take this job and shove it before they've found another job."

Doctors diagnose adults with methods similar to those used with children. Patients are sometimes asked to dig up old report cards for clues to their childhood behavior—an essential indicator. Many adults seek help only after one of their children is diagnosed. Such was the case with Chuck Pearson of Birmingham, Michigan, who was diagnosed three years ago, at 54. Pearson had struggled for decades in what might be the worst possible career for someone with ADD: accounting. In the first 12 years of his marriage, he was fired from 15 jobs. "I was frightened," says Zoe, his wife of 35 years. "We had two small children, a mortgage. Bill collectors were calling perpetually. We almost lost the house." Chuck admits he had trouble focusing on

HAIL TO THE HYPERACTIVE HUNTER

Why is attention deficit hyperactivity disorder so common? Is there an evolutionary reason why these traits are found in as many as 1 in 20 American youngsters? Such questions have prompted intriguing speculation. Harvard psychiatrist John Ratey finds no mystery in the prevalence of ADHD in the U.S. It is a nation of immigrants who, he notes, "risked it all and left their homelands." Characteristics like impulsiveness, high energy and risk taking are therefore highly represented in the U.S. gene pool. "We have more Nobel laureates and more criminals than anywhere else in the world. We have more people who absolutely push the envelope."

But why would ADHD have evolved in the first place? perhaps, like the sickle-cell trait, which can help thwart malaria, attention deficit confers an advantage in certain circumstances. In *Attention Deficit Disorder: A Different Perception,* author Thom Hartmann has laid out a controversial but appealing theory that the characteristics known today as ADHD were vitally important in early hunting societies. They became a mixed blessing only when human societies turned agrarian, Hartmann suggests. "If you are walking in the night and see a little flash, distractibility would be a tremendous asset. Snap decision making, which we call impulsiveness, is a survival skill if you are a hunter." For a farmer, however, such traits can be disastrous. "If this is the perfect day to plant the crops, you can't suddenly decided to wander off into the woods."

Modern society, Hartmann contends, generally favors the farmer mentality, rewarding those who develop plans, meet deadlines and plod through schedules. But there's still a place for hunters, says the author, who counts himself as one: they can be found in large numbers among entrepreneurs, police detectives, emergency-room personnel, race-care drivers and, of course, those who stalk the high-stakes jungle known as Wall Street.

DO YOU HAVE ATTENTION DEFICIT?

If eight or more of the following statements accurately describe your child or yourself as a child, particularly before age 7, there may be reason to suspect ADHD. A definitive diagnosis requires further examination.

1. Often fidgets or squirms in seat.

2. Has difficulty remaining seated.

3. Is easily distracted.

4. Has difficulty awaiting turn in groups.

5. Often blurts out answers to questions.

6. Has difficulty following instructions.

7. Has difficulty sustaining attention to tasks.

8. Often shifts from one

uncompleted activity to another.

9. Has difficulty playing quietly.

10. Often talks excessively.

11. Often interrupts or intrudes on others.

12. Often does not seem to listen.

13. Often loses things necessary for tasks.

14. Often engages in physically dangerous activities without considering consequences.

Source: *The ADHD Rating Scale: Normative Data, Reliability, and Validity*

details, completing tasks and judging how long an assignment would take. He was so distracted behind the wheel that he lost his license for a year after getting 14 traffic tickets. Unwittingly, Pearson began medicating himself: "In my mid-30s, I would drink 30 to 40 cups of coffee a day. The caffeine helped." After he was diagnosed, the Pearsons founded the Adult Attention Deficit Foundation, a clearinghouse for information about ADD; he hopes to spare others some of his own regret: "I had a deep and abiding sadness over the life I could have given my family if I had been treated effectively."

PERSONALITY OR PATHOLOGY? While Chuck Pearson's problems were extreme, many if not all adults have trouble at times sticking with boring tasks, setting priorities and keeping their minds on what they are doing. The furious pace of society, the strain on families, the lack of community support can make anyone feel beset by ADD. "I personally think we are living in a society that is so out of control that we say, 'Give me a stimulant so I can cope.' " says Charlotte Tomaino, a clinical neuropsychologist in White Plains, New York. As word of ADHD spreads, swarms of adults are seeking the diagnosis as an explanation for their troubles. "So many really have symptoms that began in adulthood and reflected depression or other problems," says psychiatrist Silver. In their best-selling new book, *Driven to Distraction,* Edward Hallowell and John Ratey suggest that American life is "ADD-ogenic": "American society tends to create ADD-like symptoms in us all. The fast pace. The sound bite. The quick cuts. The TV remote-control clicker. It is important to keep this in mind, or you may start thinking that everybody you know has ADD."

And that is the conundrum. How do you draw the line between a spontaneous, high-energy person who is feeling overwhelmed by the details of life and someone afflicted with a neurological disorder? Where is the boundary between personality and pathology? Even an expert in the field like the University of Chicago's Mark Stein admits, "We need to find more pre-

cise ways of diagnosing it than just saying you have these symptoms." Barkley also concedes the vagueness. The traits that constitute ADHD "are personality characteristics," he agrees. But it becomes pathology, he says, when the traits are so extreme that they interfere with people's lives.

THE RISKS There is no question that ADHD can disrupt lives. Kids with the disorder frequently have few friends. Their parents may be ostracized by neighbors and relatives, who blame them for failing to control the child. "I've got criticism of my parenting skills from strangers," says the mother of a hyperactive boy in New Jersey. "When you're out in public, you're always on guard. Whenever I'd hear a child cry, I'd turn to see if it was because of Jeremy."

School can be a shattering experience for such kids. Frequently reprimanded and tuned out, they lose any sense of self-worth and fall ever further behind in their work. More than a quarter are held back a grade; about a third fail to graduate from high school. ADHD kids are also prone to accidents, says neurologist Roseman. "These are the kids I'm going to see in the emergency room this summer. They rode their bicycle right into the street and didn't look. They jumped off the deck and forgot it was high."

But the psychological injuries are often greater. By ages five to seven, says Barkley, half to two-thirds are hostile and defiant. By ages 10 to 12, they run the risk of developing what psychologists call "conduct disorder"—lying, stealing, running away from home and ultimately getting into trouble with the law. As adults, says Barkley, 25% to 30% will experience substance-abuse problems, mostly with depressants like marijuana and alcohol. One study of hyperactive boys found that 40% had been arrested at least once by age 18—and these were kids who had been treated with stimulant medication; among those who had been treated with the drug plus other measures, the rate was 20%—still very high.

It is an article of faith among ADHD researchers that the right interventions can prevent such dreadful outcomes. "If you

can have an impact with these kids, you can change whether they go to jail or to Harvard Law School," says psychologist James Swanson at the University of California at Irvine, who co-authored the study of arrest histories. And yet, despite decades of research, no one is certain exactly what the optimal intervention should be.

TREATMENT The best-known therapy for ADHD remains stimulant drugs. Though Ritalin is the most popular choice, some patients do better with Dexedrine or Cylert or even certain antidepressants. About 70% of kids respond to stimulants. In the correct dosage, these uppers surprisingly "make people slow down," says Swanson. "They make you focus your attention and apply more effort to whatever you're supposed to do." Ritalin kicks in within 30 minutes to an hour after being taken, but its effects last only about three hours. Most kids take a dose at breakfast and another at lunchtime to get them through a school day.

When drug therapy works, says Utah's Wender, "it is one of the most dramatic effects in psychiatry." Roseman tells how one first-grader came into his office after trying Ritalin and announced, "I know how it works." "You do?" asked the doctor. "Yes," the child replied. "It cleaned out my ears. Now I can hear the teacher." A third-grader told Roseman that Ritalin had enabled him to play basketball. "Now when I get the ball, I turn around, I go down to the end of the room, and if I look up, there's a net there. I never used to see the net, because there was too much screaming."

For adults, the results can be just as striking. "Helen," a 43-year-old mother of three in northern Virginia, began taking the drug after being diagnosed with ADD in 1983. "The very first day, I noticed a difference," she marvels. For the first time ever, "I was able to sit down and listen to what my husband had done at work. Shortly after, I was able to sit in bed and read while my husband watched TV."

Given such outcomes, doctors can be tempted to throw a little Ritalin at any problem. Some even use it as a diagnostic tool, believing—wrongly—that if the child's concentration improves with Ritalin, then he or she must have ADD. In fact, you don't have to have an attention problem to get a boost from Ritalin. By the late 1980s, over-prescription became a big issue, raised in large measure by the Church of Scientology, which opposes psychiatry in general and launched a vigorous campaign against Ritalin. After a brief decline fostered by the scare, the drug is now hot once again. Swanson has heard of some classrooms where 20% to 30% of the boys are on Ritalin. "That's just ridiculous!'" he says.

Ritalin use varies from state to state, town to town, depending largely on the attitude of the doctors and local schools. Idaho is the No. 1 consumer of the drug. A study of Ritalin consumption in Michigan, which ranks just behind Idaho, found that use ranged from less than 1% of boys in one county to as high as 10% in another, with no correlation to affluence.

Patients who are taking Ritalin must be closely monitored, since the drug can cause loss of appetite, insomnia and occasionally tics. Doctors often recommend "drug holidays" during school vacations. Medication is frequently combined with other treatments, including psychotherapy, special education and cognitive training, although the benefits of such expensive measures are unclear. "We really haven't known which treatment to use for which child and how to combine treatments," says Dr. Peter Jensen, chief of NIMH's Child and Adolescent Disorders Research Branch. His group has embarked on a study involving 600 children in six cities. By 1998 they hope to have learned how medication alone compares to medication with psychological intervention and other approaches.

BEYOND DRUGS A rough consensus has emerged among ADHD specialists that whether or not drugs are used, it is best to teach kids—often through behavior modification—how to gain more control over their impulses and restless energy. Also recommended is training in the fine art of being organized: establishing a predictable schedule of activities, learning to use a date book, assigning a location for possessions at school and at home. This takes considerable effort on the part of teachers and parents as well as the kids themselves. Praise, most agree, is vitally important.

Within the classroom "some simple, practical things work well," says Reid. Let hyperactive kids move around. Give them stand-up desks, for instance. "I've seen kids who from the chest up were very diligently working on a math problem, but from the chest down, they're dancing like Fred Astaire." To minimize distractions, ADHD kids should sit very close to the teacher and be permitted to take important tests in a quiet area. "Unfortunately," Reid

observes, "not many teachers are trained in behavior management. It is a historic shortfall in American education."

In Irvine, California, James Swanson has tried to create the ideal setting for teaching kids with ADHD. The Child Development Center, an elementary school that serves 45 kids with the disorder, is a kind of experiment in progress. The emphasis is on behavior modification: throughout the day students earn points—and are relentlessly cheered on—for good behavior. High scorers are rewarded with special privileges at the end of the day, but each morning kids start afresh with another shot at the rewards. Special classes also drill in social skills: sharing, being a good sport, ignoring annoyances rather than striking out in anger. Only 35% of the kids at the center are on stimulant drugs, less than half the national rate for ADHD kids.

Elsewhere around the country, enterprising parents have struggled to find their own answers to attention deficit. Bonnie and Neil Fell of Skokie, Illinois, have three sons, all of whom have been diagnosed with ADD. They have "required more structure and consistency than other kids," says Bonnie. "We had to break down activities into clear time slots." To help their sons, who take Ritalin, the Fells have employed tutors, psychotherapists and a speech and language specialist. None of this comes cheap: they estimate their current annual ADD-related expenses at $15,000. "Our goal is to get them through school with their self-esteem intact," says Bonnie.

The efforts seem to be paying off. Dan, the eldest at 15, has become an outgoing A student, a wrestling star and a writer for the school paper. "ADD gives you energy and creativity," he says. "I've learned to cope. I've become strong." On the other hand, he is acutely aware of his disability. "What people don't realize is that I have to work harder than everyone else. I start studying for finals a month before other people do."

COPING Adults can also train themselves to compensate for ADHD. Therapists working with them typically emphasize organizational skills, time management, stress reduction and ways to monitor their own distractibility and stay focused.

I N HER OFFICE IN WHITE PLAINS, Tomaino has a miniature Zen garden, a meditative sculpture and all sorts of other items to help tense patients relax. Since many people with ADHD also have learning disabilities, she tests each patient and then often uses computer programs to strengthen weak areas. But most important is helping people define their goals and take orderly steps to reach them. Whether working with a stockbroker or a homemaker, she says, "I teach adults basic

rewards and goals. For instance, you can't go out to lunch until you've cleaned the kitchen."

Tomaino tells of one very hyperactive and articulate young man who got all the way through college without incident, thanks in good measure to a large and tolerant extended family. Then he flunked out of law school three times. Diagnosed with ADHD, the patient took stock of his goals and decided to enter the family restaurant business, where, Tomaino says, he is a raging success. "ADHD was a deficit if he wanted to be a lawyer, but it's an advantage in the restaurant business. He gets to go around to meet and greet."

For neurologist Roseman, the same thing is true. With 11 offices in four states, he is perpetually on the go. "I'm at rest in motion," says the doctor. "I surround myself with partners who provide the structure. My practice allows me to be creative." Roseman has accountants to do the bookkeeping. He starts his day at 6:30 with a hike and doesn't slow down until midnight. "Thank God for my ADD," he says. But, he admits, "had I listened to all the negative things that people said when I was growing up, I'd probably be digging ditches in Idaho."

LESSONS Whether ADHD is a brain disorder or simply a personality type, the degree to which it is a handicap depends not only on the severity of the traits but also on one's environment. The right school, job or home situation can make all the difference. The lessons of ADHD are truisms. All kids do not learn in the same way. Nor are all adults suitable for the same line of work.

Unfortunately, American society seems to have evolved into a one-size-fits-all system. Schools can resemble factories: put the kids on the assembly line, plug in the right components and send 'em out the door. Everyone is supposed to go to college; there is virtually no other route to success. In other times and in other places, there have been alternatives: apprenticeships, settling a new land, starting a business out of the garage, going to sea. In a conformist society, it becomes necessary to medicate some people to make them fit in.

This is not to deny that some people genuinely need Ritalin, just as others need tranquilizers or insulin. But surely an epidemic of attention deficit disorder is a warning to us all. Children need individual supervision. Many of them need more structure than the average helter-skelter household provides. They need a more consistent approach to discipline and schools that tailor teaching to their individual learning styles. Adults too could use a society that's more flexible in its expectations, more accommodating to differences. Most of all, we all need to slow down. And pay attention.   *—With reporting by Hannah Bloch/New York, Wendy Cole/Chicago and James Willwerth/Irvine*

Learning from Asian Schools

American schools could benefit from the teaching styles and institutional structures used in Asia—many of which were pioneered here

Harold W. Stevenson

Harold W. Stevenson is professor of psychology at the University of Michigan, Ann Arbor. He received his Ph.D. from Stanford University. Since 1979, he has been conducting a series of cross-national studies of children's academic achievement. Stevenson has earned several distinctions, including a Guggenheim fellowship and the American Psychological Association's G. Stanley Hall award for research in developmental psychology.

During the past decade, it has become a truism that American students are not being adequately prepared to compete in a global economy. The latest research shows that the deficiencies become apparent as early as kindergarten and persist throughout the school years. These deficiencies have been most evident when the students are compared with their peers in East Asia. Yet contrary to popular stereotypes the high levels of achievement in Asian schools are not the result of rote learning and repeated drilling by overburdened, tense youngsters. Children are motivated to learn; teaching is innovative and interesting. Knowledge is not forced on children; instead the students are led to construct their own ways of representing this knowledge. The long school days in Asia are broken up by extensive amounts of recess. The recess in turn fosters a positive attitude toward academics.

My colleagues and I gained these insights in a series of five collaborative, large cross-national studies begun in 1980. We explored the children's experiences both at home and at school in the U.S., China, Taiwan and Japan. We found that there is nothing mysterious about the teaching styles and techniques used in Asian schools. Rather these societies embody many of the ideals Americans have for their own schools. They just happen to apply them in an interesting, productive way that makes learning enjoyable.

The vast cultural differences preclude direct translation of many of the practices and beliefs from those cultures to our own. But these comparative data have helped us realize how far Americans have strayed from the effective application of well-known teaching methods. The studies have revealed new perspectives about our own culture and fresh ideas about how our educational system might be improved. Indeed, simply increasing the length of school days would be meaningless if there were no change in the way American teachers are asked to perform their jobs.

Results from cross-national studies can be greatly distorted if the research procedures are not comparable in each area and if the test materials are not culturally appropriate. We avoided the first potential problem by selecting a full range of schools in five metropolitan areas: Minneapolis, Chicago, Sendai, Beijing and Taipei. These cities are similar in size and cultural status within their own countries. In each metropolitan region, we selected from 10 to 20 elementary schools that represented a range of students from different socioeconomic backgrounds. (Because socioeconomic status is not easy to define, we used the parents' educational level as the basis for selection.) We then randomly chose two first-grade and two fifth-grade classrooms in each school.

To avoid the difficulty in translating materials developed in one culture for use in another, we constructed our own tests. We began by compiling computer files of every concept and skill included in the students' mathematics textbooks and of every word and grammatical structure in their reading material. With these files, we were able to create test items that were relevant to each culture and that were at the appropriate levels of difficulty.

Armed with these materials, we administered mathematics and reading tests to thousands of students in the first- and fifth-grade classrooms. Later we randomly selected samples of six boys and six girls from each classroom for more in-depth testing and interviews. In one of the studies, we visited a total of 204 classrooms in 11 schools in Beijing, 10 in Taipei, 10 in Sendai and 20 in Chicago.

The test results confirmed what has become common knowledge: schoolchildren in Asia perform better academically than do those in the U.S. In mathematics the average scores of the Asian first graders were above the American average, but scores of some of the American schools were as high as some of those in Sendai and Taipei. By fifth grade, however, the American students lost much ground: the average score of only one of the Chicago-area schools was as high as the worst of the Asian schools. On a computation test, for example, only 2.2 percent of the Beijing first graders and 1.4 percent of the fifth graders scored as low as the mean for their Chicago counterparts. On a test of word problems, only 2.6 percent of the Beijing first graders and 10 percent of the fifth graders scored at or below corresponding American means.

The deficiencies of American children appear to build throughout the school years. When we compared the scores of kindergarten children and of first, fifth and 11th graders in Minneapolis, Sendai, and Taipei, we found a relative decline in the scores among the American students, improvement in Taiwan and steady high performance in Japan.

American students' shortcomings are not limited to mathematics. Although Americans performed the best on read-ing in the first grade, the Asian students had caught up by the fifth grade. The rise is remarkable when one considers the reading demands of Asian languages. Chinese students had to learn several thousand characters by the fifth grade,

and Japanese students had to learn Chinese characters, two syllabaries (symbols for the syllables in Japanese) and the roman alphabet.

Because of the early onset and pervasiveness of cross-cultural differences in academic achievement, it seemed obvious that we would have to investigate attitudes, beliefs and practices related to children's success. We spent hundreds of hours observing in the classrooms, interviewed the teachers, children and mothers and gave questionnaires to the fathers.

American parents show a surprisingly high level of satisfaction with their children's level of academic performance. From kindergarten through the 11th grade, more than three times as many Minneapolis mothers as Asian mothers said they were very satisfied with their child's current level of achievement.

The U.S. students were also very positive about their abilities. More than 30 percent of the Chicago fifth graders considered themselves to be "among the best" in mathematics, in reading, in sports and in getting along with other children. Such self-ratings were significantly higher than those made by Sendai and Taipei children for mathematics and by Sendai children for reading. Taipei children gave the highest self-ratings for reading. Except for social skills, many fewer Beijing children gave themselves such positive ratings.

In another set of questions, we asked the mothers how well the school was educating their own children. More than 80 percent of the American mothers expressed a high level of satisfaction. Except at kindergarten, when mothers in all four societies were quite satisfied, Minneapolis mothers felt much better about their children's schools than did mothers in Taipei and Sendai.

Why should American mothers be so positive? One likely explanation is that they lack clear standards to which they can refer. No national or state curricula define what children should learn at each grade, and few mothers receive more than vague reports about their children's performance. American mothers also seem to place a lesser emphasis on academic achievement. In the U.S., childhood is a time for many different types of accomplishment. Doing well in school is only one of them.

Asian mothers, on the other hand, have told us repeatedly that their chil-

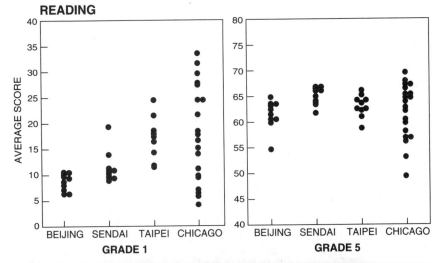

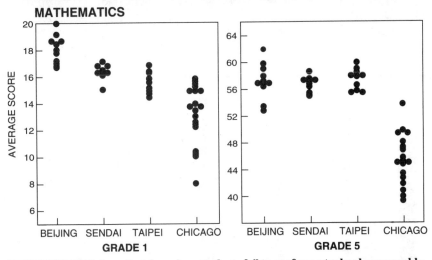

TEST RESULTS show that American students fail to perform at a level comparable to that of their peers in Asia. The data plotted are mean scores from various schools (dots). Although Americans performed best in reading in the first grade, they lost the advantage by the fifth grade. In mathematics, American students in both the first and fifth grades on average scored the poorest.

dren's primary task is to do well in school. The mothers' own job is to try to do everything possible to ensure that success. They regarded education as critical for their children's future. Thus, Asian mothers find it more difficult to be satisfied with moderate levels of performance.

The American mothers' contentment had clearly been transmitted to their children. Fifth graders were asked whether they agreed with the statement, "I am doing as well in school as my parents want me to." American children thought this statement was more true of them than did the Asian children. We obtained similar results when we asked the question in terms of their teachers' satisfaction.

The American mothers we interviewed apparently were not strongly impressed by recent criticisms of U.S. education. As far as they were concerned, the relatively poor academic showing of U.S. students did not reflect the abilities of their own children or their children's schools. For American mothers, problems existed at other schools and with other children. Our interviews revealed little evidence that American mothers were motivated to seek improvements in the quality of their children's education or that American children believed they were doing anything but a satisfactory job in school.

We explored academic motivation in another way by posing a hypothetical question to the children: "Let's say there is a wizard who will let you make a wish about anything you want. What would you wish?" The most frequent wishes fell into four categories: money; material objects, such as toys or pets; fantasy, such as wanting to be sent to the moon, or to have more wishes; and educational aspirations, such as doing well in school

How Parents and Students See the System

Satisfaction with academic performance of students (a) and their children's schools (b) is higher among American mothers that it is among Asian mothers. Children seem to reflect their parents' attitudes: more American students rated themselves "among the best" in several categories than did children from Beijing (c).

or going to college. Almost 70 percent of the Chinese children focused their wishes on education. American children were more interested in receiving money and material objects. Fewer than 10 percent of the American children expressed wishes about education.

The enthusiasm Asian children express about school comes in part, of course, from the well-known societal emphasis on education. Several studies of immigrants have documented the willingness of Asian children to work hard [see "Indochinese Refugee Families and Academic Achievement," by Nathan Caplan, Marcella H. Choy and John K. Whitmore; SCIENTIFIC AMERICAN, February 1992]. This attitude stems from Confucian beliefs about the role of effort and ability in achievement. The malleability of human behavior has long been emphasized in Chinese writings, and a similar theme is found in Japanese philosophy. Individual differences in potential are deemphasized, and great importance is placed on the role of effort and diligence in modifying the course of human development.

In contrast, Americans are much more likely to point to the limitations imposed by an assumed level of innate ability. This belief has potentially devastating effects. When parents believe success in school depends for the most part on ability rather than effort, they are less likely to foster participation in activities related to academic achievement. Such parents may question whether spending time in academic pursuits after school is useful for children of presumed low ability. They may readily accept poor performance. Furthermore, if the parents believe the child has high ability, they may question whether such activities are needed.

It is relatively easy to demonstrate the greater emphasis placed by Americans on innate ability. One approach is to ask children to rate the importance of certain factors for doing well in school. Beijing children emphasized effort rather than ability. Chicago children thought both to be of near-equal importance.

In another approach we asked Taipei, Sendai and Minneapolis children to indicate the degree to which they agreed with the statement that "everybody in the class has about the same amount of ability in math." American children expressed less strong agreement than did the Chinese and Japanese children. Mothers follow the same pattern of re-

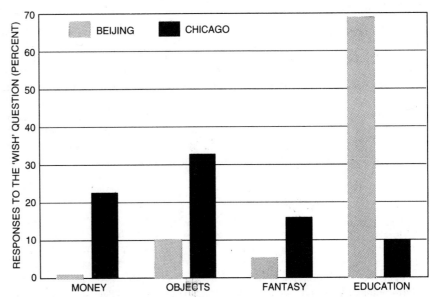

WISHFUL THINKING seems to reflect cultural priorities. Chicago children tended to wish for money and material objects, such as toys or pets. Beijing children wished for educational goals, such as going to college.

sponse. When asked about the degree to which they agreed that "any student can be good at math if he/she works hard enough," Minneapolis mothers expressed less agreement than did Sendai or Taipei mothers.

Children may work harder because they believe achievement depends on diligence. The idea that increased effort will lead to improved performance is an important factor in accounting for the willingness of Chinese and Japanese children, teachers and parents to spend so much time and effort on the children's academic work.

The enthusiasm for school also seems to come from the happy times that Asian children appear to have there. That these children regard school as pleasant— rather than as regimented, austere and demanding—surprises most Americans. Our stereotype is that the intense quest for academic excellence reduces the possibilities of making school a place that children enjoy. This clearly is not the case.

When we compare the daily routine in Asian and American schools, we realize how easy it is to overlook the constraints of American schools. Classes begin shortly after the students arrive, and the children leave just after their last class ends. Rarely is there more than a single recess. The lunch period—a potential time for play and social interaction—is usually limited to half an hour or less. As a consequence, American children spend most of their time at school in the classroom.

In contrast, the daily routine in Asian schools offers many opportunities for social experience. There are frequent recesses, long lunch periods and after-school activities and clubs. Such opportunities make up about one fourth of the time spent during the eight hours at school. The school day is longer in Asia mainly because of the time devoted to these nonacademic periods. Play, social interaction and extracurricular activity may not contribute directly to academic success, but they make school an enjoyable place. The enjoyment likely creates cooperative attitudes.

The relative lack of nonacademic activities in American schools is reflected in greater amounts of time spent in play after school. American mothers estimated that their elementary school children spend nearly 25 hours a week playing. We found this surprisingly high until we considered how little time was available for play at school. Estimates for Chinese children were much lower— their social life at school is reflected in the shorter amounts of time they play after returning home.

Chicago children also spent nearly twice as much time as Beijing children watching television. But compared with Americans, Japanese students from kindergarten through high school spent even more time watching television. The difference in this case appears to be that Japanese children are more likely to watch television after they had completed their homework.

American children were reported to

spend significantly less time than Asian children in doing homework and reading for pleasure—two pursuits that are likely to contribute to academic achievement. Mothers estimated that the Taipei children spent about four times as much time each day doing homework as did American children and over twice as much time as did Japanese children. American children were estimated to spend less time reading for pleasure than their Asian peers throughout their school years.

The enjoyment Asian students have at school may be the reason they appear to Western visitors as well behaved and well adjusted. These observations, however, have always been informal, and no data exist to support or refute them. So we decided to ask mothers and teachers in Beijing and Chicago about these matters. In particular, we questioned them about physical symptoms of tension, which we thought would be a good indicator of adjustment.

Chinese mothers reported fewer complaints by their children of stomachaches and headaches, as well as fewer requests to stay home from school than did American mothers. The Chinese mothers also more frequently described their children as happy and obedient. Only 4 percent of the Chinese mothers, but 20 percent of the American mothers, said their children encountered problems in getting along with other children.

The intense dedication of Chinese elementary school children to schoolwork did not appear to result in tension and maladjustment. Nor have we found patterns of psychological disturbance

among several thousand Chinese and Japanese 11th graders in self-evaluations of stress, depression, academic anxiety or psychosomatic complaints. Our data do not support the Western assumption that Asian children must experience extraordinary stress from their more demanding curriculum. The clear academic goals and the enthusiastic support given by family, teachers and peers may reduce the strain from working so hard.

The achievement of Asian students is facilitated by the extensive amount of attention teachers can give the children. Indeed, one of the biggest differences we found was the amount of time teachers had. Beijing teachers were incredulous after we described a typical day in American schools. When, they asked, did the teachers prepare their lessons, consult with one another about teaching techniques, grade the students' papers and work with individual students who were having difficulties? Beijing teachers, they explained, are responsible for classes for no more than three hours a day; for those with homeroom duties, the total is four hours. The situation is similar in Japan and Taiwan, where, according to our estimates, teachers are in charge of classes only 60 percent of the time they are at school.

Teaching is more of a group endeavor in Asia than it is in the U.S. Teachers frequently consult with one another, because, in following the national curriculum, they are all teaching the same lesson at about the same time. More

experienced teachers help newer ones. Head teachers in each grade organize meetings to discuss technique and to devise lesson plans and handouts. The group may spend hours designing a single lesson or discussing how to frame questions that will produce the greatest understanding from their pupils. They also have a teachers' room, where all the instructors have desks and where they keep their books and teaching materials. They spend most of the time there when not teaching.

American teachers have neither the time nor the incentive to share experiences with one another or to benefit from hearing about the successes and failures of other instructors. Each teacher's desk is in the classroom, and little space is allocated specifically for informal discussions and meetings. The teachers' room in American schools is typically a place to rest rather than to work. As a result, American teachers spend most of their time at school isolated in their own classrooms, with few opportunities for professional interaction or consultation.

With no national curriculum or guidelines, American schools typically develop their own agenda. In any year the curriculum may not be consistent within a city or even within a single school. Adding further to the diversity in the curricula among American classrooms is the fact that teachers are free to proceed through textbooks at any rate they wish, skipping the parts they do not find especially interesting or useful.

The demanding daily schedule places serious constraints on the ability of

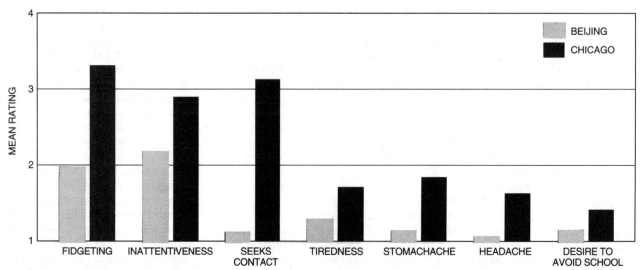

SYMPTOMS OF STRESS in U.S. classrooms exceed those in Asian schools. First-grade teachers in Chicago and Beijing estimated the frequency of physical complaints among students. They rated their impressions on a scale from 1 (seldom complained) to 5 (often complained). American schoolchildren expressed symptoms more often than did Beijing students.

American teachers to create exciting, well-organized lessons. They usually must prepare for their classes at home during evenings and weekends. Furthermore, they must cover all elementary school subjects, because teachers for specific academic subjects typically do not appear until junior high school. Evenings are not the most appropriate time to begin such a difficult task, for teachers are tired from the demands of school and their own affairs. There are, of course, excellent American teachers. And there are individual differences among Asian teachers. But what has impressed us in our observations and in the data from our studies is how remarkably well most East Asian teachers do their jobs.

Asian teachers can be described best as well-informed, well-prepared guides. They do not see themselves primarily as dispensers of information and arbiters of what is correct but rather as persons responsible for guiding students skillfully through the material. Each lesson typically begins with a statement of its purpose and ends with a summary of its content. The lesson follows a well-planned script in which children are led through a series of productive interactions and discussions. Teachers regard children as active participants in the learning process who must play an important role in producing, explaining and evaluating solutions to problems.

The skill shown by Asian teachers is not acquired in college. In fact, some teachers in China have only a high school education. The pattern for training teachers resembles that provided to other professionals: in-service training under the supervision of skilled models. Colleges are assumed to provide basic knowledge about subject matter, as well as about child development and theories of learning. But Asian instructors believe the art of teaching can be accomplished better in classrooms of elementary schools than in lecture halls of colleges. This approach stands in sharp contrast to that taken in the U.S., where teaching skill is generally thought to be best acquired through several specialized courses in teaching methods.

The skills employed by Asian teachers are also more effective in attracting and maintaining children's attention. We found Asian children listening to the teacher more frequently than American children—at least 80 percent of the time versus approximately 60 percent. This finding may also result from differences

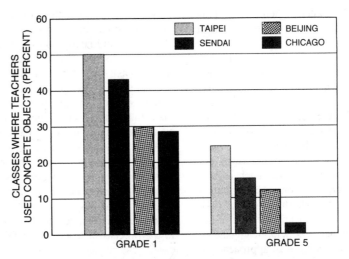

USING OBJECTS to teach young children is often more effective than verbal instruction. In mathematics classes, teachers in Asia use concrete materials more frequently than do American teachers.

in the number of recesses in Asian and American schools. Attention is more likely to falter after several hours of classes than it is if opportunities for play and relaxation precede each class, as is the case in Asian schools.

Another likely reason for the American children's lack of attention lies in the manner in which U.S. teachers often structure the lessons. Because of the time spent on seatwork—exercises or assignments children are to complete at their desks—and the way in which seatwork is used, American children have fewer opportunities to interact with the teacher than do children in Asian classrooms. American teachers rely more heavily on seatwork than do Asian teachers, which is not surprising. Giving children such tasks is one of the few ways American teachers can gain some free time in their grueling daily schedule.

In the U.S., teachers usually explain the concepts during the early part of the lesson and then assign seatwork during the later part. Asian teachers, on the other hand, intersperse brief periods of seatwork throughout the class period. Seatwork is a means of getting children to practice what they have just learned and of quickly spotting difficulties the children might be encountering. American teachers are less likely to take advantage of the diagnostic value of seatwork.

Children's attention also increases when they receive feedback. If students do not receive some type of acknowledgment from the teacher or some indication of whether their work is correct, they are more likely to lose interest. In a sur-

prisingly large number of classes, Chicago teachers failed to provide feedback to the children, especially when the children were doing seatwork. In nearly half of the 160 class periods we observed in the Chicago fifth grades, teachers failed to offer any type of evaluation as the children worked alone at their desks. In striking contrast, lack of such acknowledgment was practically never observed in Sendai and only infrequently in Taipei.

In addition, Asian teachers make more frequent use of materials that can be manipulated. Jean Piaget and other psychologists (as well as most parents and teachers) have discovered that young children enjoy manipulating concrete objects, which is often a more effective way to learn than is listening to verbal instruction. Even so, American teachers were much less likely than Asian teachers to provide concrete objects for manipulation in mathematics classes.

Finally, Asian teachers make the subjects interesting by giving them some meaningful relation to the children's everyday lives. In mathematics, word problems often serve this function. They can transform mathematics from a subject of dull computation to one requiring active problem solving. We found that American teachers were much less likely than Asian teachers to introduce word problems. Fifth-grade American teachers presented word problems in less than one out of five class periods; Sendai teachers included word problems in more than eight out of every 10 lessons. Similar differences emerged when we calculated how often children were asked to construct word problems themselves. This exercise rarely occurred in American classrooms.

Asian teachers are able to engage children's interest not because they have insights that are unknown in the U.S. but because they take well-known principles and have the time and energy to apply them with remarkable skill. They incorporate a variety of teaching techniques within each lesson, rely more frequently on discussion than on lectures, teach children how to make smooth transitions from one type of activity to another and seldom engage in irrelevant discussions—all approaches to teaching that American instructors would agree are reasonable and effective.

Perhaps the most pointed difference between the goals of Asian and American teachers emerged when we asked teachers in Beijing and Chicago what they considered to be the most-important characteristics of a good instructor. "Clarity," said nearly half of the Beijing teachers. "Sensitivity to the needs of individuals" was the most common response of the Chicago teachers. Beijing teachers were also more likely to emphasize enthusiasm, and Chicago teachers were more likely to stress patience.

Have the goals of education diverged to such a degree in Eastern and Western cultures that American teachers see their main tasks as those of evaluating and meeting the needs of individuals, while Asian teachers can devote their attention to the process of teaching? If this is the case, the academic achievement of American children will not improve until conditions are as favorable as those provided in Asia. Clearly, a challenge in the U.S. is to create a greater cultural emphasis on education and academic success. But we must also make changes in their teaching schedules, so that they, too, will be able to incorporate sound teaching practices into their daily routines.

FURTHER READING

PRESCHOOL IN THREE CULTURES: JAPAN, CHINA, AND THE UNITED STATES. J. J. Tobin, D. Y. H. Wu and D. H. Davidson. Yale University Press, 1989.

JAPANESE EDUCATIONAL PRODUCTIVITY. Edited by R. Leestma and H. J. Walberg. University of Michigan, Center for Japanese Studies, 1992.

LEARNING TO GO TO SCHOOL IN JAPAN: THE TRANSITION FROM HOME TO PRESCHOOL LIFE. L. Peak. University of California Press, 1992.

THE LEARNING GAP: WHY OUR SCHOOLS ARE FAILING AND WHAT WE CAN LEARN FROM JAPANESE AND CHINESE EDUCATION. H. W. Stevenson and J. W. Stigler. Summit Books, 1992.

Tracked to Fail

In today's schools, children who test poorly may lose the chance for a quality education. Permanently.

Sheila Tobias

Sheila Tobias is the author of Breaking the Science Barrier *(1992),* Succeed With Math *(1987) and* Overcoming Math Anxiety *(1978).*

No one who has ever read Aldous Huxley's anti-utopian novel, *Brave New World,* can forget the book's opening scene, a tour of the "Hatchery and Conditioning Centre." There human embryos in their first hours of existence are transformed into Alphas, Betas, Gammas, Deltas and Epsilons—the five social classes that collectively meet the economy's manpower needs. Arrested in their development, the Gamma, Delta and Epsilon embryos are programmed *in vitro* for a lower-class future. After "birth," whatever individuality remains with these pre-ordained proletarians will be conditioned out of each child, until there is no one in this brave new world who does not grow up accepting and even loving his bleak servitude.

Huxley's totalitarian embryology may seem fanciful to us, but his real message was political, not technological. Huxley understood, as he wrote in the foreword to the 1946 edition of *Brave New World,* that any "science of human differences" would enable the authorities to assess the relative capacities of each of us and then assign everybody his or her appropriate place in society. Huxley's vision of the modern state, with its desire for social control, implies that the discovery that ability can be measured will suggest that it *should* be. Similarly, the knowledge that people can be sorted by ability will lead irresistibly to the belief that they ought to be.

Today, many educators contend that a "science of human differences" does exist in the form of standardized tests for intelligence and ability. And, as Huxley foresaw, the pressures have grown to put these discriminating instruments to use. Education in this country is becoming a process of separating the "gifted" from the "average," the "intelligent" from the "slow"—one is tempted to say, the wheat from the chaff. From an early age, children are now ranked and sorted (a process known variably as tracking, ability grouping or screening) as they proceed through school. Those who test well are encour-

aged and expected to succeed and offered the most challenging work. Those who do not, get a watered-down curriculum that reflects the system's minimal expectations of them.

All this is a far cry from the vision of schooling that America's founding educators had in mind. Horace Mann, the father of American public education and the influential first secretary of the Massachusetts board of education from 1837 to 1848, thought public education would be "the great equalizer" in a nation of immigrants. For over a century now, Mann's egalitarian vision, translated into educational policy, has helped millions of immigrants to assimilate and to prosper here. But this vision is now threatened by a competing view of individual potential—and worth. We are becoming a society where test-taking skills are the prerequisites for a chance at getting a good education, and where hard work, hope and ambition are in danger of becoming nothing more than meaningless concepts.

A poor showing on tests was once a signal to all concerned—child, teacher, parents—that greater effort was needed to learn, or to teach, what was required. It didn't mean that a child *couldn't* learn. But the damaging assumption behind testing and tracking as they are now employed in many schools is that *only* those who test well are capable of learning what is needed to escape an adult life restricted to menial, dead-end jobs. This new message imparted by our schools is profoundly inegalitarian: that test-measured ability, not effort, is what counts. What many students are learning is that they are *not* equal to everybody else. Gammas, Deltas and Epsilons shouldn't even try to compete with Alphas. Alphas are better, *born* better, and it is impossible for others to catch up. What's tragic about this change is not just that it's unjust—but that it's untrue.

A Lifetime of Testing

In a private Los Angeles primary school, a 4-year-old is being taught to play a game-like test he is going to have to pass to show that he is ready for kindergarten. This is the first in an endless series of evaluations that will determine who he is, what he can learn and how far he will go in school. Just before the test begins, the counselor hands him the red plastic cube he will use. But he doesn't need her cube. He has taken this test so often, as his parents drag him around from his preschool admissions screenings, that when the time comes to play, he pulls his *own* bright red cube out of his pocket. Whether or not he is ready for this particular school, he is more than ready for the test.

Each year after this child's admission to kindergarten, he will take "norm-referenced tests" to show his overall achievement against those of his age group and "criterion-referenced tests," which examine the specific skills he is supposed to have learned in each grade. Even if he and his parents are not told his test scores (a practice that varies from school to school), ability-grouping in elementary school will soon let him know where he stands. "By the second or third grade," says Susan Harter, a psychology professor at the University of Denver who studies social development in children, "children know precisely where they stand on the 'smart or dumb' continuum, and since most children at this age want to succeed in school, this knowledge profoundly affects their self-esteem."

The point is that today "smart or dumb" determinations are made very early. "Those who come to school knowing how to read or who learn very quickly are pronounced bright," says Jeannie Oakes, author of *Keeping Track: How Schools Structure Inequality*. "Those for whom reading is still a puzzle at the end of the first grade are judged slow." And these early decisions stick. As children proceed through the elementary grades, more and more of their course work is grouped by ability. By ninth grade, 80% to 90% of students are in separate classes determined by whether they are judged to be "fast," "average" or "slow."

Magnifying Our Differences

Tracking in all its variants is rarely official policy, and the validity and fairness of standardized testing have long been under fire. Nevertheless, both tracking and testing are becoming more common. As a result, argues University of Cincinnati education professor Joel Spring (in unwitting resonance with Huxley), education in America has become a "sorting machine."

Moreover, the stunting effects of this machine may remain with students for a lifetime. "Adults can remember well into middle age whether they were 'sharks' or 'goldfish' in reading," says Bill Kelly, professor of education at Regis College in Denver. Students learn whether they have good verbal skills or mathematical ones. They learn whether or not they are musically or mechanically inclined, and so on. There are millions of adults who carry with them the conviction that they "can't do math" or play an instrument or write well. And it may all be the result of assessments made of them and internalized as children — long before they had any idea of what they wanted from life. Their sense of inadequacy may prevent them from exploring alternative careers or simply narrow their experiences.

Why are testing and tracking on the rise? Oakes, who has studied more than 13,000 junior- and senior-high-school students, their schools and their teachers, suggests that the answer has several components. They range from the focus on educational excellence during the last decade to widespread public confidence that testing is an accurate, appropriate way of gauging educational potential. Oakes also believes that testing and tracking comprise a not-so-subtle effort to resegregate desegregated schools. But they reflect as well a preference among teachers for "homogeneous groupings" of students, which are easier to teach than classes composed of students of varying abilities.

Whatever the motives, Oakes is convinced that the basic premise of the whole system is wrong. There is no way, she says, to determine accurately the potential of young or even older children by standardized tests. One key reason: Such examinations are always fine-tuned to point out differences, not similarities. They eliminate those items that everyone answers the same way — either right or wrong. Thus, small differences that may or may not measure ability in general are amplified to give the test makers what they want, namely ease of sorting. Test results, then, will make any group of individuals appear to be more different than they really are.

Benjamin Bloom, Distinguished Service Professor Emeritus of Education at the University of Chicago, agrees. "I find that many of the individual differences in school learning are man-made and accidental rather than fixed in the individual at the time of conception," he writes in his book *All Our Children Learning*. "When students are provided with unfavorable learning conditions, they become even more dissimilar." Bloom concedes that some longitudinal studies show that between grades 3 and 11, for example, children's rank in class remains virtually the same. But this is not because intelligence is fixed, he argues. It is the result of the unequal, unsupportive education the schools provide. So long as schools think there is little they can do about "learning ability," says Bloom, they will see their task as weeding out the poorer learners while encouraging the better learners to get as much education as they can.

Watered-Down Education

Research generated by Oakes and others supports Bloom, revealing that placement in a low track has a corroding impact on students' self esteem. Worse yet, because there are real differences not just in level but in the *content* of what is being taught, tracking may in fact contribute to academic failure.

Students in low-track courses are almost never exposed to what educators call "high-status knowledge," the kind that will be useful in colleges and universities. They do not read works of great literature in their English classes, Oakes's team found, and instead of critical-thinking skills and expository writing, low-track students are taught standard English usage and "functional literacy," which involves mainly filling out forms, job applications and the like. In mathematics, high-track students were exposed to numeration, computational systems, mathematical models, probability and statistics in high school. "In contrast," writes Oakes, "low-track classes focused grade after grade on basic computational skills and arithmetic facts" and sometimes on simple measurement skills and converting English to metric.

More generally, Oakes's team also found that high-track classes emphasize reasoning ability over simple memorization of disembodied facts. Low-track students, meanwhile, are taught by rote, with an emphasis on conformity. "Average" classes — the middle track — resembled those in the high track, but they are substantially "watered down."

Is this discriminatory system the only way to handle differences in ability among students? One innovative program is challenging that notion. Called "accelerated learning," it is the creation of Henry M. Levin, a professor of education and economics at Stanford University. Levin, an expert on worker-managed companies, decided to apply the principles of organizational psychology to an analysis of the crisis in education. He began with a two-year-study, during which he surveyed the literature on education and looked at hundreds of evaluations of at-risk students at elementary and middle schools. Fully one-third of all students, he estimated, were "educationally disadvantaged" in some way, were consigned to a low track and were falling farther and farther behind in one or more areas. These children needed remedial help, but that help, Levin writes, treated "such students and their educators as educational discards, marginal to mainstream education." For them, the pace of instruction was slowed to a crawl and progressed by endless repetition. The whole system seemed designed to demoralize and fail everyone who was a part of it. As Levin told one reporter, "As soon as you begin to talk about kids needing remediation, you're talking about damaged merchandise. And as soon as you have done that, you have lost the game."

To try to change the game, Levin designed and is helping to implement the Accelerated Schools Program. Now being tested in California, Utah, Missouri and (this fall) Illinois, the project accepts that elementary school children who are having academic problems *do* need special assistance, but it departs radically from traditional tracking in every other respect. First, Accelerated Schools are expected to have all their students learning at grade level by the time they reach the sixth grade. In other words, the remedial track exists only to get students off it. Collectively, the teachers and administrators at each school are allowed to design their own curricula, but they must create a clear set of measurable (and that means testable) goals for students to meet each year they are in the program. Finally, it is expected that the curriculum, whatever its specifics, will be challenging and fast-paced and will emphasize abstract reasoning skills and a sophisticated command of English.

Levin's program reflects the current administration's view that business practice has much to contribute to schooling. Levin wants schools to find a better way to produce what might be called their product — that is, children willing and able to get the quality education they will need in life. To do this, he recognizes that schools must offer better performance incentives to students, teachers and administrators. "Everyone benefits from the esprit de corps," explains Levin, "and the freedom to experiment with curriculum and technique — which we also encourage — is an incentive for teachers." By insisting upon school and teacher autonomy, the regular attainment of measurable goals and the development of innovative, engaging curricula, Accelerated Schools also hope to erase the stigma associated with teaching or needing remediation. The early results of this six-year test program are encouraging: The Hoover Elementary School in Redwood City, CA, one of the first schools to embark on the project, is reporting a 22 percentile increase in sixth-grade reading scores, actually outperforming state criteria. Both Levin and Ken Hill, the district superintendent, caution that these results are preliminary and the improved scores could be due to many factors other than the Accelerated Schools Program. But regardless of the program's measurable impact, Hill sees real changes in the school. "Teachers are now working with the kids on science projects and developing a literature-based reading program. There's a positive climate, and all the kids are learners."

Another alternative to tracking is what Bloom calls "mastery learning." He believes that it is the rate of learning, not the capacity to learn, that differentiates students with "high" or "low" abilities. This is a critical distinction, for we are rapidly approaching the day when all but the most menial jobs will require relatively complex reasoning and technical skills.

In a mastery class, children are given as much time as they need to become competent at a certain skill or knowledge level.

Teachers must take 10% to 15% more time with their classes and break the class down into small groups in which the fast learners help their peers along. In time, the slower students catch up both in the amount of knowledge acquired and in the rate at which they learn. Though slow students may start out as much as five times slower than their classmates, Bloom says, "in mastery classes, fast and slow students become equal in achievement and increasingly similar in their learning rates."

At present, fewer than 5% of the nation's schools are following either of these promising strategies, estimates Gary Fenstermacher, dean of the University of Arizona's College of Education. He is a firm believer that de-tracking in some form must be the educational wave of the future. "There are ethical and moral imperatives for us to do whatever we can to increase the equality of access to human knowledge and understanding," he says.

Second Class and Dropping Out

Until society responds to those ethical and moral imperatives, however, the educational system, with its testing, tracking and discriminatory labeling, will continue on its questionable course. Today, around 25% of America's teenagers — 40% to 60% in inner-city schools — do not graduate from high school, according to Jacqueline P. Danzberger of the Institute for Educational Leadership in Washington, DC. Most of the attrition occurs by the third year of high school, and many educators believe increased testing is a contributing factor.

Norman Gold, former director of research for the District of Columbia's public school system, says school dropouts are linked to the raising of standards (with no compensatory programs) in the late 1970s and the end of "social promotions"—the habit of routinely allowing failing students to move to a higher grade. "Studies show," he says, "that the risk of dropping out goes up 50% if a child fails one school year." Neil Shorthouse, executive director of Atlanta's Cities in Schools, which enrolls 750 teenagers on the point of dropping out, agrees. "Most of these kids quit school," he says of his students, "because they repeatedly get the message that they are bad students, 'unteachables.' "

Ending social promotions was long overdue. What purpose is served by graduating high-school students who can't read, write or do simple arithmetic? But schools have done little to help these failing students catch up. The present system is continuing to produce a whole class of people, particularly inner-city blacks and Hispanics, who have little economic role in our society. High school, Gold observes, has become an obstacle course that a significant number of young people are unable to negotiate. "We expect them to fail. We have to have greater expectations, and equally great support."

These failing students are missing what John Ogbu, an educational anthropologist at the University of California, Berkeley, calls "effort optimism," the faith that hard work will bring real rewards in life. Ogbu's ethnographic studies of black and Hispanic schoolchildren in Stockton, CA, suggest that one reason today's inner-city children do poorly in tests is that "they do not bring to the test situation serious attitudes and do not persevere to maximize their scores." The fault lies neither with their intelligence, Ogbu argues, nor with the absence of the "quasi-academic training" that middle-class children experience at home. Rather, it is their lower caste status and the limited job prospects of their parents that lower their sights. Tracking formalizes this caste humiliation and leads to disillusionment about school and what school can do for their lives.

What Parents Can Do

If you are worried that your own child is losing his or her enthusiasm for schoolwork as a result of being put in a lower, "dumber" track, Susan Harter of the University of Denver advises you to watch for the following signs of trouble:

Decline in intrinsic motivation, the kind of curiosity and involvement in school work that promises long-term academic success, and its replacement with *extrinsic* motivation, doing just enough to get by while depending too much on the teacher for direction and help.

Indifference to school and schoolwork; losing homework on the way to school, or homework assignments on the way back; delivering homework that is crumpled, dirty or incomplete.

Constant self-deprecation: "I'm no good." "I can't do long division."

Signs of helplessness: unwillingness to try a task, especially new ones; starting but not finishing work; difficulty in dealing with frustration.

Avoiding homework, or school, altogether. (The most frequent cause of truancy, says Olle Jane Sahler of the pediatrics department at the University of Rochester, is low self-esteem with regard to school subjects.)

Should parents whose kids have problems undertake compensatory home instruction? Sherry Ferguson and Lawrence E. Mazin, authors of *Parent Power: A Program to Help Your Child Succeed in School,* think so, not because parents can make their children "smart," but because they have the power to make their kids persistent, competitive and eager. Here are some specific steps parents can take at home to achieve this end, according to Abigail Lipson, Ph.D., a clinical psychologist at the Harvard University Bureau of Study Counsel:

Praise your child for effort, not just for achievement. Children learn about persistence from many contexts, not just academic ones, so praise your child for hard work at any task: developing a good hook shot, painting a picture, etc.

Ask your child to explain her homework, or the subjects she is studying at school, to you. Try to learn *from* your child, don't just instruct her.

Find a regular time when you and your child can work in the same space. When children are banished to their rooms to do homework, they are cut off from social interaction. It can be very lonely. Setting up a special study time together can help both (or all) of you focus on accomplishing difficult or onerous tasks. While your child is doing homework, you can balance your checkbook, pay bills, whatever.

Help your child find a learning activity he feels good about. If the subject is animals, go to a zoo. If it's cars, select some car books together from the library. Encourage him to pursue his natural interests.

Games of all kinds are good for teaching children about persistence and achievement. Competitive games emphasize strategies for competing effectively and fairly, while noncompetitive games provide children with a sense of accomplishment through perseverance.

—S.T.

Who Is "Smart"?
Who Will "Succeed"?

The consequences of increased testing and tracking are only now beginning to be felt. First there is personal trauma, both for students who do reasonably well but not as well as they would like, and for those who fail. "When a child is given to understand that his or her worth resides in what he or she achieves rather than in what he or she is, academic failure becomes a severe emotional trauma," David Elkind writes in *The Child and Society.*

But the most severe consequence may be what only dropouts are so far demonstrating—an overall decline in Ogbu's effort optimism. Its potential social effects extend well beyond the schoolroom. Intelligence and ability, says writer James Fallows, have become legally and socially acceptable grounds for discrimination, and both are measured by the testing and tracking system in our schools. Doing well in school has thus come to be the measure of who is intelligent and who has ability. Beyond that, Fallows writes, our culture increasingly accepts that "he who goes further in school will go further in life." Many of the best jobs and most prestigious professions are restricted to those with imposing academic and professional degrees, thus creating a monopoly on "positions of privilege."

At a time when our economy requires better-educated workers than ever before, can we afford to let abstract measures of ability curtail the educational aspirations and potential accomplishments of our children? Quite aside from questions of national prosperity, do we really want to become a culture whose fruits are not available to most of its citizens? Despite income disparities and more classism than many observers are willing to admit, there has always been the *belief* in America that success, the good life, is available to all who are willing to work for it. But with our current fixation on testing and tracking, and what Fallows calls credentialism, we may be abandoning that belief and, with it, the majority of our young people.

The Good, The Bad
And The
DIFFERENCE

BARBARA KANTROWITZ

Like many children, Sara Newland loves animals. But unlike most youngsters, she has turned that love into activism. Five years ago, during a trip to the zoo, the New York City girl learned about the plight of endangered species, and decided to help. With the aid of her mother, Sara—then about 4 years old—baked cakes and cookies and sold them on the sidewalk near her apartment building. She felt triumphant when she raised $35, which she promptly sent in to the World Wildlife Fund.

A few weeks later, triumph turned into tears when the fund wrote Sara asking for more money. "She was devastated because she thought she had taken care of that problem," says Polly Newland, who then patiently told her daughter that there are lots of big problems that require continual help from lots of people. That explanation worked. Sara, now 9, has expanded her causes. Through her school, she helps out at an inner-city child-care center; she also regularly brings meals to homeless people in her neighborhood.

A sensitive parent can make all the difference in encouraging—or discouraging—a child's developing sense of morality and values. Psychologists say that not only are parents important as role models, they also have to be aware of a child's perception of the world at different ages and respond appropriately to children's concerns. "I think the capacity for goodness is there from the start," says Thomas Lickona, a professor of education at the State University of New York at Cortland and author of "Raising Good Children." But, he says, parents must nurture those instincts just as they help their children become good readers or athletes or musicians.

That's not an easy task these days. In the past, schools and churches played a key role in fostering moral development. Now, with religious influence in decline and schools wavering over

> **A sensitive parent is crucial in encouraging a child's sense of morality and values**
> ——

the way to teach values, parents are pretty much on their own. Other recent social trends have complicated the transmission of values. "We're raising a generation that is still groping for a good future direction," says psychologist William Damon, head of Brown University's education department. Many of today's parents were raised in the '60s, the age of permissiveness. Their children were born in the age of affluence, the '80s, when materialism was rampant. "It's an unholy combination," says Damon.

These problems may make parents feel they have no effect on how their children turn out. But many studies show that parents are still the single most important influence on their children. Lickona says that the adolescents most likely to follow their consciences rather than give in to peer pressure are those who grew up in "authoritative" homes, where rules are firm but clearly explained and justified—as opposed to "authoritarian" homes (where rules are laid down without explanation) or "permissive" homes.

The way a parent explains rules depends, of course, on the age of the child. Many adults assume that kids see right and wrong in grown-up terms. But what may be seen as "bad" behavior by an adult may not be bad in the child's eyes. For example, a young child may not know the difference between a fanciful tale and a lie, while older kids—past the age of 5—do know.

Many psychologists think that in children, the seeds of moral values are emotional, not intellectual. Such traits as empathy and guilt—observable in the very young—represent the beginning of what will later be a conscience. Even newborns respond to signs of distress in others. In a hospital nursery, for example, a bout of crying by one infant will trigger wailing all around. Research on children's attachment to their mothers shows that babies who are most secure (and those whose mothers are most responsive to their needs) later turn out to be leaders in school: self-directed and eager to learn. They are also most likely to absorb parental values.

The first modern researcher to describe the stages of a child's moral development was Swiss psychologist Jean Piaget. In his groundbreaking 1932 book, "The Moral Judgment of the Child," he described three overlapping phases of childhood, from 5 to 12. The first is the "morality of constraint" stage: children accept adult rules as absolutes. Then comes the "morality of cooperation," in which youngsters think of morality as equal treatment. Parents of siblings will recognize this as the "If he got a new Ninja Turtle, I want one, too," stage. In the third, kids can see complexity in moral situations. They can understand extenuating circumstances in which strict equality might not necessarily mean fairness ("He got a new Ninja Turtle, but I got to go to the ball game, so it's OK.")

Although Piaget's conclusions have been expanded by subsequent researchers, his work forms the basis for most current theories of moral development. In a study begun in the 1950s, Lawrence Kohlberg, a Harvard professor, used "moral dilemmas" to define six phases. He began with 50 boys who were 10, 13 and 16. Over the next 20 years, he asked them their reactions to carefully constructed dilemmas. The most famous concerns a man named Heinz, whose wife was dying of cancer. The boys were told, in part, that a drug that might save her was a form of radium discovered by the town pharmacist. But the pharmacist was charging 10 times the cost of manufacture for the drug and Heinz could not afford it—although he tried to borrow money from everyone he knew. Heinz begged the pharmacist to sell it more cheaply, but he refused. So Heinz, in desperation, broke into the store and stole the drug. Kohlberg asked his subjects: Did Heinz do the right thing? Why?

Kohlberg and others found that at the first stage, children base their answers simply on the likelihood of getting caught. As they get older, their reasons for doing the right thing become more complex. For example, Lickona says typical 5-year-olds want to stay out of trouble. Kids from 6 to 9 characteristically act out of self-interest; most 10- to 13-year-olds crave social approval. Many 15- to 19-year-olds have moved on to thinking about maintaining the social system and being responsible.

Over the years, educators have used these theories to establish new curricula at schools around the country that emphasize moral development. The Lab School, a private preschool in Houston, was designed by Rheta DeVries, a student of Kohlberg's. The teacher is a "companion/guide," not an absolute authority figure. The object of the curriculum is to get kids to think about why they take certain actions and to think about consequences. For example, if two children are playing a game and one wants to change the rules, the teacher would ask the other child if that was all right. "Moral development occurs best when children live in an environment where fairness and justice is a way of life," says DeVries.

Not everyone agrees with the concept of moral development as a series of definable stages. Other researchers say that the stage theories downplay the role of emotion, empathy and faith. In "The Moral Life of Children," Harvard child psychiatrist Robert Coles tells the story of a 6-year-old black girl named Ruby, who braved vicious racist crowds to integrate her New Orleans school—and then prayed for her tormentors each night before she went to bed. Clearly, Coles says, she did not easily fall into any of Kohlberg's or Piaget's stages. Another criticism of stage theorists comes from feminist psychologists, including Carol Gilligan, author of "In a Different Voice." Gilligan says that the stages represent only *male* development with the emphasis on the concepts of justice and rights, not female development, which, she says, is more concerned with responsibility and caring.

But many psychologists say parents can use the stage theories to gain insight into their children's development. At each phase, parents should help their children make the right decisions about their behavior. In his book, Lickona describes a typical situation involving a 5-year-old who has hit a friend over the head with a toy while playing at the friend's house. Lickona suggests that the parents, instead of simply punishing their son, talk to him about why he hit his friend (the boy played with a toy instead of with him) and about what he could do next time instead of hitting. The parents, Lickona says, should also discuss how the friend might have felt about being hit. By the end of the discussion, the child should realize that there are consequences to his behavior. In Lickona's example, the child decides to call his friend and apologize—a positive ending.

For older children, Lickona suggests family "fairness meetings" to alleviate tension. If, for example, a brother and sister are constantly fighting, the parents could talk to both of them about what seem to be persistent sources of irritation. Then, youngsters can think of ways to bring about a truce—or at least a cease-fire.

Children who learn these lessons can become role models for other youngsters—and for adults as well. Sara Newland tells her friends not to be scared of homeless people (most of them rush by without even a quick glance, she says). "Some people think, 'Why should I give to them?' " she says. "But I feel that you should give. If everyone gave food, they would all have decent meals." One recent evening, she and her mother fixed up three plates of beef stew to give out. They handed the first to the homeless man who's always on their corner. Then, Sara says, they noticed two "rough-looking guys" down the block. Sara's mother, a little scared, walked quickly past them. Then, she changed her mind and asked them if they'd like some dinner. "They said, 'Yes, God bless you'," Sara recalls. "At that moment, they weren't the same people who were looking through a garbage can for beer bottles a little while before. It brought out a part of them that they didn't know they had."

With TESSA NAMUTH *in New York and* KAREN SPRINGEN *in Chicago*

Trying to Explain AIDS

This is a good time to educate kids about AIDS, before they hit puberty and decide, as adolescents, that their parents don't know much. Kids this age are able to understand how a virus enters the body. They are ready for information about respecting differences in people, homosexuality, drug use, and, of course, prevention.

Deborah Berger

Last year, as part of his job with the Seattle-King County Health Department, Larry Ray-Keil began talking to kids about AIDS. And he brought his work home with him. "I asked my six-year-old daughter if she knew anything about AIDS. She said no. Then I asked her if she wanted to know anything about AIDS. She said no, she didn't want to know." And that was the end of that particular conversation.

But not the end of the subject. About three weeks later, Erin was ready to ask questions, and her father was prepared to answer. By opening the door to the topic, by showing his child it was okay to talk about AIDS, "I let her know I was approachable," says Ray-Keil.

The openness is essential to talking to kids about sexually transmitted diseases, says Katharine Knowles, project director of the Health Information Network, a nonprofit agency. Knowles, who has worked on AIDS education since 1983, believes that parents must begin early to offer children information about sexuality and sexually transmitted diseases.

That approach is one Dawn English understands. When she volunteers at the Northwest AIDS Foundation, Dawn often brings her four-year-old daughter with her. Darting between the cubicles, playing on the floor at her mother's feet, or waving hello to a friend, Amy is perfectly at home at the Madison Street offices. And she understands what a four-year-old can about AIDS. "She knows it's something that makes a person get sick and die," says Dawn.

Amy also knows that her mother, who routinely spends more than ten hours a week at the Northwest AIDS Foundation, is one of the many working to help people with AIDS.

Sometimes Dawn brings work home and in the process educates her older children about AIDS. The teens help out by putting condoms in matchbox covers. "They like the idea of saving lives. It's a very effective way of educating them," says Dawn.

Not all families, of course, have a parent directly involved in AIDS programs, but AIDS hits all of us where we live. Some of us already have lost friends or relatives to this dread disease; many more will in the future. Experts estimate that about 20,000 people in Washington state are infected with the virus. On the average, it takes seven years for AIDS to appear after a person is infected. More than 80 percent of people with AIDS die within three years of the onset of the disease, which destroys the immune system.

Some parents are reluctant to educate their kids about AIDS. The topic forces us to confront our own feelings about difficult issues: sexuality, homosexuality, drug use, and mortality. "A lot of parents don't have models for being open. There's a wall of fear because we haven't been recipients ourselves of this kind of openness," says Ann Downer, a health education and training consultant who serves on the faculty of the University of Washington's AIDS Education and Training Center.

The temptation may be to say nothing, perhaps out of a desire to protect our children (and ourselves) from some of the more painful aspects of reality. Ignoring the problem, however, simply doesn't work. Says Ray-Keil, "Silence is not the answer," a view shared by other health and education experts.

"Besides the emotional and moral reasons to talk to kids about AIDS, parents have a responsibility to keep their kids safe," says Ray-Keil. "Information is the only vaccine we have now."

And parents who believe that AIDS education is not the issue for younger children need to think again. "We have to face the fact that kids find used condoms, and IV needles in schoolyards and parks. We have to teach kids to not pick them up," says Pamela Hillard, AIDS education coordinator for the Seattle Public Schools. "Sometimes kids confuse condoms with balloons and try to blow them up."

Resources for Parents

With AIDS education, you're not on your own. You don't need to know all the answers, although some basic information is essential. To get started:

AIDS: What Parents Need to Know, by Larry Ray-Keil, is a useful one-page guide.

Ideas for Talking to Your Children about AIDS, by Ann Downer, is a wonderful reference that is organized by age group and gives examples of typical questions and answers.

Another useful publication is *AIDS and Children: Information for Parents,* published by the Washington State Department of Social and Health Services.

These resources and others are available from the AIDS Prevention Project (296-4999). The AIDS Hotline (1-800-ARC-AIDS) also is a good source of information.

Reprinted with permission from *Seattle's Child,* April 1989, pp. 1, 4-5.

135

Downer points out another reason to start talking with kids early: "If you ignore the subject until they're too old, they won't bring it up," says Downer. Ignoring AIDS takes work: the subject is on the television news, in the newspapers, on street posters. And if you travel through Tacoma (or get lost going to the Point Defiance Zoo), you may see some of the six billboards the Tacoma-Pierce County Health Department has put up as part of an educational campaign to prevent the spread of AIDS.

All of the AIDS coverage means parents have lots of opportunities to initiate discussions. A good first step is to ask your child, as Larry Ray-Keil did, if she wants to know about AIDS, or what she has heard about it. How much information you provide depends on the age and development of the child. "There's a point at which kids don't have a frame of reference; you need to explain things in stages," says Dawn English.

Important information for all children (of, say, five years and older) includes these points, says Ann Downer:
- AIDS is hard to get, and we're happy about that.

- AIDS is spread in limited ways.
- Being infected with AIDS can be prevented in almost all cases.

For young children five through seven or eight years of age, "Your primary goal should be to alleviate anxiety," says Ann Downer. Use a simple definition, such as "AIDS is a serious disease some people, mostly adults, get." Explain that kids don't have to be afraid of touching or hugging people with AIDS, and that AIDS is difficult to get. You can also tell your children that you will tell them when they are older, how *not* to get AIDS. Answer their questions simply and directly.

"Besides the emotional and moral reasons to talk to kids about AIDS, parents have a responsibility to keep their kids safe," says Ray-Keil. "Information is the only vaccine we have now."

It's important to incorporate AIDS into what a child is learning about sexuality and his own body. Children at this age are old enough to know the correct words for body parts, such as vagina, penis, breast, and so forth.

When children are nine or ten, they can handle and may actively seek out more detailed information. Kids can learn what AIDS stands for—Acquired Immune Deficiency Syndrome—and what those words mean. (The Seattle School District pamphlet, "AIDS: Facts for Elementary-Aged Students," includes a clear explanation.)

This is a good time to educate kids about AIDS, before they hit puberty and decide, as adolescents, that their parents don't know much. Kids this age are able to understand how a virus enters the body. They are ready for information about respecting differences in people, homosexuality, drug use, and, of course, prevention.

Kids reaching puberty often get uptight about the subject of sex. (One mother recalled how her son used to quash any discussions about sex. Now a college student, he is "like another per-

---

AIDS Education in the Public Schools

Teaching kids about AIDS is no longer only a parent's responsibility. AIDS education is now required, by law, for all Washington state public-school students in grades five through twelve.

Why begin in the fifth grade? "We already have a good family life program that starts in the fifth grade, so it's a natural beginning point," says Pamela Hillard, the school district's AIDS education coordinator. "The whole curriculum is meant to be empowering, so kids develop good decision-making skills. We must give our kids information so they can protect themselves. Our goal is to make kids aware of risky behaviors."

That kids desperately need such information is borne out by statistics. American teens make some of the worst choices, says Hillard. She cites the numbers: the U.S. has the highest pregnancy rate of any industrialized Western country; we have one of the highest rates of sexually transmitted diseases among teens. Twenty-five percent of all teens

have some STD before graduating from high school.

"We have the facts to show us kids are not making good choices," says Hillard. "Faced with a new and fatal illness, we need to give kids information and skills to enable them to make better decisions."

Seattle is one of sixteen school districts to receive funding for AIDS education from the Centers for Disease Control. The Seattle curriculum includes information about safe and risky behaviors, how the virus is transmitted, and prevention. Optional family homework exercises seem a sure bet to generate lively discussions. (One example: a friend had a blood transfusion in 1983, before screening for the AIDS virus was available. The exercise concludes with the question: If it turns out that the friend does have the AIDS virus, what will our family do?)

Parents can preview AIDS educational materials, and are notified in advance when the curriculum will be taught.

Contact your child's principal or teacher for information.

Many communities continue to ignore or resist AIDS education. In Seattle, however, the vast majority of parents apparently want their kids to know about AIDS. Only 29 children have been waived from the education by parents, says Hillard.

The Bellevue School District also has had few children waived from the AIDS education program, says Bob Collins, health education curriculum specialist. Bellevue schools are using "Here's Looking at AIDS and You," a multimedia curriculum developed by the Comprehensive Health Education Foundation, a Seattle-based nonprofit organization.

In Bellevue, the AIDS education program started early this year, so it's a bit early to gauge parents' reaction. Collins points out that the curriculum was picked because it could influence kids' behavior, to make it "not as cool to take risks with drug and sex experimentation, because those risks are not worth it."

son: he comes home and talks about why there should be condom machines in the dorms.")

Some middle school-aged kids want to be included in adult discussions. "We talk about how AIDS is transmitted and the main ways it's caught," says Rosemary Mayo, an English teacher whose youngest child is a seventh grader at Eckstein Middle School in Seattle. "We talk about normal hygiene, things like washing hands and covering cuts with bandages to keep out infection. And we include our twelve-year-old son in adult discussions, so he hears my husband and I talking about AIDS."

Downer notes that teens often deny their vulnerability to the disease because they typically think of themselves as invincible. That's a good reason why AIDS education should take place before children hit puberty. (Incorrectly describing AIDS as a disease of only gay people or drug users perpetuates the view that people in other groups don't need to be concerned. Remind children that viruses do *not* discriminate.)

Sometimes it helps to have the same-sex parent talk with the child before both parents and the child discuss AIDS. "It's important to give a clear message that sex is not bad, but that the risks are high. Sex, like all good things, has physical and emotional risks," says Downer.

And if your palms sweat and you find yourself stumbling a bit over certain words, that's all right. "It's okay if it feels difficult, it *is* difficult," says Larry Ray-Keil. "It's all right to feel not quite sure. Be honest if you need a time out when they ask a difficult question. Kids get sex information—they want information and they will get it somewhere. The information they find may not be accurate, it may not reflect your values, so parents need to be responsible for conveying information and values." Surrounded by AIDS posters and pamphlets in his First Hill office, Ray-Keil speaks as a professional and as a parent. "Kids learn what they live. If they live with people responsible about sex and drugs they will be responsible, too. Effective parenting is good modeling."

Editor's note: "AIDS-Wise, No Lies," a special AIDS program for middle-school through college students, aired on KCTS/9, April 1, [1989] at 8:30 p.m. The video may be previewed for purchase or rental. Contact Current-Rutledge, [206] 324-7530, for more information.

Development during Childhood – Family and Culture

- Family (Articles 27–32)
- Culture (Articles 33–37)

The personal and social skills developed during infancy and early childhood are modified and expanded during childhood. Two of the most important influences on personal-social growth and change are physical development and cognitive development. The world looks different to the bigger, stronger, cognitively more "reasonable" child. A third very important influence on personal and social change is the child's entrance into the subculture of childhood, which includes school, peers, and clubs. While family is still of vital importance to the school-age child, peers grow in importance, as do teachers and extracurricular activity leaders. The culture, especially as seen through the eyes of peers and close friends, becomes more meaningful. Cultural influences include multiple factors that interact with each other, such as family, friends, schools, parents' jobs, television, exposure to sex, drugs, violence in society, popular music, faddish clothing, language, and behavior.

Erik Erikson proposed that psychosocial development in school-age children followed the psychosexual stage of latency proposed by Sigmund Freud earlier in the century. Freud believed that school-age children sublimate their libidinous (sexual) urges. They become calmer and steadier as they bury their phallic drives in their unconscious and concentrate more on school concerns and same-sex friendships.

Erikson expanded Freud's beliefs about the sexually latent stage to include cultural influences on personal-social skills. Erikson proposed that the nuclear (central) conflict of the school-age child is learning to be industrious vs. feeling inferior to others. Caregivers and teachers who give systematic instruction in skills and tasks and who recognize the progress and productions of children, foster the growing sense of industry. Industry and a sense of competence foster self-esteem.

Many other theorists have attempted to explain the personal and social growth and change of children in relation to family and cultures. Lawrence Kohlberg combined cognitive changes with social changes to propose a social-cognitive theory of moral development. Initially infants and young children are amoral, or base right and wrong decisions on simple criteria such as avoiding punishment, pleasing themselves, or pleasing significant others. By school-age, the concrete cognitive operations of children allow them to make more sophisticated decisions about right and wrong. They use criteria such as the approval of others, maintaining good relationships with others, maintaining the social order, and respect for authority to decide if behavior is moral and ethical. When role models condone a social environment that includes drugs, violence, and sexual promiscuity, children are apt to view these behaviors as acceptable. Some children experience a great deal of stress trying to discern right from wrong in relation to maintaining good relationships with others in the rapidly changing social climate.

Families are crucial to the healthy social and personality development of school-age children. Much research has been directed to family "risk factors" that may disrupt social and emotional health. All too often, oversimplistic generalizations are made about families. A school-age child is not necessarily at risk of becoming socially and emotionally disturbed if the mother is employed, the father is absent, the family lives in poverty, the parents divorce, the family is homeless, the child is abused, the child witnesses too much violence, or if the child is exposed to negative peer influence or drugs. Some children are very resilient despite multiple stresses and cultural adversities. Other children seem to wilt with only a minimal amount of stress. A working mother or a working father can be a good parent. Likewise, a single parent, a poor parent, a divorced parent, or a homeless parent can be a good parent. Recent research suggests that parental affection coupled with family togetherness and family democracy can go a long way toward ameliorating some of the adversities of the external environment. Adequate health care and nutrition also contribute to more resilient children. Children with a positive resolution of Erikson's conflict of trust, autonomy, initiative, and industry have higher self-esteem and are more tenacious in the face of the troubles and pressures of the times.

Peer pressures increase as children move through the school years. While much has been written about negative peer influences like drugs, violence, and delinquency, peers also can have positive influences on each other. In general, children prefer same-sex friends during the school years. Friendships are usually based more on shared activities at first and become more intimate as children move closer to puberty. Friends provide a forum for self-disclosure in late childhood. They are often more important than families for decisions about the culture of childhood (e.g., dress, behavior codes, vocabulary, television viewing, choice of music).

The articles selected for this unit focus on new concerns about family and culture as they relate to child development. Two-income families are now the norm. The first article addresses some of the family risk factors associated with workaholic parents and latchkey children. How can working parents still be good parents? How can the workplace support parenting? The second article describes the shift in fathering that is occurring as both parents work outside the home. Fathers are very important sources of support for school-age children. The third article helps to explain why siblings are different despite similar parenting practices. The next two articles describe the risks to children from divorce and maltreatment. Finally, the family subsection of this unit ends with an upbeat article about the benefits of family love. The five articles in the culture subsection of this unit discuss America's rapidly changing social climate: alienation, sex, peer pressures, divorce, child abuse, televised violence, and homelessness. Each article summarizes some of the societal problems that may cause stress in school-age children and describes some factors that help to alleviate the effects of stress.

Looking Ahead: Challenge Questions

Can occupational pressures of parents be harmful to children?

Describe the family role of the 1990s father.

Why is each child in a family different despite similar parenting?

Is divorce always bad for children? Explain your answer.

Does maltreatment in childhood have effects that last into adulthood? Support your answer.

Why is affection so important in childhood?

What are the four "worlds," of childhood and how do they relate to alienation?

What do today's children have to cry about?

Why are some children more resilient to stress and cultural adversity?

Do you agree that television fosters violence? Why, or why not?

What is the impact of homelessness on children?

CAN YOUR CAREER HURT YOUR KIDS?

Mommy often gets home from work too tired to talk. Daddy's almost never around. Says one expert: "We can only guess at the damage being done to the very young."

Kenneth Labich

BECAUSE CHILDREN are the future, America could be headed for bad bumps down the road. Some of the symptoms are familiar—rising teenage suicides and juvenile arrest rates, average SAT scores lower than 30 years ago. But what is the disease festering beneath that disturbing surface? Says Alice A. White, a clinical social worker who has been counseling troubled children in Chicago's prosperous North Shore suburbs for nearly two decades: "I'm seeing a lot more emptiness, a lack of ability to attach, no sense of real pleasure. I'm not sure a lot of these kids are going to be effective adults."

Not all children, or even most of them, are suffering from such a crisis of the spirit. In fact, some trends are headed in a promising direction. For example, drug use among young people has fallen sharply since the 1970s. But a certain malaise does seem to be spreading. Far more and far earlier than ever before, kids are pressured to take drugs, have sex, deal with violence. In a world ever more competitive and complex, the path to social and economic success was never more obscure.

And fewer traditional pathfinders are there to show the way. Divorce has robbed millions of kids of at least one full-time parent. With more and more women joining the work force, and many workaholic parents of both sexes, children are increasingly left in the care of others or allowed to fend for themselves. According to a University of Maryland study, in 1985 American parents spent on average just 17 hours a week with their children.

This parental neglect would be less damaging if better alternatives were widely available, but that is decidedly not the case. Families that can afford individual child care often get good value, but the luxury of a compassionate, full-time, \$250-a-week nanny to watch over their pride and joy is beyond the reach of most American parents. They confront a patchwork system of informal home arrangements and more structured day care centers. In far too many cases, parents with infants or toddlers cannot feel secure about the care their children get. Says Edward Zigler, a professor of child development at Yale, who has spent much of his career fighting the abuses of child care: "We are cannibalizing children. Children are dying in this system, never mind achieving optimum development."

For older children with no parental overseer, the prospects can be equally bleak. Studies are beginning to show that preteens and teenagers left alone after school, so-called latchkey children, may be far more prone than other kids to get involved with alcohol and illegal drugs.

For some experts in the field, the answer to all this is to roll back the clock to an idyllic past. Mom, dressed in a frilly apron, is merrily stirring the stew when Dad gets home from work. Junior, an Eagle Scout, and Sally—they call her Muffin—greet him with radiant smiles. Everybody sits down for dinner to talk about schoolwork and Mom's canasta party.

For others more in touch with the economic temper of the times—especially the financial realities behind the rising number of working mothers—the solution lies in improving the choices available to parents. Government initiatives to provide some financial relief may help, but corporations could make an even greater difference by focusing on the needs of employees who happen to be parents. Such big companies as IBM and Johnson & Johnson have taken the lead in dealing with employee child care problems, and many progressive corporations are discovering the benefits of greater flexibility with regard to family issues. At the same time, an array of professional child care organizations has sprung up to help big corporations meet their employees' demands.

Without doubt, helping improve child care is in the best interest of business—today's children, after all, are tomorrow's labor pool. Says Sandra Kessler Hamburg, director of education studies at the Committee for Economic Development, a New York research group that funnels corporate funds into education projects: "We can only guess at the damage being done to very young children right now. From the perspective of American business, that is very, very disturbing. As jobs get more and more technical, the U.S. work force is less and less prepared to handle them."

The state of America's children is a political mine field, and threading through the research entails a lot of gingerly probing as well as the occasional explosion. Much work in the field is contradictory, and many additional longer-range studies need to be done before anyone can say precisely what is happening.

Moreover, any researcher who dwells on the problems of child care—of infants in particular—risks being labeled antiprogressive by the liberal academic establishment. If the researcher happens to be male, his motives may seem suspect. If he says babies are at risk in some child care settings, he may be accused of harboring the wish that women leave the work force and return to the kitchen. Much valid research may be totally ignored because it has been deemed politically incorrect.

For example: Jay Belsky, a Penn State professor specializing in child development, set off a firestorm in 1986 with an article in *Zero to Three*, an influential journal that summarizes existing academic re-

REPORTER ASSOCIATE *Jung Ah Pak*

search. His conclusions point to possible risks for very small children in day care outside the home. Though he scrupulously threw in a slew of caveats and even went so far as to confess a possible bias because his own wife stayed home with their two children, Belsky came under heavy attack. Feminist researchers called his scholarship into question. Says Belsky: "I was flabbergasted by the response. I felt like the messenger who got shot."

Belsky's critics charged, among other things, that he had ignored studies that document some more positive results from infant day care. Since then, for example, a study conducted by researchers at the University of Illinois and Trinity College in Hartford, Connecticut, found that a child's intellectual development may actually be helped during the second and third years of life if the mother works. The study, which tracked a nationwide sample of 874 children from ages 3 to 4, determined that the mental skills of infants in child care outside the home were lower than those of kids watched over by their mothers during the first year, but then picked up enough at ages 2 and 3 to balance out.

Whatever the merits of his critics' assault, Belsky presents a disturbing picture of the effects on infants of nonparental child care outside the home. In a 1980 study he cited in the article, involving low-income women in the Minneapolis-St. Paul area, infants in day care were disproportionately likely to avoid looking at or approaching their mothers after being separated from them for a brief period.

ANOTHER STUDY, conducted in 1974, concluded that 1-year-olds in day care cried more when separated from their mothers than those reared at home; still another, in 1981, found that day care infants threw more temper tantrums. To at least some extent, the observations seem to apply across socioeconomic boundaries. A 1985 University of Illinois study of infants from affluent Chicago families showed that babies in the care of full-time nannies avoided any sort of contact with their mothers more often than those raised by moms during their first year.

An infant's attachment, or lack of it, to the mother is especially crucial because it can portend later developmental problems. In the Minnesota study, toddlers who had been in day care early on displayed less enthusiasm when confronted with a challenging task. They were less likely to follow their mothers' instructions and less persistent in dealing with a difficult problem. Another study, which took a look at virtually all 2-year-olds on the island of Bermuda, found more poorly adjusted children among the early day care group regardless of race, IQ, or socioeconomic status.

Researchers in Connecticut investigating 8- to 10-year-old children in 1981 found higher levels of misbehavior and greater

withdrawal from the company of others among those who had been in day care as infants, no matter what the educational level of their parents. In a study of kindergarten and first-grade children in North Carolina, the early day care kids were found more likely than others to hit, kick, push, threaten, curse, and argue with their peers.

What we should take away from the research, says an unrepentant Belsky, is this: "There is an accumulating body of evidence that children who were cared for by people other than their parents for 20 or more hours per week during their first year are at increased risk of having an insecure relationship with their parents at age 1— and at increased risk of being more aggressive and disobedient by age 3 to 8."

Belsky adds several "absolutely necessary caveats": First, the results of all these studies must be viewed in light of the added stress that many families experience when both parents work and of the fact that affordable high-quality day care is not always available. Belsky agrees with some of his academic opponents that the quality of day care matters. His second warning: The results of these studies are generalizations and do not apply to every single child. Third, he says, nobody really knows what causes underlie the findings.

Research on older children who spend at least part of the day on their own is far less controversial, though no less disturbing. A recent study by the American Academy of Pediatrics focused on substance abuse by nearly 5,000 eighth-graders around Los Angeles and San Diego. The sample cut across a wide range of ethnic and economic backgrounds and was split about half and half between boys and girls. The researchers concluded that 12- and 13-year-olds who were latchkey kids, taking care of themselves for 11 or more hours a week, were about twice as likely as supervised children to smoke, drink alcohol, and use marijuana. About 31% of the latchkey kids have two or more drinks at a time; only about 17% of the others do. Asked whether they expected to get drunk in the future, 27% of the latchkey kids and 15% of the others said yes.

Increasingly, isolation from parents is a problem even when the family is physically together. Beginning in infancy, children are highly attuned to their parents' moods. And when parents have little left to give to their offspring at the end of a stressful day, the kids' disappointment can be crushing. Says Eleanor Szanton, executive director of the National Center for Clinical Infant Programs, a nonprofit resource center in Virginia: "What happens between parents and children during the first hour they are reunited is as important as anything that happens all day. If the mother is too exhausted to be a mother, you've got a problem."

When children become adolescents and begin to test their wings by defying their

parents' authority, stressed-out families may break down completely because no strong relationship between parents and children has developed over the years. In high-achiever families, says Chicago social worker Alice White, family life can become an ordeal where children must prove their worth to their parents in the limited time available. Conversation can be a series of "didjas"—Didja ace that test, win the election, score the touchdown? What's missing is the easygoing chatter, the long, relaxed conversations that allow parents and children to know each other.

White says that many of today's kids don't understand how the world works because they haven't spent enough time with their parents to understand how decisions are made, careers are pursued, personal relationships are formed. She finds herself spending more and more time acting as a surrogate mother for the seemingly privileged kids she counsels, advising them on everything from sexual issues to recipes for a small dinner party. Says White: "The parents serve as a model of success, but the kids are afraid they won't get there because nobody has shown them how."

JUST ABOUT EVERYONE in the child-development field agrees that all this adds up to a discouraging picture, but opinions vary wildly as to what ought to be done about it—and by whom. For a growing band of conservative social thinkers, the answer is simple: Mothers ought to stay home. These activists, working at private foundations and conservative college faculties, rail against what they see as the permissiveness of recent decades. They save their most lethal venom for organized child care, blaming it for everything from restraining kids' free will to contributing to major outbreaks of untold diseases. One conservative researcher, Bryce Christensen of the Rockford Institute in Illinois, has likened day care to the drug Thalidomide. Day care, he writes, is "a new threat to children that not only imperils the body, but also distorts and withers the spirit."

Gary L. Bauer, president of a conservative Washington research outfit called the Family Research Council, is among the most visible of these social activists. Bauer, a domestic-policy adviser in the Reagan White House, believes strongly that the entry of great numbers of women into the work force has harmed America's children. He says the importance of bonding between a mother and her children became clear to him and his wife one morning several years ago when they were dropping their 2-year-old daughter at a babysitter's home. The child went immediately to the sitter, calling her "Mommy." That was something of an epiphany for Bauer's wife, Carol: She quit her job as a government employment counselor soon after and has since stayed home to raise the couple's three children.

Still, the dual-career trend continues. No

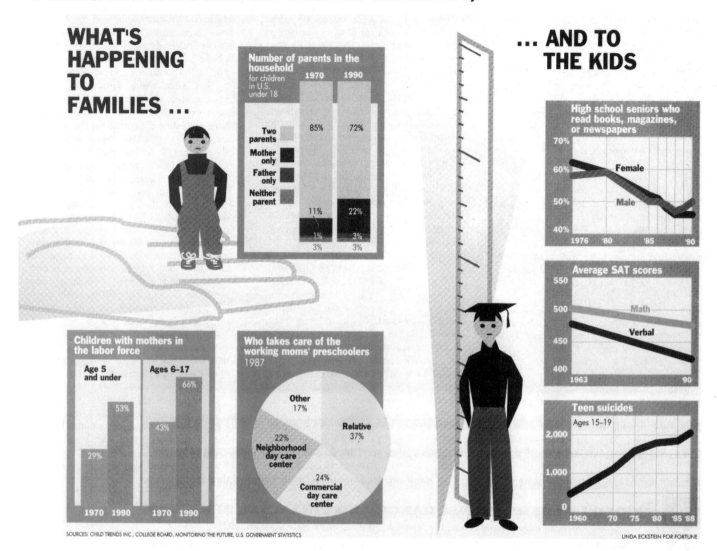

WHAT'S HAPPENING TO FAMILIES ...

Number of parents in the household
for children in U.S. under 18

	1970	1990
Two parents	85%	72%
Mother only	11%	22%
Father only	1%	3%
Neither parent	3%	3%

Children with mothers in the labor force

Age 5 and under: 1970 29%, 1990 53%
Ages 6–17: 1970 43%, 1990 66%

Who takes care of the working moms' preschoolers
1987

- Other 17%
- Relative 37%
- Commercial day care center 24%
- Neighborhood day care center 22%

... AND TO THE KIDS

High school seniors who read books, magazines, or newspapers
Female, Male — 1976 '80 '85 '90

Average SAT scores
Math, Verbal — 1963 '90

Teen suicides
Ages 15–19 — 1960 70 75 80 '85 '88

SOURCES: CHILD TRENDS INC., COLLEGE BOARD, MONITORING THE FUTURE, U.S. GOVERNMENT STATISTICS

LINDA ECKSTEIN FOR FORTUNE

wonder. Most American families could not afford to forfeit a second income, a fact that renders the conservatives' yearning for a simpler past quixotic at best. Real weekly earnings for workers declined 13% from 1973 to 1990. So in most cases two paychecks are a necessity. Also, about a quarter of American children—and about half of black children—live in single-parent homes. Those parents are nearly all women. Though some receive child support or other income, their wages are usually their financial lifeblood. About half the mothers who have been awarded child support by the courts do not get full payments regularly.

From the standpoint of the national economy, a mass exodus of women from the work force would be a disaster: There simply won't be enough available males in the future. Women now make up over 45% of the labor force, and they are expected to fill about 60% of new jobs between now and the year 2000.

EVEN IF a child's welfare were the only consideration, in many cases full-time motherhood might not be the best answer. Children whose mothers are frustrated and angry about staying home might be better off in a high-quality day care center. And many kids may well benefit from the socializing and group activities available in day care. A mother and child alone together all day isn't necessarily a rich environment for the child.

In the end, the short supply of high-quality day care is the greatest obstacle to better prospects for America's children. Experts agree on what constitutes quality in child care—a well-paid and well-trained staff, a high staff-child ratio, a safe and suitable physical environment. They also generally concur that if those criteria are met, most children will not just muddle through but prosper. Says Barbara Reisman, executive director of the Child Care Action Campaign, a nonprofit educational and advocacy organization in New York: "Despite all the questions that have been raised, the bottom line is that if the quality is there, and the parents are comfortable with the situation, the kids are going to be fine."

But even tracking, much less improving, child care quality is a monumental task. Something like 60% of the approximately 11 million preschool kids whose mothers work are taken care of in private homes. That can be a wonderful experience: Grandma or a warm-hearted neighbor spends the day with the wee ones baking cookies and imparting folk wisdom. Or it can be hellish. Yale's Edward Zigler speaks in horror of the home where 54 kids in the care of a 16-year-old were found strapped into car seats all day. Low pay and the lack of status associated with organized day care centers make it tough to recruit and retain qualified workers. A study by a research group called the Child Care Employee Project in Oakland revealed an alarming 41% annual turnover rate at day care operations across the U.S. One big reason: an average hourly salary of $5.35. Says Zigler: "We pay these people less than we do zoo keepers—and then we expect them to do wonders."

The experts have floated various schemes to make more money available. The Bush Administration has offered $732 million in block grants to the states for child care and has also proposed increasing the modest tax credits (current maximum: $1,440) for lower-income parents using most kinds of day care. Another current idea: increase the personal exemption. If it had kept pace with inflation since 1950, it would be about $7,000 instead of $2,050. Zigler has proposed that couples be allowed to dip into their Social Security accounts for a short while when their children are young. Under his plan families would be limited to tapping the accounts for up to three years per child, and their retirement benefits would be reduced or delayed proportionately. Zigler would also limit the amount of money withdrawn to some reasonable maximum.

Under all these proposals, parents—especially women—could more easily afford to pay for high-quality day care, scale back their work hours, or even stay at home longer with a newborn if they wished. A 1989 Cornell University study found that about two-thirds of mothers who work full time would cut their hours if they didn't need the extra income. In other surveys, even greater percentages of working mothers with infants say they would reduce their hours or stay home if money were no problem.

In his recent book, *Child Care Choices*, Zigler presents some innovative notions about improving care for older children. He would start organized classes in the public school system beginning at age 3, and keep schools open in the afternoon and early evening for the use of kids with working parents. School libraries, gyms, music rooms, and art rooms would be available. Says Zigler: "All you need is a traffic cop." The city of Los Angeles and the entire state of Hawaii have begun after-school programs along these lines.

BUSINESS has a crucial role to play in helping employees who are parents cope with their responsibilities. The U.S. Congress is currently considering legislation that would guarantee 12 weeks of unpaid leave in the event of a family illness or the birth of a child. According to a study conducted by economics professors at Cornell University and the University of Connecticut, the costs of allowing such leaves for most workers is less than letting them quit and hiring permanent replacements. Companies can provide big-time relief with smaller gestures as well: making a telephone available to assembly-line workers so they can check up on their latchkey kids, say, or letting office workers slip out for a parent-teacher conference without a hassle.

As the competition for good workers heats up, many companies will be forced to grapple with the problems working parents face, or risk losing desirable employees. Says Douglas Besharov, a resident scholar at the American Enterprise Institute in Washington: "If you need workers, you will do what has to be done."

Many corporations have already taken the plunge. IBM, among other companies, offers employees a free child-care referral service; IBM uses 250 different organizations. The company has also pledged $22 million over five years to improve the quality of day care available in the towns and cities where most of its employees live. Johnson & Johnson provides an array of goodies: one-year unpaid family care leaves, an extensive referral network, dependent care reimbursement accounts so that employees can pay child care expenses with pretax dollars, and up to $2,000 toward the cost of adoption.

J&J also supports an on-site day care center at its headquarters in New Brunswick, New Jersey. The company subsidizes part of the cost, but employees using the center still pay $110 to $130 a week depending on the age of the child. Depending on the region, average charges for a preschooler range from $67 to $115 a week. Infant care can cost up to $230 a week, and the affluent few with a full-time nanny pay $200 to $600.

Some smaller companies are paying attention as well. American Bankers Insurance Group, based in Miami, maintains a day care center for employees' children ages 6 weeks to 5 years. After that the child can attend a company-run private school for an additional three years. The school takes care of the child from 8 A.M. to 6:15 P.M. and keeps its doors open during school holidays and summer vacations.

The child care business is growing rapidly. Approximately 77,000 licensed child care centers now serve about four million children daily. Financially troubled Kinder-Care Learning Centers of Montgomery, Alabama, is the industry giant, with 1,257 centers around the country and revenues of $396 million a year. The runner-up is a Kansas City, Missouri, outfit called La Petite Academy Inc. It operates about 750 centers and did $201 million worth of business in 1990.

ServiceMaster, the widely diversified management company based near Chicago, jumped into the field last year and now runs three centers in suburban office parks, with four more under construction. The beauty part of the business is that ServiceMaster typically gets some form of financial help from a landlord or corporate client—reduced rent or lower occupancy costs—and then charges market rates for its services.

Parents working at companies such as Sears, Abbott Laboratories, Ameritech, and Mobil pay about $140 to $150 a week for infants and about $95 a week for 3- to 5-year-olds. ServiceMaster executives consider this a business with splendid growth prospects: They plan to open another half-dozen centers by the end of 1991 and then begin expanding beyond the Chicago area.

Child-development experts admire a relatively new and growing company, Bright Horizons Children's Centers of Cambridge, Massachusetts, for the innovative on-site day care it provides for major corporations including IBM, Prudential, and Dun & Bradstreet. Founded in 1986 by Linda Mason and her husband, Roger Brown, both former economic development workers in Africa, Bright Horizons now operates 38 centers up and down the East Coast. In most cases the corporate client donates space for child care in or near its office building, providing Bright Horizons with a handsome cost advantage. Fees can be steep—up to $225 per week for infants—but companies often subsidize the payments for employees low on the wage scale.

Because the centers are close to the workplace, parents are encouraged to drop in throughout the day. Bright Horizons' teaching staff members earn up to $20,000 per year, far more than most day care centers pay, plus a full benefits package. They can pursue a defined career track and move into management ranks if they qualify. As a result, turnover runs at a relatively low 16% to 24%.

Brown and Mason concede that many children might be damaged by second-rate child care, but they contend that parents rarely have anything to fear from the kind of high-quality attention their centers provide. Says Mason: "It's very much like health care. If you can afford to pay for it, you can receive the best child care in the world in this country."

For business, helping employees find their way through the child care thicket makes increasing sense—and not only as a method of keeping today's work force happy. More and more companies with an eye on the future recognize the importance of early childhood development, and many are alarmed by the discouraging signals they see in the upcoming generation of workers. At BellSouth in Atlanta, for instance, only about one job applicant in ten passes a battery of exams that test learning ability; ten years ago, twice as many did. Even those who make it through the tests often require extensive training and carry heavy personal baggage: A startling 70% of BellSouth's unmarried employees support at least one child.

More companies are finding that they have to help employees cope not just with their children but also with the gamut of life's vicissitudes. Says Roy Howard, BellSouth's senior vice president for corporate human resources: "Business used to feel that you ought to leave your personal problems at home. We can no longer afford to take that view." The psychic welfare of workers—and of their children—is increasingly a legitimate management concern, and companies that ignore it risk their employees' future as well as their own.

BRINGING UP FATHER

The message dads get is that they are not up to the job. And a record number don't stick around—even as fathers are needed more than ever.

NANCY R. GIBBS

"I don't have a dad," says Megan, 8, a tiny blond child with a pixie nose who gazes up at a visitor and talks of her hunger. "Well, I do have a dad, but I don't know his name. I only know his first name, Bill."

Just what is it that fathers do?

"Love you. They kiss you and hug you when you need them. I had my mom's boyfriend for a while, but they broke up." Now Megan lives with just her mother and older brother in Culver City, California.

What would you like to do with your dad?

"I'd want him to talk to me." She's hurting now. "I wish I had somebody to talk to. It's not fair. If two people made you, then you should still be with those two people." And she's sad. "I'm not so special," she says, looking down at the floor. "I don't have two people."

She imagines what it would be like for him to come home from work at night.

"It would be just like that commercial where the kids say, 'Daddy, are you all right?' " She smiles, dreaming. "The kids show the daddy that they care for him. They put a thermometer in his mouth. They think he's sick because he came home early. They are sitting on the couch watching TV, and it's like, wow, we can play with Dad!"

Megan thinks her father is in the Navy now. "One day when I get older, I'm gonna go back to Alabama and try to find him."

More children will go to sleep tonight in a fatherless home than ever in the nation's history. Talk to the experts in crime, drug abuse, depression, school failure, and they can point to some study somewhere blaming those problems on the disappearance of fathers from the American family. But talk to the fathers who do stay with their families, and the story grows more complicated. What they are hearing, from their bosses, from institutions, from the culture around them, even from their own wives, very often comes down to a devastating message: We don't really trust men to be parents, and we don't really need them to be. And so every day, everywhere, their children are growing up without them.

Corporate America, for a start, may praise family life but does virtually nothing to ease it. Managers still take male workers aside and warn them not to take a paternity leave if they want to be taken seriously. On TV and in movies and magazine ads, the image of fathers over the past generation evolved from the stern, sturdy father who knew best to a helpless Homer Simpson, or some ham-handed galoot confounded by the prospect of changing a diaper. Teachers call parent conferences but only talk to the mothers. When father arrives at the doctor's office with little Betsy, the pediatrician offers instructions to pass along to his wife, the caregiver presumptive. The Census Bureau can document the 70 million mothers age 15 or older in the U.S. but has scant idea how many fathers there are. "There's no interest in fathers at all," says sociologist Vaughn Call, who directs the National Survey of Families and Households at the University of Wisconsin. "It's a nonexistent category. It's the ignored half of the family."

Mothers themselves can be unwitting accomplices. Even women whose own progress in public life depends on sharing the workload in private life act as "gatekeepers" in the home, to use Harvard pediatrician T. Berry Brazelton's description. Dig deeply into household dynamics, and the tensions emerge. Women say they need and want their husbands to be more active parents but fear that they aren't always reliable. Men say they might like to be more involved, but their wives will not make room for them, and jealously guard their domestic power.

Most troubling of all to some social scientists is the message men get that being a good father means learning how to mother. Among child-rearing experts, the debate rages over whether men and women parent differently, whether there is some unique contribution that each makes to the emotional health of their children. "Society sends men two messages," says psychologist Jerrold Lee Shapiro, father of two and the author of *A Measure of the Man*, his third book on fatherhood. "The first is, We want you to be involved, but you'll be an inadequate mother. The second is, You're invited into the birthing room and into the nurturing process—but we don't want all of you. We only want your support. We're not really ready as a culture to accept men's fears, their anger or their sadness. This is the stuff that makes men crazy. We want men to be the protectors and providers, but we are scared they won't be if they become soft."

So now America finds its stereotypes crushed in the collision between private needs and public pressures. While some commend the nurturing nature of the idealized New Father, others cringe at the idea

From *Time*, June 28, 1993, pp. 52-56, 58, 61. © 1993 by Time Inc. Magazine Company. Reprinted by permission.

of genderless parenting and defend the importance of men being more than pale imitations of mothers. "If you become Mr. Mom," says Shapiro, "the family has a mother and an assistant mother. That isn't what good fathers are doing today." And fathers themselves wrestle with memories of their own fathers, vowing to do it differently, and struggling to figure out how.

THE DISAPPEARING DAD

Well into the 18th century, child-rearing manuals in America were generally addressed to fathers, not mothers. But as industrialization began to separate home and work, fathers could not be in both places at once. Family life of the 19th century was defined by what historians call the feminization of the domestic sphere and the marginalization of the father as a parent. By the 1830s, child-rearing manuals, increasingly addressed to mothers, deplored the father's absence from the home. In 1900 one worried observer could describe "the suburban husband and father" as "almost entirely a Sunday institution."

What alarms modern social scientists is that in the latter part of this century the father has been sidelined in a new, more disturbing way. Today he's often just plain absent. Rising divorce rates and out-of-wedlock births mean that more than 40% of all children born between 1970 and 1984 are likely to spend much of their childhood living in single-parent homes. In 1990, 25% were living with only their mothers, compared with 5% in 1960. Says David Blankenhorn, the founder of the Institute for American Values in New York City: "This trend of fatherlessness is the most socially consequential family trend of our generation."

Credit Dan Quayle for enduring the ridicule that opened the mainstream debate over whether fathers matter in families. In the year since his famous Murphy Brown speech, social scientists have produced mounting evidence that, at the very least, he had a point. Apart from the personal politics of parenting, there are larger social costs to reckon in a society that dismisses fathers as luxuries.

Studies of young criminals have found that more than 70% of all juveniles in state reform institutions come from fatherless homes. Children from broken families are nearly twice as likely as those in two-parent families to drop out of high school. After assessing the studies, economist Sylvia Hewlett suggested that "school failure may well have as much to do with disintegration of families as with the quality of schools."

Then there is the emotional price that children pay. In her 15 years tracking the lives of children of divorced families, Judith Wallerstein found that five years af-

ter the split, more than a third experienced moderate or severe depression. After 10 years a significant number of the young men and women appeared to be troubled, drifting and underachieving. At 15 years many of the thirtyish adults were struggling to create strong love relationships of their own. Daughters of divorce, she found, "often experience great difficulty establishing a realistic view of men in general, developing realistic expectations and exercising good judgment in their choice of partners."

For boys, the crucial issue is role modeling. There are psychologists who suggest that boys without fathers risk growing up with low self-esteem, becoming overly dependent on women and emotionally rigid. "Kids without fathers are forced to find their own ways of doing things," observes Melissa Manning, a social worker at the Boys and Girls Club of Venice, Cali-

It Takes Two

WOMEN'S VOICES ARE MORE SOOTHING. THEY CAN READ THE SIGNALS A CHILD SENDS BEFORE HE OR SHE CAN TALK. BUT AS TIME PASSES, THE STRENGTHS THAT FATHERS MAY BRING TO CHILD REARING BECOME MORE IMPORTANT.

fornia. "So they come up with their own ideas, from friends and from the gangs. Nobody is showing them what to do except to be drunk, deal drugs or go to jail." Then there are the subtler lessons that dads impart. Attorney Charles Firestone, for instance, recently decided it was time to teach his 11-year-old son how to play poker. "Maybe it will help if he knows when to hold 'em, when to fold 'em," he says.

THE ANTI-FATHER MESSAGE

Given the evidence that men are so vital to a healthy home, the anti-father messages that creep into the culture and its institutions are all the more troubling. Some scholars suggest that fatherhood is by its very biological nature more fragile than motherhood, and needs to be encouraged by the society around it. And yet for all the focus on the New Father (the kind who skips the corporate awards dinner to attend the school play), the messages men receive about how

they should act as parents are at best mixed and often explicitly hostile.

Employers that have been slow to accommodate the needs of mothers in their midst are often even more unforgiving of fathers. It is a powerful taboo that prevents men from acknowledging their commitment to their children at work. A 1989 survey of medium and large private employers found that only 1% of employees had access to paid paternity leave and just 18% could take unpaid leave. Even in companies like Eastman Kodak, only 7% of men, vs. 93% of women, have taken advantage of the six-year-old family-leave plan.

Those who do soon discover the cost. "My boss made me pay a price for it emotionally," says a prominent Washington executive who took leaves for both his children. "He was very generous with the time, but he never let me forget it. Every six seconds he reminded me what a great guy he was and that I owed him really, really big. You don't get a lot of points at the office for wanting to have a healthy family life." Men, like women, are increasingly troubled by the struggle to balance home and work; in 1989, asked if they experienced stress while doing so, 72% of men answered yes, compared with 12% a decade earlier, according to James Levine of the Fatherhood Project at the Families and Work Institute of New York City.

Many men will freely admit that they sometimes lie to employers about their commitments. "I announced that I was going to a meeting," shrugged a Washington journalist as he left the office in midafternoon one day recently. "I just neglected to mention that the 'meeting' was to watch my daughter play tennis." Now it is the fathers who are beginning to ask themselves whether their careers will stall and their incomes stagnate, whether the glass ceiling will press down on them once they make public their commitment as parents, whether today's productivity pressures will force them to work even harder with that much less time to be with their kids. In the higher reaches of management, there are not only few women, there are also few men in dual-income families who take an active part in raising their children. "Those who get to the top today," says Charles Rodgers, owner of a 10-year-old family-research organization in Brookline, Massachusetts, called Work/Family Directions, "are almost always men from what used to be the traditional family, men with wives who don't work outside the home."

Many men insist that they long to veer off onto a "daddy track." In a 1990 poll by the Los Angeles *Times,* 39% of the fathers said they would quit their jobs to have more time with their kids, while another survey found that 74% of men said they would rather have a daddy-track job than a fast-track job. But in real life, when they are not talking to pollsters, some fathers recognize the power of their atavistic impulses to earn bread and compete, both of which often leave them ambivalent about their obligations as fathers.

George Ingram, 48, lives on Capitol Hill with his sons Mason, 15, and Andrew, 10. He is the first to admit that single fatherhood has not helped his career as a political economist. "We're torn between working hard to become Secretary of State and nurturing our kids," he says. "You make the choice to nurture your kids, and people think it's great. But does it put a crimp on your career? Yes, very definitely. When I finish this process, I will have spent 15 years on a professional plateau." Ingram finds that his colleagues accept his dual commitments, his leaving every night before 6, or by 5 if he has a soccer practice to coach. In fact they are more accepting of his choices than those of his female colleagues. "I get more psychic support than women do," he says. "And I feel great about spending more time with my kids than my father did."

MATERNAL GATEKEEPERS

The more surprising obstacle men say, arises in their own homes. Every household may be different, every division of labor unique, but sociologists do find certain patterns emerging when they interview groups of men and women about how they view one another's parenting roles. Men talk about their wife's unrealistic expectations, her perfectionism, the insistence on dressing, feeding, soothing the children in a certain way. "Fathers, except in rare circumstances, have not yet become equal partners in parenthood," says Frank Furstenberg, professor of sociology at the University of Pennsylvania. "The restructuring of the father role requires support and encouragement from wives. Presumably, it is not abnormal for wives to be reluctant to give up maternal prerogatives."

Many men describe in frustration their wife's attitude that her way of doing things is the only way. "Dad is putting the baby to bed," says Levine. "He's holding his seven-month-old on his shoulders and walking around in circles. Mom comes in and says, 'She likes it better when you just lay her down on her stomach and rub her back.' Dad gets mad that Mom is undermining his way of doing things, which he thinks works perfectly well."

In most cases, it is still the mother who carries her child's life around in her head, keeping the mental daybook on who needs a lift to piano practice and who needs to get the poetry folder in on time. After examining much of the research on men's housework and child care, Sylvia Hewlett concluded that married men's average time in household tasks had increased only 6% in 20 years, even as women have flooded the workplace. Psychologists Rosalind Barnett and Grace Baruch found that fathers were often willing to perform the jobs they were assigned but were not responsible for remembering, planning or scheduling them.

Women often respond that until men prove themselves dependable as parents, they can't expect to be trusted. A haphazard approach to family responsibilities does nothing to relieve the burdens women carry. "Men haven't been socialized to think about family appointments and how the household runs for kids," notes Marie Wilson of the Ms. Foundation for Women, who constantly hears of the hunger women feel for their husbands to participate more fully at home. "They don't really get in there and pay attention. Mothers often aren't sure they can trust them—not just to do it as they do it, but to do it at a level that you can get away with without feeling guilty."

Some women admit that their own feelings are mixed when it comes to relinquishing power within the family. "I can probably be overbearing at times as far as wanting to have it my way," says the 35-year-old wife of a St. Louis, Missouri, physician. "But I would be willing to relax my standards if he would be more involved. It would be a good trade-off." Here again the attitude is changing with each generation. Women under 35, researchers find, seem more willing than older women, whose own fathers were probably less engaged, to trust men as parents. Also, as younger women become more successful professionally, they are less fearful of relinquishing power at home because their identity and satisfaction come from many sources.

THE NEW FATHER

The redefinition of fatherhood has been going on in virtually every arena of American life for well over 20 years. As women worked to broaden their choices at home and work, the implicit invitation was for men to do likewise. As Levine has observed, Dr. Spock had carefully revised his advice on fathers by 1974. The earlier version suggested that fathers change the occasional diaper and cautioned mothers about "trying to force the participation of fathers who get gooseflesh at the very idea of helping to take care of a baby." The new version of *Baby and Child Care*, by contrast, offered a prescription for the New Fatherhood: "The father—any father—should be sharing with the mother the day-to-day care of their child from birth onward ... This is the natural way for the father to start the relationship, just as it is for the mother."

By the '80s, bookstores were growing fat with titles aimed at men: *How to Father,* *Expectant Father, Pregnant Fathers, The Birth of a Father, Fathers Almanac* and *Father Power.* There were books about child-and-father relations, like *How to Father a Successful Daughter,* and then specific texts for part-time fathers, single fathers, stepfathers and homosexual fathers. Bill Cosby's *Fatherhood* was one of the best-selling books in publishing history, and *Good Morning, Merry Sunshine,* by Chicago *Tribune* columnist Bob Greene, a journal about his first year of fatherhood, was on the New York *Times* best-seller list for almost a year. Parents can now pick up *Parents' Sports,* a new magazine dedicated to reaching the dad market with stories on the joys of soccer practice.

Institutions were changing too. In his book *Fatherhood in America,* published this month, Robert L. Griswold has traced the history of a fast-changing role that today not only allows men in the birthing room (90% of fathers are in attendance at their child's birth) but also offers them

Mixed Emotions

"WE'RE NOT READY TO ACCEPT MEN'S FEARS . . . OR THEIR SADNESS. WE WANT MEN TO BE THE PROTECTORS . . . BUT WE ARE SCARED THEY WON'T BE IF THEY BECOME SOFT."

postpartum courses in which new fathers learn how to change, feed, hold and generally take care of their infant. Some fathers may even get in on the pregnancy part by wearing the "empathy belly," a bulge the size and weight of a third-trimester fetus. Suddenly available to men hoping to solidify the father-child bond are "Saturday with Daddy Outings," special songfests, field trips and potlucks with dads. Even men behind bars could get help: one program allows an inmate father to read children's stories onto cassette tapes that are then sent, along with the book and a Polaroid picture of Dad, to his child.

"It's become cool to be a dad," says Wyatt Andrews, a correspondent for CBS News who has three children: Rachel, 8, Averil, 7, and Conrad, 5. "Even at dinner parties, disciplinary techniques are discussed. Fathers with teenagers give advice about strategies to fathers with younger kids. My father was career Navy. I don't think he ever spent two seconds thinking about strategies of child rearing. If he said anything, it was 'They listen to me.'"

BRING BACK DAD

These perceptual and behavioral shifts have achieved enough momentum to trigger a backlash of their own. Critics of the New Fatherhood are concerned that something precious is being lost in the revolution in parenting—some uniquely male contribution that is essential for raising healthy kids. In a clinical argument that sends off political steam, these researchers argue that fathers should be more than substitute mothers, that men parent differently than women and in ways that matter enormously. They say a mother's love is unconditional, a father's love is more qualified, more tied to performance; mothers are worried about the infant's survival, fathers about future success. "In other words, a father produces not just children but socially viable children," says Blankenhorn. "Fathers, more than mothers, are haunted by the fear that their children will turn out to be bums, largely because a father understands that his child's character is, in some sense, a measure of his character as well."

When it comes to discipline, according to this school of thought, it is the combination of mother and father that yields justice tempered by mercy. "Mothers discipline children on a moment-by-moment basis," says Shapiro. "They have this emotional umbilical cord that lets them read the child. Fathers discipline by rules. Kids learn from their moms how to be aware of their emotional side. From dad, they learn how to live in society."

As parents, some psychologists argue, men and women are suited for different roles at different times. The image of the New Fatherhood is Jack Nicholson surrounded by babies on the cover of *Vanity Fair,* the businessman changing a diaper on the newly installed changing tables in an airport men's room. But to focus only on infant care misses the larger point. "Parenting of young infants is not a natural activity for males," says David Popenoe, an associate dean of social studies at Rutgers University who specializes in the family. He and others argue that women's voices are more soothing; they are better able to read the signals a child sends before he or she can talk. But as time passes, the strengths that fathers may bring to child rearing become more important.

"At a time when fatherhood is collapsing in our society," warns Blankenhorn, "when more children than ever in history are being voluntarily abandoned by their fathers, the only thing we can think of talking about is infant care? It's an anemic, adult-centered way of looking at the problem." Why not let mothers, he says, do more of the heavy lifting in the early years and let fathers do more of the heavy lifting after infancy when their special skills have more relevance? As children get older, notes William Maddox, director of research and policy at the Washington-based Family Research Council, fathers become crucial in their physical and psychological development. "Go to a park and watch father and mother next to a child on a jungle gym," he said. "The father encourages the kid to challenge himself by climbing to the top; the mother tells him to be careful. What's most important is to have the balance of encouragement along with a warning."

This notion that men and women are genetically, or even culturally, predisposed to different parenting roles strikes other researchers as misguided. They are quick to reject the idea that there is some link between X or Y chromosomes and, say, conditional or unconditional love. "To take something that is only a statistical tendency," says historian E. Anthony Rotundo, "and turn it into a cultural imperative—fathers must do it this way and mothers must do it that way—only creates problems for the vast number of people who don't fit those tendencies, without benefiting the children at all." While researchers have found that children whose fathers are involved in their early rearing tend to have higher IQs, perform better in school and even have a better sense of humor, psychologists are quick to say this is not necessarily a gender issue. "It has to do with the fact that there are two people passionately in love with a child," says Harvard's Brazelton.

The very fact that psychologists are arguing about the nature of fatherhood, that filmmakers are making movies based entirely on fatherlove, that bookstores see a growth market in father guides speaks not only to children's well-being but to men's as well. As much as families need fathers, men need their children in ways they are finally allowed to acknowledge, to learn from them all the secrets that children, with their untidy minds and unflagging hearts, have mastered and that grownups, having grown up, long to retrieve.

—Reported by Ann Blackman/Washington, Priscilla Painton/New York and James Willwerth/Los Angeles

Same Family, Different Lives

Family experiences may make siblings different, not similar

BRUCE BOWER

Psychologists uncovered a curious feature of military morale during World War II. Those in branches of the service handing out the most promotions complained the most about their rank. The investigators cited "relative deprivation" as an explanation for the trend — it's not what you have, but what you have compared with others in the same situation.

Relative deprivation achieves a more profound influence through the daily battles and negotiations that constitute life in the nuclear family, maintain researchers in human behavioral genetics. Each child in a family harbors an exquisite sensitivity to his or her standing with parents, brothers and sisters, and thus essentially grows up in a unique psychological environment, according to these investigators. The result: Two children in the same family grow to differ from one another in attitudes, intelligence and personality as much as two youngsters randomly plucked from the population at large.

While one-of-a-kind experiences and perceptions of family life combine with each child's genetic heritage to create pervasive sibling differences, shared genes — which account for half the genes possessed by all siblings save for identical twins — foster whatever similarities they display, argue scientists who apply behavioral genetics to child development.

The emphasis on children's diverse experiences cultivating sibling differences seems ironic coming from scientists dedicated to estimating the genetic contribution to individual development. Yet behavioral genetic data provide a

compelling antidote to the increasingly influential notion among psychiatrists that defective genes and broken brains primarily cause mental disorders, asserts psychologist Robert Plomin of Pennsylvania State University in University Park, a leading researcher in human behavioral genetics. Ongoing studies also challenge the assumption of many developmental psychologists that important family features, such as parental education, child-rearing styles and the quality of the marital relationship, affect all siblings similarly, Plomin adds.

"What runs in families is DNA, not shared experiences," Plomin contends. "Significant environmental effects are specific to each child rather than common to the entire family."

In a further challenge to child development researchers, Plomin and psychologist Cindy S. Bergeman of the University of Notre Dame (Ind.) contend that genetic influences substantially affect common environment measures, such as self-reports or experimenter observations of family warmth and maternal affection. "Labeling a measure environmental does not make it environmental," they conclude in the September BEHAVIORAL AND BRAIN SCIENCES. "We need measures ... that can capture the individual's active selection, modification and creation of environments."

Not surprisingly, the trumpeting of "non-shared" sibling environments and the questioning of traditional measures of the family milieu have drawn heated rebukes from some psychologists. In particular, critics claim that behavioral genetics studies rely on statistical techniques that inappropriately divvy up

separate genetic and environmental effects on individual traits, rather than examining more important interactions between genes and environment.

Human behavioral genetics use family, adoption and twins studies to estimate the importance of genes and environment to individual development. Family studies assess the similarity among genetically related family members on measures of intelligence, extroversion, verbal ability, mental disturbances and other psychological traits. Adoption studies obtain psychological measures from genetically related individuals adopted by different families, their biological parents, and their adoptive parents and siblings. Researchers assume that similar scores between adoptees and biological parents reflect a greater genetic contribution, while adoptees showing similarity to adoptive parents and their children illuminate environmental effects. Twin studies compare the resemblance of identical twins on various measures to the resemblance of fraternal twins on the same measures. If heredity shapes a particular trait, identical twins display more similarity for it than fraternal twins, behavioral geneticists maintain.

Psychologist John C. Loehlin of the University of Texas at Austin directed a twin study published in 1976 that greatly influenced human behavioral genetics. Averaging across a broad range of personality measures obtained from 514 identical and 336 fraternal pairs of twins culled from a national sample of high school seniors, Loehlin's group found a correlation of 0.50 for identical twins and 0.28 for fraternal twins.

Correlations numerically express associations between two or more variables. The closer to 1.0 a correlation figure reaches, the more one variable resembles another — say, one twin's IQ and the corresponding twin's IQ. A correlation of zero between twin IQs would signify a complete lack of resemblance, with twin pairs as different in intelligence scores as randomly selected pairs of youngsters.

The Texas researchers doubled the difference between identical and fraternal twin correlations to obtain a "heritability estimate" of 0.44, or 44 percent, an estimate of how much genes contribute to individual differences. This means that genes accounted for just under half of the individual personality differences observed in the sample of twins. Thus, environment accounted for slightly more than half of the twin's personality variations.

A further finding intrigued the scientists. The correlation on personality measures for identical twins only reached 0.50, suggesting the environment orchestrated one-half of their personality differences. Since these twins carried matching sets of genes and grew up in the same families, only "non-shared" family experiences could account for such differences, Loehlin's group argued.

Subsequent twin and adoption studies carried out in Colorado, Minnesota, Sweden and England confirmed the importance of the non-shared environment for most aspects of personality, as well as intelligence and mental disorders such as schizophrenia, Plomin asserts. He and psychologist Denise Daniels of Stanford University reviewed much of this data in the March 1987 BEHAVIORAL AND BRAIN SCIENCES, followed by a book on the subject written with Penn State psychologist Judy Dunn titled *Separate Lives: Why Siblings Are So Different* (1990, Basic Books).

All the correlations and heritability estimates boil down to a simple point, Plomin maintains: Allegedly shared family influences, such as parent's emotional warmth or disciplinary practices, get filtered through each child's unique perceptions and produce siblings with strikingly diverse personalities. For example, a shy 9-year-old who gets picked on by schoolmates will react differently to an emotional, permissive mother than a gregarious 7-year-old sibling who attracts friends easily.

Many factors divide sibling's perceptions of family life, Plomin says, including age spacing, peer and school experiences, accidents, illnesses, random events and — to a lesser extent — birth order and sex differences.

Each sibling's temperament and behavior also generate specific perceptions and responses from parents that further shape non-shared environments, he argues.

As researchers in molecular genetics vigilantly pursue genes that predispose people to a variety of mental disorders, psychiatrists should not neglect the importance of the environment specific to each child in a family, contends Plomin and two colleagues — psychiatrist David Reiss of George Washington University in Washington, D.C., and psychologist E. Mavis Hetherington of the University of Virginia in Charlottesville — in the March AMERICAN JOURNAL OF PSYCHIATRY.

The three researchers bluntly warn psychiatrists enamored of the new genetic techniques that biology alone cannot explain the development of serious mental disorders. For example, a large, ongoing study in Sweden — conducted by Plomin and several other researchers — has found that when one identical twin develops schizophrenia, the other twin contracts the disorder about one-third of the time. Heredity shoulders considerable responsibility for fomenting schizophrenia, Plomin acknowledges, but an individual's experience of family life, peers and chance events plays at least as strong a role in triggering the devastating fragmentation of thought and emotion that characterizes the disorder.

Research directed by George Washington's Reiss, and described in his article with Plomin and Hetherington, suggests non-shared experiences protect some siblings, but not others, from alcoholism when one or both parents drink alcohol uncontrollably. Family members often shield the protected child from alcoholic behavior during that child's most cherished family practices, such as Christmas celebrations, Reiss' team finds. In this way, the protected sibling gradually learns to minimize brushes with the corrosive effects of alcoholism within and outside the family, the investigators observe. Upon reaching adolescence and adulthood, the protected sibling maintains limited family contacts to avoid the influence of an alcoholic parent and often marries a non-alcoholic person.

Given the importance of non-shared environments, developmental researchers need to study more than one child per family and devise better measures of children's perceptions of family experiences, Plomin contends. He and Bergeman find that several self-report tests currently used to assess the home environment largely ignore unique individual experiences within the family and rely on measures that show substantial genetic influence. In one case they cite,

unpublished data from a study of 179 reared-apart twin pairs (both identical and fraternal) and 207 reared-together twin pairs indicate that genes account for one-quarter of the individual differences plumbed by the widely used Family Environment Scales, which is generally regarded to measure environmental influences. These scales include ratings of emotional warmth, conflict, cohesion and cultural pursuits within the family.

Even the time children spend watching television — a seemingly vacuum-sealed environmental measure employed in many studies — significantly stems from genetically influenced characteristics, Plomin and his colleagues argue in the November 1990 PSYCHOLOGICAL SCIENCE. Parental restrictions do not exert strong effects on children's television viewing, since about 70 percent of parents put no limits on how much time their offspring can spend watching the tube, they state.

Plomin's team tested 220 adopted children three times, at 3, 4 and 5 years of age, as well as their biological and adoptive parents, younger adopted and non-adopted siblings, and control families with no adopted children. Biological parents and their children adopted by others spent a surprisingly similar amount of time watching television, indicating an important genetic influence on the behavior, Plomin's team asserted. Shared home environment, such as the television viewing habits of parents, also influenced children's television time, but to a lesser extent.

The results do not imply that some people follow a genetic imperative to sit glassy-eyed in front of the television for hours, day after day. "We can turn the television on or off as we please, but turning it off or leaving it on pleases individuals differently, in part due to genetic factors," the investigators conclude.

Some scientists who have long labored to understand family influences on psychological development take no pleasure in the conclusions of behavioral genetics researchers. Psychologist Lois W. Hoffman of the University of Michigan in Ann Arbor offers a critique of research highlighting sibling differences in the September PSYCHOLOGICAL BULLETIN.

Behavioral genetics tends to overestimate sibling differences because it concentrates on self-reports of personality traits, rather than on observations of coping skills and social behavior typically relied upon by developmental psychologists, Hoffman holds. A child may exaggerate differences from siblings on self-reports, whereas behavioral observations by experimenters may turn up sibling similarities in aggression or other attributes, she maintains.

Even in behavioral genetics research, significant sibling similarities apparently due to shared family environment turn up in political and religious beliefs and in general interests such as music, Hoffman adds.

Some family environments may more easily produce similarities among siblings than others, she argues. When both parents share the same values, attitudes and child-rearing styles, the chances increase that their pattern of behavior will rub off on all their children, in Hoffman's opinion.

Behavioral genetics researchers also incorrectly assume that only strong correlations between the personalities of adoptive parents and their adopted children reflect an environmental influence, the Michigan psychologist contends. Parental influences can weaken parent-child correlations on all sorts of personality measures, she points out. For instance, domineering, powerful parents may produce an anxious child, and an extremely self-assured, professionally successful parent may make a child feel inadequate.

Behavioral genetics comes under additional fire for its reliance on statistics that treat genetic and environmental influences on personality separately. This approach simply lacks the statistical power to pick up the interactions between genes and environment that primarily direct physical and psychological development, rendering current research in human behavioral genetics meaningless, argues Canadian psychologist Douglas Wahlsten of the University of Alberta in Edmonton. Much larger samples might begin to pick up such interactions, he adds.

Behavioral geneticists rely on statistics derived from a technique known as analysis of variance (ANOVA). This method is used throughout psychology to calculate whether a significant relationship, or correlation, exists between experimental variables by comparing variations in individual scores from a group's average value. Statisticians developed ANOVA in the 1920s as a way to estimate whether different types and amounts of fertilizer substantially increased the yield of various agricultural crops.

When applied to human personality and behavior, an ANOVA-based approach treats heredity and environment as mutually exclusive influences on personality, Wahlsten argues. Psychologists possess no conclusive test of interactions between genes and environments. But evidence of their interplay — as in the widely accepted theory that specific genes combine with particular family experiences to produce a psychotic disorder — may begin to emerge in behavioral genetics studies employing samples of 600 or more individuals, Wahlsten maintains. Mathematical formulas used in conjunction with ANOVA stand a better chance of ferreting out gene-environment interactions in extremely large samples, Wahlsten concludes in the March 1990 BEHAVIORAL AND BRAIN SCIENCES.

Psychologist Daniel Bullock of Boston University takes a bleaker view of ANOVA, citing its neglect of the intertwined forces guiding personality development. "The special status of ANOVA in psychology is an utter anachronism," he contends. "Many past claims by behavioral geneticists are unreliable."

Plomin rejects such charges. "To say that genetic and environmental effects interact and therefore cannot be disentangled is wrong," he states.

Twin and adoption studies consistently find strong separate effects of genes and non-shared environments on personality and other developmental measures, even when researchers painstakingly seek out possible interactions of nature and nurture, Plomin points out. Investigators may devise more sensitive statistical tests to illuminate cooperative ventures between genes and family experiences, but that will not invalidate the insights of behavioral genetics, he maintains.

That includes the discovery that what parents do similarly to two children does not importantly influence personality or problem behavior in the long run; rather, each child's perceptions of what goes on in the family prove critical. Appreciating the differences of offspring based on their individual qualities, with minimal preferential treatment of one child over another, seems a good general rule for concerned parents, Plomin says. Parents should recognize that siblings as well as "only children" harbor a keen sensitivity to their standing within the family, he adds.

"If we are reasonable, loving, but not perfect parents, the children will grow up to be themselves — all different but okay," says psychologist Sandra Scarr of the University of Virginia, a behavioral genetics researcher. "Children experience us as different parents, depending on their own characteristics, and we simply cannot make them alike or easily spoil their chances to be normal adults."

Longitudinal Studies of Effects of Divorce on Children in Great Britain and the United States

Andrew J. Cherlin, Frank F. Furstenberg, Jr., P. Lindsay Chase-Lansdale, Kathleen E. Kiernan, Philip K. Robins, Donna Ruane Morrison, Julien O. Teitler

National, longitudinal surveys from Great Britain and the United States were used to investigate the effects of divorce on children. In both studies, a subsample of children who were in two-parent families during the initial interview (at age 7 in the British data and at ages 7 to 11 in the U.S. data) were followed through the next interview (at age 11 and ages 11 to 16, respectively). At both time points in the British data, parents and teachers independently rated the children's behavior problems, and the children were given reading and mathematics achievement tests. At both time points in the U.S. data, parents rated the children's behavior problems. Children whose parents divorced or separated between the two time points were compared to children whose families remained intact. For boys, the apparent effect of separation or divorce on behavior problems and achievement at the later time point was sharply reduced by considering behavior problems, achievement levels, and family difficulties that were present at the earlier time point, before any of the families had broken up. For girls, the reduction in the apparent effect of divorce occurred to a lesser but still noticeable extent once preexisting conditions were considered.

At current rates, about 40% of U.S. children will witness the breakup of their parents' marriages before they reach 18 (1). The research literature leaves no doubt that, on average, children of divorced parents experience more emotional and behavioral problems and do less well in school than children who live with both biological parents (2). But much less is known about why children whose parents divorce do less well. Most observers assume that their troubles stem mainly from the difficult adjustment children must make after their parents separate. Studies emphasize how difficult it can be for a recently separated mother or father to function effectively as a parent. "Put simply," wrote

A. J. Cherlin and D. R. Morrison are in the Department of Sociology, Johns Hopkins University, Baltimore, MD 21218. F. F. Furstenberg, Jr., and J. O. Teitler are in the Department of Sociology, 3718 Locust Walk, University of Pennsylvania, Philadelphia, PA 19104. P. L. Chase-Lansdale is at the Chapin Hall Center for Children, University of Chicago, 1155 East 60 Street, Chicago, IL 60637. K. E. Kiernan is at the Family Policy Studies Centre, 231 Baker Street, London NW1 6XE, United Kingdom. P. K. Robins is in the Department of Economics, University of Miami, Coral Gables, FL 33124.

Wallerstein and Kelly, "the central hazard which divorce poses to the psychological health and development of children and adolescents is in the diminished or disrupted parenting which so often follows in the wake of the rupture and which can become consolidated within the post-divorce family" (3). Largely because of the widespread perception that marital disruption makes children more vulnerable to problems, a series of social policies and legal reforms were enacted in the 1970s and 1980s to increase and enforce child support payments and to encourage new custody practices that promote contact and cooperation between divorced parents (4).

We agree that events occurring after the separation can be critical for children's adjustment and that adequate child support payments and workable custody arrangements are indispensable. However, we present evidence that, at least for boys, tempers the conclusion that the aftermath of divorce is the major factor in children's adjustment. Our evidence, which comes from statistical analyses of national, longitudinal studies of children in both Great Britain and the United States, indicates that a substantial portion of what is usually considered the effect of divorce on children is visible before the parents separate. For boys, the apparent effect of divorce on behavior problems and school achievement falls by about half to levels that are not significantly different from zero, once preexisting behavior problems, achievement test scores, and family difficulties evident before the separation are taken into account. For girls, the same preexisting conditions reduce the effects of divorce to a lesser but still noticeable degree.

The observed differences between children from families in which the parents have separated or divorced and children from two-parent families may be traced to three distinct sources. The first source is the effect of growing up in a dysfunctional family—a home where serious problems of the parents or the children make normal development difficult. Parents with psychological impairments are reportedly more prone to divorce and their children are more likely to experience developmental difficulties (5). A second source, often accompanying the first, is severe and protracted marital conflict, which is known to harm children's development and often leads to divorce (6). The third source is the difficult transition that occurs only after couples separate—the emotional upset, fall in income, diminished parenting, continued conflict, and so forth. Although some researchers acknowledge the potentially adverse contribution of each source (7), nearly all empirical studies have focused exclusively on the third—the period after the separation—and have collected information only after the separation occurred (8).

Moreover, the current understanding of the effects of divorce on children is largely based on intensive, observational studies of a

From *Science*, Vol. 252, 1991, pp. 1386-1389. © 1991 by the American Association for the Advancement of Science. Reprinted by permission.

relatively small number of families (9). These studies are invaluable because of the detailed observations of family interaction and child development they provide, but they typically are based on nonrandom samples of the population. In some influential clinical studies, there has not been a comparison group of intact families (3).

The British National Child Development Study

We describe two prospective studies that began with large samples of intact families. The British data come from the National Child Development Study (NCDS). Originally a study of perinatal mortality, the NCDS began as a survey of the mothers of all children born in England, Scotland, and Wales during the week of 3 to 9 March 1958 (10). Interviews were completed with 17,414 mothers, representing 98% of all women giving birth (11). In 1965, when the children were 7, the parents (usually the mothers) of 14,746 children were successfully reinterviewed. Local authority health visitors (trained nurses who normally saw every family before and after the birth of a child and frequently conducted follow-up visits, especially to families with difficulties) asked the mothers the majority of questions from the Rutter Home Behaviour Scale, which measured the children's behavior problems (12), and reported on the family's difficulties and use of social welfare services.

Our factor analyses of the Rutter items identified the two clusters of behavior problems typical of assessments such as these: "externalizing disorders" (aggression, disobedience) and "internalizing disorders" (depression, anxiety). However, the reliability of the internalizing subscale was considerably lower than that of the externalizing subscale. Consequently, we constructed a single, 18-item summated scale (α reliability = 0.72). The items were: temper tantrums, reluctance to go to school, bad dreams, difficulty sleeping, food fads, poor appetite, difficulty concentrating, bullied by other children, destructive, miserable or tearful, squirmy or fidgety, continually worried, irritable, upset by new situations, twitches or other mannerisms, fights with other children, disobedient at home, and sleepwalking.

In addition, the children's teachers filled out a detailed behavioral assessment at age 7, the Bristol Social Adjustment Guide (BSAG) (13). Again, our factor analyses showed the externalizing versus internalizing distinction, but the internalizing subscale was weaker. So again we constructed a single scale (α = 0.68). The children also were given reading and mathematics tests (14) and physical examinations at age 7. Then in 1969, when the children were 11, another round of interviews and testing was undertaken. Parents again were asked questions on children's behavior problems, and teachers once again filled out the BSAG (15). The reading and mathematics tests that had been given earlier were not appropriate for 11-year-olds; instead, the study used reading and mathematics achievement tests constructed specifically for this round of the NCDS, and standardized against normal populations, by the National Foundation for Educational Research in England and Wales (16).

Divorce and Children's Adjustment

We use parent-rated and teacher-rated behavior problems and reading and mathematics achievement, all measured at age 11, as the four outcome measures of children's adjustment in our analyses. In order to evaluate the relative contributions of pre- and post-separation sources of children's adjustment at age 11, we restricted our analyses to children whose parents were in an intact, first marriage in 1965, when the children were 7—the first time we have

detailed information about the children's behavior and achievement. Then we followed these children as they split into two groups by age 11: those whose parents had divorced or separated and those who parents had remained together (17). (Henceforth by "divorce" we mean divorce or marital separation; we do not distinguish between them.)

The number of children living with both parents at age 7 and for whom outcome variables were observed at age 11 ranged from 11,658 to 11,837 for the four outcome variables. Among these, there were 239 instances of a divorce occurring between ages 7 and 11. A remarriage before age 11 occurred in only 47 of these instances, so we have not analyzed separately data on non-remarried and remarried cases but rather have combined them. One limitation of the NCDS is that it did not obtain the exact date at which a marital disruption occurred. We can determine whether or not a divorce occurred between the age 7 and age 11 interviews, but we cannot determine the exact timing of the divorce. We conducted all analyses separately by the child's gender because of evidence in the literature that the effect of divorce is different for boys than for girls (2).

As expected, we found that boys and girls whose parents had divorced between the age 7 and age 11 interviews showed more behavior problems at age 11, as rated by parents and by teachers, and scored lower than other children on reading and mathematics achievement tests at age 11, even after controlling for predictors such as social class and race (18) (model 1 in Fig. 1). On average, the magnitude of the differences was modest, although significantly different from zero. For example, boys whose parents divorced showed 19% [standard error (SE) = 8%] more behavior problems at age 11, according to ratings by their parents, than did boys whose

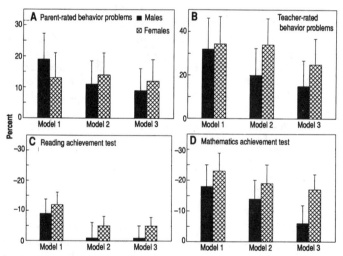

Fig. 1. Effects of a parental divorce or separation between ages 7 and 11 on four outcome measures for children age 11 in 1969 from the National Child Development Study, Great Britain (estimates restricted to children living with two married parents in 1965). (**A**) Behavior problems scale score as reported by parents. (**B**) Behavior problems scale score as reported by teachers. (**C**) Reading achievement test score. (**D**) Mathematics achievement test score. The height of the boxes shows the percentage by which the score of children whose parents divorced or separated between ages 7 and 11 was greater or less than the score of children whose parents remained married. In each of the four diagrams, three estimates of the effects of divorce are shown. Model 1 controls only for the social class and race of the child; model 2 controls additionally for the child's score on the same outcome measure at age 7, before anyone's parents were divorced; and model 3 adds further controls for characteristics of the child and family when he or she was 7. These included scales of family problems and difficulties from the Health Visitor's report and physician's reporting of physical handicap, mental retardation, or emotional maladjustment. Error bars represent one standard error.

parents were together, controlling for social class and race (Fig. 1A).

Unlike nearly all previous studies, we were able to introduce information on the children and parents before any of the families broke up. The measures we introduce may be proxies for family dysfunction and marital conflict. We first added the comparable 7-year-old behavior problems scale or achievement test score of the child (model 2 in Fig. 1). This step essentially adjusted the estimated effect of divorce for preexisting differences in behavior or achievement between children whose families would later divorce and children whose families would remain intact. For boys, the apparent effects of divorce dropped for all four outcome measures; for girls there was a drop in reading and mathematics achievement test scores. Finally, we controlled for other age 7 characteristics of the child and his or her family, such as the physician's rating of the child's mental and physical health and the Health Visitor's rating of the family's difficulties and use of social services (19) (model 3 in Fig. 1). After all the preseparation characteristics were taken into account, the apparent effect of divorce for boys fell by about half to levels that no longer were significantly different from zero for all four outcomes. For example, boys whose parents divorced now showed just 9% (SE = 7%) more behavior problems, according to parent ratings. For girls, the decline was smaller, and the remaining effect was significantly different from zero for two of the four outcomes (20).

The U.S. National Survey of Children

In order to determine whether these findings were generalizable beyond Great Britain in the 1960s, we estimated a similar set of models from U.S. data from the National Survey of Children (NSC), which began in 1976 with a random-sample survey of 2279 children aged 7 to 11 from 1747 families (21). In 1981, when the children were ages 11 through 16, additional interviews were conducted with parents and children in all families in which there already had been a separation or a divorce by 1976 or in which there was substantial marital conflict in 1976, and in a randomly selected subsample of intact, low-conflict families in 1976.

In both waves of the survey, a parent, usually the mother, was asked a series of questions about behavior problems similar in content to the Rutter Home Behaviour Scale in the NCDS (12) and to items in the Achenbach Child Behavior Checklist (22). In parallel with the procedure for the NCDS, we constructed single-factor scales from nine items in the 1976 data ($\alpha = 0.69$) and 24 items in the 1981 data ($\alpha = 0.90$). The items in the 1976 scale are fights too much, cannot concentrate, often tells lies, easily confused, breaks things, acts too young, very timid, has strong temper, and steals things. The items in the 1981 scale are changes in mood, feels no one loves him or her, high strung, tells lies, too fearful, argues too much, difficulty concentrating, easily confused, cruel to others, disobedient at home, disobedient at school, impulsive, feels inferior, not liked by other children, has obsessions, restless, stubborn or irritable, has strong temper, sad or depressed, withdrawn, feels others are out to get him or her, hangs around with kids who get into trouble, secretive, and worries too much.

Married parents in 1976 also were asked questions about conflict with their spouses covering nine areas, as follows: "Most married couples have some arguments. Do you ever have arguments about (i) chores and responsibilities, (ii) your children, (iii) money, (iv) sex, (v) religion, (vi) leisure time, (vii) drinking, (viii) other women or men, or (ix) in-laws?" We constructed a scale of marital conflict, which was the number of affirmative responses; scores ranged from 0 to 8 with a mean of 2.26 ($\alpha = 0.63$).

As with the British data, we restricted our analyses to children who were living with both of their parents at the first interview in 1976. As in the British study, these children were followed as their families split into divorced and nondivorced groups by 1981. Parent-rated behavior problems was the only outcome that could be compared adequately with the British findings (Fig. 2). The results for U.S. boys are similar to the results for British boys. Controlling for social class, race, and whether the mother was employed outside the home in 1976, boys whose parents had divorced between 1976 and 1981 showed 12% (SE = 4%) more behavior problems, on average (model 1). But when a control was added for behavior problems in 1976, before any of the parents divorced, the effect of divorce fell (model 2). And after a second control was introduced for the amount of marital conflict that was present in the home in 1976, the effect of divorce had fallen by approximately half, as in the British data, to 6% (SE = 4%), and it was no longer significantly different from zero.

For girls, however, the results are different from the British study. Controlling for class and race (model 1), there is little difference between girls from divorced families and girls from intact families. But with controls for 1976 behavior problems (model 2) and 1976 marital conflict (model 3), girls whose parents had divorced were showing somewhat fewer behavior problems than girls from intact families. In view of the inconsistency with the British data, we think it is prudent to be skeptical of this finding until it can be confirmed.

Conclusion

Overall, the evidence suggests that much of the effect of divorce on children can be predicted by conditions that existed well before the separation occurred. These predivorce effects were stronger for boys than for girls. Just when children begin to experience the process that precedes a divorce we cannot say. Our survey-based studies do not allow us to differentiate between a generally dysfunctional family and a family that has functioned adequately until the time that marital conflict becomes acute and the divorce process begins. It is also possible that the effects of divorce may differ for children older or younger than the ones in our studies or that divorce may have long-term effects on adult behavior. Nevertheless, the British and U.S. longitudinal studies suggest that those concerned with the effects of divorce on children should consider reorienting their thinking. At least as much attention needs to be paid to the processes that occur in troubled, intact families as to the trauma that children suffer after their parents separate.

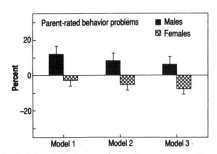

Fig. 2. Effects of a parental divorce between 1976 and 1981 on the behavior problems of children in 1981, when the children were ages 11 to 16, based on a behavior problems scale score as reported by parents from the U.S. National Survey of Children (estimates are restricted to children living with two married parents in 1976). The height of the boxes shows the percentage by which the score of children whose parents divorced between 1976 and 1981 was greater (or less) than the score of children whose parents remained married. Three estimates of the effects of divorce are shown: model 1 controls only for social class, race, and whether the mother was employed outside the home in 1976; model 2 controls additionally for the child's score on the behavior problems scale in 1976, as reported by parents, before anyone's parents were divorced; and model 3 adds further controls for the parents' score on a nine-item marital conflict scale in 1976. Error bars represent one standard error.

REFERENCES AND NOTES

1. L. L. Bumpass, *Demography* **21**, 71 (1984).
2. R. E. Emery, *Marriage, Divorce, and Children's Adjustment* (Sage, Beverly Hills, CA, 1988); P. L. Chase-Lansdale and E. M. Hetherington, in *Life-Span Development and Behavior*, P. B. Baltes, D. L. Featherman, R. M. Lerner, Eds. (Erlbaum, Hillsdale, NJ, 1990), vol. 10, pp. 105–150; S. S. McLanahan, *Am. J. Sociol.* **94**, 130 (1988).
3. J. S. Wallerstein and J. B. Kelly, *Surviving the Breakup: How Children and Parents Cope with Divorce* (Basic Books, New York, 1980), p. 316.
4. See, for example, L. J. Weitzman, *The Divorce Revolution: The Unexpected Consequences for Women and Children* (Free Press, New York, 1985); M. A. Glendon, *Abortion and Divorce in Western Law* (Harvard Univ. Press, Cambridge, MA, 1987); I. Garfinkel and S. S. McLanahan, *Single Mothers and Their Children: A New American Dilemma* (The Urban Institute Press, Washington, DC, 1986).
5. K. E. Kiernan, *Popul. Stud.* **40**, 1 (1986).
6. R. E. Emery, *Psychol. Bull.* **92**, 310 (1982).
7. E. M. Hetherington, M. Cox, R. Cox, in *Mother-Child, Father-Child Relations*, J. H. Stevens and M. Mathews, Eds. (National Association for the Education of Young Children Press, Washington, DC, 1978); E. M. Hetherington and K. Camara, in *Review of Child Development Research*, R. D. Parke, Ed. (Univ. of Chicago Press, Chicago, 1984), vol. 7.
8. But see J. H. Block, J. Block, P. F. Gjerde, *Child Dev.* **57**, 827 (1986); N. Baydar, *J. Marriage Family* **50**, 967 (1988).
9. The leading set of studies of this type have been conducted by E. M. Hetherington, M. Cox, and R. Cox [in *Nontraditional Families, Parenting, and Child Development*, M. E. Lamb, Ed. (Erlbaum, Hillsdale, NJ, 1982); *J. Am. Acad. Child Psychiatr.* **24**, 518 (1985)] and E. M. Hetherington [in *Remarriage and Stepparenting Today*, K. Pasley and M. Ihinger-Tallman, Eds. (Guilford Press, New York, 1987)].
10. The NCDS is described in a paper by P. M. Shepherd, "The National Child Development Study: An introduction to the background to the study and the methods of data collection" (Social Statistics Research Unit, City University, London, October 1985).
11. Information in medical records at birth also was recorded. Between 1958 and 1965, a supplementary sample was added consisting of 1142 children from recent immigrant families who had 3 to 9 March 1958 birth dates. We include this sample in our analyses.
12. M. Rutter, J. Tizard, K. Whitmore, Eds., *Educaton, Health, and Behaviour* (Longman, London, 1970).
13. D. H. Stott, *The Social Adjustment of Children* (Univ. of London Press, London, 1969).
14. V. Southgate, *Southgate Group Reading Tests: Manual of Instructions* (Univ. of London Press, London, 1962); M. L. K. Pringle, in *The Sixth Mental Measurements Yearbook*, O. K. Buros, Ed. (Gryphon Press, Highland Park, NJ, 1965). The mathematics test was developed for the NCDS by M. L. K. Pringle, N. Butler, and R. Davie [*11,000 Seven Year Olds* (Longman, London, 1966)].
15. Ten of the 11 items in the parent-rated scale ($\alpha = 0.68$) were identical to the items in the age 7 parent-rated scale (*12*). For the BSAG scale at age 11, $\alpha = 0.71$.
16. K. Fogelman, *Br. J. Educ. Psychol.* **48**, 148 (1978).
17. There are two sources of nonrandomness that could have arisen with respect to the sample of families analyzed in 1969, when the children were 11: (i) the restriction that when the child was 7 the family was intact, was successfully found and reinterviewed, and had valid data on behavior and achievement; and (ii) the restriction that when the child was 11 the family was successfully reinterviewed and had valid data on behavior and achievement. To determine whether these sources of nonrandomness could possibly have biased our results, we specified and estimated several selection models. [G. S. Maddala, *Limited Dependent and Qualitative Variables in Econometrics* (Cambridge Univ. Press, Cambridge, 1983).] The coefficients for the effect of divorce were nearly identical in the selection models and the ordinary least squares (OLS) models we present here.
18. Among boys, the coefficient for the effect of divorce on three of the four outcomes was positive and at least twice its standard error in model 1 of Fig. 1 (for the reading test, the coefficient was 1.8 times its standard error). Among girls, all the coefficients for the effect of divorce, except on parent-rated behavior problems, were more than twice their standard errors in model 1. As in any nonexperimental study, it is possible that the variables we "control" for are actually markers for other, unmeasured variables. However, we have relied on a large literature in sociology and developmental psychology to guide our choice of variables. In the OLS regressions (*17*) for the NCDS, which form the basis for Fig. 1, we used the natural logarithms of the outcomes as dependent variables because the logarithmic transformation resulted in a more normally shaped distribution of the scale scores. The key independent variable was a dummy variable that indicated whether or not a divorce occurred during the time between the age 7 and age 11 interviews . Let β be the coefficient for the divorce dummy variable. Then, for the logarithmically transformed outcomes, the percentage change in the scale score produced by the occurrence of a divorce is $(e^\beta - 1) \cdot 100$. In model 1, the only additional independent variables in the equation (all measured at age 7) were father's social class (six-category classification), housing tenure (whether renting from a public agency, renting in the private market, or owning one's home), number of persons per room, and race (white, Asian, black, mixed). In our regression models, mean values were imputed for missing information on independent variables.
19. From the health visitor's report at age 7 we constructed five scales: use of children's services (five items, $\alpha = 0.56$), family conflict (two items, $\alpha = 0.44$), family problems (two items, $\alpha = 0.64$), and use of mental health services (three items, $\alpha = 0.60$). For models in which behavior problems were the dependent variables, the age 7 reading test score was entered at this stage; and for models in which age 11 achievement tests were the dependent variables, age 7 teacher-rated behavior problems were added at this stage.
20. For boys, none of the model 3 estimates in Fig. 1 was twice its standard error; for girls, two of four were twice their standard errors. The death of a parent between the ages of 7 and 11 had no significant effects for girls on any of the four outcome measures and no significant effect on behavior problems for boys, even before controls for age 7 characteristics. The death of a parent did have a negative effect on reading and mathematics achievement at 11 for boys; this effect was reduced by age 7 controls but remained statistically significant.
21. See F. F. Furstenberg, Jr., C. W. Nord, J. L. Peterson, N. Zill, *Am. Sociol. Rev.* **48**, 656 (1983). We restricted the sample to include only families that were intact in 1976, in which the biological mother of the child or children was the parent respondent at both times and was living with the target child or children, and in which the father was not reported to have died between 1976 and 1981. Among this subsample of 822 children, there were 65 cases of a divorce or separation occurring between the 1976 and 1981 interviews.
22. T. M. Achenbach and C. S. Edelbrock, *Monogr. Soc. Res. Child Dev.* **33** (no. 166) (1981).
23. Supported primarily by NICHHD grant HD25936, with additional support from NSF grant SES-8908503. We thank M. Trieb for computer programming assistance. Complete sets of the estimated coefficients and other detailed documentation are available from A.J.C.

THE LASTING EFFECTS OF CHILD MALTREATMENT

Raymond H. Starr, Jr.

Raymond H. Starr, Jr., is a developmental psychologist on the faculty of the University of Maryland, Baltimore County. He has been conducting research with maltreated children and their families for more than sixteen years and was also a founder and first president of the National Down Syndrome Congress.

Every day, the media contain examples of increasingly extreme cases of child abuse and neglect and their consequences. The cases have a blurring sameness. Take, for example, the fourteen-year-old crack addict who lives on the streets by selling his body. A reporter befriends him and writes a vivid account of the beatings the boy received from his father. There is the pedophile who is on death row for mutilating and murdering a four-year-old girl. His record shows a sixth-grade teacher threatened to rape and kill him if he told anyone what the teacher had done to him. There is the fifteen-year-old girl who felt that her parents didn't love her. So she found love on the streets and had a baby she later abandoned in a trash barrel. And there are the prostitutes on a talk show who tell how the men their mothers had trusted sexually abused them as children. These and hundreds more examples assault us and lead us to believe that abused children become problem adolescents and adults.

Are these incidents the whole story? Case examples are dramatic, but have you ever wondered how such maltreatment changes the course of a child's life? In this sound-bite era, most of us rarely stop to think about this important question. We seldom ask why trauma should play such an important role in shaping the course of a child's life.

To examine these questions, we need to understand what psychologists know about the course of lives and how they study them—the subject of the field of life-span developmental psychology.

LIFE-SPAN DEVELOPMENT

Understanding why people behave the way they do is a complex topic that has puzzled philosophers, theologians, and scientists. The course of life is so complex that we tend to focus on critical incidents and key events. Most of us can remember a teacher who played an important role in our own development, but we have to consider that other teachers may have been important. If his seventh-grade civics teacher, Ms. Jones, is the person Bill says showed him the drama of the law, leading him to become a lawyer, does this mean that his sixth-grade English teacher, Ms. Hazelton, played no role in his career choice? An outside observer might say that Ms. Hazelton was the key person because she had a debate club and Bill was the most able debater in his class.

Case descriptions fascinate us, but it is hard to divine the reasons for life courses from such examples. It is for this reason that scientists studying human behavior prefer to use prospective studies. By following people from a certain age, we can obtain direct evidence about the life course and factors that influence it. However, most of our information comes from retrospective studies in which people are asked what has happened to them in the past and how it relates to their present functioning.

Life-span developmental theory seeks to explain the way life events have influenced individual development. Of necessity, such explanations are complex; lives themselves are complex. They are built on a biological foundation, shaped by genetic characteristics, structured by immediate events, and indirectly influenced by happenings that are external to the family. As if this were not complex enough, contemporary theory holds that our interpretation of each event is dependent on the prior interactions of all these factors.

Hank's reaction to the loss of his wife to cancer will differ from George's reaction to his wife's death from a similar cancer. Many factors can contribute to these differing reactions. Hank may have grown up with two parents who were loving and attentive, while George may never have known his father. He may have had a mother who was so depressed that from the time he was two, he had lived in a series of foster homes, never knowing a secure, loving, consistent parent.

MALTREATED CHILDREN AS ADULTS

Research has shown that there is a direct relation between a child's exposure to negative emotional, social, and environmental events and the presence of problems during adulthood. Psychiatrist Michael Rutter compared young women who were removed from strife-filled homes and who later came back to live with their parents to women from more harmonious homes.[1] The women from discordant homes were more likely to become pregnant as teens, were less skilled in parenting their children, and had unhappy marriages to men who also had psychological and social problems. Adversity begat adversity.

Do the above examples and theoretical views mean that abused and neglected children will, with great certainty, become adults with problems? Research on this issue has focused on three questions: First, do maltreated children grow up to

tween 25 percent and 35 percent.[2] Thus, it is far from certain that an abused child will grow up to be an abusive parent. Physical abuse should be seen as a risk factor for becoming an abusive adult, not as a certainty. Many abusive adults were never abused when they were children.

Researchers have also taken a broader approach by examining the cycle of family violence. Sociologist Murray Straus surveyed a randomly selected national sample of families about the extent of violence between family members.[3] Members of the

as a training ground for later child abuse.

To summarize, this evidence suggests that maltreatment during childhood is but one of many factors that lead to a person's becoming an abusive parent. Being abused as a child is a risk marker for later parenting problems and not a cause of such difficulties. It accounts for, at most, less than a third of all cases of physical abuse. Research suggests that a number of other factors, such as stress and social isolation, also play a role as causes of child abuse.[4]

Research has shown that there is a direct relation between a child's exposure to negative emotional, social, and environmental events and the presence of problems during adulthood.

---

maltreat their children? Second, are yesterday's maltreated children today's criminals? Third, are there more general effects of abuse and neglect on later psychological and social functioning? A number of research studies have examined these questions.

The cycle of maltreatment. It makes logical sense that we tend to raise our own children as we ourselves were raised. Different theoretical views of personality development suggest that this should be the case. Psychoanalytic theorists think that intergenerational transmission of parenting styles is unconscious. Others, such as learning theorists, agree that transmission occurs but differ about the mechanism. Learning parenting skills from our parents is the key mode by which childrearing practices are transmitted from one generation to the next, according to members of the latter group of theorists.

Research suggests that the correspondence between being maltreated as a child and becoming a maltreating adult is far from the one-to-one relationship that has been proposed. Studies have focused on physical abuse; data are not available for either sexual abuse or neglect. In one recent review, the authors conclude that the rate of intergenerational transmission of physical abuse is be-

surveyed families were asked about experiences of violence when they were children and how much husband-wife and parent-child violence there had been in the family in the prior year.

Straus concluded that slightly fewer than 20 percent of parents whose mothers had been violent toward them more than once a year during childhood were abusive toward their own child. The child abuse rate for parents with less violent mothers was less than 12 percent. Having or not having a violent father was less strongly related to whether or not fathers grew up to be abusive toward their own children. Interestingly, the amount of intergenerational transmission was higher if a parent was physically punished by his or her opposite-sex parent.

Straus also found that the abusive adults in his study did not have to have been abused in childhood to become abusive adults. A violent home environment can lead a nonabused child to become an abusive adult. Boys who saw their fathers hit their mothers were 38 percent more likely to grow up to be abusive than were boys who never saw their father hit their mother (13.3 vs. 9.7 percent). Similarly, mothers who saw their mothers hit their fathers were 42 percent more likely to become abusive mothers (24.4 vs. 17.2 percent). Straus views seeing parents fight

Maltreatment and later criminality. Later criminal behavior is one of the most commonly discussed consequences of child abuse. Research on this subject has examined the consequences of both physical abuse and sexual abuse. Maltreatment has been linked to both juvenile delinquency and adult criminality.

It is difficult to do research on this topic. Furthermore, the results of studies must be carefully interpreted to avoid overstating the connection between maltreatment and criminality. For example, researchers often combine samples of abused and neglected children, making it hard to determine the exact effects of specific forms of maltreatment.

Two types of study have typically been done. Retrospective studies examine the family backgrounds of criminals and find the extent to which they were maltreated as children. It is obvious that the validity of the results of such studies may be compromised by the criminals' distortion of or lack of memory concerning childhood experiences. Prospective studies, in which a sample of children is selected and followed through childhood and into adolescence or adulthood, are generally seen as a more valid research strategy. Such studies are expensive and time-consuming to do.

One review of nine studies concluded that from 8 to 26 percent of delinquent youths studied retrospectively had been abused as children.[5] The rate for prospective studies was always found to be less than 20 percent. In one of the best studies, Joan McCord analyzed case records for more than 250 boys, almost 50 percent of whom had been abused by a parent.[6] Data were also collected when the men were in middle age. McCord found that 39 percent of the abused boys had been convicted of a crime as juveniles, adults, or at both ages, compared to 23 percent of a sample of 101 men who, as boys, had been classified as loved by their parents. The crime rate for both sets of boys is higher than would be expected because McCord's sample lived in deteriorated, urban areas where both crime and abuse are common.

Researchers have also examined the relationship between abuse and later violent criminality. Research results suggest that there is a weak relationship between abuse and later violence. For example, in one study, 16 percent of a group of abused children were later arrested —but not necessarily convicted—as suspects in violent criminal cases.[7] This was twice the arrest rate for nonabused adolescents and adults. Neglected children were also more likely to experience such arrests. These data are higher than would be the case in the general population because the samples contained a disproportionately high percentage of subjects from low-income backgrounds.

The connection between childhood sexual abuse and the commission of sex crimes in adolescence and adulthood is less clear. Most of the small number of studies that have been done have relied upon self-reports of childhood molestation made by convicted perpetrators. Their results show considerable variation in the frequency with which childhood victimization is reported. Incidence figures range from a low of 19 percent to a high of 57 percent. However, we should look at such data with suspicion. In an interesting study, perpetrators of sex crimes against children were much less likely to report that they had been sexually abused during their own childhood when they knew that the truthfulness of their answers would be validated by a polygraph examination and that lies were likely to result in being sent to jail.[8] Thus, people arrested for child sexual abuse commonly lie, claiming that they were abusing children because they themselves had been victims of sexual abuse as children.

To summarize, there is a link between childhood abuse and later criminality. Although some studies lead to a conclusion that this relationship is simple, others suggest that it is really quite complex. The latter view is probably correct.

The case of neglect is an example of this complexity. Widom, in her study discussed above, found that 12 percent of adolescents and adults arrested for violent offenses were neglected as children and 7 percent experienced both abuse and neglect (compared to 8 percent of her nonmaltreated control adolescents and adults).

Psychoanalytic theorists think that intergenerational transmission of parenting styles is unconscious.

These data raise an interesting question: Why is neglect, typically considered to be a nonviolent offense, linked to later criminality? Poverty seems to be the mediating factor. Neglect is more common among impoverished families. Poor families experience high levels of frustration, known to be a common cause of aggression. Similarly, we know that lower-class families are, in general, more violent.[9] For these reasons, all the forms of maltreatment we have considered make it somewhat more likely that a maltreated child will grow up to commit criminal acts.

Maltreatment in context. Research suggests that maltreatment during childhood has far-reaching consequences. These are best seen as the results of a failure to meet the emotional needs of the developing child. Indeed, in many cases, the trust the child places in the parent is betrayed by the parent.

This betrayal has been linked to many and varied consequences. The greatest amount of research has focused on the long-term effects of sexual abuse. Studies have looked at samples that are representative of the normal population and also at groups of adults who are seeking psychotherapy because of emotional problems. The most valid findings come from the former type of study. One review of research concluded that almost 90 percent of studies found some lasting effect of sexual abuse.[10]

Sexual abuse has been linked to a wide variety of psychological disturbances. These include depression, low self-esteem, psychosis, anxiety, sleep problems, alcohol and drug abuse, and sexual dysfunction (including a predisposition to revictimization during adulthood). As was true for the research reviewed in the preceding two sections of this article, any particular problem is present in only a minority of adult survivors of childhood sexual victimization.

We know less about the long-term effects of physical abuse. Most of the limited amount of available research has used data obtained from clinical samples. Such studies have two problems. First, they rely on retrospective adult reports concerning events that happened during childhood. Second, the use of such samples results in an overestimate of the extent to which physical abuse has long-term consequences. Compared with a random sample of the general population, clinical samples contain individuals who are already identified as having emotional difficulties, regardless of whether or not they have been abused.

Researchers in one study found that more than 40 percent of inpatients being treated in a psychiatric hospital had been sexually or physically abused as children, usually by a family member.[11] Also, the abuse was typically chronic rather than a onetime occurrence. The abused patients were almost 50 percent more likely to have tried to commit suicide, were 25 percent more likely to have been violent toward others, and were 15 percent more likely to have had some involvement with the criminal justice system than were other patients at the same hospital who had not experienced childhood maltreatment.

Much research remains to be done in this area. We know little about the long-term consequences of particular forms of abuse. The best that we can say is that many victims of physical and sexual abuse experience psychological trauma lasting into adulthood.

The lack of universal consequences. The above analysis suggests that many victims of childhood maltreatment do *not* have significant problems functioning as adults. Researchers are only beginning to ask why many adult victims apparently have escaped unsullied. Factors that mediate and soften the influence of abuse and neglect are called buffers.

The search for buffers is a difficult one. Many of the negative outcomes that have been discussed in the preceding sections may be the result of a number of factors other than maltreatment itself. For example, abused children commonly have behavior problems that are similar to those that have been reported in children raised by drug addicts or adults suffering from major psychological disturbances. Abused children do not exhibit any problems that can be attributed only to abuse. A given behavior problem can have many causes.

One view of the way in which buffers act to limit the extent to which physical abuse is perpetuated across succeeding generations has been proposed by David Wolfe.[12] He believes that there is a three-part process involving the parent, the child, and the relationships between the two. In the first stage, factors predisposing a parent to child abuse (including stress and a willingness to be aggressive toward the child) are buffered by such factors as social support and an income adequate for the purchase of child-care services. Next, Wolfe notes that children often do things that annoy parents and create crises that may lead to abuse because the parent is unprepared to handle the child's provocative behavior. Amelior-

ating factors that work at this level include normal developmental changes in child behavior, parental attendance at child management classes, and the development of parental ability to cope with the child's escalating annoying actions. Finally, additional compensatory factors work to limit the ongoing use of aggression as a solution to parenting problems.

The amount of intergenerational transmission was higher if a parent was physically punished by his or her opposite-sex parent.

Parents may realize that researchers are indeed correct when they say that physical punishment is an ineffective way of changing child behavior. In addition, children may respond positively to parental use of nonaggressive disciplinary procedures and, at a broader level, society or individuals in the parents' circle of friends may inhibit the use of physical punishment by making their disapproval known. Parents who were abused as children are therefore less likely to abuse their own children if any or all of these mediating factors are present.

Research suggests that the factors

Physical abuse should be seen as a risk factor for becoming an abusive adult, not as a certainty.

mentioned by Wolfe and other influences all can work to buffer the adult effects of childhood maltreatment. These include knowing a nurturing, loving adult who provides social support, intellectually restructuring the maltreatment so that it is not seen so negatively, being altruistic and giving to others what one did not get as a child, having good skills for coping with stressful events, and getting psychotherapy.

One study compared parents who broke the cycle of abuse to those who did not.[13] Mothers who were not abusive had larger, more supportive social networks. Support included help with child care and financial assistance during times of crisis. Mothers who did not continue the abusive cycle also were more in touch with their own abuse as children and expressed doubts about their parenting ability. This awareness made them more able to relive and discuss their own negative childhood experiences.

To summarize, investigators have gone beyond just looking at the negative consequences of childhood maltreatment. They are devoting increasing attention to determining what factors in a child's environment may inoculate the child against the effects of maltreatment. While research is starting to provide us with information concerning some of these mediating influences, much more work needs to be done before we can specify the most important mediators and know how they exert their influences.

CONCLUSIONS

We know much about the intergenerational transmission of childhood physical and sexual abuse. Research suggests that abused children are (1) at an increased risk of either repeating the acts they experienced with their own children or, in the case of sexual abuse, with both their own and with unrelated children; (2) more likely to be involved with the criminal justice system as adolescents or adults; and (3) likely to suffer long-lasting emotional effects of abuse even if they do not abuse their own children or commit criminal acts.

This does not mean that abused chil-

People arrested for child sexual abuse commonly lie, claiming that they were abusing children because they themselves had been victims of sexual abuse as children.

dren invariably grow up to be adults with problems. Many adults escape the negative legacy of abuse. They grow up to be normal, contributing members of society. Their escape from maltreatment is usually related to the presence of factors that buffer the effects of the physical blows and verbal barbs.

The knowledge base underlying these conclusions is of varied quality. We know more about the relationship of physical and sexual abuse to adult abusiveness and criminality, less about long-term psychological problems and buffering factors, and almost nothing about the relationship of neglect to any of these outcomes. Almost no research has been done on neglect, a situation leading to a discussion of the reasons behind our "neglect of neglect."[14] Our ignorance is all the more surprising when we consider that neglect is the most common form of reported maltreatment.

The issues involved are complex. We can no longer see the development of children from a view examining such simple cause-effect relationships as exemplified by the proposal that abused children grow up to be abusive adults. Contemporary developmental psychology recognizes that many interacting forces work together to shape development. Children exist in a context that contains their own status as biological beings, their parents and the background they bring to the task of child-rearing, the many and varied environments such as work and school that exert both direct and indirect influences on family members, and the overall societal acceptance of violence.

Advances in research methods allow us to evaluate the interrelationships of all the above factors to arrive at a coherent view of the course of development. Appropriate studies are difficult to plan and expensive to conduct. Without such research, the best that we can do is to continue performing small studies that give us glimpses of particular elements of the picture that we call the life course.

Research is necessary if we are to develop and evaluate the effectiveness of child maltreatment prevention and treatment programs. Our existing knowledge base provides hints that are used by program planners and psychotherapists to find families where there is a high risk of maltreatment and to intervene early. But when such hints are all we have to guide us in working to break the cycle of maltreatment, there continues to be risk of intergenerational perpetuation.

1. Michael Rutter, "Intergenerational Continuities and Discontinuities in Serious Parenting Difficulties," in *Child Maltreatment: Theory and Research on the Causes and Consequences of Child Abuse and Neglect*, ed., Dante Cicchetti and Vicki Carlson (New York: Cambridge University Press, 1989), 317–348.

2. Joan Kaufman and Edward Zigler, "Do Abused Children Become Abusive Adults?" *American Journal of Orthopsychiatry* 57 (April 1987): 186–192.

3. Murray A. Straus, "Family Patterns and Child Abuse in a Nationally Representative American Sample," *Child Abuse and Neglect* 3 (1979): 213–225.

4. Raymond H. Starr, Jr., "Physical Abuse of Children," in *Handbook of Family Violence* ed. Vincent B. Van Hasselt, et al. (New York: Plenum Press, 1988): 119–155.

5. Cathy Spatz Widom, "Does Violence Beget Violence? A Critical Examination of the Literature," *Psychological Bulletin* 106 (1989): 3–28.

6. Joan McCord, "A Forty-year Perspective on Effects of Child Abuse and Neglect," *Child Abuse and Neglect* 7 (1983): 265–270. Joan McCord, "Parental Aggressiveness and Physical Punishment in Long-term Perspective," in *Family Abuse and Its Consequences*, ed. Gerald T. Hotaling, et al. (Newbury Park, Calif.: Sage Publishing, 1988): 91–98.

7. Cathy Spatz Widom, "The Cycle of Violence," *Science*, 14 April 1989.

8. Jan Hindman, "Research Disputes Assumptions about Child Molesters," *National District Attorneys' Association Bulletin* 7 (July/August 1988): 1.

9. Murray A. Straus, Richard J. Gelles, and Suzanne K. Steinmetz, *Behind Closed Doors: Violence in the American Family* (New York: Anchor Press, 1980).

10. David Finkelhor and Angela Browne, "Assessing the Long-term Impact of Child Sexual Abuse: A Review and Conceptualization," in *Family Abuse and Its Consequences*, ed. Gerald T. Hotaling, et al.: 270–284.

11. Elaine (Hilberman) Carmen, Patricia Perri Rieker, and Trudy Mills, "Victims of Violence and Psychiatric Illness," *American Journal of Psychiatry* 141 (March 1984): 378–383.

12. David A. Wolfe, *Child Abuse: Implications for Child Development and Psychopathology* (Newbury Park, Calif.: Sage Publishing, 1987).

13. Rosemary S. Hunter and Nancy Kilstrom, "Breaking the Cycle in Abusive Families," 136 (1979): 1320–22.

14. Isabel Wolock and Bernard Horowitz, "Child Maltreatment as a Social Problem: The Neglect of Neglect," *American Journal of Orthopsychiatry* 54 (1984); 530–543.

Your Loving Touch

The hugs, cuddles, and kisses you give your children will benefit
them throughout their lives.

Janice T. Gibson, Ed.D.

Janice T. Gibson, Ed.D., is a contributing
editor of Parents Magazine.

Like most mothers, I remember vividly the births of my two children, Robin and Mark. Each time I cuddled my newborn children in my arms—snuggling them gently against my skin and caressing them with my hands and lips—I felt peace and an extraordinary personal happiness. For each child, born four years apart, it took only an instant for me to fall in love! My joy made me want to continue cuddling and, in the process, strengthened a learned need to hug. Years later, when Mark was in fourth grade, I would hide behind the kitchen door and nab him for a hug when he came home from school. (He always put up with me, except in front of his friends.) And when Robin dressed for the prom, I zipped her gown, patted her on the shoulders, and wrapped my arms around her before she left with her date.

The power of touch.

Affectionate physical contact is meaningful at all age levels. Everyone needs affection, especially when frightened, insecure, or overtired. But particularly for children who cannot yet talk or understand words, cuddling and other forms of affectionate touch convey strong nonverbal messages and serve as important means of communication. When your baby is tired and snuggles in your arms, the gentle body-to-body contact relaxes him and communicates, "You're special. I love you."

Cuddling teaches infants about their environment and the people in it. They explore by touching with their fingers and tongue. Since touching is a reciprocal act, by cuddling your child you teach him to cuddle back. And by responding to his actions, you teach your baby to feel good about himself.

As your child grows older and snuggles with you after a frightening experience, a gentle hug that says "You are safe" will relieve him of his anxiety and help him to feel secure. If during a tantrum he lets you pick him up and hold him on your lap, he will be able to calm down and gain control of his emotions. Furthermore, your affectionate touch can help if your child misbehaves. If he hits his baby brother, for example, you can hold him on your lap as you tell him, "Hitting your brother is not okay." These words, together with the affectionate actions, tell him that although his behavior is not acceptable, you still love him. And when your child exhibits positive behavior, by praising him with a hug and a kiss or an enthusiastic high five, you will convey the message "I'm proud of you."

Why touch is so important.

Physical affection is crucial to a child's development. First of all, parents form strong affectional ties to their children by cuddling and touching them. Gary Johnson, of Delavan, Wisconsin, recalls how he felt after the birth of his first child, Jake: "I got to hold him in my arms for the first twenty minutes of his life. From those first moments together, I never felt strange with him. He was this little helpless creature who needed to be held, cuddled, and protected."

Whether an attachment such as the one Gary describes occurs immediately or over time, it increases the probability that parents will respond to their children's needs. Later, this strong attachment increases the child's psychological well-being.

For babies whose parents don't respond to their signals for close bodily contact, the result is what Mary Ainsworth, Ph.D., professor of psychology emeritus at the University of Virginia, in Charlottesville, has termed "anxious avoidance attachment." She and her colleagues found that babies whose mothers seldom pick them up to comfort them, and who rebuff their attempts to snuggle and cuddle, eventually learn to mask their emotions. When these babies are anxious and upset and most want their mother, they will avoid her so as not to risk being rejected again. "These babies often become adults who don't trust people and find it difficult to form close attachments," remarks Ainsworth. Thus the cycle becomes vicious and self-perpetuating.

The results of a recently completed 36-year study further demonstrate that the effects of parental affection are lifelong. In 1951 a team of psychologists from Harvard University, in Cambridge, Massachusetts, studied 379 five-year-olds in Boston. They asked the children's mothers about their own and their husband's child-rearing practices, including how the mothers responded when their child cried and whether they played with him; whether the father hugged and kissed the child when he came home from work; and whether he spent free time with the child. The researchers found that kindergartners whose parents were warm and

From Parents, March 1992, pp. 65-69. © 1992 by Gruner & Jahr USA Publishing. Reprinted from Parents Magazine by permission.

affectionate and cuddled them frequently were happier, played better, and had fewer feeding, behavior, and bed-wetting problems than did their peers raised by colder and more reserved parents.

In a 1987 follow-up study involving 76 of the original subjects, researchers found that as adults, those who were raised by warm, nurturing parents tended to have longer, happier marriages and better relationships with close friends than did adult peers whose early child rearing was not so warm. According to psychologist Carol Franz, Ph.D., one of the study's researchers, "Affectionate touching was always associated with a lot of warmth. The more warmth parents exhibited, the more socially adjusted their child was at midlife."

Cuddling barriers.

Most parents provide what their babies need and want. Holding, carrying, rocking, and caressing are part of child rearing in most societies. Infant massage, in which babies are systematically touched and stroked in caring ways, is practiced throughout the world. In some countries, such as India, mothers massage with scented oils. And in China, moms not only massage their youngsters but also use acupuncture to relax them.

But in contrast with people from other countries, Americans, in general, aren't "touchy." In my own cross-cultural studies of child rearing, I've found that although mothers and fathers in the United States are basically as affectionate as other parents, they tend to refrain from physical expressions of love. Although a baby's need for constant physical attention is obvious, the need is less obvious for older children and adults. Consequently, as U.S. children grow older, touching becomes less a part of parent-child interaction.

Some parents are uncomfortable behaving affectionately because they are afraid that it will spoil their children. Far from spoiling children, however, it teaches them to trust you and to view the world as a safe place to explore. Youngsters whose parents pick them up and hug them when they are hurt, frightened, or insecure develop feelings of security that make it easier for them to do things on their own.

Although there has been a lot of talk about how much more involved dads are today, many fathers still have a problem touching their children affectionately. Ronald Levant, Ed.D., former director of Boston University's Fatherhood Project and coauthor of *Between Father and Child* (Penguin), explains that today's generation of men have been raised to be like their fathers, who were the family breadwinners, and as a result they have grown up to be stoic. "As boys, they did not learn the basic psychological skills that girls did—such as self-awareness and empathy—which are necessary to nurture and care for children."

Furthermore, when dads do give their children affection, they tend to give more hugs and kisses to their daughters than to their sons. Why? Some fathers think that cuddling is not masculine and that too much physical affection will turn boys into "sissies." One dad admitted that when his wife was pregnant with their first child, he secretly hoped for a girl. "My father was not a very tactile person. We mostly shook hands. So I was concerned that if I had a son, I'd be too reserved. I was afraid to touch a son." Levant assures, however, that boys who are cuddled by their dads will not become "sissies" but will learn to be nurturing themselves. And more good news: The fathers of this generation are recognizing that they missed affection from their dads and, says Levant, are "breaking the old molds" of masculine reserve.

Some women also feel uncomfortable kissing and hugging their children because their parents weren't comfortable showing affection. One mother says that on the surface, her parents were warm and loving and she was well taken care of, "but I was rarely touched, hugged, or kissed." She wasn't comfortable cuddling with her children until she went into therapy and talked about her feelings. Now, she says, "I don't even think about it anymore. Hugging comes very naturally."

The high rate of divorce today, and the large number of single-parent homes in which the head of the household must work outside the home, also make it more difficult for some parents to provide the physical affection that their children may want or need at any given time. The recent concern raised by the specter of child abuse hasn't made it easier either. Highly publicized cases of purported sexual abuse of children by caregivers or estranged parents make some adults afraid that cuddling and touching may be construed as sexual and harmful. So what can be done? Although it is critical to protect children from sexual abuse, it is equally important to show all children that they are loved and needed. Children need healthy affection, and parents need to find ways to provide it.

Some parents are uncomfortable behaving affectionately with their children because they are afraid it will spoil them. On the contrary, it will help them develop feelings of security.

There are 1,001 ways to demonstrate affection, and not everyone needs to do it the same way. Parents who aren't comfortable giving their children big hugs and kisses shouldn't feel obliged to do so. Patting on the hand or back—or giving a squeeze—plus some loving words, can convey affection if it is done in a meaningful way.

Cuddling comfort.

Like some parents, some children are uncomfortable about being held closely, not because they don't want affection, but because they are uncomfortable feeling physically constrained. For such children, you can stroke their shoulders or back gently, give them lots of kisses, or tickle them gently so that they don't feel entrapped. Eventually they may even like to be cuddled. Gary Johnson's four-year-old daughter, Hallie, and one-year-old son, Nate, weren't as cuddly from the beginning with their father as was their older brother, Jake. But now Hallie is "Daddy's little girl and a permanent fixture on my lap." And Nate has just recently started to want Gary to cuddle him. "It's a real thrill to me to have him reach out for a hug from Dad," he says.

If you work outside the home and are away for most of the day, be sure that your caregiver supplies all the physical love your child needs. The Johnsons were concerned about leaving their kids in somebody else's care. "Becky and I believe that kids need plenty of physical love and affection, and we were afraid that someone else might not give them enough," says Gary. So they searched carefully. "We were fortunate to find a warm, loving, and wonderful caregiver. We can tell the kids are happy."

When peers become important to your child, he may start to shun your affections, particularly if his friends are present. Statements of rejection, such as "Yuck, Mom, don't kiss me" and "Leave my hair alone," do sting, but they signal that your child is growing up and striving for independence. Because he still needs your affection, you might try hugging him at bedtime when his friends aren't around.

As boys and girls reach puberty, touching becomes charged with sexual meaning, making it hard for many adolescents even to acknowledge the desire to touch or be touched in nonsexual ways. Parents should respect their teens' discomfort. When a hug may be too threatening, you can still express your love with a squeeze of the hand or a pat on the back.

If you are divorced, your child needs love from both you and your ex-spouse, even more than before the separation. So, if possible, work together with your ex-spouse to help your child to understand that both of you care. Sometimes boys raised in fatherless households, interpreting the loss of their father as making them the "man of the house," decide that permitting their mother to hug or kiss them makes them less manly. Mothers should respect these feelings but should not stop showing affection: A hug at bedtime or a lingering pat on the arm while going over homework will do wonders.

A recent experience underscored the message for me that even in adulthood, we still need, and benefit from, touch. It was while my now adult children and I were mourning their father's death. We stood silently for some minutes in a circle, our arms around one another, holding on tightly. The feel of our bodies touching consoled us and gave us strength. It convinced us, in a very concrete way, that we would be able to get on with our lives.

ALIENATION

AND THE FOUR WORLDS OF CHILDHOOD

The forces that produce youthful alienation are growing in strength and scope, says Mr. Bronfenbrenner. And the best way to counteract alienation is through the creation of connections or links throughout our culture. The schools can build such links.

Urie Bronfenbrenner

Urie Bronfenbrenner is Jacob Gould Shurman Professor of Human Development and Family Studies and of Psychology at Cornell University, Ithaca, N.Y.

To be alienated is to lack a sense of belonging, to feel cut off from family, friends, school, or work—the four worlds of childhood.

At some point in the process of growing up, many of us have probably felt cut off from one or another of these worlds, but usually not for long and not from more than one world at a time. If things weren't going well in school, we usually still had family, friends, or some activity to turn to. But if, over an extended period, a young person feels unwanted or insecure in several of these worlds simultaneously or if the worlds are at war with one another, trouble may lie ahead.

What makes a young person feel that he or she doesn't belong? Individual differences in personality can certainly be one cause, but, especially in recent years, scientists who study human behavior and development have identified an equal (if not even more powerful) factor: the circumstances in which a young person lives.

Many readers may feel that they recognize the families depicted in the vignettes that are to follow. This is so because they reflect the way we tend to look at families today: namely, that we see parents as being good or not-so-good without fully taking into account the circumstances in their lives.

Take Charles and Philip, for example. Both are seventh-graders who live in a middle-class suburb of a large U.S. city. In many ways their surroundings seem similar; yet, in terms of the risk of alienation, they live in rather different worlds. See if you can spot the important differences.

CHARLES

The oldest of three children, Charles is amiable, outgoing, and responsible. Both of his parents have full-time jobs outside the home. They've been able to arrange their working hours, however, so that at least one of them is at home when the children return from school. If for some reason they can't be home, they have an arrangement with a neighbor, an elderly woman who lives alone. They can phone her and ask her to look after the children until they arrive. The children have grown so fond of this woman that she is like another grandparent—a nice situation for them, since their real grandparents live far away.

Homework time is one of the most important parts of the day for Charles and his younger brother and sister. Charles's parents help the children with their homework if they need it, but most of the time they just make sure that the children have a period of peace and quiet—without TV—in which to do their work. The children are allowed to watch television one hour each night—but only after they have completed their homework. Since Charles is doing well in school, homework isn't much of an issue, however.

Sometimes Charles helps his mother or father prepare dinner, a job that everyone in the family shares and enjoys. Those family members who don't cook on a given evening are responsible for cleaning up.

Charles also shares his butterfly collection with his family. He started the collection when he first began learning about butterflies during a fourth-grade science project. The whole family enjoys picnicking and hunting butterflies together, and Charles occasionally asks his father to help him mount and catalogue his trophies.

Charles is a bit of a loner. He's not a very good athlete, and this makes him somewhat self-conscious. But he does have one very close friend, a boy in his class who lives just down the block. The two boys have been good friends for years.

Charles is a good-looking, warm, happy young man. Now that he's beginning to be interested in girls, he's gratified to find that the interest is returned.

PHILIP

Philip is 12 and lives with his mother, father, and 6-year-old brother. Both of his parents work in the city, commuting more than an hour each way. Pandemonium strikes every weekday morning as

From *Phi Delta Kappan,* February 1986, pp. 430-436. © 1986 by Phi Delta Kappa, Inc. Reprinted by permission of the author and *Phi Delta Kappan.*

the entire family prepares to leave for school and work.

Philip is on his own from the time school is dismissed until just before dinner, when his parents return after stopping to pick up his little brother at a nearby day-care home. At one time, Philip took care of his little brother after school, but he resented having to do so. That arrangement ended one day when Philip took his brother out to play and the little boy wandered off and got lost. Philip didn't even notice for several hours that his brother was missing. He felt guilty at first about not having done a better job. But not having to mind his brother freed him to hang out with his friends or to watch television, his two major after-school activities.

The pace of their life is so demanding that Philip's parents spend their weekends just trying to relax. Their favorite weekend schedule calls for watching a ball game on television and then having a cookout in the back yard. Philip's mother resigned herself long ago to a messy house; pizza, TV dinners, or fast foods are all she can manage in the way of meals on most nights. Philip's father has made it clear that she can do whatever she wants in managing the house, as long as she doesn't try to involve him in the effort. After a hard day's work, he's too tired to be interested in housekeeping.

Philip knows that getting a good education is important; his parents have stressed that. But he just can't seem to concentrate in school. He'd much rather fool around with his friends. The thing that he and his friends like to do best is to ride the bus downtown and go to a movie, where they can show off, make noise, and make one another laugh.

Sometimes they smoke a little marijuana during the movie. One young man in Philip's social group was arrested once for having marijuana in his jacket pocket. He was trying to sell it on the street so that he could buy food. Philip thinks his friend was stupid to get caught. If you're smart, he believes, you don't let that happen. He's glad that his parents never found out about the incident.

Once, he brought two of his friends home during the weekend. His parents told him later that they didn't like the kind of people he was hanging around with. Now Philip goes out of his way to keep his friends and his parents apart.

THE FAMILY UNDER PRESSURE

In many ways the worlds of both

> **I**nstitutions that play important roles in human development are rapidly being eroded, mainly through benign neglect.

teenagers are similar, even typical. Both live in families that have been significantly affected by one of the most important developments in American family life in the postwar years: the employment of both parents outside the home. Their mothers share this status with 64% of all married women in the U.S. who have school-age children. Fifty percent of mothers of preschool children and 46% of mothers with infants under the age of 3 work outside the home. For single-parent families, the rates are even higher: 53% of all mothers in single-parent households who have infants under age 3 work outside the home, as do 69% of all single mothers who have school-age children.[1]

These statistics have profound implications for families — sometimes for better, sometimes for worse. The determining factor is how well a given family can cope with the "havoc in the home" that two jobs can create. For, unlike most other industrialized nations, the U.S. has yet to introduce the kinds of policies and practices that make work life and family life compatible.

It is all too easy for family life in the U.S. to become hectic and stressful, as both parents try to coordinate the disparate demands of family and jobs in a world in which everyone has to be transported at least twice a day in a variety of directions. Under these circumstances, meal preparation, child care, shopping, and cleaning — the most basic tasks in a family — become major challenges. Dealing with these challenges may sometimes take precedence over the family's equally important child-rearing, educational, and nurturing roles.

But that is not the main danger. What threatens the well-being of children and young people the most is that the external havoc can become internal, first for parents and then for their children. And that is exactly the sequence in which the psychological havoc of families under stress usually moves.

Recent studies indicate that conditions at work constitute one of the major sources of stress for American families.[2] Stress at work carries over to the home, where it affects first the relationship of parents to each other. Marital conflict then disturbs the parent/child relationship. Indeed, as long as tensions at work do not impair the relationship between the parents, the children are not likely to be affected. In other words, the influence of parental employment on children is indirect, operating through its effect on the parents.

That this influence is indirect does not make it any less potent, however. Once the parent/child relationship is seriously disturbed, children begin to feel insecure — and a door to the world of alienation has been opened. That door can open to children at any age, from preschool to high school and beyond.

My reference to the world of school is not accidental, for it is in that world that the next step toward alienation is likely to be taken. Children who feel rootless or caught in conflict at home find it difficult to pay attention in school. Once they begin to miss out on learning, they feel lost in the classroom, and they begin to seek acceptance elsewhere. Like Philip, they often find acceptance in a group of peers with similar histories who, having no welcoming place to go and nothing challenging to do, look for excitement on the streets.

OTHER INFLUENCES

In contemporary American society the growth of two-wage-earner families is not the only — or even the most serious — social change requiring accommodation through public policy and practice in order to avoid the risks of alienation. Other social changes include lengthy trips to and from work; the loss of the extended family, the close neighborhood, and other support systems previously available to families; and the omnipresent threat of television and other media to the family's traditional role as the primary transmitter of culture and values. Along with most families today, the families of Charles and Philip are experiencing the unraveling and disintegration of social institutions that in the past were central to the health and well-being of children and their parents.

Notice that both Charles and Philip come from two-parent, middle-class families. This is still the norm in the U.S. Thus neither family has to contend with two changes now taking place in U.S. society that have profound implications for the future of American families and the well-being of the next generation. The first of these changes is the increasing number of single-parent families. Although the divorce rate in the U.S. has been leveling off of late, this decrease has been more than compensated for by a rise in the number of unwed mothers, especially teenagers. Studies of the children brought up in single-parent families indicate that they are at greater risk of alienation than their counterparts from two-parent families. However, their vulnerability appears to have its roots not in the single-parent family structure as such, but in the treatment of single parents by U.S. society.[3]

In this nation, single parenthood is almost synonymous with poverty. And the growing gap between poor families and the rest of us is today the most powerful and destructive force producing alienation in the lives of millions of young people in America. In recent years, we have witnessed what the U.S. Census Bureau calls "the largest decline in family income in the post-World War II period." According to the latest Census, 25% of all children under age 6 now live in families whose incomes place them below the poverty line.

COUNTERING THE RISKS

Despite the similar stresses on their families, the risks of alienation for Charles and Philip are not the same. Clearly, Charles's parents have made a deliberate effort to create a variety of arrangements and practices that work against alienation. They have probably not done so as part of a deliberate program of "alienation prevention" — parents don't usually think in those terms. They're just being good parents. They spend time with their children and take an active interest in what their children are thinking, doing, and learning. They control their television set instead of letting it control them. They've found support systems to back them up when they're not available.

Without being aware of it, Charles's parents are employing a principle that the great Russian educator Makarenko employed in his extraordinarily success-

ful programs for the reform of wayward adolescents in the 1920s: "The maximum of support with the maximum of challenge."[4] Families that produce effective, competent children often follow this principle, whether they're aware of it or not. They neither maintain strict control nor allow their children total freedom. They're always opening doors — and then giving their children a gentle but firm shove to encourage them to move on and grow. This combination of support and challenge is essential, if children are to avoid alienation and develop into capable young adults.

From a longitudinal study of youthful alienation and delinquency that is now considered a classic, Finnish psychologist Lea Pulkkinen arrived at a conclusion strikingly similar to Makarenko's. She found "guidance" — a combination of love and direction — to be a critical predictor of healthy development in youngsters.[5]

No such pattern is apparent in Philip's family. Unlike Charles's parents, Philip's parents neither recognize nor respond to the challenges they face. They have dispensed with the simple amenities of family self-discipline in favor of whatever is easiest. They may not be indifferent to their children, but the demands of their jobs leave them with little energy to be actively involved in their children's lives. (Note that Charles's parents have work schedules that are flexible enough to allow one of them to be at home most afternoons. In this regard, Philip's family is much more the norm, however. One of the most constructive steps that employers could take to strengthen families would be to enact clear policies making such flexibility possible.)

But perhaps the clearest danger signal in Philip's life is his dependence on his peer group. Pulkkinen found heavy reliance on peers to be one of the strongest predictors of problem behavior in adolescence and young adulthood. From a developmental viewpoint, adolescence is a time of challenge — a period in which young people seek activities that will serve as outlets for their energy, imagination, and longings. If healthy and constructive challenges are not available to them, they will find their challenges in such peer-group-related behaviors as poor school performance, aggressiveness or social withdrawal (sometimes both), school absenteeism or dropping out, smoking, drinking, early and promiscuous sexual activity, teenage parenthood, drugs, and juvenile delinquency.

This pattern has now been identified in a number of modern industrial societies, including the U.S., England, West Germany, Finland, and Australia. The pattern is both predictable from the circumstances of a child's early family life and predictive of life experiences still to come, e.g., difficulties in establishing relationships with the opposite sex, marital discord, divorce, economic failure, criminality.

If the roots of alienation are to be found in disorganized families living in disorganized environments, its bitter fruits are to be seen in these patterns of disrupted development. This is not a harvest that our nation can easily afford. Is it a price that other modern societies are paying, as well?

A CROSS-NATIONAL PERSPECTIVE

The available answers to that question will not make Americans feel better about what is occurring in the U.S. In our society, the forces that produce youthful alienation are growing in strength and scope. Families, schools, and other institutions that play important roles in human development are rapidly being eroded, *mainly through benign neglect.* Unlike the citizens of other modern nations, we Americans have simply not been willing to make the necessary effort to forestall the alienation of our young people.

As part of a new experiment in higher education at Cornell University, I have been teaching a multidisciplinary course for the past few years titled "Human Development in Post-Industrial Societies." One of the things we have done in that course is to gather comparative data from several nations, including France, Canada, Japan, Australia, Germany, England, and the U.S. One student summarized our findings succinctly: "With respect to families, schools, children, and youth, such countries as France, Japan, Canada, and Australia have more in common with each other than the United States has with any of them." For example:

• The U.S. has by far the highest rate of teenage pregnancy of any industrialized nation — twice the rate of its nearest competitor, England.

• The U.S. divorce rate is the highest in the world — nearly double that of its nearest competitor, Sweden.

• The U.S. is the only industrialized society in which nearly one-fourth of all infants and preschool children live in families whose incomes fall below the poverty line. These children lack such basics as adequate health care.

• The U.S. has fewer support systems for individuals in all age groups, including adolescence. The U.S. also has the highest incidence of alcohol and drug abuse among adolescents of any country in the world.[6]

All these problems are part of the unraveling of the social fabric that has been going on since World War II. These problems are not unique to the U.S., but in many cases they are more pronounced here than elsewhere.

WHAT COMMUNITIES CAN DO

The more we learn about alienation and its effects in contemporary post-industrial societies, the stronger are the imperatives to counteract it. If the essence of alienation is disconnectedness, then the best way to counteract alienation is through the creation of connections or links.

For the well-being of children and adolescents, the most important links must be those between the home, the peer group, and the school. A recent study in West Germany effectively demonstrated how important this basic triangle can be. The study examined student achievement and social behavior in 20 schools. For all the schools, the researchers developed measures of the links between the home, the peer group, and the school. Controlling for social class and other variables, the researchers found that they were able to predict children's behavior from the number of such links they found. Students who had no links were alienated. They were not doing well in school, and they exhibited a variety of behavioral problems. By contrast, students who had such links were doing well and were growing up to be responsible citizens.[7]

In addition to creating links within the basic triangle of home, peer group, and school, we need to consider two other structures in today's society that affect the lives of young people: the world of work (for both parents and children) and the community, which provides an overarching context for all the other worlds of childhood.

Philip's family is one example of how the world of work can contribute to alienation. The U.S. lags far behind other industrialized nations in providing child-care services and other benefits designed to promote the well-being of children and their families. Among the most needed benefits are maternity and paternity leaves, flex-time, job-sharing

> ## Caring is surely an essential aspect of education in a free society; yet we have almost completely neglected it.

arrangements, and personal leaves for parents when their children are ill. These benefits are a matter of course in many of the nations with which the U.S. is generally compared.

In contemporary American society, however, the parents' world of work is not the only world that both policy and practice ought to be accommodating. There is also the children's world of work. According to the most recent figures available, 50% of all high school students now work part-time — sometimes as much as 40 to 50 hours per week. This fact poses a major problem for the schools. Under such circumstances, how can teachers assign homework with any expectation that it will be completed?

The problem is further complicated by the kind of work that most young people are doing. For many years, a number of social scientists — myself included — advocated more work opportunities for adolescents. We argued that such experiences would provide valuable contact with adult models and thereby further the development of responsibility and general maturity. However, from their studies of U.S. high school students who are employed, Ellen Greenberger and Lawrence Steinberg conclude that most of the jobs held by these youngsters are highly routinized and afford little opportunity for contact with adults. The largest employers of teenagers in the U.S. are fast-food restaurants. Greenberger and Steinberg argue that, instead of providing maturing experiences, such settings give adolescents even greater exposure to the values and lifestyles of their peer group. And the adolescent peer group tends to emphasize immediate gratification and consumerism.[8]

Finally, in order to counteract the

mounting forces of alienation in U.S. society, we must establish a working alliance between the private sector and the public one (at both the local level and the national level) to forge links between the major institutions in U.S. society and to re-create a sense of community. Examples from other countries abound:

• Switzerland has a law that no institution for the care of the elderly can be established unless it is adjacent to and shares facilities with a day-care center, a school, or some other kind of institution serving children.

• In many public places throughout Australia, the Department of Social Security has displayed a poster that states, in 16 languages: "If you need an interpreter, call this number." The department maintains a network of interpreters who are available 16 hours a day, seven days a week. They can help callers get in touch with a doctor, an ambulance, a fire brigade, or the police; they can also help callers with practical or personal problems.

• In the USSR, factories, offices, and places of business customarily "adopt" groups of children, e.g., a day-care center, a class of schoolchildren, or a children's ward in a hospital. The employees visit the children, take them on outings, and invite them to visit their place of work.

We Americans can offer a few good examples of alliances between the public and private sectors, as well. For example, in Flint, Michigan, some years ago, Mildred Smith developed a community program to improve school performance among low-income minority pupils. About a thousand children were involved. The program required no change in the regular school curriculum; its principal focus was on building links between home and school. This was accomplished in a variety of ways.

• A core group of low-income parents went from door to door, telling their neighbors that the school needed their help.

• Parents were asked to keep younger children out of the way so that the older children could complete their homework.

• Schoolchildren were given tags to wear at home that said, "May I read to you?"

• Students in the high school business program typed and duplicated teaching materials, thus freeing teachers to work directly with the children.

• Working parents visited school classrooms to talk about their jobs and about how their own schooling now helped them in their work.

WHAT SCHOOLS CAN DO

As the program in Flint demonstrates, the school is in the best position of all U.S. institutions to initiate and strengthen links that support children and adolescents. This is so for several reasons. First, one of the major — but often unrecognized — responsibilities of the school is to enable young people to move from the secluded and supportive environment of the home into responsible and productive citizenship. Yet, as the studies we conducted at Cornell revealed, most other modern nations are ahead of the U.S. in this area.

In these other nations, schools are not merely — or even primarily — places where the basics are taught. Both in purpose and in practice, they function instead as settings in which young people learn "citizenship": what it means to be a member of the society, how to behave toward others, what one's responsibilities are to the community and to the nation.

I do not mean to imply that such learnings do not occur in American schools. But when they occur, it is mostly by accident and not because of thoughtful planning and careful effort. What form might such an effort take? I will present here some ideas that are too new to have stood the test of time but that may be worth trying.

Creating an American classroom. This is a simple idea. Teachers could encourage their students to learn about schools (and, especially, about individual classrooms) in such modern industrialized societies as France, Japan, Canada, West Germany, the Soviet Union, and Australia. The children could acquire such information in a variety of ways: from reading, from films, from the firsthand reports of children and adults who have attended school abroad, from exchanging letters and materials with students and their teachers in other countries. Through such exposure, American students would become aware of how attending school in other countries is both similar to and different from attending school in the U.S.

But the main learning experience would come from asking students to consider what kinds of things *should* be happening — or not happening — in American classrooms, given our nation's values and ideals. For example, how should children relate to one another and to their teachers, if they are doing things in an *American* way? If a student's idea seems to make sense, the American tradition of pragmatism makes the next step obvious: try the idea to see if it works.

The curriculum for caring. This effort also has roots in our values as a nation. Its goal is to make caring an essential part of the school curriculum. However, students would not simply learn about caring; they would actually engage in it. Children would be asked to spend time with and to care for younger children, the elderly, the sick, and the lonely. Caring institutions, such as day-care centers, could be located adjacent to or even within the schools. But it would be important for young caregivers to learn about the environment in which their charges live and the other people with whom their charges interact each day. For example, older children who took responsibility for younger ones would become acquainted with the younger children's parents and living arrangements by escorting them home from school.

Just as many schools now train superb drum corps, they could also train "caring corps" — groups of young men and women who would be on call to handle a variety of emergencies. If a parent fell suddenly ill, these students could come into the home to care for the children, prepare meals, run errands, and serve as an effective source of support for their fellow human beings. Caring is surely an essential aspect of education in a free society; yet we have almost completely neglected it.

Mentors for the young. A mentor is someone with a skill that he or she wishes to teach to a younger person. To be a true mentor, the older person must be willing to take the time and to make the commitment that such teaching requires.

We don't make much use of mentors in U.S. society, and we don't give much recognition or encouragement to individuals who play this important role. As a result, many U.S. children have few significant and committed adults in their lives. Most often, their mentors are their own parents, perhaps a teacher or two, a coach, or — more rarely — a relative, a neighbor, or an older classmate. However, in a diverse society such as ours, with its strong tradition of volunteerism, potential mentors abound. The schools need to seek them out and match them with young people who will respond positively to their particular knowledge and skills.

The school is the institution best suited to take the initiative in this task, because the school is the only place in which all children gather every day. It is also the only institution that has the right (and the responsibility) to turn to the community for help in an activity that represents the noblest kind of education: the building of character in the young.

There is yet another reason why schools should take a leading role in rebuilding links among the four worlds of childhood: schools have the most to gain. In the recent reports bemoaning the state of American education, a recurring theme has been the anomie and chaos that pervade many U.S. schools, to the detriment of effective teaching and learning. Clearly, we are in danger of allowing our schools to become academies of alienation.

In taking the initiative to rebuild links among the four worlds of childhood, U.S. schools will be taking necessary action to combat the destructive forces of alienation — first, within their own walls, and thereafter, in the life experience and future development of new generations of Americans.

1. Urie Bronfenbrenner, "New Worlds for Families," paper presented at the Boston Children's Museum, 4 May 1984.
2. Urie Bronfenbrenner, "The Ecology of the Family as a Context for Human Development," *Developmental Psychology*, in press.
3. Mavis Heatherington, "Children of Divorce," in R. Henderson, ed., *Parent-Child Interaction* (New York: Academic Press, 1981).
4. A.S. Makarenko, *The Collective Family: A Handbook for Russian Parents* (New York: Doubleday, 1967).
5. Lea Pulkkinen, "Self-Control and Continuity from Childhood to Adolescence," in Paul Baltes and Orville G. Brim, eds., *Life-Span Development and Behavior*, Vol. 4 (New York: Academic Press, 1982), pp. 64-102.
6. S.B. Kamerman, *Parenting in an Unresponsive Society* (New York: Free Press, 1980); S.B. Kamerman and A.J. Kahn, *Social Services in International Perspective* (Washington, D.C.: U.S. Department of Health, Education, and Welfare, n.d.); and Lloyd Johnston, Jerald Bachman, and Patrick O'Malley, *Use of Licit and Illicit Drugs by America's High School Students — 1975-84* (Washington, D.C.: U.S. Government Printing Office, 1985).
7. Kurt Aurin, personal communication, 1985.
8. Ellen Greenberger and Lawrence Steinberg, *The Work of Growing Up* (New York: Basic Books, forthcoming).

Why kids have a lot to cry about

David Elkind, Ph.D.

David Elkind, Ph.D., professor of child study at Tufts University, is the author of more than 400 articles. He is perhaps best known for his books The Hurried Child; All Grown Up and No Place to Go *and* Ties That Stress: Childrearing in a Postmodern Society. *He is an active consultant to government agencies, private foundations, clinics, and mental-health centers.*

"MOMMY," THE FIVE-YEAR-OLD GIRL asked her mother, "why don't you get divorced again?" Her thrice-married mother was taken aback and said in return, "Honey, why in the world should I do that?" To which her daughter replied, "Well, I haven't seen you in love for such a long time."

This young girl perceives family life and the adult world in a very different way than did her counterpart less than

half a century ago. Likewise, the mother perceives her daughter quite differently than did a mother raising a child in the 1940s. Although this mother was surprised at her daughter's question, she was not surprised at her understanding of divorce, nor at her familiarity with the symptoms of romance.

As this anecdote suggests, there has been a remarkable transformation over the last 50 years in our children's perceptions of us, and in our perceptions of our children. These altered perceptions are a very small part of a much larger tectonic shift in our society in general and in our families in particular. This shift is nothing less than a transformation of the basic framework, or paradigm, within which we think about and thus perceive our world. To understand the changes in the family, the perceptions of family members, and of parenting that have been brought about, we first have to look at this broader "paradigm shift" and what it has meant for family sentiments, values, and perceptions.

FROM MODERN TO POSTMODERN

Without fully realizing it perhaps, we have been transported into the postmodern era. Although this era has been called "postindustrial" and, alternatively, "information age," neither of these phrases is broad enough to encompass the breadth and depth of the changes that have occurred. The terms modern and postmodern, in contrast, encompass all aspects of society and speak to the changes in science, philosophy, architecture, literature, and the arts—as well as in industry and technology—that have marked our society since mid-century.

THE MODERN AND THE NUCLEAR FAMILY

The modern era, which began with the Renaissance and spanned the Industrial Revolution, was based upon three related assumptions. One was the idea of *human progress*—the notion that the natural direction of human and societal development is toward a more equitable, peaceful, and harmonious world in which every individual would be entitled to life, liberty, and the pursuit of happiness. A second assumption is *universality*. There were, it was taken as given, universal laws of nature of art, science, economics, and so on that transcended time and culture. The third basic assumption was that of *regularity*—the belief that the world is an orderly place, that animals and plants, geological layers and chemical elements could be classified in an orderly hierarchy. As Einstein put it, "God does not play dice with the universe!"

These assumptions gave a unique character and distinctiveness to modern life. Modern science, literature, architecture, philosophy, and industry all embodied these premises. And they were enshrined in the Modern Family as well. The modern nuclear family, for example, was seen as the end result of a progressive evolution of family forms. Two parents, two or three children, one parent working and one staying home to rear the children and maintain the home was thought to be the ideal family form toward which all prior, "primitive" forms were merely preliminary stages.

SENTIMENTS OF THE NUCLEAR FAMILY

The Modern Family was shaped by three sentiments that also reflected the underlying assumptions of modernity. One of these was Romantic Love. In premodern times, couples married by familial and community dictates. Considerations of property and social position were paramount. This community influence declined in the modern era, and couples increasingly came to choose one another on the basis of mutual attraction. This attraction became idealized into the notion that "Some enchanted evening, you will meet a stranger" for whom you and only you were destined ("You were meant for me, I was meant for you"), and that couples would stay together for the rest of their lives, happily "foreveraftering."

A second sentiment of the Modern Family was that of Maternal Love—the idea that women have a maternal "instinct" and a need to care for children, particularly when they are small. The idea of a maternal instinct was a thoroughly modern invention that emerged only after modern medicine and nutrition reduced infant mortality. In premodern times, infant mortality was so high that the young were not even named until they were two years old and stood a good chance of surviving. It was also not uncommon for urban parents to have their infants "wet-nursed" in the country. Often these

infants died because the wet-nurse fed her own child before she fed the stranger, and there was little nourishment left. Such practices could hardly be engaged in by a mother with a "maternal instinct."

The third sentiment of the Modern Family was Domesticity, a belief that relationships within the family are always more powerful and binding than are those outside it. The family was, as Christopher Lasch wrote, "a haven in a heartless world." As a haven, the nuclear family shielded and protected its members from the evils and temptations of the outside world. This sentiment also extended to the family's religious, ethnic, and social-class affiliations. Those individuals who shared these affiliations were to be preferred, as friends and spouses, over those with different affiliations.

PARENTING THE INNOCENT

The modern perceptions of parenting, children, and teenagers grew out of these family sentiments. Modern parents, for example, were seen as intuitively or instinctively knowledgeable about child-rearing. Professional help was needed only to encourage parents to do "what comes naturally." In keeping with this view of parenting was the perception of children as innocent and in need of parental nurturance and protection. Teenagers, in turn, were seen as immature and requiring adult guidance and direction. Adolescence, regarded as the age of preparation for adulthood, brought with it the inevitable "storm and stress," as young people broke from the tight nuclear family bonds and became socially and financially independent.

These modern perceptions of parenting

and of children and youth were reinforced by the social mirror of the media, the law and the health professions. Motion pictures such as the Andy Hardy series (starring Mickey Rooney) depicted a teenage boy getting into youthful scrapes at school and with friends from which he was extricated by his guardian the judge, played by Harlan Stone. Fiction similarly portrayed teenagers as immature young people struggling to find themselves. Mark Twain's Huck Finn was an early version of the modern immature adolescent, while J. D. Salinger's Holden Caulfield is a modern version.

Modern laws, such as the child-labor laws and compulsory-education statutes were enacted to protect both children and adolescents. And the health professions attributed the mental-health problems of children and youth to conflicts arising from the tight emotional bonds of the nuclear family.

POSTMODERNITY AND THE POSTMODERN FAMILY

The postmodern view has largely grown out of the failure of modern assumptions about progress, universality, and regularity. Many of the events of this century have made the idea of progress difficult to maintain. Germany, one of the most educationally, scientifically, and culturally advanced countries of the world, engaged in the most heinous genocide. Modern science gave birth to the atomic bomb that was dropped on Hiroshima and Nagasaki. Environmental degradation, pollution, population explosions, and widespread famine can hardly be reconciled with the notion of progress.

Secondly, the belief in universal principles has been challenged as the "grand"

We are so caught up in our perception of kids' competence that we teach five-year-olds about AIDS and child abuse, and give them toys that simulate pregnancy and dismemberment.

theories of the modern era—such as those of Marx, Darwin, and Freud—are now recognized as limited by the social and historical contexts in which they were elaborated. Modern theorists believed that they could transcend social-historical boundaries; the postmodern worker recognizes that he or she is constrained by the particular discourse of narrative in play at the time. Likewise, the search for abiding ethical, moral, and religious universals is giving way to a recognition that there are many different ethics, moralities, and religions, each of which has a claim to legitimacy.

Finally, the belief in regularity has given way to a recognition of the importance of irregularity, indeterminacy, chaos, and fuzzy logic. There is much in nature, such as the weather, that remains unpredictable—not because it is perverse, but only because the weather is affected by non-regular events. Sure regularity appears, but irregularity is now seen as a genuine phenomenon in its own right. It is no longer seen, as it was in the modern era, as the result of some failure to discover an underlying regularity.

In place of these modern assumptions, a new, postmodern paradigm with its own basic premises has been invented. The assumption of progress, to illustrate, has given way to the presumption of *difference*. There are many different forms and types of progress, and not all progressions are necessarily for the better. Likewise, the belief in universals has moved aside for the belief in *particulars*. Different phenomena may have different rules and principles that are not necessarily generalizable. For example, a particular family or a particular class of children is a non-replicable event that can never be exactly duplicated and to which universal principles do not apply. Finally, the assumption of regularity moved aside to make room for the principle of *irregularity*. The world is not as orderly and as logically organized as we had imagined.

As the societal paradigm has shifted, so has the structure of the family. The ideal nuclear family, thought to be the product of progressive social evolution, has given way to what might be called the *Permeable Family* of the postmodern era. The Permeable Family encompasses many different family forms: traditional or nuclear, two-parent working, single-parent, blended, adopted child, test-tube, surrogate mother, and co-parent families. Each of these is valuable and a potentially successful family form.

Rapid social change is a catastrophe for children and youths, who require stability and security for healthy growth and development.

The family is permeable in other ways as well. It is no longer isolated from the larger community. Thanks to personal computers, fax and answering machines, the workplace has moved into the homeplace. The homeplace, in turn, thanks to childcare facilities in office buildings and factories, has moved into the workplace. The home is also permeated by television, which brings the outside world into the living room and bedrooms. And an ever-expanding number of TV shows (*Oprah, Donahue, Geraldo, and Sally Jessy Raphael*), all detailing the variety of family problems, brings the living room and the bedroom into the outside world.

Quite different sentiments animate the postmodern Permeable Family than animated the modern nuclear family. The transformation of family sentiments came about in a variety of ways, from the civil-rights movement, the women's movement, changes in media, and laws that were part of the postmodern revolution. Because there is a constant interaction between the family and the larger society, it is impossible to say whether changes in the family were brought about by changes in society or vice versa. Things moved in both directions.

For a number of reasons, the Modern Family sentiment of Romantic Love has been transformed in the Postmodern era into the sentiment of *Consensual Love*. In contrast to the idealism and perfectionism of Romantic Love, consensual love is realistic and practical. It recognizes the legitimacy of premarital relations and is not premised on long-term commitment. Consensual Love is an agreement or contract between the partners; as an agreement it can be broken. The difference between Romantic Love and Consensual Love is summed up in the prenuptial agreement, which acknowledges the possible rupture of a marriage—before the marriage actually occurs. The current emphasis upon safe sex is likewise a symptom of consensual, not romantic, love.

The Modern Family sentiment of ma-

ternal love has yielded to other changes. Today, more than 50 percent of women are in the workforce, and some 60 percent of these women have children under the age of six. These figures make it clear that non-maternal and non-parental figures are now playing a major role in child-rearing. As part of this revision of child-rearing responsibilities, a new sentiment has emerged that might be called *shared parenting*. What this sentiment entails is the understanding that not only mothers, but fathers and professional caregivers are a necessary part of the child-rearing process. Child-rearing and childcare are no longer looked upon as the sole or primary responsibility of the mother.

The permeability of the Postmodern Family has also largely done away with the Modern Family sentiment of domesticity. The family can no longer protect individuals from the pressures of the outside world. Indeed, the impulse of the Permeable Family is to move in the other direction. Permeable Families tend to thrust children and teenagers forward to deal with realities of the outside world at ever earlier ages. This has resulted in what I have called the "hurrying" of children to grow up fast. Much of the hurrying of children and youth is a well-intentioned effort on the part of parents to help prepare children and youth for the onrush of information, challenges, and temptations coming at them through the now-permeable boundaries of family life.

POSTMODERN PARENTS OF KIDS WITHOUT INNOCENCE

These new, postmodern sentiments have given rise to new perceptions of parenting, of children, and of adolescents. Now that parenting is an activity shared with non-parental figures, we no longer regard it as an instinct that emerges once we have become parents; it is now regarded as a matter of learned *technique*.

Postmodern parents understand that doing "what comes naturally" may not be good for children. There are ways to say things to children that are less stressful than others. There are ways of disciplining that do not damage the child's sense of self esteem. The problem for parents today is to choose from the hundreds of books and other media sources bombarding them with advice on child-rearing. As one mother said to me, "I've read your books and they sound okay, but what if you're wrong?"

With respect to children, the perception of childhood innocence has given way to the perception of childhood competence. Now that children are living in Permeable Families with—thanks to television—a steady diet of overt violence, sexuality, substance abuse, and environmental degradation, we can no longer assume they are innocent. Rather, perhaps to cover our own inability to control what our children are seeing, we perceive them as competent to deal with all of this material. Indeed, we get so caught up in this perception of competence that we teach four- and five-year-olds about AIDS and child abuse and provide "toys" that simulate pregnancy or the dismemberment that accidents can cause unbuckled-up occupants. And the media reinforce this competence perception with films such as *Look Who's Talking* and *Home Alone*.

If children are seen as competent, teenagers can no longer be seen as immature. Rather they are now seen as sophisticated in the ways of the world, knowledgeable about sex, drugs, crime, and much more. This is a convenient fiction for parents suffering a time-famine. Such parents can take the perception of teenage sophistication as a rationale to abrogate their responsibility to provide young people with limits, guidance, and supervision. Increasingly, teenagers are on their own. Even junior and senior high schools no longer provide the social programs and clubs they once did.

This new perception of teenagers is also reflected in the social mirror of media, school and law. Postmodern films like *Risky Business* (in which teenager runs a bordello in the parents' home) and *Angel* (demure high school student by day, avenging hooker by night) are a far cry from the Andy Hardy films. Postmodern TV sitcoms such as *Married with Children* and *Roseanne* present images of teenage sophistication hardly reconcilable with the teenagers portrayed in modern TV shows such as *My Three Sons* or *Ozzie and Harriet*. Postmodern legal thinking is concerned with protecting the *rights* of children and teenagers, rather than protecting children themselves. Children and teenagers can now sue their parents for divorce, visitation rights, and for remaining in the United States when the family travels overseas.

REALITY IS HERE TO STAY

The postmodern perceptions of children as competent and of teenagers as sophisticated did not grow out of any injustices nor harm visited upon children and youth. Rather they grew out of a golden era for young people that lasted from the end of the last century to the middle of this one. Society as a whole was geared to regard children as innocent and teenagers as immature, and sought to protect children and gradually inculcate teenagers into the ways of the world.

In contrast, the perceptions of childhood competence and teenage sophistication have had detrimental effects upon children and youth. Indeed, these perceptions have placed children and teenagers under inordinate stress. And it shows. On every measure that we have, children and adolescents are doing less well today than they did a quarter century ago, when the new postmodern perceptions were coming into play. While it would be unwise to attribute all of these negative effects to changed perceptions alone—economics and government policy clearly played a role—it is also true that government policy and economics are affected by the way young people are perceived.

The statistics speak for themselves. There has been a 50-percent increase in obesity in children and youth over the past two decades. We lose some ten thousand teenagers a year in substance-related accidents, not including injured and maimed. One in four teenagers drinks to excess every two weeks, and we have two million alcoholic teenagers.

Teenage girls in America get pregnant at the rate of one million per year, twice the rate of the next Western country, England. Suicide has tripled among teenagers in the last 20 years, and between five and six thousand teenagers take their own lives each year. It is estimated that one out of four teenage girls manifests at least one symptom of an eating disorder, most commonly severe dieting. The 14- to 19-year-old age group has the second-highest homicide rate of any age group.

These are frightening statistics. Yet they are not necessarily an indictment of the postmodern world, nor of our changed perceptions of children and youth. We have gone through enormous social changes in a very brief period of time. No other society on Earth changes, or can change, as rapidly as we do. That is both our strength and our weakness. It has made us, and will keep us, the leading industrial nation in the world because we are more flexible than any other society, including Japan.

But rapid social change is a catastrophe for children and youth, who require stability and security for healthy growth and development. Fortunately, we are now moving toward a more stable society. A whole generation of parents was caught in the transition between Modern and Postmodern Family sentiments; among them, divorce, open marriage, and remarriage became at least as commonplace as the permanent nuclear family. The current generation of parents have, however, grown up with the new family sentiments and are not as conflicted as their own parents were.

As a result, we are slowly moving back to a more realistic perception of both children and teenagers, as well as toward a family structure that is supportive of all family members. We are moving towards what might be called the *Vital Family*. In the Vital Family, the modern value of togetherness is given equal weight with the Postmodern Family value of autonomy. Children are seen as *growing into competence* and as still needing the help and support of parents. Likewise, teenagers are increasingly seen as *maturing into sophistication*, and able to benefit from adult guidance, limits, and direction.

These new perceptions pop up in the media. Increasingly, newspapers and magazines feature articles on the negative effects pressures for early achievement have upon children. We are also beginning to see articles about the negative effects the demands for sophistication place upon teenagers. A number of recent TV shows (such as *Beverly Hills 90210*) have begun to portray children and youth as sophisticated, but also as responsible and accepting of adult guidance and supervision. There is still much too much gratuitous sex and violence, but at least there are signs of greater responsibility and recognition that children and adolescents may not really be prepared for everything we would like to throw at them.

After 10 years of traveling and lecturing all over the country, I have an impression that the American family is alive and well. It has changed dramatically, and we are still accommodating to the changes. And, as always happens, children and youths are more harmed by change than are adults. But our basic value system remains intact. We do have a strong Judeo-Christian heritage; we believe in hard work, democracy, and autonomy. But our sense of social and parental responsibility, however, was temporarily deadened by the pace of social change. Now that we are getting comfortable in our new Permeable Family sentiments and perceptions, we are once again becoming concerned with those who are young and those who are less fortunate.

As human beings we all have a need to become the best that we can be. But we also have a need to love and to be loved, to care and to be cared for. The Modern Family spoke to our need to belong at the expense, particularly for women, of the need to become.

The Permeable Family, in contrast, celebrates the need to become at the expense of the need to belong, and this has been particularly hard on children and youth. Now we are moving towards a Vital Family that ensures both our need to become and our need to belong. We are not there yet, but the good news is, we are on our way.

the MIRACLE OF RESILIENCY

DAVID GELMAN

There are sharp differences in the way children bear up under stress
—

A prominent child psychiatrist, E. James Anthony, once proposed this analogy: there are three dolls, one made of glass, the second of plastic, the third of steel. Struck with a hammer, the glass doll shatters; the plastic doll is scarred. But the steel doll proves invulnerable, reacting only with a metallic ping.

In life, no one is unbreakable. But child-health specialists know there are sharp differences in the way children bear up under stress. In the aftermath of divorce or physical abuse, for instance, some are apt to become nervous and withdrawn; some may be illness-prone and slow to develop. But there are also so-called resilient children who shrug off the hammer blows and go on to highly productive lives. The same small miracle of resiliency has been found under even the most harrowing conditions—in Cambodian refugee camps, in crack-ridden Chicago housing projects. Doctors repeatedly encounter the phenomenon: the one child in a large, benighted brood of five or six who seems able to take adversity in stride. "There are kids in families from very adverse situations who really do beautifully, and seem to rise to the top of their potential, even with everything else working against them," says Dr. W. Thomas Boyce, director of the division of behavioral and developmental pediatrics at the University of California, San Francisco. "Nothing touches them; they thrive no matter what."

Something, clearly, has gone right with these children, but what? Researchers habitually have come at the issue the other way around. The preponderance of the literature has to do with why children fail, fall ill, turn delinquent. Only

recently, doctors realized they were neglecting the equally important question of why some children *don't* get sick. Instead of working backward from failure, they decided, there might be as much or more to be learned from studying the secrets of success. In the course of looking at such "risk factors" as poverty, physical impairment or abusive parents, they gradually became aware that there were also "protective factors" that served as buffers against the risks. If those could be identified, the reasoning went, they might help develop interventions that could change the destiny of more vulnerable children.

At the same time, the recognition that many children have these built-in defenses has plunged resiliency research into political controversy. "There is a danger among certain groups who advocate nonfederal involvement in assistance to children," says Duke University professor Neil Boothby, a child psychologist who has studied children in war zones. "They use it to blame people who don't move out of poverty. Internationally, the whole notion of resiliency has been used as an excuse not to do anything."

The quest to identify protective factors has produced an eager burst of studies in the past 10 or 15 years, with new publications tumbling off the presses every month. Although the studies so far offer no startling insights, they are providing fresh perspectives on how nature and nurture intertwine in childhood development. One of the prime protective factors, for example, is a matter of genetic luck of the draw: a child born with an easygoing disposition invariably handles stress better than one with a nervous, overreactive temperament. But even highly reactive children can acquire resilience if they have a consistent, stabilizing element in their young lives—something like an attentive parent or mentor.

The most dramatic evidence on that score comes not from humans but from their more researchable cousins, the apes. In one five-year-long study, primate researcher Stephen Suomi has shown that by putting infant monkeys in the care of supportive mothers, he could virtually turn their lives around. Suomi, who heads the Laboratory of Comparative Ethology at the National Institute of Child Health and Human Development, has been comparing "vulnerable" and "invulnerable" monkeys to see if there are useful nurturing approaches to be learned. Differences of temperament can be spotted in monkeys before they're a week old. Like their human counterparts, vulnerable monkey infants show measurable increases in heart rate and stress-hormone production in response to threat situations. "You see a fairly consistent pattern of physiological arousal, and also major behavioral differences," says Suomi. "Parallel patterns have been found in human-developmental labs, so we feel we're looking at the same phenomena."

Left alone in a regular troop, these high-strung infants grow up to be marginal figures in their troops. But by putting them in the care of particularly loving, attentive foster mothers within their first four days of life, Suomi turns the timid monkeys into social lions. Within two months, they become bold and outgoing. Males in the species Suomi has been working with normally leave their native troop at puberty and eventually work their way into a new troop. The nervous, vulnerable individuals usually are the last to leave home. But after being "cross-fostered" to loving mothers, they develop enough confidence so that they're first to leave.

Once on their own, monkeys have complicated (but somehow familiar) patterns of alliances. Their status often depends on whom they know and to whom they're related. In squabbles, they quickly generate support among friends and family members. The cross-fostered monkeys grow very adept at recruiting that kind of support. It's a knack they somehow get through interaction with their foster mothers, in which they evidently pick up coping styles as well as information. "It's essentially a social-learning phenomenon," says Suomi. "I would argue that's what's going on at the human level, too. Evidently, you can learn styles in addition to specific information."

In the long run, the vulnerable infants not only were turned around to normality, they often rose to the top of their hierarchies; they became community leaders. Boyce notes there are significant "commonalities" between Suomi's findings and studies of vulnerable children. "The implications are that vulnerable children, if placed in the right social environment, might become extraordinarily productive and competent adult individuals," he says.

Children, of course, can't be fostered off to new parents or social conditions as readily as monkeys. Most resiliency research is based on children who have not had such interventions in their lives. Nevertheless, some of the findings are revealing. One of the definitive studies was conducted by Emmy E. Werner, a professor of human development at the University of California, Davis, and Ruth S. Smith, a clinical psychologist on the Hawaiian island of Kauai. Together,

they followed 698 children, all descendants of Kauaiian plantation workers, from their birth (in 1955) up to their early 30s. About half the children grew up in poverty; one in six had physical or intellectual handicaps diagnosed between birth and age 2. Of the 225 designated as high risk, two thirds had developed serious learning or behavior problems within their first decade of life. By 18 they had delinquency records, mental-health problems or teenage pregnancies. "Yet one out of three," Werner and Smith noted, "grew into competent young adults who loved well, worked well, played well and expected well."

Some of the protective factors the two psychologists identified underscore the nature-nurture connection. Like other researchers, they found that children who started out with robust, sunny personalities were often twice lucky: not only were they better equipped to cope with life to begin with, but their winning ways made them immediately lovable. In effect, the "nicer" the children, the more readily they won affection—both nature and nurture smiled upon them. There were also other important resiliency factors, including self-esteem and a strong sense of identity. Boyce says he encounters some children who even at 2 or 3 have a sense of "presence" and independence that seem to prefigure success. "It's as if these kids have had the 'Who am I' questions answered for them," he says.

One of the more intriguing findings of the Kauai research was that resilient children were likely to have characteristics of both sexes. Boys and girls in the study tended to be outgoing and autonomous, in the male fashion, but also nurturant and emotionally sensitive, like females. "It's a little similar to what we find in creative children," observes Werner. Some other key factors were inherent in the children's surroundings rather than their personalities. It helped to have a readily available support network of grandparents, neighbors or relatives. Others note that for children anywhere, it doesn't hurt at all to be born to well-off parents. "The advantage of middle-class life is there's a safety net," says Arnold Sameroff, a developmental psychologist at Brown University's Bradley Hospital. "If you screw up, there's someone to bail you out."

In most cases, resilient children have "clusters" of protective factors, not just one or two. But the sine qua non, according to Werner, is a "basic, trusting relationship" with an adult. In all the clusters in the Kauai study, "there is not one that didn't include that one good relationship, whether with a parent, grandparent, older sibling, teacher or mentor—someone consistent enough in that person's life to say, 'You count,' and that sort of begins to radiate other support in their lives." Even children of abusive or schizophrenic parents may prove resilient if they had at least one caring adult looking out for them—someone, as Tom Boyce says, "who serves as a kind of beacon presence in their lives."

Such relationships do the most good when they are lasting. There is no lasting guarantee for resiliency itself, which is subject to change, de-

Researchers can spot differences of temperament in monkeys before they're a week old

pending on what sort of ups and downs people encounter. Children's ability to cope often improves naturally as they develop and gain experience, although it may decline after a setback in school or at home. Werner notes that around half the vulnerable children in the Kauai study had shaken off their previous problems by the time they reached their late 20s or early 30s. "In the long-term view, more people come through in spite of circumstances. There is an amazing amount of recovery, if you don't focus on one particular time when things are falling apart."

Ironically, this "self-righting" tendency has made the resiliency issue something of a political football. Conservatives have seized on the research to bolster their case against further social spending. "It's the politics of 'It's all within the kid'," says Lisbeth Schorr, a lecturer in social medicine at Harvard Medical School whose book, "Within Our Reach: Breaking the Cycle of Disadvantage," has had a wide impact in the field. "The conservative argument against interventions like Operation Head Start and family-support programs is that if these inner-city kids and families just showed a little grit they would pull themselves up by their own bootstraps. But people working on resilience are aware that when it comes to environments like the inner city, it really doesn't make a lot of sense to talk about what's intrinsic to the kids, because the environment is so overwhelming."

So overwhelming, indeed, that some researchers voice serious doubts over how much change can be brought about in multiple-risk children. Brown's Sameroff, who has been dealing with poor inner-city black and white families in Rochester, N.Y., says the experience has left him "more realistic" about what is possible. "Interventions are important if we can target one or two things wrong with a child. So you provide psychotherapy or extra help in the classroom, then there's a lot better chance." But the children he deals with usually have much more than that going against them—not only poverty but large families, absent fathers, drug-ridden neighborhoods and so on. "We find the more risk factors the worse the outcome," says Sameroff. "With eight or nine, *nobody* does well. For the majority of these children, it's going to involve changing the whole circumstance in which they are raised."

Others are expressing their own reservations, as the first rush of enthusiasm in resiliency research cools somewhat. "A lot of the early intervention procedures that don't follow through have been oversold," says Emmy Werner. "Not every-

one benefited equally from such programs as Head Start." Yet, according to child-development specialists, only a third of high-risk children are able to pull through relatively unaided by such interventions. Says Werner: "At least the high-risk children should be guaranteed basic health and social programs."

Interestingly, when Suomi separates his vulnerable monkeys from their foster mothers at 7 months—around the same time that mothers in the wild go off to breed, leaving their young behind—the genes reassert themselves, and the monkeys revert to fearful behavior. According to Suomi, they do recover again when the mothers return and their new coping skills seem to stay with them. Yet their experience underscores the frailty of change. Boyce, an admirer of Suomi's work, acknowledges that the question of how lasting the effects of early interventions are remains open. But, he adds, programs like Head Start continue to reverberate as much as 15 years later, with reportedly higher school-completion rates and lower rates of delinquency and teen pregnancies.

Boyce recalls that years ago, when he was at the University of North Carolina, he dealt with an 8-year-old child from an impoverished, rural black family, who had been abandoned by his mother. The boy also had "prune-belly syndrome," an anomaly of the abdominal musculature that left him with significant kidney and urinary problems, requiring extensive surgery. But he also had two doting grandparents who had raised him from infancy. They showered him with love and unfailingly accompanied him on his hospital visits. Despite his physical problems and loss of a mother, the boy managed to perform "superbly" in school. By the age of 10, when Boyce last saw him, he was "thriving."

Children may not be as manageable or resilient as laboratory monkeys. If anything, they are more susceptible in the early years. But with the right help at the right time, they can overcome almost anything. "Extreme adversity can have devastating effects on development," says psychologist Ann Masten, who did some of the groundbreaking work in the resiliency field with her University of Minnesota colleague Norman Garmezy. "But our species has an enormous capacity for recovery. Children living in a hostile caregiving environment have great difficulty, but a lot of ability to recover to better functioning if they're given a chance. That's a very important message from the resiliency literature." Unfortunately, the message may not be getting through to the people who can provide that chance.

> **There are kids from adverse situations who do beautifully and seem to rise to their potential**

TELEVISED VIOLENCE AND KIDS:
A PUBLIC HEALTH PROBLEM?

When Leonard Eron surveyed every 8-year-old child in Columbia County, New York, in 1960, he found something he wasn't looking for: an astonishing, and unmistakable, correlation between the amount of violence the youngsters saw on television and the aggressiveness of their behavior.

More than three decades and two follow-up studies later, after several related research projects and countless hearings and conferences, the work of Eron and his ISR colleague, L. Rowell Huesmann, has become an "overnight sensation." As leading researchers on the effects of media violence on the young, they have been making the rounds of TV talk and news programs and radio call-in shows, while fielding almost daily calls from reporters.

Their message is ultimately a simple one: Aggression is a learned behavior, it is learned at an early age, and media violence is one of its teachers. But because it is a learned behavior, there is hope that it can be unlearned, or never taught in the first place.

Both Eron and Huesmann are professors of psychology at the University of Michigan and research scientists at ISR's Research Center for Group Dynamics. Huesmann is also a professor of communication and acting chair of the Department of Communication. Their talents and interests have complemented each other since they met at Yale in the early 1970s. Eron's research interest is aggression, while Huesmann, who minored in mathematics as a U-M undergraduate in the early '60s, brings his prowess in data analysis and expertise in cognitive mechanisms and development to the team.

"I wanted to measure child-rearing practices as they related to aggression" in the 1960 survey, says Eron. "The parents knew what the study was about and, in the interviews, we were asking sensitive questions about how parents punished their children, what their disagreements were, and so forth. So we wanted to buffer those with what we called 'Ladies' Home Journal' questions — Had they read Dr. Spock? How often did their child watch TV? What were his or her favorite shows?

"But the computer was unaware of our humor and analyzed those TV programs," he adds. "And, lo and behold, the more aggressive that kids were in school, the higher the violence content of the shows they watched."

But that still left the chicken-and-egg ambiguity. Did watching violent TV make kids more aggressive, or did more aggressive kids watch violent TV?

That's where time, and Huesmann, came in. In 1970, the U.S. Surgeon General formed a committee on television and social behavior, and asked Eron to re-survey as many of the Columbia County kids as he could find. Eron, in turn, sought the services of Huesmann, then an assistant professor at Yale.

> "How can they say their programs have no effect on behavior when they're in the business of selling ads?"
>
> —Leonard Eron

"The analysis of long-term data on children's behavior required some sophisticated mathematical and statistical analysis," says Huesmann, "and that was the area in which I was trained."

The project also struck another responsive chord, he says: "The models that had been advanced to explain the long-terms effects of television violence were lacking an explanation of how the effects of watching television violence could last way into adulthood."

So it was back to the Hudson Valley of upstate New York in 1971. They found about 500 of

From *ISR Newsletter,* Vol. 18, No. 1, February 1994, pp. 5-7. © 1994 by the Regents of the University of Michigan Institute for Social Research. Reprinted by permission.

the now 19-year-olds from the original sample of 875 youngsters. The results were just as powerful, if not more so.

"The correlation between violence-viewing at age 8 and how aggressive the individual was at 19 was higher than the correlation between watching violence at age 8 and behaving aggressively at age 8," says Eron. "There was no correlation between violence-viewing at age 19 and aggressiveness at 19. It seems there was a cumulative effect going on here."

Its persistence was documented once more in 1981, when 400 of the subjects were surveyed again, along with 80 of their offspring. The 30-year-old men who had been the most aggressive when they were 8 had more arrests for drunk

---

"The evidence is overwhelming. The strength of the relationship is the same as cigarettes causing lung cancer. Is there any doubt about that?"

—Leonard Eron

---

driving, more arrests for violent crime, were more abusive to their spouses . . . and had more aggressive children. And of the 600 subjects whose criminal justice records were reviewed, those who watched more violence on TV when they were 8 had been arrested more often for violent crimes, and self-reported more fights when consuming alcohol.

In other words, their viewing choices and behavior as 8-year-olds were better predictors of their behavior at age 30 than either what they watched on TV or how aggressively they behaved later in life.

"Children learn programs for how to behave that I call scripts," says Huesmann. "In a new social situation, how do

you know how to behave? You search for scripts to follow. Where is a likely place for those scripts to come from? From what you've observed others doing in life, films, TV. So, as a child, you see a Dirty Harry movie, where the heroic policeman is shooting people right and left. Even years later, the right kind of scene can trigger that script and suggest a way to behave that follows it. Our studies have come up with a lot of evidence that suggests that's very possible. Moreover, we find that watching TV violence affects the viewer's beliefs and attitudes about how people are going to behave."

The longitudinal data were so compelling that the 1993 report of the American Psychological Association's Commission on Violence and Youth, which Eron chaired, stated unequivocally that there is "absolutely no doubt that higher levels of viewing violence on television are correlated with increased acceptance of aggressive attitudes and increased aggressive behavior."

"The evidence is overwhelming," says Eron. "The strength of the relationship is the same as cigarettes causing lung cancer. Is there any doubt about that?"

Only among those who profit from tobacco, just as TV and movie industry executives have generated most of the criticism of the ISR colleagues' work. While the media in general were fascinated by the damning data, especially after the APA report was released last August, the visual media in particular were equally eager to defend themselves and defuse the evidence.

This is not a message the industry wants to hear. Its position is that the off-on switch is the ultimate defense, and parents wield it. Eron says that's unrealistic.

"Parents can't do it all by themselves, especially in these days

of single-parent families and two parents working," he says. "They can't be with their children all the time."

If the industry can't or won't regulate itself, should the government intervene? It's an obvious question to ask and a difficult one to answer, especially for believers in the First Amendment.

"The scientific evidence clearly shows that long-term exposure to TV violence makes kids behave more aggressively," says Huesmann, "but it doesn't show the same effect on adults. What you watch now won't have nearly the effect of what you saw when you were 8. What we're talking about is regulating what kids see, not adults, and there are reasonable precedents for this — alcohol and tobacco regulations, for example."

"What we're talking about is regulating what kids see, not adults, and there are reasonable precedents for this—alcohol and tobacco regulations, for example."

—L. Rowell Huesmann

In their view, watching TV violence is every bit as dangerous to kids as smoking and drinking. They see it as a matter of public health, not free speech. And they are grimly amused by the industry's protestations of exculpability. "How can they say their programs have no effect on behavior when they're in the business of selling ads?" Eron asks.

Then there are those who wonder how it is that Detroit and Windsor, Ontario, which face each other across the Detroit River and receive the same TV signals, have such disparate crime rates. "If we said TV violence is the only cause, then they'd have an argument," says Eron. "But we don't say that."

They are, in fact, well aware that any number of psychological, physiological and macro-social factors are simmering in the stew of violence. "TV is really a minor part of our research," says Eron, "although it's gotten the most play. We're interested in how children learn aggression. Violence on TV is only one cause, but it's a cause we can do something about."

Two projects they are currently involved in show signs of making progress toward that end. Huesmann is directing the second phase of a study begun in 1977 that looks, he says, at "whether the effects of media violence generalize across different countries and cultures."

Researchers are collecting longitudinal data on subjects in Poland, Australia, Finland and Israel, as well as the United States. Meanwhile, Eron, Huesmann and three researchers at the University of Illinois (where Huesmann spent 20 years before returning to U-M in 1992) are conducting an ambitious study of inner-city schools "in which we are trying to change the whole school atmosphere," says Eron.

In the former study, almost 2,000 children were interviewed and tested in either first or third grade and for two consecutive years thereafter. "In all countries, the children who watched more violence were the more aggressive," says Huesmann. "This was a study showing that this was a real effect across countries and not a special, one-time study of Columbia County."

The only exceptions were found in Australia and Israel. In Australia, there was a correlation between watching violence and behaving aggressively, but it was not as persistent as in other countries. In Israel, the correlation was stronger for city-raised children than for those growing up in kibbutzes. Huesmann suspects that the communal nature of the kibbutz, with its attendant reinforcement of pro-social behaviors, neutralized the effect of televised violence. And Australia? "We have no good explanation," he says.

"As a child, you see a Dirty Harry movie, where the heroic policeman is shooting people right and left. Even years later, the right kind of scene can trigger that script and suggest a way to behave that follows it."

—L. Rowell Huesmann

Perhaps the second phase, revisiting subjects who are now in their early 20s, will provide one. Interviewing is almost complete in the United States and Finland and began in Poland this winter as one of the collaborative projects between ISR and ISS [Institute for Social Studies], its Polish sibling. Work will begin in Israel near the end of 1994.

The project in Illinois attempts to measure the relative influence of multiple contexts, including schools, peers, families, and neighborhoods, and the cost-effectiveness of targeting each. "This is a public health model," says Eron, "from primary prevention to tertiary prevention."

Both teachers and students will be taught techniques for handling aggression and solving problems. Youngsters who are believed to be at high risk for becoming aggressive will also be seen in groups of six by research staffers. And half of those youngsters will receive family therapy as well, what Eron calls "an increased dosage" of treatment.

"We don't think just working with kids in the schools will help much," Eron says. "Studies show kids change attitudes, but there's no data to show they change behavior. In this program, we're trying to change the whole school atmosphere. We're also trying to see what the cost-effectiveness is. Is it enough to have a school program? Or do you always have to do family therapy, which is the most costly? Does it really add to the effectiveness of the treatment?"

The problem clearly isn't simple, but some of the data are nonetheless clear. "Over the years, Rowell and I have testified at many congressional hearings," says Eron, "and now it's having an effect. The public sentiment is there's too much of this stuff, and we've got the data to show it. I think we are having an impact, finally."

Eron himself estimates that TV is only responsible for perhaps 10% of the violent behavior in this country. "But," he says, "if we could reduce violence by 10%, that would be a great achievement."

The Impact of Homelessness on Children

Yvonne Rafferty
Marybeth Shinn
Advocates for Children, Long Island City, NY
New York University

This article reviews and critiques community-based research on the effects of homelessness on children. Homeless children confront serious threats to their ability to succeed and their future well-being. Of particular concern are health problems, hunger, poor nutrition, developmental delays, anxiety, depression, behavioral problems, and educational underachievement. Factors that may mediate the observed outcomes include inadequate shelter conditions, instability in residences and shelters, inadequate services, and barriers to accessing services that are available. Public policy initiatives are needed to meet the needs of homeless children.

Research on the impact of homelessness on children indicates that homeless children (generally identified as those in emergency shelter facilities with their families) confront serious threats to their well-being. Of particular concern are health problems, hunger and poor nutrition, developmental delays, psychological problems, and educational underachievement. This article examines the problems faced by homeless children in each of these areas. Where possible, we describe the extent to which homeless children are at a disadvantage, relative not only to the population at large but to other poor children. That is, we attempt to understand to what extent problems are associated with homelessness per se and to what extent they are linked with extreme poverty.

A second task of this article is to understand how homelessness leads to the outcomes we document and to identify which conditions in the lives of homeless children lead to particular adverse effects. As Molnar and Rubin (1991) pointed out, homelessness is a composite of many conditions and events, such as poverty, changes in residence, schools, and services, loss of possessions, disruptions in social networks, and exposure to extreme hardship. Effects of homelessness on children may be mediated by any of these ecological conditions and by their effects on parents and the family system. Research on homeless children, however, has not generally examined mediating mechanisms. We focus on mechanisms that can be influenced by social policy, namely, inadequate shelter conditions, instability of shelters and residences, lack of adequate services, and barriers to accessing available services. A final section describes linkages among outcomes and discusses implications for public policy.

Health Problems

Studies have consistently found that homeless children experience elevated levels of acute and chronic health problems. Risk for health problems begins before birth. Chavkin, Kristal, Seabron, and Guigli (1987) compared the reproductive experience of 401 homeless women in welfare hotels in New York City with that of 13,249 women in public housing and with all live births in New York City during the same time period. Significantly more of the homeless women (16%, compared with 11% of women in public housing and 7% of all women) had low birth-weight babies. Infant mortality was also extraordinarily high: 25 deaths per 1,000 live births among the homeless women, compared with 17 per 1,000 for housed poor women and 12 per 1,000 for women citywide.

Wright (1987, 1990, 1991) examined the medical records of 1,028 homeless children under 15 years of age who were treated in the Robert Wood Johnson Health Care for the Homeless programs in 16 cities. He compared the occurrence of various diseases and disorders among homeless children with rates reported in the National Ambulatory Medical Care Survey for U.S. ambulatory patients ages 15 and under. All of the disorders studied were more common among homeless children, often occurring at double the rate observed in the general pediatric caseload. The most common disorders among homeless children were upper respiratory infections (42% vs. 22% in the national sample), minor skin ailments (20% vs. 5% in the national sample), ear disorders (18% vs. 12% in the national sample), chronic physical disorders (15% vs. 9% in the national sample), and gastrointestinal disorders (15% vs. 4% in the national sample). Infestational ailments, although less common than other disorders among homeless children (7%), occurred at more than 35 times the rate of those in the national sample. The Health Care for the Homeless and National Ambulatory Medical Care Survey samples differ along several dimensions. Members of the homeless sample are more likely to be poor, members of minority groups, and urban dwellers. Also, both surveys assess prevalence among those who use health services rather than among the general population. Al-

Preparation of this article was supported in part by grants from the Edna McConnell Clark Foundation and the Robert Sterling Clark Foundation to Advocates for Children, and Grant RO1MH46116 from the National Institute of Mental Health to the second author.

The first author gratefully acknowledges numerous insightful discussions with Norma Rollins, which resulted in *Learning in Limbo: The Educational Deprivation of Homeless Children*, published in September of 1989. The authors thank Andrea Solarz for her helpful comments on an earlier draft of this article.

Correspondence concerning this article should be addressed to Yvonne Rafferty, Advocates for Children of New York, Inc., 24-16 Bridge Plaza South, Long Island City, NY 11101.

though one might expect homeless families to wait until problems become serious before seeking treatment (leading to higher prevalence rates for many disorders), differences in utilization patterns are unlikely to account for the high prevalences observed. As Wright (1987) concluded, "Among the many good reasons to do something about homelessness is . . . that homelessness makes people ill; in the extreme case, it is a fatal condition" (p. 80).

Alperstein and Arnstein (1988) and Alperstein, Rappaport, and Flanigan (1988) made several comparisons between the health of homeless children in New York City and that of poor housed children receiving health care there. Using clinic records, they found that 27% of 265 homeless children under the age of 5 who were living in a "welfare" hotel were late in getting necessary immunizations, compared with 8% of 100 poor children attending the same outpatient clinic. Twice as many homeless children (4%) as members of the population of 1,072 children whose blood was tested that year by the clinic (2%), had elevated lead levels in the blood. (The comparison group may have included some homeless children.) Rates of hospital admission among a larger sample of 2,500 homeless children under the age of 18 were almost twice as high as for 6,000 children of the same age living in the same area (11.6 vs. 7.5 per thousand, respectively).

Bernstein, Alperstein, and Fierman (1988) compared the clinic charts of 90 homeless children aged 6 months to 12 years with those of a matched cohort of housed children whose family incomes were below the federal poverty level. Nearly one half (48%) of the homeless children under age 2 were delayed in their immunizations, compared with 16% of the housed children. Fifty percent of the homeless children, compared with 25% of the housed group, had iron deficiencies, which may be related to other unmeasured nutritional deficiencies. Most of these studies are based on families who use health care services, so that differential patterns in the use of services could account for some of the differences in health status.

Other studies that are based on self-reported health status or that lack comparison groups paint a consistent picture. Homeless children's health problems include immunization delays, asthma, ear infections, overall poor health, diarrhea, and anemia (Dehavenon & Benker, 1989; Miller & Lin, 1988; New York City Department of Health, 1986; Paone & Kay, 1988; Rafferty & Rollins, 1989; Redlener, 1989; Roth & Fox, 1988; Wright, 1990, 1991; but not Wood, Valdez, Hayashi, & Shen, 1990a).

Both inadequate emergency shelter conditions and lack of adequate preventive and curative health services are prime mechanisms by which homelessness leads to poor health. A third factor, poor nutrition, is discussed in the next section.

The conditions in many private and public shelters place children at risk of lead poisoning and other environmental hazards. Congregate living environments in many shelters present optimal conditions for the transmission of infectious and communicable diseases such as upper respiratory infections, skin disorders, and diarrhea. These conditions include close proximity of beds, use of bathrooms by many people, inadequate facilities to change and bathe infants, unsanitary conditions, and noise and light that disrupt sleep (cf. Citizens Committee

for Children, 1988; Gross & Rosenberg, 1987; Jahiel, 1987). According to the New York City Department of Health (1986), "There appears to be no basis for concluding that congregate family shelters can be operated in compliance with basic principles of public health" (p. 5). Regulations in 50% of cities require families to leave shelters during daytime hours (U.S. Conference of Mayors, 1989). This policy means that children are exposed to the elements, and it makes daytime naps for preschoolers and adequate care of sick children impossible.

Another important mediator of health problems is the lack of adequate primary and preventive health care services. Research has demonstrated that poor children have less access to quality health care than do middle-class children (Newacheck & Starfield, 1988); children who are both poor and homeless are at an even greater disadvantage. Access to timely and consistent health care is compromised by extreme poverty, removal from community ties, frequent disruptions in family life, and lack of health insurance (Angel & Worobey, 1988; Rafferty & Rollins, 1989; Roth & Fox, 1988).

The scarcity of adequate health care for homeless children begins with the paucity of prenatal care available to their mothers. Chavkin et al. (1987) found that 40% of 401 homeless women received no prenatal care compared with 14.5% of public housing residents and 9% of all women in New York who gave birth during the same period. This may help to explain the higher risk of negative birth outcomes, previously described, for homeless women.

As noted earlier, most research focuses on homeless children in emergency shelters because they are easier to study and identify. Many health problems may predate shelter entry, including crowding in doubled-up situations, as well as exposure and lack of sanitary facilities in public places.

Hunger and Poor Nutrition

In their survey of 26 cities, the U.S. Conference of Mayors (1987) described a variety of negative effects of homelessness on physical and emotional well-being. The factors mentioned most frequently by city officials were lack of food and poor nutrition. The struggle to maintain an adequate and nutritionally balanced diet while living in a welfare hotel was described by Simpson, Kilduff, and Blewett (1984), who surveyed 40 heads of families (representing 194 people). Overall, 92% had no refrigerator in the hotel room, no family had a stove, 80% reported eating less food and food of lesser quality than they previously had, and 67% said they "felt hungrier" since moving to the hotel. Similarly, Wood et al. (1990a) compared the dietary intake and episodes of hunger among 192 homeless and 194 stably housed poor children in Los Angeles. Homeless children were significantly more likely to have gone hungry during the prior month (23% vs. 4%, respectively); more than one fifth (21% vs. 7%, respectively) did not have enough to eat because of lack of money.

Dehavenon and Benker (1989) found that nonpregnant adults in 202 families requesting shelter in New York City reported eating only once per day over the previous three days, on average; pregnant women ate twice per day. Although children were reported to have eaten three times per day, suggesting that adults gave up food for them, it appears unlikely that the children's food intake was adequate, given the bleak nutritional picture for their families. Among those in the shelter system for at least a week, nonpregnant women lost a median of eight pounds; of 98 pregnant women, 22% reported losing weight during their pregnancy and an additional 8% reported no weight gain. Nine of 26 families reported stretching infants' formula with water.

Anecdotal observations of homeless children in day care settings also suggest that they are hungry. Molnar (1988) reported that some homeless children threw tantrums until they were fed. Grant (1989) noted that most "ate enthusiastically, asking for second helpings" but "nearly all lacked previous experience in eating at a table and sharing food family-style" (p. 30). Many had not used utensils or cups.

Inadequate benefits and difficulties in accessing food and entitlements are the major mediators of hunger and poor nutrition. The vast majority of homeless families are headed by women who rely on Aid to Families with Dependent Children (AFDC) as their primary source of income (Bassuk & Rosenberg, 1988; Rafferty & Rollins, 1989). However, benefit levels have been described as "woefully inadequate" (National Coalition for the Homeless, 1988) and a main cause of hunger (U.S. Conference of Mayors, 1989).

The difficulties homeless families have in trying to manage on benefits that generally fall below 70% of the federal poverty line (Community Food Resource Center, 1989) are frequently compounded by failure to receive benefits to which they are entitled, erroneous case closings, and benefit reductions (National Coalition for the Homeless, 1988). The U.S. House of Representatives Select Committee on Hunger (1987) surveyed 2,112 individuals in emergency shelters in New York City in 1987 and found that 49% of those who were eligible for food stamps were not receiving them. In addition, more than 50% of all New York City residents who were eligible for the federally funded Special Supplemental Food Program for Women, Infants, and Children (WIC) in 1988 did not receive benefits (New York State Department of Health, 1988). Among New York City families with a pregnant mother or a newborn, only 44% of 385 families seeking shelter were receiving WIC benefits, compared with 60% of 83 families randomly sampled from the public assistance caseload (Knickman & Weitzman, 1989).

Homeless families are also more likely than housed families to have had their welfare (AFDC) cases closed and benefits reduced. In one study conducted in California, 43% of 196 homeless families reported losing or being removed from the welfare rolls during the past year, often contributing to their loss of housing. In contrast, 23% of 194 stably housed poor families had *ever* lost their AFDC benefits (Wood, Valdez, Hayashi, & Shen, 1990b). In addition, homeless families were less likely to be receiving food stamps or WIC (62% vs. 81%, respectively).

Families with limited resources are often left with no other alternative than emergency food assistance facilities. However, in almost 20 of 27 cities surveyed, emergency food programs reported that they turned away people in need because of lack of resources. Emergency food programs in 17 of the cities reported being unable to provide adequate quantities of food (U.S. Conference of Mayors, 1989).

Developmental Delays

Molnar (1988) documented observational and teachers' anecdotal accounts of distressing behaviors of homeless preschoolers aged 2½ to 5 years. The behaviors most frequently mentioned include short attention span, withdrawal, aggression, speech delays, sleep disorders, "regressive" toddlerlike behaviors, inappropriate social interaction with adults, immature peer interaction contrasted with strong sibling relationships, and immature motor behavior.

Whitman and her colleagues (Whitman, 1987; Whitman, Accardo, Boyert, & Kendagor, 1990) observed severe language disabilities and impaired cognitive ability among 88 children living in a dormitory style shelter for homeless families in St. Louis. Overall, 35% of these children scored at or below the borderline/slow-learner range on the Slosson Intelligence Test (Jensen & Armstrong, 1985), and 67% were delayed in their capacity to use and produce language as judged by the Peabody Picture Vocabulary Test (Dunn & Dunn, 1981).

Using the Denver Developmental Screening Test (DDST; Frankenburg, Goldstein, & Camp, 1971), Bassuk and her colleagues (Bassuk & Rosenberg, 1988; Bassuk & Rubin, 1987; Bassuk, Rubin, & Lauriat, 1986) assessed the development of 81 children (age 5 or younger) living in family shelters in Massachusetts. Overall, 36% of the children demonstrated language delays, 34% could not complete the personal and social developmental tasks, 18% lacked gross motor skills, and 15% lacked fine motor coordination. Almost one half (47%) manifested at least one developmental lag, 33% had two or more, and 14% failed in all four areas. A subgroup of the sample (those sheltered in the Boston area) was subsequently compared with poor housed children. When compared with 75 housed preschoolers, the 48 homeless preschoolers tested were significantly more likely to manifest at least one developmental lag (54% vs. 16%, respectively), to lack personal and social development (42% vs. 3%, respectively), to demonstrate language delays (42% vs. 13%, respectively), to lack gross motor skills (17% vs. 4%, respectively), and to lack fine motor skills (15% vs. 1%, respectively; Bassuk & Rosenberg, 1988, 1990).

In contrast, more recent studies of homeless children in Ohio, Los Angeles, Philadelphia, and New York City, have not found such severe developmental problems. Wagner and Menke (1990), also using the DDST to assess 162 homeless children age 5 or younger in Ohio, found that 23% demonstrated language delays, 12% could not complete the personal and social developmental tasks, and 17% lacked gross motor skills. However, twice as many children in this sample lacked fine motor coordination as in the Boston sample (30% vs. 15%, respectively). Although Wagner and Menke (1990) had no comparison group, overall, their homeless children were more similar to the homeless than to the housed children in Bassuk and Rosenberg's (1988) study. Of the Ohio children, 44% manifested at least one developmental lag and 24% had two or more.

Wood et al. (1990b) studied developmental lags (as assessed by the DDST) in a sample of preschoolers in

Los Angeles. Although overall performance was worse than in the general child population, only 15% manifested at least one delay and 9% had two or more. The most common delay was language (13%), then fine motor coordination (11%), gross motor coordination (6%), and personal–social development (5%).

Rescorla, Parker, and Stolley (1991) compared the cognitive ability of 40 homeless children between the ages of 3 and 5 with 20 housed children of the same age awaiting treatment at a pediatric clinic in Philadelphia. Significant delays were found for receptive vocabulary as assessed by the Peabody Picture Vocabulary Test (M score of 68 for homeless children vs. 78 for housed children) and visual motor development as assessed by the Beery (1989) Developmental Test of Visual Motor Integration (82 vs. 90, respectively). However, no differences were found for vocabulary (using the Stanford-Binet [Thorndike, Hagen, & Sattler, 1986]), visual motor development (using the Draw-a-Person clinical technique [Harris, 1963]), or developmental ability (using the Cubes Test [Yale Child Study Center, 1986]).

When they assessed speech, language, cognition, perception, and gross and fine motor coordination using the Early Screening Inventory (Meisels & Wiske, 1988), Molnar and Rath (1990) found no significant differences between 84 homeless and 76 poor housed children between the ages of 3 and 5. Children in both groups scored poorly. Note that the only significant difference to emerge in this New York City sample was between children who did and those who did not receive day care services.

Although many of the instruments used to assess development have not been standardized for poor and minority children, the strong differences between homeless and comparison samples in several studies suggests that the problems are significant. In fact, problems may be underestimated because the commonly used DDST is a conservative screening instrument and because families in some studies had been in shelters for only short periods of time.

The poor performance of both homeless and comparison samples suggests that poverty may be a key mediator of developmental problems. Other influential mediating factors include inadequate shelter conditions, lack of access to quality day care services, instability in child care arrangements, and effects of homelessness on parents.

Media accounts detail the brutal and shocking conditions in welfare hotels and in other shelters for homeless families (Kozol, 1988). Berezin (1988) described how restrictive physical environments in emergency shelters make physical exploration virtually impossible: "There is little opportunity for the kind of exploration and interactive play that we know lay the foundation for healthy physical, emotional, and cognitive growth" (p. 3).

Despite the abundance of literature documenting the importance of high quality day care services for social and intellectual stimulation (Consortium for Longitudinal Studies, 1983; Haskins, 1989; Phillips, McCartney, & Scarr, 1987; Scarr & Weinberg, 1986), there is a paucity of such programs for homeless children (Berezin, 1988; Molnar, 1988). In New York City, for example, the percentage of homeless children reported to be enrolled in early childhood programs ranges from 15% (Vanderbourg & Christofides, 1986) to 20% (Molnar, 1988). Similarly,

15% of 40 homeless preschoolers in Philadelphia were enrolled in early childhood programs, in contrast to 65% of the 20 housed children in the comparison group (Rescorla et al., 1991).

Instability in shelter placements and other disruptions in child care and schooling may also impede children's development. For example, stability in child care arrangements for domiciled children is related to competent play with peers and toys in day care settings and to academic competence in first grade (Howes, 1988; Howes & Stewart, 1987). Finally, Molnar and Rubin (1991) extrapolate from research on poverty to posit that effects of homelessness on children's development and psychological functioning (reviewed next) are mediated by parental distress and its effect on parenting behaviors.

Psychological Problems

Psychological problems identified most often among homeless children include depression, anxiety, and behavioral problems. Bassuk and her colleagues (Bassuk & Rubin, 1987; Bassuk et al., 1986) studied 156 children from 82 families sheltered in Massachusetts. On the Children's Depression Inventory (CDI; Kovacs, 1983), 54% of the 44 homeless children over the age of 5 scored above the cutoff score of 9, indicating a need for mental health evaluation; 31% were clinically depressed. In fact, the mean score of 10.4 was higher than the mean for six of eight clinical comparison groups studied during the development of the test. In a subsequent comparison of a subgroup of this sample, 16 of 31 children (52%) sheltered in Boston scored in the clinical range, compared with 16 of 33 (48%) housed poor children. Although mean scores for the children who were homeless were higher than were those for the housed group (10.3 vs. 8.3, respectively), the difference was not significant (Bassuk & Rosenberg, 1990). The 50 school-aged children's average score on the Children's Manifest Anxiety Scale (Reynolds & Richmond, 1985) was 14.4, and 30% scored in the clinical range (a T score of 60 or higher), indicating a need for mental health evaluation. In a subsequent comparison of a subgroup of this sample, 9 of 29 children (31%) sheltered in Boston scored in the clinical range compared with 3 out of 34 (9%) housed children ($p = .06$). No mean scores are presented (Bassuk & Rosenberg, 1990).

Two other studies also used the CDI to assess depression. Wagner and Menke (1990) found that 50% of 76 homeless children between the ages of 7 and 12 years manifested a need for mental health evaluation, and 35% were clinically depressed; boys scored slightly higher than did girls (11.3 vs. 10.3, respectively). Masten (1990) found that 159 homeless children and 62 poor housed children ages 8–17 years did not differ significantly from each other (9.45 vs. 8.13, respectively) or from normative levels either in mean scores or in the proportion of children in the clinical range.

Several studies have examined parents' reports of their children's behavior using the Achenbach Behavior Problem Checklist (CBCL; Achenbach & Edelbrock, 1981, 1983). Overall, mean differences between homeless and poor housed children are somewhat elusive, but more homeless children tend to score in the clinical range. Wood, Hayashi, Schlossman, and Valdez (1989) found no differences between 194 homeless and 193 stably housed poor children on the Behavior Problems Scale (adapted from the CBCL). Mean scores were quite similar, and only a minority of both groups displayed a significant number of behavior problems, primarily aggressive behaviors. Similarly, Masten (1990) found no difference in mean scores of 159 homeless children between the ages of 8 and 17 years and 62 housed children, although both groups had mean scores above normative levels. Also, the means for the externalizing subscale (reflecting acting-out behavior problems) were significantly higher for the homeless sample, and significantly more homeless children scored in the clinical range on both internalizing (reflecting emotional problems like anxiety and depression) and externalizing.

Rescorla et al. (1991) found marginally significant differences on the CBCL between 43 homeless and 25 housed children between the ages of 6 and 12 years. More homeless school-age children (30%) than housed children (16%) had scores above 65; however, differences between the proportions of extreme scores were significant only for externalization (35% vs. 12%, respectively). Finally, Bassuk and Rosenberg (1990) found that a greater proportion of 31 homeless children between the ages of 6 and 16 years exceeded the cutoff point than did a comparison group of 54 housed children (39% vs. 26%, respectively). However, this difference was not significant.

Only two studies have used the CBCL among preschool children. Rescorla et al. (1991) found that their sample of 40 preschoolers between the ages of 3 and 5 scored significantly higher than did the comparison group of 20 housed children of the same age, and 20% of the homeless children (vs. 5% of the housed children) had scores in the clinical range. Molnar and Rath (1990) found no mean differences on the CBCL between 84 homeless and 76 poor housed children between the ages of 3 and 5 years; neither group differed from a nonclinical, normative group. However, once again, significantly more homeless children than housed comparison peers scored above the clinical cutoff point (33% vs. 11%, respectively).

Other, primarily descriptive, studies of behavioral problems also yield inconsistent findings. Bassuk and Rosenberg (1988) found that 55 homeless preschool children scored significantly higher ($M = 5.6$) on the Simmons Behavior Checklist (Reinherz & Gracey, 1982) than did both a sample of 17 "normal" children ($M = 1.9$) and a sample of 17 "disturbed" children ($M = 2.3$). When compared with the housed normal children, the homeless children had poorer attention, more trouble sleeping, delayed speech, and were more likely to exhibit aggressive behaviors, shyness, and withdrawal. The only area in which homeless children scored significantly lower than both comparison groups was in being less afraid of new things. Note that a subsequent analysis compared a subgroup of this sample ($n = 21$) with 33 permanently housed poor children and found no significant differences on any of the aforementioned measures (Bassuk & Rosenberg, 1990).

A study of 83 families sheltered in New York City (Citizen's Committee for Children, 1988) revealed that 66% of parents had observed adverse behavioral changes in their children since becoming homeless. Among the most frequent changes were increased acting out, fighting, restlessness, depression, and moodiness. Molnar, Rath, and Klein (1991) cited parent reports of withdrawal, exaggerated fears, disobedience, and destructiveness.

In sum, several studies show that homeless children are more likely than are housed poor children or normative groups to have clinical levels of depression, anxiety, or behavior problems. Research findings, however, have not been entirely consistent. Possible explanations include small sample sizes and the lack of adequate comparison groups in some studies. In addition, several researchers suggest that other methodological issues need to be considered. For example, Cohen and Schwab-Stone (1990) noted the inadequacy of available instruments to assess the mental health of children generally, and additional limitations in making valid assessments of homeless children (e.g., lack of appropriate places to carry out interviews, families' greater involvement in problems connected to daily living than to the interview). The fact that families are often in an acutely stressful situation may temporarily inflate children's scores on measures of depression and anxiety. Molnar and Rubin (1991) also discussed how the chaotic life arrangements of homeless families are not conducive to lengthy interviews. They also address the limitations of assessment instruments in ethnic minority groups and suggest the use of multiple informants.

Finally, the fact that both homeless and poor housed children perform poorly, relative to normative samples, in more recent studies also implicates poverty, as well as specific conditions of homelessness, in the development of psychological problems. In fact, many of the risk factors previously discussed also prevail in extremely poor families. Homeless families, however, are even more likely to be deprived of some essential requirements for child rearing. These include adequate health care, nutrition, housing, employment, and status for parenthood (Bronfenbrenner, 1986).

In addition, the emergency shelter needs of families frequently go unmet. For example, 21 of 27 cities turn away homeless families because of a lack of resources (U.S. Conference of Mayors, 1989). Birmingham, Alabama, for example, turns away 25% of the families requesting emergency shelter each day (National Coalition for the Homeless, 1989a). In other cases in which shelter is available, fathers and older boys are separated from their families. Overall, 17 of the cities reported being unable to keep homeless families intact in emergency shelters.

For families who manage to obtain emergency shelter, other obstacles prevail. Unsafe, chaotic, unpredictable shelter placements are not conducive to normal psychological development. Rafferty and Rollins (1989) found that families in New York City shelters were routinely bounced from one facility to another, compounding stress for children already struggling to master their environments. According to Neiman (1988), the resiliency literature indicates that children are not particularly at risk from any single stressor, but when two stressors occur together, the risk quadruples. Thus, she argued, if even a portion of the multiple stressors that plague homeless families were substantially alleviated, the psychological risk for children would be greatly reduced.

Finally, homeless parents often encounter difficulties balancing their own physical, social, and personal needs and those of their children. The loss of control over their environment and their lives place them at increased risk for learned helplessness and depression. Drawing on Maslow's hierarchy of needs, Eddowes and Hranitz (1989) suggested that deprivation of basic needs and lack of security often lead to mistrust, apathy, and despair in homeless parents. Maternal depression, in turn, places children at increased risk for depressive disorders, behavior problems, anxiety, attention problems, insecure attachment, and social incompetence (cf. Dodge, 1990; Rutter, 1990).

Educational Underachievement

Little research has focused on the educational achievement of homeless children. What has been undertaken, however, indicates that homeless children score poorly on standardized reading and mathematics tests and are often required to repeat a grade.

Rafferty and Rollins (1989) examined the educational records of the entire population of 9,659 homeless school-age children identified by the New York City Board of Education between September 1987 and May 1988. Of the 3,805 homeless children in Grades 3 through 10 who took the Degrees of Reading Power test in the spring of 1988, 42% scored at or above grade level, compared with 68% citywide. Although these findings may reflect effects of poverty as well as homelessness, findings in the three school districts that served the greatest numbers of homeless children (45% of the total) were consistent. The percentages of homeless children scoring at or above grade level were 36%, 40%, and 41%, compared with 57%, 74%, and 68% for all children. Furthermore, of the 73 schools composing these three school districts, only 1 school had a lower proportion of students reading at or above grade level than did the overall proportion for homeless children attending schools in that district.

Results were similar for the Metropolitan Achievement Test in mathematics, which 4,203 homeless children in Grades 2 through 8 took in the spring of 1988. Homeless students were less than half as likely to score at or above grade level as were all students both citywide (28% vs. 57%, respectively) and in the three districts with the most homeless children (22%, 24%, and 23% vs. 48%, 70%, and 60%, respectively).

Several other studies have found that homeless children are more likely than are housed poor children to have repeated grades (Masten, 1990: 38% vs. 24%, respectively; Wood et al., 1989: 30% vs. 18%, respectively) or to be currently repeating a grade (Rafferty & Rollins, 1989: 15% vs. 7%, respectively). Other studies without comparison groups also found high rates of grade retention (Dumpson & Dinkins, 1987: 50%; Maza & Hall, 1988: 30%). In contrast, Rescorla et al. (1991) found similar retention rates among homeless and housed children (35% vs. 32%, respectively). The excessive rate of holdovers among homeless children will, no doubt, have long-term repercussions. Students who are overage for their grade are more likely than are others to drop out of school, get into trouble with the law, learn less the following year, and develop negative self-concepts (Hess, 1987).

Several factors appear to mediate the educational underachievement of homeless children. These include poor school attendance, lack of adequate educational services, inadequate shelter conditions, and shelter instability.

Government estimates of the number of homeless school-aged children who do not regularly attend school range from 15% (U.S. General Accounting Office, 1989) to 30% (U.S. Department of Education, 1989). In contrast, the National Coalition for the Homeless (1987a) estimated that 57% of homeless school-aged children do not regularly attend school. Two additional studies have evaluated the school attendance of homeless children. Homeless students in Los Angeles (Wood et al., 1989) missed more days in the prior three months than did poor housed children (8–9 vs. 5–6, respectively), and were more likely to have missed more than one week of school (42% vs. 22%, respectively). For housed children, the primary reason for absence was illness; for homeless children, it was family transience. In a New York City study of 6,142 homeless students (Rafferty & Rollins, 1989), homeless high school students had the poorest rate of attendance (51% vs. 84% citywide), followed by junior high school students (64% vs. 86% citywide) and children in elementary schools (74% vs. 89% citywide).

Many homeless children experience difficulty obtaining and maintaining access to a free public education. Major barriers include residency requirements, guardianship requirements, special education requirements, inability to obtain school records, transportation problems, lack of clothing and supplies, inadequate health care services, and lack of day care for teenage parents (Center for Law and Education, 1987; National Coalition for the Homeless, 1987a; Rafferty, 1991; U.S. Department of Education, 1990).

School is especially crucial for homeless children because it may instill a sense of stability that they otherwise lack (National Coalition for the Homeless, 1987a). Given the disruptions associated with homelessness and the excessive number of school transfers, homeless children may also need remedial educational services to address academic deficits, preschool enrichment services to prevent academic failure, psychological support services to respond to emotional problems, and greater sensitivity from school personnel who often stigmatize them (cf. Eddowes & Hranitz, 1989; Gewirtzman & Fodor, 1987; Horowitz, Springer, & Kose, 1988; National Association of State Coordinators for the Education of Homeless Children and Youth, 1990). Despite these needs, homeless children are likely to lose educational services with the onset of homelessness. Of 97 children who were receiving remedial assistance, bilingual services, or gifted and talented programs in New York City prior to their loss of permanent housing, only 54% continued to receive them while they were homeless (Rafferty & Rollins, 1989).

Environmental conditions within emergency shelters are hardly conducive to education. In addition, families entering the emergency shelter system are often placed in temporary facilities without consideration of the educational needs of the children or the impact of their being moved to unfamiliar and often distant communities. For example, 71% of 277 homeless families interviewed by Rafferty and Rollins (1989) were in temporary shelter facilities in a different borough than that of their last permanent home. Bouncing families from one facility to another compounded the disruptions in their lives and in their children's schooling. Overall, 66% of families had been in at least two shelters, 29% in at least four, and 10% in seven or more. The resulting school transitions significantly hindered children's continuity of education and disrupted their social relationships with classmates and friends.

Conclusion and Social Policy Implications

Homeless children confront abject poverty and experience a constellation of risks that have a devastating impact on their well-being. The research reviewed here links homelessness among children to hunger and poor nutrition, health problems and lack of health and mental health care, developmental delays, psychological problems, and academic underachievement. These consequences of homelessness often compound one another as well. When young children's nutritional needs are not met, growth is affected (Jahiel, 1987), physical health deteriorates (Acker, Fierman, & Dreyer, 1987), mental health is adversely affected (Winick, 1985), behavioral problems increase (Lazoff, 1989), the ability to concentrate is compromised (Jahiel, 1987), and academic performance suffers (Galler, 1984).

The paucity of prenatal care available to homeless women places unborn homeless children at risk of low birth weight (Buescher et al., 1988), subsequent health problems and chronic diseases (Hack, Caron, Rivers, & Fanaroff, 1983), cognitive and developmental problems (Resnick, Armstrong, & Carter, 1988), and academic problems (Russell & Williams, 1988). Delays in language development, motor skills, cognitive ability, and personal and social development place children at risk for academic failure (Molnar, 1988). Health problems are associated with psychological problems, classroom performance, and dropout rates (Needleman, Gunnoe, & Leviton, 1979; Needleman, Schell, Bellinger, Leviton, & Allred, 1990). Anxiety, depression, and behavioral problems engendered by destructive psychological environments interfere with one's capacity to learn (Jahiel, 1987). Thus, the risks we have identified may snowball to seriously compromise the future of homeless children.

Any list of solutions to homelessness must begin with decent, permanent, and affordable housing (National Alliance to End Homelessness, 1988; National Coalition for the Homeless, 1987b; Partnership for the Homeless, 1989; U.S. Conference of Mayors, 1988). National policy must focus both on rehousing those who are currently homeless and on preventing additional homelessness (National Coalition for the Homeless, 1989b). However, although affordable permanent housing is the fundamental issue of homelessness, it is not the sole need of homeless families with children. The research we have surveyed suggests that homeless families also have special needs in the areas of adequate shelter facilities, stability, and adequate services without barriers to access.

At the very least, homeless children and their families need access to safe, clean emergency shelters for transitional use while they are without homes. Shelters must provide privacy so that children are not exposed to communicable diseases, control over light and noise so that children can sleep and do homework, and enough space so that young children can explore their environments. Shelters must provide nutritious meals, or they must have refrigeration and cooking facilities so that families can prepare nutritious meals.

Emergency shelter placements must be designed to create stability, not chaos, in children's lives. Families and their children should not be required to leave shelters during the day or to move from shelter to shelter (or back to the street) because of administrative convenience or arbitrary limits on length of stay. Families must be accommodated as families and not be forced to separate in order to obtain shelter. To minimize disruptions in schools and services, shelters should be in the neighborhoods from which families came or in the neighborhoods in which they will be housed permanently.

In the realm of services, homeless families need adequate health care, including prenatal, mental health, pediatric, and preventive care, and they need continuity of care. Children need day care and early intervention programs (to prevent the onset of developmental delays), after-school programs, and the same or better standard of public education received by other children. Children should continue to receive the bilingual, special education, or gifted and talented services they obtained previously. They should have the option of continuing at the schools they attended before becoming homeless. By maintaining stability for children and offering new services to help them cope with the trauma of homelessness, schools can play an important role in tertiary prevention and in preventing residual damage from homelessness.

Our poorest families with children, inside or outside of shelter, also need adequate levels of benefits to meet basic needs—a public assistance grant at least at the federal poverty level, food stamps, the WIC program—and the assurance of receiving, without interruption, benefits to which they are entitled. More adequate and continuous benefits, along with an increase in the supply of affordable housing, would prevent many families from ever becoming homeless.

Recent studies have emphasized similarities, rather than differences, between homeless and poor housed children on measures of development and psychological problems. Both groups are at high risk. Even in health and education, where homeless children clearly fare worse than do their housed peers, the profile of both groups is grim. These findings indicate the need for a public policy agenda that addresses poverty among children, in addition to providing housing, stability, and services for those who are homeless.

In conclusion, an entire generation of children faces truly unacceptable risks that jeopardize their future potential. In the long run, the monetary costs of neglecting children's needs are likely to substantially exceed the costs of combating poverty and homelessness. The human costs will be much more tragic. Our cities and our nation must develop an appropriate and effective response.

REFERENCES

Achenbach, T. M., & Edelbrock, C. S. (1981). Behavioral problems and competencies reported by parents of normal and disturbed children aged four through sixteen. *Monograph of the Society for Research in Child Development, 46,* 1–82.

Achenbach, T. M., & Edelbrock, C. S. (1983). *Manual for the Child Behavior Checklist and Revised Child Behavior Profile.* Burlington, VT: University of Vermont, Department of Psychiatry.

Acker, P. J., Fierman, A. H., & Dreyer, B. P. (1987). An assessment of parameters of health care and nutrition in homeless children. *American Journal of Diseases of Children, 141,* 388.

Alperstein, G., & Arnstein, E. (1988). Homeless children—A challenge for pediatricians. *Pediatric Clinics of North America, 35,* 1413–1425.

Alperstein, G., Rappaport, C., & Flanigan, J. M. (1988). Health problems of homeless children in New York City. *American Journal of Public Health, 78,* 1232–1233.

Angel, R., & Worobey, J. (1988). Single motherhood and children's health. *Journal of Health and Social Behavior, 29,* 38–52.

Bassuk, E. L., & Rosenberg, L. (1988). Why does family homelessness occur? A case-control study. *American Journal of Public Health, 78,* 783–788.

Bassuk, E. L., & Rosenberg, L. (1990). Psychosocial characteristics of homeless children and children with homes. *Pediatrics, 85,* 257–261.

Bassuk, E. L., & Rubin, L. (1987). Homeless children: A neglected population. *American Journal of Orthopsychiatry, 57,* 279–286.

Bassuk, E. L., Rubin, L., & Lauriat, A. (1986). Characteristics of sheltered homeless families. *American Journal of Public Health, 76,* 1097–1101.

Beery, K. E. (1989). *The Developmental Test of Visual Motor Integration.* Cleveland, OH: Modern Curriculum Press.

Berezin, J. (1988). *Promises to keep: Child care for New York City's homeless children.* New York: Child Care.

Bernstein, A. B., Alperstein, G., & Fierman, A. H. (1988, November). *Health care of homeless children.* Paper presented at the meeting of the American Public Health Association, Chicago.

Bronfenbrenner, U. (1986). Ecology of the family as a context for human development: Research perspectives. *Developmental Psychology, 22,* 723–742.

Buescher, P. A., Meis, P. J., Ernest, J. M., Moore, M. L., Michielutte, R., & Sharp, P. (1988). A comparison of women in and out of a prematurity prevention project in a North Carolina perinatal care region. *American Journal of Public Health, 78,* 264–267.

Center for Law and Education (1987). Homelessness: A barrier to education for thousands of children. *Newsnotes, 38,* 1–3.

Chavkin, W., Kristal, A., Seabron, C., & Guigli, P. E. (1987). Reproductive experience of women living in hotels for the homeless in New York City. *New York State Journal of Medicine, 87,* 10–13.

Citizens Committee for Children (1988). *Children in storage: Families in New York City's barracks-style shelters.* New York: Author.

Cohen, P., & Schwab-Stone, M. (1990). Assessing mental health status among children who are homeless. In J. Morrissey & D. Dennis (Eds.), *Proceedings of a NIMH sponsored conference* (pp. 78–87). Rockville, MD: National Institute of Mental Health, Office of Programs for the Homeless Mentally Ill.

Community Food Resource Center (1989). *Who are New York City's hungry?* New York: Author.

Consortium for Longitudinal Studies. (1983). *As the twig is bent: Lasting effects of preschool programs.* Hillsdale, NJ: Erlbaum.

Dehavenon, A. L., & Benker, K. (1989). *The tyranny of indifference: A study of hunger, homelessness, poor health and family dismemberment in 818 New York City households with children in 1988–1989.* New York: East Harlem Interfaith Welfare Committee.

Dodge, K. (1990). Developmental psychopathology in children of depressed mothers. *Developmental Psychology, 26,* 3–6.

Dumpson, J. R., & Dinkins, D. N. (1987). *A shelter is not a home: Report of the Manhattan borough president's task force on housing for homeless families.* New York: Author.

Dunn, L., & Dunn, L. (1981). *Peabody Picture Vocabulary Test—Revised manual.* Circle Pines, MN: American Guidance Service.

Eddowes, A., & Hranitz, J. (1989). Childhood education: Infancy through early adolescence. *Journal of the Association for Childhood Education International, 65,* 197–200.

Frankenburg, W. K., Goldstein, A., & Camp, P. (1971). The revised Denver Development Screening Test: Its accuracy as a screening instrument. *Journal of Pediatrics, 79,* 988–995.

Galler, J. R. (Ed.). (1984). Human nutrition: A comprehensive treatise. *Nutrition and behavior.* New York: Plenum Press.

Gewirtzman, R., & Fodor, I. (1987). The homeless child at school: From welfare hotel to classroom. *Child Welfare, 66,* 237–245.

Grant, R. (1989). *Assessing the damage: The impact of shelter experience on homeless young children.* New York: Association to Benefit Children.

Gross, T., & Rosenberg, M. (1987). Shelters for battered women and their children: An under-recognized source of communicable disease transmission. *American Journal of Public Health, 77,* 1198–1201.

Hack, M., Caron, B., Rivers, A., & Fanaroff, A. (1983). The very low birth weight infant: The broader spectrum of morbidity during infancy and early childhood. *Developmental and Behavioral Pediatrics, 4,* 243–249.

Harris, D. B. (1963). *Children's drawings as measures of intellectual maturity.* New York: Harcourt, Brace & World.

Haskins, R. (1989). Beyond metaphor: The efficacy of early childhood education. *American Psychologist, 44,* 274–282.

Hess, G. A. (1987). *Schools for early failure: The elementary years and dropout rates in Chicago.* Chicago: Chicago Panel on Public School Finances.

Horowitz, S., Springer, C., & Kose, G. (1988). Stress in hotel children: The effects of homelessness on attitudes toward school. *Children's Environments Quarterly, 5,* 34–36.

Howes, C. (1988). Relations between early child care and schooling. *Developmental Psychology, 24,* 53–57.

Howes, C., & Stewart, P. (1987). Child's play with adults, peers, and toys. *Developmental Psychology, 23,* 423–430.

Jahiel, R. I. (1987). The situation of homelessness. In R. D. Bingham, R. E. Green, & S. E. White (Eds.), *The homeless in contemporary society* (pp. 99–118). Newbury Park, CA: Sage.

Jensen, J. A., & Armstrong, R. J. (1985). *Slosson Intelligence Test (SIT) for Children and Adults: Expanded norms, tables, application, and development.* East Aurora, NY: Slosson Educational Publications.

Knickman, J. R., & Weitzman, B. C. (1989). *Forecasting models to target families at high risk of homelessness* (Final report; Vol. 3). New York: New York University Health Research Program.

Kovacs, M. (1983). *The Children's Depression Inventory: A self-rated depression scale for school age youngsters.* Pittsburgh, PA: University of Pittsburgh, School of Medicine.

Kozol, J. (1988). *Rachel and her children: Homeless families in America.* New York: Crown.

Lazoff, B. (1989). Nutrition and behavior. *American Psychologist, 44,* 231–236.

Masten, A. S. (1990, August). *Homeless children: Risk, trauma and adjustment.* Paper presented at the 98th Annual Convention of the American Psychological Association, Boston.

Maza, P. L., & Hall, J. A. (1988). *Homeless children and their families: A preliminary study.* Washington, DC: Child Welfare League of America.

Meisels, S. J., & Wiske, M. S. (1988). *Early Screening Inventory: Test and manual (2nd ed.).* New York: Teachers College Press.

Miller, D. S., & Lin, E. H. B. (1988). Children in sheltered homeless families: Reported health status and use of health services. *Pediatrics, 81,* 668–673.

Molnar, J. (1988). *Home is where the heart is: The crisis of homeless children and families in New York City.* New York: Bank Street College of Education.

Molnar, J., & Rath, W. (1990, August). *Beginning at the beginning: Public policy and homeless children.* Paper presented at the 98th Annual Convention of the American Psychological Association, Boston.

Molnar, J., Rath, W., & Klein, T. (1991). Constantly compromised: The impact of homelessness on children. *Journal of Social Issues, 46,* 109–124.

Molnar, J., & Rubin, D. H. (1991, March). *The impact of homelessness on children: Review of prior studies and implications for future research.* Paper presented at the NIMH/NIAAA research conference organized by the Better Homes Foundation, Cambridge, MA.

National Alliance to End Homelessness. (1988). *Housing and homelessness.* Washington, DC: Author

National Association of State Coordinators for the Education of Homeless Children and Youth. (1990). *Position document on the re-authorization of Subtitle VII-B of the Stewart B. McKinney Homeless Assistance Act.* Austin, TX: State Department of Education.

National Coalition for the Homeless. (1987a). *Broken lives: Denial of education to homeless children.* Washington, DC: Author.

National Coalition for the Homeless. (1987b). *Homelessness in the United States: Background and federal response. A briefing paper for presidential candidates.* Washington, DC: Author.

National Coalition for the Homeless. (1988). *Over the edge: Homeless families and the welfare system.* Washington, DC: Author.

National Coalition for the Homeless. (1989a). *American nightmare: A decade of homelessness in the United States.* Washington, DC: Author.

National Coalition for the Homeless. (1989b). *Unfinished business: The Stewart B. McKinney Homeless Assistance Act after two years.* Washington, DC: Author.

Needleman, H. L., Gunnoe, C., & Leviton, A. (1979). Deficits in psychological and classroom performance of children with elevated dentine lead levels. *The New England Journal of Medicine, 300,* 689–695.

Needleman, H. L., Schell, A., Bellinger, D., Leviton, A., & Allred, E. N. (1990). The long-term effects of exposure to low doses of lead in childhood: An 11-year follow-up report. *The New England Journal of Medicine, 322,* 83–88.

Neiman, L. (1988). A critical review of resiliency literature and its relevance to homeless children. *Children's Environments Quarterly, 5*(1), 17–25.

Newacheck, P. W., & Starfield, B. (1988). Morbidity and use of ambulatory care services among poor and non-poor children. *American Journal of Public Health, 78,* 927–933.

New York City Department of Health. (1986). *Diarrhea in the family congregate shelters of New York City* (Draft No. 5). Unpublished manuscript, New York City Department of Health.

New York State Department of Health. (1988). *WIC state plan.* New York: Author.

Paone, D., & Kay, K. (1988, November). *Immunization status of homeless preschoolers.* Paper presented at the meeting of the American Public Health Association, Boston.

Partnership for the Homeless. (1989). *Moving forward: A national agenda to address homelessness in 1990 and beyond.* New York: Author.

Phillips, D. A., McCartney, K., & Scarr, S. (1987). Child care quality and children's social development. *Developmental Psychology, 23,* 537–543.

Rafferty, Y. (1991). *Homeless children in New York City: Barriers to academic achievement and innovative strategies for the delivery of educational services.* Long Island City, NY: Advocates for Children.

Rafferty, Y., & Rollins, N. (1989). *Learning in limbo: The educational deprivation of homeless children.* New York: Advocates for Children. (ERIC Document Reproduction No. ED 312 363)

Redlener, I. (1989, October 4). *Unacceptable losses: The consequences of failing America's homeless children* (Testimony presented before the U.S. Senate Committee on Labor and Human Resources Subcommittee on Children, Family, Drugs and Alcoholism). Washington, DC: U.S. Government Printing Office.

Reinherz, H., & Gracey, C. A. (1982). *The Simmons Behavior Checklist: Technical information.* Boston: Simmons School of Social Work.

Rescorla, L., Parker, R., & Stolley, P. (1991). Ability, achievement, and adjustment in homeless children. *American Journal of Orthopsychiatry, 61,* 210–220.

Resnick, M. B., Armstrong, S., & Carter, R. (1988). Developmental intervention program for high-risk premature infants: Effects on development and parent–infant interactions. *Developmental and Behavioral Pediatrics, 9*(2), 73–78.

Reynolds, C. R., & Richmond, B. O. (1985). *Revised Children's Manifest Anxiety Scale manual.* Los Angeles: Western Psychological Services.

Roth, L., & Fox, E. R. (1988, November). *Children of homeless families: Health status and access to health care.* Paper presented at the meeting of the American Public Health Association, Boston.

Russell, S., & Williams, E. (1988). Homeless handicapped children: A special education perspective. *Children's Environments Quarterly, 5*(1), 3–7.

Rutter, M. (1990). Commentary: Some focus and process considerations regarding effects of parental depression on children. *Developmental Psychology, 26,* 60–67.

Scarr, S., & Weinberg, R. (1986). The early childhood enterprise: Care and education for the young. *American Psychologist, 41,* 1140–1146.

Simpson, J., Kilduff, M., & Blewett, C. D. (1984). *Struggling to survive in a welfare hotel.* New York: Community Service Society.

Thorndike, R. L., Hagen E. P., & Sattler, J. M. (1986). *Stanford Binet Intelligence Scale* (4th ed). Chicago: Riverside Publishing.

U.S. Conference of Mayors. (1987). *The continuing growth of hunger, homelessness and poverty in America's cities: 1987, A 26-city survey.* Washington, DC: Author.

U.S. Conference of Mayors. (1988). *A status report on the Stewart B. McKinney Homeless Assistance Act of 1987.* Washington, DC: Author.

U.S. Conference of Mayors. (1989). *A status report on hunger and homelessness in America's cities—A 27-city survey.* Washington, DC: Author.

U.S. Department of Education. (1989, February 15). *Report to Congress on state interim reports on the education of homeless children.* Washington, DC: Author.

U.S. Department of Education. (1990, March 29). *Report to Congress on state interim reports on the education of homeless children.* Washington, DC: Author.

U.S. General Accounting Office. (1989). *Children and youths: Report to congressional committees.* Washington, DC: Author.

U.S. House of Representatives Select Committee on Hunger. (1987). *Hunger among the homeless: A survey of 140 shelters, food stamp participants and homelessness.* Washington, DC: U.S. Government Printing Office.

Vanderbourg, K., & Christofides, A. (1986, June). *Children in need: The child care needs of homeless families in temporary shelter in New York City* (Report prepared for Ruth W. Messinger, New York City Council member, 4th District). (Available from Office of the President of the Borough of Manhattan, Municipal Building, New York, NY 10007).

Wagner, J., & Menke, E. (1990). *The mental health of homeless children.* Paper presented at the meeting of the American Public Health Association, New York City.

Whitman, B. (1987, February 24). *The crisis in homelessness: Effects on children and families* (Testimony presented before the U.S. House of Representatives Select Committee on Children, Youth, and Families). Washington, DC: U.S. Government Printing Office.

Whitman, B., Accardo, P., Boyert, M., & Kendagor, R. (1990). Homelessness and cognitive performance in children: A possible link. *Social Work, 35,* 516–519.

Winick, M. (1985). Nutritional and vitamin deficiency states. In P. Brickner, L. Scharer, B. Conanan, A. Elvy, & M. Savarese (Eds.), *Health care of homeless people* (pp. 103–108). New York: Springer.

Wood, D., Hayashi, T., Schlossman, S., & Valdez, R. B. (1989). *Over the brink: Homeless families in Los Angeles.* Sacramento, CA: State Assembly Office of Research, Box 942849.

Wood, D., Valdez, R. B., Hayashi, T., & Shen, A. (1990a). The health of homeless children: A comparison study. *Pediatrics, 86,* 858–866.

Wood, D., Valdez, R. B., Hayashi, T., & Shen, A. (1990b). Homeless and housed families in Los Angeles: A study comparing demographic, economic and family function characteristics. *American Journal of Public Health, 80,* 1049–1052.

Wright, J. (1987, February 24). *The crisis in homelessness: Effects on children and families* (Testimony presented before the U.S. House of Representatives Select Committee on Children, Youth, and Families, pp. 73–85). Washington, DC: U.S. Government Printing Office.

Wright, J. (1990). Homelessness is not healthy for children and other living things. *Child and Youth Services.* 14(1), 65–88.

Wright, J. (1991). Poverty, homelessness, health, nutrition, and children. In J. H. Kryder-Coe, L. M. Salamon, & J. M. Molnar (Eds.), *Homeless children and youth: A new American dilemma* (pp. 71–104). New Brunswick, NJ: Transaction.

Yale Child Study Center. (1986). *Cubes test.* Unpublished manuscript. New Haven, CT: Author.

Development during Adolescence and Early Adulthood

- Adolescence (Articles 38–41)
- Early Adulthood (Articles 42–45)

Adolescence, from the Latin word meaning to grow up, is a fairly prolonged period of time in American culture. For most of recorded history, the stage was not acknowledged. Children underwent puberty and then were considered to be mature—or in the adult stage of life. G. Stanley Hall coined the term adolescence at the turn of the twentieth century to describe the period of time from the onset of puberty until the culturally realistic accomplishment of maturity, or adulthood. This is usually marked by independence from the family of origin and creation of a family of procreation. Hall saw adolescence as roughly equivalent to the teenage years. Today the period of adolescence usually extends well into the twenties as youths find reasons to postpone marriage, permanent jobs, and parenting.

Early adulthood is also becoming a prolonged period of time in American culture. The boundary between adolescence and early adulthood is vague. Although adolescence ends with complete independence from one's family of origin, young adulthood is claimed by many youths who are still financially and socially dependent on their families. Some independence, such as living at school or holding a part-time job, is usually reason enough for claiming early adult status.

The end of early adulthood and the advent of middle adulthood is also vague. Some writers prefer to attach chronological age to middle adulthood so that middle age equals 40, 45, or 50 years. Most adults view themselves as still in early adulthood when they are navigating the complicated course of child rearing. Middle age arrives when they begin launching their offspring and have more time for themselves. This may be at 30 years of age for some, and not until 50 plus years of age for others.

The biological changes of puberty that bring about adolescent status are legion. Sexual maturation is primary and noted by menarche and sperm in semen, but rapid secondary sexual changes in physical growth and development are what outsiders notice.

During puberty, every organ system matures in structure and function. The skeleton, skin, muscles, brain and spinal cord, heart and blood vessels, endocrine glands and hormones, lymph nodes and lymphatic system, lungs and respiratory structures, digestive structures, urinary system, and sensory organs all join the reproductive system in rapid growth. Each of these systems reaches final adult maturity by the early 20s. After that, age and health related changes cause a very slow reduction in the functioning of each system. Young adults who exercise, follow nutritional guidelines, practice health and safety precautions, and manage their stresses can maintain the vigor and vitality of all their organ systems longer.

Sexual maturation and increased sexual libido have profound effects on the cognitive and personal-social aspects of adolescence and early adulthood. The sex urge is powerful. The social pressures to postpone marriage and child bearing, and to practice celibacy or responsible sexuality are also powerful. Youths today have many more socially accepted sexual options than did their parents, or grandparents: virtual reality, single parenthood, no children, same-sex families, nontraditional families, and singlehood. The terms spinster, old maid, old bachelor, and celibate have fallen into disuse. Youths today also have many more troublesome sexual concerns: rape, date rape, sexually transmitted diseases, and AIDS.

Jean Piaget described the cognitive stage of adolescence and adulthood as formal operations. As the central nervous system reaches full maturity, the brain can deal with abstractions, unlimited possibilities, and all combinations of logic. Not every adult reaches full formal operations, and not every adult has the same capabilities for logic. Some researchers have suggested cognitive developmental stages beyond those that Piaget described: post-formal operations, practical operations, and dialectic operations. K. Warner Schaie proposed that different experiences trigger different cognitions. Childhood and adolescence equate with cognitive acquisition; late adolescence and early adulthood equate with cognitive achieving; early and middle adulthood equate with responsibility or perhaps executive functioning; and late adulthood equates with reintegrative cognitions.

Lawrence Kohlberg proposed that mature cognitive functioning can lead to high levels of moral and ethical reasoning. However, personal and social factors may outweigh cognitions. Not all adolescents and young adults subscribe to the moral codes of their society or agree that their society is moral.

Physical and cognitive maturity can lead to high levels

of personal and social maturity and integrity. However, not all adolescents and young adults achieve healthy psychosocial development.

Erik Erikson proposed that the nuclear conflict of adolescence is achieving a sense of identity vs. role confusion. The nuclear conflict of young adulthood is achieving a sense of intimacy vs. isolation. Youths who have opportunities to pursue a choice of activities in keeping with their aptitudes and endowments, and who succeed in activities with social reinforcement, usually have a strong sense of self-identity. Youths who experience cooperative and intimate sharings and interactions with others, who see that mutuality of efforts is beneficial, and who succeed in making sacrifices and compromises to maintain relationships have a better sense of intimacy. Unfortunately, many adolescents and young adults feel both confused about their identity and life roles, and isolated from others.

The isolation of adolescents and young adults often leads to abuse of alcohol and drugs, thoughts of suicide, and irresponsible sexual and violent behaviors. Many youths spend considerable amounts of time plugged into Walkmans, or watching television, videos, and movies with themes of sex and violence. Many youths fear forming their own families of procreation after having witnessed dysfunction in their families of origin. Self-esteem is hard to achieve when surrounded by such adversities.

The articles selected to portray contemporary adolescence reiterate the cultural pressures that make healthy maturation difficult: increased stress, problems with self-esteem, the threat of AIDS, unwanted sex and violence. The articles selected to portray early adulthood focus on new social trends, young marriage, raising children, and increased intrafamilial violence.

Looking Ahead: Challenge Questions

What do you think will happen to today's adolescents who feel unloved and unwanted?

Why do you think female adolescents have lower self-esteem than males?

How can the transmission of AIDS among teenagers be halted?

What is the effect of acquaintance rape on the teenage psyche?

What will sexuality and family life be like in the future?

Is there love after a couple has children? How can a relationship change?

What is the effect of adoption on biological parents, the adopted child, and adoptive parents?

Why are crimes of passion increasing within the home?

A Much
RISKIER
PASSAGE

DAVID GELMAN

There was a time when teenagers believed themselves to be part of a conquering army. Through much of the 1960s and 1970s, the legions of adolescence appeared to command the center of American culture like a victorious occupying force, imposing their singular tastes in clothing, music and recreational drugs on a good many of the rest of us. It was a hegemony buttressed by advertisers, fashion setters, record producers suddenly zeroing in on the teen multitudes as if they controlled the best part of the country's wealth, which in some sense they did. But even more than market power, what made the young insurgents invincible was the conviction that they were right: from the crusade of the children, grown-ups believed, they must learn to trust their feelings, to shun materialism, to make love, not money.

In 1990 the emblems of rebellion that once set teenagers apart have grown frayed. Their music now seems more derivative than subversive. The provocative teenage styles of dress that adults assiduously copied no longer automatically inspire emulation. And underneath the plumage, teens seem to be more interested in getting ahead in the world than in clearing up its injustices. According to a 1989 survey of high-school seniors in 40 Wisconsin communities, global concerns, including hunger, poverty and pollution, emerged last on a list of teenage worries. First were personal goals: getting good grades and good jobs. Anything but radical, the majority of teens say they're happy and eager to get on with their lives.

One reason today's teens aren't shaking the earth is that they can no longer marshal the demographic might they once could. Although their sheer numbers are still growing, they are not the illimitably expanding force that teens appeared to be 20 years ago. In 1990 they constitute a smaller percentage of the total population (7 percent, compared with nearly 10 percent in 1970). For another thing, almost as suddenly as they became a highly visible, if unlikely, power in the world, teenagers have reverted to anonymity and the old search for identity. Author Todd Gitlin, a chronicler of the '60s, believes they have become "Balkanized," united less by a common culture than by the commodities they own. He says "it's impossible to point to an overarching teen sensibility."

But as a generation, today's teenagers face more adult-strength stresses than their predecessors did—at a time when adults are much less available to help them. With the divorce rate hovering near 50 percent, and 40 to 50 percent of teenagers living in single-parent homes headed mainly by working mothers, teens are more on their own than ever. "My parents let me do anything I want as long as I don't get into trouble," writes a 15-year-old high-schooler from Ohio in an essay submitted for this special issue of NEWSWEEK. Sociologists have begun to realize, in fact, that teens are more dependent on grown-ups than was once believed. Studies indicate that they are shaped more by their parents than by their peers, that they adopt their parents' values and opinions to a greater extent than anyone realized. Adolescent specialists now see real hazards in lumping all teens together; 13-year-olds, for instance, need much more parental guidance than 19-year-olds.

These realizations are emerging just when the world has become a more dangerous place for the young. They have more access than ever to fast cars, fast drugs, easy sex—"a bewildering array of options, many with devastating outcomes," observes Beatrix Hamburg, director of Child and Adolescent Psychiatry at New York's Mount Sinai School of Medicine. Studies indicate that while overall drug abuse is down, the use of lethal drugs like crack is up in low-income neighborhoods, and a dangerous new kick called ice is making inroads in white high schools. Drinking and smoking rates remain ominously high. "The use of alcohol appears to be normative," says Stephen Small, a developmental psychologist at the University of Wisconsin. "By the upper grades, everybody's doing it."

Sexual activity is also on the rise. A poll conducted by Small suggests that most teens are regularly having sexual intercourse by the 11th grade. Parents are generally surprised by the data, Small says. "A lot of parents are saying, 'Not my kids . . .' They just don't think it's happening." Yet clearly it is: around half a million teenage girls give birth every year, and sexually transmitted diseases continue to be a major problem. Perhaps the only comforting note is that teens who are given AIDS education in schools and clinics are more apt to use condoms—a practice that could scarcely be mentioned a few years ago, let alone surveyed.

One reliable assessment of how stressful life has become for young people in this country is the Index of Social Health for Children and Youth. Authored by social-policy analyst Marc Miringoff, of Fordham University at Tarrytown, N.Y., it charts such factors as poverty, drug-abuse and high-school dropout rates. In 1987, the latest year for which statistics are available, the index fell to its lowest point in two decades. Most devastating, according to Miringoff, were the numbers of teenagers living at poverty levels—about 55 percent for single-parent households—and taking their own lives. The record rate of nearly 18 suicides per 100,000 in 1987—a total of 1,901—was double that of 1970. "If you take teens in the '50s—the 'Ozzie and Harriet' generation—those kids lived on a less complex planet," says Miringoff. "They could be kids longer."

The social index is only one of the yardsticks used on kids these days. In fact, this generation of young people is surely one of the most closely watched ever. Social scientists are tracking nearly everything they do or think about, from dating habits (they prefer going out in groups) to extracurricular activities (cheerleading has made a comeback) to general outlook (45 percent think the world is getting worse and 62 percent believe life will be harder for them than it was for their parents). One diligent prober, Reed Larson of the University of Illinois, even equipped his 500 teen subjects with beepers so he could remind them to fill out questionnaires about how they are feeling, what they are doing and who they are with at random moments during the day. Larson, a professor of human development, and psychologist Maryse Richards of Loyola University, have followed this group since grade school. Although the results of the high-school study have not been tabulated yet, the assumption is that young people are experiencing more stress by the time they reach adolescence but develop strategies to cope with it.

Without doubt, any overview of teenage problems is skewed by the experience of the inner cities, where most indicators tilt sharply toward the negative. Especially among the minority poor, teen pregnancies continue to rise, while the institution of marriage has virtually disappeared. According to the National Center for Vital Statistics, 90 percent of black teenage mothers are unmarried at the time of their child's birth, although about a third eventually marry. Teenage mothers, in turn, add to the annual school-dropout rate, which in some cities reaches as high as 60 percent. Nationwide, the unemployment rate for black teenagers is 40 to 50 percent; in some cities, it has risen to 70 percent. Crack has become a medium of commerce and violence. "The impact of crack is worse in the inner city than anywhere else," says psychiatrist Robert King, of the Yale Child Study Center. "If you look at the homicide rate among young, black males, it's frighteningly high. We also see large numbers of young mothers taking crack."

Those are realities unknown to the majority of white middle-class teenagers. Most of them are managing to get through the adolescent years with relatively few major problems. Parents may describe them as sullen and self-absorbed. They can also be secretive and rude. They hang "Do Not Disturb" signs on their doors, make phone calls from closets and behave churlishly at the dinner table if they can bring themselves to sit there at all. An earlier beeper study by Illinois's Larson found that in the period between ages 10 and 15, the amount of time young people spend with their families decreases by half. "This is when the bedroom door becomes a significant marker," he says.

Yet their rebelliousness is usually overstated. "Arguments are generally about whether to take out the garbage or whether to wear a certain hairstyle," says Bradford Brown, an associate professor of human development at the University of Wisconsin. "These are not earth-shattering issues, though they are quite irritating to parents." One researcher on a mission to destigmatize teenagers is Northwestern University professor Ken Howard, author of a book, "The Teenage World," who has just completed a study in Chicago's Cook County on where kids go for help. The perception, says Howard, is that teenagers are far worse off than they really are. He believes their emotional disturbances are no different from those of adults, and that it is only 20 percent who have most of the serious problems, in any case.

The findings of broad-based studies of teenagers often obscure the differences in their experience. They are, after all, the product of varied ethical and cultural influences. Observing adolescents in 10 communities over the past 10 years, a team of researchers headed by Frances Ianni, of Columbia University's Teachers College, encountered "considerable diversity." A key finding, reported Ianni in a 1989 article in Phi Delta Kappan magazine, was that the people in all the localities reflected the ethnic and social-class lifestyles of their parents much more than that of a universal teen culture. The researchers found "far more congruence than conflict" between the views of parents and their teenage children. "We much more frequently hear teenagers preface comments to their peers with 'my mom says' than with any attributions to heroes of the youth culture," wrote Ianni.

For years, psychologists also tended to overlook the differences between younger and older adolescents, instead grouping them together as if they all had the same needs and desires. Until a decade ago, ideas of teen behavior were heavily influenced by the work of psychologist Erik Erikson, whose own model was based on older adolescents. Erikson, for example, emphasized their need for autonomy—appropriate, perhaps, for an 18-year-old preparing to leave home for college or a job, but hardly for a 13-year-old just beginning to experience the confusions of puberty. The Erikson model nevertheless was taken as an across-the-board prescription to give teenagers independence, something that families, torn by the domestic upheavals of the '60s and '70s, granted them almost by forfeit.

In those turbulent years, adolescents turned readily enough to their peers. "When there's turmoil and social change, teenagers have a tendency to break loose and follow each other more," says Dr. John Schowalter, president of the American Academy of Child and Adolescent Psychiatry. "The leadership of adults is somewhat splintered and they're more on their own—sort of like 'Lord of the Flies'."

That period helped plant the belief that adolescents were natural rebels, who sought above all to break free of adult influence. The idea persists to this day. Says Ruby Takanishi, director of the Carnegie Council on Adolescent Development: "The society is still permeated by the notion that adolescents are different, that their hormones are raging around and they don't want to have anything to do with their parents or other adults." Yet research by Ianni and others suggests the contrary. Ianni points also to studies of so-called invulnerable adolescents—those who develop into stable young adults in spite of coming from troubled homes, or other adversity. "A lot of people have attributed this to some inner resilience," he says. "But what we've seen in practically all cases is some caring adult figure who was a constant in that kid's life."

Not that teenagers were always so dependent on adults. Until the mid-19th century, children labored in the fields alongside their parents. But by the time they were 15, they might marry and go out into the world. Industrialization and compulsory education ultimately deprived them of a role in the family work unit, leaving them in a state of suspension between childhood and adulthood.

To teenagers, it has always seemed a useless period of waiting. Approaching physical and sexual maturity, they feel capable of doing many of the things adults do. But they are not treated like adults. Instead they must endure a prolonged childhood that is stretched out even more nowadays by the need to attend college—and then possibly graduate school—in order to make one's way in the world. In the family table of organization, they are mainly in charge of menial chores. Millions of teenagers now have part-time or full-time jobs, but those tend to be in the service industries, where the pay and the work are often equally unrewarding.

If teenagers are to stop feeling irrelevant, they need to feel needed, both by the family and by the larger world. In the '60s they gained some sense of empowerment from their visibility, their music, their sheer collective noise. They also joined and swelled the ranks of Vietnam War protesters, giving them a feeling of importance that evidently they have not had since. In the foreword to "Student Service," a book based on a 1985 Carnegie Foundation survey of teenagers' attitudes toward work and community service, foundation director Ernest Boyer wrote: "Time and time again, students complained that they felt isolated, unconnected to the larger world . . . And this detachment occurs at the very time students are deciding who they are and where they fit." Fordham's Miringoff goes so far as to link the rising suicide rate among teens to their feelings of disconnection. He recalls going to the 1963 March on Washington as a teenager, and gaining "a sense of being part of something larger. That idealism, that energy, was a very stabilizing thing."

Surely there is still room for idealism in the '90s, even if the causes are considered less glamorous. But despite growing instances of teenagers involving themselves in good works, such as recycling campaigns, tutorial programs or serving meals at shelters for the homeless, no study has yet detected anything like a national groundswell of volunteerism. Instead, according to University of Michigan social psychologist Lloyd Johnston, teens seem to be taking their cues from a culture that, up until quite recently at least, has glorified self-interest and opportunism. "It's fair to say that young people are more career oriented than before, more concerned about making money and prestige," says Johnston. "These changes are consistent with the Me Generation and looking for the good life they see on television."

Some researchers say that, indeed, the only thing uniting teenagers these days are the things they buy and plug into. Rich or poor, all have their Walkmans, their own VCRs and TVs. Yet in some ways, those marvels of communication isolate them even more. Teenagers, says Beatrix Hamburg, are spending "a lot of time alone in their rooms."

Other forces may be working to isolate them as well. According to Dr. Elena O. Nightingale, author of a Carnegie Council paper on teen rolelessness, a pattern of "age segregation" is shrinking the amount of time adolescents spend with grown-ups. In place of family outings and vacations, for example, entertainment is now more geared toward specific age groups. (The teen-terrorizing "Freddy" flicks and their ilk would be one example.) Even in the sorts of jobs typically available to teenagers, such as fast-food chains, they are usually supervised by people close to their age, rather than by adults, notes Nightingale. "There's a real need for places for teenagers to go where there's a modicum of adult involvement," she says.

Despite the riskier world they face, it would be a mistake to suggest that all adolescents of this generation are feeling more angst than their predecessors. Middle-class teenagers, at least, seem content with their lot on the whole: According to recent studies, 80 percent—the same proportion as 20 years ago—profess satisfaction with their own lives, if not with the state of the world. Many teenagers, nevertheless, evince wistfulness for what they think of as the more heroic times of the '60s and '70s—an era, they believe, when teenagers had more say in the world. Playwright Wendy Wasserstein, whose Pulitzer Prize-winning "The Heidi Chronicles" was about coming of age in those years, says she has noticed at least a "stylistic" nostalgia in the appearance of peace-sign earrings and other '60s artifacts. "I guess that comes from the sense of there having been a unity, a togetherness," she says. "Today most teens are wondering about what they're going to do when they grow up. We

had more of a sense of liberation, of youth—we weren't thinking about getting that job at Drexel." Pop-culture critic Greil Marcus, however, believes it was merely the "self-importance" of the '60s generation—his own contemporaries—"that has oppressed today's kids into believing they've missed something. There's something sick about my 18-year-old wanting to see Paul McCartney or the Who. We would never have emulated our parents' culture."

But perhaps that's the point: the teens of the '90s do emulate the culture of their parents, many of whom are the very teens who once made such an impact on their own parents. These parents no doubt have something very useful to pass on to their children—maybe their lost sense of idealism rather than the preoccupation with going and getting that seems, so far, their main legacy to the young. Mom and Dad have to earn a living and fulfill their own needs—they are not likely to be coming home early. But there must be a time and place for them to give their children the advice, the comfort and, most of all, the feelings of possibility that any new generation needs in order to believe in itself.

With MARY TALBOT *and* PAMELA G. KRIPKE

Teenage Turning Point

Does adolescence herald the twilight of girls' self-esteem?

BRUCE BOWER

Youngsters often experience a decline in self-esteem as they enter their adolescent years, a time marked by the abrupt move from the relatively cloistered confines of elementary school to the more complex social and academic demands of junior high. Social scientists have documented this trend — often more pronounced among girls — over the past 20 years through questionnaires and interviews aimed at gauging how adolescents feel about themselves.

But a new survey of U.S. elementary and secondary students bears the worst news yet about plummeting self-esteem among teenage girls. The controversial findings, released in January by the American Association of University Women (AAUW), have refocused researchers' attention on long-standing questions about the meaning of such studies and their implications, if any, for educational reform and for male and female psychological development.

The concept of self-esteem itself remains vague, contends psychiatrist Philip Robson in the June 1990 HARVARD MEDICAL SCHOOL MENTAL HEALTH LETTER. Some researchers assess a person's "global" self-esteem with questions about general feelings of worth, goodness, health, attractiveness and social competence. Others focus on people's evaluations of themselves in specific situations. Robson, of Oxford University in England, notes that an individual might score high on one type of test but not on another, presumably because the measures reflect different aspects of self-esteem.

Moreover, he argues, high test scores may sometimes indicate conceit, narcissism or rigidity rather than healthy feelings of self-worth.

Despite the complexities involved in determining how people truly regard themselves, the AAUW survey suggests that adolescent girls experience genuine, substantial drops in self-esteem that far outpace those reported by boys. Girls also reported much less enthusiasm for math and science, less confidence in their academic abilities and fewer aspirations to professional careers.

The survey, conducted last fall by a private polling firm commissioned by AAUW, involved 2,400 girls and 600 boys from 36 public schools throughout the United States. Black and Hispanic students made up almost one-quarter of the sample. Participants, whose ages ranged from 9 to 16 (fourth through tenth grades), responded to written statements probing global self-esteem, such as "I like the way I look" and "I'm happy the way I am."

In a typical response pattern, 67 percent of the elementary school boys reported "always" feeling "happy the way I am," and 46 percent still felt that way by tenth grade. For girls, the figures dropped from 60 percent to 29 percent.

For both sexes, the sharpest declines in self-esteem occurred at the beginning of junior high.

Compared with the rest of the study sample, students with higher self-esteem liked math and science more, felt better about their schoolwork and grades, considered themselves more important and felt better about their family relationships, according to the survey.

Boys who reported doing poorly in math and science usually ascribed their performance to the topics' lack of usefulness, whereas girls who reported a lack of success in these areas often attributed the problem to personal failure.

Although the survey included too few boys to allow a racial breakdown for males, race did appear to play an important role in the strength of self-esteem among girls. White and Hispanic girls displayed sharp drops in all the measured areas of self-esteem — appearance, confidence, family relationships, school, talents and personal importance — as they grew older. In contrast, more than half the black girls reported high levels of self-confidence and personal importance in both elementary and high school, and most attributed this to strong family and community support, says psychologist

Janie Victoria Ward of the University of Pennsylvania in Philadelphia, an adviser to the study. Their confidence in their academic abilities, however, dropped substantially as they passed through the school system, Ward says.

"Something is going on in the schools that threatens the self-esteem of girls in general," asserts psychologist Nancy Goldberger, another adviser to the survey. "A lot of girls come to doubt their own intelligence in school."

Goldberger, who teaches psychology at the Fielding Institute in Santa Barbara, Calif., calls for intensive, long-term studies to address how schools shortchange female students.

An AAUW pamphlet published last August argues that school-age girls represent the proverbial square peg attempting to fit into the round hole of most educational programs.

Starting early in life, societal pressures urge girls and boys to think and behave in contrasting ways that create gender-specific learning styles, according to the AAUW pamphlet. Schools, however, generally tailor instructional techniques to the learning style of boys, leaving girls with a tattered education and doubts about their academic abilities, the pamphlet contends.

This argument rests heavily on research directed by Harvard University psychologist Carol Gilligan. In her much-praised and much-criticized book, *In a Different Voice* (1982, Harvard University Press), Gilligan asserted that girls and boys generally follow divergent paths of moral development. She based her contention on several studies of Harvard undergraduates, men and women at different points in the life cycle, and women considering abortion.

In Gilligan's view, females respond to an inner moral voice emphasizing human connections and care, and they attempt to solve moral dilemmas by responding to the needs and situations of those affected by the problem. Males, on the other hand, focus on abstract principles such as justice and follow a moral code centered on the impartial application of rules of right and wrong.

Gilligan's most recent research, described in *Making Connections: The Relational Worlds of Adolescent Girls at Emma Willard School* (1990, Harvard University Press), draws on findings collected over a three-year period among 34 students at a private girls' school in Troy, N.Y. Gilligan and her co-workers argue that many girls, at least in this predominantly white, privileged sample, show an aggressive confidence in their identities and ideas around age 11, only to find their self-assurance withering by age 15 or 16.

During this period of increasing separation from parents, marked by a search for an independent identity and future career possibilities, girls feel torn between responding to others and caring for themselves, the Harvard researchers maintain. In addition, they say, adolescent girls encounter more pressure from parents and teachers to keep quiet and not make a fuss than do adolescent boys or younger girls.

The gender gap seen in academic achievement during early adolescence arises largely because a social and educational emphasis on career development and personal advancement clashes with girls' distinctive sense of connection to others, Gilligan's team asserts. The researchers maintain that girls often learn best and gain increased self-confidence through collaboration with other students and faculty, not through competition among individuals as practiced in most schools.

Boys, in contrast, often perform best on competitive tasks or in games with a strict set of prescribed rules, the investigators contend.

Some adolescence researchers argue that Gilligan paints too stark a contrast between the moral development of boys and girls. Others say Gilligan's ideas have an intuitive appeal, but her small studies lack a sound empirical foundation on which to build educational reforms. These researchers see Gilligan's work as a preliminary corrective for previous studies, based largely on male participants, that suggested the ability to reason from abstract principles represented the pinnacle of moral development.

Similarly, social scientists differ over the extent to which self-esteem dips during adolescence and the meaning of the AAUW survey data. In fact, some investigators question whether a significant gender gap in self-esteem exists at all.

Most surveys of teenagers' self-esteem, including the AAUW project, focus on students and neglect school dropouts. This approach may lead to overestimates of self-esteem among boys, argues sociologist Naomi Gerstel of the University of Massachusetts in Amherst. More boys than girls drop out of school, and male dropouts may regard themselves in an especially poor light, Gerstel points out.

Furthermore, she says, since no one has examined the moral "voice" of boys in the intensive way Gilligan studied her group of girls, Gilligan's theory has yet to meet a scientifically rigorous test. Gilligan's ideas prove "problematic" when educators attempt to use them to formulate specific educational reforms, Gerstel writes in the Jan. 4 SCIENCE.

The self-esteem reports gathered in the AAUW survey fail to provide evidence for any particular need to change school instruction, contends psychologist Joseph Adelson of the University of Michigan in Ann Arbor. "It's been known for some time that girls report greater self-esteem declines in adolescence, but the reasons for those declines are unclear," he says. "It's inappropriate to take the correlations in this survey to politicized conclusions about educational reform."

In his view, gender differences in mathematics achievement remain particularly mysterious and probably stem from a number of as-yet-unspecified social or family influences (SN: 12/6/86, p.357). Preliminary studies directed by Carol S. Dweck, a psychologist at Columbia University in New York City, suggest that bright girls show a stronger tendency than bright boys to attribute their difficulty or confusion with a new concept — such as mathematics — to a lack of intelligence. Thus, when bright girls confront mathematics, initial confusion may trigger a feeling of helplessness, Dweck writes in *At The Threshold* (1990, S. Shirley Feldman and Glen R. Elliot, editors, Harvard University Press).

Many girls with considerable potential in mathematics may deal with this sense of helplessness by throwing their energies into already mastered verbal skills, Dweck suggests. Rather than indict their intelligence, both boys and girls who shrink from challenging new subjects may need to learn how to channel initial failures into a redoubled effort to master the material, she says.

Gender differences in reported well-being — an aspect of personal experience closely related to self-esteem — also prove tricky to study, Adelson observes. A statistical comparison of 93 independent studies, directed by psychologist Wendy Wood of Texas A&M University in College Station, serves as a case in point. In examining these studies, which focused on well-being and life satisfaction among adult men and women, Wood and her colleagues found that women reported both greater happiness *and* more dissatisfaction and depression than men. Wood contends that societal influences groom women for an acute emotional responsiveness, especially with regard to intimate relationships, and that this helps explain why women report more intense emotional highs and lows than men.

"No clear advantage can be identified in the adaptiveness and desirability of [men's and women's] styles of emotional life," she and her colleagues write in the March 1989 PSYCHOLOGICAL BULLETIN.

Researchers have yet to conduct a similar statistical comparison of the literature on adolescent self-esteem and well-being. But according to Adelson, a persistent problem plagues the interpretation of all such studies. If females generally show more sensitivity to and awareness of emotions than males, they may more easily offer self-reports about disturbing feelings, creating a misimpression that large sex differences exist in self-esteem, he suggests.

Although this potential "response bias" muddies the research waters, psychologist Daniel Offer of Northwestern University in Evanston, Ill., cites several possible explanations for the tendency among early-adolescent girls to report more self-dissatisfaction than boys.

One theory holds that since girls experience the biological changes of puberty up to 18 months before boys, they may suffer earlier and more pronounced self-esteem problems related to sexual maturity. Several studies have found that early-maturing girls report the most dissatisfaction with their physical appearance, a particularly sensitive indicator of self-esteem among females. Social pressures to begin dating and to disengage emotionally from parents may create additional problems for early-maturing girls, Offer says.

Other research suggests that, unlike their male counterparts, adolescent girls often maintain close emotional ties to their mothers that interfere with the development of a sense of independence and self-confidence, Offer says. In addition, parents may interrupt and ignore girls more than boys as puberty progresses, according to observational studies of families, directed by psychologist John P. Hill of Virginia Commonwealth University in Richmond.

Despite these findings, the director of the most ambitious longitudinal study of adolescent self-esteem to date says her findings provide little support for the substantial gender gap outlined in the AAUW survey, which took a single-point-in-time "snapshot" of self-esteem.

During the 1970s, sociologist Roberta G. Simmons of the University of Pittsburgh and her co-workers charted the trajectory of self-esteem from grades 6 through 10 among more than 1,000 youngsters attending public schools in Milwaukee and Baltimore. Simmons discusses the research in *Moving Into Adolescence* (1987, Aldine de Gruyter).

Overall, adolescents reported a gradual increase in self-esteem as they got older, she says, but many girls entering junior high and high school did experience drops in feelings of confidence and self-satisfaction.

Simmons agrees with Gilligan that adolescent girls increasingly strive for intimacy with others. Large, impersonal junior high schools throw up a barrier to intimacy that initially undermines girls' self-esteem, Simmons asserts. As girls find a circle of friends and a social niche, their self-esteem gradually rebounds, only to drop again when they enter the even larger world of high school.

"We don't know if that last self-esteem drop [in high school] was temporary or permanent," Simmons points out.

As in the AAUW survey, Simmons' team found that black girls, as well as black boys, consistently reported positive and confident self-images.

But given the increased acceptance of women in a wide variety of occupations since the 1970s, Simmons expresses surprise at how much the self-esteem of girls lagged behind that of boys in the AAUW survey.

A new study of 128 youngsters progressing through junior high, described in the February JOURNAL OF YOUTH AND ADOLESCENCE, also contrasts with the AAUW findings. The two-year, longitudinal investigation reveals comparable levels of self-esteem among boys and girls, notes study director Barton J. Hirsch, a psychologist at Northwestern University. Hirsch and his colleagues used a global self-esteem measure much like the one in the AAUW survey.

The researchers gathered self-reports from boys and girls as the students neared the end of sixth grade, then repeated the process with the same youngsters at two points during seventh grade and at the end of eighth grade. Students lived in a midwestern city and came from poor or middle-class families. Black children made up about one-quarter of the sample.

In both sexes, about one in three youngsters reported strong self-esteem throughout junior high school, the researchers report. These individuals also did well in school, maintained rewarding friendships and frequently participated in social activities.

Another third of the sample displayed small increases in self-esteem, but their overall psychological adjustment and academic performance were no better than those of the group with consistently high self-esteem.

Chronically low self-esteem and school achievement dogged 13 percent of the students, who probably suffered from a long history of these problems, Hirsch says.

But the most unsettling findings came from the remaining 21 percent of the youngsters. This group — composed of roughly equal numbers of boys and girls — started out with high self-esteem, good grades and numerous friends, but their scores on these measures plunged dramatically during junior high, eventually reaching the level of the students with chronically low self-esteem.

The data offer no easy explanations for the steep declines seen among one in five study participants, Hirsch says. An examination of family life might uncover traumatic events that influenced the youngsters' confidence and motivation, but this remains speculative, he says.

One of the most comprehensive longitudinal studies of the relation between child development and family life (SN: 8/19/89, p. 117) suggests that particular parenting styles produce the most psycho-logically healthy teenagers. The findings indicate that parents who set clear standards for conduct and allow freedom within limits raise youngsters with the most academic, emotional and social competence.

Directed by psychologist Diana Baumrind of the University of California, Berkeley, the ongoing study has followed children from 124 families, most of them white and middle-class. At three points in the youngsters' lives — ages 3, 10 and 15 — investigators assessed parental styles and the children's behavior at home and school.

Baumrind assumes that self-esteem emerges from competence in various social and academic tasks, not vice versa. For that reason, she and her colleagues track achievement scores and trained observers' ratings of social and emotional adjustment, not children's self-reports of how they feel about themselves.

In fact, Baumrind remains unconvinced that girls experience lower self-esteem than boys upon entering adolescence. Her study finds that girls in elementary grades show a more caring and communal attitude toward others, while boys more often strive for dominance and control in social encounters. But by early adolescence, she maintains, such differences largely disappear.

The gender-gap debate, however, shows no signs of disappearing. In a research field characterized by more questions than answers, most investigators agree on one point. "Most kids come through the years from 10 to 20 without major problems and with an increasing sense of self-esteem," Simmons observes.

Yet that trend, too, remains unexplained. "Perhaps the steady increase in self-esteem noted in late adolescence results more from progressive indoctrination into the values of society than from increasing self-acceptance," says Robson. "We simply do not have the empirical data necessary to resolve this question."

TEENAGERS AND AIDS

'Do you want to put your life in that other person's hands? Is that boy or girl worth dying for? I doubt it . . . Every one of my dreams was shattered, blown away.'

The din inside the downtown Seattle video arcade is overpowering: guns blasting away, bells ringing wildly. None of the 50 or so teens inside notices the tall kid with a Falcons cap who walks in. He steps up to two boys engrossed in a shooting game. "Hey, brothers, you using condoms?" he asks. They nod, barely looking his way. "Need some?" he says, shoving a handful toward them. The boys grab the condoms and stuff them into their pockets. The intruder isn't finished with them. "Know much about AIDS and HIV?" he continues, with the patter of a door-to-door salesman. "Yeah," they answer, in unison. "Then you know you can get it from unprotected sex and sharing needles?" They nod. He quickly hands them a brochure: "This will answer any other questions you have."

The kid in the Falcons cap is Kevin Turner and at 19, he is already an experienced warrior on the front lines of the battle against AIDS. He carries his weapon of choice, condoms, in a black leather bag strapped around his chest. Turner works for POCAAN (People of Color Against AIDS Network). Officially, he's a peer educator; unofficially, he's "Mr. Condom," on call 24 hours a day. He gives out hundreds of condoms every week and has been known to burst into conservations when he hears someone talking about sex. "You're going to use condoms, aren't you?" he'll ask. "Here, have a few."

It's a tough sell, even though it's literally a matter of life and death. A congressional report issued in April warned that HIV, the virus that causes AIDS, is "spreading unchecked among the nation's adolescents, regardless of where they live or their economic status." Since the beginning of the epidemic, more than 5,000 children and young adults have died of AIDS; it is now the sixth leading cause of death among 15- to 24-year-olds. No one knows exactly how many teens are HIV-positive, but during the past three years, the cumulative number of 13- to 24-year-olds diagnosed with AIDS increased 77 percent. By the end of last year, AIDS cases in that age group had been reported in almost every state and the District of Columbia. Nearly half of the afflicted teenagers come from just six places: New York, New Jersey, Texas, California, Florida and Puerto Rico.

No one has yet managed to screen a true cross section of any community's adolescents, but Dr. Lawrence D'Angelo has come close. Since late 1987, the Washington, D.C., pediatrician has tested virtually all the blood samples drawn from 13- to 20-year-olds at Children's National Medical Center, a large public hospital serving kids from all over the metropolitan area. Of the samples drawn between October 1987 and January 1989, one in 250 tested positive. During the next study period (through October 1991), the infection rate rose to one in 90. D'Angelo predicts that one sample in 50 will test positive this year.

Up to now, the majority of afflicted teens have been males, minorities and older adolescents—who, given the long incubation period, probably got the virus in their early teens. But the future holds the frightening prospect of much more widespread illness. A 1990 study of blood samples drawn from college students on 19 campuses found that one student in 500 tested positive. In 1991, the rate among 137,000 Job Corps participants was closer to one in 300. According to U.S. Surgeon General Antonia Novello, the ratio of female to male AIDS patients has doubled in the last four years, with females going from 17 percent of adolescent cases in 1987 to 39 percent of cases last year.

The virus is spreading because adolescent sexual behavior is risky. Some studies have suggested that up to a quarter of teenagers report engaging in rectal intercourse, sometimes to avoid pregnancy or to retain their virginity. But that practice is more likely to cause the cuts and tears that invite infection. Many adolescents also report having multiple partners, again increasing their chances of infection.

The most effective ammunition against AIDS for other high-risk groups—gays, drug users, hemophiliacs—has been education: blunt talk, reinforced by peer support groups. But this approach isn't working for teens. High-risk adults are free to seek any information they want. But teens are at the mercy of adults—parents, teachers, politi-

Kaye Brown, Houston
19 Years Old

AIDS also kills dreams.

At 18, Kaye Brown was ready for the world. The bubbly honor student was looking forward to life in the army. Last March, she signed up at a recruiting office in Houston and took a mandatory AIDS test. A week later she learned she was HIV-positive, and the world was no longer a sure thing. "I was really, really angry," she says. "My career had been snatched away from me."

Though doctors estimated that she had contracted the virus recently, they recommended that she get in touch with anyone she had had sex with in the previous year. The list was long. "It was easy for me to list the guys I had slept with," she says, "but when I counted 24, I was like, gosh!" Brown chose to tell them personally. One former partner said, "But you don't look like you're that way." Brown shot back, "What is *that way*? HIV doesn't mean that I'm dirty or low. It just means that I made a mistake." Her boyfriend couldn't cope with the news, and they split up. Not one man was willing to be tested. "They were too scared,"

Brown says.

Brown blames only herself; she never insisted on condoms. "It makes me angry that I allowed this to happen," she says. "Choices I made have stolen away the choices that I might have had in the future." Now she's turning her anger to good use by working at the AIDS Foundation Houston Inc., talking to teens. "Kids see people who have HIV as bad," she says. "I'm out there to prove that it does happen to good, everyday people." Most teenagers, says Brown, won't practice safe sex unless someone really close to them becomes ill. HIV, she tells them, "doesn't discriminate. It doesn't care how old you are or who you are." She refuses to put her life on hold, and next fall she'll attend Texas Southern University. She gobbles up romance novels ("If you can't live it, read it, " she jokes) and lives a day at a time: "That way, worry won't kill me before HIV does." AIDS, she says, has given her a purpose: "I feel responsible for educating other young people. That's my big mission; that's why I'm here."

cians—who often won't give young people the information they desperately need to make the right choices about their sexual behavior. Even in areas where AIDS is widely acknowledged as a serious problem, there's powerful resistance to frank discussion of teenage sexuality—as if avoiding the issue will make it go away. Many communities avoid the issue altogether, says Rep. Patricia Schroeder, because "they know they are going to raise a firestorm" about whether discussing sex and AIDS will "degenerate morals and values." Jerry Permenter, an AIDS educator in east Texas, has offered to teach in many schools in his area, but few have taken him up on his offer, and he is frustrated. "Some people don't want to talk about issues below the waistline," says Permenter. "That is the conservative mind-set that exists right now in east Texas and that is the mind-set that will bury the next generation."

Clearly, teenagers aren't getting the safe-sex message—either at home or in school. Although many adolescents say they use condoms, experts think most don't. According to the congressional study, only 47 percent of females and 55 percent of males used condoms the first time they had intercourse. Roger Bohman, who teaches a popular course on AIDS at the University of California, Los Angeles, takes surveys of students' condom use before and after the course. He found that students didn't really change their behavior—even when they knew all the dangers. Says Bohman: "They think it can't happen to them."

Teenagers' feelings of invulnerability make them even

more difficult to reach than other at-risk groups. Emotionally, they are still children and they still think they are going to be "rescued" from disaster. "We have a hard time gaining compliance from teens," says Dr. E. Richard Stiehm of the Los Angeles Pediatric AIDS Consortium. "They don't watch out for their own health care. I don't think it's ignorance of the consequences so much as the fallacy that it can only happen to someone else." Wendy Arnold, director of the Peer Education Program in Los Angeles, says that a typical attitude is: "I'm practically a virgin. He couldn't have HIV. He drives a nice car and I just had lunch with him."

That attitude is deadly. Bridgett Pederson always made her boyfriends use condoms until she met Alberto Gonzalez, then a 24-year-old bartender in Portland, Ore. Pederson, then 17, didn't protest when Gonzalez refused; he told her he was "safe." He was a clean, good-looking guy, so she went along. They began living together when she was 19; a year later, she says, he lost his job and they went to a plasma center to sell their blood. The doctors there told Pederson and Gonzalez that they were both HIV-positive. There was worse news to come. Gonzalez's brother told Pederson that Alberto had known for years that he had the virus—and had already infected a previous girlfriend, Shawn Hop. Armed with that information, Pederson went to the authorities and last October, Gonzalez became the first person in the nation to be convicted on assault charges for passing the virus. He's now in a detention center in Portland.

As for Pederson, she has a new mission: getting the

word out. She has become an AIDS activist, appearing on television and speaking to school groups. Her message is simple: "Don't trust someone, even someone you love, to come clean. People aren't always honest about their past sex life or HIV status. I'm a white, middle-class female who is well educated. I didn't fall into any of the high-risk groups, and it happened to me." Pederson, now 23, doesn't have any symptoms yet, but she knows her good health won't last forever. Although she's comfortable talking frankly to groups of teens about the virus, it was painful to visit Shawn Hop, Gonzalez's previous girlfriend, who died June 15. In her last days, Shawn was pale, gaunt and bedridden. Seeing her scared Pederson: "I wonder if I'm looking into my future."

Pederson's story is shocking—and when the young people she talks to hear it, they can't ignore the message. But AIDS educators say that while first-person testimony is important, teens also need careful instruction in how to prevent the disease. A recent study of 100 programs that reduced high-risk behavior among teens indicated that young people need more than good medical information, they also need training in how to stand up to peer pressure. Other reports indicate that each at-risk group has different needs. For example, heterosexual teenagers need to understand that they are not immune just because they're straight. Gay teens, on the other hand, need special support as they cope with accepting their sexuality and the possibility of disease. Dr. June Osborn, chair

of the National Commission on AIDS, says that kids want frank answers from someone who is not judgmental or condemnatory. "They know their peers are sexually active and they know there's something out there they don't know enough about," she says. "They know the adult world is quarreling about condoms, and they are terribly eager to ask questions."

But getting those questions answered has not been simple—even in supposedly "liberal" areas of the country where AIDS among adults is openly discussed. For example, New York leads the nation in the number of AIDS cases among teenagers and the state's schools and health facilities have pioneered approaches to AIDS education. Since 1987, all public schools in New York have been required to include HIV/AIDS instruction as part of their sex-education and family-planning programs. And last fall, New York City became the first major city to begin giving out free condoms to high-school students despite pressure from religious groups and others opposed to the program.

But last May, after 92 of the city's 120 high schools had implemented condom-distribution plans, the city school board voted to bar a state-approved video and city-produced pamphlet used in the schools. The board members said the materials did not place enough emphasis on abstinence, and they required all AIDS educators to devote "substantially" more time and attention to abstinence than to other methods of prevention. The restric-

---

Wally Hansen, San Francisco, 24 Years Old

Getting a driver's license was a liberating experience for 16-year-old Wally Hansen, who grew up in a household so "normal [it was] almost like 'Leave It to Beaver'." He and some buddies in suburban Pinole, Calif., would cut classes and drive to the woods near a gay beach in San Francisco, where they would "frolic" with each other and the men they met there. Hansen never considered using a condom—this was the mid-'80s, when safe sex meant not getting caught by your parents.

Hansen eventually joined the air force. But in 1987, he was discharged after the service discovered he was a homosexual. Routine exit exams revealed the presence of the AIDS virus. Hansen, now 24, is almost certain he was first exposed to HIV during his hooky-playing days. Had he known about the growing epidemic, he says, he might have altered his behavior. He is convinced that education is the key to stopping the spread of AIDS among young people. The effort, he says, should begin in junior high. And since teenagers "are going to have sex no matter what," it's important, "especially in high school, to hand out condoms, anything." Hansen, an administrative assistant at the Bay

Area Reporter, a gay paper in San Francisco, is active in the AIDS war. For two years he was a driver for Rubbermen, an organization that donates condoms to city bars, and now volunteers at AIDS fund-raisers.

But when it comes to his own health—and sometimes that of others—Hansen is reckless. He says he has used speed intermittently for two years. Though he knows that unprotected sex brings the risk of more infections with more strains of the AIDS virus, he doesn't always use a condom. He admits that many of his peers who are HIV-positive don't always inform their partners of their condition, in the assumption that they are infected, too. Some may see it as the behavior of the doomed, but to Hansen, "it basically comes down to what you think it's worth." He insists he wouldn't be happy if he restricted his activities. "I can only think positively. I do anything I want. I feel like I'd do more damage to myself by stressing my system out of worry." His family has taken his illness in stride. "My mom and dad told me they may not love the things I do," says Hansen, "but they love me." And that, sad to say, makes him luckier than many.

Krista Blake, Columbiana, Ohio
20 Years Old

In the fall of 1990, Krista Blake was 18 and looking forward to her first year at Youngstown State University in Ohio. She and her boyfriend were talking about getting married. Her life, she says, was "basic, white-bread America." Then she went to the doctor, complaining about a backache, and found out she had the AIDS virus.

Blake had been infected with HIV, the virus that causes AIDS, two years earlier by an older boy, a hemophiliac. "He knew that he was infected, and he didn't tell me," she says. "And he didn't do anything to keep me from getting infected, either." When she first heard the diagnosis, Blake felt as though she had just walked into a brick wall. Suddenly, she couldn't envision her future. She found herself thinking things like "There are 50 states out there. I don't want to just live and die in Ohio." Her doctor sent her to University Hospital in Cleveland, 90 minutes from home, for treatment. She has taken AZT and is now on the new antiviral DDI. Although she needed frequent transfusions to counteract the effects of AZT, she is relatively healthy. "I am living with AIDS, not dying from AIDS," she says. "I do all of the same things I used to do. That doesn't mean I can run the Boston Marathon, but my mind is still 20." She reads everything from Danielle Steel to "Life 101," a popular advice book. She makes a point of going out at least once every day, even if it's just down to the park to watch a softball game. "It gets those juices moving," she says.

Still, she doesn't know how long her good health will last—a month, a year, five years. She doesn't make long-term commitments. Blake and her fiancé broke off their engagement, because, she says, "I love him enough that I want him to have his options for a life open." However, they are still very good friends. Blake also dropped out of school. "A bachelor's degree wouldn't do much for me," she says with a rueful laugh.

Since the spring of 1991, Blake has spent as many as four or five days a week doing the one thing she believes is really important—talking to other teens about HIV and how to avoid infection. The first thing the kids ask about is her sex life. "I don't have a sex life," she tells them, "but that's because I don't have any energy to have a sex life." The kids usually start laughing. Then she says: "I have just so much energy and I have to decide, do I come out here and talk to you, or do I have sex? I pick what's important, and you won." After one presentation, a student came up to Blake and told her: "I had an uncle who came home at Easter one year, and he had AIDS. This was in 1988. My mom was afraid. We didn't go see him. She wouldn't let us go. He died the next year, at Easter. I never got to say goodbye to my uncle. Would it be OK if I came up and gave you a hug?"

LUCILLE BEACHY

tions went even further, requiring outside AIDS groups working with the schools to abide by the rules as well. The board's actions have been challenged by the New York Civil Liberties Union; to date, there has been no ruling. In the meantime, the city's AIDS educators complain that they can't work under censorship. "This is a disaster for us," says Cydelle Berlin, coordinator of the adolescent AIDS-prevention program at Mount Sinai Medical Center. "We're talking life and death. We can't submit our work to the sex police."

Sessions at clinics like Berlin's go far beyond technical descriptions of the virus—and discussions of abstinence seem beside the point. On one recent afternoon, 20-year-old Jerome Bannister held up a pink plastic penis for a group of inner-city teens. "Anybody wanna touch this?" he asked. "His name is Johnson." Bannister's 20-year-old partner, Diana Hernandez, flicked open a flesh-colored condom. "We've got a little friend here," she said. Bannister went next. "You wanna put a little jelly inside," he said, gesturing toward the condom. "There are a lot of nerve endings in the penis. That way you get that wet, hot feeling when it's in the vagina where it's warm. But lubrication's not only for that warm feeling. It's also a backup. If you use nonoxynol-9, it can kill the sperm—and the HIV virus." Many experts believe that nonoxynol-9 helps prevent transmission. Bannister and Hernandez then demonstrated exactly how to slip the condom on the penis. The team went through equally detailed descriptions of dental dams and the new female condom, which is inserted like a diaphragm. Their audience took the session very seriously, asking questions about where to buy condoms and grabbing handfuls of free samples.

Buying condoms isn't enough; kids also need help persuading partners to use them. Many AIDS programs focus on role-playing, giving teens practical strategies for dealing with social pressure. "All these kids want to do is fit in with their peers," says Dr. Marvin Belzer of Children's Hospital in Los Angeles. "If a young woman thinks she'll lose her boyfriend if she insists on condoms, and feels that he is the only reason she is somebody, she's not going to use them." There are mixed cultural messages to deal with, too. A boy who is told that having sex with multiple partners is dangerous is also being told that more sexual conquests make him more of a man. "In this society, if we want to make a difference, we have to stop the mixed message between parental and community values versus the values portrayed in the media," says Belzer.

Straight teens have a difficult time sorting out conflicting values; gay teens have even fewer resources—and they have to contend with cultural prejudices and their own mixed emotions about their emerging sexual identity. "Nobody wants to talk about male-to-male sex in the teen population," says Rene Durazzo of the San Francisco AIDS Foundation. AIDS experts say that prevention campaigns designed for older gay men don't help teenagers. "Education efforts to date assume youths have choices and are free agents," says Barry Lawlor of the Haight Ashbury Free Clinic in San Francisco. "Many youths do not have choices . . . They're new to sexual behavior and they can be exploited." The likelihood of exploitation increases among runaways who are desperate for money. "On the streets, when a teen says he's not going to have sex without a condom and the other guy says he'll pay $20 more if he does, that's a lot of pressure," Lawlor says. But even teens still at home take risks when they know they shouldn't. The need for love and affection overwhelms the fear of getting sick. Scott Miller, 24, of San Francisco, discovered he was HIV-positive in college. He says that when he was a teenager, his sense of self-worth was low; witnessing a particularly violent gay-bashing incident made him feel even more vulnerable. "Unsafe behavior was OK if it would make you my friend," he says. "If this person wouldn't want me because I wanted to use a condom, well, I'd rather have him like me."

Gay teens who discover they are HIV-positive must tell their parents—often in the same conservation—that they're gay and that they're infected. Sue Beardsley, a volunteer with Rest Stop, a San Francisco support center for people with AIDS, still remembers the phone call she got from 16-year-old David on the last night of his life. His family was thousands of miles away and he didn't want to be alone. She rushed to his hospital room; a few hours later he died in her arms. Beardsley telephoned David's mother to tell her that her son was gone. "My son David doesn't exist," the mother said. "He died a year ago." That was when David had told his mother he was gay.

Fear of such rejection compels many gay teens to keep both their sexual identity and their HIV status a secret. They're desperate for a "safe place" where they can talk freely. One such place is Bay Positives in San Francisco, a peer support group for HIV-positive young people. Jim Neiss, 21, a Bay Positives member, says that even though his family is behind him, he needs the group as well. "In the middle of the night, if I'm really upset or traumatized about something, I don't hesitate to call a member." They

share a tragic bond: confronting the prospect of an unnaturally early death before they have even embarked on their adult lives. Support groups for adult AIDS sufferers often seem irrelevant because the adult agenda is so different. In adult groups, says therapist Julie Graham, a founder of Bay Positives, "People talk about stuff . . . they'll never have. Like wills. Young people with HIV often don't have enough material possessions to need a will. Or relationships. Young people with HIV feel like they're never going to get the chance to have a relationship."

Knowing that life will be short gives other HIV-positive young people a special sense of purpose. Amy Dolph grew up in the quintessential small town of Katy, Texas. In the spring of 1987, she seemed to be just a typical all-American girl: blond, blue-eyed, with nothing more serious on her mind than going steady and heading for college in the fall. But when she donated blood to help her ailing great-grandmother, she found out that the second man she slept with had given her HIV. She was shocked and confused. The last of her friends to lose her virginity, she didn't sleep around. "Every one of my dreams was shattered, blown away," she says. To this day she isn't sure how the man who infected her contracted the virus; she knew that he had been sexually active at an early age and had experimented with drugs. Later she found out that he was also bisexual. She is past the stage of blaming him but says she wishes she had known more and had understood that she could be at risk. "Back then we were always reading that you're only at high risk if you're this group, this group or this group," she says. "And you're at low risk if you're a sexually active heterosexual. And everyone saw that 'low risk' as 'no risk'."

Dolph, now 23, works with the AIDS Foundation Houston Inc. in its education program, traveling to urban and rural high schools and junior highs to talk about AIDS. She's trying to give the kids something she never got—a warning. She tells teenagers that they shouldn't allow their sex partners, no matter how close they are to them, to have control over when they're going to die. "Do you want to put your life in that other person's hands? Is that boy or girl worth dying for? I doubt it." Dolph doesn't dwell on the past and she doesn't look too far ahead into the future. Her present is full—and, for the moment, that has to be enough.

Barbara Kantrowitz *with* Mary Hager *in Washington,*
Geoffrey Cowley *and* Lucille Beachy *in New York,*
Melissa Rossi *in Seattle,* Brynn Craffey
in San Francisco,
Peter Annin *in Houston,* Rebecca Crandall
in Los Angeles
and bureau reports

Date and Acquaintance Rape among a Sample of College Students

Crystal S. Mills
Barbara J. Granoff

Crystal S. Mills, PhD, is Associate Professor, Department of Social Work, Eastern Michigan University, 411 King Hall, Ypsilanti, MI 48197. Barbara J. Granoff, ACSW, is Prevention-Education Coordinator, Sex Abuse Treatment Center, Honolulu. The research reported here was a collaborative effort between the Sex Abuse Treatment Center, Kapiolani Medical Center for Women and Children, Honolulu, HI, and the University of Hawaii School of Social Work.

This article reports on a date and acquaintance rape needs-assessment survey of 106 male and 113 female students in undergraduate English courses at the University of Hawaii–Manoa. The sample was ethnically mixed, with Japanese being the largest ethnic group represented. Unduplicated counts showed that 28 percent (n = 32) of the women acknowledged that they were victims of rape or attempted rape, and the majority reported multiple victimizations. One-sixth (n = 18) of the men admitted to committing acts that meet the legal definition of sexual assault in Hawaii, and about one-third (29.2 percent, n = 31) admitted that they continue to make sexual advances even after a woman says no. Implications for date and acquaintance rape prevention programs are discussed.

THIS STUDY was undertaken as part of a needs-assessment survey of the incidence of date and acquaintance rape among students at the University of Hawaii–Manoa. The needs assessment was initiated in response to the noted increase in college-age women receiving services through the Sex Abuse Treatment Center (SATC) in Honolulu for sexual assaults by people whom they knew. (On the basis of SATC statistics for 1987, 75 percent of the college-age clients had reported being victimized by people they knew.)

The SATC staff noted that many of these women had difficulty labeling the experience as an assault, which not only delayed their receipt of treatment, but compounded their trauma. In addition, fewer Japanese women sought SATC services than would be expected, given that one out of three women are victims of rape or attempted rape sometime during their lives (Russell, 1984) and given the size of the Japanese population on the island of Oahu. Thus, the purpose of this study was twofold: to document the prevalence of sexual assaults among a sample of college students at the University of Hawaii–Manoa and to determine the relationship between reported victimizations and ethnicity.

According to the Bureau of Justice Statistics (1984), acquaintance rape occurs most frequently among females ages 16 to 24. Because this population largely comprises college students, research has focused on college students in an attempt to document the prevalence of sexual assaults among this age group (Ehrhart & Sandler, 1985; Koss, Gidycz, & Wisniewski, 1987; Koss, Leonard, Beezley, & Oros, 1985; Parrot, 1985). The findings underscore the prevalence of sexual victimizations among college-age women. Koss et al. (1987) found that approximately 28 percent of college-age women reported having experienced at least one sexual victimization (since age 14) that met the legal definition of rape, and almost 8 percent of college-age men reported perpetrating such acts. Some researchers (Koss, 1985; Parrot, 1985) have speculated that approximately one in every five female college students will be victims of sexual assault before they graduate.

Using self-reported statistics from students representing 32 mainland colleges, Koss and associates (1987) found that one-eighth of the female students in their study had been raped. According to *Ms.* survey statistics, 84 percent of the college-age women surveyed in Koss et al.'s study knew their assailants and 57 percent of the rapes occurred on dates (Warshaw, 1988). Rapaport and Burkhart (1984) found that 15 percent of their sample of college men reported forcing sex on their dates. Miller and Marshall's (1987) survey of 795 undergraduate and graduate students found that 27 percent of the women and 15 percent of the men indicated that they were involved in forced sexual intercourse while dating. These results, along with others, only begin to describe the full extent of sexual assault among college-age students.

Compared with sexual assaults by strangers, sexual assaults by dates and acquaintances are reported less often (Burkhart, 1983; Koss, 1985). Many of these assaults are never reflected in official statistics because women generally consider encounters of this type private, personal, and embarrassing. In addition, the inability to identify such encounters as sexual assaults is a major problem for many women (Koss, 1985). In an article entitled "The Hidden Rape Victim," Koss (1985) reported that none of the unacknowledged rape victims (those who were unable to label the experience as rape) in her study reported the experience to the police, a rape crisis center, or a hospital emergency room. Even among the women who were able to recognize their experiences as sexual assault, only 8 percent made police reports and only 13 percent went to a rape crisis center.

Many women who have been victimized are unable to validate their feelings or label the experience as a sexual assault because of their lack of information about sex and sexual assault and their confusion about changing sexual norms. Nonetheless, women who are victimized by dates and acquaintances—whether or not they are able to label the experience as an assault—manifest the same, or perhaps stronger, physical and emotional reactions as do those women who are raped by strangers. The feelings that sexual assault victims frequently express, such as guilt, shame, fear, anger, and impaired trust, are often strongest in the case of acquaintance rape (Grossman & Sutherland, 1983).

Despite the proliferation of the literature on date and acquaintance rape, little attention has been given to ethnic–cultural differences in the prevalence of sexual assault. Studies that have addressed ethnicity have looked at prevalence on the mainland among large concentrations of ethnic groups such as blacks, Hispanics, and Native Americans (Koss et al., 1987). These groups are underrepresented among the population of Hawaii, which consists mainly of people whose ethnic backgrounds are from Asia and the Pacific Islands. Consequently, the literature on prevalence provides little from which to generalize about date and acquaintance rape in Hawaii. For these reasons, the study presented here sought to document the prevalence of sexual assaults among a sample of college students on this unique ethnocultural island campus.

Method

Subjects

The subjects for the study were a sample of 106 males and 113 females who were enrolled in undergraduate English courses during the spring 1988 semester at the University of Hawaii–Manoa. The sample was ethnically mixed, with Japanese being the largest ethnic group represented. Table 1 presents the distribution of subjects across ethnic groups by gender.

Approximately 59 percent ($n = 129$) of the subjects were born and raised in Hawaii. Eighty percent ($n = 175$) were ages 18 to 23, with an average age of 22 years, and approximately 28 percent ($n = 61$) were first-year students, 15.5 percent ($n = 34$) were sophomores, 19.6 percent ($n = 43$) were juniors, and 32.4 percent ($n = 71$) were seniors. Although undergraduate courses were selected for sampling, 4.6 percent ($n = 10$) of the subjects were graduate students.

Instruments

The instruments related to prevalence and reporting behaviors were administered as part of a larger package. Prevalence was assessed through the use of a progressive series of ques-

Table 1.
Ethnicity by Gender

Ethnic Group	Men		Women		Total	
	%	n	%	n	%	n
Caucasian	9.13	20	8.22	18	17.4	38
Hawaiian	2.74	6	6.39	14	9.1	20
Japanese	12.32	27	18.26	40	30.6	67
Chinese	5.02	11	5.02	11	10.0	22
Filipino	3.65	8	1.83	4	5.5	12
Black	.46	1	.46	1	.9	2
Mixed Asian	10.05	22	8.22	18	18.3	40
Other	5.02	11	3.20	7	8.2	18

tions regarding sexually assaultive experiences, three of which met the legal definition of sexual assault in Hawaii (State of Hawaii Penal Code 707-730 to 707-734). Male and female versions of this instrument were administered.

Limitations

Recognizing the need to develop and implement a date rape prevention project at the university, the authors designed the survey as the basis for determining the program's components. Certain temporal and logistical considerations precluded the use of random probability sampling. The sampling procedures used facilitated the collection of information within a relatively short period. Because of the limitations imposed by these sampling procedures, the data reported here are viewed as suggestive and may have limited generalizability.

Procedures

An invitation to participate was extended to the English department at the university. Interest in the project was high, and the department offered class time (with instructors' approval) for the data collection. Instructors were contacted by a member of the research team, informed of the study, and asked to cooperate. Students were informed by their instructors the week before data were to be collected that regularly scheduled class time would be used and that participation was voluntary.

Immediately before the survey was administered, the subjects were read

an introduction to the study and their written consent was obtained. Classes ranged in size from 10 to 35. Out of 222 students, 219 agreed to participate.

Given the sensitive nature of the content and the potential for unresolved trauma to resurface among subjects with a history of victimization, each class was informed, after the data were collected, that resources were available to them through the SATC. The name of a person to contact and the phone number of the center were provided to all the classes that were surveyed.

Results

Victims

The female subjects were asked a series of questions regarding various forms of personal victimization, along a continuum of the degree of sexually abusive experiences. They were not asked the age at which they were victimized. However, their comments suggested that a few had experienced incestuous relationships in childhood and adolescence. In addition, many subjects were not sure about labeling certain interactions as sexual assaults and thus responded "never" to questions about personal victimization. Therefore, unacknowledged victimizations may not be included in the data. The subjects' responses are organized according to those who reported only one victimization and those who reported multiple victimizations. These results are summarized in Table 2.

Twenty-eight percent ($n = 32$) of the 113 women acknowledged that they

Table 2.
Women Reporting Victimizations, by Type of Victimization (N = 113)

Question[a]	Once		Multiple		Total	
	n	%	n	%	n	%
Have you ever been raped or sexually assaulted?	5	4.4	15	13.3	20	17.7
Has anyone ever attempted unsuccessfully to sexually assault you?	17	15.0	8	7.1	25	22.1
Has anyone ever touched you sexually or forced you to touch them sexually against your will?	12	10.6	24	21.2	36	31.8
Have you ever been tricked into a sexual act?	6	5.3	5	4.4	11	9.7
Have you ever felt unable to say no to sexual advances because of the other person's status, size, relationship to you, and so forth?	6	5.3	24	21.2	30	26.5
Have you ever found yourself in sexual situations that you were uncomfortable with but you were not sure that it was a sexual assault?	10	8.8	20	17.7	30	26.5
Have you ever felt "taken advantage of" sexually when you were under the influence of alcohol or drugs?	3	2.6	11	9.7	14	12.3
Have you ever had sex because you felt that saying no would not have made a difference?	4	3.5	8	7.1	12	10.6
Have you ever had sex because you felt it had "gone too far" to say no?	5	4.4	13	11.5	18	15.9

[a]The first three questions meet the legal definition of sexual assault, as defined in the state of Hawaii penal code.

were victims of rape or attempted rape, and the majority reported multiple victimizations. Table 3 summarizes the percentage of women who reported victimizations by age.

With regard to ethnicity, the results suggest that the Caucasian and Japanese women experienced more victimizations of all forms than did the other women. For example, 39 percent (n = 7) of the Caucasian women and 17 percent (n = 7) of the Japanese women reported having been raped at least once. Table 4 summarizes the Caucasian and Japanese women's responses to questions about different forms of victimization.

Only 15 percent (n = 3) of the 20 female students who were raped told someone, and none reported the offense to the police. Of the 25 women reporting attempted rape, 40 percent (n = 10) told someone about the incident, but only one woman reported the incident to the police. (In this instance, n values reflect duplicate classification.) Thus, victims seemed to be more likely to tell in instances of attempted rape than of actual rape.

Subjects who had been victims of sexual assault were asked to identify their assailants. Although it was anticipated that only women would respond, a small percentage of men reported victimizations by strangers (8 percent, n = 8), acquaintances (6 percent, n = 6), and lovers (2 percent, n = 2). Eleven percent (n = 12) of all the female subjects reported victimizations by strangers; 17 percent (n = 19) by acquaintances; 6 percent (n = 7) by dates; 10 percent (n = 11) by lovers; and 3 percent (n = 3) by spouses. Of the 40 women who knew their assailant, 45 percent (n = 18) reported that when there was a relationship with the assailant, that relationship continued after the assault.

Perpetrators

The male students were asked a series of questions regarding their offense behavior. Although few admitted to having perpetrated rape or attempted rape (1.9 percent [n = 2] and 8.5 percent [n = 9], respectively), many admitted to other types of sexually abusive behavior. The findings are summarized in Table 5.

Whereas 97.2 percent (n = 103) of the men stated that they would be unlikely to force sex if they thought they could get away with it, 10.4 percent (n = 11) thought that women want men to be forceful, and 50.9 percent (n = 54) believed that women sometimes say no to sex when they really mean yes. Those who thought that woman say no when they mean yes stated that a woman needs to say no an average of 2.6 times before they would believe she really means it. Even those who said a woman needs to say no only once tended to qualify their responses with comments regarding the forcefulness of the protest.

The Caucasian and Japanese men reported sexually assaultive behaviors more than did men of other ethnic groups. Data for Caucasian and Japanese men are summarized in Table 6.

Discussion and Implications

These findings regarding date and acquaintance rape suggest that sexual victimization is a real problem among

Table 3.
Women Reporting Rapes or Attempted Rapes, by Age

		Women Reporting Rape/Attempted Rape (n = 32)	
Age (yrs.)	N	n	%
18	31	7	23
19	17	5	29
20	22	6	27
21	19	7	37
22	14	4	29
23	10	3	30

Table 4.
Caucasian and Japanese Women Reporting at Least One Victimization, by Type of Victimization

Question[a]	Caucasian ($n = 18$)		Japanese ($n = 40$)	
	n	%	n	%
Have you ever been raped or sexually assaulted?	7	39	7	18
Has anyone ever attempted unsuccessfully to sexually assault you?	7	39	11	28
Has anyone ever touched you sexually or forced you to touch them sexually against your will?	11	61	14	35
Have you ever been tricked into a sexual act?	6	33	3	8
Have you ever felt unable to say no to sexual advances because of the other person's status, size, relationship to you, and so forth?	10	56	10	25
Have you ever found yourself in sexual situations that you were uncomfortable with but you were not sure that it was a sexual assault?	10	56	11	28
Have you ever felt "taken advantage of" sexually when you were under the influence of alcohol or drugs?	7	39	2	5
Have you ever had sex because you felt that saying no would not have made a difference?	4	22	4	10
Have you ever had sex because you felt it had "gone too far" to say no?	5	28	7	18

[a]The first three questions meet the legal definition of sexual assault, as defined in the state of Hawaii penal code.

the ethnic groups represented on this campus. Unduplicated counts suggest that as many as 28 percent ($n = 32$) of the female subjects had been victims of rape or attempted rape. Although victimizations were highest among Caucasian and Japanese women, the native Hawaiians and the mixed Asians in the study also reported being victimized. Two of the native Hawaiian–part Hawaiian women reported having been raped, and four reported attempted rape. Only one mixed Asian reported having been raped and three reported attempted rape. Curiously, the Chinese and Filipino women did not report victimizations.

Some of the written responses suggested that a significant number of the women in the study had difficulty labeling certain interactions sexual assaults, even though the interactions may have met the legal definition of a sexual assault in Hawaii. On the basis of unduplicated responses ($n = 52$) to the three questions that meet the legal definition of sexual assault, one out of three ($n = 17$) of the women correctly labeled the experience and acknowledged having been victims of some form of sexual abuse.

In addition, approximately 77 percent ($n = 40$) of the 52 reported victimizations were perpetrated by people whom the victims knew. Almost half the women ($n = 18$) who were victim-

ized by people known to them continued the relationship with their perpetrators after they were victimized. This finding suggests that these women are perhaps mislabeling the experiences and normalizing abusive situations or interactions. Another possibility is that such women perceived themselves as damaged or soiled and stayed with their abusers because no one else would want them.

The incidence of sexual offenses perpetrated by the men in this study is alarming. One out of six ($n = 18$) of the male students admitted to committing

acts that meet the legal definition of sexual assault in Hawaii. Moreover, about one-third ($n = 31$) continue to make sexual advances even after a woman says no. Thus, the men in this study seem to hold attitudes that support a rape culture, of which miscommunication between the sexes appears to be a key element.

These findings were used to demonstrate the need to develop an educational program at the university that would increase awareness of the problem of sexual assault among college students, dispel common myths,

Table 5.
Men Reporting Sexually Assaultive Behavior ($N = 106$)

Question	Men Admitting Offense	
	n	%
Have you ever had intercourse with someone against their will?	2	1.9
Have you ever attempted to force intercourse with someone who didn't want to cooperate?	9	8.5
Have you ever touched someone sexually or forced someone to touch you sexually against their will?	15	14.2
Have you ever made use of your size, status, or relationship to obtain sex?	11	10.4
Have you ever continued to make sexual advances after your partner said no?	31	29.2
Have you ever given or encouraged the use of drugs or alcohol to obtain sex?	17	16.0
Have you ever told someone that the foreplay had gone "too far" for you to be able to stop?	11	10.4

Table 6.
Caucasian and Japanese Men Reporting Sexually Assaultive Behavior

Question	Caucasian (n = 20)		Japanese (n = 26)	
	n	%	n	%
Have you ever had intercourse with someone against their will?	2	10	0	0
Have you ever attempted to force intercourse with someone who didn't want to cooperate?	3	15	1	3.8
Have you ever touched someone sexually or forced someone to touch you sexually against their will?	2	10	4	15.4
Have you ever made use of your size, status, or relationship to obtain sex?	4	20	1	3.8
Have you ever continued to make sexual advances after your partner said no?	5	25	6	23.1
Have you ever given or encouraged the use of drugs or alcohol to obtain sex?	5	25	2	7.7
Have you ever told someone that the foreplay had gone "too far" for you to be able to stop?	1	5	3	11.5

explore sex-role socialization, assist students in identifying abusive and potentially abusive situations, promote the development of healthy nonabusive relationships, and provide information about services that are available to victims. Because of the sampling procedures used, the generalizability of these findings is limited. However, this and other research conveys the pervasiveness of sexual assault among students on college campuses across the nation (Koss et al., 1987).

Many colleges have established programs to prevent and educate students about sexual assault. Unfortunately, few, if any, have established evaluation procedures to support the benefit of educational programs of this type (Mills, Granoff, & Anderson, 1990). Unlike most college-based educational programs on date and acquaintance rape, the peer education program at the University of Hawaii gathered data on specific outcomes using a before–after design. The findings support the benefit of peer education in dispelling common myths and promoting a rape-free culture (Mills & Granoff, 1990).

Notwithstanding the increasing recognition of the need to prevent date rape among college-age people, many colleges and universities have yet to develop such programs. Colleges and universities cannot afford to ignore that their students are at high risk. Programs and services to address the needs

in this area must be developed, implemented, and supported within the university and college system.

Cultural sensitivity is essential to the development of such programs, especially at universities and colleges that have large Asian populations. The findings from this study revealed that a substantial number of the female Japanese students had been victimized. Written comments on the questionnaires suggested that an additionally large number of these women were unable to label and acknowledge their victimizations. If this group is taken into consideration, then it is possible that the victimization rate among the Japanese women would be comparable to that of the Caucasian women in this study. Thus, among these Japanese women, there may have been a number of hidden victims.

The number of hidden victims identified among the Japanese women in this study may be related to cultural traditions that normalize the status of "victim" among these women. In the traditional East Asian family, women's status is low: in their youth, they must obey their fathers; in adulthood, their husbands; and in old age, their eldest sons (Shon & Ja, 1982). These culturally ascribed attitudes and behaviors may increase the women's vulnerability and decrease the likelihood that they will correctly label sexual assaults and disclose that they have been victimized. In addition, the whats and hows of appropriate communication

are determined largely by the characteristics of the individuals involved and their relationship (Shon & Ja, 1982). Because of the higher status of men, women from traditional Japanese families may be less likely to communicate their sexual desires or to challenge male behaviors openly. Their vulnerability may also be increased by the value placed on harmony in interpersonal relationships. To avoid direct confrontation, these women may submit to unwanted advances. Finally, the taboo on the discussion of sexual matters (the fact that they are too personal and may bring shame) may decrease the likelihood that victims from many Asian cultures will disclose and seek needed services (Shon & Ja, 1982).

Similarly, men's lack of acknowledgment of themselves as perpetrators of sexual assault may be tied to their culture. Just as Japanese women may be more likely not to acknowledge abusive experiences and to normalize them, Japanese men may be more likely to fail to perceive or acknowledge abusive behaviors, thus normalizing their behavior. This normalization of behavior may explain why the Caucasian men reported greater perpetrator behavior than did the Japanese men.

As was stated earlier, the proportional representation of Japanese women seeking sexual assault recovery services through the SATC is substantially lower than would be expected, given their representation on Oahu, perhaps because these women are reluctant to disclose their victimization or are unable to label the experience as sexual assault. Though the ability to generalize beyond this sample is limited, the findings suggest that the incidence of sexual assault in the Japanese culture needs closer empirical scrutiny, as do culturally derived definitions of sexual assault. For example, do Japanese women hold views of sexual involvement that make it difficult for them to label assaultive sexual interactions?

Information on programs should be presented in a culturally unbiased manner; attempts should be made to create a safe atmosphere in which students, regardless of their cultural orientation, are willing to explore new ideas and behaviors that would support a rape-free environment; and outreach programs should be developed to help the hidden victims to identify themselves. Many components, such as assertiveness training, that are typically included in such prevention programs may conflict with the cultural values of Asian students. Therefore, it is important to respect cultural values and to present new ideas as choices that can be used when and where they are warranted.

With regard to treatment, it is imperative that sexual assault support services be available to college students. Programs that cannot incorporate a treatment component should at least provide referral services. Given that a substantial number of young women may be hidden victims, symptoms such as depression, the inability to concentrate, and difficulty with trust and intimacy may be presenting problems. Direct practitioners in clinical settings should be familiar with the clinical symptoms of the rape-trauma syndrome and should assess the possibility that women who display such symptoms have a history of victimization. A thorough assessment should include a sexual history and direct and indirect questions regarding sexual victimization, especially in working with Japanese women. Care should be taken to create a therapeutic relationship in which the woman feels safe to acknowledge her victimization and to take the risk to disclose it.

References

Bureau of Justice Statistics. (1984). *Criminal victimization in the United States, 1982* (Publication No. NCJ 92820). Washington, DC: U.S. Department of Justice.

Burkhart, B. (1983, November). *Acquaintance rape strategies and prevention.* Paper presented at the conference on Acquaintance Rape and Rape Prevention on Campus, Louisville, KY.

Ehrhart, J., & Sandler, B. (1985, November). *Campus gang rape: Party games.* Washington, DC: Project on the Status and Education of Women, Association of American Colleges.

Grossman, R., & Sutherland, J. (1983). *Surviving sexual assault.* New York: Congdon & Weed.

Koss, M. (1985). The hidden rape victim. *Psychology of Women Quarterly, 9,* 193–209.

Koss, M., Gidycz, C., & Wisniewski, N. (1987). The scope of rape: Incidence and prevalence of sexual aggression and victimization in a national sample of higher education students. *Journal of Consulting and Clinical Psychology, 55,* 162–170.

Koss, M., Leonard, K., Beezley, D., & Oros, C. (1985). Nonstranger sexual aggression. *Sex Roles, 12,* 981–992.

Miller, B., & Marshall, J. (1987, January). Coercive sex on the university campus. *Journal of College Student Personnel,* pp. 38–47.

Mills, C., & Granoff, B. (1990). *An evaluation of a date rape prevention program.* Unpublished manuscript, University of Hawaii School of Social Work, Honolulu.

Mills, C., Granoff, B., & Anderson, W. (1990). *A survey of acquaintance rape prevention programs on college campuses.* Unpublished manuscript, University of Hawaii School of Social Work, Honolulu.

Parrot, A. (1985). *Comparison of acquaintance rape patterns among college students in a large co-ed university and a small women's college.* Paper presented at the 1985 National Conference for the Society for the Scientific Study of Sex, San Diego, CA.

Rapaport, K., & Burkhart, B. (1984). Personality and attitudinal characteristics of sexually coercive college males. *Journal of Abnormal Psychology, 93,* 216–221.

Russell, D. (1984). *Sexual exploitation, rape, child sexual abuse, and workplace harassment.* Beverly Hills, CA: Sage Publications.

Shon, S., & Ja, D. (1982). Asian families. In M. McGoldrick, J. Pearce, & J. Giordano (Eds.), *Ethnicity and family therapy* (pp. 208–228). New York: Guilford Press.

Warshaw, R. (1988). *I never called it rape: The Ms. report on recognizing, fighting and surviving date and acquaintance rape.* New York: Harper & Row.

PSYCHOTRENDS

Taking Stock of Tomorrow's Family and Sexuality

Where are we going and what kind of people are we becoming? Herewith, a road map to the defining trends in sexuality, family, and relationships for the coming millenium as charted by the former chair of Harvard's psychiatry department. From the still-rollicking sexual revolution to the painful battle for sexual equality to the reorganization of the family, America is in for some rather interesting times ahead.

Shervert H. Frazier, M.D.

Has the sexual revolution been side-tracked by AIDS, and the return to traditional values we keep hearing about? In a word, no. The forces that originally fueled the revolution are all still in place and, if anything, are intensifying: mobility, democratization, urbanization, women in the workplace, birth control, abortion and other reproductive interventions, and media proliferation of sexual images, ideas, and variation.

Sexuality has moved for many citizens from church- and state-regulated behavior to a medical and self-regulated behavior. Population pressures and other economic factors continue to diminish the size of the American family. Marriage is in sharp decline, cohabitation is growing, traditional families are on the endangered list, and the single-person household is a wave of the future.

AIDS has generated a great deal of heat in the media but appears to have done little, so far, to turn down the heat in the bedroom. It is true that in some surveys people *claimed* to have made drastic changes in behavior—but most telling are the statistics relating to marriage, divorce, cohabitation, teen sex, out-of-wedlock births, sexually transmitted diseases (STDs), contraception,

and adultery. These are far more revealing of what we *do* than what we *say* we do. And those tell a tale of what has been called a "postmarital society" in continued pursuit of sexual individuality and freedom.

Studies reveal women are more sexual now than at any time in the century.

Arguably there are, due to AIDS, fewer visible sexual "excesses" today than there were in the late 1960s and into the 1970s, but those excesses (such as sex clubs, bathhouses, backrooms, swinging singles, group sex, public sex acts, etc.) were never truly reflective of norms and were, in any case, greatly inflated in the media. Meanwhile, quietly and without fanfare, the public, even in the face of the AIDS threat, has continued to expand its interest in sex and in *increased,* rather than decreased, sexual expression.

Numerous studies reveal that women are more sexual now than at any time in the century. Whereas sex counselors used to deal with men's complaints about their wives' lack of "receptivity," it is now more often the women complaining about the men. And women, in this "postfeminist"

era, are doing things they never used to believe were "proper." Fellatio, for example, was seldom practiced (or admitted to) when Kinsey conducted his famous sex research several decades ago. Since that time, according to studies at UCLA and elsewhere, this activity has gained acceptance among women, with some researchers reporting that nearly all young women now practice fellatio.

Women's images of themselves have also changed dramatically in the past two decades, due, in large part, to their movement into the workplace and roles previously filled exclusively by men. As Lilian Rubin, psychologist at the University of California Institute for the Study of Social Change and author of *Intimate Strangers,* puts it, "Women feel empowered sexually in a way they never did in the past."

Meanwhile, the singles scene, far from fading away (the media just lost its fixation on this subject), continues to grow. James Bennett, writing in *The New Republic,* characterizes this growing population of no-reproducers thusly: "Single adults in America display a remarkable tendency to multiply without being fruitful."

Their libidos are the target of million-dollar advertising budgets and entrepreneurial pursuits that seek to put those sex drives on line in the information age. From video dating to computer coupling to erotic faxing, it's now "love at first

From *Psychology Today*, January/February 1994, pp. 32-37, 64, 66. Excerpted from *Psychotrends: What Kind of People Are We Becoming?* by Shervert H. Frazier, M.D. © 1994 by Shervert H. Frazier, M.D. Reprinted by permission of Simon & Schuster, Inc.

byte," as one commentator put it. One thing is certain: the computer is doing as much today to promote the sexual revolution as the automobile did at the dawn of that revolution.

Political ideologies, buttressed by economic adversities, *can* temporarily retard the sexual revolution, as can sexually transmitted diseases. But ultimately the forces propelling this revolution are unstoppable. And ironically, AIDS itself is probably doing more to promote than impede this movement. It has forced the nation to confront a number of sexual issues with greater frankness than ever before. While some conservatives and many religious groups have argued for abstinence as the only moral response to AIDS, others have lobbied for wider dissemination of sexual information, beginning in grade schools. A number of school districts are now making condoms available to students—a development that would have been unthinkable before the outbreak of AIDS.

Despite all these gains (or losses, depending upon your outlook) the revolution is far from over. The openness that it has fostered is healthy, but Americans are still ignorant about many aspects of human sexuality. Sexual research is needed to help us deal with teen sexuality and pregnancies, AIDS, and a number of emotional issues related to sexuality. Suffice it to say for now that there is still plenty of room for the sexual revolution to proceed—and its greatest benefits have yet to be realized.

THE REVOLUTION AND RELATIONSHIPS

The idea that the Sexual Revolution is at odds with romance (not to mention tradition) is one that is widely held, even by some of those who endorse many of the revolution's apparent objectives. But there is nothing in our findings to indicate that romance and the sexual revolution are inimical—unless one's defense of romance disguises an agenda of traditional male dominance and the courtly illusion of intimacy and communication between the sexes.

The trend now, as we shall see, is away from illusion and toward—in transition, at least—a sometimes painful reality in which the sexes are finally making an honest effort to *understand* one another.

But to some, it may seem that the sexes are farther apart today than they

ever have been. The real gender gap, they say, is a communications gap so cavernous that only the most intrepid or foolhardy dare try to bridge it. Many look back at the Anita Hill affair and say that was the open declaration of war between the sexes.

The mistake many make, however, is saying that there has been a *recent* breakdown in those communications, hence all this new discontent. This conclusion usually goes unchallenged, but there is nothing in the data we have seen from past decades to indicate that sexual- and gender-related communication were ever better than they are today. On the contrary, a more thoughtful analysis makes it very clear they have always been *worse.*

What has changed is our *consciousness* about this issue. Problems in communication between the sexes have been masked for decades by a rigid social code that strictly prescribes other behavior. Communication between the sexes has long been preprogrammed by this code to produce an exchange that has been as superficial as it is oppressive. As this process begins to be exposed by its own inadequacies in a rapidly changing world, we suddenly discover that we have a problem. But, of course, that problem was there for a long time, and the discovery does not mean a decline in communication between the sexes but, rather, provides us with the potential for better relationships in the long run.

Thus what we call a "breakdown" in communications might more aptly be called a *breakthrough.*

Seymour Parker, of the University of Utah, demonstrated that men who are the most mannerly with women, those who adhere most strictly to the "code" discussed above, are those who most firmly believe, consciously or unconsciously, that women are "both physically and psychologically weaker (i.e., less capable) than men." What has long passed for male "respect" toward women in our society is, arguably, *disrespect.*

Yet what has been learned can be unlearned—especially if women force the issue, which is precisely what is happening now. Women's views of themselves are changing and that, more than anything, is working to eliminate many of the stereotypes that supported the image of women as weak and inferior. Women, far from letting men continue to dictate to them, are making it clear they want more *real* respect from men and will accept

nothing less. They want a genuine dialogue; they want men to recognize that they speak with a distinct and equal voice, not one that is merely ancillary to the male voice.

The sexual revolution made possible a serious inquiry into the ways that men and women are alike and the ways that each is unique. This revolutionary development promises to narrow the gender gap as nothing else can, for only by understanding the differences that make communication so complex do we stand any chance of mastering those complexities.

SUBTRENDS

Greater Equality Between the Sexes

Despite talk in the late 1980s and early 1990s of the decline of feminism and declarations that women, as a social and political force, are waning, equality between the sexes is closer to becoming a reality than ever before. Women command a greater workforce and wield greater political power than they have ever done. They are assuming positions in both public and private sectors that their mothers and grandmothers believed were unattainable (and their fathers and grandfathers thought were inappropriate) for women. Nonetheless, much remains to be achieved before women attain complete equality—but movement in that direction will continue at a pace that will surprise many over the next two decades.

Women voters, for example, who have long outnumbered male voters, are collectively a sleeping giant whose slumber many say was abruptly interrupted during the Clarence Thomas–Anita Hill hearings in 1991. The spectacle of a political "boy's club" raking the dignified Hill over the coals of sexual harassment galvanized the entire nation for days.

On another front, even though women have a long way to go to match men in terms of equal pay for equal work, as well as in equal opportunity, there is a definite *research* trend that shows women can match men in the skills needed to succeed in business. This growing body of data will make it more difficult for businesses to check the rise of women into the upper echelons of management and gradually help to change the corporate consciousness that still heavily favors male employees.

As for feminism, many a conservative wrote its obituary in the 1980s, only to find it risen from the dead in the 1990s. Actually, its demise was always imaginary. Movements make headway only in a context of dissatisfaction. And, clearly, there is still plenty for women to be dissatisfied about, particularly in the wake of a decade that tried to stifle meaningful change.

The "new feminism," as some call it, is less doctrinaire than the old, less extreme in the sense that it no longer has to be outrageous in order to call attention to itself. The movement today is less introspective, more goal oriented and pragmatic. Demands for liberation are superseded—and subsumed—by a well-organized quest for power. Women no longer want to burn bras, they want to manufacture and market them.

The New Masculinity

To say that the men's movement today is confused is to understate mercifully. Many men say they want to be more "sensitive" but also "less emasculated," "more open," yet "less vulnerable." While the early flux of this movement is often so extreme that it cannot but evoke guffaws, there is, nonetheless, something in it that commands some respect—for, in contrast with earlier generations of males, this one is making a real effort to examine and redefine itself. The movement, in a word, is *real.*

Innumerable studies and surveys find men dissatisfied with themselves and their roles in society. Part of this, undoubtedly, is the result of the displacement men are experiencing in a culture where *women* are so successfully transforming themselves. There is evidence, too, that men are dissatisfied because their own fathers were so unsuccessful in their emotional lives and were thus unable to impart to their sons a sense of love, belonging, and security that an increasing number of men say they sorely miss.

The trend has nothing to do with beating drums or becoming a "warrior." It relates to the human desire for connection, and this, in the long run, can only bode well for communications between humans in general and between the sexes in particular. Many psychologists believe men, in the next two decades, will be less emotionally closed than at any time in American history.

More (and Better) Senior Sex

People used to talk about sex after 40 as if it were some kind of novelty. Now it's sex after 60 and it's considered not only commonplace but healthy.

Some fear that expectations among the aged may outrun physiological ability and that exaggerated hopes, in some cases, will lead to new frustrations—or that improved health into old age will put pressure on seniors to remain sexually active beyond any "decent" desire to do so.

But most seem to welcome the trend toward extended sexuality. In fact, the desire for sex in later decades of life is *heightened,* studies suggest, by society's growing awareness and acceptance of sexual activity in later life.

Diversity of Sexual Expression

As sex shifts from its traditional reproductive role to one that is psychological, it increasingly serves the needs of the individual. In this context, forms of sexual expression that were previously proscribed are now tolerated and are, in some cases, increasingly viewed as no more nor less healthy than long-accepted forms of sexual behavior. Homosexuality, for example, has attained a level of acceptance unprecedented in our national history.

More Contraception, Less Abortion

Though abortion will remain legal under varying conditions in most, if not all, states, its use will continue to decline over the next two decades as more—and better-contraceptives become available. After a period of more than two decades in which drug companies shied away from contraceptive research, interest in this field is again growing. AIDS, a changed political climate, and renewed fears about the population explosion are all contributing to this change.

Additionally, scientific advances now point the way to safer, more effective, more convenient contraceptives. A male contraceptive that will be relatively side-effect free is finally within reach and should be achieved within the next decade, certainly the next two decades. Even more revolutionary in concept and probable impact is a vaccine, already tested in animals, that some predict will be available within 10 years—a vaccine that safely stops ovum maturation and thus makes conception impossible.

Religion and Sex: A More Forgiving Attitude

Just a couple of decades ago mainstream religion was monolithic in its condemnation of sex outside of marriage. Today the situation is quite different as major denominations across the land struggle with issues they previously wouldn't have touched, issues related to adultery, premarital sex, homosexuality, and so on.

A Special Committee on Human Sexuality, convened by the General Assembly of the Presbyterian Church (USA), for example, surprised many when it issued a report highly critical of the traditional "patriarchal structure of sexual relations," a structure the committee believes contributes, because of its repressiveness, to the proliferation of pornography and sexual violence.

All this will surely pale alongside the brave new world of virtual reality.

The same sort of thing has been happening in most other major denominations. It is safe to say that major changes are coming. Mainstream religion is beginning to perceive that the sexual revolution must be acknowledged and, to a significant degree, accommodated with new policies if these denominations are to remain in touch with present-day realities.

Expanding Sexual Entertainment

The use of sex to sell products, as well as to entertain, is increasing and can be expected to do so. The concept that "sex sells" is so well established that we need not belabor the point here. The explicitness of sexual advertising, however, may be curbed by recent research finding that highly explicit sexual content is so diverting that the viewer or reader tends to overlook the product entirely.

Sexual stereotyping will also be less prevalent in advertising in years to come. All this means, however, is that women will not be singled out as sex objects; they'll have plenty of male company, as is already the case. The female "bimbo" is now joined by the male "himbo" in ever-increasing numbers. Sexist advertising is still prevalent (e.g., male-oriented beer commercials) but should diminish as women gain in social and political power.

There's no doubt that films and TV have become more sexually permissive in the last two decades and are likely to continue in that direction for some time to come. But all this will surely pale alongside the brave (or brazen) new world of "cybersex" and virtual reality, the first erotic emanations of which may well be experienced by Americans in the coming two decades. Virtual reality aims to be just that—artificial, electronically induced experiences that are virtually indistinguishable from the real thing.

The sexual revolution, far from over, is in for some new, high-tech curves.

FROM BIOLOGY TO PSYCHOLOGY: THE NEW FAMILY OF THE MIND

Despite recent pronouncements that the traditional family is making a comeback, the evidence suggests that over the next two decades the nuclear family will share the same future as nuclear arms: there will be fewer of them, but those that remain will be better cared for.

Our longing for sources of nurturance has led us to redefine the family.

Demographers now believe that the number of families consisting of married couples with children will dwindle by yet another 12 percent by the year 2000. Meanwhile, single-parent households will continue to increase (up 41 percent over the past decade.) And household size will continue to decline (2.63 people in 1990 versus 3.14 in 1970). The number of households maintained by women, with no males present, has increased 300 percent since 1950 and will continue to rise into the 21st century.

Particularly alarming to some is the fact that an increasing number of people are choosing *never* to marry. And, throughout the developed world, the one-person household is now the fastest growing household category. To the traditionalists, this trend seems insidious—more than 25 percent of all households in the United States now consist of just one person.

There can be no doubt: the nuclear family has been vastly diminished, and it will continue to decline for some years, but at a more gradual pace. Indeed, there is a good chance that it will enjoy more stability in the next two decades than it did in the last two. Many of the very forces that were said to be weakening the traditional family may now make it stronger, though not more prevalent. Developing social changes have made traditional marriage more elective today, so that those who choose it may, increasingly, some psychologists believe, represent a subpopulation better suited to the situa-

tion and thus more likely to make a go of it.

As we try to understand new forms of family, we need to realize that the "traditional" family is not particularly traditional. Neither is it necessarily the healthiest form of family. The nuclear family has existed for only a brief moment in human history. Moreover, most people don't realize that no sooner had the nuclear family form peaked around the turn of the last century than erosion set in, which has continued ever since. For the past hundred years, reality has chipped away at this social icon, with increasing divorce and the movement of more women into the labor force. Yet our need for nurturance, security, and connectedness continues and, if anything, grows more acute as our illusions about the traditional family dissipate.

Our longing for more satisfying sources of nurturance has led us to virtually redefine the family, in terms of behavior, language, and law. These dramatic changes will intensify over the next two decades. The politics of family will be entirely transformed in that period. The process will not be without interruptions or setbacks. Some lower-court rulings may be overturned by a conservative U.S. Supreme Court, the traditional family will be revived in the headline from time to time, but the economic and psychological forces that for decades have been shaping these changes toward a more diverse family will continue to do so.

SUBTRENDS

Deceptively Declining Divorce Rate

The "good news" is largely illusory. Our prodigious national divorce rate, which more than doubled in one recent 10-year period, now shows signs of stabilization or even decline. Still, 50 percent of all marriages will break up in the next several years. And the leveling of the divorce rate is not due to stronger marriage but to *less* marriage. More people are skipping marriage altogether and are cohabiting instead.

The slight dip in the divorce rate in recent years has caused some prognosticators to predict that younger people, particularly those who've experienced the pain of growing up in broken homes, are increasingly committed to making marriage stick. Others, more persuasively, predict the opposite, that the present lull precedes a storm in which the divorce rate will soar to 60 percent or higher.

Increasing Cohabitation

The rate of cohabitation—living together without legal marriage—has been growing since 1970 and will accelerate in the next two decades. There were under half a million cohabiting couples in 1970; today there are more than 2.5. The trend for the postindustrial world is very clear: less marriage, more cohabitation, easier and—if Sweden is any indication—less stressful separation. Those who divorce will be less likely to remarry, more likely to cohabit. And in the United States, cohabitation will increasingly gather about it both the cultural acceptance and the legal protection now afforded marriage.

We need to realize the "traditional family" is not particularly traditional.

More Single-Parent Families and Planned Single Parenthood

The United States has one of the highest proportions of children growing up in single-parent families. More than one in five births in the United States is outside of marriage—and three quarters of those births are to women who are not in consensual unions.

What is significant about the single-parent trend is the finding that many single women with children now *prefer* to remain single. The rush to the altar of unwed mothers, so much a part of American life in earlier decades, is now, if anything, a slow and grudging shuffle. The stigma of single parenthood is largely a thing of the past—and the economic realities, unsatisfactory though they are, sometimes favor single parenthood. In any case, women have more choices today than they had even 10 years ago; they are choosing the psychological freedom of single parenthood over the financial security (increasingly illusory, in any event) of marriage.

More Couples Childless by Choice

In the topsy-turvy 1990s, with more single people wanting children, it shouldn't surprise us that more married couples *don't* want children. What the trend really comes down to is increased freedom of choice. One reason for increasing childlessness among couples has to do with the aging of the population, but many of the reasons are more purely psychological.

With a strong trend toward later marriage, many couples feel they are "too old" to have children. Others admit they like the economic advantages and relative freedom of being childless. Often both have careers they do not want to jeopardize by having children. In addition, a growing number of couples cite the need for lower population density, crime rates, and environmental concerns as reasons for not wanting children. The old idea that "there must be something wrong with them" if a couple does not reproduce is fast waning.

The One-Person Household

This is the fastest growing household category in the Western world. It has grown in the United States from about 10 percent in the 1950s to more than 25 percent of all households today. This is a trend that still has a long way to go. In Sweden, nearly *40 percent* of all households are now single person.

"Mr. Mom" a Reality at Last?

When women began pouring into the work force in the late 1970s, expectations were high that a real equality of the sexes was at hand and that men, at last, would begin to shoulder more of the household duties, including spending more time at home taking care of the kids. Many women now regard the concept of "Mr. Mom" as a cruel hoax; but, in fact, Mr. Mom *is* slowly emerging.

Men *are* showing more interest in the home and in parenting. Surveys make clear there is a continuing trend in that direction. Granted, part of the impetus for this is not so much a love of domestic work as it is a distaste for work outside the home. But there is also, among many men, a genuine desire to play a larger role in the lives of their children. These men say they feel "cheated" by having to work outside the home so much, cheated of the experience of seeing their children grow up.

As the trend toward more equal pay for women creeps along, gender roles in the home can be expected to undergo further change. Men will feel less pressure to take on more work and will feel more freedom to spend increased time with their families.

More Interracial Families

There are now about 600,000 interracial marriages annually in the United States, a third of these are black-white, nearly triple the number in 1970, when 40 percent of the white population was of the opinion that such marriages should be illegal. Today 20 percent hold that belief. There is every reason to expect that both the acceptance of and the number of interracial unions will continue to increase into the foreseeable future.

Recognition of Same-Sex Families

Family formation by gay and lesbian couples, with or without children, is often referenced by the media as a leading-edge signifier of just how far society has moved in the direction of diversity and individual choice in the family realm. The number of same-sex couples has steadily increased and now stands at 1.6 million such couples. There are an estimated 2 million gay parents in the United States.

And while most of these children were had in heterosexual relationships or marriages prior to "coming out," a significant number of gay and lesbian couples are having children through adoption, cooperative parenting arrangements, and artificial insemination. Within the next two decades, gays and lesbians will not only win the right to marry but will, like newly arrived immigrants, be some of the strongest proponents of traditional family values.

The Rise of Fictive Kinships

Multiadult households, typically consisting of unrelated singles, have been increasing in number for some years and are expected to continue to do so in coming years. For many, "roommates" are increasingly permanent fixtures in daily life.

In fact housemates are becoming what some sociologists and psychologists call "fictive kin." Whole "fictive families" are being generated in many of these situations, with some housemates even assigning roles ("brother," "sister," "cousin," "aunt," "mom," "dad," and so on) to one another. Fictive families are springing up among young people, old people, disabled people, homeless people, and may well define one of the ultimate evolutions of the family concept, maximizing, as they do, the opportunities for fulfillment of specific social and economic needs outside the constraints of biological relatedness.

THE BREAKUP OF THE NUCLEAR FAMILY

It's hard to tell how many times we've heard even well-informed health professionals blithely opine that "the breakup of the family is at the root of most of our problems." The *facts* disagree with this conclusion. Most of the social problems attributed to the dissolution of the "traditional" family (which, in reality, is *not* so traditional) are the product of other forces. Indeed, as we have seen, the nuclear family has itself created a number of economic, social, and psychological problems. To try to perpetuate a manifestly transient social institution beyond its usefulness is folly.

What *can* we do to save the nuclear family? Very little.

What *should* we do? Very little. Our concern should not be the maintenance of the nuclear family as a *moral* unit (which seems to be one of the priorities of the more ardent conservative "family values" forces), encompassing the special interests and values of a minority, but, rather, the strengthening of those social contracts that ensure the health, well-being, and freedom of individuals.

Is There Love After Baby?

Why the passage to parenthood rocks even the best of couples today: A cautionary tale.

Carolyn Pape Cowan, Ph.D., and Philip A. Cowan, Ph.D.

Carolyn Pape Cowan, Ph.D., and Philip A. Cowan, Ph.D., are co-directors of the Becoming a Family Project at the University of California at Berkeley. Carolyn codirects the Schoolchildren and Their Families Project and is the co-editor of Fatherhood Today: Men's Changing Roles in the Family. *Philip is the author of* Piaget: With Feeling, *and co-editor of* Family Transitions: Advances in Family Research, Vol. 2. *They are the parents of three grown children.*

Babies are getting a lot of bad press these days. Newspapers and magazine articles warn that the cost of raising a child from birth to adulthood is now hundreds of thousands of dollars. Television news recounts tragic stories of mothers who have harmed their babies while suffering from severe postpartum depression. Health professionals caution that child abuse has become a problem throughout our nation. Several books on how to "survive" parenthood suggest that parents must struggle to keep their marriage alive once they become parents. In fact, according to recent demographic studies, more than 40 percent of children born to two parents can expect to live in a single-parent family by the time they are 18. The once-happy endings to family beginnings are clouded with strain, violence, disenchantment, and divorce.

What is so difficult about becoming a family today? What does it mean that some couples are choosing to remain "child-free" because they fear that a child might threaten their well-established careers or disturb the intimacy of their marriage? Is keeping a family together harder than it used to be?

Over the last three decades, sociologists, psychologists, and psychiatrists have begun to search for the answers. Results of the most recent studies, including our own, show that partners who become parents describe:

• an ideology of more equal work and family roles than their mothers and fathers had;

• actual role arrangements in which husbands and wives are sharing family work and care of the baby less than either of them expected;

• more conflict and disagreement after the baby is born than they had reported before;

• and increasing disenchantment with their overall relationship as a couple.

To add to these disquieting trends, studies of emotional distress in new parents suggest that women and possibly men are more vulnerable to depression in the early months after having a child. Finally, in the United States close to 50 percent of couples who marry will ultimately divorce.

We believe that children are getting an unfair share of the blame for their parents' distress. Based on 15 years of research that includes a three-year pilot study, a 10-year study following 72 expectant couples and 24 couples without children, and ongoing work with couples in distress, we are convinced that the seeds of new parents' individual and marital problems are sown long before baby arrives. Becoming parents does not so much raise new problems as bring old unresolved issues to the surface.

Our concern about the high incidence of marital distress and divorce among the parents of young children led us to study systematically what happens to partners when they become parents. Rather than simply add to the mounting documentation of family problems, we created and evaluated a new preventive program, the Becoming a Family Project, in which mental-health professionals worked with couples during their transition to parenthood, trying to help them get off to a healthy start. Then we followed the families as the first children progressed from infancy through the first year of elementary school.

What we have learned is more trou-

From *Psychology Today*, July/August 1992, pp. 59-63, 78-79. Excerpted from *When Partners Become Parents: The Big Life Change for Couples*, by C. Philip and Carolyn Pape Cowan. © 1992 by Basic Books, Inc. Reprinted by permission.

bling than surprising. The majority of husbands and wives become more disenchanted with their couple relationship as they make the transition to parenthood. Most new mothers struggle with the question whether and when to return to work. For those who do go back, the impact on their families depends both on what mothers do at work and what fathers do at home. The more unhappy parents feel about their marriage, the more anger and competitiveness and the less warmth and responsiveness we observe in the family during the preschool period—between the parents as a couple and between each parent and the child. The children of parents with more tension during the preschool years have a harder time adjusting to the challenges of kindergarten.

or couples who thought having a baby was going to bring them closer together, the first few months are especially confusing and disappointing.

On the positive side, becoming a family provides a challenge that for some men and women leads to growth—as individuals, as couples, as parents. For couples who work to maintain or improve the quality of their marriage, having a baby can lead to a revitalized relationship. Couples with more satisfying marriages work together more effectively with their children in the preschool period, and their children tend to have an easier time adapting to the academic and social demands of elementary school. What is news is that the relationship *between* the parents seems to act as a crucible in which their relationships with their children take place.

The transition to parenthood is stressful even for well-functioning couples. In addition to distinctive inner changes, men's and women's roles change in very different ways when partners become parents. It seems to come as a great surprise to most of them that changes in some of their major roles affect their feelings about their overall

relationship. Both partners have to make major adjustments of time and energy as individuals at a time when they are getting less sleep and fewer opportunities to be together. They have less patience with things that didn't seem annoying before. Their frustration often focuses on each other. For couples who thought that having a baby was going to bring them closer together, this is especially confusing and disappointing.

Why does becoming a parent have such a powerful impact on a marriage? We have learned that one of the most difficult aspects of becoming a family is that so much of what happens is unexpected. Helping couples anticipate how they might handle the potentially stressful aspects of becoming a family can leave them feeling less vulnerable, less likely to blame each other for the hard parts, and more likely to decide that they can work it out before their distress permeates all of the relationships in the family.

But when things start to feel shaky, few husbands and wives know how to tell anyone, especially each other, that they feel disappointed or frightened. "This is supposed to be the best time of our lives; what's the matter with me?" a wife might say through her tears. They can't see that some of their tension may be attributable to the conflicting demands of the very complex stage of life, not simply to a suddenly stubborn, selfish, or unresponsive spouse.

Becoming a family today is more difficult than it used to be. Small nuclear families live more isolated lives in crowded cities, often feeling cut off from extended family and friends. Mothers of young children are entering the work force earlier; they are caught between traditional and modern conceptions of how they should be living their lives. Men and women are having a difficult time regaining their balance after having babies, in part because radical shifts in the circumstances surrounding family life in America demand new arrangements to accommodate the increasing demands on parents of young children. But new social arrangements and roles have simply not kept pace with the changes, leaving couples on their own to manage the demands of work and family.

News media accounts imply that as mothers have taken on more of a role in the world of paid work, fathers have taken on a comparable load of family work. But this has just not happened. It is not simply that men's and women's

roles are unequal that seems to be causing distress for couples, but rather that they are so clearly discrepant from what both spouses expected them to be. Women's work roles have changed, but their family roles have not. Well-intentioned and confused husbands feel guilty while their overburdened wives feel angry. It does not take much imagination to see how these emotions can fuel the fires of marital conflict.

Separate (Time)Tables

As they bring their first baby home from the hospital, new mothers and fathers find themselves crossing the great divide. After months of anticipation, their transition from couple to family becomes a reality. Entering this unfamiliar territory, men and women find themselves on different timetables and different trails of a journey they envisioned completing together.

Let's focus on the view from the inside, as men and women experience the shifting sense of self that comes with first-time parenthood. In order to understand how parents integrate Mother or Father as central components of their identity, we give couples a simple pie chart and ask them to think about the various aspects of their lives (worker, friend, daughter, father, so on) and mark off how large each portion feels, not how much time they spend "being it." The size of each piece of the pie reflects their psychologic involvement or investment in that aspect of themselves.

Almost all show pieces that represent parent, worker or student, and partner or lover. The most vivid identity changes during the transition to parenthood take place between pregnancy and six months postpartum. The part of the self that women call Mother takes up 10 percent of their pictures of themselves in late pregnancy. It then leaps to 34 percent six months after birth, and stays there through the second year of parenthood. For some women, the psychological investment in motherhood is much greater than the average.

Most of the husbands we interviewed took on the identity of parent more slowly than their wives did. During pregnancy, Father takes half as much of men's pie as their wives' Mother sections do, and when their children are 18 months old, husbands identity as parent is still less than one third as large as their wives'. We find that the larger the difference between husbands and wives in the size of their parent piece of the pie when their babies are six months old, the less satisfied both spouses are with the marriage, and the more their satisfaction declines over the next year.

The Big Squeeze

Men's and women's sense of themselves as parents is certainly expected to increase once they have had a baby. What comes as a surprise is that other central aspects of the self are getting short shrift as their parent piece of the pie expands. The greatest surprise—for us and for the couples—is what gets squeezed as new parents' identities shift. Women apportion 34 percent to the Partner or Lover aspect of themselves in pregnancy, 22 percent at six months after the birth, and 21 percent when their children are 18 months. Men's sense of themselves as Partner or Lover also shows a decline—from 35 percent to 30 percent to 25 percent over the two-year transition period.

The size of the Partner piece of the pie is connected to how new parents feel about themselves: A larger psychological investment in their relationship seems to be good for both of them. Six months after the birth of their first child, both men and women with larger Partner/Lover pieces have higher self-esteem and less parenting stress. This could mean that when parents resist the tendency to ignore their relationship as a couple, they feel better about themselves and less stressed as parents. Or that when they feel better about themselves they are more likely to stay moderately involved in their relationship.

At our 18-month follow-up, Stephanie and Art talk about the consequences for their marriage of trying to balance—within them and between them—the pulls among the Parent, Worker, and Partner aspects.

Stephanie: We're managing Linda really well. But with Art's promotion from teacher to principal and my going back to work and feeling guilty about being away from Linda, we don't get much time for *us*. I try to make time for the two of us at home, but there's no point in making time to be with somebody if he doesn't want to be with you. Sometimes when we finally get everything done and Linda is asleep, I want to sit down and talk, but Art says this is a perfect opportunity to get some prepara-

tion done for one of his teachers' meetings. Or he starts to fix one of Linda's toys—things that apparently are more important to him than spending time with me.

Art: That does happen. But Stephanie's wrong when she says that those things are more important to me than she is. The end of the day is just not my best time to start a deep conversation. I keep asking her to get a sitter so we can go out for a quiet dinner, but she always finds a reason not to. It's like being turned down for a date week after week.

Stephanie: Art, you know I'd love to go out with you. I just don't think we can leave Linda so often.

Stephanie and Art are looking at the problem from their separate vantage points. Art is very devoted to fatherhood, but is more psychologically invested in his relationship with Stephanie than with Linda. In his struggle to hold onto himself as Partner, he makes the reasonable request that he and Stephanie spend some time alone so they can nurture their relationship as a couple. Stephanie struggles with other parts of her shifting sense of self. Although Art knows that Stephanie spends a great deal of time with Linda when she gets home from work, he does not understand that juggling her increasing involvement as Mother while trying to maintain her investment as Worker is creating a great deal of internal pressure for her. The Partner/Lover part of Stephanie is getting squeezed not only by time demands but also by the psychological reshuffling that is taking place inside her. Art knows only that Stephanie is not responding to his needs, and to him her behavior seems unreasonable, insensitive, and rejecting.

Stephanie knows that Art's view of himself has changed as he has become a parent, but she is unaware of the fact that it has not changed in the same way or to the same degree as hers. In fact, typical of the men in our study, Art's psychological investment in their relationship as couple has declined slightly since Linda was born, but his Worker identity has not changed much. He is proud and pleased to be a father, but these feelings are not crowding out his sense of himself as a Partner/Lover. All Stephanie knows is that Art is repeatedly asking her to go out to dinner and ignoring her inner turmoil. To her, his behavior seems unreasonable, insensitive, and rejecting.

It might have been tempting to con-

clude that it is natural for psychological involvement in one's identity as Partner or Lover to wane over time—but the patterns of the childless couples refute that. The internal changes in each of the new parents begin to have an impact on their relationship as a couple. When women add Mother to their identity, *both* Worker and Partner/Lover get squeezed. As some parts of identity grow larger, there is less "room" for others. The challenge, then, is how to allow Parent a central place in one's identity without abandoning or neglecting Partner. We find that couples who manage to do this feel better about themselves as individuals and as couples.

Who Does What?

How do new parents' internal shifts in identity, and their separate timetables, play out in their marriage? We find that "who does what?" issues are central not only in how husbands and wives feel about themselves, but in how they feel about their marriage. Second, there are alternations in the emotional fabric of the couple's relationship; how caring and intimacy get expressed and how couples manage their conflict and disagreement have a direct effect on their marital satisfaction.

Husbands and wives, different to begin with, become even more separate and distinct in their years after their first child is born. An increasing specialization of family roles and emotional distance between partners-become-parents combine to affect their satisfaction with the relationship.

Behind today's ideology of the egalitarian couple lies a much more traditional reality. Although more than half of mothers with children under five have entered the labor force and contemporary fathers have been taking a small but significantly greater role in cooking, cleaning, and looking after their children than fathers used to do, women continue to carry the overwhelming responsibility for managing the household and caring for the children. Women have the primary responsibility for family work even when both partners are employed full time.

Couples whose division of household and family tasks was not equitable when they began our study tended to predict that it would be after the baby was born. They never expected to split baby care 50-50 but to work as a team in rearing their children. Once the babies are born, however, the women do more of the housework than before they became mothers, and the men do much less of the care of the baby than they or their wives predicted they would. After children appear, a couple's role arrangements—and how both husband and wife feel about them—become entwined with their intimacy.

Ideology vs Reality

In both expectant and childless couples, spouses divide up the overall burden of family tasks fairly equitably. But new parents begin to divide up these tasks in more gender-stereotyped ways. Instead of both partners performing some of each task, he tends to take on a few specific household responsibilities and she tends to do most of the others. His and her overall responsibility for maintaining the household may not shift significantly after having a baby, but it feels more traditional because each has become more specialized.

In the last trimester of pregnancy, men and women predict that the mothers will be responsible for more of the baby care tasks than the father. Nine months later, when the babies are six months old, a majority describe their arrangements as even more Mother's and less Father's responsibility than either had predicted. Among parents of six-month-old babies, mothers are shouldering more of the baby care than either parent predicted on eight of 12 items on our questionnaire: deciding about meals, managing mealtime, diapering, bathing, taking the baby out, playing with the baby, arranging for baby sitters, and dealing with the pediatrician. On four items, women and men predicted that mothers would do more and their expectations proved to be on the mark: responding to baby's cries, getting up in the middle of the night, doing the child's laundry, and choosing the baby's toys.

From this we contend that the ideology of the new egalitarian couple is way ahead of the reality. The fallout from their unmet expectations seems to convert both spouses' surprise and disappointment into tension between them.

Jackson and Tanya talked a lot about their commitment to raising Kevin together. Three months later, when the baby was six months old, Tanya explained that Jackson had begun to do more housework than ever before but

that he wasn't available for Kevin nearly as much as she would have liked.

Tanya: He wasn't being a chauvinist or anything, expecting me to do everything and him nothing. He just didn't *volunteer* to do things that obviously needed doing, so I had to put down some ground rules. Like if I'm in a bad mood, I may just yell: "I work eight hours just like you. This is half your house and half your child, too. You've got to do your share!" Jackson never changed the kitty litter box once in four years, but he changes it now, so we've made great progress. I just didn't expect it to take so much work. We planned this child together and we went through Lamaze together, and Jackson stayed home for the first two weeks. But then—wham—the partnership was over.

Tanya underscores a theme we hear over and over: The tension between new parents about the father's involvement in the family threatens the intimacy between them.

The fact that mothers are doing most of the primary child care in the first months of parenthood is hardly news. What we are demonstrating is that the couples' arrangements for taking care of their infants are *less equitable* than they expected them to be. They are amazed they became so traditional so fast.

It's not just that couples are startled by how the division of labor falls along gender lines, but they describe the change as if it were a mysterious virus they picked up while in the hospital having their baby. They don't seem to view their arrangements as *choices* they have made.

Husbands' and wives' descriptions of their division of labor are quite similar but they do shade things differently: Each claims to be doing more than the other gives him or her credit for. The feeling of not being appreciated for the endless amount of work each partner actually does undoubtedly increases the tension between them. Compared with the childless couples, new parents' overall satisfaction with their role arrangements (household tasks plus decision making plus child care) declined significantly—most dramatically between pregnancy and six months after baby's birth.

Parents who had been in one of our couples groups maintained their satisfaction with the division of household and family tasks. This trend is particularly true for women. Since the actual role arrangement in the group and non-

group participants were very similar, we can see that men's and women's satisfactions with who does what is, at least in part, a matter of perspective.

Some men and women are happy with traditional arrangements. Most of the men in our study, however, wanted desperately to have a central role in their child's life.

Is There Sex after Parenthood?

Most new parents feel some disenchantment in their marriage. It is tempting to blame this on two related facts reported by every couple. First, after having a baby, *time* becomes their most precious commodity. Second, even if a couple can eke out a little time together, the effort seems to require a major mobilization of forces. They feel none of the spontaneity that kept their relationship alive when they were a twosome.

We asked husbands and wives what they do to show their partners that they care. It soon became clear that different things feel caring to different people: bringing flowers or special surprises,

The division of workload in the family wins hands down as the issue most likely to cause conflict in the first two years.

being a good listener, touching in certain ways, picking up the cleaning without being asked.

New parents describe fewer examples of caring after having a baby compared to before, but as we keep finding in each domain of family life, men's and women's changes occur at different times. Between the babies' six- and 18-month birthdays, wives and husbands report that the women are doing fewer caring things for their husbands than the year before. In the parents' natural preoccupation with caring for baby, they seem less able to care for each other.

Both husbands and wives also report a negative change in their sexual relationship after having a baby. The frequency of lovemaking declines for almost all couples in the early months of parenthood.

There are both physical and psychological deterrents to pleasurable sex for new parents. Probably the greatest interference with what happens in the bedroom comes from what happens between the partners outside the bedroom. Martin and Sandi, for example, tell us that making love has become problematic since Ellen's birth. To give an example of a recent disappointment, Martin explains that he had had an extremely stressful day at work. Sandi greeted him with a "tirade" about Ellen's fussy day, the plumber failing to come, and the baby-sitter's latest illness. Dinnertime was tense, and they spent the rest of the evening in different rooms. When they got into bed they watched TV for a few minutes, and then Martin reached out to touch Sandi. She pulled away, feeling guilty that she was not ready to make love.

Like so many couples, they were disregarding the tensions that had been building up over the previous hours. They had never had a chance to talk in anything like a collaborative or intimate way. This is the first step of the common scenario for one or both partners to feel "not in the mood."

Ninety-two percent of the men and women in our study who became parents described more conflict after having their baby than before they became parents. The division of workload in the family wins hands down as the issue most likely to cause conflict in the first two years. Women feel the impact of the transition more strongly during the first six months after birth, and their husbands feel it more strongly in the following year.

Why does satisfaction with marriage go down? It begins, we think, with the issue of men's and women's roles. The new ideology of egalitarian relationships between men and women has made some inroads on the work front. Most couples, however, are not prepared for the strain of creating more egalitarian relationships at home, and it is this strain that leads men and women to feel more negatively about their partners and the state of their marriage.

Men's increasing involvement in the preparation for the *day* of the baby's birth leads both spouses to expect that he will be involved in what follows—— the ongoing daily care and rearing of the children. How ironic that the recent widespread participation of fathers in the births of their babies has become a source of new parents' disappointment when the men do not stay involved in their babies' early care.

The transition to parenthood heightens the differences between men and women, which leads to more conflict between them. This, in turn, threaten the equilibrium of their marriage.

Needed: Couples Groups

Family making is a joint endeavor, not just during pregnancy, but in the years to come. Men simply have little access to settings in which they can share their experiences about intimate family matters. Given how stressful family life is for so many couples, we feel it is important to help them understand how their increasing differences during this transition may be generating more distance between them. Most couples must rebalance of the relationship.

Our results show that when sensitive group leaders help men and women focus on what is happening to them as individuals and as a couple during their transition to parenthood, it buffers them from turning their strain into dissatisfaction with each other. Why intervene with couples in *groups*? We find that a group setting provides the kind of support that contemporary couples often lack.

Groups of people going through similar life experiences help participants "normalize" some of their strain and adjustment difficulties; they discover that the strain they are experiencing is expectable at this stage of life. This can strengthen the bond between husbands and wives and undercut their tendency to blame each other for their distress.

Group discussions, by encouraging partners to keep a focus on their couple relationship, help the women maintain their identity as Partner/Lover while they are taking on Motherhood and returning to their jobs and careers. Fathers become painfully aware of what it takes to manage a demanding job and the day-to-day care of a household with baby.

The modern journey to parenthood, exciting and fulfilling as it is, is beset with many roadblocks. Most couples experience stress in the early years of family life. Most men and women need to muster all the strength and skills they have to make this journey. Almost all of the parents in our studies say that the joyful parts outweigh the difficult ones. They also say that the lessons they learn along the way are powerful and well worth the effort.

The Lifelong Impact of ADOPTION

In many cases, birthparents have trouble dealing with giving up their offspring; adoptees want to know more about their biological roots and genetic history; and adoptive parents are being confronted with issues concerning the raising of their adopted children that no one had warned them about.

Marlou Russell

Dr. Russell is a clinical psychologist in private practice in Santa Monica, Calif., specializing in adoption. She is an adoptee who has been reunited with her birthmother and two brothers.

IMAGINE BEING an adoptive parent who has gone through years of infertility treatment. You recently have adopted an infant and are at a party with it. Someone exclaims, "What a cute baby. Why, I didn't even know you were pregnant!" You wonder if you need to explain.

Now, try to imagine being a birthmother who relinquished a child 25 years ago. You since have married and had two more offspring. You strike up a conversation with someone you've just met. She asks, "How many children do you have?" You hesitate for a moment, then answer, "Two."

Finally, imagine that you were adopted as an infant. You have an appointment to see a new physician for the first time. When you arrive at the office, you are given a two-page form asking for your medical history. When you meet the doctor, he asks, "Does cancer run in your family?" You respond, "I don't know."

The adoption triad has three elements: the adoptive parent or parents, the birthparents, and the adoptee. All members are

necessary and all depend on each other, as in any triangle.

There have been many changes in adoption over the years. The basic premise of adoption in the past was that it was a viable solution to certain problem situations. The infertile parents wanted a child; a birthparent was pregnant and unable to raise her offspring; and the infant needed available parents. It was thought that all the triad members would get their needs met by adoption. The records were amended, sealed, and closed through legal proceedings, and the triad members were expected never to see each other again.

It was discovered, however, that there were problems with closed adoption. Some birthparents began having trouble "forgetting" that they had had a child and were finding it hard "getting on with their lives," as suggested by those around them. There were adoptees who wanted to know more about their biological roots and had questions about their genetic history. Some adoptive parents were having difficulties raising their adopted children and were being confronted with parenting issues that no one had told them about.

Clinicians and psychotherapists became involved because more and more adopted children were being brought in for psychotherapy and being seen in juvenile deten-

tion facilities, inpatient treatment centers, and special schools. Questions began to be raised about the impact and process of closed adoption.

From these questions, it became clear that there are new basic tenets in adoption. One is that adoption usually is a second choice for all the triad members. For example, most people don't imagine that they will grow up, get married, and adopt children. They expect that they will grow up, get married, and have kids of their own. Girls and/or women also don't expect to get pregnant and give their child to strangers to raise.

Coping with loss

A second basic tenet of adoption is that it involves loss for all involved. A birthparent loses a child; the adoptee loses biological connections; and infertile adoptive parents lose the hope for biological children. Those indirectly involved in adoption also experience loss. The birthparents' parents lose a grandchild, while the siblings of the birthparent lose a niece or nephew.

Since loss is such a major part of adoption, grieving is a necessary and important process. The five stages of normal grief and mourning, as set forth by psychologist

Elisabeth Kübler-Ross, are denial—feeling shocked, numbed, and detached; anger—maintaining that the situation is unfair; bargaining—wanting to make a deal or trade-off; depression—feeling helpless and hopeless; and acceptance—integrating and resolving the loss enough to function.

For triad members, grief holds a special significance. They may not even be aware that they are grieving or mourning their loss. Adoption can create a situation where grieving is delayed or denied. Because adoption has been seen as such a positive solution, it may be difficult for a triad member to feel that it is okay to grieve when everything is "working out for the best."

There are no rituals or ceremonies for the loss of adoption. In the case of death, society provides the rituals of funerals and the gathering of people to support the person who is mourning. If the adoption process is secret, as was the case in many adoptions of the past, there is even less opportunity for mourning. In addition, with adoption, much attention is given to the next step of raising the child or getting on with one's life.

Some triad members resolve their grief by trying to find the person they are grieving for. Search and reunion offers the opportunity to address the basic and natural curiosity that all people have in their inheritance and roots. The missing pieces can be put in the puzzle, and lifelong questions can be answered. In addition, there is an empowering aspect to search and reunion and an internal sense of timing that brings with it a feeling of being in control and trusting one's own judgment. For most people who search, knowing—even if they find uncomfortable information—is better than not knowing.

Whether someone actively searches or not, there usually is some part of the person that is searching internally. A common experience among adoptees and birthparents is scanning crowds, looking for someone who could be their parent or their child. Even triad members who say they aren't interested in seeking will express curiosity and react to the idea of search and reunion.

What holds many triad members back from searching or admitting they are doing so is the fear of causing pain to one of the other triad members. Adoptees may worry about hurting their adoptive parents' feelings and appearing to be ungrateful, while birthparents may be concerned that their child wasn't told of the adoption or that he or she will reject them.

Reunion between triad members is the beginning of a previous relationship. It is where fantasy meets reality. Reunions impact all triad members and those close to them. As with other relationships, there has to be nurturing, attention, and a respect for people's boundaries and needs. Reunions and the interactions within them show that adoption was not just a simple solution, but a process that has lifelong impact.

WHEN VIOLENCE HITS HOME

Suddenly, domestic abuse,
once perniciously silent, is
exposed for its brutality in the
wake of a highly public scandal

JILL SMOLOWE

DANA USED TO HIDE THE BRUISES ON HER neck with her long red hair. On June 18, her husband made sure she could not afford even that strand of camouflage. Ted ambushed Dana (not their real names) as she walked from her car to a crafts\store in Denver. Slashing with a knife, Ted, a pharmaceutical scientist, lopped off Dana's ponytail, then grabbed her throat, adding a fresh layer of bruises to her neck.

Dana got off easy that time. Last year she lost most of her hearing after Ted slammed her against the living-room wall of their home and kicked her repeatedly in the head, then stuffed her unconscious body into the fireplace. Later, he was tearfully despondent, and Dana, a former social worker, believed his apologies, believed he needed her, believed him when he whispered, "I love you more than anything in the world." She kept on believing, even when more assaults followed.

Last Tuesday, however, Dana finally came to believe her life was in danger. Her change of mind came as she nursed her latest wounds, mesmerized by the reports about Nicole Simpson's tempestuous marriage to ex-football star O.J. "I grew up idolizing him," she says. "I didn't want to believe it was O.J. It was just like with my husband." Then, she says, "the reality hit me. Her story is the same as mine—except she's dead."

THE HORROR HAS ALWAYS BEEN WITH US, A PERSIStent secret, silent and pernicious, intimate and brutal. Now, however, as a result of the Simpson drama, Americans are confronting the ferocious violence that may erupt when love runs awry. Women who have clung to destructive relationships for years are realizing, like Dana, that they may be in dire jeopardy. Last week phone calls to domestic-violence hot lines surged to record numbers; many battered women suddenly found the strength to quit their homes and seek sanctuary in shelters. Although it has been two years since the American Medical As-

❝Women are at more risk of being killed by their

sociation reported that as many as 1 in 3 women will be assaulted by a domestic partner in her lifetime—4 million in any given year—it has taken the murder of Nicole Simpson to give national resonance to those numbers.

"Everyone is acting as if this is so shocking," says Debbie Tucker, chairman of the national Domestic Violence Coalition on Public Policy. "This happens all the time." In Los Angeles, where calls to abuse hot lines were up 80% overall last week, experts sense a sort of awakening as women relate personally to Simpson's tragedy. "Often a woman who's been battered thinks it's happening only to her. But with this story, women are saying, 'Oh, my God, this is what's happening to me,'" says Lynn Moriarty, director of the Family Violence Project of Jewish Family Services in Los Angeles. "Something as dramatic as this cracks through a lot of the denial."

Time and again, Health and Human Services Secretary Donna Shalala has warned, "Domestic violence is an unacknowledged epidemic in our society." Now, finally, lawmakers are not only listening—they are acting. In New York last week, the state legislature unanimously passed a sweeping bill that mandates arrest for any person who commits a domestic assault. Members of the California legislature are pressing for a computerized registry of restraining orders and the confiscation of guns from men arrested for domestic violence. This week Colorado's package of anti-domestic-violence laws, one of the nation's toughest, will go into effect. It not only compels police to take abusers into custody at the scene of violence but also requires arrest for a first violation of a restraining order. Subsequent violations bring mandatory jail time.

Just as women's groups used the Anita Hill–Clarence Thomas hearings as a springboard to educate the public about sexual harassment, they are now capitalizing on the Simpson controversy to further their campaign against domestic violence. Advocates for women are pressing for passage of the Violence Against Women Act, which is appended to the anticrime bill that legislators hope to have on President Clinton's desk by July 4. Modeled on the Civil Rights Act of 1964, it stipulates that gender-biased crimes violate a woman's civil rights. The victims of such crimes would therefore be eligible for compensatory relief and punitive damages.

Heightened awareness may also help add bite to laws that are on the books but are often underenforced. At present, 25 states require arrest when a reported domestic dispute turns violent. But police often walk away if the victim refuses to press charges. Though they act quickly to separate strangers, law-enforcement officials remain wary of interfering in domestic altercations, convinced that such battles are more private and less serious.

Yet, of the 5,745 women murdered in 1991, 6 out of 10 were killed by someone they knew. Half were murdered by a spouse or someone with whom they had been intimate. And that does not even hint at the level of violence against women by loved ones: while only a tiny percentage of all assaults on women result in death, the violence often involves severe physical or psychological damage. Says psychologist Angela Browne, a pioneering researcher in partner violence: "Women are at more risk of being killed by their current or former male partners than by any other kind of assault."

AFTER DANA DECIDED TO LEAVE TED IN MAY, SHE used all the legal weapons at her disposal to protect herself. She got a restraining order, filed for a divorce and found a new place to live. But none of that gave her a new life. Ted phoned repeatedly and stalked her. The restraining order seemed only to provoke his rage. On Memorial Day, he trailed her to a shopping-mall parking garage and looped a rope around her neck. He dragged her along the cement floor and growled, "If I can't have you, no one will." Bystanders watched in shock. But no one intervened.

After Ted broke into her home while she was away, Dana called the police. When she produced her protective order, she was told, "We don't put people in jail for breaking a restraining order." Dana expected little better after Ted came at her with the knife on June 18. But this time a female cop, herself a battering victim, encouraged Dana to seek shelter. On Tuesday, Dana checked herself into a shelter for battered women. There, she sleeps on a floor with her two closest friends, Sam and Odie—two cats. Odie is a survivor too. Two months ago, Ted tried to flush him down a toilet.

THOUGH DOMESTIC VIOLENCE USUALLY GOES UNDETECTED by neighbors, there is a predictable progression to relationships that end in murder. Typically it begins either with a steady diet of battery or isolated incidents of violence that can go on for years. Often the drama is fueled by both parties. A man wages an assault. The woman retaliates by deliberately trying to provoke his jealousy or anger. He strikes again. And the cycle repeats, with the two locked in a sick battle that binds—and reassures—even as it divides.

When the relationship is in risk of permanent rupture, the violence escalates. At that point the abused female may seek help outside the home, but frequently the man will refuse counseling, convinced that she, not he, is at fault. Instead he will reassert his authority by stepping up the assaults. "Battering is about maintaining power and dominance in a relationship," says Dick Bathrick, an instructor at the Atlanta-based Men Stopping Violence, a domestic-violence intervention group. "Men who batter believe that they have the right to do whatever it takes to regain control."

When the woman decides she has had enough, she may move out or demand that her partner leave. But "the men sometimes panic about losing [their women] and will do anything to prevent it from happening," says Deborah Burk, an Atlanta prosecutor.

male partners than by any other kind of assault.

"The men who batter believe that they have the

To combat feelings of helplessness and powerlessness, the man may stalk the woman or harass her by phone.

Women are most in danger when they seek to put a firm end to an abusive relationship. Experts warn that the two actions most likely to trigger deadly assault are moving out of a shared residence and beginning a relationship with another man. "There aren't many issues that arouse greater passion than infidelity and abandonment," says Dr. Park Dietz, a forensic psychiatrist who is a leading expert on homicide.

Disturbingly, the very pieces of paper designed to protect women—divorce decrees, arrest warrants, court orders of protection—are often read by enraged men as a license to kill. "A restraining order is a way of getting killed faster," warns Dietz. "Someone who is truly dangerous will see this as an extreme denial of what he's entitled to, his God-given right." That slip of paper, which documents his loss, may be interpreted by the man as a threat to his own life. "In a last-ditch, nihilistic act," says Roland Maiuro, director of Seattle's Harborview Anger Management and Domestic Violence Program, "he will engage in behavior that destroys the source of that threat." And in the expanding range of rage, victims can include children, a woman's lawyer, the judge who issues the restraining order, the cop who comes between. Anyone in the way.

For that reason, not all battered women's organizations support the proliferating mandatory arrest laws. That puts them into an unlikely alliance with the police organizations that were critical of New York's tough new bill. "There are cases," argues Francis Looney, counsel to the New York State Association of Chiefs of Police, "where discretion may be used to the better interest of the family."

Proponents of mandatory-arrest laws counter that education, not discretion, is required. "I'd like to see better implementation of the laws we have," says Vickie Smith, executive director of the Illinois Coalition Against Domestic Violence. "We work to train police officers, judges and prosecutors about why they need to enforce them."

"I TOOK IT VERY SERIOUSLY, THE MARRIAGE, THE commitment. I wanted more than anything to make it work." Dana's eyes are bright, her smile engaging, as she sips a soda in the shelter and tries to explain what held her in thrall to Ted for so many years. Only the hesitation in her voice betrays her anxiety. "There was a fear of losing him, that he couldn't take care of himself."

Though Dana believed the beatings were unprovoked and often came without warning, she blamed herself. "I used to think, 'Maybe I could have done things better. Maybe if I had bought him one more Mont Blanc pen.'" In the wake of Nicole Simpson's slaying, Dana now says that she was Ted's "prisoner." "I still loved him," she says, trying to explain her servitude. "It didn't go away. I didn't want to face the fact that I was battered."

IT IS IMPOSSIBLE TO CLASSIFY THE WOMEN WHO are at risk of being slain by a partner. Although the men who kill often abuse alcohol or drugs, suffer from personality disorders, have histories of head injuries or witnessed abuse in their childhood homes, such signs are often masterfully cloaked. "For the most part, these are people who are functioning normally in the real world," says Bathrick of Men Stopping Violence. "They're not punching out their bosses or jumping in cops' faces. They're just committing crimes in the home."

The popular tendency is to dismiss or even forgive the act as a "crime of passion." But that rush of so-called passion is months, even years, in the making. "There are few cases where murder comes out of the blue," says Sally Goldfarb, senior staff attorney for the NOW Legal Defense and Education Fund. "What we are talking about is domestic violence left unchecked and carried to its ultimate outcome." Abuse experts also decry the argument that a man's obsessive love can drive him beyond all control. "Men who are violent are rarely completely out of control," psychologist Browne argues. "If they were, many more women would be dead."

Some researchers believe there is a physiological factor in domestic abuse. A study conducted by the University of Massachusetts Medical Center's domestic-violence research and treatment center found, for instance, that 61% of men involved in marital violence have signs of severe head trauma. "The typical injuries involve the frontal lobe," says Al Rosenbaum, the center's director. "The areas we suspect are injured are those involved in impulse control, and reduce an individual's ability to control aggressive impulses."

Researchers say they can also distinguish two types among the men most likely to kill their wives: the "loose cannon" with impulse-control problems, and those who are calculated and focused, whose heart rate drops even as they prepare to do violence to their partners. The latter group may be the more dangerous. Says Neil Jacobson, a psychology professor at the University of Washington: "Our research

right to do whatever it takes to regain control."

"I didn't want to face the fact I was battered."

shows that those men who calm down physiologically when they start arguing with their wives are the most aggressive during arguments."

There may be other psycho-physiological links to violence. It is known, for instance, that alcohol and drug abuse often go hand in hand with spousal abuse. So does mental illness. A 1988 study by Maiuro of Seattle's domestic-violence program documented some level of depression in two-thirds of the men who manifested violent and aggressive behavior. Maiuro is pioneering work with Paxil, an antidepressant that, like Prozac, regulates the brain chemical serotonin. He reports that "it appears to be having some benefits" on his subjects.

Most studies, however, deal not with battering as an aftereffect of biology but of violence as learned behavior. Fully 80% of the male participants in a Minneapolis, Minnesota, violence-control program grew up in homes where they saw or were victims of physical, sexual or other abuse. Women who have witnessed abuse in their childhood homes are also at greater risk of reliving such dramas later in their lives, unless counseling is sought to break the generational cycle. "As a child, if you learn that violence is how you get what you want, you get a dysfunctional view of relationships," says Barbara Schroeder, a domestic-violence counselor in Oak Park, Illinois. "You come to see violence as an O.K. part of a loving relationship."

The cruelest paradox is that when a woman is murdered by a loved one, people are far more inclined to ask, "Why didn't she leave?" than "Why did he do that?" The question of leaving not only reflects an ingrained societal assumption that women bear primary responsibility for halting abuse in a relationship; it also suggests that a battered woman has the power to douse a raging man's anger—and to do it at a moment when her own strength is at an ebb. "It's quite common with women who have been abused that they don't hold themselves in high esteem," says Dr. Allwyn Levine, a Ridgewood, New Jersey, forensic psychiatrist who evaluates abusers for the court system. "Most of these women really feel they deserve it." Furthermore, says Susan Forward, the psychoanalyst who counseled Nicole Simpson on two occasions, "too many therapists will say, 'How did it feel when he was hitting you?' instead of addressing the issue of getting the woman away from the abuser."

Most tragically, a woman may have a self-image that does not allow her to see herself—or those nearby to see her—as a victim. Speaking of her sister Nicole Simpson, Denise Brown told the New York *Times* last week, "She was not a battered woman. My definition of a battered woman is somebody who gets beat up all the time. I don't want people to think it was like that. I know Nicole. She was a very strong-willed person."

Such perceptions are slowly beginning to change, again as a direct result of Simpson's slaying. "Before, women were ashamed," says Peggy Kerns, a Colorado state legislator. "Simpson has almost legitimized the concerns and fears around domestic violence. This case is telling them, 'It's not your fault.'" The women who phoned hot lines last week seemed emboldened to speak openly about the abuse in their lives. "A woman told me right off this week about how she was hit with a bat," says Carole Saylor, a Denver nurse who treats battered women. "Before, there might have been excuses. She would have said that she ran into a wall."

Abusive men are also taking a lesson from the controversy. The hot lines are ringing with calls from men who ask if their own conduct constitutes abusive behavior, or who say that they want to stop battering a loved one but don't know how. Others have been frightened by the charges against O.J. Simpson and voice fears about their own capacity to do harm. "They're worried they could kill," says Rob Gallup, executive director of AMEND, a Denver-based violence prevention and intervention group. "They figure, 'If [O.J.] had this fame and happiness, and chose to kill, then what's to prevent me?'"

EVEN IF DANA IS ABLE TO HOLD TED AT BAY, THE DAMage he has inflicted on her both physically and psychologically will never go away. Doctors have told her that her hearing will never be restored and that she is likely to become totally deaf within the decade. She is now brushing up the sign-language skills she learned years ago while working with deaf youngsters. At the moment, she is making do with a single set of hearing aids. Ted stole her other pair.

Dana reflects on her narrow escape. But she knows that her refuge in the shelter is only temporary. As the days go by, she grows increasingly resentful of her past, fearful of her present, and uncertain about her future. "I don't know when I'll be leaving, or where I'll be going."

And Ted is still out there.

—Reported by

Ann Blackman/Washington, Wendy Cole/Chicago, Scott Norvell/Atlanta, Elizabeth Rudulph and Andrea Sachs/ New York and Richard Woodbury/Denver

Development during Middle and Late Adulthood

- **Middle Adulthood (Articles 46–49)**
- **Late Adulthood (Articles 50–53)**

Middle and late adulthood are characterized by very gradual physical decline. The "use it or lose it" theory of decline probably has some merit physically. Research suggests that people who use their muscles retain more strength; people who exercise regularly retain more stamina for exertion; and people who engage in more frequent sex retain the ability to have sex throughout their lives. Despite retention related to exercise, there is a gradual slowing of the rate at which the cells of all the organ systems (except the central nervous system) replace themselves by mitosis. Thus, senses, cardiovascular fitness, respiratory fitness, the immune response, the skin, the digestive processes, the hormone responses, the urinary efficiency, and even the skeleton show aging changes. The spinal column "settles" slightly as the connective tissues and spinal disks lose materials, causing a decrease in height. The decreased height associated with aging is also related to weakening back muscles and demineralization of bones. The bones of women tend to lose minerals and become brittle more rapidly than the bones of men. This is believed to be related to the loss of estrogenic hormones that comes with age, especially after menopause. Women can reduce the bone demineralization (osteoporosis) by increasing their calcium intake throughout their lives, and especially after menopause.

Nutrition is quite clearly related to the changes of aging. Not only do persons with more adequate calcium intake retain bone strength longer, but persons with more adequate fruit, vegetable, and complex carbohydrate (starch) intake retain general good health longer. Diets high in refined sugars and saturated fats are associated with many human disease processes, such as cardiovascular illness and cancer, and with earlier death.

There are sex differences in morbidity (illness) and mortality (death) favoring women. Men tend to have more serious health problems, especially cardiovascular disease, and earlier death. While some environmental factors are probably involved, this seems to be, at least in part, genetically preprogrammed. The females of most species outlive the males.

Many theories have been advanced to try to explain physical aging in humans. Some researchers believe that the maximum number of years a healthy old human can live is between 100 and 120 years. Other researchers believe that with improved nutrition, improved health care, and the knowledge of how to genetically alter aging cells, the human life span could be extended to 150 or 200 years. This, of course, would bring about incredible social changes: social security, jobs, housing, environmental impact.

The cognitive changes that accompany middle and late adulthood follow the general pattern of physical decline. All the neurons (brain cells) that a person will ever have are present at birth. There is no mitosis (replacement) of neurons once they die. And neurons do die. By middle adulthood, a typical human can lose hundreds of neurons each day. However, this loss of brain cells is not necessarily associated with a decline in intellectual abilities. The brain has a sufficient supply of neurons to last a lifetime. Neurons continue to grow larger and add materials to their cell processes (axons and dendrites) throughout life. Recent research has demonstrated that neurons of old animals will continue to add dendritic branches if they are needed and used. The "use it or lose it" hypothesis also seems to be true for human brain cells.

Intelligence is a concept without a clear definition. It certainly seems to be multifactorial. Recently, several hypotheses have been put forward to explain the types of factors involved in intelligence. It can be subdivided into fluid (abstract) reasoning and crystallized (accumulation of facts) knowledge. It can be subdivided into metacomponents, contextual components, and experiential components. It can be viewed as having at least six autonomous factors: self-understanding, social understanding, logical-mathematical abilities, musical abilities, body kinesthetic abilities, and language skills. It can be divided into general and specific abilities, or ken (range of knowledge) and practical intelligence (common sense). Creativity is often viewed as a special form of intelligence. One hypothetical construct views intelligence as having 120 separate components. Regardless of how one looks at the definition of intelligence, it is clear that it is not all lost in healthy aging humans. The accumulation of facts continues with age. Practical intelligence grows with experience. Humans can become expert at the tasks that they do frequently, even in old age. Finally, many persons honor the wisdom of old age, based on accumulated memories, experiences, and strategies.

Erik Erikson suggested that the psychosocial nuclear conflict of middle age is generating vs. stagnating. Persons who use their skills and abilities, who are concerned about guiding the next generation, and who feel productive achieve a sense of generativity. Erikson proposed that the psychosocial nuclear conflict of late adulthood is achieving a sense of ego integrity vs. feeling a sense of despair about one's life. A healthy feeling of ego integrity is fostered by love of self and others, acceptance of the ups and downs of one's life, and a sense of assurance that one's life had order and meaning. While Erikson proposed that different conflicts are nuclear (central) at different ages, he felt that all humans worked on all conflicts throughout life. Thus, the human being in middle and late adulthood is continuing to work at having positive senses of trust, autonomy, initiative, industry, identity, intimacy, generativity, and ego integrity.

Many recent researchers have suggested that middle-aged adults go through a midlife crisis associated with career stagnation, launching children, menopause, and signs of physical aging. Other researchers have suggested that middle-aged adults go through a midlife transition associated with the same factors, but which is gradual and does not qualify as a crisis. Many persons feel that life is sweeter and more enjoyable after a midlife transition.

The articles selected for this unit stress the positive aspects of aging. Each offering presents a constructive view of the third third of life.

Looking Ahead: Challenge Questions

Is midlife a crisis or a time of glorious rebirth?

What factors can prolong the healthy life span of the human species?

How soon will we put together the complex puzzle pieces of senescence and have a complete picture of human aging?

Why do many adults equate getting older with getting better?

the new
MIDDLE AGE

MELINDA BECK

A generation verges toward a mass midlife crisis. But wait: it can be a lot better than you think.

The names are culled from driver's license records, credit-card applications, magazine-subscription forms—any place an unsuspecting consumer might have listed his birth date somewhere along the line. They pour into a data-management firm, where they are standardized, merged and purged of duplications. From there, they are assigned one of several different solicitation packets, then bundled and shipped nationwide. It's a point of great pride with the American Association of Retired Persons that on or about their birthdays, roughly 75 percent of the 2.7 million Americans who turned 50 this year received an offer to partake—for just $8!—in all the benefits of membership in the AARP.

Not since the Selective Service Board sent "greetings" to 18-year-old men during the Vietnam War has a birthday salutation been so dreaded by so many. True, the leading edge of the baby boom won't get the official invitations into the quagmire of the 50s for four more years—but these things are always worse in anticipation than in reality. And the icons of the baby boom are already there. Paul McCartney turned 50 this year; so did Aretha Franklin. Bob Dylan is 51, as are Frank Zappa, Paul Simon and Art Garfunkel. Even the heartthrobs have crossed the great divide: Raquel Welch is pinned up at 51, Robert Redford at 55.

Month by month, individually and collectively, the generation that refused to grow up is growing middle aged. The reminders are everywhere—from the gracefully aging Lauren Hutton (49) in the J. Crew catalog to the now ubiquitous prefix *"aging* baby boomers" to the Oval Office itself. Sure, Bill Clinton and Al Gore will breathe new youth into the presidency that has been held for three decades by the PT-109 crowd. But for many in this competitive cohort, their ascension is just one more reminder of time marching on and leaving accomplishment victims in its wake. See—*the president is 46. You're 49. Weren't you supposed to be CEO by now, or at least know what you want to DO with your life?*

To be sure, this is hardly the first generation to hit or anticipate the Big Five-Oh. The baby boomers' group obsession with aging is already sounding, well, old, to everybody else, and, by conventional definitions at least, most boomers have been "middle aged" since they turned 40. But raised with such outsize expectations of life, they may have a tougher time accepting the age of limitations than other generations. "This group was somehow programmed to never get older—that sets us up for a whole series of disappointments," says psychiatrist Harold Bloomfield in Del Mar, Calif. Rice University sociologist Chad Gordon has another take on the angst that is seizing baby boomers. "Let's face it—aging sucks," he says. "It's filled with all those D words—decay, decrepitude, degeneration, dying . . . Then there's balding, paunchiness, losing sex drives and capabilities, back trouble, headaches, cholesterol and high blood pressure—they all go from the far horizon to close up. Then you worry about worrying about those things."

In truth, authorities on aging and ordinary people who've been there say that middle age isn't so bad. "It's the most powerful and glorious segment of a person's life," says Ken Dychtwald, whose company, Age Wave, counsels businesses on how to serve the needs of the aging population. Dychtwald admits, however, that American culture hasn't universally embraced this idea and that most of the soon-to-be-middle-aged themselves haven't gotten into the swing of it yet.

Instead, they are responding with ever more exaggerated forms of foreboding. Bloomfield says he sees an increase in a once rare condition called *dysmorphophobia*—the intense but unfounded fear of looking ugly. In Hollywood, not only do actresses try desperately to disguise their age, but so do agents, scriptwriters and studio executives. "It's hard to age gracefully out here," says Dr. Mel Bircoll, 52, considered the father of the cosmetic pectoral implant, the calf implant and the fat implant (which he layers into face-lifts to add contour and avoid the "overstretched look"). Bircoll says his clients used to start at 55. Now they come to him at about 45.

All of this might have been grist for a great TV series, but when producer Stan Rogow tried it this season, it flopped. Rogow intended "Middle Ages" to be an upbeat portrayal—"pretty hip, pretty life affirming, not angst-ridden. What we tried to do with the show was to say, 'This is OK. It's better than OK'." Critics liked it but viewers never gave it a chance and, in retrospect, Rogow understands why: "The name was a colossal mistake. 'Middle age' is this horrible-sounding thing you've heard throughout your life and hated." As the low ratings piled up, Rogow said to himself: "We have a problem here, and it's called denial."

But the funny thing about denial is that sometimes it works. In the very act of staving off physical aging through exercise, diet and dye, the StairMaster set has actually succeeded in pushing back the boundaries of "middle age." Boomers will look, act and feel younger at 50 than previous generations did. "Fifty will be like 40," says UCLA gerontologist Fernando Torres-Gil, who predicts that this generation won't confront "old age" until well into their 70s. The broad concept of middle age is starting later and lasting longer—and looking better than ever before. "We're seeing that 50 means all kinds of very vibrant, alive, sexy, dynamic people," says June Reinisch, director of the Kinsey Institute for Research in Sex, Gender and Reproduction at Indiana University. "I'm 49 this year. I wear clothes that my mother never would have thought of wearing when she was this age. When skirts went up, my skirts went up." Rogow, 44, says: "I'd really be shocked if I'm wearing plaid golf pants at 60. I suspect I'll be wearing the same ripped jeans I've been wearing for 20 years. They'll be much cooler then."

The new middle age also features more children than ever before, since this generation has delayed marriage and childbearing. Many men are having second families, with even younger children, well into their 50s. Some may be pushing strollers *and* paying college tuition just when psychologists say they should be busting loose and fulfilling themselves. At the same time, today's middle-agers have aging parents who are starting to need care. "For many people, 50 will be just like 20, 30 and 40—tied to providing basic subsistence needs," says University of Texas psychologist David Drum. "They won't see a chance to change, to repattern their lives."

Yet even as they postponed family responsibilities, many people in this fast-track generation reached the peaks of their careers much earlier than their parents did—and are wondering, "Is that all there is?" even in their 30s and 40s. Many of them will top out earlier, too, as record numbers of middle managers chase fewer and fewer promotions. While previous generations worried about sex and marriage, "career crashes are the baby boom's version of midlife crisis," says Barry Glassner, a University of Southern California sociologist. Women, having forged careers of their own in record numbers, may face the same kind of professional crisis traditionally reserved for men—and their incomes will still be needed to make ends meet. "Lose a job—have any piece of the puzzle taken out—and the whole thing falls apart," says Andrea Saveri, a research fellow at the Institute for the Future in Menlo Park, Calif.

The cruel demographic joke is that just as this generation is hitting middle age with unprecedented family responsibilities, corporate America is mustering legions of fiftysomethings out of the work force through early-retirement plans and less compassionate methods. "There is tremendous doubt about the future," says Saveri. "People see their friends getting pink slips. Their M.B.A.s aren't doing them any good now." Retiring earlier—and living longer—will bring a host of financial, emotional and psychological problems in the years ahead. Today's 50-year-olds still have 20 or 30 more years to live. What are they going to do—and how are they going to pay for it? "The 50s are not the beginning of the end—you have an awful long way to go," says University of Chicago gerontologist Bernice Neugarten, now 76. And that may be the most frightening thought of all.

Midway life's journey I was made aware
  That I had strayed into a dark forest,
And the right path appeared not anywhere.

Dante was 35 years old and frustrated in his quest for political position in 1300 when he wrote the first lines of "The Inferno"—describing perhaps the first midlife crisis in Western literature. Shakespeare charted similar midlife muddles in "King Lear," "Macbeth," "Hamlet" and "Othello" in the early 1600s, though he barely used the phrase "middle age." Sigmund Freud and Carl Jung studied midlife transitions around the turn of the 20th century. But then "midlife" came much earlier in time. In 1900, average life expectancy in the United States was 47 and only 3 percent of the population lived past 65. Today average life expectancy is 75—and 12 percent of the U.S. population is older than 65.

The longer life gets, the harder it is to plot the midpoint and define when middle age begins and ends. "We've broken the evolutionary code," says Gail Sheehy, author of "Passages" and "The Silent Passage." "In only a century, we've added 30 years to the life cycle." Statistically, the middle of life is now about 37, but what we think of as middle age comes later—anywhere from 40 to 70. As chronological age has less and less meaning, experts are groping for other definitions. When the American Board of Family Practice asked a random sampling of 1,200 Americans when middle age begins, 41 percent said it was when you worry about having enough money for health-care concerns, 42 percent said it was when your last child moves out and 46 percent said it was when you don't recognize the names of music groups on the radio anymore.

However it is defined, middle age remains one of the least studied phases in life. "It's the last uncharted territory in human development," said MacArthur Foundation president Adele Simmons in 1989, announcing a $10 million grant to fund the largest scholarly look ever at the period. Team leader Gilbert Brim and his colleagues at the Research Network on Successful Midlife Development are now partway through their eight-year effort, trying to answer, among other things, why some people hit their

> # How do I know if what I achieve in life should be called serenity and not surrender?
> **—JUDITH VIORST, 61**

■ **Percentage of baby boomers who say they have been through midlife crisis: 27**
■ **Average age of men who marry for second time: 39.2**
■ **Average age of women who marry for second time: 34.8**

SOURCE: GALLUP, NATIONAL CENTER FOR HEALTH STATISTICS

strides at midlife and others hit the wall. To date, they have concluded that there are no set stages or transition points—that what happens to people is more the result of accident, personal experiences and the historical period in which they live. "Midlife is full of changes, of twists and turns; the path is not fixed," says Brim. "People move in and out of states of success."

In particular, Brim's group debunks the notion of a "midlife crisis." "It's such a mushy concept—not like a clinical diagnosis in the medical field," he says. But, Brim adds, "what a wonderful idea! You could load everything on that—letting people blame something external for what they're feeling." Other scholars agree that very few people suffer full-blown crackups—and that dumping the spouse for a bimbo is more the stuff of fiction—or fantasy— than reality. So is the Gauguin syndrome: running off to Tahiti at 43. People do have affairs and end up with different mates—but that is often after marriages have failed for reasons other than midlife malaise.

Still, the mythology persists. "You ask people if they've had a midlife crisis and some say they have," says sociologist Ronald Kessler at the University of Michigan's Institute for Social Research. "Then you ask them what it was and they'll say that they didn't get to be vice president. So what did they do—try to kill themselves? Buy a sports car? Well no, people come to terms with getting older in a most gradual way." The idea of a crisis sometimes provides an excuse for wild and outrageous behavior, says psychologist Susan Krauss Whitbourne at the University of Massachusetts at Amherst: "It sounds romantic and fun—certainly better than complete boredom." She also suspects it's a class phenomenon: well-educated people with money "have the luxury to reflect on these things."

What does commonly happen, experts say, is a more subtle acceptance of life's limitations. One key task may be to change your self-image. "A lot of the more tangible rewards come in the first half of life, such as good grades, first jobs, early promotions, marriage, first children," says psychologist Robert E. Simmons in Alexandria, Va. After that, "it's harder and harder to rely on external gratifications because there aren't as many. So one is thrown back more on one's internal self-esteem system." That can mean finding new forms of satisfaction—from coaching Little League to taking up the saxophone to tutoring kids in school.

The sooner you accept the idea that life may not turn out as you planned, the easier the transition will be. "It's the person who has just been driving himself and getting burnt out, who is starting to turn 50 and who feels like, 'My God, my life is over'," says Bloomfield. Gail Sheehy agrees: "For those who deny, postpone, elude or fantasize to escape coming to terms with [reality], it comes up again around 50 with a double whammy." Sheehy can see this now, at 54. She barely mentioned life past 50 in "Passages" because she was only 35 at the time and couldn't visualize herself at an older age. Now she says she knows that "you have to work your way up to saying 'I'm not going to go backward. I'm not going to try to stay in the same place. That way lies self-torture and eventually

foolishness. I'm going to have the courage to go forward'."

Contrary to conventional wisdom, many people find that the 50s is actually a period of reduced stress and anxiety. "In terms of mental health, midlife is the best time," says Ronald Kessler. One tantalizing bit of biomedical research has found that between 40 and 60, people actually lose cells in the locus coeruleus, the part of the brain that registers anxiety, which may help explain the "mellowing" many people feel in middle age. Depression does tend to peak in this period, however, which may also be linked to biochemical changes in the aging brain.

Not all mood shifts are biochemical. There are definite life events that can bring about profound changes of heart and direction. The list includes divorce; illness; losing a job; the kids leaving home (or returning); the death of parents, spouses and friends. Those can happen at any point in life, but they begin to mount up in the 50s. Any kind of change is stressful and simply fearing these things can bring tension. "It also happens when mentors retire," says University of North Carolina sociologist Glen Elder. "You have to think about yourself playing that role. It's a major transition, one that is hard to come to terms with."

Professional disappointments weigh especially heavily on men, and they are inevitable even for the most successful, from George Bush to laid-off steelworkers. Being forced out of a job in midlife can be devastating—or liberating, if it brings about a rethinking of what's most important. Men (and increasingly, women) who sacrificed time with their families for their careers in their younger years may be particularly regretful when success proves as empty as the nest. "Men our age have lived such a macho fake life," says Rogers Brackmann, 61, a former advertising executive in Chicago. "When I was in the agency business, I was up at 5 o'clock, home at 7:30. For the first 15 years I worked every Saturday. I didn't make it to my kid's Little League games. When I left that environment I realized how hard and unproductive the work was." Rogers packed it in five years ago and says, "I was so happy to get out I can't describe it." Since then he has turned to other new businesses, including inventing, and now holds five patents—including one for a golf-ball washer that doesn't get your hands wet.

Can I ask you a question? Why do men chase women?... I think it's because they fear death.
—Rose (Olympia Dukakis) in "Moonstruck"

Typically, men and women cross paths, psychologically, in middle age. Men become more nurturing and family-oriented. Women become more independent and aggressive. Jung described this as the "contrasexual transition." Northwestern University psychologist David Gutmann found the phenomenon not only in American culture, but also in Navajo, Mayan and Middle Eastern Druze societies he studied for his book "Reclaimed Powers: Toward a New Psychology of Men and Women in Later Life"—suggesting that it is more biological than cultural. Much

---

I live like a monk, almost. A monk with red lips, short dresses and big hair.

—TINA TURNER, 53

■ Percentage of men aged 40 to 49 who say their lives are exciting: 52.4
■ Percentage aged 50 to 59: 43.3
■ Percentage of women aged 40 to 49 who find their lives exciting: 45.6
■ Percentage aged 50 to 59: 40.7

SOURCE: NATIONAL OPINION RESEARCH CENTER

of it has to do with the demands of child rearing, Gutmann explains, in which men provide for the family's physical needs and women do the emotional work, each suppressing the other parts of their personalities. When the children leave home, those submerged forces tend to reassert themselves, Gutmann says.

Ideally, that crossing should be liberating for both halves of the couple and bring them closer together. But often the transition is rocky. "It can be very threatening for men to see their women soar," says counselor Sirah Vettese, Bloomfield's wife. Some men are so unnerved that they do seek out younger, more compliant women, Gutmann says. He thinks Ernest Hemingway is a prime example: devastated after his third wife left him to pursue her own career, the author became increasingly alcoholic. He took another younger wife and killed himself at 61.

It doesn't help that many men wrestling with self-image adjustments in midlife must also accept declining sexual performance. Testosterone levels gradually drop, which can diminish their libido. Erections are less full, less frequent and require more stimulation to achieve. Researchers once attributed that to psychological factors, but increasingly they find that 75 percent of erection dysfunctions stem from physiological problems. "Smoking, diabetes, hypertension, elevated cholesterol—without a doubt, those are the four erection busters," says University of Chicago urologist Laurence A. Levine. Still, psychology does play a role. "If you think you're going to have a problem, suddenly you're going to begin having a problem," says psychologist Jan Sinnott at Towson State University in Baltimore, Md.

Inevitably, pharmaceutical manufacturers have sensed that there's money to be made in the fear of flaccidity. Gynex Pharmaceuticals is researching a daily under-the-tongue testosterone-replacement product called Androtest-SL and already markets an injectable version that is used every two weeks. But there may be considerable side effects. Excessive use of testosterone may lead to testicular atrophy and infertility and spur the growth of some cancers. Too much testosterone can cause some men to grow small breasts, too.

A better remedy for men who find their potency declining is to change the way they think about sex—to take things slower, more romantically and not mourn the seemingly instant erections of their youth. "The midlife male has to finally get the idea that his primary sex organ is not his penis. It's his heart and his brain," says Bloomfield, author of "Love Secrets for a Lasting Relationship." Talking helps, too, though most men are not accustomed to such openness. "It's really important that men and women sit down and say to each other, 'Our lives are changing'," says Vettese.

In many ways, women have it easier in midlife. For all the new willingness to discuss the hot flashes and mood swings some feel during menopause, many women feel a surge of sexual and psychological freedom once their shifting hormones rebalance and they are no longer concerned about getting pregnant. "With each pass-

ing generation, women feel sexier and more desire after menopause," says June Reinisch at the Kinsey Institute. Sheehy says that based on studies she has seen, about one third of women have some noticeable diminution of desire after menopause. That can be rectified with hormone supplements or accepted as it is, if the woman doesn't mind.

What many women do mind is finding themselves alone and lost in the discouraging midlife singles scene. Zella Case, co-owner of the Someone Special dating service in Dallas, says, "We have hundreds of women who want in, but so few men." The numbers are right there in the census statistics: there are 14 million single women older than 55, and only 4 million single men. Just ask Victoria Anderson, a Dallas private investigator who turned 50 last month. Divorced 13 years, she's been losing confidence and gaining weight and she frets that she'll never fit into the size 3s in her closet again. She despairs of meeting a new mate on the job—"I deal with criminals and jerks," she says. And as far as the bar scene goes, Anderson says ruefully, the typical question now is not "what's your sign, but what's your cholesterol level?"

Women with stable marriages may find other tensions mounting in midlife. With delayed childbirth, kids may be hitting adolescence just when their mothers are in menopause—a volatile combination. Some women desperately fear losing their faces and their figures—especially if those have been the focus of their self-esteem. But the new burst of postmenopausal independence some feel may help to compensate.

Bobbi Altman literally took flight at midlife. "Turning 50 was the best thing that ever happened to me. I could do anything I wanted to," she says. After suffering through a divorce in her early 40s and raising three children, Altman took up aviation, bought an airplane and, at 59, went to aircraft-mechanic school. Last April she graduated and in June she flew cross-country solo. Now 61, she lives in Laguna Beach, Calif., and is involved with a man who finished law school at 70. Altman flies to work every day at the Santa Monica Museum of Flying, where she is helping to restore a World War II P-39. "Aging is not a loss of youth—it's another stage," she says.

I remember now that the toughest birthday I ever faced was my fortieth. It was a big symbol because it said goodbye, goodbye, goodbye to youth. But I think that when one has passed through that age it's like breaking the sound barrier.
> —Writer and director NORMAN CORWIN, 82
> quoted in the 1992 book "The Ageless Spirit"

Baby boomers who dread what will happen to them beyond the age of 50 have only to look at what older people are doing with their lives today. The generation preceding them—the first to enjoy the longevity revolution—are going back to school in record numbers, forging new careers and still making great strides in their old ones. Lydia Bronte, a research fellow at the Phelps Stokes Institute in New York, recently com-

> ## I feel exactly the same as I've always felt: a lightly reined-in voracious beast.
> **—JACK NICHOLSON, 55**

■ Percentage of married men aged 40 to 49 who admit to infidelity: 28.4
■ Percentage aged 50 to 59: 24.3
■ Percentage of married women aged 40 to 49 who admit to infidelity: 15.21
■ Percentage aged 50 to 59: 3.3

SOURCE: NATIONAL OPINION RESEARCH CENTER

■ **Total face-lifts in U.S., 1990: 48,743 (91% women) percentage aged 35 to 50: 27 percentage aged 51 to 64: 58**
■ **Total tummy tucks in U.S., 1990: 20,213 (93% women) percentage aged 35 to 50: 64 percentage aged 51 to 64: 15**
■ **Total hair transplants in U.S., 1990: 3,188 (100% men) percentage aged 35 to 50: 57 percentage aged 51 to 64: 10**
■ **Median age of an American using hair-color product: women: 43.14, men: 43.02**

SOURCE: AMERICAN SOCIETY OF PLASTIC & RECONSTRUCTIVE SURGEONS, SIMMONS 1992

pleted a five-year study of the work lives of 150 people 65 to 102, and concludes that "many people are as active as they've ever been during those years . . . The single most important thing was that they found work that they loved." Some of Bronte's subjects switched jobs many times over in their lives. Some found their true calling only in their later years. Julia Child, now 80, learned French cooking after her husband took a job in France and started her TV career in her 50s. The late Millicent Fenwick won her first race for Congress at 65.

Still, the image of elderly people as desperate, frail and unproductive prevails, and that brings an unrealistic fear of growing middle aged and older. "People need to profoundly rethink what aging means, not only for themselves as individuals, but for the whole society," says Harry Moody, deputy director of the Brookdale Center on Aging at Hunter College in New York. By 2030, when the oldest boomers are 84 and the youngest have turned 65, thee will be an estimated 65 million Americans 65 and older—more than twice as many as today.

To find more satisfaction and hope in that future, aging baby boomers need to bust out of the rigid "three boxes of life" mentality that has governed the pattern of American lives for so long. Confining education to youth, work and child rearing to the middle years, and retirement to old age makes less and less sense—and it simply won't fly in an economy that is dismissing people from the work world in their 50s, with an ever-longer stretch of life ahead. "We desperately need some real, contributing roles for people in the third third of life," says New York management consultant Bill Stanley. He argues that the whole concept of "retirement" should be retired.

Some change in the image of aging will come about naturally in the decades ahead. Baby boomers, by sheer force of numbers, have always made their stage in life the hip stage to be in. The generation that thought it could change the world overnight has only a few years left before its members become elders themselves. While some of their frantic efforts to stave off aging may constitute denial, some go hand in hand with forging a healthier, more constructive vision of old age that could last even longer than we now suspect. The boomers will go there, riding Stair-Masters to heaven, and that may be their most lasting legacy of all.

With GINNY CARROLL *in Houston,* PATRICIA KING *in San Francisco,* KAREN SPRINGEN *and* TODD BARRETT *in Chicago,* LUCILLE BEACHY *in New York,* JEANNE GORDON *in Los Angeles and* CAROLYN FRIDAY *in Boston*

Building a Better Brain

Evidence is accumulating that the brain works a lot like a muscle—the harder you use it, the more it grows. Although scientists had long believed the brain's circuitry was hard-wired by adolescence and inflexible in adulthood, its newly discovered ability to change and adapt is apparently with us well into old age. Best of all, this research has opened up an exciting world of possibilities for treating strokes and head injuries—and warding off Alzheimer's disease.

Daniel Golden

The party last year was as rowdy as it gets in a convent. Celebrating her 100th birthday, Sister Regina Mergens discarded her habit in favor of a daring red gown, downed two glasses of champagne and proclaimed her intention to live to 102. She didn't quite make it. Now, at vespers on a March afternoon in Mankato, Minn., dozens of nuns file past the open casket where Mergens, 101, lies, rosary beads in her hands.

Concealed from view is an incision in the back of Mergens's head through which her brain has been removed. Mergens and nearly 700 elderly sisters in her order are the largest group of brain donors in the world. By examining these nuns, as well as thousands of stroke victims, amputees and people with brain injuries, researchers are living up to the promise of a presidential proclamation that the 1990s be the Decade of the Brain. Scientists are beginning to understand that the brain has a remarkable capacity to change and grow, even in old age, and that individuals have some control over how healthy and alert their brains remain as the years go by. The Sisters of Mankato, for example, lead an intellectually challenging life, and recent research suggests that stimulating the mind with mental exercise may cause brain cells, called neurons, to branch wildly. The branching causes millions of additional connections, or synapses, between brain cells. Think of it, says Arnold Scheibel, director of UCLA's Brain Research Institute, as a computer with a bigger memory board: "You can do more things more quickly."

The capacity of the brain to change offers new hope for preventing and treating brain diseases. It helps explain why some people can:

■ Delay the onset of Alzheimer's disease symptoms for years. Studies now show that the more educated a person is, the less likely he or she is to show symptoms of the disease. The reason: Intellectual activity develops surplus brain tissue that compensates for tissue damaged by the disease.

■ Make a better recovery from strokes. Research indicates that even when areas of the brain are permanently damaged by stroke, new message routes can be created to get around the roadblock or to resume the function of that area.

■ Feel sensation in missing limbs. Scientists no longer think that complaints of pain in amputated body parts are psychosomatic. The feelings, which eventually fade, turn out to be the brain's way of keeping once-busy neurons active, evidence that the brain's plasticity can trick as well as treat and that areas of the brain no longer useful can be taken over by nearby regions of the cortex.

New knowledge about the brain may emerge from the obscure convent in Minnesota, a place where Ponce de León might have been tempted to test the waters. Mankato is the site of the northwest headquarters of the School Sisters of Notre Dame, where a long life is normal. In part because the nuns of this order don't drink much, smoke or die in childbirth, they live to an average age of 85, and many live far beyond that. Of the 150 retired nuns residing in this real-life *Cocoon,* 25 are older than 90.

But longevity is only part of the nuns' story. They also do not seem to suffer from dementia, Alzheimer's and other debilitating brain diseases as early or as severely as the general population. David Snowdon of the Sanders-Brown Center on Aging at the University of Kentucky, the professor of preventive medicine who

How to Make Your Dendrites Grow and Grow

What can the average person do to strengthen his or her mind? "The important thing is to be actively involved in areas unfamiliar to you," says Arnold Scheibel, head of UCLA's Brain Research Institute. "Anything that's intellectually challenging can probably serve as a kind of stimulus for dendritic growth, which means it adds to the computational reserves in your brain."

So pick something that's diverting and, most important, unfamiliar. A computer programmer might try sculpture; a ballerina might try marine navigation. Here are some other stimulating suggestions from brain researchers:

■ Do puzzles. "I can't stand crosswords," says neuroscientist Antonio Damasio of the University of Iowa, "but they're a good idea." Psychologist Sherry Willis of Pennsylvania State University says, "People who do jigsaw puzzles show greater spatial ability, which you use when you look at a map."

■ Try a musical instrument. "As soon as you decide to take up the violin, your brain has a whole new group of muscle-control problems to solve. But that's nothing compared with what the brain has to do before the violinist can begin to read notes on a page and correlate them with his or her fingers to create tones. This is a remarkable, high-level type of activity," says Scheibel.

■ Fix something. Learn to reline your car's brakes or repair a shaver, suggests Zaven Khachaturian, a brain expert at the National Institute of Aging. "My basement is full of electronic gadgets, waiting to be repaired. The solution is not the important thing. It's the challenge."

■ Try the arts. If your verbal skills are good, buy a set of watercolors and take a course. If your drawing skills are good, start a journal or write poetry.

■ Dance. "We keep seeing a relationship between physical activity and cognitive maintenance," says Harvard brain researcher Marilyn Albert. "We suspect that moderately strenuous exercise leads to the development of small blood vessels. Blood carries oxygen, and oxygen nourishes the brain." But be sure the activity is new and requires thinking. Square dancing, ballet or tap is preferable to twisting the night away.

■ Date provocative people. Better yet, marry one of them. Willis suggests that the most pleasant and rewarding way to increase your dendrites is to "meet and interact with intelligent, interesting people." Try tournament bridge, chess, even sailboat racing.

And remember, researchers agree that it's never too late. Says Scheibel: "All of life should be a learning experience, not just for the trivial reasons but because by continuing the learning process, we are challenging our brain and therefore building brain circuitry. Literally. This is the way the brain operates."

---

has been studying the nuns for several years, has found that those who earn college degrees, who teach, who constantly challenge their minds, live longer than less-educated nuns who clean rooms or work in the kitchen. He suspects the difference lies in how they use their heads.

Within the human brain each neuron contains at one end threadlike appendages called axons, which send signals to other nearby neurons. At the other end of the neuron are similar threadlike appendages called dendrites, which receive messages from nearby cells. Axons and dendrites tend to shrink with age, but experiments with rats have shown that intellectual exertion can spur neurons to branch like the roots of a growing tree, creating networks of new connections. Once a skill becomes automatic, the extra connections may fade, but the brain is so plastic that they can be tapped again if needed. Like the power grid of an electric company, the branching and connections provide surplus capacity in a brownout. Snowdon and some neuroscientists believe that people with such a surplus who find their normal neural pathways

blocked by the tangles that characterize Alzheimer's disease can reroute messages. To be sure, every brain is limited by genetic endowment, and flexibility does decrease with age. But new thinking in brain science suggests that whether someone hits that wall at age 65 or at age 102 may be partly up to the individual. Even Harvard's David Hubel, who shared a Nobel prize just 13 years ago for vision experiments showing that parts of the brain become fixed in infancy, is surprised that new research shows the brain "is much more modifiable than we ever suspected."

Professor Snowdon says the nuns of Mankato demonstrate this. He expects to prove that the better-educated sisters have significantly more cortex and more synaptic branching of neurons than their less-educated counterparts, which would allow the former to cope better with Alzheimer's disease, dementia and stroke.

Brain exercising is a way of life at the nunnery, where the sisters live by the principle that an idle mind is the devil's plaything. They write spiritual meditations in their journals and letters to their congressmen about the blockade of Haiti, and do puzzles of

The Brain of a Child

"It's crazy," says Pasko Rakic, a Yale neurobiologist. "Americans think kids should not be asked to do difficult things with their brains while they are young: 'Let them play; they'll study at the university.' The problem is, if you don't train them early, it's much harder."

It is never too early for a child to exercise his mind. Some of the benefits of early brain workouts have been known for centuries. Teachers of music, gymnastics and chess, for example, have long insisted that practicing begin early. Linguists have marveled that children can learn a new language without an accent, while adults cannot. "In order to pronounce certain words, you have to put the vocal cord in a certain tension," Rakic says. "To do that, you have to contract throat muscles. Control of these muscles is in the synapses that were formed before puberty."

There is, says Rakic, a fairly simple scientific explanation: Children's brains can make far more synaptic connections than can adults'. Shortly after birth, the brain makes connections at an incredible pace. As puberty approaches, the number tapers off. Then two processes begin–functional validation, in which the connections the brain finds useful are made permanent, and selective elimination, in which those that are not useful, not continually used, are eliminated. Says Rakic: "We chisel our brain from the larger stone, so to speak." The greatest chiseling is accomplished between the ages of two and 11.

"Of course," Rakic adds, "this doesn't mean you cannot learn in later life. You can learn tremendously. But in childhood there is an ability to learn quickly which is unparalleled."

all sorts. Although more than a few were born when Grover Cleveland was President, they are adept at debating Bill Clinton's health-reform proposals. Current-events seminars are held every week. Raised before radio, the nuns are more skilled at answering questions on the TV program *Jeopardy* than the actual contestants. One 99-year-old, Sister Mary Esther Boor, takes advantage of slow minutes while working as the complex's receptionist to solve brainteasers–some with words in Spanish.

And Willard Scott, take note: Five nuns in Mankato will turn 100 within a few months. One, Sister Matthia Gores, will hit 101. Like many of the sisters, she taught school into her seventies, and she is still sharp enough to recite her rosary and knit gloves for poor children at the same time, without missing a stitch. "I pray for a happy death," she says. "That's the most important thing in life–to die well." But she is in no hurry for that prayer to be answered. Having overcome cancer and a recent nasty bout with the flu, she looks forward to daily exercise sessions. Born two years after Dr. James Naismith invented basketball, she likes the geriatric version of the sport: shooting a Nerf ball through a hoop. Leaning on her walker one afternoon, she swishes three in a row.

Like the aging nuns of Mankato, Henry Carr is determined to exercise his brain. The 81-year-old stroke victim's chances of recovery depend on his brain's ability to redesign itself and grow new routes of communication.

His body motionless, his face straining with determination, Carr lies in a metal doughnut known as a Positron Emission Tomograph (PET) scanner as a tech-

nician comes rushing into the room with a syringe of radioactive water. He injects it into Carr's arm, and the scan begins to track the radioactivity, which has a half-life of only two minutes. Wasting no time, Dr. Holley Dey begins to rub a toothbrush against the fingertips of Carr's left hand.

"Can you feel that?" asks Dey, clinical director of the Yale/Veterans Affairs PET Center in West Haven, Conn. "Try and move your left hand. Try and move your fingers, Mr. Carr." Carr, who suffered a stroke two weeks earlier that paralyzed most of his left side, tries. Instead, his right hand makes a fist–involuntarily. This may indicate, scientists say, that Carr's brain is trying to use its left hemisphere, which normally controls the right side of the body, to find new neural pathways to move the left arm. Scan results confirm this.

Most of the 500,000 Americans who have a stroke each year recover some lost function. Before the development of advanced imaging techniques, neurologists thought stroke victims regained use of bruised brain tissue as swelling in the area subsided. PET scans now show that a stroke victim may recover even if the neurons in the affected part of the brain are permanently damaged. Scientists like Dr. Lawrence Brass, associate professor of neurology at Yale, believe that the brains of stroke patients may form new dendritic connections, indicating that even an aging adult's brain can grow in response to injury. Recovery depends in part on the type and location of the stroke, and the patient's age and medical history. In some patients, scientists believe, nearby neurons enlarge their networks and take over for the damaged tissue, or other brain centers that govern involuntary actions expand their role. In Carr's case, for example, the left side of his mouth still droops. But when he smiles without thinking, it rises as readily as the right. The reflexive system that raises his mouth involuntarily may find a way to take over other movements.

The plasticity of the brain can be a burden as well as a blessing, especially in cases of amputation. Then, a whole area of the cortex previously devoted to a part of the body has nothing to respond to. Derek Steen learned to compensate after his left arm was amputated above the elbow following a motorcycle crash in 1985. Before long he could tie his shoelaces with one hand and shoot pool so well with one arm that his friends in Poway, Calif., began calling him "the Bandit." But the 27-year-old hasn't been able to adjust to the mysterious aching in his lost limb. It hurts so much that Steen has often been unable to sleep. His happy-go-lucky personality has turned sour, and his temper has cost him one job after another. "I'm not the same Derek I was," he says. Until recently no one was able to explain why the pain was intense when he was shaving his left cheek or when his face was buffeted by wind.

For centuries phantom pain has puzzled researchers. Some have interpreted it as psychosomatic, others as a cry of protest from truncated nerve endings in the stump. Now research links phantom pain, like recovery from stroke, to the brain's capacity to flex and grow. In the cortex, each area of the body is represented in proportion to its importance as a sensory receptor. Fingers take up more neurons than do shoulders. But boundaries in the brain can shift as often as they do in the Balkans, and each section of cortex can control its neighbor's territory.

Not long ago it was believed that when a limb was amputated, the corresponding brain cells withered away. Then professor Michael Merzenich of the University of California at San Francisco severed the nerve of the middle finger in an adult monkey. Deprived of normal stimuli, the related cortex did not die. Instead, nearby neurons activated by other fingers filled in the dormant region. In effect, the brain tried to compensate for lost feeling in the finger by reallocating its share of cortex to the rest of the hand.

Merzenich's finding inspired professor Vilayanur Ramachandran of the University of California at San Diego to study human amputees. Last year he began seeing Derek Steen, the one-armed pool player. Ramachandran asked Steen to close his eyes. Then the doctor touched Steen's cheek, asking where he felt a sensation. In his phantom hand, Steen said. When Ramachandran stroked Steen's jaw with a cotton swab, the patient felt movement across his missing limb.

Ramachandran was not surprised. In the cortex, neurons for the face are next to those for the arm. Once Steen's brain stopped receiving signals from the arm,

Century of Mind Gains

1901	Russian physiologist Ivan Pavlov coins the term "conditioned reflex" to describe why his dogs salivate at the sound of a bell.
1906	Alois Alzheimer discovers a severe age-related neurological disorder that leads to dementia and death.
1906	Anatomist Santiago Ramón y Cajal wins a Nobel for showing that neurons are separate cells connected by synapses.
1911	Eugen Bleuler identifies schizophrenia, a major mental disease.
1929	German psychiatrist Hans Berger uses the electroencephalograph to discover human brain waves.
1952	Two French psychiatrists, Jean Delay and Pierre Deniker, introduce chlorpromazine to treat psychoses, ushering in the age of psychopharmacology.
1971	A new tool is made available for imaging the brain: computerized axial tomography (CAT scan).
1988	Prozac is introduced by Eli Lilly and Co. as an antidepressant. Patients report unparalleled improvement, and before long it is prescribed for everything from panic attacks to dieting.
1991	Nitric oxide is found to be a neurotransmitter and a key compound in stroke damage. The discovery may lead to effective drug therapy for strokes.

stimuli from the cheek filled in, a development confirmed by magnetic mapping of Steen's brain waves. Yet Steen's mind attributed the sensations to the phantom limb, indicating that some higher centers of the brain that coordinate sensory information cannot easily adjust to something as drastic as an amputation.

And the effects of filling in are not always predictable. Most amputees, for example, feel pain in their missing limbs, but not all do. Deborah Finnegan-Ling, a graduate student in neuroscience at the University of Vermont, is a disciple of Ramachandran. She is writing her dissertation on phantom pain, a phenomenon with which she is familiar: Her lower left leg was amputated after a farming accident three years ago. Because the area of the brain for the foot is adjacent to the area for genitalia, Finnegan-Ling's missing limb aches when she makes love. I consider myself tough," she says. "But the pain is so acute that I'll cry." Nobody knows why, but some amputees feel phantom pleasure rather than pain. Told about a man who feels an orgasmic sensation in his lost foot during sex, Finnegan-Ling sighs. "I wish," she says.

As David Snowdon table-hops in the Mankato cafeteria, greeting nuns by name and inquiring after their health, his interest is professional as well as personal. Someday soon the researcher likely will be looking at their brains under a microscope, but that prospect, like death itself, doesn't seem to bother anyone, and the nuns continue to tease the 41-year-old about his long hair and his bachelor lifestyle. "I've spent so much time in convents lately," he jests, "that it has kind of crimped my social life." He was less at ease three years ago when he first stood up and described his study. Snowdon worried that asking nuns to give their brains to science was like asking them to boo Notre Dame.

"The sisters talked about it seriously and severely," says Sister Matthia Gores. But the nuns' intellectual curiosity prevailed. As a gerontologist intrigued by aging, Snowdon wanted only the brains of nuns who were 75 years or older, and most agreed to participate. Other School Sisters across the country followed. Every year they undergo a battery of mental and physical tests.

So far, Snowdon's team has examined the brains of 90 nuns for signs of dementia. He has found Alzheimer's in about 40 percent of the brains. In the general population, Alzheimer's is found in as many as 50 percent of those over 85. Soon researchers will look for proof of dendritic growth in the nuns' brains.

Of the 678 subjects in Snowdon's study, Regina Mergens was the 95th to die. Just before viewing her body, 30 nuns past the age of 85, all in the nursing home wing, gathered to celebrate St. Patrick's Day. Entering the room, they were given cardboard shamrocks to pin on their habits beside their purple ribbons for Lent.

Accompanied by an accordion-playing nun in a green hat, they sang, "When Irish Eyes Are Smiling." Just for fun, the activities director asked them to name as many green foods as they could. They reeled off 25 answers.

"See," the director cried. "Nothing wrong with our memories."

Additional reporting by **Anne Hollister**
and **Sasha Nyary**

The Myth of the Miserable Working Woman

She's Tired, She's Stressed Out, She's Unhealthy, She Can't Go Full Speed at Work or Home. Right? Wrong.

Rosalind C. Barnett and Caryl Rivers

Rosalind C. Barnett is a psychologist and a senior research associate at the Wellesley College Center for Research on Women. Caryl Rivers is a professor of journalism at Boston University and the author of More Joy Than Rage: Crossing Generations With the New Feminism.

"You Can't Do Everything," announced a 1989 USA Today *headline on a story suggesting that a slower career track for women might be a good idea. "Mommy Career Track Sets Off a Furor," declaimed the* New York Times *on March 8, 1989, reporting that women cost companies more than men. "Pressed for Success, Women Careerists Are Cheating Themselves," sighed a 1989 headline in the* Washington Post, *going on to cite a book about the "unhappy personal lives" of women graduates of the Harvard Business School. "Women Discovering They're at Risk for Heart Attacks," Gannett News Service reported with alarm in 1991. "Can Your Career Hurt Your Kids? Yes, Say Many Experts," blared a* Fortune *cover just last May, adding in a chirpy yet soothing fashion, "But smart parents—and flexible companies—won't let it happen."*

If you believe what you read, working women are in big trouble—stressed out, depressed, sick, risking an early death from heart attacks, and so overcome with problems at home that they make inefficient employees at work.

In fact, just the opposite is true. As a research psychologist whose career has focused on women and a journalist-critic who has studied the behavior of the media, we have extensively surveyed the latest data and research and concluded that the public is being engulfed by a tidal wave of disinformation that has serious consequences for the life and health of every American woman. Since large numbers of women began moving into the work force in the 1970s, scores of studies on their emotional and physical health have painted a very clear picture: Paid employment provides substantial health *benefits* for women. These benefits cut across income and class lines; even women who are working because they have to—not because they want to—share in them.

There is a curious gap, however, between what these studies say and what is generally reported on television, radio, and in newspapers and magazines. The more the research shows work is good for women, the bleaker the media reports seem to become. Whether this bizarre state of affairs is the result of a backlash against women, as *Wall Street Journal* reporter Susan Faludi contends in her new book, *Backlash: The Undeclared War Against American Women,* or of well-meaning ignorance, the effect is the same: Both the shape of national policy and the lives of women are at risk.

Too often, legislation is written and policies are drafted not on the basis of the facts but on the basis of what those in power believe to be the facts. Even the much discussed *Workforce 2000* report, issued by the Department of Labor under the Reagan administration—hardly a hotbed of feminism—admitted that "most current policies were designed for a society in which men worked and women stayed home." If policies are skewed toward solutions that are aimed at reducing women's commitment to work, they will do more than harm women—they will damage companies, managers and the productivity of the American economy.

THE CORONARY THAT WASN'T

One reason the "bad news" about working women jumps to page one is that we're all too willing to believe it. Many adults today grew up at a time when soldiers were returning home from World War II and a way had to be found to get the women who replaced them in industry back into the kitchen. The result was a barrage of propaganda that turned at-home moms into saints and backyard barbecues and station wagons into cultural icons. Many of us still have that outdated postwar map inside our heads, and it leaves us more willing to believe the horror stories than the good news that paid employment is an emotional and medical plus.

In the 19th century it was accepted medical dogma that women should not be educated because the brain and the ovaries could not develop at the same time. Today it's PMS, the wrong math genes or rampaging hormones. Hardly anyone points out the dire predictions that didn't come true.

You may remember the prediction that career women would start having more heart attacks, just like men. But the Framingham Heart Study—a federally funded cardiac project that has been studying 10,000 men and women since 1948—reveals that working women are not having more heart attacks. They're not dying any earlier, either. Not only are women not losing their health advantages; the lifespan gap is actually widening. Only one group of working women suffers more heart attacks than other women: those in low-paying clerical jobs with many demands on them and little control over their work pace, who also have several children and little or no support at home.

As for the recent publicity about women having more problems with heart disease, much of it skims over the important underlying reasons for the increase: namely, that by the time they have a heart attack, women tend to be a good deal older (an average of 67, six years older than the average age for men), and thus frailer, than males who have one. Also, statistics from the National Institutes of Health show that coronary symptoms are treated less aggressively in women—fewer coronary bypasses, for example. In addition, most heart research is done on men, so doctors do not know as much about the causes—and treatment—of heart disease in women. None of these factors have anything to do with work.

But doesn't working put women at greater risk for stress-related illnesses? No. Paid work is actually associated with *reduced* anxiety and depression. In the early 1980s we reported in our book, *Lifeprints* (based on a National Science Foundation–funded study of 300 women), that working women were significantly higher in psychological well-being than those not employed. Working gave them a sense of mastery and control that homemaking didn't provide. More recent studies echo our findings. For example:

• A 1989 report by psychologist Ingrid Waldron and sociologist Jerry Jacobs of Temple University on nationwide surveys of 2,392 white and 892 black women, conducted from 1977 to 1982, found that women who held both work and family roles reported better physical and mental health than homemakers.

• According to sociologists Elaine Wethington of Cornell University and Ronald Kessler of the University of Michigan, data from three years (1985 to 1988) of a continuing federally funded study of 745 married women in Detroit "clearly suggests that employment benefits women emotionally." Women who increase their participation in the labor force report lower levels of psychological distress; those who lessen their commitment to work suffer from higher distress.

• A University of California at Berkeley study published in 1990 followed 140 women for 22 years. At age 43, those who were homemakers had more chronic conditions than the working women and seemed more disillusioned and frustrated. The working mothers were in good health and seemed to be juggling their roles with success.

In sum, paid work offers women heightened self-esteem and enhanced mental and physical health. It's unemployment that's a major risk factor for depression in women.

DOING IT ALL—AND DOING FINE

This isn't true only for affluent women in good jobs; working-class women share the benefits of work, according to psychologists Sandra Scarr and Deborah Phillips of the University of Virginia and Kathleen McCartney of the University of New Hampshire. In reviewing 80 studies on this subject, they reported that working-class women with children say they would not leave work even if they didn't need the money. Work offers not only income but adult companionship, social contact and a connection with the wider world that they cannot get at home.

Doing it all may be tough, but it doesn't wipe out the health benefits of working.

Looking at survey data from around the world, Scarr and Phillips wrote that the lives of mothers who work are not more stressful than the lives of those who are at home. So what about the second shift we've heard so much about? It certainly exists: In industrialized countries, researchers found, fathers work an average of 50 hours a week on the job and doing household chores; mothers work an average of 80 hours. Wethington and Kessler found that in daily "stress diaries" kept by husbands and wives, the women report more stress than the men do. But they also handle it better. In short, doing it all may be tough, but it doesn't wipe out the health benefits of working.

THE ADVANTAGES FOR FAMILIES

What about the kids? Many working parents feel they want more time with their kids, and they say so. But does maternal employment harm children? In 1989 University of Michigan psychologist Lois Hoffman reviewed 50 years of research and found that the expected negative effects never materialized. Most often, children of employed and unemployed mothers didn't differ on measures of child development. But children of both sexes with working mothers have a less sex-stereotyped view of the world because fathers in two-income families tend to do more child care.

However, when mothers work, the quality of non-parental child care is a legitimate worry. Scarr, Phillips and McCartney say there is "near consensus among developmental psychologists and early-childhood experts that child care per se does not constitute a risk factor in children's lives." What causes problems, they report, is poor-quality care and a troubled family life. The need for good child care in this country has been obvious for some time.

What's more, children in two-job families generally don't lose out on one-to-one time with their parents. New studies, such as S. L. Nock and P. W. Kingston's *Time with Children: The Impact of Couples' Work-Time Commitments,* show that when both parents of preschoolers are working, they spend as much time in direct interaction with their children as families in which only the fathers work. The difference is that working parents spend more time with their kids on weekends. When only the husband works, parents spend more leisure time with each other. There is a cost to two-income families—the couples lose personal time—but the kids don't seem to pay it.

One question we never used to ask is whether having a working mother could be *good* for children. Hoffman, reflecting on the finding that employed women—both blue-collar and professional—register higher life-satisfaction scores than housewives, thinks it can be. She cites studies involving infants and older children, showing that a mother's satisfaction with her employment status relates positively both to "the quality of the mother-child interaction and to various indexes of the child's adjustment and abilities." For example, psychologists J. Guidubaldi and B. K. Nastasi of Kent State University reported in a 1987 paper that a mother's satisfaction with her job was a good predictor of her child's positive adjustment in school.

Again, this isn't true only for women in high-status jobs. In a 1982 study of sources of stress for children in low-income families, psychologists Cynthia Longfellow and Deborah Belle of the Harvard University School of Education found that employed women were generally less depressed than unemployed women. What's more, their children had fewer behavioral problems.

But the real point about working women and children is that work *isn't* the point at all. There are good mothers and not-so-good mothers, and some work and some don't. When a National Academy of Sciences panel reviewed the previous 50 years of research and dozens of studies in 1982, it found no consistent effects on children from a mother's working. Work is only one of many variables, the panel concluded in *Families That Work,* and not the definitive one.

What is the effect of women's working on their marriages? Having a working wife can increase psychological stress for men, especially older men, who grew up in a world where it was not normal for a wife to work. But men's expectations that they will—and must—be the only provider may be changing. Wethington and Kessler found that a wife's employment could be a significant buffer *against* depression for men born after 1945. Still, the picture of men's psychological well-being is very mixed, and class and expectations clearly play a role. Faludi cites polls showing that young blue-collar men are especially angry at women for invading what they see as their turf as breadwinners, even though a woman with such a job could help protect her husband from economic hardship. But in highly educated, dual-career couples, both partners say the wife's career has enhanced the marriage.

THE FIRST SHIFT: WOMEN AT WORK

While women's own health and the well-being of their families aren't harmed by their working, what effect does this dual role have on their job performance? It's assumed that men can compartmentalize work and home lives but women will bring their home worries with them to work, making them distracted and inefficient employees.

Perhaps the most dangerous myth is that the solution is for women to drop back—or drop out.

The only spillover went in the other direction: The women brought their good feelings about their work home with them and left a bad day at home behind when they came to work. In fact, Wethington and Kessler found that it was the *men* who brought the family stresses with them to work. "Women are able to avoid bringing the contagion of home stress into the workplace," the researchers write, "whereas the inability of men to prevent this kind of contagion is pervasive." The researchers speculate that perhaps women get the message early on that they can handle the home front, while men are taking on chores they aren't trained for and didn't expect.

THE PERILS OF PART-TIME

Perhaps the most dangerous myth is that the solution to most problems women suffer is for them to drop back – or drop out. What studies actually show is a significant connection between a reduced commitment to work and increased psychological stress. In their Detroit study, Wethington and Kessler noted that women who went from being full-time employees to full-time housewives reported increased symptoms of distress, such as depression and anxiety attacks; the longer a woman worked and the more committed she was to the job, the greater her risk for psychological distress when she stopped.

What about part-time work, that oft-touted solution for weary women? Women who work fewer than 20 hours per week, it turns out, do not get the mental-health work benefit, probably because they "operate under the fiction that they can retain full responsibility for child care and home maintenance," wrote Wethington and Kessler. The result: Some part-timers wind up more stressed-out than women working full-time. Part-time employment also provides less money, fewer or no benefits and, often, less interesting work and a more arduous road to promotion.

That doesn't mean that a woman shouldn't cut down on her work hours or arrange a more flexible schedule. But it does mean she should be careful about jumping on a poorly designed mommy track that may make her a second-class citizen at work.

Many women think that when they have a baby, the best thing for their mental health would be to stay home. Wrong once more. According to Wethington and Kessler, having a baby does not increase psychological distress for working women – *unless* the birth results in their dropping out of the labor force. This doesn't mean that any woman who stays home to care for a child is going to be a wreck. But leaving the work force means opting out of the benefits of being in it, and women should be aware of that.

As soon as a woman has any kind of difficulty – emotional, family, medical – the knee-jerk reaction is to get her off the job. No such solution is offered to men, despite the very real correlation for men between job stress and heart attacks.

What the myth of the miserable working woman obscures is the need to focus on how the *quality* of a woman's job affects her health. Media stories warn of the alleged dangers of fast-track jobs. But our *Lifeprints* study found that married women in high-prestige jobs were highest in mental well-being; another study of life stress in women reported that married career women with children suffered the least from stress. Meanwhile, few media tears are shed for the women most at risk: those in the word-processing room who have no control at work, low pay and little support at home.

Women don't need help getting out of the work force; they need help staying in it. As long as much of the media continues to capitalize on national ignorance, that help will have to come from somewhere else. (Not that an occasional letter to the editor isn't useful.) Men need to recognize that they are not just occasional helpers but vital to the success of the family unit. The corporate culture has to be reshaped so that it doesn't run totally according to patterns set by the white male workaholic. This will be good for men *and* women. The government can guarantee parental leave and affordable, available child care. (It did so in the '40s, when women were needed in the factories.) Given that Congress couldn't even get a bill guaranteeing *unpaid* family leave passed last year, this may take some doing. But hey, this is an election year.

*Far from being the slough of despond it is considered, middle age
may be the very best time of life, researchers say—the "it" we work toward*

MIDLIFE MYTHS

WINIFRED GALLAGHER

Winifred Gallagher ("Midlife Myths") is a senior editor of
American Health. *Her latest book [is]* The Power of Place:
How Our Surroundings Shape Our Thoughts, Emotions, and
Actions.

According to the picture of human development drawn by traditional scientific literature, after a busy childhood and adolescence young adults launch their careers and social lives and then stride into a black box, from which they hobble some forty years later to face a darkly eventful senescence. According to popular literature, what takes place inside the box is an anticlimactic, unsatisfying, and even traumatic march over the hill and toward the grave—or, worse, the nursing home. This scenario complements the anecdotes that often figure in conversations about middle age: that friend of a friend whose lifetime investment in career and family went up in the flames of a passion for the au pair, or that second cousin rumored to have gone off the deep end during the "change of life" when the kids left for college.

So entrenched is the idea that middle age is bad or boring or both that the almost 80 million members of the graying Baby Boom generation won't use the term except in referring to Ozzie and Harriet Nelson or Ward and June Cleaver. "We have a problem here, and it's called denial," the television producer Stan Rogow, whose 1992 series *Middle Ages* was a critical success, recently told *Newsweek*. He blames the show's title for its commercial failure: "'Middle age' is this horrible-sounding thing you've heard throughout your life and hated." The denial he describes frustrates the efforts of researchers who are conducting the first comprehensive, multidisciplinary studies of middle age. They are finding that it is not just an aging process but life's peak experience.

The study of development concentrates mostly on life's early stages, when behavioral and physiological growth and change are simultaneous. In the 1960s the new discipline of gerontology revealed that as people lived much further into old age, a reverse synchrony obtained toward life's end. Looking back from studies of the elderly and, to a lesser extent, forward from studies of the young, researchers began to suspect that middle age might be not simply a long interval during which things are worse than they are in youth and better than they are

in old age but a developmental process in its own right—albeit one not particularly tied to changes in the body. Common perceptions of middle age are that it occurs from roughly forty to sixty; in the future, increased longevity and better health may push back the period of middle age even further. The scientists and scholars exploring this part of life, which is probably better described experientially than chronologically—the very concept of middle age itself is something of a cultural artifact, with social and economic components—range from the medically, sociologically, and psychologically oriented John D. and Catherine T. MacArthur Foundation Research Network on Successful Midlife Development (MIDMAC), administered from Vero Beach, Florida, to the psychoanalytically and spiritually grounded C. G. Jung Foundation's Center for Midlife Development in New York City.

Although there are plenty of exceptions, "the data show that middle age is the very best time in life," says Ronald Kessler, a sociologist and MIDMAC fellow who is a program director in the survey research center of the University of Michigan's Institute for Social Research. "When looking at the total U.S. population, the best year is fifty. You don't have to deal with the aches and pains of old age or the anxieties of youth: Is anyone going to love me? Will I ever get my career off the ground? Rates of general distress are low—the incidences of depression and anxiety fall at about thirty-five and don't climb again until the late sixties. You're healthy. You're productive. You have enough money to do some of the things you like to do. You've come to terms with your relationships, and the chance of divorce is very low. Midlife is the 'it' you've been working toward. You can turn your attention toward being rather than becoming."

Whereas Kessler's picture of middle age is drawn from facts and figures, the image in most Americans' minds is based on myths, derived not from the ordinary experiences of most people but from the unusual experiences of a few. Although these make for livelier reading and conversation, they generate an unnecessarily gloomy attitude about the middle years which limits people's horizons, according to Margie Lachman, a psychologist, a MIDMAC fellow, and the director of the Life-span Developmental Psychology Laboratory at Brandeis University. When Lachman asked young adults what it means to be middle-aged, they gave such answers as "You think more

The overwhelming majority of people, surveys show, accomplish the task of coming to terms with the realities of middle age through a long, gentle process—not an acute, painful crisis.

about the past than the future" and "You worry about money for health care." They also assumed that the stress experienced in middle age came from the desire to be young again. Older subjects Lachman surveyed, who knew better, attributed stress to coping with the many demands of the busiest time in life. And whereas the older group saw their lives as generally stable, the younger expected to experience a lot of change—and a crisis—in midlife. "The images and beliefs we have about middle age are the guideposts for our planning, evaluation, and goal-setting," Lachman says. "Are they accurate? Or negative self-fulfilling prophesies?"

Gilbert Brim, a pioneer in the study of social development through the life-span and the director of MIDMAC, agrees. "Passed on from generation to generation," he says, "widely shared cultural beliefs and untested theories about middle age put forward in the media continue to be played out in society. But they're likely to be wrong. There are probably as many myths about midlife now as there were about aging thirty years ago, before the advent of gerontology. The time has come to rid ourselves of these obsolete ideas."

The Inexorable Midlife Crisis?

MOST YOUNGER ADULTS ANTICIPATE THAT BEtween their late thirties and their early fifties a day will come when they suddenly realize that they have squandered their lives and betrayed their dreams. They will collapse into a poorly defined state that used to be called a nervous breakdown. Escape from this black hole will mean either embracing an un-American philosophy of eschatological resignation or starting over—jaded stockbrokers off to help Mother Teresa, phlegmatic spouses off to the StairMaster and the singles scene. In short, they will have a midlife crisis.

If youth's theme is potential, midlife's is reality: childhood fantasies are past, the fond remembrances of age are yet to be, and the focus is on coming to terms with the finite resources of the here and now. The overwhelming majority of people, surveys show, accomplish this devel-

opmental task, as psychologists put it, through a long, gentle process—not an acute, painful crisis. Over time the college belle or the high school athlete leans less on physical assets, the middle manager's horizons broaden beyond the corner office, and men and women fortunate enough to have significant others regard the rigors of courtship with indulgent smiles. In relying on brains and skill more than beauty and brawn, diffusing competitive urges to include the tennis court or a community fundraising project, and valuing long-term friendship and domestic pleasures over iffy ecstasies, these people have not betrayed their youthful goals but traded them in for more practical ones that bring previously unsuspected satisfaction. Ronald Kessler says, "The question to ask the middle-aged person isn't just What has happened to you? but also How has your experience changed your thinking?"

The middle-aged tend to be guided not by blinding revelations associated with emotional crisis but by slowly dawning adaptive insights into the self and others, which Kessler calls "psychological turning points." Early in midlife these usually involve a recognition of limitations: the local politician realizes that she'll never make it to the U.S. Senate, and the high school English teacher accepts that he's not going to be a famous man of letters. In the middle period of middle age the transitions usually concern what Kessler calls a redirection of goals: "You say to yourself, 'I'm killing myself at work, but the thing that really satisfies me is my family. I'm not going to change jobs, but from now on I'm going to focus more on home, and career will mean something different to me.'" In later middle age, turning points, especially for women, often involve a recognition of strength—"just the opposite of what you'd suppose," Kessler says. "The shy violet, for example, finds herself chairing a committee." These soundings taken and adjustments made prompt not dramatic departures from one's life course but gentle twists and curves.

"Mastery experiences," the more robust versions of which figure in Outward Bound–type adventure vacations, can be catalysts for middle-aged people in their ordinary settings as well. One of Kessler's subjects finally got his college diploma at fifty-eight, observing that he

"Mastery experiences," the more robust versions of which figure in Outward Bound–type vacations, can be catalysts for middle-aged people in their ordinary settings as well.

had thereby "resolved a lot of things and completed something important"; in almost the same language, a man of fifty said that he had "done something important" when he became proficient enough in his hobby of electronics to tutor others. Overcoming her lifelong fear of water, one woman learned to swim at the age of forty-five. "One day her family went to the pool, and she just jumped in," Kessler says. "This was a very powerful experience for her, not because she wanted to be a lifeguard but because she had mastered her anxiety as well as a new skill."

Even an apparently negative turning point can have benefits. Quite a few of Kessler's subjects, when asked if they had realized a dream in the past year, said yes, "but quite a few said they had given up on one," he says. "When the folks who have dreamed for years about a big summer house where all the kids would flock finally accept that they don't have the money and the kids have other plans, they release a lot of tension. This kind of surrender is very productive, because dreams that run counter to reality waste a lot of energy."

Although all people make psychological transitions and adjustments in the course of middle age, relatively few experience these as catastrophic. In surveys 10 to 12 percent of respondents report that they have had a midlife crisis, Kessler says. "What they often mean is that the kind of disaster that can happen at other times in life—divorce, or being fired, or a serious illness—happened to them during their middle years." An unusual convergence of such unhappy events can push even a hardy middle-aged person into a state of emotional emergency. "First you notice that your hair is falling out," Gilbert Brim says. "Then you go to the office and learn you didn't get that raise, and when you get home, your wife says she's leaving." But most of those who have a true psychological crisis in middle age—according to MIDMAC, about five percent of the population—have in fact experienced internal upheavals throughout their lives. "They see the world in those terms," says David Featherman, a MIDMAC fellow and the president of the Social Science Research Council, in New York City. "They aren't particularly good at absorbing or rebounding from life's shocks."

People prone to midlife crisis score low on tests of introspection, or reflecting on one's self and on life, and high in denial, or coping with trouble by not thinking about it. "Take the guy who still thinks he's a great athlete," Kessler says. "Somehow he hasn't let reality intrude on his boyhood fantasy. But one day something forces him to wake up. Maybe he's at a family reunion playing ball with his twelve-year-old nephew and he can't make his shots. Suddenly he's an old man, a failure." Heading for the same kind of shock are the people banking on the big promotion that their colleagues know will never happen, along with those who believe that hair transplants and breast implants mean eternal youth. "Such individuals have to work hard to maintain their illusions," Kessler says. "They spend a lot of energy on the cogni-

tive effort of self-delusion, until reality finally intervenes." Because most middle-aged people have grown skilled at monitoring changes in reality—the jump shot isn't what it used to be, the figure has changed for good—they are spared the abrupt, traumatic run-ins with reality that result in a psychic emergency.

Midlife crises are an affliction of the relatively affluent: rosy illusions are easier to maintain when a person is already somewhat shielded from reality. Just as childhood is often constricted among the poor, who early in life face adult realities and burdens, so middle age may be eclipsed by a premature old age brought on by poverty and poor health. Among working-class people, for whom strength and stamina mean earning power, middle age may begin at thirty-five rather than the forty-five often cited in studies by respondents drawn from the sedentary middle class. Because any fanciful notions that poor and blue-collar people might have are rigorously tested by daily life, Kessler says, they rarely dwell in fantasy. "In terms of career, factory workers are likelier to be wherever they're going to be at thirty than executives," he says. "In terms of mental health, being disappointed at what *is* is a better kind of problem to have than being anxious about what will be. Once you know the reality, you can say, 'I can't afford to buy a boat, so I'll rent one for vacations.' Being up in the air is the big problem."

Despite the lurid tales of fifty-year-olds who run off with their twenty-five-year-old secretaries, such events are relatively rare in real-life midlife. Most couples who divorce break up in the first six or eight years of matrimony, and by midlife the majority report being more or less content. "The family-demography side of the midlife crisis just isn't there," says Larry Bumpass, a MIDMAC fellow and a professor of sociology at the University of Wisconsin at Madison, who directs the federally funded National Survey of Families and Households, the largest demographic study of its kind. "After ten or fifteen years together, the probability that a couple will split up is low. I've looked at the data every way possible to see if there's even a blip in the divorce rate when the children leave home, but that's just folklore too."

Even the nature of the difficulties most commonly reported suggests that the majority of the middle-aged operate from a position of strength. "The problems mentioned usually concern not the self but someone else—a child or parent," Kessler says. "Part of the reason for this outward focus is that the middle-aged person has secured his or her own situation and can afford to pay attention to others. Compared with the issues that arise in youth and old age, for most people the management-type problems that crop up in midlife aren't nearly as emotionally devastating."

Carl Jung divided life into halves—the first devoted to forming the ego and getting established in the world, the second to finding a larger meaning for all that effort. He then took the unorthodox step of paying more attention to the second. When shifting from one stage to the other, Jung observed, people experience an external loss of some kind—physical prowess or upward mobility or a relationship. When they treat this loss as a signal that it's time to develop new dimensions, Jung thought, transformation is in store. However, he predicted stagnation or even a breakdown if the loss is met with denial, fear, or a sense of defeat. Aryeh Maidenbaum, the executive director of the C. G. Jung Foundation's Center for Midlife Development, offers the Jungian rule of thumb for midlife crises: "The greater the disparity between the outer and inner person, the greater the chance for trouble. The most important inner need people have is to be seen for who they are. If that's what's happening at midlife, there's no crisis."

The Change for the Worse

IF THERE'S ONE ISSUE REGARDING WHICH MISINFORMATION feeds mounting hysteria about middle age, it's menopause. After finishing any of a number of recent books and articles, a reader might conclude that for a few years a middle-aged woman might as well choose between sobbing alone and riding around on a broom. One of the few people who have gleaned their own hard data on the subject is Karen Matthews, a professor of psychiatry, epidemiology, and psychology at the University of Pittsburgh School of Medicine, who has conducted a longitudinal survey of the psychological and physical changes experienced by 500 women passing through menopause. "The fact is that most women do very well in the menopausal transition," she says, refuting the popular image of women who are invariably depressed, extremely unpleasant, or both. "There are some common physical symptoms that aren't fun, notably hot flashes, but only a minority of women—about ten percent—have a tough time psychologically."

Matthews has identified the characteristics of those who experience few problems in menopause and those who experience many. "The women who do well respond to the menopause with action," she says. "That may not be their direct intention, but they end up coping with the stressor by making positive changes. Those who, say, step up their exercise regimen don't even show the biological changes, such as the adverse shifts in lipids implicated in coronary disease, that others do. These 'active copers' say, 'Hey, I look a little different, feel a little less energetic. Why don't I . . .'"

Try hormone-replacement therapy? In evaluating its effects on physical health, women and doctors must juggle evidence suggesting that while HRT cuts the number of hot flashes by about half and reduces vulnerability to osteoporosis and perhaps coronary disease, it may raise the risk of breast cancer and, if estrogen is taken without progestin, uterine cancer. The National Institutes of Health is now conducting a badly needed controlled long-term clinical trial of large numbers of women on HRT which should provide some answers. Meanwhile, some doctors, confronted with incomplete data, tell women that the decision is up to them. Considering the threat of osteoporosis and of coronary disease, which is the leading cause of death for women over fifty, many other doctors recommend HRT to those whose risk of breast cancer is low. Still others regard its widespread use with dismay. Their concerns range from the fact that only one in three women is vulnerable to osteoporosis to a flaw in the argument that hormones can prevent heart disease. In part because doctors are cautious about prescribing HRT for women with illnesses such as hypertension and diabetes, the population that takes it is healthier to begin with—a built-in selection bias that skews studies of the therapy's effects. Among HRT's vocal critics are the doctors Sonja and John McKinlay, epidemiologists at the New England Research Institute, in Watertown, Massachusetts. "HRT is inappropriate for the vast majority of women, who shouldn't use it," John McKinlay says. "Yet the pharmaceutical industry's goal is to have every post-menopausal woman on it until death." Having surveyed the literature on menopause and HRT, Alice Rossi, a MIDMAC fellow and an emeritus professor of sociology at the University of Massachusetts at Amherst, says, "I wish we had a better scientific foundation for deciding if it's appropriate for women to take hormones for decades. At this point there's no strong evidence for a pro or anti position."

Although the process of weighing HRT's effects on physical health continues, Matthews has determined that as far as behavioral effects are concerned, HRT is "*not* the most important factor in most women's psychological well-being during menopause." For that matter, she says, women who do and don't use HRT may report differing experiences because they are different types of people to begin with. In Matthews's study the typical user was not only better educated and healthier but also likely to be a hard-driving "Type A" person, less content with the status quo. "These women are up on the literature," Matthews says, "more aware of HRT, and more interested in seeking treatment."

If active copers, whether or not they take hormones, fare best during menopause, Matthews says, the women likely to have the worst time have two disparate things in common: HRT and a low regard for themselves. "Women who have poor self-esteem but don't use hormones don't have a hard time," she says. One hypothesis is that reproductive hormones, particularly progesterone, cause some women to become dysphoric, or moody; if a woman who has this adverse reaction to HRT also has a poor self-image, she is likely to be more upset by a stressor such as a menopausal symptom than a woman with a sturdier ego.

"The idea that most women have a hard time psychologically is the major myth our data have dispelled," Matthews says. "Eighty percent of our subjects thought they were going to become depressed and irritable at menopause, but only ten percent did. Those who had a rough time had showed signs long before of being anxious, depressed, or pessimistic. Menopause makes women with that pre-existing set of characteristics, which are not age-related, more emotionally vulnerable."

Much of the dark mythology of menopause derives not from the thing itself but from simultaneous aspects of the aging process. "It's the physical manifestation of aging—and a woman's reaction to it—that's critical in predicting whether the years from forty-five to fifty-five will be difficult or not," Alice Rossi says. "Society's image of an attractive woman is ten years younger than that of an attractive man. Graying at the temples and filling out a bit can be attractive in a man—look at Clinton and Gore. But their wives are still trying to look twenty-eight." Rossi isn't necessarily advocating the grin-and-bear-it attitude toward aging favored by Barbara Bush. Seeming ten years younger than you are can be a good thing, she says, if it means a concern for good health and well-being, rather than an obsession with youth.

Matthews considers a lot of the anxiety expressed by women about menopause to be unnecessary. In response to the often-heard complaint that there has been no good research on the subject, she points to several major long-term investigations—including hers, one by Sonja and John McKinlay, and one conducted in Sweden—that independently show that the majority of women have no serious problems making the transition.

In discussing a recent bestseller on the subject, Gail Sheehy's *The Silent Passage*, she says, "Ms. Sheehy interviewed me at length, but the experience of menopause she describes in her book is not the one that emerges as typical in the three major studies. Some women have a very difficult menopause, and Ms. Sheehy feels there's a message there. We need to figure out why some women do have problems, so that we can help. "There has been no generation of women like this one. They're better educated. They're healthier to the point that they now live half their adult lives after the menopause. For them, the menopausal transition is best characterized as a time of optimism. It's a bridge—an opportunity for women to think about what they want to do next."

Despite persistent rumors, there's probably no such thing as male menopause. Men simply don't experience a midlife biological change equivalent to the one women undergo. Whereas nature is responsible for that inequity, culture is at the bottom of a far more destructive one. For a research project, John McKinlay videotaped visits to doctors' offices made by patients matched for every variable but gender. The films showed that a man and a woman who complained of the same symptoms were often treated very differently: men were twice as likely to be referred to a medical specialist, and women were much likelier to be referred to a psychotherapist; men were urged toward health-enhancing behavior such as dieting and exercise, but women rarely were. ("This is particularly unfortunate where smoking is concerned," McKinlay says, "because the health benefits for women who give it up may be greater than those for men.") He concludes that the gender-related disparities apparent in much medical literature may reflect what doctors see more than actual physiological differences. Accordingly,

Many studies show that satisfaction with the marital relationship climbs again after couples weather the labor-intensive period of launching careers and babies.

he suspects that when middle-aged men complain of bad moods and decreased libido and energy, most doctors see a need for behavioral change. When women report the same symptoms, many doctors attribute them to menopause and prescribe hormones. "Don't forget that most women get their primary health care from a gynecologist," McKinlay says, "which would be like most men getting theirs from a urologist."

Among endocrinologists outside the United States there is more support for the notion of a male climacteric, in which older men's lower testosterone levels cause decreased fertility, increased body fat, bone loss, and skin-tone changes, along with the same behavioral symptoms that are often attributed to female menopause. While allowing that a small percentage of older men suffer from an endocrinological problem and can benefit from hormone-replacement therapy, McKinlay insists that there is no evidence that the majority would benefit. For that matter, he says, testosterone has little effect on the sexuality of those over fifty or fifty-five, and taking it as a supplement may in fact increase the risk of prostate cancer. Having conducted a study of the sex lives of 1,700 men aged forty to seventy which is considered by many to be the best information on the subject, he says, "There's no physiological, endocrinological, psychological, or clinical basis for a male menopause. Whether or not people believe in it has nothing to do with whether it exists, only with whether the pharmaceutical industry can persuade them that it does. In ten years male climacteric clinics will sprout up to treat a condition that may or may not exist—but, of course, they'll make money."

McKinlay's major reservation about most of the existing research on the effects of reproductive hormones is that it has been conducted with "small, atypical" samples of people who are seeking treatment in the health-care system. "What's talked about in the literature—both professional and popular—is the experience of *patients*," he says, "not healthy people, about whom we know very little."

The Best Years of Your Life Are Over

MANY PEOPLE HAVE A MEMORY FROM ADOLES-
cence of gazing around a gathering of adults,
no longer in the green days of their youth
yet dressed to kill and living it up, and
thinking the equivalent of "How valiant they are to make
an effort at their age." Because Hollywood and Madison
Avenue project this same juvenile notion, many of the
middle-aged are surprised and relieved to find that their
lives aren't nearly so dreary as they expected. After analyzing decades of social research for his 1992 book *Ambition*, Gilbert Brim found that a person's zest for and satisfaction with life don't depend on youth—or on status,
sexuality, health, money, or any of the other things one
might expect. "What people really want out of life are action and challenge—to be in the ballgame," he says. "To
feel satisfied, we must be able to tackle a task that's hard
enough to test us, but not so difficult that we'll repeatedly fail. We want to work hard, then succeed."

This maxim has a special resonance for today's middle-
aged, career-oriented middle class, often portrayed as be-
leaguered victims of "role strain" or burnt-out cases operating on automatic pilot. In fact, Brim says, most are
instinctively seeking the level of "just manageable difficulty"—an optimum degree of effort that taps about 80
percent of a person's capacity and generates that satisfied,
job-well-done feeling. Pushing beyond that level for prolonged periods leaves people stressed and anxious; falling
below it leaves them bored. Because what is just manageable at forty might not be at sixty, people rearrange their
lives, often unconsciously, to balance capacities and challenges. When one does well at something, one ups the
ante; when one fails, one lowers the sights a bit or even
switches arenas. Brim draws an illustration from a study
of AT&T executives: over time the most successful grew
more work-oriented; the others began to turn more to
their families and social lives—educating the children or
lowering the golf handicap—for feelings of accomplishment. The key point, he says, is that neither group was
more satisfied than the other. "This intuitive process by
which we constantly reset our goals in response to our
gains and losses is one of the most overlooked aspects of
adult development."

One way in which the middle-aged are particularly
skilled in adjusting their goals is in choosing which Joneses
to keep up with. "Our mental health is very much affected by our estimation of how we're doing in terms of the
people around us," says Carol Ryff, a psychologist and a
MIDMAC fellow who is the associate director of the Institute on Aging and Adult Life, at the University of Wisconsin at Madison. "We all make these important measurements, even though we're often barely conscious of
doing so." Whereas the young person launching a career
might try to outdo Maurizio Pollini or Donna Karan, the
savvy middle-aged one knows that holding to this standard beyond a certain point ensures misery—or a genuine

midlife crisis. Particularly when faced with a difficult situation, the mature person makes a "downward comparison" that puts his own problems in a different perspective and helps him soldier on. Thus the executive who
has just been laid off compares his finances not with the
Rockefellers' but with those of the couple across the
street who are both on unemployment, and reminds himself that at least his wife's position is secure. "The better
your mental health, the less often you measure yourself
against people who make you feel crummy," Ryff says.
"In midlife you begin to say, 'Well, so I'm not in the
same category as the Nobelists. That's just not an expectation I'm going to drag around anymore.'"

By middle age most people destined for success have
achieved it, which erects some special hurdles in the just-
manageable course of life. "Winning is not simply the opposite of losing," Brim says. "It creates its own disruptions." If a person becomes psychologically trapped by
the need to do better, go higher, and make more, for example, he can end up operating at 90 to 100 percent of his
capacity—a level at which stress makes life very uncomfortable. At this level, too, Brim says, he will begin to lose
more than he wins. Burdened with more roles than he can
handle, or promoted beyond the level of just-manageable
difficulty, he may end up "held together by a thin paste
of alcohol, saunas, and antibiotics." Brim says that because our society does not supply many ways to step
down gracefully, it "pays the price in burnout and incompetence in high places."

Even those who can sustain Hollywood-style success
must do some internal retooling in order to maintain the
charge of the just-manageable mode. To keep life interesting, Brim says, the people who handle winning best
don't merely raise the challenge in the same area but go
into a new one—a sport, a hobby, a community project—
where they again find a lot of room for moving up. "Certain professional athletes are good examples," he says.
"Because they know that their peak will be short-lived, at
a certain point they diversify their aspirations to include
family, business interests, and volunteer activities."

So skilled are most people at maintaining a just-manageable life through the years that Brim finds no appre-
ciable differences in the sense of well-being reported by
different age groups. Indeed, he says, despite the insis-
tent propaganda to the contrary, "except for concerns
about health, most research shows that older people are
as happy as younger ones."

Midlife Romance:
The Bloom Is Off the Rose

IF MIDDLE AGE IS SEEN AS A DULL BUSINESS, ITS RELA-
tionships are imagined to be the dreariest part. In the
course of studying beliefs about and images of
midlife, Margie Lachman compared the experiences
of a group of Boston-area people aged eighteen to eighty-
five, and found no evidence that the middle-aged are less

loving. In fact, steady levels of intimacy and affection were two of the few constants she tracked. Largely because married people make up the majority of the middle-aged—about 75 percent—most of the data about life relationships concern them. Then too, less is known about other bonds because until the mid-seventies studies of midlife focused on the experience of white middle-class heterosexual men. Although there is still very little information about gay midlife, some data are emerging about how single people in general fare socially during middle age.

It's about time, according to Alice Rossi. "Considering the longer life-span, a person may be without a partner at many points in life," she points out. "We not only marry later today but often have intervals between relationships, and perhaps lengthy spells as widows and widowers." She thinks that the stereotype of the aging spinster who is unfulfilled without a man is heading into the realm of midlife mythology. "There's recent evidence that single women have better mental and physical health and social lives than single men," she says. "Rather than being all alone, they have friends and close family ties, not only with parents but also with young nieces and nephews, with whom they may enjoy special relationships."

As for the married, many studies show that satisfaction with the relationship is lower throughout the child-rearing years that it had been, but climbs again after couples weather the labor-intensive period of launching careers and babies. In Lachman's Boston survey, reports of stress related to marriage decreased steadily from youth through old age. Although divorce and death may account for some of that decline, she says, "people may in fact grow more skilled in handling their relationships." Observing that by midlife couples have fewer fights and more closeness, Ron Kessler says, "Once they get the little kids out of their hair, husbands and wives catch their breath, look at each other, and ask, 'What are we going to talk about now? What was it all about twenty years ago?'"

In his study of sexuality John McKinlay found that only two percent of the 1,700 middle-aged and older men reported having more than one current sexual partner. This figure, vastly lower than the usual guesstimates, challenges the stereotype of the bored middle-aged philanderer. Moreover, although McKinlay recorded steady declines in the men's sexual activity, from lusty thoughts to erections, he found no decrease in their sexual satisfaction—a phenomenon Gilbert Brim calls "a triumph of the adaptation of aspirations to realities." Equivalent data about women have not been gathered, but McKinlay's findings complement other surveys that show that aging has little impact on people's enjoyment of sex.

People and their doctors, McKinlay says, should distinguish between sexual problems caused by aging and those caused by things that often get lumped with it, such as poor health, weight gain, lack of exercise, and the use of nicotine or too much alcohol. Compared with a healthy nonsmoking peer, for example, a smoker who has heart disease has a sevenfold greater risk of impotence.

Psychological fitness, too, plays a vital role. A man may think his primary problem is impotence caused by age when in fact his sexual trouble is a symptom of a very treatable depression. "We must not resort to biological reductionism, which is what women have been struggling against," McKinlay says.

Widely publicized conclusions drawn from the sex lives of the ill—that a vigorous sex life is not a reasonable expectation in middle age, for instance—may cast their pall on the well. "When I hear a healthy fifty-year-old man say, 'That sexy stuff is for kids,' I feel sorry for him," McKinlay says. "Only five percent of the women in our institute's long-term study of menopause reported suffering from vaginal dryness, but women are told it's a very common problem after a certain age." Contrary to the stereotype of the asexual older woman, he says, some women feel liberated by menopause and the end of birth control. If older women have a problem with their sex lives, according to McKinlay, it may be that their husbands aren't in good health. His prescription for a vital midlife: "If I were feeling troubled about aging, I'd look first at the behavioral modifications I could make—diet, exercise, alcohol-monitoring, and so on. If they didn't work, then I'd think about treatments."

Having edited a book about sexuality through the course of life, Alice Rossi observes that although the mature expression of eroticism remains poorly understood by science, let alone by our youth-oriented culture, middle-aged people are likely to expand their definition of sex to include sensual, not just reproductive, acts. "If the message we get from society is that we have to keep on acting as we did at thirty," she says, "a lot of us are going to feel that we have a sexual disorder at some point." After a certain age, for example, men in particular may require physical stimulation to feel aroused. An awareness of this normal tendency, Rossi says, added to modern women's generally greater assertiveness, lays the groundwork for a new kind of relationship for older couples—one in which women have a more active role. "If the middle-aged don't feel pressured to conform to a youthful stereotype," she says, "I think we can predict some good things for their sex lives."

The Empty Nest and the Sandwich Generation

WHEN THE ROLE OF FAMILY IN THE EXPERIENCE of middle age is mentioned, one of two scenarios usually comes to mind. In the better established, the abandoned mother waves a tearful good-bye to her last chick and dully goes through the motions of life in the "empty nest." According to Larry Bumpass's demographic survey, however, the nest may be anything but empty: expensive housing and a weak economy and job market mean that the young delay their own marriages and are likelier to return home after a brief foray outside.

The more contemporary midlife family myth concerns the plight of the "sandwich generation": in a recent *Doonesbury* cartoon starring a professional couple, the forty-something husband tells his wife, busy juggling the needs of her children and their grandmother, "Don't die. Everyone's counting on you." Women's entry into the job market has focused much attention on a purported host of adults who make the circuit from the day-care center to Gramps's place to the office with nary a moment for themselves. "It's true that there's a lot going on in your life in middle age and you have little time for leisure," Margie Lachman says. "Fortunately, you're also at your peak in terms of competence, control, the ability to handle stress, and sense of responsibility. You're *equipped* for overload." According to Carol Ryff, people busy with both careers and relationships enjoy not only greater financial security and intellectual and social stimulation but also a psychological benefit. The eminent behavioral scientist Bernice Neugarten thinks that the hallmark of healthy middle age is "complexity," or a feeling of being in control of a crowded life and involved in the world at the same time. Ryff found in the course of one of her studies that this quality was most marked among the first generation to combine family and career. "It seems," she says, "that all the role-juggling that middle-aged people complain about actually makes them feel more engaged in life."

Rossi is dubious that the sandwich-generation problem is either new or widespread. "This phenomenon is a lot like the supposed midlife crisis," she says. "There are people who think that spending two hours a week with Mother is a big deal. But the fact is that very few men or women are caring both for little children and for elderly parents." One reason for this is that the "old old" who need considerable care are still a small group, and few of them are a daily drain on their children. Then, too, as Bumpass says, "over the past several decades the elderly have increasingly lived independently. They're economically more able to do so, and both sides prefer things that way." According to research conducted by Glenna Spitze, of the State University of New York at Albany, close involvement by the middle-aged with their parents—usually with a mother who has already cared for and buried her own husband—is likeliest to occur when the middle-aged person's children are older and need less attention. "For that matter," Rossi says, "rather than being a drain, the children are likely to be a comfort and help. It's important to remember that intimacy with children, which bottoms out from ages fifteen to nineteen, climbs steeply through the twenties and thirties. One of the things to look forward to in midlife is the continuity and shared interests that will come as your children in turn become parents."

To the list of underestimated family pleasures Ryff adds the satisfaction that parents take in knowing that grown-up children have turned out all right. She found that adult offspring are a vital if underrecognized element in middle-aged well-being, and that adjusting to how well or poorly they have matured is another of midlife's important developmental tasks. After studying 215 parents, Ryff found that their adult children's level of psychological adjustment was a major predictor for almost all aspects of both fathers' and mothers' mental health—although mothers took more credit for it. "The literature on parenting includes very little on what *parents* get out of it," she says, "or on how it affects their self-image, especially when the kids are older. Parenting never ends."

At Last, the Reward: Wisdom

LONG ON THE PROCESS OF BECOMING, THE LITERature of human development remains short on the business of being. That adults don't grow and change in the predictable, simultaneously physiological and behavioral fashion that children do partly explains why. So tidy is early development by comparison that it's even possible to link certain ages to certain behavioral stages, such as the "terrible twos" and the "temperamental teens." Although Gail Sheehy's bestseller *Passages* (described by Gilbert Brim as focused on "selected case studies that illustrate a theory that has no broad empirical support") advanced an adult model of such "age-stage" development, research continues to show that the ways in which adults evolve are not universal, not likely to occur in clear-cut stages, and not tied to particular ages. So poorly do the middle-aged fit into developmental patterns, in fact, that the huge National Survey of Families and Households revealed that of more than forty projected "typical midlife events," none was likely to happen at a certain, predictable age.

Biologically oriented behavioral scientists argue that at the individual level certain basic tendencies evident at birth or shortly after are the immutable building blocks of personality. The aversion to novel stimuli which becomes shyness, denoted by a low score in extroversion, is one such element. Some claim, moreover, that anyone can be defined even in early childhood in terms of how high or low he or she scores in tests that measure the "big five"

Most middle-aged adults benefit from knocking about in the world. When they go down a blind alley, they soon recognize the mistake, and save themselves much time and energy.

traits: neuroticism, extroversion, openness, agreeableness, and conscientiousness. This largely biological programming, trait theorists believe, means that personality is set in concrete around the time that physical development ceases. Afterward one may grow in terms of changing attitudes, skills, interests, and relationships, but only in ways consistent with one's big-five template.

Environment-minded researchers, including the MIDMAC team, take the influence of things like attitudes, interests, and relationships more seriously. They're working on a different, flexible model of adult development, based not on genes but on experience. Brim and his colleagues don't dispute that someone born shy or dutiful may very well stay that way, but they stress that whether he or she is raised in a sociable or a reclusive family, has a happy or an unhappy marriage, gets an exciting or a dull job, and has good or poor health will have considerable impact on identity. Bringing up reports of "aberrant outcomes"—people who early in life seem destined for success or failure yet somehow turn out the other way—Brim observes that adult change is shaped not just by the characteristics a person brings to bear on life but also by what life brings to bear on him or her, from family feuds to fatal attractions, religious experiences to traffic accidents. Accordingly, the MIDMAC group and others interested in tracking adult development focus on the ways in which, as a result of the depth and variety of their experience, their subjects' goals and values alter over time.

To illustrate experiential midlife development, Ron Kessler points to ways in which people are shaped by the influence of the workplace. "During early life you're socially segregated—all your school companions are also eight- or twelve-year-olds from the same neighborhood," he says. "Then comes adulthood, and suddenly you're working alongside different kinds of people of different ages. You can look around and say to yourself, 'In twenty years, if I act like him, I could have a heart attack, or end up divorced.' Or 'Sure, she makes a lot of money, but do I really want to work sixty hours a week?'"

Most middle-aged adults benefit from knocking about in the world, a process that greatly increases their efficiency in managing life. When they go down a blind alley, they soon recognize the mistake, and save themselves much time and energy. "Because they have all this material to plot trajectories with, the middle-aged are equipped to do an enormous amount of internal reshuffling," Kessler says. "Unlike younger people, they don't have to test everything themselves in the real world. Adults who learn from their mistakes change and grow, and those who don't, don't." Kessler describes a bright corporate lawyer who remains developmentally stalled in the "becoming" phase appropriate to youth: "He goes around saying '*This* is being a lawyer? I'd rather be a kid *wanting* to be a lawyer.'"

Perhaps the best refutation of the myths that adults don't develop and that adults do develop but only in rigid stages is a new body of research on the genesis of a psychological and cognitive capacity that scientists can only call wisdom. As is often the case in science, this inquiry began with the investigation of a mistaken premise. Assuming that the formalistic SAT-type process was the human norm in solving problems, those studying the effects of aging concluded that older people suffer a cognitive deficit, because they do worse than the young on such tests. The more researchers explored this apparently biological decline, however, the more they had to consider another possibility: people of different ages may perceive the same problem differently.

Any adult who has debated with a bright adolescent about, say, the likelihood that the world's nations will erase their boundaries and create a passportless global citizenry knows that there are two types of intelligence: the abstract, objective, Platonic-dualism sort that peaks early, and the practical, subjective type, born of shirtsleeves experience, which comes later. When asked the way to Rome, the young trace the most direct route very quickly, while their elders ponder: "Why Rome? Is this trip really a good idea? At what time of year? For business or pleasure? Alone or with others?"

The pre-eminent wisdom researcher is Paul Baltes, a MIDMAC fellow and a co-director of the Max Planck Institute for Human Development and Education, in Berlin. Baltes conducts studies of "whether living long can produce a higher level of mental functioning." The cognitive mechanics of the brain—the speed and accuracy with which we process information—are biological and subject to decline, he finds. But the brain's pragmatics—our knowledge and skill in using information—are not. When Baltes's subjects take the intellectual equivalent of a medical stress test, the young do in two seconds what the older do, with many more mistakes, in eight. But, Baltes says, unlike other species, ours can compensate for biological deficits. "If people have hearing problems, society develops hearing aids, and if I train an older subject in test-taking skills, he'll outperform an untutored younger person. By providing knowledge and strategies for using it, culture outwits biology. In all the areas of functioning in which age means more access to information, older people may be better off than young ones." In short, the middle-aged may be slower but they're smarter.

Beyond the commonsensical savvy acquired through daily experience lies a rarefied ability to deal with the fundamental problems of the human condition: matters ambiguous and existential, complex and conflicted, which call for the wisdom of Solomon. Using literary analysis, Baltes finds evidence in all cultures of people equipped to deal with these difficult issues, and he has devised several ways to test for the presence of this ability. In one type of study, subjects read vignettes of difficult situations—for example, a person pondering how to respond to a friend who has decided to commit suicide—and then "think aloud" through their decision-making process to a resolution of the problem. In another type, people with many contacts in the world of high achievers are asked to nominate those they consider especially wise; researchers then monitor how these candidates think about difficult problems. Both forms of testing allow Baltes to score subjects on his "wisdom criteria," which include great factual and procedural knowledge, the capacity to cope with uncertainty, and the ability to frame an event in its larger context. "Those who have these attributes are the people we call wise," he says, "and they are easily recognized. People who are said to have this quality do score higher than others."

To sense the difference between the wise and the hoi polloi, one might imagine a successful fifty-year-old urban lawyer who announces that she is going to quit her job, move to the country, and start a mail-order seed and bulb business. Most listeners will think, if not say, something like "What a crazy idea." But there might be someone who says, "Wait. What are the circumstances? Maybe this lawyer feels that her life has grown sterile. Maybe she has some solid plans for this change. Let's talk some more." According to Baltes's statistics, this wise person is probably neither young nor very old but somewhere between the ages of forty and seventy. "The highest grades we record occur somewhere around sixty," he says. "Wisdom peaks in midlife or later."

While intelligence is essential to wisdom, certain personal qualities predict with greater accuracy who will be wise. Thoreau observed, "It is a characteristic of wisdom not to do desperate things," and Baltes agrees. "Modulation and balance are crucial elements," he says, "because wisdom has no extremes. You can't be passionate or dogmatic and wise at the same time." Just as the Lao-tzus and Lincolns among us are likely to be reasonable and open-minded, they are not likely to be motivated by selfish concerns, at least not markedly so: Machiavelli was clever but not wise.

"At some point in middle age," says David Featherman, of the Social Science Research Council, "we're inclined to become more tolerant of the uncertain, the complex, and the impossible, and even to learn to dismiss some problems as unsolvable or not worth our effort. Perhaps most important, we grow more interested in how our solutions affect others. Along with being good at figuring out what to do in real-life situations themselves, the wise are skilled in advising others—in sharing their wisdom. Unfortunately, Americans' Lone Ranger mentality about solving everything on our own means we don't always profit from this resource." The concern for others that is a hallmark of wisdom seems to augur well for those who have it as well as for its beneficiaries. The evolutionary neurobiologist Paul D. MacLean once observed, "We become nicer mammals as we age." Featherman points out that the benignity integral to wisdom seems characteristic of people who enjoy a happy, healthy old age.

In a youth-obsessed culture the suggestion that at least one element of character emerges only in middle age is both appealing and iconoclastic. "Wisdom doesn't happen at the age of six, or eighteen," Featherman says. "It may take a long time for all of its components to be in place. The timing of its emergence means that in maturity we get a new start—a new way of understanding life that's more apt to benefit others. It may turn out that caring about people is the capstone of the process of living."

The Prime of Our Lives

*WHAT SEEMS TO MARK OUR ADULT YEARS
MOST IS OUR SHIFTING PERSPECTIVE
ON OURSELVES AND OUR WORLD. IS THERE A
COMMON PATTERN TO OUR LIVES?*

Anne Rosenfeld
and Elizabeth Stark

*Anne Rosenfeld and Elizabeth Stark, both
members of* Psychology Today's *editorial staff,
collaborated across cohorts to write this article.*

My parents had given me everything they could possibly owe a child and more. Now it was my turn to decide and nobody ... could help me very far...." That's how Graham Greene described his feelings upon graduation from Oxford. And he was right. Starting on your own down the long road of adulthood can be scary.

But the journey can also be exciting, with dreams and hopes to guide us. Maybe they're conventional dreams: getting a decent job, settling down and starting to raise a family before we've left our 20s. Or maybe they're more grandiose: making a million dollars by age 30, becoming a movie star, discovering a cure for cancer, becoming President, starting a social revolution.

Our youthful dreams reflect our unique personalities, but are shaped by the values and expectations of those around us—and they shift as we and our times change. Twenty years ago, college graduates entered adulthood with expectations that in many cases had been radically altered by the major upheavals transforming American society. The times were "a-changin'," and almost no one was untouched. Within a few years many of the scrubbed, obedient, wholesome teenagers of the early '60s had turned into scruffy, alienated campus rebels, experimenting with drugs and sex and deeply dissatisfied with their materialistic middle-class heritage.

Instead of moving right on to the career track, marrying and beginning families, as their fathers had done, many men dropped out, postponing the obligations of adult life. Others traveled a middle road, combining "straight" jobs with public service rather than pursuing conventional careers. And for the first time in recent memory, large numbers of young men refused to serve their country in the military. In the early 1940s, entire fraternities went together to enlist in World War II. In the Age of Aquarius, many college men sought refuge from war in Canada, graduate school, premature marriages or newly discovered medical ailments.

Women were even more dramatically affected by the social changes of the 1960s. Many left college in 1967 with a traditional agenda—work for a few years, then get married and settle down to the real business of raising a family and being a good wife—but ended up following a different and largely unexpected path. The women's movement and changing economics created a whole new set of opportunities. For example, between 1967 and 1980, women's share of medical degrees in the United States rocketed from 5 percent to 26 percent, and their share of law degrees leaped from 4 percent to 22 percent.

A group of women from the University of Michigan class of 1967 who were interviewed before graduation and again in 1981 described lives very different from their original plans. Psychologists Sandra Tangri of Howard University and Sharon Jenkins of the University of California found that far more of these women were working in 1981 than had expected to, and far more had gotten advanced degrees and were in "male" professions. Their home lives, too, were different from their collegiate fantasies: Fewer married, and those who did had much smaller families.

Liberation brought problems as well as opportunities. By 1981, about 15 percent of the women were divorced (although some had remarried), and many of the women who "had it all" told Tangri and Jenkins that they felt torn between their careers and their families.

Living out our dreams in a rapidly changing society demands extreme flexibility in adjusting to shifting social realities. Our hopes and plans, combined with the traditional rhythms of the life course, give some structure, impetus and predictability to our lives. But each of us must also cope repeatedly with the unplanned and unexpected. And in the process, we are gradually transformed.

For centuries, philosophers have been trying to capture the essence of how people change over the life course by focusing on universally experienced stages of life, often linked to specific ages. Research on child development, begun earlier in this century, had shown that children generally pass through an orderly succession of stages that correspond to fairly specific ages. But recent studies have challenged some of the apparent orderliness of child development, and the pattern of development among adults seems to be even less clear-cut.

When we think about what happens as we grow older, physical changes leap to mind—the lessening of physical prowess, the arrival of sags, spreads and lines. But these take a back seat to psychological changes, according to psychologist Bernice Neugarten of Northwestern University, a pioneer in the field of human development. She points out that although biological maturation heavily influences childhood development, people in young and middle adulthood are most affected by their own experiences and the timing of those experiences, not by biological factors. Even menopause, that quintessentially biological event, she says, is of relatively little psychological importance in the lives of most adult women.

In other words, chronological age is an increasingly unreliable indicator of what people will be like at various points. A group of newborns, or even 5-year-olds, shows less variation than a group of 35-year-olds, or 50-year-olds.

What seems to mark our adult years most is our shifting perspective on ourselves and our

STAGE THEORIES ARE A LITTLE LIKE HOROSCOPES— VAGUE ENOUGH TO LET EVERYONE SEE SOMETHING OF THEMSELVES IN THEM. THAT'S WHY THEY'RE SO POPULAR.

world—who we think we are, what we expect to get done, our timetable for doing it and our satisfactions with what we have accomplished. The scenarios and schedules of our lives are so varied that some researchers believe it is virtually impossible to talk about a single timetable for adult development. However, many people probably believe there is one, and are likely to cite Gail Sheehy's 1976 best-seller *Passages* to back them up.

Sheehy's book, which helped make "midlife crisis" a household word, was based on a body of research suggesting that adults go through progressive, predictable, age-linked stages, each offering challenges that must be met before moving on to the next stage. The most traumatic of these transitions, Sheehy claimed, is the one between young and middle adulthood—the midlife crisis.

Sheehy's ideas were based, in part, on the work of researchers Daniel Levinson, George Vaillant and Roger Gould, whose separate studies supported the stages of adult development Erik Erikson had earlier proposed in his highly influential model (see "Erikson's Eight Stages," next page).

Levinson, a psychologist, had started his study in 1969, when he was 49 and intrigued with his own recent midlife strains. He and his Yale colleagues intensively interviewed 40 men between the ages of 35 and 45 from four occupational groups. Using these interviews, bolstered by the biographies of great men and the development of memorable characters in literature, they described how men develop from 17 to 65 years of age (see "Levinson's Ladder," this article).

At the threshold of each major period of adulthood, they found, men pass through predictably unstable transitional periods, including a particularly wrenching time very close to age 40. At each transition a man must confront issues that may involve his career, his marriage, his family and the realization of his dreams if he is to progress successfully to the next period. Seventy percent to 80 percent of the men Levinson interviewed found the midlife transition (ages 40 to 45) tumultuous and psychologically painful, as most aspects of their lives came into question. The presumably universal timetable Levinson offered was very rigid, allowing no more than four years' leeway for each transition.

Vaillant's study, although less age-bound than Levinson's, also revealed that at midlife men go through a period of pain and preparation—"a time for reassessing and reordering the truth about adolescence and young adulthood." Vaillant, a psychiatrist, when he conducted his study at Harvard interviewed a group of men who were part of the Grant Study of Adult Development. The study had tracked almost 270 unusually accomplished, self-reliant and healthy Harvard freshmen (drawn mostly from the classes of 1942 to 1944) from their college days until their late 40s. In 1967 and 1977 Vaillant and his team interviewed and evaluated 94 members of this select group.

They found that, despite inner turmoil, the men judged to have the best outcomes in their late 40s "regarded the period from 35 to 49 as the happiest in their lives, and the seemingly calmer period from 21 to 35 as the unhappiest." But the men least well adapted at midlife "longed for the relative calm of their young adulthood and regarded the storms of later life as too painful."

While Levinson and Vaillant were completing their studies, psychiatrist Roger Gould and his colleagues at the University of California, Los Angeles, were looking at how the lives of both men and women change during young and middle adulthood. Unlike the Yale and Harvard studies, Gould's was a one-time examination of more than 500 white, middle-class people from ages 16 to 60. Gould's study, like those of Levinson and Vaillant, found that the time around age 40 was a tough one for many people, both personally and maritally. He stressed that people need to change their early expectations as they develop. "Childhood delivers most people into adulthood with a view of adults that few could ever live up to," he wrote. Adults must

confront this impossible image, he said, or be frustrated and dissatisfied.

The runaway success of *Passages* indicated the broad appeal of the stage theorists' message with its emphasis on orderly and clearly defined transitions. According to Cornell historian Michael Kammen, "We want predictability, and we desperately want definitions of 'normality.'" And almost everyone could find some relationship to their own lives in the stages Sheehy described. Stage theories, explains sociologist Orville Brim Jr., former president of the Russell Sage Foundation, are "a little like horoscopes. They are vague enough so that everyone can see something of themselves in them. That's why they're so popular."

But popularity does not always mean validity. Even at the time there were studies contradicting the stage theorists' findings. When sociologist Michael Farrell of the State University of New York at Buffalo and social psychologist Stanley Rosenberg of Dartmouth Medical School looked for a crisis among middle-aged men in 1971 it proved elusive. Instead of finding a "universal midlife crisis," they discovered several different developmental paths. "Some men do appear to reach a state of crisis," they found, "but others seem to thrive. More typical than either of these responses is the tendency for men to bury their heads and deny and avoid all the pressures closing in on them."

Another decade of research has made the picture of adult development even more complex. Many observations and theories accepted earlier as fact, especially by the general public, are now being debated. Researchers have espe-

Erikson's Eight Stages

According to Erik Erikson, people must grapple with the conflicts of one stage before they can move on to a higher one.

BONNIE SCHIFFMAN

SOURCE: ADAPTED FROM "REFLECTION ON DR. BORG'S LIFE CYCLE": ERIK H. ERIKSON, DAEDALUS, SPRING 1976.

							Old Age — Integrity vs. Despair, Disgust
						Maturity — Generativity vs. Self-absorption	
				Young Adulthood — Intimacy vs. Isolation			
			Adolescence — Identity vs. Identity Confusion				
		School Age — Industry vs. Inferiority					
	Play Age — Initiative vs. Guilt						
Early Childhood — Autonomy vs. Shame, Doubt							
Infancy — Trust vs. Mistrust							
1	2	3	4	5	6	7	8

Oh, God, I'm only twenty and I'll have to go on living and living and living.
—Jean Rhys, *Diary*

At thirty a man should know himself like the palm of his hand, know the exact number of his defects and qualities, know how far he can go, foretell his failures—be what he is. And above all accept these things.
—Albert Camus *Carnets.*

cially challenged Levinson's assertion that stages are predictable, tightly linked to specific ages and built upon one another.

In fact, Gould, described as a stage theorist in most textbooks, has since changed his tune, based upon his clinical observations. He now disagrees that people go through "formal" developmental stages in adulthood, although he says that people "do change their ways of looking at and experiencing the world over time." But the idea that one must resolve one stage before going on to the next, he says, is "hogwash."

Levinson, however, has stuck by his conceptual guns over the years, claiming that no one has evidence to refute his results. "The only way for my theory to be tested is to study life structure as it develops over adulthood," he says. "And by and large psychologists and sociologists don't study lives, they study variables."

Many researchers have found that changing times and different social expectations affect how various "cohorts"—groups of people born in the same year or time period—move through the life course. Neugarten has been emphasizing the importance of this age-group, or cohort, effect since the early 1960s. Our values and expectations are shaped by the period in which we live. People born during the trying times of the Depression have a different outlook on life from those born during the optimistic 1950s, according to Neugarten.

The social environment of a particular age group, Neugarten argues, can influence its so-

*W*HAT WAS TRUE FOR PEOPLE BORN IN THE DEPRESSION ERA MAY NOT HOLD FOR TODAY'S 40-YEAR-OLDS, BORN IN THE UPBEAT POSTWAR YEARS.

cial clock—the timetable for when people expect and are expected to accomplish some of the major tasks of adult life, such as getting married, having children or establishing themselves in a work role. Social clocks guide our lives, and people who are "out of sync" with them are likely to find life more stressful than those who are on schedule, she says.

Since the 1960s, when Neugarten first measured what people consider to be the "right" time for major life events, social clocks have changed (see "What's the Right Time?" this article), further altering the lives of those now approaching middle age, and possibly upsetting the timetable Levinson found in an earlier generation.

As sociologist Alice Rossi of the University of Massachusetts observes, researchers trying to tease out universal truths and patterns from

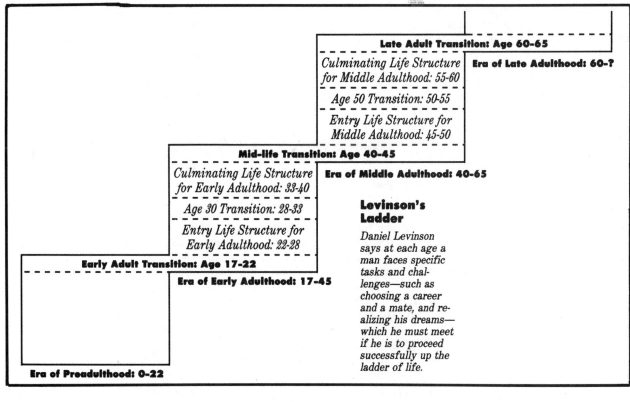

Late Adult Transition: Age 60-65

Culminating Life Structure for Middle Adulthood: 55-60

Era of Late Adulthood: 60-?

Age 50 Transition: 50-55

Entry Life Structure for Middle Adulthood: 45-50

Mid-life Transition: Age 40-45

Culminating Life Structure for Early Adulthood: 33-40

Era of Middle Adulthood: 40-65

Age 30 Transition: 28-33

Entry Life Structure for Early Adulthood: 22-28

Levinson's Ladder

Daniel Levinson says at each age a man faces specific tasks and challenges—such as choosing a career and a mate, and realizing his dreams—which he must meet if he is to proceed successfully up the ladder of life.

Early Adult Transition: Age 17-22

Era of Early Adulthood: 17-45

Era of Preadulthood: 0-22

SUDDENLY I'M THE ADULT?

BY RICHARD COHEN

Several years ago, my family gathered on Cape Cod for a weekend. My parents were there, my sister and her daughter, too, two cousins and, of course, my wife, my son and me. We ate at one of those restaurants where the menu is scrawled on a blackboard held by a chummy waiter and had a wonderful time. With dinner concluded, the waiter set the check down in the middle of the table. That's when it happened. My father did not reach for the check.

In fact, my father did nothing. Conversation continued. Finally, it dawned on me. Me! I was supposed to pick up the check. After all these years, after hundreds of restaurant meals with my parents, after a lifetime of thinking of my father as the one with the bucks, it had all changed. I reached for the check and whipped out my American Express card. My view of myself was suddenly altered. With a stroke of the pen, I was suddenly an adult.

Some people mark off their life in years, others in events. I am one of the latter, and I think of some events as rites of passage. I did not become a young man at a particular year, like 13, but when a kid strolled into the store where I worked and called me "mister." I turned around to see whom he was calling. He repeated it several times—"Mister, mister"—looking straight at me. The realization hit like a punch: Me! He was talking to me. I was suddenly a mister.

There have been other milestones. The cops of my youth always seemed to be big, even huge, and of course they were older than I was. Then one day they were neither. In fact, some of them were kids—short kids at that. Another milestone.

The day comes when you suddenly realize that all the football players in the game you're watching are younger than you. In-

Richard Cohen is a syndicated columnist for The Washington Post.

stead of being big men, they are merely big kids. With that milestone goes the fantasy that someday, maybe, you too could be a player—maybe not a football player but certainly a baseball player. I had a good eye as a kid—not much power, but a keen eye—and I always thought I could play the game. One day I realized that I couldn't. Without having ever reached the hill, I was over it.

For some people, the most momentous milestone is the death of a parent. This happened recently to a friend of mine. With the burial of his father came the realization that he had moved up a notch. Of course, he had known all along that this would happen, but until the funeral, the knowledge seemed theoretical at best. As long as one of your parents is alive, you stay in some way a kid. At the very least, there remains at least one person whose love is unconditional.

For women, a milestone is reached when they can no longer have children. The loss of a life, the inability to create one—they are variations on the same theme. For a childless woman who could control everything in life but the clock, this milestone is a cruel one indeed.

I count other, less serious milestones—like being audited by the Internal Revenue Service. As the auditor caught mistake after mistake, I sat there pretending that really knowing about taxes was for adults. I, of course, was still a kid. The auditor was buying none of it. I was a taxpayer, an adult. She all but said, Go to jail.

There have been others. I remember the day when I had a ferocious argument with my son and realized that I could no longer bully him. He was too big and the days when I could just pick him up and take him to his room/isolation cell were over. I needed to persuade, reason. He was suddenly, rapidly,

the lives of one birth cohort must consider the vexing possibility that their findings may not apply to any other group. Most of the people studied by Levinson, Vaillant and Gould were born before and during the Depression (and were predominantly male, white and upper middle class). What was true for these people may not hold for today's 40-year-olds, born in the optimistic aftermath of World War II, or the post baby-boom generation just approaching adulthood. In Rossi's view, "The profile of the

midlife men in Levinson's and Vaillant's studies may strike a future developmental researcher as burned out at a premature age, rather than reflecting a normal developmental process all men go through so early in life."

Based on her studies of women at midlife, Nancy Schlossberg, a counselor educator at the University of Maryland, also disagrees that there is a single, universal timetable for adult development—or that one can predict the crises

older. The conclusion was inescapable: So was I.

One day you go to your friends' weddings. One day you celebrate the birth of their kids. One day you see one of their kids driving, and one day those kids have kids of their own. One day you meet at parties and then at weddings and then at funerals. It all happens in one day. Take my word for it.

I never thought I would fall asleep in front of the television set as my father did, and as my friends' fathers did, too. I remember my parents and their friends talking about insomnia and they sounded like members of a different species. Not able to sleep? How ridiculous. Once it was all I did. Once it was what I did best.

I never thought that I would eat a food that did not agree with me. Now I meet them all the time. I thought I would never go to the beach and not swim. I spent all of August at the beach and never once went into the ocean. I never thought I would appreciate opera, but now the pathos, the schmaltz and, especially, the combination of voice and music appeal to me. The deaths of Mimi and Tosca move me, and they die in my home as often as I can manage it.

I never thought I would prefer to stay home instead of going to a party, but now I find myself passing parties up. I used to think that people who watched birds were weird, but this summer I found myself watching them, and maybe I'll get a book on the subject. I yearn for a religious conviction I never thought I'd want, exult in my heritage anyway, feel close to ancestors long gone and echo my father in arguments with my son. I still lose.

One day I made a good toast. One day I handled a headwaiter. One day I bought a house. One day—what a day!—I became a father, and not too long after that I picked up the check for my own. I thought then and there it was a rite of passage for me. Not until I got older did I realize that it was one for him, too. Another milestone.

in people's lives by knowing their age. "Give me a roomful of 40-year-old women and you have told me nothing. Give me a case story about what each has experienced and then I can tell if one is going to have a crisis and another a tranquil period." Says Schlossberg: "What matters is what transitions she has experienced. Has she been 'dumped' by a husband, fired from her job, had a breast removed, gone back to school, remarried, had her first book published. It is what has happened or not happened

to her, not how old she is, that counts. . . . There are as many patterns as people."

Psychologist Albert Bandura of Stanford University adds more fuel to the anti-stage fire by pointing out that chance events play a big role in shaping our adult lives. Careers and marriages are often made from the happenstance of meeting the right—or wrong—person at the right—or wrong—time. But, says Bandura, while the events may be random, their effects are not. They depend on what people do with the chance opportunities fate deals them.

The ages-and-stages approach to adult development has been further criticized because it does not appear to apply to women. Levinson claims to have confirmed that women do follow the same age-transition timetable that men do. But his recent study of women has yet to be published, and there is little other evidence that might settle the case one way or the other.

Psychologists Rosalind Barnett and Grace Baruch of the Wellesley Center for Research on Women say, "It is hard to know how to think of women within this [stage] theory—a woman may not enter the world of work until her late 30s, she seldom has a mentor, and even women with lifelong career commitments rarely are in a position to reassess their commitment pattern by age 40."

But University of Wisconsin-Madison psychologist Carol Ryff, who has directly compared the views of men and women from different age groups, has found that the big psychological issues of adulthood follow a similar developmental pattern for both sexes.

Recently she studied two characteristics highlighted as hallmarks of middle age: Erikson's "generativity" and Neugarten's "complexity." Those who have achieved generativity, according to Ryff, see themselves as leaders and decision makers and are interested in helping and guiding younger people. The men and women Ryff studied agreed that generativity is at its peak in middle age.

Complexity, which describes people's feeling that they are in control of their lives and are actively involved in the world, followed a somewhat different pattern. It was high in young adulthood and stayed prominent as people matured. But it was most obvious in those who are now middle-aged—the first generation of middle-class people to combine family and work in dual-career families. This juggling of roles, although stressful, may make some men and women feel actively involved in life.

Psychologist Ravenna Helson and her colleagues Valory Mitchell and Geraldine Moane at the University of California, Berkeley, have recently completed a long-term study of the lives of 132 women that hints at some of the forces propelling people to change psychologically during adulthood. The women were studied as seniors at Mills College in California in the late 1950s, five years later and again in 1981, when they were between the ages of 42 and 45.

Helson and her colleagues distinguished three main groups among the Mills women: family-oriented, career-oriented (whether or not they also wanted families) and those who followed neither path (women with no children who pursued only low-level work). Despite their different profiles in college, and their diverging life paths, the women in all three groups underwent similar broad psychological changes over time, although those in the third group changed less than those committed to career or family.

Personality tests given through the years revealed that from age 21 to their mid-40s, the Mills women became more self-disciplined and committed to duties, as well as more independent and confident. And between age 27 and the early 40s, there was a shift toward less traditionally "feminine" attitudes, including greater dominance, higher achievement motivation, greater interest in events outside the family and more emotional stability.

To the Berkeley researchers, familiar with the work of psychologist David Gutmann of Northwestern University, these changes were not surprising in women whose children were mostly grown. Gutmann, after working with Neugarten and conducting his own research, had theorized that women and men, largely locked into traditional sex roles by parenthood, become less rigidly bound by these roles once the major duties of parenting decline; both are then freer to become more like the opposite sex—and do. Men, for example, often become more willing to share their feelings. These changes in both men and women can help older couples communicate and get along better.

During their early 40s, many of the women Helson and Moane studied shared the same midlife concerns the stage theorists had found in men: "concern for young and old, introspectiveness, interest in roots and awareness of limitation and death." But the Berkeley team described the period as one of midlife "consciousness," not "crisis."

In summing up their findings, Helson and Moane stress that commitment to the tasks of young adulthood—whether to a career or family (or both)—helped women learn to control impulses, develop skills with people, become independent and work hard to achieve goals.

According to Helson and Moane, those women who did not commit themselves to one of the main life-style patterns faced fewer challenges and therefore did not develop as fully as the other women did.

The dizzying tug and pull of data and theories about how adults change over time may frustrate people looking for universal principles or certainty in their lives. But it leaves room for many scenarios for people now in young and middle adulthood and those to come.

People now between 20 and 60 are the best-educated and among the healthiest and most fit of all who have passed through the adult years. No one knows for sure what their lives will be like in the years to come, but the experts have some fascinating speculations.

For example, Rossi suspects that the quality of midlife for baby boomers will contrast sharply with that of the Depression-born generation the stage theorists studied. Baby boomers, she notes, have different dreams, values and opportunities than the preceding generation. And they are much more numerous.

Many crucial aspects of their past and future lives may best be seen in an economic rather than a strictly psychological light, Rossi says. From their days in overcrowded grade schools, through their struggles to gain entry into college, to their fight for the most desirable jobs, the baby boomers have had to compete with one another. And, she predicts, their competitive struggles are far from over. She foresees that many may find themselves squeezed out of the workplace as they enter their 50s—experiencing a crisis at a time when it will be difficult to redirect their careers.

But other factors may help to make life easier for those now approaching midlife. People are on a looser, less compressed timetable, and no longer feel obliged to marry, establish their careers and start their families almost simultaneously. Thus, major life events may not pile up in quite the same way they did for the older generation.

Today's 20-year-olds—the first wave of what some have labeled "the baby busters"—have a more optimistic future than the baby boomers who preceded them, according to economist Richard Easterlin of the University of Southern California. Easterlin has been studying the life patterns of various cohorts, beginning with the low-birthrate group born in the 1930s—roughly a decade before the birthrate exploded.

The size of a birth cohort, Easterlin argues, affects that group's quality of life. In its simplest terms, his theory says that the smaller the cohort the less competition among its members and the more fortunate they are; the larger the cohort the more competition and the less fortunate.

Compared with the baby boomers, the smaller cohort just approaching adulthood "will have much more favorable experiences as they grow

WHAT'S THE RIGHT TIME?

Two surveys asking the same questions 20 years apart (late 1950s and late 1970s) have shown a dramatic decline in the consensus among middle-class, middle-aged people about what's the right age for various major events and achievements of adult life.

SOURCE: ADAPTED FROM "AGE NORMS AND AGE CONSTRAINTS TWENTY YEARS LATER," P. PASSUTH, D. MAINES AND B.L. NEUGARTEN. PAPER PRESENTED AT THE MIDWEST SOCIOLOGICAL SOCIETY MEETING, CHICAGO, APRIL 1984

Activity/Event	Appropriate Age Range	Late '50s Study % Who Agree Men	Late '50s Study % Who Agree Women	Late '70s Study % Who Agree Men	Late '70s Study % Who Agree Women
Best age for a man to marry	20-25	80%	90%	42%	42%
Best age for a woman to marry	19-24	85	90	44	36
When most people should become grandparents	45-50	84	79	64	57
Best age for most people to finish school and go to work	20-22	86	82	36	38
When most men should be settled on a career	24-26	74	64	24	26
When most men hold their top jobs	45-50	71	58	38	31
When most people should be ready to retire	60-65	83	86	66	41
When a man has the most responsibilities	35-50	79	75	49	50
When a man accomplishes most	40-50	82	71	46	41
The prime of life for a man	35-50	86	80	59	66
When a woman has the most responsibilities	25-40	93	91	59	53
When a woman accomplishes most	30-45	94	92	57	48

up—in their families, in school and finally in the labor market," he says. As a result, they will "develop a more positive psychological outlook."

The baby busters' optimism will encourage them to marry young and have large families—producing another baby boom. During this period there will be less stress in the family and therefore, Easterlin predicts, divorce and suicide rates will stabilize.

Psychologist Elizabeth Douvan of the University of Michigan's Institute for Social Research shares Easterlin's optimistic view about the future of these young adults. Surprisingly, she sees as one of their strengths the fact that, due to divorce and remarriage, many grew up in reconstituted families. Douvan believes that the experience of growing up close to people who are not blood relatives can help to blur the distinction between kinship and friendship, making people more open in their relationships with others.

Like many groups before them, they are likely to yearn for a sense of community and ritual, which they will strive to fulfill in many ways, Douvan says. For some this may mean a turn toward involvement in politics, neighborhood or religion, although not necessarily the religion of their parents.

In summing up the future quality of life for today's young adults and those following them, Douvan says: "Life is more open for people now. They are judging things internally and therefore are more willing to make changes in the external aspects. That's pretty exciting. It opens up a tremendous number of possibilities for people who can look at life as an adventure."

ON GROWING OLD

Not Every Creature Ages, But Most Do. The Question Is Why

ROBERT M. SAPOLSKY *and*
CALEB E. FINCH

ROBERT M. SAPOLSKY is an assistant professor of biology and neuroscience at Stanford University. CALEB E. FINCH is professor of gerontology at the University of Southern California in Los Angeles. His book LONGEVITY, SENESCENCE, AND THE GENOME *was recently published by University of Chicago Press.*

> *I can do anything now at age ninety that I could when I was eighteen. Which shows you how pathetic I was at eighteen.*
> —George Burns

I T HAS BEEN OBSERVED more than once that human beings are the only creatures on earth haunted by an awareness of their own mortality. People know that life is desperately fragile and that any of myriad intrusions can kill them instantly: an aneurysm, a cerebral hemorrhage or a heart attack; a fire, an earthquake, a traffic accident or a mugger's bullet. And they know that even should they escape sudden disaster, the end remains inevitable. If nothing else, the years themselves take a fatal toll. Muscles weaken, eyesight dims, memories fade, and people become ever more conscious of the discrepancy between what they were and what they have become. In short, they senesce: they age.

To the gerontologist seeking to understand the aging process, the phenomenon of senescence is defined in terms of vulnerability: a "pathetic" eighteen-year-old college student is more likely to survive a certain challenge or insult than is a ninety-year-old curmudgeon. Each one may slip and fall on ice or play host to a single cancerous cell or contract a dangerous fever. Yet the older person is more likely to suffer a broken pelvis from the fall, to develop a malignant tumor from the cancerous cell, to perish from the fever. The risk that an illness or an injury will prove fatal increases with age.

Given such dark prospects, one is tempted to fantasize about living in a sort of never-never land where there is no such thing as senescence, no increase in vulnerability with each passing year. There would be no more crow's feet, sagging jowls or thinning hair and, more to the point, no degenerative heart disease, hardened arteries or Alzheimer's disease. We would all look great and feel wonderful. And we would live forever. Or would we?

The overall risk of mortality in the population at large is lowest at around age eleven. Suppose, magically, that the entire population, with every succeeding year, were somehow able to retain the adolescent's physiological near-invulnerability—in other words, suppose no one ever aged. Then half the people would still be alive by their 600th birthday, but by the same token half would be gone. Certainly that is an improvement, but immortality it is not. The point is that physiological invulnerability goes only so far. Even in a world populated solely with nonsenescing creatures there would be some constant mortality rate, one dependent entirely on the rate of external insults or ecological danger. Such a hypothetical population of Dorian Grays (or Dick Clarks, perhaps) would slowly but steadily decline in size with the passage of time because of airplane crashes, earthquakes or substance abuse. In some unit of time (600 years, for instance) half the population would die from extrinsic causes, in the next unit half the survivors would die, and so on.

For a real aging population the mortality rate increases with time because of an interaction between the rate of extrinsic insults and the extent of internal senescence. As the anatomy deteriorates with age, the person becomes increasingly vulnerable to intrusions by the outside world. Organs, bones and muscles wear out with time, and at age sixty, seventy or eighty, one cannot withstand the same kinds of stresses one sloughed off at eleven. It is all depressingly tragic but certainly not surprising. Things fall apart. How could life be otherwise?

S TARTLINGLY ENOUGH, for many species things *are* otherwise. Bristlecone pine trees and rockfish, certain parameciums and some social insect queens, to name just a few, do not senesce. Populations of such plants and animals suffer constant attrition from extrinsic threats. In some insect species a queen dies at the proverbial hands of her minions: when her nuptial sperm supply runs out after many years, she is killed by the workers. But even at an advanced age those organisms do not show any of the usual signs of internal deterioration associated with other representatives of their phyla. For example, unlike most other trees, a bristlecone pine shows no increased sensitivity to insect infestations with age. Although it is unclear how many species are nonsenescers, it is known that there are a great many of them, particularly in groups such as bony fishes, sea anemones and bivalve mollusks.

One might very well wonder what stroke of evolutionary good fortune, what extraordinary biological innovation, has allowed those species to evade decrepitude. What feature have they evolved that humans and most other animals have not? On closer examination, however, it becomes clear that rockfish, parameciums, mollusks and the like are not the real innovators. Quite to the contrary, such perennially youthful species are typically among the most ancient, primitive organisms. Indeed it appears that nonsenescence was the original state of living things on earth. The mammalian line, one of the latest and certainly the most sophisticated of the chordate classes, can be considered an island of senescence among most of its evolutionary relatives. If, then, aging is a relatively recent development, another question arises: What possible evolutionary advantages are conferred by such a dismal characteristic?

THE ATTEMPT to understand the adaptive benefits of senescence is almost as old as the idea of evolution itself. One of the first to explore the issue was the English naturalist Alfred Russel Wallace, who shares with Darwin the credit for having founded the theory of evolution by natural selection. Darwin and Wallace established that the driving force of evolution is the quest for optimizing reproductive success, a goal best realized by leaving the maximum number of copies of one's own genes for future generations. (As the sociobiologists say, "A chicken is an egg's way of making another egg.")

There are two fundamental strategies for ensuring the proliferation of one's genes: either reproducing a lot or, failing that, doing whatever is possible to increase the reproduction of one's relatives—a kind of genetic altruism known as kin selection. Wallace speculated that aging is a kin-selection strategy; in other words, at some stage in its life the best way for an organism to pass on its genes is for it to senesce and get out of the way, leaving the resources it would otherwise consume behind for its descendants to share as they multiply the genetic line.

Since Wallace's day many other theories of adaptive senescence have been advanced, based on studies of aging patterns in a range of living things. To illustrate one popular recent theory, compare the extremely long lived, nonsenescing rockfish with the short-lived, senescing guppy. As one might expect, the guppy population, subject to both external insult and internal deterioration, dies off at a much faster rate than the rockfish population does. Still, guppies enjoy one crucial advantage over rockfish: earlier in life they fare substantially better at reproduction. In general, species that age follow the same pattern: they die off sooner, but they reproduce earlier in life and more successfully than their nonsenescing counterparts.

For a number of years many biologists have recognized that in senescing species the enhanced fecundity earlier in life and the increased mortality rate later on might express an evolutionary trade-off. The essence of the idea, which has acquired the forbidding label "negative pleiotropy," is that genes have evolved that confer marked advantages on an organism at certain stages in its life, only to extract a cost at certain other stages. Unlike Wallace's

notion of altruistic kin selection, negative pleiotropy is a genetically "selfish" mechanism: it would operate solely to maximize the reproductive potential of individual organisms, without regard for the greater good of subsequent generations of the species.

When genes are viewed as negatively pleiotropic, they are double-edged swords. Perhaps the best-known example of this kind of duality—though one not related to aging—is the gene for sickle-cell anemia. The sickle-cell gene can bring about a dreadful, life-threatening disease, in which insufficient oxygen is delivered to the cells of the body. Yet the same gene confers resistance to malaria, a disease that takes a horrendous toll in Africa, where sickle-cell anemia evolved. Whereas senescence may be an instance of negative pleiotropy over time, sickle-cell anemia can be thought of as negative pleiotropy over space: thus the sickle-cell gene offers advantages only in those environments in which malaria is rampant. In the evolution of such trade-offs the critical issue becomes how often the advantage is conferred compared with how often the deleterious bill arrives. Apparently, with sickle-cell anemia the payoffs have led to widespread selection for the trait. That is small comfort to sickle-cell victims who live in, say, urban America, where shored-up resistance to malaria is of little use. Betrayed by geography, American carriers of the sickle-cell gene are forced to pay its price without enjoying any of its benefits.

ALTHOUGH THE IDEA of negative pleiotropy as a driving force in aging looks good on paper, specific examples of the phenomenon have been surprisingly hard to track down. One instance may be Huntington's disease, best known for having afflicted the folksinger Woody Guthrie. People stricken with Huntington's disease generally begin sometime during their forties to suffer from a variety neurological symptoms: flailing and spasms of the limbs, paralysis, rigidity and dementia. Death usually comes after about fifteen years.

A subtle, intriguing feature of Huntington's disease usually manifests itself early on. The illness initially appears to be a psychiatric disorder: the victim's behavior and personality begin to change dramatically before the neurological symptoms emerge. In a few years a quiet and uncontentious person might begin to lose self-control, becoming loud, uninhibited and more aggressive. Clinical lore also holds that a behavioral feature of early Huntington's is hypersexuality; in fact, one recent study indicates that Huntington's patients outreproduce their unaffected siblings. No one has a clue to just how the disease works —especially to why some of the behavioral traits and the neurological symptoms should emerge from the same disorder. Nevertheless, one can speculate that if the gene that accelerates mortality at age sixty also confers increased reproduction by age forty, the gene would work to the overall advantage of the organism in the evolutionary sense. Such a mechanism for the disease would constitute a neat illustration of negative pleiotropy at work in the aging process.

One can imagine any number of other negatively pleiotropic scenarios that give rise to senescence. There could be many genes that confer early advantages in exchange for later costs, each affecting discrete organ systems. One feature of human aging, for instance, is that older men have a much greater chance than younger men of developing prostate cancer. What if such a tendency toward uncontrolled carcinogenic growth were a side effect of a gene that, earlier in life, increased the rate of prostate metabolism and cell division? One result might be that the younger man could produce more seminal fluid, having greater sperm mobility, and thus be a more fertile individual. If the reproductive advantages of better sperm at age thirty outweigh the reproductive disadvantages of dying from prostate cancer at sixty-five, the gene will be selected. Some investigators already consider senescent increases in the frequency of prostate cancer to be a valid example of negative pleiotropy.

Another, more hypothetical example is the potentially adaptive effect of fat stored on the body early in life. In periods of drought or famine fat might act as a buffer, thereby keeping the individual alive through the reproductive years. As a person grows older, however, the advantages of that storage tendency begin to be counterbalanced by the accompanying risk of heart disease and diabetes. In physiology, as in so many other spheres, there are no free lunches; ultimately, the check arrives.

IF NEGATIVE PLEIOTROPY is to account for the emergence of senescence in humans, one would expect to find that certain advantageous traits of youth are genetically linked to whatever turn out to be the mechanisms of decline. Understanding those mechanisms, of course, is one of the central aims of gerontological research. Gerontologists have searched for a single cause of aging—a critical gene, hormone or organ that goes awry. But in the light of the rather sparse evidence in support of that idea, many investigators have adopted another hypothesis: that senescence results from the gradual but steady deterioration of cells, which over time become less proficient at maintenance and self-repair. After all, there is no question that the lives of cells are finite; a cell divides a fixed number of times and then dies. What causes that abrupt cessation? What changes take place in a cell as it approaches the end of its line? These questions are of central concern to gerontologists. And it is becoming increasingly clear that there are no easy answers and that if the key to aging is cellular deterioration, aging is a complex, multifaceted process, perhaps involving not one but a host of regulatory genes.

In the past decade or so a number of theories have been put forward that try to explain what causes cells to wear down. According to one such theory, as it ages a lineage of cells accumulates harmful metabolic "garbage," which can damage nucleic acids, proteins and other vital cellular building blocks. One class of physiological debris may be the oxygen-free radicals: such molecules can lodge in the cell membrane, disrupt and destroy fats and protein by linking them inappropriately, and perhaps impair the functioning of DNA.

Another line of investigation implicates glucose in a process that is severely destructive to animal cells. Glucose can attach itself to proteins via a process called nonenzymatic glycosylation, which binds the proteins together into a nonfunctional yellowish brown mess. (The biochemist Anthony Cerami of Rockefeller University in New York has named such accumulations of dis-

abled proteins "advanced glycosylation endproducts," allowing the acronym AGE.) As animals age, AGE proteins appear to damage vital organs and connective tissue. There is also speculation that, like the oxygen-free radicals, AGE proteins may somehow interact with DNA, causing mutations and obstructing the cell's ability both to repair damage and to replicate. The role of AGE proteins in aging is an intriguing subject for future research. At this point, however, they have been studied only in people and in laboratory rodents. Whether and to what degree other animals accumulate these protein masses may say a great deal about aging patterns across the various species.

TO THE AVERAGE, reluctantly senescing person, aging connotes a gradual, albeit inexorable, slide from summer into autumn and, with any luck, on to winter. But not all the earth's aging creatures necessarily decline and fall in the same way people do. Even in some relatively long-lived species senescence and death can come in a flash, sometimes in a matter of weeks or days. Well-known victims of such sudden death are the five species of Pacific salmon. In the mating season the adult fish heroically fight their way upstream to the pools where they were born in order to spawn—only to die off, en masse, a few days later. Fish captured during the dying-off period typically display enlarged adrenal glands, ulcers and kidney lesions; their immune systems have collapsed and they are teeming with parasites and opportunistic infections.

A similar pattern occurs in about a dozen species of marsupial mice in Australia. Those animals have an annual, synchronized mating season after which, in the course of a few weeks, all the males die. Remarkably the mice exhibit symptoms nearly identical with the symptoms of the salmon. People seemingly age by going to pieces idiosyncratically over decades; one person gets arthritis, another gets diabetes, a third gets cancer. Here instead, an identical pathological switch is thrown in each individual of the species, causing a kind of pansenescence: the population ages almost overnight.

Studies over the past thirty years have traced the sudden-death switch to the adrenal glands, which in times of physical or psychological stress secrete hormones belonging to a class known as the glucocorticoids. Such hormones come in many varieties; in humans they take the form of hydrocortisone, also known as cortisol. Glucocorticoids can be extremely handy in a physical emergency: a lot of energy must be released suddenly when one is, say, sprinting away from an onrushing predator. The hormones work by mobilizing glucose, freeing it from storage sites in the body and sending it into the blood. At the same time they increase the heart rate and raise blood pressure to speed the delivery of the glucose to the muscles. Glucocorticoids also turn off all kinds of long-term, energy consumptive building projects that can be put on hold until the emergency has passed: digestion, growth, reproduction, tissue repair and the maintenance of the immune system, among others.

All these effects are wonderful when you are running for your life, but they are disastrous at other times. In long periods of chronic psychological stress, for instance, the constant mobilization of energy at the cost of storage can waste the muscles away. An increase in cardiovascular tone for a long enough period brings about hypertension. By repeatedly deferring long-term building projects, the body eventually deteriorates: stomach walls ulcerate; growth, reproduction and immunity are irreparably impaired. To a large extent the illnesses that accompany chronic stress are consequences of an overexposure to glucocorticoids.

Pacific salmon and marsupial mice meet sudden death when their bodies loose a veritable flood of glucocorticoids. The phenomenon has been most thoroughly observed in marsupials. Around the mating period three changes take place that guarantee catastrophe. First, far more glucocorticoids than normal are secreted. Second, the concentration of proteins in circulation that can bind glucocorticoids—in effect sponging them up and buffering organs from the effects of the hormones—falls sharply, allowing the glucocorticoids unrestrained access to target tissues. Finally, parts of the brain, as yet unknown, that normally curtail glucocorticoid secretion before too much damage is done, fail to function. How all these steps work is poorly understood, but the result is that massive, pathological levels of glucocorticoids pummel the body. The Pacific salmon and the marsupial mice die from the effects of half the stress-related illnesses on earth, packed into a few miserable weeks.

The most dramatic proof of this account is that if, just after the salmon or the mice have mated, one blocks the secretion of glucocorticoids by removing the adrenal glands, the animals will live on for a year or more instead of the usual few weeks. The procedure demonstrates how drastically the aging process can be accelerated in otherwise diverse creatures that happen to have evolved the same hormonal death switch.

THE EVOLUTIONARY PURPOSE served by such abrupt pansenescence remains unclear. From one point of view Pacific salmon and marsupial mice can be regarded as classic examples of negative pleiotropy: they reproduce in abundance and then pay for their fecundity with their lives. But whether or not there is a pure trade-off of enhanced reproduction for greater mortality later on has not been established. There has been some speculation—and it is no more than that—that ties the Pacific salmon to Wallace's theory of kin selection. Some investigators have suggested that by quickly dying and decomposing in the water, the salmon are contributing nutrients to the ecosystem and hence improving the lot of future generations. The hypothesis is certainly intriguing, but it is still unsubstantiated by experimental evidence.

Are there any examples of greatly accelerated senescence in people? No doubt, devotees of the lurid tabloids ever present at supermarket checkout counters will immediately recall one possibility. Publications of that stripe have a morbid fascination with progeria, a supremely rare hereditary disease that afflicts children. Progerics appear to age incredibly prematurely. By the age of twelve, shortly before their deaths, they may have gray hair or be completely bald, and they manifest the bony chins, beaked noses and dry, scratchy voices common to elderly people. Children stricken with progeria can also

suffer from hearing loss, arteriosclerosis or heart disease. When an attempt is made to grow certain cells from their bodies in a laboratory dish, the cells act like the well-worn tissue of a seventy-year-old—that is, they divide very infrequently. The implication seems to be that for a progeric the body's rate of aging has run amuck.

Progeric children, however, are not aged in every respect. For example, they do not show increased tendencies toward dementia or cancer, two major diseases strongly linked to aging. Thus even in progerics there is no single aging clock gone mad, and by the same token, there is no one such timepiece ticking at a normal pace in the rest of us. Instead the development of progeria suggests a mosaic of aging mechanisms, a variety of clocks of which only some are out of joint. Although the macabre disease gives rise to certain features associated with senescence, it is not, by itself, accelerated aging. Almost certainly, many nonprogerics also suffer dire but less spectacular consequences that have been brought on because some, but not all, of their aging clocks have sped out of control: witness the early onset of certain types of cancer in some people. But on the whole there remains sparse evidence of accelerated aging in humans, and even that is not at all like the affliction that befalls Pacific salmon and Australian marsupial mice.

SALMON, MICE AND PROGERICS notwithstanding, there are some species in nature that display determinedly more upbeat patterns of senescence, creatures for which the aging process is greatly slowed down. In spite of our own species' chronic despair about the ephemerality of life, a typical human being comes off next to immortal compared with an average laboratory rat. After only two years the rat is plagued by cataracts, reproductive problems and memory loss. Indeed the maximum human life span of 120 years or so is impressive in almost any context. (Notice that the occasional claims for the existence of substantially older populations such as one in Soviet Georgia usually prove attributable to some blend of bemused exaggeration and the inhabitants' lack of rigor about personal chronology.) There are other species in the range of human longevity —notably apes, elephants, sturgeons, clams and Galápagos tortoises. And there are some that far outstrip us, particularly certain trees such as conifers that can live for more than a millennium. The point is not that such species do not senesce; they do, but they also happen to be long-lived. The decline of a given population comes about quite slowly, over a great many years.

In a few cases species can temporarily arrest the encroachments of age and physical decline and, in effect, achieve suspended animation. One familiar example is hibernation, a dormant state during which the mortality rate of an entire population of animals is essentially frozen. Hibernation has been thoroughly studied in Turkish hamsters. The investigators manipulated the length of hibernation in the laboratory by adjusting the environmental temperature and found, remarkably, that for every day the hamsters hibernated, the animals' life spans were extended by about a day. The hamsters had managed to stop their aging clocks.

Hibernation is only one of several ways senescence can

be temporarily slowed or halted by dormancy. A somewhat more exotic example is the diapause, a holding stage in the development of certain organisms—particularly some insects such as worker bees—which can last for more than a year. If an insect enters diapause, its life span is extended by an equal amount of time. Various African and South American fishes can enter diapause even before they have hatched. As it turns out, the fishes' behavior is opportunistic: They live in ponds that disappear during dry seasons. Rather than start off life just as their homes have been turned into mud flats, unhatched eggs go into diapause amid the dried mud and await the return of the waters—perhaps for a year or more.

People, of course, are desperate for news of any intervention that might forestall decline. Newspapers have recently been filled with reports that the administration of growth hormone apparently reverses some aspects of human aging, in particular the loss of muscle mass and diminution of organ size that typically occur in the elderly. Despite this good news, growth hormone treatment has not been shown to increase the life span. Is there anything in the works, then, that can actually help us live longer?

At the moment, unfortunately, the answer is no. That fact notwithstanding, there are a number of entrepreneurial biologists who—for a handsome price—will contract to freeze you after you die, in the optimistic hope that future scientists will be able to effect your resurrection. Some of these so-called cryobiologists are even lobbying to freeze live but terminally ill patients on the assumption that some later generation of physicians might be able to revive them when a cure is available. (That approach is currently illegal, though a California man with terminal cancer recently initiated a court challenge.) Nevertheless, there is precious little experimental evidence to support any attempt to induce suspended animation in mammals. And there are many reasons such an effort would fail in any organism as large as a human being; for one, the cells could not be frozen quickly enough to avoid severe tissue damage. Even if suspended life were possible, it might not be all that desirable, especially if the hibernation worked as it does in hamsters. It is a safe bet that few of us would care to live on for centuries if all but seventy-two of those years were spent packed in ice. What we presumably want is a full, decidedly nondormant life that lasts beyond the present limits.

REMARKABLY there is one technique that for the past half-century has been known to extend mammalian life. It is not, however, what one would call an inviting alternative. In the 1930s it was discovered that if rats are deprived of nourishment (in this case, 30 percent of calories) indefinitely, beginning just after weaning, they live as much as one-third longer than rats given unrestricted access to food—the equivalent of extending human life expectancy from seventy-five years to a century. Before long a number of investigators had replicated the finding in other rodents, and today an entire branch of gerontology is devoted to studying the benefits of what is variously called dietary restriction or diet optimization.

It is now known that most of what tends to fall apart in

an unmolested aging rat does so more slowly in a diet-restricted rat: organs such as the liver, the immune and reproductive systems and possibly parts of the brain such as the hippocampus. Dietary restriction also protects the rat from tumor growth, to which the animal normally becomes progressively susceptible as it grows older. One relatively recent discovery is that dietary restriction need not be as severe as it was in the initial studies in order to prolong an animal's life. Other strategies can be just as effective: cutting back calorie consumption by as little as 30 percent; beginning restriction in adulthood instead of after weaning; or restricting only some dietary constituents such as protein intake instead of the total number of calories consumed.

Gerontologists in this subfield spend most of their time trying to figure out precisely why cutting back on food leads to longevity. One of many attractive answers is that decreasing the diet may slow the accumulation of AGE proteins, the dysfunctional mess slung together over time by glucose. If AGE accumulation is, in fact, one of the basic cellular pacemakers of aging, a delay in its generation might well account for the deceleration of the aging process that dietary restriction seems to effect in so many organ systems.

A number of investigators, however, have raised a somewhat more deflating explanation for the effect. In their view the average laboratory rat, confined to a cage and given unrestricted access to food, eats far more than a normal wild rat does, simply for lack of anything better to do. In the process the animal drives itself into an early grave by contracting some of the diseases that kill millions of Americans. It may well be that dietary restriction is merely a means of getting a bored and gluttonous rat to adopt wild eating habits and thereby live a normal life span. In that circumstance dietary restriction would not change the basic nature of aging, but it would reduce the impact of diet-associated diseases on the aging process. Clarification will come once investigators know more about the eating habits of wild rodents. Only then can one know whether the normal laboratory rat gorges itself on an unrestricted diet.

Assuming, for the moment, that dietary restriction does extend the maximal life span of rodents, should we all start limiting our diets? How general is the phenomenon? Clearly such questions are hard to resolve. For rats or mice that live just a few years it is tedious (not to mention expensive) to manipulate diet over the lifetime of a population. To do the same for creatures that live for decades is far more difficult, and it makes the optimistic assumption that the investigator will live long enough to complete the project. Thus no one knows whether food restriction will work for our pets, our livestock or ourselves.

One observation offers little hope. Actuarial tables show that people with extreme body weights—the thinnest as well as the stoutest—tend to live shorter lives than people who stand somewhere in between. On the other hand, one can retort that some people are thin not because of a lifetime of restricted eating but because of genetics, chronic diseases or any number of other confounding characteristics. At bottom no one yet knows whether eating less means living longer. Nevertheless, the rodent data are sufficiently convincing to have motivated at least one respected gerontologist, Roy L. Walford of the University of California at Los Angeles, to keep himself on a restricted diet for years. Walford's colleagues eagerly—but not too eagerly, of course—await the results of his self-experimentation.

Any review of aging research is necessarily somewhat disjointed, an account of what is currently a rather disparate patchwork of unconnected studies. The hope is that a unified theory of senescence will one day emerge. Perhaps there is some thread that draws together AGE production in people, pansenescence in salmon, negative pleiotropy and other anecdotal and hypothetical aspects of aging into the wider context of evolution. On the other hand, senescence may turn out to be resolutely untidy, as complex and varied in its mechanisms as the aging species themselves. Further-

more, all the many lines of inquiry into senescence, even if they converge on a fundamental understanding of the phenomenon, may not add a day to human life expectancy. Perhaps we will have to content ourselves with curing the prevalent diseases of aging, such as Alzheimer's or atherosclerosis, rather than aging itself. That alone would obviously be of incalculable benefit.

But if bristlecone pines, marsupial mice and fishes tell us nothing about our aging problems, why study them? One could as easily ask why anatomists pass their lifetimes documenting the ways the primate pelvis can be constructed, why ethologists catalogue dialects of bird songs or why geneticists devote study to the hereditary patterns of worms. If we are to understand our place in the scheme of nature, it is perhaps important for us to realize that ours is not the only way to evolve, appear or behave. Or even to grow old.

Unlocking the Secrets of Aging

Scientists are deciphering genetic codes they say will lead to keeping people alive much longer. But the social and ethical implications of sharing the Fountain of Youth are impossible to ignore.

Sheryl Stolberg

Times Medical Writer

In his laboratory at the University of Colorado, molecular biologist Thomas Johnson is studying a translucent worm no bigger than a printed comma. In this simple animal, composed of just 959 cells, Johnson believes he may find the answers to complex questions that have eluded scientists for centuries:

What makes us grow old? Can we stop aging, or at least slow it down?

By breeding tens of thousands of these nematodes, Johnson has created a strain that can live for about five weeks—about 70% longer than the worm's average three-week life span. It appears that the difference between the elderly worms and their shorter-lived counterparts lies in a single gene. Now, Johnson is trying to isolate that gene, and he says he is close.

And if genes can be manipulated to extend the lives of worms, the 48-year-old researcher asks, might not the same be true of people?

"Maybe there are major genes in humans that, if we alter [them], we could project a longer human life span," Johnson said. "This would be an absolutely tremendous sociological finding. It would affect . . . every aspect of the way we live our lives if we all of a sudden had average life spans of 120 years instead of 70 years."

Tremendous indeed. Johnson's work is on the cutting edge of a fascinating scientific sojourn, a modern-day quest for the legendary Fountain of Youth. He is among a growing corps of 2,000 molecular biologists, geneticists, immunologists and other researchers across the United States who are trying to unlock the secrets of aging.

They are tinkering with genes, human growth hormones and new drugs, and with strategies of diet, nutrition and exercise. They are studying patterns of survival in worms, fruit flies, mice and people. They are examining the links between aging and illness—cancer, Alzheimer's, Parkinson's, osteoporosis, heart disease, stroke—as well as the effect of environment on aging.

Their strides in recent years have been so significant that a startling new body of thought has emerged, one that says humans may one day live much longer than anyone dreamed possible. Some go so far as to say that the maximum life span, now at 120 years, and average life expectancy, about 75 years in the United States, could double or triple.

"The ideal of all our work is that sometime in the future, we would take pills that would slow or postpone our aging," said UC Irvine biologist Michael Rose, who is breeding fruit flies that can live up to three times as long as the average fly. "That's the ultimate goal, the man on the moon for all this research. We're not going to have that in five years. But someday it will happen."

Michal Jazwinski, a Louisiana State University biologist who has isolated "longevity assurance genes" in yeast, said: "In the next 30 to 50 years, we will in fact have in hand many of the major genes that determine longevity in humans. What we have been able to see with our yeast is a doubling of the life span. So that could be something that we might aim for in the future."

Scientists are pondering the social and ethical implications of their work. They raise a litany of questions: If the research is successful, what would happen to the nation's overburdened health care and Social Security systems? Would the work

From the *Los Angeles Times*, November 17, 1992, pp. A1, A25-A27. © 1992 by the Los Angeles Times Company. Reprinted by permission.

force be so crowded with elderly people who have postponed retirement that young people will not be able to find jobs? Would a population boom cause a housing crunch? What would be the effect on our fragile environment?

And, perhaps most important, will living longer also mean living healthier?

"If we are able to produce 150-year-old people but those 150-year-old people spend the last 40 years of their life in a nursing home, we would have created a disaster," said Dr. Richard Sprott, a top official at the National Institute on Aging. "The big public worry is that by increasing the number of people who make it [to advanced ages] we will produce this huge increase in the amount of disease."

In some respects, that is occurring. As the population has grown older, the incidence of age-related diseases such as Alzheimer's and osteoporosis has skyrocketed. The Alliance for Aging Research estimates that it costs the nation $90-billion a year to treat people with Alzheimer's, which affects at least 2 million and possibly 4 million Americans. As these costs continue to rise, experts say, society has a vested interest in finding ways to keep older people healthier.

What we have to do as a society is come to the realization of how much money is going into the medical care of the elderly," said Raymond Daynes, a cellular immunologist at the University of Utah. "We are becoming incredibly sophisticated in preventing individuals who have some acute, devastating illnesses from dying. But we are way behind in providing preventive measures so that [illness] doesn't happen in the first place."

Life expectancy in the United States has increased dramatically since 1900, from 47.3 years to 75.4 years. The greatest gains occurred during the first half of this century, largely because of dramatic reductions in infant mortality and infectious diseases. More recently, as

Daynes notes, smaller gains have resulted from progress against major fatal illnesses, such as heart disease, cancer and stroke.

Improvements in sanitation and living conditions have also made a big difference, and are likely to continue to do so, said James R. Carey, a medical demographer at UC Davis whose recent work with fruit flies has been cited as evidence that there is no arbitrary cap on human life span.

"The people that are 100 years old today were born in 1892," Carey said. "Think about all the things they went through, in terms of lack of medicine and nutrition. They were working hard to make it to 100. Now think about a newborn of today, with the emphasis on nutrition and exercise and medical advances. I would bet that we are going to find 125-, 130-year-olds by the 22nd Century just because of these changes in conditions."

Whether the pace proceeds more quickly than Carey suggests will depend on the outcome of the research being conducted in laboratories today—particularly in the area of genetics, scientists say. Few researchers, however, are willing to make predictions about how soon a breakthrough might come.

Yet as demographic shifts create an older society, and as scientific advances continue, the study of gerontology is enjoying an unprecedented boom. Once suspiciously regarded as the province of charlatans and snake-oil salesmen, longevity research is gaining attention and respect. Now, top-flight scientists are flocking to a field that, as little as five years ago, failed to draw the best and the brightest.

"Aging," said Daynes, "is finally coming of age."

This trend is reflected in funding: The federal government's National Institute on Aging is among the fastest-growing branches of the National Institutes of Health, with a budget that has nearly doubled in the past three years—from $222 million in 1989 to $402 million this year.

However, the budget is still small compared to that of some other arms of NIH—the National Cancer Institute has an annual budget of nearly $2 billion.

Much of the growth in aging research has been fueled by intense interest in Alzheimer's and other age-related diseases. The media have lavished much attention on the subject, particularly since a highly publicized 1990 study in which doses of a synthetic form of human growth hormone were reported to restore youthful vigor to elderly people.

Within the past decade new technologies—such as the ability to conduct transgenic experiments, in which a gene can be transferred from one organism into another—have become available to biologists, making possible certain types of gene research that used to be unthinkable.

"For the last 20 years, a lot of the research has been simply trying to characterize aging in a descriptive way," said Huber Warner, deputy associate director of the NIA's Biology of Aging program. "Now people are beginning to find out what the mechanisms of the aging process are so that they can then try to develop interventions that will slow the process down or prevent it altogether."

Judith Campisi is among those whose work is funded by the National Institute on Aging. At UC's Lawrence Berkeley Laboratory she is studying cellular senescence, the process by which cells keep dividing until they grow old and die. When she entered the field five years ago, she said, science had barely begun to examine the basic mechanisms that control aging.

"Before," she said, "nobody quite knew how to ask critical questions about aging. That has changed dramatically in the past five years. The field has now reached a level of maturity where . . . we are beginning to see a path to at least dream about approaching some answers. Until recently, that dream was not a very viable one."

The answers remain elusive. Aging is an extraordinarily complex puzzle—affected by genetics and the environment and individual habits, such as cigarette smoking and diet and exercise—and Campisi said she and her compatriots each hold only one small piece of it. "We all need each other terribly," she said.

Research is proceeding on many different—albeit interwoven—fronts:

At Bemidji State University in Minnesota, biochemist Gary W. Evans recently reported that dietary supplements of the metal chromium can extend the life span of rats by one-third, and may do the same for humans. At USC, noted gerontologist Caleb Finch is exploring new terrain with his studies on how aging affects the brain.

In Irvine, biologist Rose is breeding red-eyed fruit flies that can live 80 days—double the life span of an average fly—by mating selected flies that are able to reproduce late in life. Rose theorizes that these elderly flies, some of which live six months, are passing longevity genes to their offspring. But a key question remains: Which genes are responsible?

At the University of Colorado, Johnson, the biochemist who is breeding round worms, is taking a slightly different tack. He is mating long-lived nematodes with short-lived ones in an effort to follow the worms' DNA trails. Through a process by which he marks the DNA of the elderly worms, Johnson can see which genetic patterns reappear in the offspring. He has narrowed his search for a "longevity assurance gene" down to a 50-gene region of a single, 3,000-gene chromosome.

In Kentucky, pharmacologist John Carney has learned that when a synthetic compound known as PBN—phenyl butyl nitrone—is injected into gerbils, certain proteins in the brain that deteriorate with age are restored, resulting in improved short-term memory for the animals.

PBN works by combatting the effects of "free radicals"—damaging oxygen byproducts that occur natu-

rally in the body, destroying fats and proteins that are crucial to the way cells function. In certain diseases such as Alzheimer's and Parkinson's, researchers believe, these free radicals run amok.

In addition, scientists at the National Institute on Aging say they have evidence that free radicals speed the aging process. The theory is that if free radicals can be controlled, so too can aging. Researchers are also exploring the effects of "dietary antioxidants"—foods and vitamins including Vitamins C and E, and beta-carotene, a compound that turns into Vitamin A in the body—that may help combat free radicals.

Soon, Carney hopes, PBN will be tried in humans. He and his partner, a biochemist at the University of Oklahoma, have set up a pharmaceutical company to manufacture the drug and are hoping to gain government approval for testing within the next two years.

While Carney studies how a synthetic drug might slow the aging of the brain, Dr. Daniel Rudman of the Veterans Administration Medical Center in Milwaukee has spent the past five years examining how human growth hormones, which occur naturally in the body but decline in secretions as people grow older, affect aging.

Rudman has administered a synthetic form of the hormones to 42 men, ages 60 to 90, and the results have been nothing short of dramatic. Some signs of old age—the shrinking of certain organs, such as the spleen and liver, and the increase of fatty tissue in the body—were reversed by the hormones. After a few months of therapy, Rudman said, 70-year-old men looked as though they were 55.

But a growth hormone is not a cure-all. Given in doses that are too large, it can cause carpal tunnel syndrome, a repetitive stress disorder that commonly affects the wrists of computer users, breast enlargement and a rise in blood sugar. Moreover, it failed to curb other factors associated with aging, such as memory loss and softening of bones. "This,"

Rudman said, "is by no means a total reversal of the aging process."

Another promising hormone is DHEA, a steroid whose natural secretions decline with age. At the University of Utah, immunologist Daynes has discovered that when laboratory mice are given small amounts of DHEA-Sulfate—a water-soluble form of the hormone that had been thought to be irrelevant to the functioning of the body—their immune systems work better and their skin looks more youthful.

Over the long term, Daynes hopes that the hormone might be used as a sort of vitamin for the elderly. "I believe that over the next few years, we are going to prove beyond a shadow of a doubt that some of the physiological changes which are used to define old age are totally preventable," he said. "They don't have to happen."

In the Arizona desert, meanwhile, UCLA Prof. Roy Walford is trying to delay the onset of old age through his diet.

Walford and seven other scientists who are living in a glass-enclosed three-acre greenhouse known as Biosphere II are engaged in the first human version of a well-known study in which Walford found that a severely restricted, low-calorie diet could double the life expectancy of rats and mice.

Now, Walford and the other biospherians are subsisting on 1,800 calories per day, compared to the usual 2,500. According to Walford, the group eats only what is grown in the dome—grains, vegetables, fruit and one serving of meat per week.

According to the 68-year-old Walford, who has been following the diet for more than five years, the group is exhibiting the same changes as the rodents. Each has dropped an average of 14% in body weight since the experiment began 13 months ago. Their cholesterol is lower—an average of 130, down from 200—and their blood sugar has declined.

"This is the first well-monitored human application of the idea," Walford said, "and it indicates that humans respond the same as animals."

But be it gene manipulation, hormones, drugs or nutrition, researchers agree that if their work proves anything, it is that there is no Fountain of Youth, no single elixir that has the power to stop or even slow the aging process.

Instead, they say, advances that come in disparate arenas will over time be put together to create a greater understanding of the aging process. And only when the age-old mystery of aging is unraveled will scientists figure out ways to stop it, or slow it down.

"There is no silver bullet," said Edward Schneider, dean of USC's Andrus Center of Gerontology. Instead, Schneider likens the state of aging research to the decades-old search for a cure for cancer.

"Picture cancer research 30 years ago," he said. "People thought it's simple, we'll give one drug and it will cure all cancer. Well, it didn't work. In the next 10 or 20 years we'll have specific therapies for specific cancers, because cancer is a complex process.

"Imagine cancer being a 1,000-piece puzzle and we have a third of the pieces. Aging is a 100,000-piece puzzle, and we maybe have a tenth of the pieces."

Getting Older and Getting Better

When senior volunteers are included in educational settings, the schools truly mirror the community, Mr. Armengol reminds us.

RONALD ARMENGOL

RONALD ARMENGOL (Montclair State College Chapter) is an associate professor in the Department of Counseling, Human Development, and Educational Leadership at Montclair State College, Upper Montclair, N.J.

A T ALL levels of government, officials, planners, and demographers cite the burgeoning number of older citizens. For the future, this trend means more nursing homes and more beds in existing ones, soaring costs for Medicare and private health insur-ance plans, and Social Security and private pension funds struggling to stay solvent. And, the pessimists say, that's the good news.

The growth of the elderly population affects education as well. It is the rare school district that has not been caught between the rock of spiraling costs and declining revenues and the hard place of student/faculty needs. School budget increases in some of these districts have gone down to defeat at the hands of the older segment of the population, which sees no reason to support a system it neither needs nor wants and from which it derives no benefits. An administrator might well conclude that the situation is hopeless.

But the problem may already contain at least part of its own solution. Personnel costs — even just for basic staffing — take the lion's share of any budget. Meanwhile, it is also clear that classroom aides, part-time specialists, and visiting artists/lecturers all add immeasurably to the richness of the curriculum and provide vital assistance to overburdened teachers. No one questions the importance of individual attention. The only question is how to pay for it.

More and more schools are discovering that there is a wealth of experience and expertise available in their communities' senior populations. Moreover, they have learned to tap those riches through volunteer programs, with the happy result of high returns for negligible costs.

AN INEXHAUSTIBLE RESOURCE

Retirees live in every part of the country and are becoming increasingly active in organizations as well as in their communities.[1] And the graying of the American population guarantees their continuing availability as a volunteer force. The U.S. Census Bureau projects a 14% decrease during the 1990s in that segment of the population between the ages of 20 and 29, along with a 40% increase in the number of individuals between the ages of 50 and 59. The number of people between the ages of 65 and 74 will remain about the same (approximately 7.5% of the population). By 2010, however, when the baby boomers are reaching their golden years, their numbers will have increased 15%. By 2030 those 65 years of age and older are expected to constitute about 20% of the population. Both now and well into the 21st century, there will be no lack of older people.

Senior citizens have the time, the resources, the experience, and the energy to help the schools. They are capable of assisting in classrooms and offices, taking care of the nitty-gritty routines that dissipate the time and energy of teachers, thereby allowing schools to maximize their potential through the improved management of time, personnel, and money. Teachers who have welcomed senior volunteers into their classrooms as aides have been pleasantly surprised to discover that their assistants often have a wealth of skills and experience that they are willing to share with the students.

Another major benefit of involving seniors in the schools is the creation of intergenerational programs to bring young and old together. At a time when the multigenerational family living under one roof is a rarity, intergenerational programs in the schools give students experiences that they might otherwise miss. There was a time when grandparents in the home were respected role models; they assisted parents in the clarification of family values and shared

a sense of history and cultural heritage. Their wealth of life experiences enriched not only the family unit but each individual as well. The American family is poorer now that grandparents are less frequently members of the same households as their children and grandchildren. Grandparents' experiences give them a perspective on life that no amount of formal education can replace.

While deprived of the benefits of associating intimately with older people, students of all ages have acquired a view of them that is stereotypical and distorted. A major cause of the generation gap is the unfavorable image of senior citizens, which affects both the young and the old.[2] These misconceptions and misperceptions of older people cause us to see them as unproductive, always in need, and narrow and rigid in their thinking. Until these negative attitudes can be changed, the valuable legacy of the elderly will remain untouched. Yet the key to unlocking this resource is so simple: provide opportunities for young and old to meet and come to know each other as individuals.

Schools can make these meetings possible. Moreover, as the nation is recognizing the value of parent and community involvement in the schools, it is also slowly awakening to the enormous pool of talent and energy that exists in the large senior population.

DEVELOPING INTERGENERATIONAL PROGRAMS

What is required is a way to involve these valuable resources in our education system. Any teacher, backed by an innovative and committed administration, can establish an intergenerational program. It takes effort, sincerity, a belief in the value of elderly volunteers, and sensible planning. However, a truly effective intergenerational program requires a districtwide commitment in order to have access to the entire pool of potential senior volunteers in the community. The first step should be the drafting of a formal resolution on the part of the board of education and the superintendent, endorsing and encouraging the implementation of an intergenerational program in the schools.

The flip side of involving senior volunteers in the schools is enlightening stu-

> **V**olunteers want to know what the job is, when they are needed and for how long, and what they need to know.

dents with regard to the elderly. Schools need to develop a gerontology curriculum to enable the students to learn more about aging and encourage sensitivity and awareness. Students need to learn that aging does not eliminate a person's strength, agility, perception, or hearing — though it may indeed alter all of them. Moreover, it must be emphasized that these changes do not happen to everyone at the same age, nor do they all occur at once. This approach clears up the misconception that it isn't possible for younger people to relate to older ones because the latter are too feeble, hard of hearing, and so on. Through involvement and interaction with a cross-section of older people that includes those who are healthy and energetic, educators can encourage more positive attitudes toward the elderly. Bringing the young and the old together explodes myths and leads each to a greater appreciation of the other.

Planning is as important to a successful intergenerational program as it is to any other program. The plan of action must include a needs assessment, job descriptions, and provisions for recruitment, screening, orientation, and training. The plan should also state the objectives that are to be met and the specific outcomes that are desired. An important part of this process is determining what benefits for students, teachers, volunteers, and the schools will be derived from the program. In addition, a mechanism for evaluating the program should be in place before implementation begins.[3]

(United Nations photo)

Intergenerational programs are worthwhile for everyone. When seniors are included in the educational setting, it mirrors the community—all age groups and a rich variety of lifestyles, cultures, languages, motivations, and ideas.

As the initial step in the development of an intergenerational program, the needs assessment should be stated in clear, concise, and specific terms. A survey of each school's needs, a statement of what the regulations permit the volunteers to do, and a list of what they can contribute will be necessary.

When the needs assessment has been completed, a job description must be drawn up, clearly detailing the teacher's expectations, the intent of the program, the skills needed, and the amount of time to be volunteered; this should not be a difficult task for administrators or teachers.

The recruitment process need not be complicated. Those experienced in recruiting volunteers say that the best method is simply to ask for them. Potential volunteers will usually accept if they are approached by people they know. The idea of community networking is also effective for this purpose. Once staff members are committed to the idea that senior volunteers are valuable to the schools, everyone should be on the lookout for potential volunteers at social gatherings, civic meetings, and community activities. An administrator or a coordinator of special programs should be assigned to set up a communications network with the senior citizen organizations in the community and the county and with representatives of the Retired Senior Volunteer Program (RSVP) so that schools and volunteers can be matched.

In the 1988 Independent Sector Survey conducted by the Gallup Organization, which studied volunteering and charitable giving in the U.S., three-fourths of the respondents indicated that they did not refuse to volunteer when asked.[4] Volunteers want to know what the job is, when they are needed and for how long, and what they need to know. Respondents between the ages of 55 and 64 reported a 47.1% rate of volunteerism and contributed 4.7 hours of work each week. Forty percent of the 65- to 74-year-olds surveyed volunteer six hours a week, while 28.6% of those 75 years of age and older reported 4.4 hours of volunteer work each week.

The provision of transportation for seniors who need it is an important consideration and will affect the number of volunteers available to the program. It is possible that school district vehicles or the community's senior citizen transportation service could be used. Parents are another potential source of transportation. If public transportation is available, the volunteers' travel costs could be underwritten by the school district.

After volunteers have indicated their interest in working, a screening meeting is a productive and logical next step. A sincere welcome extended by the person doing the screening helps to get the conference off to a good start. Both the school's and the volunteer's expectations should be discussed to eliminate misconceptions at the outset and avoid future disillusionment. This is the time to assess the volunteer's health, physical needs, communication skills, and preferences for working with particular age groups. All these factors should be taken into consideration when deciding on the volunteer's assignment, and some thought should be given to the compatibility of the teacher and the volunteer. After the initial screening process, a well-designed orientation and training program will help ensure each volunteer's success in the assignment and, ultimately, the success of the entire program.

Before senior volunteers begin their work, the students should have an orientation session so that they understand the roles of the elderly volunteers and the objectives of the intergenerational program. This lays a foundation for the volunteers to share the skills and knowledge they have acquired during their lives and for the students to become aware of the aging process and its implications. In time, friendships that bridge the generations will be made, and those involved will learn to recognize their similarities as well as to understand and appreciate their differences. An orientation for parents is also important to ensure that they are aware of and support the program.

Calling the volunteers together to tour the building and meet the staff is an effective way to recognize the volunteers and make them feel comfortable. Students, too, should be given an early opportunity to meet and socialize with the senior volunteers. The students could help plan the welcoming party and provide refreshments.

All volunteers, especially seniors, are motivated to continue by having assignments that are significant and that keep them actively involved. Senseless busywork can be deadly. Motivation can be kept high by giving recognition to the volunteers in newsletters and news releases, by presenting special awards for outstanding contributions, and by publicly acknowledging years of service. But personal gratification is the paramount motivation for senior volunteers. The satisfaction comes from enjoyable social contacts and a sense that the skills and expertise they have to give are needed and appreciated.

OUTREACH PROGRAMS

Outreach programs for seniors are another way that school districts can attract more volunteers and fulfill real needs of senior citizens. Some programs may be joint ventures between the school district and other local government agencies. The objective is to actively involve seniors in the schools and to promote their understanding of school endeavors that require community support to be successful. One district, sensitive to the ethnic makeup of the community, enlisted support for its

> Students also sponsor intergenerational proms — with all the prom trappings — which are very popular with seniors.

new middle school by including boccie courts in its outdoor athletic facilities.

These social and service programs for seniors are generally appreciated and heavily attended. Student involvement is an important part of some of the most successful activities, such as food drives, meals on wheels for the homebound, and luncheons at school with entertainment provided by the students. Students also sponsor intergenerational proms — with all the prom trappings — which are very popular with seniors. Such events, which involve not only seniors and students but faculty, administration, and parents as well, are highly effective ways to build real community spirit. Another favorite activity that invariably brings a large turnout is the dinner show. Dinner is served by the students, after which the seniors attend the dress rehearsal of a student play. Some districts provide seniors with a "gold card," which entitles them to lifetime admittance to all school-sponsored cultural and sports events. Others arrange discounts for minor auto repairs in school shops, as well as for services provided by cosmetology, home economics, and art classes and by wood and metal shops.

WHAT SENIORS CAN OFFER

The kinds of services that senior volunteers can provide are nearly limitless. As classroom aides, they make it possible for teachers to manage time more efficiently and to provide students with more individual attention. In addition to serving as classroom aides, senior volunteers can act as teacher assistants for special school projects, sharing their work skills and making presentations to classes. They can be helpful at all grade levels, as well as with special needs students.

Highly skilled volunteers have been able and willing to make display cases or bookshelves needed by a teacher or administrator, to tune pianos, to decorate for a special event, and to repair cameras and audiovisual equipment. Many are capable of tutoring non-English-speaking students and serving as translators for parent/teacher conferences. They can assist with clerical duties in offices and library media centers or act as chaperones on field trips. They have been successful at demonstrating technical skills in an industrial arts class and helping out in typing, computer, and reading labs. A volunteer mentoring program for students in math, reading, and science has had very positive results; support programs for disadvantaged youths have been equally successful. Senior volunteers are ideal for reading to students and for telling them about real-life experiences that relate to topics being studied in class, such as living in another country, having been a prisoner of war, or immigrating to the U.S. These firsthand accounts are especially appropriate for social studies programs, and there are few students who have such sources of living history at home.

Senior volunteers can be equally successful in nonacademic areas. Great numbers of seniors are involved in Child Assault Programs, helping children in a very sensitive area. Volunteers in Meals with Manners eat with students and model appropriate mealtime behavior. Athletic directors benefit from the enthusiasm and sense of responsibility that seniors bring to their work at concession stands and ticket booths and as sports announcers.

ASSESSING THE PROGRAM

Once a senior volunteer program is in place, it is important to conduct an ongoing assessment. The evaluation process should include everyone with a stake in the program: teachers, students, administrators, volunteers, and parents. The strengths and weaknesses of the program must be determined and recommendations made for improvement. Future needs of the program should be projected and steps initiated to meet them.

Students should be encouraged to log

the highlights of each day's activities with seniors and to reflect on the benefits of these relationships. The students' impressions of their daily experiences with the volunteers can be shared as part of the assessment process.

BENEFITS FOR ALL

Intergenerational programs are guaranteed to be worthwhile for everyone. Young people receive many benefits. Students from preschool through grade 12 who were interviewed about their experiences with senior volunteers responded enthusiastically. "Can they come to see us more often?" some asked. "I like hold-ing hands, and it's nice to be hugged," others said.

All students appear to be positive about their relationships, even those who originally were squeamish about the aging process and wanted to reserve judgment about the volunteers until they "got to know them better." Many long-lasting relationships developed over time, with students visiting their senior friends at their homes, taking them shopping, and making them favorite desserts. The senior volunteers will tell you, "Although I gave a lot of time and effort, the students gave me much more than I could ever imagine."

When senior volunteers are included in educational settings, the schools truly mirror the community, which is composed of all age groups and a rich variety of lifestyles, cultures, languages, motivations, and ideas.

1. Stanley B. Hoffman, "Peer Counselor Training with the Elderly," *Gerontologist*, vol. 23, 1983, pp. 358-60.

2. Taher Zandi, Joystna Mirle, and Patricia Jarvis, "Children's Attitudes Toward Elderly Individuals: A Comparison of Two Ethnic Groups," *International Journal of Aging and Human Development*, vol. 30, 1990, pp. 161-74.

3. Jane Angelis, "Bringing Old and Young Together," *Vocational Education Journal*, January/February 1990, pp. 19-21.

4. Alec M. Gallup, "Giving and Volunteering in the United States," Independent Sector Survey, 1988.